Contents

Contents

CRACKNELL'S COMPANION

CASES & STATUTES

Criminal Law

Sixth Edition

P N Hollick
JP, LLB, MEd, FCollP, of the Middle Temple, Barrister

OLD BAILEY PRESS

OLD BAILEY PRESS
200 Greyhound Road, London W14 9RY

First published 1969
Sixth edition 2000

© P N Hollick and D G Cracknell 2000

ISBN 1 85836 300 4

British Library Cataloguing-in-Publication.

A CIP Catalogue record for this book is available from the British Library.

Printed and bound in Great Britain

Contents

Contents

Preface
to the Sixth Edition

This edition brings further summaries of important cases and extracts from statutes. The cases are mostly those decided in the House of Lords and the Court of Appeal.

Cases include the decision of the Court of Appeal in *R v Thornton (No 2)* [1996] 2 All ER 1023, a murder case referred back to the Court of Appeal by the Home Secretary, which examined 'battered women syndrome' as a relevant 'characteristic' and the meaning of 'sudden and temporary loss of self-control' when considering the effect of provocation. See *R v Horrex* [1999] Crim LR 500 for a further view on 'characteristics' attributable to a defendant.

R v Preddy; *R v Slade* [1996] 3 All ER 481 confronted the issue of obtaining property by deception (s15 Theft Act 1968) and the meaning of 'property belonging to another' when the transfer of funds was executed elecronically. The Court of Appeal then considered a number of appeals brought by defendants who had been convicted prior to this ruling.

The scope of a 'joint enterprise' and the question of 'foreseeability' have arisen in a number of recent cases. Was the joint enterprise continuing when the fatal injuries were sustained? Was the defendant still acting within that joint enterprise? Were the acts which caused death within the scope of the joint enterprise? See *R v Powell and Daniels*; *R v English* [1997] 4 All ER 545, *R v Mitchell and Another* [1999] Crim LR 496 and *R v Greatrex*; *R v Bates* [1999] 1 Cr App R 126.

Can hate mail and malicious telephone calls lead to the infliction of 'grievous bodily harm'? Can silent telephone calls give rise to a conviction under s47 (common assault) of the Offences Against the Person Act 1861? These questions were answered in *R v Ireland*; *R v Burstow* [1997] 4 All ER 225.

As to the statutes, the fourteen added for this edition include relevant provisions of the Criminal Appeal Act 1995, the Knives Act 1997 and the Criminal Cases Review (Insanity) Act 1999. Amendments and additions made to earlier Acts and in force on 1 September 1999 have been reflected in the text so that those provisions are now set out in their form as at that date.

P N Hollick
November 1999

Cases

Airedale NHS Trust **v** *Bland* [1993] 1 All ER 821 (House of Lords)

When he was 17½, Anthony Bland was severely crushed in the April 1989 Hillsborough football ground disaster. Since that time he had been in a persistent vegetative state, having suffered irreversible brain damage. Would it be, inter alia, a criminal act for the applicant health authority to discontinue all life-sustaining treatment?

Held, it would not, provided responsible and competent medical opinion was of the view that it would not be in his best interests to prolong his life. Death would be regarded as being exclusively caused by the injuries to which his condition was attributable. However, as a matter of practice, doctors should seek the court's guidance in all such cases. (See also *R* v *Malcherek*.)

Attorney-General for Northern Ireland **v** *Gallagher* [1963] AC 349 (House of Lords)

The respondent was convicted of the murder of his wife. There was no doubt he killed her. The defence was insanity or alternatively that he was so drunk when he killed her as to be incapable of having any intent to kill her. The respondent appealed to the Court of Criminal Appeal in Northern Ireland on the ground of misdirection of the jury by the trial judge. The court directed a verdict of acquittal. The Attorney-General for Northern Ireland was granted leave to appeal to the House of Lords on a point of law of general public importance, ie whether a person in a psychopathic condition which is quiescent may become insane (within the meaning of the rules in *M'Naghten's* case) as the result of the voluntary consumption by him of intoxicating liquor, if the effect of that intoxicating liquor is to bring about an explosive outburst in the course of a mental disease although the disease was not itself caused by intoxicating liquor.

Held, the conviction of murder should be restored. The accused was a psychopath but he was not insane when he made up his mind, as he did before drinking whisky, to kill his wife. The drunkenness was equally no defence to the charge. LORD GODDARD took the view that neither self-imposed intoxication nor aggressive psychopathy of itself amounts to insanity, while LORD TUCKER stated that a man can produce in himself a disease of the mind by the excessive consumption of alcohol, but this was not such a case. 'A psychopath who goes out intending to kill, knowing it is wrong, and does kill, cannot escape the consequences by making himself drunk before doing it' (*per* LORD DENNING). (See also *Bratty* v *Attorney-General for Northern Ireland, Director of Public Prosecutions* v *Beard* and *R* v *Bailey*.)

Attorney-General's Reference (No 1 of 1975) [1975] 2 All ER 684 (Court of Appeal)

This was a reference to obtain a ruling on the question 'whether an accused who surreptitiously laced a friend's drinks with double measures of spirits when he knew that his friend would shortly be driving his car home, and in consequence his friend drove with an excess quantity of alcohol in his body and was convicted of the offence under the Road Traffic Act 1972, s6(1) [now s5(1) Road Traffic Act 1988] is entitled to a ruling of no case to answer on being later charged as an aider and abettor, counsellor and procurer, on the ground that there was no shared intention between the two, that the accused did not by accompanying him or otherwise positively encourage the friend to drive, or on any other ground.'

Held, the question would be answered in the negative as where a person performs some act which results in another person unwittingly committing an offence which is an absolute offence, the first person may be said to have procured the commission of the offence by the other, within s8 of the Accessories and Abettors Act 1861, even though there was no communication between them before the offence was committed. 'We think that there was a case to answer and that the trial judge should have directed the jury that an offence is committed if it is shown beyond reasonable doubt that the accused knew that his friend was going to drive, and also knew that the ordinary and natural result of the additional alcohol added to the friend's drinks would be to bring him above the recognised limit of 80 milligrammes per 100 millilitres of blood' (*per* LORD WIDGERY CJ). (See also *Blakely, Sutton* v *Director of Public Prosecutions.*)

Attorney-General's Reference (Nos 1 and 2 of 1979) [1979] 3 All ER 143 (Court of Appeal)

This was a reference on two points of law (1) 'whether a man who has entered a house as a trespasser with the intention of stealing money therein is entitled to be acquitted of an offence against s9(1)(a) of the Theft Act 1968 on the grounds that his intention to steal is conditional on his finding money in the house' and (2) 'whether a man who is attempting to enter a house as a trespasser with the intention of stealing anything of value which he may find therein is entitled to be acquitted of the offence of attempted burglary on the ground that at the time of the attempt his said intention was insufficient to amount to "the intention of stealing anything" necessary for conviction under s9 of the Theft Act 1968.'

Held, the answer was in the negative to both questions. 'The important point is that the indictment should correctly reflect that which it is alleged that the accused did, and that the accused should know with adequate detail what he is alleged to have done' (*per* ROSKILL LJ). In *R* v *Easom* [1971] 2 All ER 945 the indictment contained a single count alleging that Easom 'stole one handbag, one purse, one notebook, a quantity of tissues, a quantity of cosmetics and one pen ...'. 'Taking as an example the facts of *R* v *Easom*, plainly what the accused intended was to steal some or all of the contents of the handbag if and when he got them into his possession. It seems clear from the latter part of Edmund Davies LJ's judgment that, if he had been charged with an attempt to steal some or all the contents of the handbag, he could properly have been convicted, subject of course to a proper direction to the jury' (*per* ROSKILL LJ).

Attorney-General's Reference (No 1 of 1991) [1992] 3 All ER 897 (Court of Appeal)

The point of law raised by this reference was 'In order for a person to commit an offence under s1(1) of the Computer Misuse Act 1990 does the computer which the person causes to perform any function with the required intent have to be a different computer to the one into which he intends to secure unauthorised access to any program or data held therein?' It had been contended that in order to contravene s1(1) of the 1990 Act, and therefore in turn s2(1), it was necessary to establish that the offender had used one computer with intent to secure unauthorised access into another computer.

Held, the answer to the question was 'No'. 'It may be that the major mischief at which the 1990 Act was directed was the mischief which has become endemic of persons using one computer to hack into another computer. But ... the scope of the section is not confined to that form of access to any computer' (*per* LORD TAYLOR OF GOSFORTH CJ).

Attorney-General's Reference (No 1 of 1992) [1993] 1 WLR 62 (Court of Appeal)

This was a reference on a point of law under s36 of the Criminal Justice Act 1972 following an acquittal of the respondent charged with the attempted rape of a girl, aged 17, contrary to s1(1) of the Criminal Attempts Act 1981. The respondent submitted that the evidence was of no more than mere preparatory acts. The trial judge ruled that there was evidence that the respondent intended to have sexual intercourse but he later directed the jury that, as a matter of law, there had to be some evidence of actual physical attempt at penetration and the respondent was acquitted by direction.

Held, on a charge of attempted rape it was not necessary for the prosecution to prove, as a matter of law, that the defendant physically attempted to penetrate the woman's vagina with his penis. 'It was sufficient if there was evidence from which the intent could be inferred and there were proved acts which a jury could properly infer were more than merely preparatory to the commission of the offence' (*per* LORD TAYLOR OF GOSFORTH CJ). (Applied: *R* v *Gullefer*.)

Attorney-General's Reference (No 2 of 1992) [1993] 3 WLR 982 (Court of Appeal)

The respondent was acquitted on charges following a motorway collision in which two people were killed. He contended that he had not seen the flashing lights of the parked vehicles into which he had crashed because he had been in a state of automatism referred to as 'driving without awareness' induced by 'repetitive visual stimulus experienced on long journeys on straight flat roads'. The defence of automatism was left to the jury. The Attorney-General referred the following question for consideration by the Court of Appeal:

'Whether the state described as "driving without awareness" should, as a matter of law, be capable of founding a defence of automatism.'

Held, the defence of automatism should not have been left to the jury: the question would be answered in the negative. 'In our judgment, the "proper evidential foundation" was not laid in this case by ... [the] evidence of "driving without awareness". As the authorities ... show, the defence of automatism requires that there was a total destruction of voluntary control on the defendant's part. Impaired, reduced or partial control is not enough. Professor Brown [who gave expert evidence for the respondent] accepted that someone "driving without awareness" within his description, retains some control. He would be able to steer the vehicle and usually to react and return to full awareness when confronted by significant stimuli' *(per* LORD TAYLOR OF GOSFORTH CJ). (See also *Bratty v Attorney-General for Northern Ireland.)*

Attorney-General's Reference (No 3 of 1992) [1994] 2 All ER 121 (Court of Appeal)

The issue was whether on a charge of attempted aggravated arson, contrary to s1(2) of the Criminal Damage Act 1971, in addition to establishing a specific intent to cause damage by fire, it was sufficient to prove that the defendant was reckless as to whether life would as a result be endangered. The respondents were charged on two counts, count 1 alleging intent to endanger life and count 2 alleging recklessness as to whether life would be endangered. While the complainants were keeping a night watch over their premises following previous attacks, a petrol bomb was thrown towards them from a car carrying the defendants. The petrol bomb fell against a nearby wall. The respondents' car sped away but crashed soon after. A number of petrol bombs, matches and a petrol can and some rags were found in the car.

Held, on a charge of attempted aggravated arson contrary to s1(2) of the 1971 Act it was enough for the Crown to establish a specific intent to cause damage by fire and that the defendant was reckless as to whether life would be endangered. If the state of mind of the defendant was that he intended to damage property and was reckless as to whether the life of another would thereby be endangered and while in that state of mind he did an act which was more than merely preparatory to the offence, he was guilty of attempting to commit the offence. It was not necessary that he intended that the lives of others would be endangered by the damage which he intended. (Applied: *R v Khan*; see also *R v Caldwell* and *R v Moloney*.)

Attorney-General's Reference (No 3 of 1994) [1997] 3 All ER 936 (House of Lords)

The defendant was charged with murder but was acquitted following a direction by the trial judge. He subsequently pleaded guilty to causing grievous bodily harm. He stabbed his pregnant girlfriend, P, who was in the 23rd week of her pregnancy. She underwent an operation to repair a cut in her uterus wall. It was concluded wrongly by the doctors there had been no injury to the foetus which in fact had suffered some damage to its abdomen.

Three weeks after the operation P went into labour and gave birth to a daughter who died 120 days later. P also died some weeks after the birth. There was no evidence directly linking the injury to the child with its death, dying as she did as a result of the premature birth and complications. The Crown referred to points of law for consideration by the Court of Appeal: (1) 'Subject to proof by the prosecution of the requisite intent in either case: whether the crimes of murder or manslaughter can be committed where the unlawful injury is deliberately inflicted (i) to the child in utero; (ii) to a mother carrying a child in utero, where the child is subsequently born alive, enjoys an existence independent of its mother, thereafter dies and the injuries inflicted while in utero either caused or made a substantial contribution to the death.' (2) 'Whether the fact that the death of the child is caused solely as a consequence of injury to the mother rather than as a consequence of direct injury to the foetus can negative any liability for murder or manslaughter in the circumstances set out in question (1).' The Court of Appeal gave the answer to (1) 'yes' and (2) 'no'. On the defendant's application leave was granted for an appeal to the House of Lords.

Held, a conviction for murder could not result where D attacked a pregnant woman, intending to kill her or cause her grievous bodily harm, thereby causing her to prematurely go into labour and give birth to a child who subsequently died as a result of prenatal injuries sustained in the attack upon the mother. But, where the defendant intentionally committed a dangerous and unlawful act upon a pregnant woman that resulted in her giving birth to a child who subsequently dies as a result of prenatal injuries sustained in the attack upon the mother, a conviction for manslaughter was sustainable. The rules applicable concerning the defendant's liability for murder were considered by LORD MUSTILL: (1) It was sufficient to raise a prima facie case of murder (subject to entire or partial excuses such as self-defence or provocation) for it to be proved that the defendant did the act which caused the death intending to kill the victim or to cause him at least grievous bodily harm. (2) That if the defendant does an act with the intention of causing a particular kind of harm to B, and unintentionally does that kind of harm to V, then the intent to harm B may be added to the harm actually done to V in deciding whether the defendant has committed a crime towards V. (3) That except under statute an embryo or foetus in utero cannot be the victim of a crime of violence: '… violence to the foetus which causes its death in utero is not a murder … It is … established beyond doubt for the criminal law , as for the civil law … that the child 'en ventre sa mere' does not have a distinct human personality, whose extinguishment gives rise to any penalties or liabilities at common law.' (4) That the existence of an interval of time between the doing of an act by the defendant with the necessary wrongful intent, and its impact on the victim in a manner which leads to death, does not in itself prevent the intent, the act and the death from together amounting to murder, so long as there is an unbroken causal connection between the act and the death. (5) That violence towards a foetus which results in harm suffered after the baby has been born alive can give rise to criminal responsibility even if the harm would not have been criminal (apart from statute) if it had been suffered in utero. (See also *Director of Public Prosecutions* v *Newbury*; distinguish *R* v *Dalby*.)

Attorney General's Reference (No 3 of 1998) [1999] 3 All ER 40 (Court of Appeal)

The defendant was charged with aggravated burglary. It was common ground that he was legally insane when he entered the property. The judge was asked to rule on what had to be proved to determine whether the defendant 'did the act or made the omission charged' for the purposes of s2(1) Trial of Lunatics Act 1883. The Crown had the burden of proving all the relevant elements of the offence, including mens rea. The indictment was amended to add a count of affray. Evidence from the defendant's psychiatrist was that he had been unable to form a criminal intent at the material time. The trial judge directed the jury to acquit him on the basis that there was no evidence of the required intent for either of the alleged offences. The Attorney-General sought the opinion of the Court of Appeal under s36 Criminal Justice Act 1972 on the question of what had to be proved when an inquiry had been embarked on under the 1883 Act to determine whether a defendant 'did the act or made the omission charged'.

Held, assuming insanity, the Crown had to prove the ingredients that constituted the actus reus of the crime; it did not have to prove the mens rea of the alleged crime. Apart from insanity, the defendant's state of mind ceased to be relevant. The trial judge's reasoning had been incorrect.

Atwal v Massey [1971] 3 All ER 881 (Queen's Bench Divisional Court)

This was an appeal by way of case stated by justices who had convicted Atwal of handling stolen goods contrary to s22 of the Theft Act 1968. A stolen electric kettle was left by the roadside by the thief for collection by the appellant, who had paid him £1.50 for it. The justices had held that the appellant, from the circumstances under which he had collected the kettle, ought to have known that it had been stolen.

Held, in order to establish an offence under s22 it was not sufficient to show that the goods had been received in circumstances which would have put a reasonable man on enquiry; the question was a subjective one: was the appellant aware of the theft or did he believe the goods to be stolen or did he, suspecting the goods to be stolen, deliberately shut his eyes to the circumstances? The justices had applied the wrong test and the conviction would be quashed. (See also *R v Lincoln*.)

Beckford v R [1987] 3 All ER 425 (Privy Council)

The appellant, a police officer, was convicted of murder. He was a member of an armed posse sent to investigate a report that an armed man was terrorising his family in their home. The man ran from the house pursued by the appellant and other police officers. The appellant and another police officer shot the man who had surrendered after he had been found hiding. The Crown alleged that the man was unarmed; the appellant claimed that the man had a firearm, had fired at the police and had been fatally shot when they returned fire. The trial judge directed the jury that if the appellant had a reasonable belief that his life was in danger or that he was in danger of serious bodily harm, he was entitled to be acquitted on the grounds of self defence. The Court of Appeal of Jamaica held that the appellant's belief that he was entitled to fire in self-defence had to be reasonably, and not merely honestly held as the appellant had contended, and his appeal was dismissed.

Held, the appeal would be allowed by reason of a misdirection by the trial judge to the jury. The test for self-defence was that a person could use such force in his own or another's defence as was reasonable in the circumstances as he honestly believed them to be.

Blakely, Sutton v Director of Public Prosecutions [1991] Crim LR 763 (Queen's Bench Divisional Court)

T was an associate of the appellant B. B and another were convicted of procuring an offence, T being convicted of drunken driving. The appellants had 'laced' T's drink in the hope that he would not drive home to his wife that night. T was careful as to how much he drank if he was driving, and the appellants knew this and had intended to tell T later, believing that he would not therefore be prepared to drive home. However, T drove off before the appellants had told him. They appealed by way of case stated on the ground that it had not been their intention that T should commit the offence.

Held, the appeal would be allowed. *Attorney-General's Reference (No 1 of 1975)* was followed in which Lord Widgery CJ said that to procure meant 'to produce by endeavour. You procure a thing by setting out to see that it happens and taking the appropriate steps to produce that happening'. It was necessary to show that one who procured an offence intended to cause its commission. (See also *Attorney-General's Reference (No 1 of 1975).*)

Bratty v Attorney-General for Northern Ireland [1963] AC 386 (House of Lords)

The appellant was convicted of the murder by strangulation of an eighteen-year-old girl and his appeal was dismissed by the Court of Criminal Appeal of Northern Ireland. The defences raised at the trial were: (1) the accused was in a state of automatism; (2) his mental condition was so impaired that he was incapable of forming an intent to kill; and (3) he was insane.

Held, (1) there were in law two types of automatism, namely insane and non-insane automatism, and a judge was only under a duty to leave the issue of automatism of either type to the jury where the defence had laid a proper foundation for so doing by adducing positive evidence in respect of it, which was a question of law for the judge to decide; (2) where, as here, the only cause alleged for the 'unconscious act' in question was the same as that which formed the basis of the defence of insanity, ie a defect of reason caused by disease of the mind, namely psychomotor epilepsy, and that cause was rejected by the jury, in considering the defence of insanity there could be no room for the alternative defence of automatism, either insane or non-insane, and the trial judge was right in not leaving that defence to the jury; (3) the appellant must be deemed to have been a sane and responsible person at the time of the killing, and since there were no grounds for the view that he lacked intent to kill, there was no issue of manslaughter to be left to the jury. LORD DENNING stated that no act is punishable if it is done involuntarily. But the category of involuntary acts is very limited, so limited that until recently there was hardly any reference in the

English books to the so-called defence of automatism. The decision of the Court of Criminal Appeal in Northern Ireland was affirmed. (See also *Attorney-General for Northern Ireland* v *Gallagher, Attorney-General's Reference (No 2 of 1992)* and *R* v *Burgess*.)

C v S [1987] 1 All ER 1230 (Court of Appeal)

By s1(1) of the Infant Life (Preservation) Act 1929 it was an offence for any person, with intent to destroy the life of a child capable of being born alive, to cause it to die before it had an existence independent of its mother. The first defendant, a single woman who was between 18 and 21 weeks pregnant, wished to terminate the pregnancy. Two medical practitioners certified, in accordance with s1(1)(a) of the Abortion Act 1967 (now amended by the Human Fertilisation and Embryology Act 1990), that the continuance of her pregnancy would involve risk of injury to her physical or mental health greater than if the pregnancy were terminated. The father sought an injunction restraining the first defendant from undergoing the termination and restraining the second defendants, the area health authority, from performing the termination. He contended that a foetus of between 18 and 21 weeks was 'capable of being born alive', and that consequently termination of such a pregnancy would constitute an offence under s1(1) of the 1929 Act. The judge refused to grant an injunction, holding that the foetus had no right to be a party and that the father had failed to establish than an offence under the 1929 Act would be committed if the termination was carried out. The father appealed.

Held, although a foetus of a gestational age of between 18 and 21 weeks could be said to demonstrate real and discernible signs of life, the medical evidence was that such a foetus would be incapable of breathing either naturally or with the aid of a ventilator. It followed that such a foetus could not properly be described as being 'capable of being born alive' within s1(1) of the 1929 Act and accordingly the termination of a pregnancy of that length would not constitute an offence under that Act. The appeal would therefore be dismissed. *Per* SIR JOHN DONALDSON MR: The Court of Appeal is the final court of appeal in circumstances of real urgency and litigants are entitled to act on its judgments in such circumstances without waiting to see whether there will be an appeal to the House of Lords. *Per* HEILBRON J (at first instance): A foetus has no right of action until it is subsequently born alive and therefore while it is unborn it cannot be a party to an action.

Chamberlain v Lindon [1998] 2 All ER 538 (Queen's Bench Divisional Court)

A private prosecution against L, brought by C for criminal damage to a wall he had built, was dismissed by the justices. C had granted L a right of way across his land, so he, L, could access land he had purchased from C. L exercised his right by driving diagonally across C's land, to which C objected. He built a wall so L could not exercise his right in this way. L demolished the wall. C appealed and a question was stated for the opinion of the Divisional Court: were the justices, on the facts as found, entitled to find that L had a lawful excuse for the purposes of s5(2)(b) of the Criminal Damage Act 1971?

Held, the appeal would be dismissed. L had believed he was acting to protect his right of way and his action had succeeded in doing that (*R* v *Hill; R* v *Hall* (1989) 89 Cr App R 74.) His course of action in demolishing C's wall rather than becoming absorbed in lengthy litigation, did not mean his purpose had not been to protect his property.

Chan Wing-Siu v *The Queen* [1984] 3 All ER 877 (Privy Council)

The appellants were convicted of murder and of wounding with intent. Armed with knives they had entered the deceased's flat and while one guarded the deceased's wife the other two stabbed him; he later died of his wounds. They also slashed his wife. In the appeal to the Privy Council it was contended that the trial judge had misdirected the jury by stating that they could convict each of the accused on both counts if he was proved to have had in contemplation that a knife might be used by one of his co-accused with the intention of inflicting serious bodily harm.

Held, the appeal would be dismissed. A second person was criminally liable for an act committed by the primary offender which the second person foresaw but did not intend, if he took part in an unlawful joint enterprise and it was proved beyond reasonable doubt that he contemplated and foresaw that the primary offender's act could come about as a result of the execution of the planned joint enterprise. The second person's conduct would be taken into account in deciding what he contemplated and foresaw the act of the primary offender to be together with any other evidence which could be used to explain what he foresaw at the time. As it had been shown by the Crown that each party had contemplated that serious bodily harm could be a consequence of their common unlawful enterprise, and as there were no grounds to show that the possibility of such injury was so remote that it could be disregarded, the jury had not been misdirected. (See also *R* v *Roberts* (1993).)

Chandler v *Director of Public Prosecutions* [1962] 3 All ER 142 (House of Lords)

The question of public importance was the proper construction of the words 'for any purpose prejudicial to the safety or interests of the State' in s1 of the Official Secrets Act 1911. The appellants were anti-nuclear protesters. They planned a demonstration at an RAF station which was a prohibited place for the purposes of s1. They proposed by non-violent action to immobilise the aircraft there for a space of some six hours. At their trial the appellants were charged with conspiracy to commit a breach of s1, namely to enter a prohibited place for a 'purpose prejudicial to the safety or interests of the State.' The trial judge ruled that they were not entitled to call evidence to establish that it would be beneficial for the country to give up nuclear weapons. Evidence tendered on that issue was not admitted. In his summing-up the judge in effect directed the jury to convict if satisfied that the appellants' immediate purpose was the obstruction of the aircraft. An appeal against conviction having been dismissed by the Court of Criminal Appeal, appeal to the House of Lords was allowed.

Held, the appellants had been rightly convicted of the offence charged. The immediate (or direct or short-term) purpose of the appellants being to obstruct the operational activity of the air base, which was clearly prejudicial to the use of the base according to existing dispositions of the armed forces, evidence, such as that tendered and rejected, directed to show that it would be beneficial and not prejudicial to the interests of the state for a policy of nuclear disarmament to be adopted by the State, was inadmissible, since the disposition and armament of the armed forces was within the prerogative and exclusive discretion of the Crown, and the wisdom of the Crown's policy in exercising that discretion was not open to challenge in the courts. Although the interests of the State referred to in s1(1) of the 1911 Act were the objects of State policy and it was for the Crown, as for any other holder of discretionary power, to determine how such power should be exercised and thus to determine what the interests of the State were, yet a jury were entitled to decide whether a fact, constituted by statute as an element of a criminal charge, had been proved, and thus on a charge such as that in the present case inquiry was not wholly excluded, the measure of permissible inquiry being such as would enable the jury to intervene to reject abuse or excess in the exercise of prerogative power. In the present case, however, there was nothing to suggest that the Crown's interests in the proper operation of the air base were not what they might naturally be presumed to be and the proposed obstruction was a purpose prejudicial to the interests of the state. On the true construction, s1 was not limited to offences of spying; 'purpose' within the meaning of s1 was to be distinguished from the motive for doing an act, and the words 'any purpose' in s1 meant or included the achieving of the consequence which a person intended and desired to follow directly on his act, viz his direct or immediate purpose as opposed to his ultimate aim; and even if a person had several purposes, his immediate purpose remained one of them and was within the words 'any purpose' in s1(1). In the phrase 'interests of the State' in s1(1) the word 'State' meant the organised community or the organs of government of a national community; and the 'interests of the State' meant such interests according to the policies of the State as they in fact were, not as it might be argued that they ought to be.

Cox v Riley (1986) 83 Cr App R 54 (Queen's Bench Divisional Court)

The defendant was convicted of criminal damage under s1(1) of the Criminal Damage Act 1971. He deliberately erased a computer program from a plastic circuit card of a computerised saw rendering the saw inoperable. He appealed on the ground that the program was not tangible within s10(1) of the 1971 Act and that erasing it did not amount to damage to property.

Held, the appeal would be dismissed. The erasing of a program from such a card constituted damage within the meaning of the Criminal Damage Act 1971. The defendant had rightly been convicted as his action necessitated time, labour and expense in restoring the relevant program on the circuit card. (See also *R v Whiteley*.)

Dawes v Director of Public Prosecutions [1994] Crim LR 604 (Queen's Bench Divisional Court)

The appellant was convicted of aggravated vehicle taking contrary to s12A of the Theft Act 1968. He had taken and been caught in a vehicle adapted by the police to trap 'joyriders'. The engine cut out after going 30 yards and the central locking system was activated trapping the appellant in the vehicle. He caused damage trying to get out of the vehicle. He contended that he had been unlawfully detained in the vehicle and s12A did not cover damage caused to a vehicle whilst trying to escape unlawful detention.

Held, the arrest was lawful (the appellant was informed of the reasons for his arrest as soon as was reasonably practicable – complying with s28 of the Police and Criminal Evidence Act 1984). He had clearly committed the offence of taking a vehicle without the owner's consent and had committed the aggravated offence when he damaged the vehicle.

Director of Public Prosecutions v Armstrong-Brown
[1999] Crim LR 416 (Queen's Bench Divisional Court)

The defendant was convicted of assault contrary to s39 Criminal Justice Act 1998. A licence had been granted to disturb and take some newts (being a protected species) to an alternative habitat, planning permission having been granted on their present site. O was doing what was necessary to comply with the terms of the licence. With a wooden stake, the defendant tried to jam the foot controls on the mechanical digger being used by O; he also struck the roll bar of the digger with the stake. O chased the defendant who struck him on the arm with the stake. The defendant said that if he struck O, he had done so in the honest belief, however misguided, that O's continued use of the digger would be a crime, or that O would hurt him. It was on this basis the defendant had used force, but no more than he genuinely thought was the minimum necessary to stop the machine or protect himself. The justices did not accept that the defendant's use of force was reasonable in the circumstances. On appeal it was submitted that the question as to whether the degree of force was reasonably necessary was to be tested subjectively, provided that the defendant recognised that the community at large would also regard the degree of force as reasonably necessary.

Held, the appeal would be dismissed. Such force used by a defendant accused of battery in self-defence was to be assessed in an objective sense as to whether it was reasonably necessary in the circumstances as the defendant subjectively believed them to be. (See also *R v Owino*.)

Director of Public Prosecutions v Bell [1992] Crim LR 176
(Queen's Bench Divisional Court)

The defendant was convicted of driving with excess alcohol. He drove away from some pursuers in terror, fearing he would suffer some serious personal injury. He had been drinking but some trouble had occurred which had caused him to run back to his car. In the process he accidentally drove over one of his passengers who had not been able to get into the car in time. The Crown Court allowed his appeal against conviction on the ground of duress. The prosecutor appealed.

Held, the appeal would be dismissed. The defence of duress was made out when fear brought about by threats caused a person to lose complete control of his will. He had only driven 'some distance' down the road so the defence of duress/necessity could still be raised. The prosecution had failed to negative the defence of duress. (See also *R v Conway* and *R v Willer*; but see *R v Cole*.)

Director of Public Prosecutions v *Camplin* [1978] 2 All ER 168 (House of Lords)

The respondent, aged 15, was convicted of murder. [The Court of Appeal substituted a verdict of manslaughter, holding that, where a person accused of murder raised the defence of provocation, the 'reasonable man' test was designed to exclude from consideration to the accused's advantage, mental or physical abnormalities which might make him exceptionally deficient in self-control. However, youth and the immaturity which goes with youth were not abnormalities.] He went to K's house, K being in his fifties. K buggered the respondent who hit him on the head with a pan, killing him. The defence of provocation under s3 of the Homicide Act 1957 was put forward. Evidence on behalf of the respondent was that: (i) K had forcibly committed the act of buggery on the respondent against his will; (ii) after the event the respondent became overwhelmed by shame; (iii) when K laughed at his 'triumph', the respondent lost his self-control and hit K.

Held, that the Crown's appeal would be dismissed. The 'reasonable man' referred to an ordinary person of either sex, not exceptionally excitable or pugnacious, but possessed of such power of self-control as everyone was entitled to expect that his fellow citizens would exercise in society as it was today. The accused's unusual characteristics (here, his age) could be taken into account by the jury; because he was only 15 the jury should not have been told to ignore his age. (See also *R* v *Ali*.)

Director of Public Prosecutions v *Daley and McGhie* [1980] AC 237 (Privy Council)

The defendants were charged with murder. The deceased had been stoned by the defendants and in running away, tripped and fallen. He was later found to be dead. The cause of death could have been a blow from one of the stones or the impact of the fall. The judge told the jury that they could return a verdict of constructive manslaughter, as had been suggested by prosecuting counsel in his final address, which they did. The Court of Appeal (Jamaica) allowed the appeal on the ground that the trial judge should not have left it open to the jury to return such a verdict.

Held, that the prosecutor's appeal would be allowed; where evidence was adduced, sufficient to support an alternative verdict of manslaughter it was open to the jury to return that alternative verdict. In regard to 'escape' cases LORD KEITH set out what the prosecution had to establish, '(1) that the victim immediately before he sustained his injuries was in fear of being hurt physically; (2) that his fear was such that it caused him to try to escape; (3) that whilst he was trying to escape, and because he was trying to escape, he met his death; (4) that his fear of being hurt there and then was reasonable and was caused by the conduct of the defendant; (5) that the defendant's conduct which caused the fear was unlawful; and (6) that his conduct was such as any sober and reasonable person would recognise as likely to subject the victim to at least the risk of some harm resulting from it, albeit not serious harm'. The convictions were restored. (See also *R* v *Williams, R* v *Davis*.)

Director of Public Prosecutions v *Doot* [1973] 1 All ER 940
(House of Lords)

The respondents, Doot and four others, all American citizens, were parties to an agreement made either in Belgium or Morocco to import cannabis resin into England with the view of re-exporting it to the United States. By s2 of the Dangerous Drugs Act 1965 (now see s3 Misuse of Drugs Act 1971) it was unlawful to import cannabis resin into the United Kingdom without a licence and the respondents did not have a licence. The cannabis resin was concealed in three separate vans and shipped to England. Customs officers discovered cannabis in one of the vans when it arrived at Southampton. The other two vans were subsequently traced and the cannabis found in them. The respondents were convicted, inter alia, of conspiracy to import dangerous drugs into the United Kingdom but the conviction was quashed by the Court of Appeal which held that the agreement was the essence of the offence and the English courts had no jurisdiction to try the charge as it had been made abroad. The Crown appealed.

Held, the appeal would be allowed and the conviction restored as (1) an agreement made outside the jurisdiction of the English courts to commit an unlawful act within the jurisdiction was a conspiracy which could be tried in England if the agreement was subsequently performed, wholly or in part, in England; (2) the crime of conspiracy is complete once the agreement has been made but the conspiratorial agreement remains in being until terminated by completion of its performance or by abandonment; (3) where acts are committed in England in performance of the agreement that will suffice to show the existence of a conspiracy within the jurisdiction triable by the English courts; (4) here, the conspiracy was committed in England.

Director of Public Prosecutions v *Majewski* [1976] 2 All ER 142
(House of Lords)

One evening a brawl broke out in a public house in Basildon between the appellant and another man. The landlord went to eject the other man and the appellant intervened to stop him. When the landlord next went to telephone for the police, the appellant butted him. Eventually the two men were ejected but fought their way back in again. During the struggle to get back the appellant cut the landlord's hand with a piece of glass and a customer sustained a grazed wrist and a cut finger. The appellant was finally overpowered and held on the floor until the police arrived. The police officer, who arrested the appellant, was kicked and abused by him and he also kicked and injured another officer whilst he was being driven to the police station. The next morning the appellant attacked a police inspector who went to his cell at the police station to see what he was doing. The appellant was charged with assault occasioning actual bodily harm and assault on a police officer in the execution of his duty. He said that for some time he had been taking a mixture of drugs and on that evening he had drunk a fair amount of alcohol whilst under the influence of the drugs. He claimed to have no recollection at all of what had happened in the public house or at the police station until he woke up there and found himself handcuffed. His conviction was confirmed by the Court of Appeal and he appealed to the House of Lords.

Held, the appeal should be dismissed as, unless the offence was one that required proof of specific or ulterior intent, it was no defence to a criminal charge that, by reason of self-induced intoxication, the appellant did not intend to do the act alleged to constitute the offence. Section 8 of the Criminal Justice Act 1967 was irrelevant since that section dealt only with matters of evidence and the rule that an accused could not excuse his conduct by relying on self-induced intoxication was a rule of substantive law. (See also *Attorney-General for Northern Ireland* v *Gallagher, R* v *Caldwell, R* v *Bailey, R* v *Culyer* and *R* v *Kingston.)*

Director of Public Prosecutions **v** *Newbury, Director of Public Prosecutions* **v** *Jones* [1976] 2 All ER 365 (House of Lords)

The train travelling from Pontypridd to Cardiff was approaching a bridge which crossed the railway line. The guard was sitting next to the driver of the train in the front cab. The driver noticed the heads of three boys above the parapet of the bridge. He saw one of the boys push something off the parapet towards the oncoming train. This proved to be part of a paving stone. It came through the glass window of the cab and struck the guard who was killed. The boys were convicted of manslaughter. They appealed and the point of law certified to be of general public importance was 'Can a defendant be properly convicted of manslaughter, when his mind is not affected by drink or drugs, if he did not foresee that his act might cause harm to another?'

Held, an accused was guilty of manslaughter if it were proved that he had intentionally done an act which was unlawful and dangerous and that the act had inadvertently caused death. It was not necessary for the prosecution to prove that the act was unlawful or dangerous; the test was not whether the accused himself recognised it was dangerous but whether sober and reasonable people would recognise its danger. The appeals would be dismissed. (See also *Attorney-General's Reference (No 3 of 1994).)*

Director of Public Prosecutions **v** *Ray* [1973] 3 All ER 131 (House of Lords)

The respondent, Ray, a university student, and three companions went to a restaurant in Gainsborough and ordered a meal to the value of 47p. When the order was given the respondent intended to pay for the meal. The meal was duly served and there were no complaints, but after it had been consumed they had a discussion and decided to leave without paying. The respondent waited until the waiter had gone out of the restaurant to the kitchen and then ran out of the restaurant without paying. He was convicted of obtaining a pecuniary advantage by deception, contrary to s16(1) of the Theft Act 1968, but the conviction was quashed by the Divisional Court and the Crown appealed.

Held, the conviction would be restored as the respondent had practised a deception on the waiter by ostensibly continuing to represent to him that he intended to pay for the meal before leaving and by that deception he had obtained a pecuniary advantage for himself by evading his obligation to pay for the meal. 'So far as the waiter was concerned the original implied representation made to him by the respondent must have been a continuing representation so long as he (the respondent) remained in the restaurant. There was nothing to alter the representation. Just as the waiter was led at the start to believe that he was dealing with a customer who by all that he did in the restaurant indicated his intention to pay in the ordinary way, so the waiter was led to believe that the state of affairs would continue' (*per* LORD MORRIS OF BORTH-Y-GEST). (See also s3 of the Theft Act 1978.)

Director of Public Prosecutions v *Smith* [1960] 3 All ER 161 (House of Lords)

The respondent Smith was driving a car containing stolen property. He was told by a police constable to draw to the kerb but accelerated. The police constable clung to the side of the car but was shaken off, falling in front of another car and receiving fatal injuries. The respondent was convicted of capital murder but the Court of Criminal Appeal substituted a verdict of manslaughter. The Crown appealed to the House of Lords.

Held, the appeal would be allowed and the conviction of murder restored. The jury must be satisfied that the accused was unlawfully and voluntarily doing an act aimed at someone, and it is immaterial what he in fact contemplated as the probable result of his action or whether he contemplated at all. Provided he was in law responsible and accountable for his actions, ie capable of forming an intent, not insane nor suffering diminished responsibility, the sole question was whether the unlawful and voluntary act was of such a kind that grievous bodily harm was the natural and probable result. The test was whether the ordinary reasonable man would have contemplated that the unlawful and voluntary act would lead to such a result. The distinction drawn between the case where serious harm was 'likely' to result was not warranted. The true question in each case is whether there is a real probability of grievous bodily harm. The expression 'grievous bodily harm' should bear its ordinary and natural meaning of 'really serious' harm. (See also s8 of the Criminal Justice Act 1967, *Hyam* v *Director of Public Prosecutions*, *R* v *Cunningham* and *R* v *Moloney*.)

Director of Public Prosecutions v *Turner* [1973] 3 All ER 124 (House of Lords)

The respondent, Turner, employed a man named Black and his brother to do some work in a house and at the end of the week he owed Black £24 in wages and Black's brother £14. When Black went to collect the money the respondent told him that he did not have any ready cash and gave him a cheque for £38, the sum due as wages. When he gave the cheque to Black the respondent knew that it would be dishonoured. The cheque was dishonoured and the respondent was convicted of obtaining a pecuniary advantage by deception, contrary to s16(1) of the Theft Act 1968. The conviction was quashed by the Court of Appeal and the Crown appealed.

Held, the conviction would be restored. 'The creditor Black was deceived by the accused into thinking that he had been paid by a cheque which the accused knew was worthless when he gave wages then due to Black and his brother, and thereby gained a pecuniary advantage within the meaning of sub-section (2)(a)' (*per* LORD MACDERMOTT). 'Normally everyone who accepts a cheque in payment takes it in discharge of the debt. But in law, unless anything is said to the contrary, the discharge is presumed to be subject to a resolutive condition that if the cheque is dishonoured the discharge is void ab initio; the condition operates retrospectively so that the debt revives in its original form' (*per* LORD REID). (See also s2 of the Theft Act 1978.)

Director of Public Prosecutions v Withers [1974] 3 All ER 984 (House of Lords)

The appellants operated an investigation agency. Its activities included making reports for clients about the status and financial standing of third parties. They made enquiries of banks, building societies, government departments and local authorities from time to time over a period of four years. The enquiries were made by telephone and to obtain information which would not normally be given (eg bank accounts and criminal records) lies were constantly told. The appellants were convicted on two counts with conspiracy to effect a public mischief by unlawfully obtaining private and confidential information by false representations that they were persons authorised to receive such information. The Court of Appeal dismissed their appeal but certified the following point of law of general public importance: 'Whether the learned judge was right in law in stating that if the jury were sure that one of the appellants agreed with another appellant to do wilfully deceitful acts themselves or agreed to procure others to do such wilfully deceitful acts for them and that such wilfully deceitful acts would cause extreme injury to the general wellbeing of the community as a whole such persons who so agreed would be guilty of the offence of conspiring to effect a public mischief'. Where a charge of conspiracy to effect a public mischief has been preferred, the question to be considered is whether the object or means of the conspiracy are in substance of such a quality or kind as has already been recognised by the law as criminal.

Held, the appeal should be allowed and both convictions quashed. 'I hope that in future such a vague expression as "public mischief" will not be included in criminal charges' (*per* VISCOUNT DILHORNE).

Director of Public Prosecutions for Northern Ireland v Maxwell [1978] 3 All ER 1140 (House of Lords)

The appellant was charged with doing an act with intent to cause an explosion by a bomb, contrary to s3(a) of the Explosive Substances Act 1883, and with possession of a bomb, contrary to s3(b) of that Act. He was a member of an illegal organisation in Northern Ireland which had been responsible for sectarian murders and bombings. He was told by a member of the organisation to guide a car at night to a public house in a remote country area. He knew that he was being sent on a terrorist attack but did not know what form it would take. Driving his own car he led another car containing three or four men to the public house. When he arrived there the appellant drove slowly past and then drove home. The other car stopped opposite the public house, one of the occupants got out, ran across to the public house and threw a pipe bomb containing 5lbs of explosive into the hallway. The attack failed due to action taken by the licensee's son. The appellant was convicted of both offences as an accomplice. He appealed contending that since he did not know what form the attack would take or of the presence of the bomb in the other car he could not properly be convicted of aiding and abetting in the commission of crimes of which he was ignorant. The Court of Criminal Appeal in Northern Ireland dismissed his appeal and he appealed to the House of Lords.

Held, the appeal would be dismissed. A person may properly be convicted of aiding and abetting the commission of a criminal offence without proof of prior knowledge of the actual crime intended if he contemplated the commission of one of a limited number of crimes by the principal and intentionally lent his assistance in the commission of such a crime. It was irrelevant that at the time of lending his assistance the accused did not know which of those crimes the principal intended to commit. On the facts, the appellant must have known when he was ordered to act as a guide for the other car that he was taking part in a terrorist attack and, although he may not have known the precise target or weapons to be used, he must have contemplated, having regard to his knowledge of the organisation's methods, that the bombing of the public house was an obvious possibility among the offences likely to be committed and consequently must have contemplated that the men in the second car had explosives. (See also *R v Rook.*)

Dobson v General Accident Fire and Life Assurance Corp plc
[1989] 3 All ER 927 (Court of Appeal)

The plaintiff's home insurance policy included cover for loss by theft. He advertised his Rolex watch and a diamond ring for sale for £5,950. A stranger telephoned and expressed interest in the articles at the advertised price, and it was provisionally agreed that the plaintiff would accept a cheque drawn by a building society in his favour. The stranger called at the plaintiff's house and received the goods in return for the cheque. It turned out that the cheque had been stolen and was worthless. The defendant insurers denied liability under the policy, contending that the circumstances in which the plaintiff had lost his watch and ring did not amount to theft within s1(1) of the Theft Act 1968.

Held, the defendant's contention would be rejected and the plaintiff's action would succeed. Property in the articles passed at the time of delivery, which was also the time of appropriation, and appropriation could occur even if the owner had consented to the property being taken. Accordingly the stranger had committed a theft, ie, he had dishonestly appropriated the plaintiff's property with the intention of permanently depriving him of it. (See also *R v Gomez.*)

Edwards v R [1973] 1 All ER 152 (Privy Council)

The appellant carried on an adulterous association with Dr Coombe's wife and followed him from Australia, where they all lived, to Hong Kong for the purpose of blackmailing him. Dr Coombe had kept a collection of indecent photographs and the appellant broke into his flat and stole one of the photographs for use in the blackmail. One evening while in Hong Kong the appellant went to Dr Coombe's hotel room, showed him a copy of the photograph and said, 'If you do not wish this to be sent around to all your friends and wish it back, it will cost you $3,000 in cash within 24 hours'. The appellant returned to his hotel, made telephone calls to Dr Coombe at intervals of between 20 and 30 minutes and was eventually told by Dr Coombe that he had agreed to pay and that the appellant should come to his hotel room for the money. The appellant went to Dr Coombe's hotel room about 2.30 am the following morning to collect the money and whilst there Dr Coombe swore at him and launched at him with a knife inflicting wounds to the ring finger and little finger of his left hand, his left arm and his left knee. The appellant wrested the knife from Dr Coombe and stabbed him, a total of 27 times, to the face, neck, arms, left hand, thighs and chest, thereby causing his death. At his trial on a charge of murder the appellant pleaded provocation and self-defence but the judge held that provocation could not be of any avail nor could self-defence and he was convicted. The Supreme Court of Hong Kong said that the trial judge erred in law in withdrawing the two defences but dismissed the appeal on the grounds that there was no substantial miscarriage of justice.

Held, the appeal would be allowed and a conviction for manslaughter should be substituted as, inter alia, Dr Coombe, the person sought to be blackmailed, did go to extreme lengths in that he made a violent attack on the appellant with a knife, inflicting painful wounds and putting the appellant's life in danger; there was evidence of provocation and it was fit for consideration by the jury. 'No authority has been cited with regard to what may be called "self-induced provocation". On principle it seems reasonable to say that (1) a blackmailer cannot rely on the predictable results of his own blackmailing conduct as constituting provocation sufficient to reduce his killing of the victim from murder to manslaughter, and the predictable results may include a considerable degree of hostile reaction by the person sought to be blackmailed, for instance vituperative words and even some hostile action such as blows with a fist; (2) but if the hostile reaction by the person sought to be blackmailed goes to extreme lengths it might constitute sufficient provocation even for the blackmailer; (3) there would in many cases be a question of degree to be decided by the jury' (*per* LORD PEARSON).

Edwards v *Toombs* [1983] Crim LR 43 (Queen's Bench Divisional Court)

The defendant was convicted of falsifying a record made for an accounting purpose contrary to s17(1)(a) of the Theft Act 1968. He was a turnstile operator. On the day in question he was only to allow through season ticket holders. The turnstile had a meter to record the number of people going through. He was seen allowing two people through in one movement of the turnstile, accepting money from them both. It was argued that the turnstile meter was not a record for an accounting purpose and that his failure to record the number of people passing through the turnstile was not an omission in a material particular capable of being treated as the falsification of an account under s17(2) of the 1968 Act.

Held, the appeal would be dismissed. The turnstile meter was a record. Section 17(2) was not a definition section but a deeming provision. If there was a conflict between s17(2) and s17(1)(a) the court would ignore s17(2) and construe the words of s17(1)(a) as they appeared.

Ferguson v *Weaving* [1951] 1 All ER 412 (King's Bench Divisional Court)

A number of people were convicted of consuming intoxicating liquor on licensed premises (an hotel) outside permitted hours and the licensee was charged with aiding and abetting them. The licensee had instructed the three waiters on duty in the concert room to collect glasses containing intoxicating liquor at ten o'clock before collecting empty glasses and to require persons having glasses containing intoxicating liquor either to drink the liquor or to give up the glasses. At five minutes before ten o'clock and again at ten o'clock she gave the signals to indicate it was closing time and the waiters called 'time'. Some time after ten o'clock police officers entered the concert room of the hotel and found a number of persons consuming intoxicating drink but the licensee, who was in another room at the time, did not know of this. She was acquitted and the prosecution appealed to the Divisional Court.

Held, the acquittal would be upheld on the ground that the knowledge of the waiters could not be imputed to her so as to make her guilty of aiding and abetting. 'In this case there is no substantive offence in the licensee at all. The substantive offence is committed only by the customers. She can aid and abet the customers if she knows that the customers are committing the offence, but we are not prepared to hold that knowledge can be imputed to her so as to make her, not a principal offender, but an aider and abettor. So to hold would be to establish a new principle in criminal law' (*per* LORD GODDARD CJ).

Gillick v *West Norfolk and Wisbech Area Health Authority* [1985] 3 All ER 402 (House of Lords)

The plaintiff sought an assurance from her local area health authority that her daughters would not be given advice and treatment on contraception without her prior knowledge and consent while they were under 16. Area health authorities received a circular from the Department of Health and Social Security in which there was advice to the effect that a doctor consulted by a girl under 16 years of age at a family planning clinic would not be acting unlawfully if he prescribed her contraceptives so long as he was acting in good faith to protect her against the harmful effects of sexual intercourse. The circular also stated that, although a doctor should proceed on the assumption that advice and treatment on contraception should not be given to a girl under 16 without parental consent and that he should try to persuade the girl to involve her parents in the matter, nevertheless the principle of confidentiality between doctor and patient applied to a girl under 16 seeking contraceptives and therefore in exceptional cases the doctor could prescribe contraceptives without consulting the girl's parents or obtaining their consent if in the doctor's clinical judgment it was desirable to prescribe contraceptives. When the authority refused to give the plaintiff the assurance she sought she brought an action against the authority and the Department seeking (1) as against them both a declaration that the advice contained in the circular was unlawful, because it amounted to advice to doctors to commit the offence of causing or encouraging unlawful sexual intercourse with a girl under 16, contrary to s28(1) of the Sexual Offences Act 1956, or the offence of being an accessory to unlawful sexual intercourse with a girl under 16, contrary to s6(1) of that Act, and (2) as against the area health authority a declaration that a doctor or other professional person employed by it in its family planning service could not give advice and treatment on contraception to any child of the plaintiff below the age of 16 without the plaintiff's consent, because to do so would be unlawful as being inconsistent with the plaintiff's parental rights. The judge held (1) that a doctor prescribing contraceptives to a girl under 16 in accordance with the advice contained in the Department's circular would not thereby be committing an offence of causing or encouraging unlawful sexual intercourse with the girl, contrary to s28(1) of the 1956 Act, and (2) that a parent's interest in his or her child did not amount to a 'right' but was more accurately described as a responsibility or duty, and accordingly giving advice to a girl under 16 on contraception without her parent's consent was not unlawful interference with parental 'rights'. He accordingly dismissed the plaintiff's action. The Court of Appeal allowed her appeal and granted the declarations sought, on the grounds that a child under 16 could not validly consent to contraceptive treatment without her parents' consent and that therefore the circular was unlawful. The Department appealed to the House of Lords against the grant of the first declaration.

Held, having regard to the reality that a child became increasingly independent as it grew older and that parental authority dwindled correspondingly, the law did not recognise any rule of absolute parental authority until a fixed age. Instead, parental rights were recognised by the law only as long as they were needed for the protection of the child and such rights yielded to the child's right to make his own decisions when he reached a sufficient understanding and intelligence to be capable of making up his own mind. Accordingly, a girl under 16 did not, merely by reason of her age, lack legal capacity to consent to contraceptive advice and treatment by a doctor. A doctor who in the exercise of his clinical judgment gave contraceptive advice and treatment to a girl under 16 without her parents' consent did not commit an offence under s6(1) or s28(1) of the 1956 Act, because the bona fide exercise by the doctor of his clinical judgment negated the mens rea which was an essential ingredient of those offences. It followed that a doctor had a discretion to give contraceptive advice or treatment to a girl under 16 without her parents' knowledge or consent provided the girl had reached an age where she had a sufficient understanding and intelligence to enable her to understand fully what was proposed, that being a question of fact in each case. It also followed that the Department's guidance could be followed by a doctor without involving him in any infringement of parental rights or breach of the criminal law. The Department's appeal would therefore be allowed, the first declaration would be set aside and (*per* LORD FRASER and LORD SCARMAN) the second declaration should be overruled as being erroneous.

Halstead v Patel [1972] 2 All ER 147 (Queen's Bench Divisional Court)

Patel, a postman, opened an account with the National Giro and arranged for his wages to be paid therein. On opening the account he was sent an explanatory booklet setting out the full instructions and regulations. He knew that overdrafts were not provided and that he was not permitted to overdraw his account. While he was on strike and no payments were being made into the account, he drew a number of cheques on the account and it became overdrawn to the amount of £108 11s (£108.55p). At all times, and in particular when he made the withdrawals, he genuinely intended to repay the National Giro as soon as he could do so after the strike was over and he was again in receipt of wages. He was charged with dishonestly obtaining specific sums from the Post Office by deception with the intention of permanently depriving it thereof, contrary to s15 of the Theft Act 1968. The justices dismissed the information on the ground that there was no intention permanently to deprive the Post Office of the sums since he honestly intended to repay the amounts drawn and the prosecutor appealed.

Held, the appeal would be allowed and the case sent back to the justices with a direction to convict as (1) he could not have intended to repay the Post Office the actual coins or notes which he had received and the justices erred in holding that he did not intend permanently to deprive the Post Office of the money which he obtained on cashing the cheques; (2) although he might have had a defence to the charge if he could have shown that he genuinely believed on reasonable grounds that by the time the respective cheques were presented for payment there would by then have been funds in his account to meet them, there was no such evidence and an honest intention to replace the money taken from the Post Office with its currency equivalent at some future date, coupled with a reasonable expectation that the money might be so replaced, was not sufficient to meet the allegation of dishonesty. (But see *R* v *Feeny*.)

Harris v Director of Public Prosecutions [1993] 1 All ER 562 (Queen's Bench Divisional Court)

The court was asked to decide whether a stipendiary magistrate had been right in law in finding that a folding knife carried in the pocket having a blade of less than three inches in length and capable of being secured in an open position by a locking device was not a folding pocketknife within the meaning of s139 of the Criminal Justice Act 1988.

Held, he had, and the possessor of such a knife had been rightly convicted of an offence, contrary to s139(1) of the 1988 Act. 'To be a folding pocketknife the knife has to be readily and indeed immediately foldable at all times, simply by the folding process. A knife of the type with which [this appeal is] concerned is not in this category because, in the first place, there is a stage, namely when it has been opened, when it is not immediately foldable simply by the folding process and, secondly, it requires that further process, namely the pressing of the button' (*per* McCOWAN LJ).

Haughton v Smith [1973] 3 All ER 1109 (House of Lords)

A quantity of corned beef was stolen from a firm in Liverpool and some days later an overloaded van travelling south was stopped by the police and the corned beef was found inside. Part of the cargo was removed but the van was allowed to proceed with the remainder of the load, two policemen concealed inside, and one disguised policeman beside the driver. The object was to catch the London receivers by using the van and its load as a decoy. When the van arrived at a rendezvous on the M1 at the Scratchwood Service Area in Hertfordshire it was met by Smith and some others by arrangement and then driven on to London under Smith's directions, but with the policemen still on board. Smith played a prominent part in assisting in the disposal of the van and its load. Finally the trap was sprung and various members of the conspiracy arrested. Smith was convicted of attempting to handle stolen goods by dishonestly attempting to assist in the disposal of the goods for the benefit of others, knowing or believing the goods to have been stolen, but the conviction was quashed by the Court of Appeal and the prosecution appealed to the House of Lords.

Held, the appeal would be dismissed as a person can only be convicted of an attempt to commit an offence in circumstances where the steps taken by him in order to commit the offence, if successfully accomplished, would have resulted in the commission of that offence. A person who carried out certain acts in the erroneous belief that those acts constituted an offence could not be convicted of an attempt to commit that offence because he had taken no steps towards the commission of an offence. Also, in order to constitute an offence under s22 of the Theft Act 1968 the goods had to be stolen goods at the time of the handling, and it was irrelevant that Smith believed them to be stolen goods. Finally, since the goods which Smith had handled were not stolen goods as they had been restored to lawful custody, he could not be convicted of attempting to commit the offence. (But see *R v Shivpuri*.)

Howker v Robinson [1972] 2 All ER 786 (Queen's Bench Divisional Court)

Weston, a barman, sold intoxicating drink to two persons under the age of 18 years who were in the lounge of licensed premises. Howker was the holder of a justices' licence in respect of the premises, but Weston had complete control over the sale of intoxicating liquor in the lounge. The responsibility of ensuring that persons under 18 years of age were not sold intoxicating liquor had been delegated to him by Howker. At the time of the sale Howker was present in another bar on the premises and had no knowledge of what took place in the lounge. Both Howker and Weston were charged with knowingly selling intoxicating liquor to a person under the age of 18 contrary to s169(1) of the Licensing Act 1964. Howker was convicted by the magistrates and appealed by way of case stated.

Held, the appeal should be dismissed as (1) even though s169(1) of the 1964 Act provided that a licensee's servant might be prosecuted for an offence under that subsection, a licensee who had no actual knowledge of the sale would also be liable for having 'knowingly' committed the offence if he had delegated his control of the premises to his servants; (2) it is possible for a licensee effectively to delegate his managerial functions and responsibilities in respect of part of the premises to his servant even though he himself remained in another part of the premises. (See also *R v Winson*; cf *Vane v Yiannopoullos*.)

Hyam v Director of Public Prosecutions [1974] 2 All ER 41
(House of Lords)

The appellant in the early hours of Saturday 15 July 1972 set fire to a dwelling-house in Coventry by deliberately pouring about half a gallon of petrol through the letterbox and igniting it by means of a newspaper and a match. The house contained four persons, presumably asleep. They were a Mrs Booth and her three children, a boy and two young girls. Mrs Booth and the boy escaped alive. The two girls died as the result of asphyxia by the fumes generated by the fire. The appellant was jealous of Mrs Booth. She believed Mrs Booth was likely to marry a Mr Jones of whom the appellant herself was the discarded mistress. Her defence was that she started the fire to frighten Mrs Booth into leaving the district. She did not intend to cause death or grievous bodily harm. The Court of Appeal dismissed the conviction for murder but certified, in giving leave to appeal to the House of Lords, the following point of law of general public importance: 'Is malice aforethought in the crime of murder established by proof beyond reasonable doubt that when doing the act which led to the death of another the accused knew that it was highly probable that that act would result in death or serious bodily harm?'

Held, the appeal would be dismissed. In order to establish the mens rea of murder it was sufficient to prove that, when the accused performed the relevant acts, he knew that it was probable that these acts would result in grievous bodily harm to somebody, even though he did not desire to bring that result about. 'Before an act can be murder it must ... be an act committed with one of the following intentions, the test of which is always subjective to the actual defendant: (1) the intention to cause death; (2) the intention to cause grievous bodily harm in the sense of that term explained in *DPP* v *Smith*, ie really serious injury; (3) where the defendant knows that there is a serious risk that death or grievous bodily harm will ensue from his acts, and commits those acts deliberately and without lawful excuse, the intention to expose a potential victim to that risk as the result of those acts. It does not matter in such circumstances whether the defendant desires those consequences to ensue or not and in none of these cases does it matter that the act and the intention were aimed at a potential victim other than the one who succumbed ... Without an intention of one of these three types the mere fact that the defendant's conduct is done in the knowledge that grievous bodily harm is likely or highly likely to ensue from his conduct is not by itself enough to convert a homicide into the crime of murder' (*per* LORD HAILSHAM). (See also *Director of Public Prosecutions* v *Smith, R* v *Vickers, R* v *Moloney* and *R* v *Nedrick*.)

JJC (A Minor) v *Eisenhower* [1983] 3 All ER 230
(Queen's Bench Divisional Court)

JJC (a minor) was found guilty of unlawfully and maliciously wounding another, contrary to s20 of the Offences against the Person Act 1861, having aimed and fired an air gun in the direction of four young people. The pellets hit one of them in the area of the left eye. The magistrates 'considered that the abnormal presence of red blood cells in the fluid of the left eye of Martin Cook, after being hit by the air gun pellet, indicated at the least the rupturing of a blood vessel or vessels internally which was sufficient to constitute a wound for the purposes of s20 of the Act.' The appellant appealed against the conviction on the ground that the justices had erred in law in concluding that the injuries suffered by the victim constituted a wound for the purpose of s20 of the 1861 Act.

Held, a 'wound' for the purposes of s20 is a break in the continuity of the whole skin. An injury where there has been internal rupturing of blood vessels is not a 'wound' for which a person may be convicted under s20. The appeal would therefore be allowed.

James & Son Ltd v *Smee* [1954] 3 All ER 273
(Queen's Bench Divisional Court)

A limited company was prosecuted for permitting one of its trailers to be used on the road with a defective braking system. When the trailer was being drawn by a motor lorry driven by one of its servants, the brake cable was not connected to the cable of the motor lorry so that the trailer brakes, which were operated by means of a lever in the driver's cabin in the lorry, were ineffective. It was proved that when the lorry and trailer left the company's premises earlier in the day the trailer brake cable was properly adjusted but the trailer boy, who was also a servant of the company, failed to reconnect it properly after the trailer had been disconnected from the lorry at a depot to be loaded with grain, and the driver had not taken any steps to check the connections. The company was convicted and appealed to the Divisional Court.

Held, the conviction would be quashed on the ground that before the company can be guilty of permitting something to be done, it must be proved that a responsible officer of the company did so permit that thing to be done. Also, the company could not be convicted of 'permitting' a user in contravention of the regulation unless it was proved that some person for whose criminal act it was responsible 'permitted', as opposed to 'committed', the user in contravention of the regulation. (See also *R v ICR Haulage Ltd*.)

Janaway v Salford Health Authority [1988] 3 All ER 1079
(House of Lords)

The appellant was employed by the health authority as a medical secretary and receptionist at a health centre. She refused to type a letter from a general practitioner at the health centre referring a patient to a consultant with a view to a possible termination of pregnancy under s1 of the Abortion Act 1967. She believed she came within s4(1) of the Act being entitled to exercise the right of conscientious objection. Refusing to type any such letters she was dismissed. In seeking judicial review she sought a declaration that by reason of her conscientious objection she was not under a duty to carry out work of such a nature. She was held by the judge not to be a person who was required to 'participate in any treatment' within the meaning of s4(1) of the Act and the Court of Appeal dismissed her further appeal.

Held, her appeal would be dismissed. The word 'participate' should be given its ordinary and natural meaning; 'participate in any treatment authorised by this Act' meant actually taking part in treatment administered in a hospital or other place approved in accordance with s1(3) of the 1967 Act for the purpose of terminating a pregnancy. (See also *Royal College of Nursing v Department of Health and Social Security*.)

Johnson v Director of Public Prosecutions [1994] Crim LR 673

The appellant, a squatter, was convicted of an offence under s1(1) of the Criminal Damage Act 1971. He broke a lock on the front door of a property, replacing it with his own. He then moved his belongings into the property. His contention was that he had a lawful excuse under s5(2)(b) of the Act believing his belongings were in need of immediate protection and that his actions were reasonable having regard to all the circumstances. The Crown Court concluded that his property had not been in need of immediate protection and that the appellant had no belief that they were.

Held, the appeal would be dismissed. Had the act of damage been committed to protect his property?; this question had to be approached on an objective basis. If 'yes', a subjective approach could be adopted to the question of whether or not the appellant honestly believed that the property was in need of immediate protection and whether or not the steps he took were reasonable having regard to all the circumstances. The Crown Court had been entitled to conclude that the appellant, in damaging the lock, has not acted in the belief that what he did was necessary to protect his property.

Johnson v Youden [1950] 1 All ER 300 (King's Bench Divisional Court)

Johnson, a solicitor, and two partners in his firm were charged with aiding and abetting. A builder had obtained a licence from a local authority to build a house, the licence providing that he should not sell at a price in excess of £1,025. In breach of the prohibition he agreed to sell the house to a railway porter for £1,275 and asked a firm of solicitors, in which Johnson and the two others were partners, to act as his solicitors for the sale. At the outset Johnson and his partners did not know of the prohibition but before completion the purchaser's solicitors pointed it out to Johnson who was dealing with the matter; nevertheless, they completed the sale of the house. The builder was convicted of the principal offence but Johnson and his partners were acquitted. The prosecution appealed to the Divisional Court.

Held, the acquittal of the two partners would be affirmed as they did not know of the essential matters which constituted the offence; but as Johnson knew of the infringement by the builder he was guilty of aiding and abetting, and the case would be remitted to the justices with a direction to convict.

Knuller (Publishing, Printing and Promotions) Ltd v Director of Public Prosecutions [1972] 2 All ER 898 (House of Lords)

The appellants, Knuller Ltd, Keen, Stansill and Hall, took part in the publication of a magazine, the *International Times*, which contained a wide variety of material thought to be of interest to those holding 'progressive views'. Much of the material was unobjectionable, but under the columns headed 'Males' there were some advertisements inserted by homosexuals with the express purpose of attracting answers from persons who would indulge in homosexual practices with the advertisers. Sometimes persons answering the advertisements were to communicate directly with the advertisers, sometimes they were to send their answers to the magazine from whence they would be forwarded to the advertisers. The magazine had a circulation of over 30,000 copies and a great many found their way into the hands of young students and schoolboys. They were convicted on two counts. First, of conspiring together and with the advertisers to induce readers to meet the advertisers for the purpose of sexual practices with intent to debauch and corrupt their morals, and second of conspiring together and with persons inserting lewd, disgusting and offensive advertisements in issues of the magazine to outrage public decency. The convictions were affirmed by the Court of Appeal and they appealed to the House of Lords contending that, inter alia, conspiracy to corrupt public morals was not an offence known to the law and *Shaw v Director of Public Prosecutions* should be reconsidered; secondly, the agreement to insert advertisements in the inside pages of a magazine which would be read by different persons individually and in different places could not amount to a conspiracy to outrage public decency.

—— 25 ——

Held, (1) the conviction on the first count would be affirmed as *Shaw's* case had established that conspiracy to corrupt public morals was an offence known to the law and should be followed. It was also stated that it would not be proper for the House in its judicial capacity to abolish the offence, Parliament alone being the proper authority to alter the law; *Shaw's* case had been properly decided and although by virtue of the Sexual Offences Act 1967 a homosexual act between adult males in private was no longer an offence, it did not follow that it was not open to a jury to say that to assist or to encourage persons to take part in such acts might be to corrupt them; and s2(4) of the Theatres Act 1968 acknowledged the existence of the offence; (2) the conviction on the second count should be quashed as, although there is an offence of outraging public decency and of conspiring to outrage public decency, the summing-up as a whole was defective and it would be unsafe to allow the conviction to stand. (See also *Shaw* v *Director of Public Prosecutions*.)

Kong Cheuk Kwan v The Queen [1985] Crim LR 787 (Privy Council)

The defendant (and others) were convicted of manslaughter following a collision between two hydrofoils. The judge had given a written direction to the jury on the ingredients of manslaughter by gross negligence stating that the relevant risk was the risk of causing some injury not necessarily serious but not so slight an ordinary prudent individual would feel justified in treating it as negligible. The Court of Appeal of Hong Kong dismissed his appeal and he appealed to the Judicial Committee of the Privy Council.

Held, allowing the appeal, the direction was wrong. One should have been given on the model of *R* v *Lawrence* [1981] 1 All ER 974. The jury should have been told to consider whether the (defendant's) navigation created an obvious and serious risk of causing physical damage to some other vessel and to persons travelling in the area of the collision. Had the defendant by his act either navigated without having given any thought to the possibility of that risk or, while recognising that the risk existed, taken that risk? The jury had been misdirected. The conviction would be quashed.

Lawrence v Commissioner of Police for the Metropolis [1971] 2 All ER 1253 (House of Lords)

On 1 September 1969 a Mr Occhi, an Italian who spoke little English, arrived at Victoria Station on his first visit to Britain. He went up to Lawrence, a taxi driver, and showed him a piece of paper on which an address in Ladbroke Grove was written. Lawrence said that it was very far and very expensive. Mr Occhi got into the taxi, took £1 out of his wallet and gave it to Lawrence who then, the wallet being still open, took a further £6 out of it. He then drove Mr Occhi to Ladbroke Grove. The correct lawful fare for the journey was in the region of 10s 6d (52½p). Lawrence was convicted of theft of the £6; the conviction was affirmed by the Court of Appeal and he appealed to the House of Lords contending that, inter alia, Mr Occhi had consented to the taking of the £6 and therefore the conviction could not stand.

Held, the appeal would be dismissed as there was a dishonest appropriation of the money with an intention permanently to deprive Mr Occhi of it. The House stated that: (1) on a charge of theft it is not necessary for the prosecution to establish that the appropriation was without the owner's consent; (2) belief, or the absence thereof, that the owner consented to the appropriation is relevant to the issue of dishonesty, not to the question whether or not there has been an appropriation; (3) proof that the owner consented to the appropriation will not suffice to show that there was no dishonesty if the owner's consent was given without full knowledge of the circumstances but it will be sufficient to show that the accused entertained the belief that in giving his consent the owner had full knowledge of the circumstances; (4) theft and obtaining by deception are not mutually exclusive and therefore a conviction for theft may be sustained even though the facts proved would also justify a conviction of obtaining by deception. (See also *R* v *Morris*, *R* v *Gomez* and *R* v *Hinks*.)

Lee Chun-Chuen v R [1963] 1 All ER 73 (Privy Council)

Lee Chun-Chuen was charged with murder and pleaded provocation. Together with the deceased, his father-in-law, he went to Hong Kong from the mainland of China and they set up business together. Some time later they quarrelled because he believed that the deceased had written to his daughter, Lee Chun-Chuen's wife, telling her that Lee Chun-Chuen was dead and that she should marry again, which she did. He wrote a letter to the deceased accusing him of malicious intervention and threatening to kill him. Finally, one day he laid in wait for him and battered him to death. In his summing-up, the trial judge told the jury that if the provocation caused Lee Chun to form an intention to kill or cause grievous bodily harm then the killing was murder. He was convicted and after an unsuccessful appeal to the Supreme Court of Hong Kong he appealed to the Privy Council.

Held, although the conviction would be affirmed on the ground that there was no substantial miscarriage of justice, there was a misdirection since the effect of what the judge said was to tell the jury that they must convict for murder or nothing.

Luc Thiet Thuan v The Queen [1996] 2 All ER 1033 (Privy Council)

The appellant was convicted of murder. He put forward evidence that following a fall that had rendered him unconscious, he was prone to explosive outbursts that temporarily rendered him incapable of controlling his temper. Expert evidence sought to show that he had suffered brain damage and he suffered from episodic dyscontrol condition. He sought to put forward the defence of provocation – his mental infirmity was a characteristic to be attributed to the reasonable person for the purposes of the objective test. The trial judge ruled that the evidence of mental infirmity was relevant only to the definition of diminished responsibility and declined to direct the jury on the basis that it formed any part of the definition of provocation.

Held, the appeal would be dismissed. Mental infirmity that impaired the appellant's power of self-control was inconsistent with the concept of the reasonable person. It could be taken into account if it formed the subject matter of taunts directed at him causing him to be provoked, and could therefore go towards determining the gravity of provocation. But if the appellant's submission was accepted it would result in diminished responsibility being imported into the definition of provocation as a characteristic to be attributed to the reasonable man, which cannot have been the intention of Parliament in enacting s3

Homicide Act 1957 when s2 introduced the new defence of diminished responsibility. (*Director of Public Prosecutions v Camplin* applied. *R v Ahluwalia*, *R v Dryden* and *R v Humphreys* doubted.)

M'Naghten's Case (1843) 10 C & F 200 (House of Lords)

M'Naghten shot Sir Robert Peel's private secretary and was charged with murder. He was acquitted on the ground of insanity. Questions were put by the House of Lords to the judges to determine the nature and extent of the unsoundness of mind which would serve as a defence to such a charge. Their reply included the following points: (1) if the accused did the act complained of knowing at the time he was acting contrary to the law, then notwithstanding a partial delusion regarding his purpose (such as acting with a view to producing some public benefit) he is nevertheless punishable; (2) the jurors should be told that every man is presumed to be sane, and to possess a sufficient degree of reason to be responsible for his crimes, until the contrary be proved to their satisfaction; and that to establish a defence on the ground of insanity, it must be clearly proved that, at the time of committing the act, the party accused was labouring under such a defect of reason, arising from disease of the mind, as not to know the nature and quality of the act he was doing, or, if he did know it, that he did not know he was doing what was wrong; (3) if a person acts under an insane delusion as to existing facts, then his responsibility must be considered as if the facts of the delusion were real; (4) that the medical expert may only be asked his opinion as to the accused's state of mind at the time of the act if the facts are admitted and the question is purely one of science. He should not be called to give evidence on matters of fact, which are for the jury to decide. (See also *Attorney-General for Northern Ireland v Gallagher* and *R v Sullivan*.)

Mancini v Director of Public Prosecutions [1941] 3 All ER 272 (House of Lords)

A fight broke out in an establishment called the Palm Beach Bottle Party and, as Mancini struggled with one Fletcher, one Distleman went to Fletcher's aid. Distleman seized Mancini's shoulder or arm, and aimed a blow at him, whereupon Mancini whipped out his dagger and inflicted a fatal blow on Distleman. Mancini was convicted of murder and appealed to the House of Lords.

Held, his appeal would be dismissed because Distleman's action did not constitute provocation of a kind which would justify a verdict of manslaughter arising from Mancini's use of the dagger. 'Provocation to have that result must be such as temporarily deprives the person provoked of the power of self-control, as the result of which he commits the unlawful act which causes death. ... The test to be applied is that of the effect of the provocation upon a reasonable man ... so that an unusually excitable or pugnacious individual is not entitled to rely on provocation which would not have led an ordinary person to act as he did. In applying the test, it is of particular importance (i) to consider whether a sufficient interval has elapsed since the provocation to allow a reasonable man time to cool, and (ii) to take into account the instrument with which the homicide was effected, for to retort in the heat of passion induced by provocation by a simple blow is a very different thing from making use of a deadly instrument like a concealed dagger. In short, the mode of resentment must bear a reasonable relationship to the provocation, if the offence is to be reduced to manslaughter' (*per* VISCOUNT SIMON LC). (See also *R* v *Brown* (1972).)

Masterson v Holden [1986] 3 All ER 39 (Queen's Bench Divisional Court)

The defendants, both men, were convicted of using insulting behaviour whereby a breach of the peace might have been occasioned contrary to s54(13) of the Metropolitan Police Act 1839 (now repealed by the Public Order Act 1986 s40(3), Sch 3). In the early hours of the morning at a bus stop they were seen by two passing couples kissing, cuddling and one was fondling the other. They appeared to be unaware of other people in the vicinity. The evidence showed that the two couples were affected by the defendant's behaviour. On appeal they contended that conduct, to be insulting, had to be directed at another person(s); since they were unaware of others, their conduct could not have been directed at another.

Held, the appeal would be dismissed. Conduct fell within s54(13) if other people were present who might be insulted by their behaviour. There was evidence to show that the behaviour had been insulting. The justices were entitled to infer that the defendants must have been aware that other people might be in the vicinity.

Metropolitan Police Commissioner v Charles [1976] 3 All ER 112 (House of Lords)

The appellant, Charles, had opened a current account at the branch of a bank. He had authority from the branch manager to overdraw his account up to £100. The manager issued him with a cheque card which contained an undertaking by the bank to honour cheques. The appellant, one evening at a gambling club, drew cheques for a total of £750, each backed by a cheque card. He had no funds on his current account to meet that sum or the amount by which it exceeded the overdraft. He was charged with obtaining a pecuniary advantage by deception contrary to s16(1) of the Theft Act 1968. He was convicted and appealed, contending that when a cheque was drawn which was backed by a cheque card there were no grounds for implying a representation to the payee that the drawer had authority from the bank to draw such a cheque, since, in view of the undertaking contained in the card, the payee had no interest in the question whether the drawer had authority to draw the cheques.

Held, where the holder of a cheque card presented the card together with a cheque made out in accordance with the conditions of the card, it was open to the court to infer that representation had been made by the drawer that he had authority as between himself and the bank to use the card in order to oblige the bank to honour the cheque. If the representation was false and the payee had accepted the cheque it was open to the court to find that the payee had been induced to accept the cheque by reason of the false representation. The drawer had thus gained a pecuniary advantage by deception. It followed the appellant had been properly convicted and the appeal would be dismissed.

National Rivers Authority v Alfred McAlpine Homes East Ltd
[1994] 4 All ER 286 (Queen's Bench Divisional Court)

The justices dismissed an information laid against the respondent company alleging pollution of controlled waters (within the meaning of s104 of the Water Resources Act 1991). In holding that there was no case to answer, the justices held that while s85 of the 1991 Act, which sets up the offence ('A person contravenes this section if he causes or knowingly permits any poisonous, noxious or polluting water ... to enter any controlled waters'), appeared to create an offence of strict liability, the appellants had failed to show that the company itself was liable. Cement had been washed into a stream when a water feature was being constructed on a residential development. The site agent and manager had both accepted responsibility for the pollution but neither was regarded as sufficiently senior to enable them to be categorised as persons whose acts were the acts of the company. The authority appealed.

Held, the appeal would be allowed. Had the company caused the pollution of the water? Had some operation or chain of operations carried out under the company's control led to the pollution? A company would be criminally liable for causing pollution which resulted from the acts or omissions of its employees acting within the course of their employment when the pollution occured. It did not matter whether it could be said they were exercising the controlling mind and will of the company, except where some third party acted in a way so as to break the chain of causation. The pollution had come about as a result of the company's operation. The justices could not properly find no case to answer. (See also *Seaboard Offshore Ltd v Secretary of State for Transport, Sherras v De Rutzen* and *Sweet v Parsley*.)

Pilgram v Rice-Smith [1977] 2 All ER 658
(Queen's Bench Divisional Court)

The defendants, a shop assistant and her friend, the customer, were convicted of theft contrary to s1(1) of the Theft Act 1968. The assistant marked a quantity of meat with an understated price being 83½p less than the price at which it should have been sold. At the checkout the customer paid one sum for all her items of shopping including the meat. The defendants were jointly charged with stealing the meat valued at 83½p, which belonged to the store. The convictions were quashed at the Crown Court on the basis that since the defendants had not been charged with the theft of the whole meat it was impossible for the prosecution to prove what part of the meat had been appropriated. The prosecutor appealed.

Held, the Crown Court had been wrong to state that there was no case to answer. The sale of meat had been a nullity as the assistant had no authority to sell the meat at an undervalue and a fraud had operated from the beginning of the transaction. Since there had been no sale it was open to the justices to convict the defendants of theft of all the meat even though they had been charged with the theft of part of it.

R v Acott [1997] 1 All ER 706 (House of Lords)

The defendant was convicted of murdering his mother, P. He stated that she had had a fall whilst under the influence of alcohol and had suffered injuries when he had tried to help her. The prosecution suggested that the defendant had argued with P. The trial judge suggested that alcohol may have caused P to act in a way that led him to lose his self-control. The Court of Appeal dismissed his appeal on the ground that the trial judge should have left the defence of provocation to the jury. Leave to appeal to the House of Lords was granted upon the following certified question: 'In a prosecution for murder, before the judge is obliged to leave the issue of provocation to the jury, must there be some evidence, either direct or inferential, as to what was either done or said to provoke the alleged loss of self-control?'

Held, the appeal would be dismissed. Evidence of specific acts or words of provocation which resulted in the defendant's loss of self-control was needed before a judge was required to leave the defence of provocation to a jury. The evidence should be such as to show that the killing might have resulted from the defendant's uncontrolled reaction to the provocation. Speculative possibility was not a sufficient ground for leaving the defence to the jury. (See *Lee Chun-Chuen* v *R* and *R* v *Marks*.)

R v Adomako [1994] 3 All ER 79 (House of Lords)

The defendant was convicted of manslaughter. He was the anaesthetist assisting during an eye operation. He failed to notice that the tube from the ventilator supplying oxygen to the patient had become disconnected before damage to the patient had become irreversible. The patient died following a cardiac arrest. An unsuccessful appeal was made to the Court of Appeal on the ground that the judge had wrongly directed the jury by applying the test of gross negligence for manslaughter. For a conviction for involuntary manslaughter by breach of duty the Crown needed to prove (i) the existence of the duty, (ii) a breach of the duty causing death, and (iii) gross negligence which a jury considered justified a criminal conviction. The judge had directed the jury properly and the evidence had justified a verdict of guilty. The following point of law of general public importance was certified for consideration by the House of Lords: 'In cases of manslaughter by gross negligence not involving driving but involving a breach of duty it is a sufficient direction to the jury to adopt the gross negligence test set out by the Court of Appeal in the present case following *R* v *Bateman* (1925) 19 Cr App R 8 and *Andrews* v *Director of Public Prosecutions* [1937] AC 576 without reference to the test of recklessness as defined in *R* v *Lawrence* [1982] AC 510 or as adapted to the circumstances of the case?'

Held, the appeal would be dismissed. A defendant was properly convicted of involuntary manslaughter by breach of duty if the jury were directed, and had found, that the defendant was in breach of a duty of care towards the victim who died, that the breach of duty caused the death of the victim, and that the breach of duty was such as amounted to gross negligence and therefore a crime. It depended upon the seriousness of the breach of duty committed by the defendant as to whether such amounted to gross negligence. Regard had to be given to all the circumstances in which the defendant was placed when the breach occurred and whether, having regard to the risk of death involved, the conduct of the defendant was so bad in all the circumstances as to amount in the jury's judgment to a criminal act or omission. On the facts the jury had been properly directed.

R v Ahluwalia [1992] 4 All ER 889 (Court of Appeal)

The appellant was convicted of murder. She had entered into an arranged marriage with her husband. From the start she had suffered from his violent and abusive behaviour; he had tried once to run her down, and threatened to kill her on other occasions. He also taunted the appellant about his affair with another woman. One evening, following threats to beat her, the appellant set fire to her husband's bedroom as he slept; he later died from burns. The trial judge directed the jury that the defence of provocation was available if there had been a sudden and temporary loss of self-control as the result of acts which would have caused a reasonable person with her characteristics as a married Asian woman to lose her self-control. On her appeal she contended that she suffered from 'battered woman syndrome', the result of years of violence and humiliation suffered at her husband's hands – this all amounted to provocation.

Held, there being fresh medical evidence as to the state of the appellant's mind at the time of the killing with reference to s2 of the Homicide Act 1957 (diminished responsibility), the verdict was unsafe, the appeal would be allowed and a retrial ordered. As to the defence of provocation – 'The phrase "sudden and temporary loss of self-control" encapsulates an essential ingredient of the defence of provocation in a clear and readily understandable phrase. It serves to underline that the defence is concerned with the actions of an individual who is not, at the moment when he or she acts violently, master of his or her own mind … it is open to the judge, when deciding whether there is any evidence of provocation to be left to the jury and open to the jury when considering such evidence, to take account of the interval between the provocative conduct and the reaction of the defendant to it … in some cases, such an interval may wholly undermine the defence of provocation; that, however, depends entirely on the facts of the individual case and is not a principle of law' *(per* LORD TAYLOR OF GOSFORTH CJ). (See also *Director of Public Prosecutions* v *Camplin* and *R* v *Thornton (No 2)*.)

R v Ali [1989] Crim LR 736 (Court of Appeal)

The defendant, A, aged 20, was convicted of murder. He was attacked by the victim who punched him and knocked him to the ground. A then saw others attacking the victim and, in his interview with the police, said that he stabbed the victim with a knife, but no one saw A do this. A argued there was no satisfactory evidence that he had stabbed the victim or that the knife had gone in; that he had been provoked. On appeal it was submitted that the judge had misdirected the jury on provocation by failing to focus the jury's attention on the reaction of a reasonable 20 year old.

Held, the appeal would be dismissed. It had been held in *Director of Public Prosecutions* v *Camplin* that the reasonable man under s3 of the Homicide Act 1957 was one having the power of self-control to be expected of an ordinary person of the same sex and age as the accused. The relevant question here was whether a 20 year old would be more likely to be influenced to react to provocation than any other reasonable man. On the present facts the court could not see that a jury would have seen any difference between a reasonable man of 20 and a reasonable man of any other age. It was not necessary for the judge to make particular mention of A's age concerning provocation.

R v Ali [1995] Crim LR 303 (Court of Appeal)

The appellant was convicted of robbery. He owed money to his drug supplier, X, who he knew to be a man of violence. X gave the appellant a gun and told him to rob a bank or building society; if he did not he would be killed or seriously injured. The trial judge asked the jury to consider whether the appellant, by buying drugs from X, had placed himself in a position where he knew he could be forced by X to commit a crime. He appealed on the basis that the trial judge had not properly addressed them on the matter of duress.

Held, the appeal would be dismissed. If the appellant associated with another committing a criminal offence and knew it was likely that this person would order the appellant to commit criminal acts, the appellant could not rely on duress if he was later ordered to commit offences. (See also *R v Hegarty* and *R v Horne*.)

R v Allen [1985] 2 All ER 641 (House of Lords)

The defendant was convicted of dishonestly making off without paying a hotel bill with intent to avoid payment, contrary to s3(1) of the Theft Act 1978. He argued that he was going to pay the bill and his intention was merely to delay or defer payment until he received the proceeds of certain business ventures. The judge directed the jury that under s3(1) a person made off 'with intent to avoid payment' if he intended to avoid payment when the bill was due, in this case when the defendant left the hotel. The Court of Appeal quashed the conviction. The Crown appealed to the House of Lords.

Held, the Crown's appeal would be dismissed. An 'intent to avoid payment' requires an intention to avoid payment permanently. An intention to delay or defer payment was not enough to establish the offence of making off without payment.

R v Allen [1988] Crim LR 698 (Court of Appeal)

The appellant was convicted of buggery and indecent assault. He argued that he was acting in a state of automatism being so drunk at the time that he was not responsible for his actions. He had taken a quantity of alcohol, the alcoholic content of some of which he had not appreciated. On appeal it was argued that the judge had been wrong in ruling that involuntary drunkenness could not be a defence to a crime of non-specific intent.

Held, the appeal would be dismissed. The judge had been correct in so far as there was no evidence that the drinking was other than voluntary. Where a defendant knows he is drinking alcohol, that drinking does not become involuntary because he does not know the exact nature or strength of the alcohol he is drinking. (See also *Director of Public Prosecutions v Majewski*.)

R v Anderson and Morris [1966] 2 All ER 644 (Court of Criminal Appeal)

Anderson was charged with murder and Morris was charged with manslaughter. One day a man named Welch met Anderson's wife and she took him back to her flat where he tried to strangle her; she ran into the street followed by Welch and told Morris what had happened, whereupon he fought with Welch. When Mrs Anderson later told her husband what had happened he became very angry and took a knife from the kitchen in the presence of Morris and another man and went with Morris and Mrs Anderson in a car to find Welch. Welch was found at an hotel and Anderson attacked him with his fists and stabbed him with the knife, causing his death; while Anderson and Welch were fighting Morris stood at Welch's back and did not take any definite part in the fight. In his summing-up the trial judge told the jury that if there was a common design to attack Welch but Anderson's act in taking the knife and deciding to kill Welch was not part of the common design, then Anderson would be guilty of murder and Morris of manslaughter since he took part in the attack on Welch. They were convicted and appealed to the Court of Criminal Appeal.

Held, a new trial would be ordered in the case of Anderson but Morris's conviction would be quashed on the ground that the summing-up was wrong and a misdirection since the principle is that where two persons embark on a joint enterprise and one goes beyond what was agreed as part of the common enterprise, his co-adventurer is not liable for the consequences of that unauthorised act. (See also *Chan Wing-Siu* v *The Queen.*)

R v Arnold [1997] 4 All ER 1 (Court of Appeal)

The defendant was convicted of theft in relation to two bills of exchange. He negotiated them with a discount house, contrary to an agreement that he would present them for payment upon maturity. He was then to have repaid H and J who had lodged the said bills with the defendant as security, enabling them to obtain fresh bills of exchange made out in his favour. This was to facilitate H and J who had greed to act as franchisees in the defendant's catering business. The bills were subsequently presented for payment with no obligation to reimburse H and J. The defendant appealed on the grounds that the paper on which the bills of exchange had been made out belonged to him and had therefore not been property belonging to another. Even if the bills of exchange had been property belonging to another, he had had no intention to permanently deprive either H or J of them.

Held, the appeal would be dismissed. The bills of exchange were, by virtue of s5(3) Theft Act 1968, property belonging to another and the defendant by negotiating them with a discount house was treating them as his own to dispose of, regardless of the rights of H and J.

R v Arobieke [1988] Crim LR 314 (Court of Appeal)

The appellant was convicted of manslaughter. The victim K, was terrified of the appellant. K seeing the appellant, made his way to the railway station and got on a train. He then saw the appellant on the platform. He sought to make his escape by getting off the train, and crossing the line, but K was electrocuted. It was said that the appellant's mere presence at the station, taking into account the history of unlawful acts and threats, was sufficient for manslaughter because it recklessly caused in K an apprehension of immediate and unlawful violence. There was some evidence that the appellant had looked into the train. The jury were told they should find certain facts before they could convict the appellant of manslaughter including (1) that the appellant had looked for K intending to physically hurt or threaten him with violence, (2) that K saw the appellant and feared a physical attack, (3) that the appellant's conduct in relation to K was such that any reasonable person would recognise it as being likely to subject K to at least the risk of some, albeit not serious, harm.

Held, the appeal would be allowed. The appellant had not carried out an unlawful act looking at the train without knowing if K was aboard, so (1) could not be shown; nor could (2) and (3) be shown against the appellant.

R v Aston; R v Hadley [1970] 3 All ER 1045 (Court of Appeal)

The appellants were convicted under s16(2)(a) of the Theft Act 1968 (see now s2 of the Theft Act 1978) of seeking to obtain a pecuniary advantage by deception. The appellants had sought to place a bet on a greyhound race due to start at 1.05 pm and they wished to place £70 for a win on the dog in trap 1. The counter clerk's limit was £10 so the matter was dealt with by the manager of the betting shop. The race had already started before the appellants had given the manager the sum of money, and the appellant Aston proceeded to count the notes with extreme slowness purporting to select £70 out of a larger total in his possession. No money was paid over to the manager and when it was obvious that the dog from trap 1 was not going to win (the race was broadcast) the appellants gathered up the money and left the betting shop. The manager caught up with them after half a mile or so and the charge of deception was preferred under s16(2)(a) which provided: 'Any debt or charge for which he makes himself liable or is or may become liable (including one not legally enforceable) is reduced or in whole or in part evaded or deferred.' The prosecution had to prove there was a debt for which the appellants had made themselves liable and that they had evaded it by deception.

Held, there was no deception, as the conduct of the appellants in the slow counting of the money could not safely or satisfactorily be presented to, or accepted by, the jury as a deception involving a representation that, as it was put, the appellants intended to pay immediately, and other difficulties arose in attempting to put the case into the framework of s16(1)(a). The court stated that if the indictment had been framed by reference to s16(2)(c) the jury might well have had no difficulty in finding that there was a deception. The appeal was allowed.

R v Attewell-Hughes (1991) 93 Cr App R 132 (Court of Appeal)

The appellant, a hotel manager, was convicted of evading a liability by deception with intent to make permanent default, contrary to s2(1)(b) of the Theft Act 1978, by dishonestly inducing the payees of cheques to wait for payment by a false representation that the cheques were valid. He opened an account in the name of the hotel at a bank, which made it clear that it would not grant an overdraft facility on the account. However, the appellant wrote a number of cheques on that account for goods and services supplied to the hotel when the funds available in the account were not sufficient to cover the cheques. At his trial the appellant submitted that the Crown's case could not be sustained because he was charged with intending to make default on his own liabilities when in fact the liabilities in the counts charged were those of the hotel owner. The judge ruled that it was irrelevant whether the liabilities were those of the appellant or the hotel owner for the purposes of a charge under s2(1)(b) and directed the jury that the question for them to decide was whether the appellant was dishonest irrespective of whether the liability he had evaded was his or another's. He appealed against his conviction on the ground that the judge had wrongly directly the jury.

Held, the appeal would be allowed. Section 2(1)(b) of the 1978 Act envisaged two different modes of committing the offence of evading a liability by deception, namely either (i) by the defendant intending to make default on his own liability or (ii) by his intending to make permanent default on behalf of another or to let another make permanent default. The question whether the liabilities were the appellant's or the hotel owner's was clearly material to the jury's consideration of the central issue of dishonesty, since the question of dishonesty might appear in quite a different light depending on whether it was being alleged that he intended to make permanent default on his own behalf or whether it was being alleged that he intended to make permanent default on behalf of another or to let another make permanent default. It followed that the judge's direction to the jury that the question was one of dishonesty and it did not matter whether the liabilities were the appellant's or the hotel owner's was incorrect.

R v Bailey [1983] 2 All ER 503 (Court of Appeal)

The appellant was convicted of causing grievous bodily harm with intent contrary to s18 of the Offences against the Person Act 1861. In the alternative he had been charged with the unlawful wounding of the victim contrary to s20 of the 1861 Act. He was a diabetic receiving insulin treatment. His girlfriend left him for another man. The appellant went round to see him; after discussing the situation he stated he felt unwell, took a mixture of sugar and water but ate nothing. A short while later he hit the other man on the head with an iron bar, severely injuring him. His defence was that he had been unable to control his actions and had acted in a state of automatism caused by hypoglycaemia which had come about following his failure to eat after drinking the sugar and water mixture; he did not have the specific intent to cause grievous bodily harm for the purpose of s18 of the 1861 Act.

Held, the appeal would be dismissed. 'It is now quite clear that, even if the incapacity of mind is self induced by the voluntary taking of drugs or alcohol, the specific intent to kill or cause grievous bodily harm may be negatived; see *DPP v Majewski* ... Automatism resulting from intoxication as a result of a voluntary ingestion of alcohol or dangerous drugs does not negative the mens rea necessary for crimes of basic intent because the conduct of the accused is reckless and recklessness is enough to constitute the necessary mens rea in assault cases where no specific intent forms part of the charge ... there may be material distinctions between a man who consumes alcohol or takes dangerous drugs and one who fails to take sufficient food after insulin to avert hypoglycaemia ... if he does appreciate the risk that such a failure may lead to aggressive, unpredictable and uncontrollable conduct and he nevertheless deliberately runs the risk or otherwise disregards it, this will amount to recklessness ... self-induced automatism, other than that due to intoxication from alcohol or drugs, may provide a defence to crimes of basic intent. The question in each case will be whether the prosecution has proved the necessary element of recklessness ... Although [in this case] an episode of sudden transient loss of consciousness or awareness was theoretically possible, it was quite inconsistent with the graphic description that the appellant gave to the police both orally and in his written statement. There was abundant evidence that he had armed himself with the iron bar and gone to [the other man's] house for the purpose of attacking him ...' (*per* GRIFFITHS LJ). (See also *Director of Public Prosecutions* v *Majewski* and *R* v *Quick; R* v *Paddison*.)

R v *Baker and Wilkins* [1997] Crim LR 497 (Court of Appeal)

The appellants were convicted of criminal damage. They were fearful that the daughter of one of the appellants was being unlawfully detained in the house occupied by the child's natural father and that the father planned to take the child out of the jurisdiction to deny her mother access. The appellants broke into the house through the front door. The trial judge rejected a submission that the desire to rescue the child could be a lawful excuse. On appeal the appellants contended the defence of necessity should have been made available, even though there was no immediate threat of death or serious physical harm; that s3 Criminal Law Act 1967 gave them justification for what they did; and that s5 Criminal Damage Act 1971 enabled them to plead 'lawful excuse' for their actions when trying to protect a child.

Held, the appeal would be dismissed. Section 5(2)(b) Criminal Damage Act 1971 related to damage caused to protect property; a child is not property. The court was not prepared to extend the defence of necessity to circumstances where the harm that the appellants contemplated and sought to prevent was psychological as opposed to physical. As to s3 Criminal Law Act 1967, there had to be some objective evidence that an offence was being committed. In this instance there had been no evidence that the detention of the appellant's daughter actually amounted to an offence. (See also *R* v *Ireland; R* v *Burstow* and *R* v *Chan-Fook*.)

R v *Ball* [1989] Crim LR 730 (Court of Appeal)

The appellant was acquitted of murder but convicted of constructive manslaughter. Following a long-running dispute between the appellant and his neighbour G, G called upon him to investigate the disappearance of her vehicle; the appellant behaved abusively and aggressively and later shot G, who died. It was the appellant's contention that he only intended to frighten G, and that he thought he had loaded the gun with a blank cartridge. He had had no intention to kill or cause harm. He appealed against his conviction of manslaughter and contended that the judge had misdirected the jury by withdrawing from them consideration of the appellant's knowledge or belief that the cartridge was only blank. While firing the gun at a range of 12 yards was an unlawful assault it was submitted that the objective assessment of danger must be based on the appellant's mistaken belief that he was firing a blank and not on the actual fact that he was firing a live cartridge. The issue of whether or not this belief was a reasonable one was relevant to the question of whether he had been guilty of manslaughter through criminal negligence, the issue the judge had not left to the jury.

Held, the appeal would be dismissed. Where the act was unlawful, the question for the jury was whether it was also dangerous in the sense that the sober and reasonable person would inevitably realise that it would subject the victim to the risk of some harm, albeit not serious harm. In manslaughter arising from an unlawful and dangerous act the accused's state of mind was relevant only to establish (a) that the act was committed intentionally and (b) that it was an unlawful act. Once (a) and (b) were established, the question whether the act was dangerous was to be judged not by what the appellant appreciated but what the sober and reasonable man would have appreciated.

R v *Bamborough* [1996] Crim LR 744 (Court of Appeal)

The appellant, B, together with T, the principal offender, were convicted of the murder of P. They went to P's house intending to effect a robbery. B knew T had a gun but did not believe it to be loaded. T shot P in the thigh; P also suffered severe head injuries during the robbery consistent to being 'pistol whipped'. P bled to death from the gunshot wound. Although B had contemplated T causing grievous bodily harm to P, he had not contemplated P being shot or suffering grievous bodily harm which was life threatening. B argued he should have been convicted of manslaughter.

Held, the appeal would be dismissed. Since B had contemplated grievous bodily harm as a possible outcome of a common design, that was sufficient to substantiate B's conviction for murder as an accomplice. (See also *Chan Wing-Siu v R.*)

R v *Baxter* [1971] 2 All ER 359 (Court of Appeal)

The appellant was charged with attempting to obtain property by deception contrary to s15 of the Theft Act 1968. He posted letters in Northern Ireland to football pool promoters in England falsely claiming that he correctly forecast the results of football matches and was entitled to winnings. He contended that when the letters were posted in Northern Ireland the attempt was complete and as he had never left this area during the relevant period the attempt had not been committed within the jurisdiction of the English courts.

Held, the attempt was committed within the jurisdiction because an offender could be said to be committing an attempt at every moment of the period between the commission of the proximate act necessary to constitute the attempt and the moment when the attempt failed; accordingly the accused was attempting to commit the offence of obtaining by deception when the letter reached its destination within England and thus the offence was committed within the jurisdiction of the English courts. Alternatively, it could be said that the accused made arrangements for the transport and delivery of the letter, essential parts of the attempt, within the jurisdiction; the presence of the accused within the jurisdiction was not an essential element of offences committed in England.

R v *Belfon* [1976] 3 All ER 46 (Court of Appeal)

The appellant attacked another man with a razor causing him serious injury. He was convicted of wounding with intent to do grievous bodily harm, contrary to s18 of the Offences against the Person Act 1861, and appealed. The basis of the appeal was that the direction of the judge was wrong in law. The judge at the trial directed the jury on the meaning of 'intent' by saying that a person intends the consequences of his voluntary act in each of two quite separate cases; first when he desires those consequences and secondly when he foresees that they are likely to follow from his act but commits the act recklessly irrespective of appreciating that those results will follow.

Held, in order to establish an offence under s18 it was necessary to prove that the acts in question had been committed by the accused with intent to cause grievous bodily harm; the fact that the accused had foreseen that such harm was likely to result from his acts, or that he had been reckless whether such harm would result, did not constitute the necessary intent. The judge's direction was therefore wrong in law. The appeal would be allowed, the conviction quashed and a conviction for unlawful wounding substituted.

R v Bevans [1988] Crim LR 236 (Court of Appeal)

The appellant was convicted of blackmail contrary to s21 of the Theft Act 1968. He threatened to shoot a doctor if he was not given an injection to ease the pain he had, being crippled with osteoarthritis. The judge directed the jury that the prosecution had to prove a demand for property; the phrase 'with a view to gain for himself' related to 'money or other property' (s34(2) of the 1968 Act) and that the drug was 'property'. It was contended that the judge had misdirected the jury.

Held, the appeal would be dismissed. The drug used in the injection was property; there was a 'gain' for the appellant in that he would get relief from pain, that there was no economic gain was immaterial.

R v Bingham [1991] Crim LR 433 (Court of Appeal)

The appellant, a diabetic, was convicted of theft. He took a can of coke and sandwiches worth £1.16 while he had £90 in his pocket. He had paid for one can of coke. When leaving the store he was stopped. His response to questions was 'no comment'. He stated he was suffering from hypoglycaemia and was unaware of his actions. The judge did not allow that defence to go before the jury.

Held, the appeal would be allowed. The judge should have decided whether, on the evidence, there was a prima facie case for the jury to decide whether the appellant was suffering from the effects of hypoglycaemia. If he was, had the Crown shown that the appellant had had the necessary intent for theft? There was some evidence that he might have been suffering from a low blood-sugar level. It should have been for the jury to weigh up the evidence. That the jury was unable to do so was a material irregularity. (See also *R v Quick*; compare *R v Bailey*.)

R v Blaue [1975] 3 All ER 446 (Court of Appeal)

A girl aged 18 was a Jehovah's Witness. She professed the tenets of the sect and lived her life by them. One evening the appellant went to her house and asked her for sexual intercourse. She refused and the appellant attacked her with a knife, inflicting four serious wounds one of which pierced her lung. She was taken to hospital and was told by the surgical registrar that she would have to have an operation, but prior to this there would have to be a blood transfusion. She was also told that if she did not have the blood transfusion she would die. The deceased refused the blood transfusion saying that it was contrary to her religious beliefs as a Jehovah's Witness and she did not care if she did die. She died the following day. The appellant was acquitted of murder but convicted of manslaughter on the ground of diminished responsibility; he was also convicted of wounding with intent to cause grievous bodily harm and indecent assault. He appealed against the conviction for manslaughter contending that the refusal to have a blood transfusion was unreasonable and broke the chain of causation between the stabbing and the death.

Held, the appeal should be dismissed as it was the policy of the law that a person who used violence on another had to take his victim as he found him, and it is not open to an assailant to assert that the victim's religious beliefs, which inhibited the victim from seeking certain kinds of treatment, were unreasonable. The court also said that the death of the victim was caused by loss of blood as a result of the stab wounds inflicted by the appellant, and refusal of the blood transfusion did not break the causal connection between the stabbing and the death. Further, the jury were entitled to find that the stab wounds were an operative or substantial cause of the death. (See also *R v Dalby* and *R v Malcherek; R v Steel*.)

R v Bloxham [1982] 1 All ER 582 (House of Lords)

The appellant pleaded guilty to handling stolen goods contrary to s22(1) of the Theft Act 1968. He sold to an unidentified third party a car which he had had to buy but had come to suspect to be stolen when the registration documents were not produced. He argued he had not disposed of or realised the car 'for the benefit of another person' and therefore there was no offence under s22(1). The car had been sold for his own benefit; the purchaser did not come within the ambit of 'another person' who would be the thief who stole the car or an original handler or receiver of it. The trial judge decided that the unknown purchaser did fall within s22(1) and that he had derived a benefit by having use of the car albeit without a valid title to it. The Court of Appeal upheld the judge's ruling.

Held, the appeal would be allowed and the decision of the Court of Appeal reversed. A purchaser, for the purposes of s22(1), could not be 'another person' for whose benefit goods were realised or sold since it was the purchase, not the sale, which was for the purchaser's benefit. The purchase of goods by a person could not be described as a disposal or realisation of the goods 'by' him.

R v Bogacki [1973] 2 All ER 864 (Court of Appeal)

At about 3.45 am on New Year's Day 1972 Bogacki, Tillwach and Cox, who had been having a lot to drink at a New Year's Eve party, went to a bus garage in London and tried to change a 50p piece in order to buy cigarettes from a machine. They were refused change and told to go away. As they went they boarded a single decker bus which was standing on the forecourt of the garage. One of them turned the engine over with the starter as if to start it. After three or four minutes they left the garage quite openly and walked to a police station where they were given change for the 50p piece which had been refused at the bus station. Very shortly thereafter they were arrested. The three men were convicted of attempting to take a motor vehicle without authority, contrary to s12 of the Theft Act 1968, and appealed.

Held, the convictions should be quashed as a result of a misdirection in his summing-up by the trial judge with regard to the meaning of the word 'take', which word, he said, suggests the acquisition of possession. The court stated that 'take' is equivalent to 'use' and should be given its ordinary and natural meaning and mere unauthorised user of itself constitutes an offence against s12. It was further held that before there can be a conviction for the complete offence it must be shown that he took the vehicle, that is, that there was an unauthorised taking of possession or control of the vehicle by him adverse to the rights of the true owner or person otherwise entitled to such possession or control, coupled with some movement, however small, of that vehicle following such unauthorised taking.

R v Bolton (1991) 84 Cr App R 74 (Court of Appeal)

The appellant was convicted on two counts of conspiracy to procure the execution of a valuable security by deception, contrary to s1(1) of the Criminal Law Act 1977. He had, with others, through false letters and documents, procured mortgage advances for others from building societies, obtaining a commission. Evidence on how the building societies might have used telegraphic or electronic transfers was unclear. The judge ruled that a telegraphic transfer did not fall within the definition of 'valuable security' in s20(3) of the Theft Act 1968. The jury needed to be satisfied that there was a conspiracy to procure the building societies to execute valuable securities representing mortgage advances; there was inadequate direction on this.

Held, the appeal would be allowed. What was agreed to be done by the conspirators was all-important. It had not been left to the jury to determine the question whether it was part of the conspiracy to execute valuable securities representing mortgage advances. Per curiam: Obtaining a mortgage advance by deception dishonestly for another could well amount to an offence under s15 of the Theft Act 1968. For an offence under s20(2) of the 1968 Act something had to be created which could be said to have been executed as a valuable security. (See also *R v Kassim*.)

R v Bonner [1970] 2 All ER 97 (Court of Appeal)

Bonner and others were convicted of theft of property from one Webb contrary to s1(1) of the Theft Act 1968. Bonner and Webb were partners and the property alleged to have been stolen was property of the partnership. It was argued for the appellant that the mere taking away of partnership property, even with the intention of keeping the other partner permanently out of possession of it, would not per se suffice to amount to theft.

Held, there may be an 'appropriation' by a partner within the meaning of the 1968 Act and that in the proper case there is nothing in law to prevent his being convicted of the theft of partnership property. Nevertheless, the court had come to the conclusion that the combination of circumstances in the case were such that the verdict of the jury was unsafe and unsatisfactory and the appeals would be allowed.

R v Bourne [1938] 3 All ER 615 (Court of Criminal Appeal)

A girl of fourteen years of age was raped with great violence and the accused, a surgeon of the highest skill, openly performed an operation of abortion on her in a London hospital. He performed the operation with the consent of the girl's parents as an act of charity, without fee or reward, and after consulting another doctor. On examining the girl he had formed the view that the continuance of her pregnancy would cause her serious injury and lead to her being a physical wreck for the rest of her life. Nevertheless he was charged under s58 of the Offences against the Person Act 1861 with unlawfully procuring the abortion. MACNAGHTEN J directed the jury: 'No person ought to be convicted under s58 of the Act of 1861 unless the jury are satisfied the act was not done in good faith for the purpose only of preserving the life of the mother ... Take a reasonable view of the words "for the preservation of the life of the mother". I do not think that it is contended that these words mean merely for the preservation of the life of the mother from instant death ... if the doctor is of opinion, on reasonable grounds and with adequate knowledge, that the probable consequence of the continuance of the pregnancy will be to make the woman a physical or mental wreck, the jury are quite entitled to take the view that the doctor, who, in these circumstances, and that honest belief, operates, is operating for the purpose of preserving the life of the woman.' The accused was found not guilty. (See now Abortion Act 1967, s1 as amended by s37 of the Human Fertilisation and Embryology Act 1990.) See also *R v Smith (John)*, *Janaway v Salford Health Authority* and *Royal College of Nursing v Department of Health and Social Security*.

R v Bowen [1996] 4 All ER 837 (Court of Appeal)

The appellant, who had an intelligence quotient of 68, was convicted of obtaining goods on credit by deception. He said he had been forced to commit the offences having been threatened by two men that his home would be petrol bombed if he did not. The trial judge followed the model direction in *R v Graham* [1982] 1 WLR 294 on the issue of duress per minas. As regards the characteristics of the accused to be attributed to the reasonable person, the trial judge did not allow the defence's argument that the appellant's low IQ was a characteristic that could have affected his ability to withstand threats.

Held, the appeal would be dismissed. A low IQ was not a characteristic that would make the reasonable person less courageous or able to resist threats. A timid or vulnerable person, not suffering from a recognised psychiatric impairment, would not be characteristics to be taken into account when attributing characteristics to the reasonable person. If there was such an impairment, it would only be taken into account if it was such as would generally render those suffering from it more susceptible to pressure and threats, and so help the jury to determine whether a reasonable person suffering from such a condition would have been impelled to act as had the appellant. (See also *R v Morhall*, *R v Hegarty*, *R v Marshall* and *R v Flatt*.)

R v Brennen [1990] Crim LR 118 (Court of Appeal)

B, a publican, was convicted on three counts of handling barrels of lager contrary to s22 of the Theft Act 1968. He thought that they were 'all right' albeit he had bought them cheaply. The judge directed the jury in accordance with the objective and subjective tests of dishonesty laid down in *R v Ghosh*, stating that if the jury found it proved that what B did was dishonest according to the ordinary standards of reasonable and honest people, B was guilty. The judge then dealt with the subjective test – whether B realised that reasonable and honest people would regard what he had done was dishonest. It was submitted that the judge had misdirected the jury on dishonesty.

Held, the appeal would be allowed. It was only necessary to give the *Ghosh* direction when a defendant was saying 'I thought that what I was doing was honest but other people and the majority of people might think that it was not honest.' It was a misdirection to deal with the objective test alone – a person is guilty if what he has done is dishonest according to the standard of reasonable and honest people. (There was also doubt as to whether the jury were properly directed as to what amounted to corroboration.) This led the court to quash the convictions.

R v Brindley; R v Long [1971] 2 WLR 895 (Court of Appeal)

Brindley and Long were convicted of impeding the apprehension of a person called Morphew knowing or believing him to be guilty of an arrestable offence contrary to s4(1) of the Criminal Law Act 1967. Two lorries containing loads of brass ingots and spirits were stolen from a yard behind a garage shortly before 10 pm. On the night the lorries were driven away across the forecourt of the garage, Brindley was on duty and she had been told by the occupier of the premises next door to the garage that strangers had got into his garden and escaped over the wall towards the yard. He offered to investigate the yard to see if everything was all right. Brindley said she would go and reported later that nothing was amiss. Two days after the theft she was interviewed by the police and said no lorries had left the yard at the material time. Long also stated that he was at the garage with Brindley, but he had not seen any lorries cross the forecourt. Later he made a statement admitting that he had seen lorries driven from the yard across the forecourt of the garage at the material time.

Held, (1) on a charge of contravening s4(1) of the Criminal Law Act 1967, proof was required that a person had committed an arrestable offence; that another person knew or believed that the first person had committed it; that the second person did an act with intent to impede the apprehension or prosecution of the first person; that the act was done without lawful authority or reasonable excuse; and that the prosecution did not have to prove that the defendants knew the identity of the person who committed the arrestable offence; (2) unless the defendants suggested that they had some intent other than that of impeding arrest or prosecution, there was no duty on the trial judge to direct the jury to consider whether they might have had such an intent. The appeals would be dismissed.

R v Broadfoot [1976] 3 All ER 753 (Court of Appeal)

The appellant was charged with two counts of attempting to procure a woman to become a common prostitute contrary to s22(1) of the Sexual Offences Act 1956. The appellant was concerned in the running of massage parlours and advertised for 'attractive young ladies with personality …' Amongst the applicants were two women journalists. Their only interest was that they were carrying out an investigation into massage parlours. They were interviewed separately by the appellant who explained the financial rewards. The appellant told each that if she provided 'extra services' she would be well paid for them, although she was not obliged to do so. The 'extra services' were such as to amount to acts of prostitution if performed for financial gain. Neither woman was willing to perform those services. The appellant was convicted on both counts and appealed against conviction contending, inter alia, that the judge had wrongly directed the jury by saying (1) that 'procure' meant to 'recruit' and (2) that the mention of possible earnings to the women without pressure or persuasion was capable of amounting to an attempt to procure.

Held, the appeal would be dismissed. 'Procure' was a word in common usage and had no special meaning in the context of s22. A jury had to use their common sense when interpreting the word and there was nothing wrong in the judge using the expression 'recruit' when directing them on the issue whether there had been a procurement or attempted procurement. An offer of a large sum of money for undertaking tasks could, in the absence of any other pressure, amount to persuasion and therefore an attempt to procure. Whether there had been such persuasion was a matter for the jury to decide on the evidence before them.

R v Brooks and Brooks (1982) 76 Cr App R 66 (Court of Appeal)

The defendants, father and daughter, were convicted of making off without payment contrary to s3(1) of the Theft Act 1978. The prosecution said that they jointly and severally intended to avoid payment and separately made off from the restaurant. They had had a meal together with S. The daughter left the premises in haste, S made off through the other door. The manager chased after him and asked him to come back. The father was coming out of the restaurant when they returned. S said he was not responsible for payment. All the father was able to offer was what turned out to be a valueless cheque made out to him. The daughter said that S had offered to treat her and her father.

Held, the father's appeal would be dismissed as there was no doubt that he had left the premises without paying the bill. However, the daughter's appeal would be allowed. The recorder told the jury that the whole essence of the offence was that people left intending, if they could, to get away without paying. He did not tell them that on the evidence she had left earlier and in haste, that she believed S would pay, and that they would have to draw the inference that at the time she left she dishonestly intended to evade payment before she could be convicted.

R v Brown [1969] 3 All ER 198 (Court of Appeal)

Holden and others broke into a cafe in Weymouth and stole a quantity of cigarettes and foodstuff. They hid the property at a flat of which Brown (B) was the tenant, and where he and some other people were sleeping. The cigarettes were taken out of their packets and placed in a plastic bag and hidden in a wardrobe in which some of B's clothes were hanging. The following morning the police went to the flat while B was still in bed and found a quantity of the foodstuffs in a refrigerator. B denied all knowledge of the theft and did not impede the search, but when he was about to be arrested he said to the officer 'Get lost'. On a second visit to the flat the police found the cigarettes. It was proved that before the police arrived Holden had told B where the cigarettes were. B was convicted of handling stolen goods (the cigarettes) by dishonestly assisting in their retention, contrary to s22(1) of the Theft Act 1968, and appealed.

Held, although the summing up was wrong the proviso would be applied and the conviction affirmed. The court said that the mere failure to tell the police that the cigarettes were in the flat coupled with the words 'Get lost' did not in themselves amount to assisting in their retention, but was strong evidence that he provided accommodation for the stolen goods in order to assist Holden to retain them.

R v Brown [1972] 2 All ER 1328 (Court of Appeal)

The appellant killed his wife with a razor, inflicting on her throat a large seven inch long wound which severed the muscles of her neck, the carotid arteries, the jugular veins, the wind-pipe and gullet. The appellant came to believe that there was an illicit association between his wife and another man, an association which according to other evidence was innocent. Early in the morning of 2 February an argument developed between the appellant and his wife about an incident that had occurred on the previous Saturday, 30 January – the appellant had found his wife and the other man in a house in which a Mrs Higgins, a crippled lady, lived; they were there quite innocently but the appellant believed otherwise. When the argument took place on 2 February the appellant's evidence was that his wife came towards him with a knife the point of which scratched his neck; he then hit her on the head with a poker twice and then he said his mind blacked out. He said that he knew that there was a fight but that he did not know what had happened; he also said that he had a cut-throat razor but he did not remember getting it or using it on his wife. Before this incident the appellant had threatened to kill his wife and on the previous Sunday he discussed his troubles with a police sergeant at the police station saying that he was frightened of what he might do to his wife. After killing his wife the appellant gave himself up to the police and amongst other things said, 'This has been going on for five years. She drove me to it. I told her not to keep seeing this fellow. She kept saying I was just talking and meant nothing by it.' The appellant was charged with murder and pleaded provocation. In his summing-up the trial judge misdirected the jury on the 'reasonable relationship rule', that is, that the mode of retaliation must bear a reasonable relationship to the provocation if the offence is to be reduced to manslaughter. The appellant was convicted.

Held, on a charge of murder s3 of the Homicide Act 1957 lays down the precise test which the jury should apply in determining whether the provocation was enough to make a reasonable man do as the accused did so as to reduce the charge of murder to manslaughter. A trial judge directing a jury on the question of provocation should avoid using the precise words of Viscount Simon LC in *Mancini* v *Director of Public Prosecutions*, 'the mode of resentment must bear a reasonable relationship to the provocation', unless he uses them in a context which makes it clear to the jury that those words do not express a rule of law which they are bound to follow, but merely a consideration which may or may not commend itself to them. There was a misdirection but, taken as a whole, the summing up was adequate and the conviction would be affirmed.

R v Brown [1993] 2 All ER 75 (House of Lords)

The appellants were charged with numerous offences contrary to s47 of the Offences against the Person Act 1861 (assault occasioning actual bodily harm) and s20 of the 1861 Act (unlawful wounding). They belonged to a group of sado-masochistic homosexuals. Over ten years they inflicted pain on each other for mutual sexual pleasure. The trial judge ruled that it was not necessary for the prosecution to prove that any victim did not consent to the infliction of bodily harm or wounding upon him – the appellants then pleaded guilty. They appealed against their convictions on the grounds that a person could not be guilty of assault occasioning actual bodily harm and wounding when the acts had been carried out with the consent of the victim, in private.

Held, the appeals would be dismissed. A person could be convicted under ss20 or 47 of the 1861 Act for committing sado-masochistic acts the results of which were neither transient nor trifling. It did not matter that these acts were committed in private, that the victim consented or that no permanent injury was sustained. 'In principle there is a difference between violence which is incidental and violence which is inflicted for the indulgence of cruelty. The violence of sado-masochistic encounters involves the indulgence of cruelty by sadists and the degradation of victims. Such violence is injurious to the participants and unpredictably dangerous. I am not prepared to invent a defence of consent for sado-masochistic encounters which breed and glorify cruelty and result in offences under ss47 and 20 of the 1861 Act' (*per* LORD TEMPLEMAN). (Compare *R v Wilson.*)

R v Brown and Stratton [1998] Crim LR 485 (Court of Appeal)

The defendants were convicted under s18 Offences Against the Person Act 1861 (grievous bodily harm with intent). The victim, Stratton's father, had had gender reassignment surgery. Stratton, and her cousin Brown, attacked Stratton's father after he visited a supermarket, where Brown worked, dressed as a woman. The cousins felt they had been shown up by Stratton's father. The victim had a broken nose, lacerations to the face and lost a number of teeth. Although the defendants had been drinking before the attack, the defence of intoxication was not raised on their behalf. The defendants offered to plead guilty to an offence under s47 of the Act (common assault). The trial judge directed the jury to determine whether the harm caused amounted to grievous bodily harm classifying it as if they were the victims. As to intent the jury were directed they could convict if there was evidence of intent to do grievous bodily harm irrespective of whether it was a sober or drunken intent. There would be a defence of intoxication only if the defendants had been so drunk that they had been rendered incapable of forming the required intent. On appeal it was contended that the trial judge had failed to direct the jury adequately on the meaning of grievous bodily harm and on the effect of intoxication on intent.

Held, the appeal would be allowed; convictions under s20 were substituted (inflicting grievous bodily harm). The determination of whether or not the harm caused was grievous bodily harm is an objective one (particular regard being had to the medical evidence). In this instance the harm suffered amounted to grievous bodily harm. As to intent the jury should have been directed to consider the possible effect of alcohol. If the defendants might not have had the requisite specific intent, they should have been acquitted.

R v Burgess [1991] 2 WLR 1206 (Court of Appeal)

The appellant was charged with wounding with intent to do grievous bodily harm contrary to s18 of the Offences against the Person Act 1861. He was found not guilty by reason of insanity in accordance with s2(1) of the Trial of Lunatics Act 1883, as amended. He visited the flat below his, being friendly with the woman there, to watch a video. She fell asleep later and was only awoken by the appellant smashing a bottle over her head. He then picked up the video recorder and brought that down on her head causing cuts and bruises. His defence was that he had been sleep walking and suffering from non insane automatism and he therefore lacked the necessary intent. The judge determined that the only defence the evidence revealed was that of insanity within the M'Naghten Rules. The appellant contended that the defence of automatism should have been put to the jury to consider.

Held, the appeal would be dismissed. On a defence of automatism the judge had to decide, first, whether a proper evidential foundation had been laid for the defence and, second, whether the evidence showed the case to be one of insane automatism within the M'Naghten Rules, or one of non-insane automatism. In the light of the medical evidence the judge had been right to conclude that this was an abnormality or disorder, albeit transitory, due to an internal factor, whether functional or organic, which had manifested itself in violence and could recur. (See also *Bratty* v *Attorney-General for Northern Ireland*.)

R v Burns (1973) 58 Cr App R 364 (Court of Appeal)

Burns and Bellis met at a party in Harlech and had a lot to drink. The party was held at the home of the housekeeper of St David's Hotel in Harlech where Burns lodged. Bellis went to sleep in the bathroom and gave evidence that he woke up to find his penis in Burns' mouth. A few days later, Bellis said that after he had finished work at the hotel he went with other waiters to drink in one of their rooms upstairs. Burns found his way there and joined the party. He appeared to be drunk and was staggering. After the party broke up the two men went out into the garden, and while they were there, Burns sitting on a seat by himself on its arm, Burns said that they were like each other, that he had read about 'body movements' and could see that he was a homosexual, that he loved him and 'wanted' him. Bellis denied he was a homosexual and said he wanted to go back into the hotel. Burns persuaded him to show him the way down the terraces and when he got as far as the grass path and turned to go back Burns jumped at him from behind in a rugby tackle, tried to kiss him and repeated that he wanted him. He laid on top of him and threatened to beat him up if he did not stop shouting; he held him by the throat until he was almost unconscious. He was finally rescued by members of the hotel staff who had heard his shouts. Burns said in evidence that he had no knowledge of the first incident and that with regard to the second, earlier that evening he went to the Castle Hotel to arrange a trip to a gold mine. He had half a pint to drink and then went to St David's Hotel where he drank one pint of bitter, and had a 'fantastic feeling'. He also said that he did not know what happened until he woke up outside his own home the next morning. He was an alcoholic and took with alcohol Mandrax tablets and other tablets. He was bisexual and had homosexual inclinations when he was drunk. He was convicted of indecent assault, the jury rejecting his defences of automatism and insanity. He appealed.

Held, the proviso to s2(1) of the Criminal Appeal Act 1968 would be applied and the conviction affirmed even though the doctor called by the defence had equated insanity with automatism and the judge had not fully distinguished the two issues in his summing-up and there had in consequence been a misdirection or non-direction with regard to automatism. Also, where there is evidence of other factors operating upon a disease of the mind (such as drink or drugs) and the possibility that the defendant did not appreciate the effect which they might have on his mind, a direction should be given to the jury that the burden lies on the prosecution to negative a defence of automatism. (See also *R v Quick; R v Paddison*.)

R v Buswell [1972] 1 All ER 75 (Court of Appeal)

Buswell, a drug addict, was prescribed 70 amphetamine tablets by his doctor in November 1969. He put the tablets in a pocket of his jeans which he placed in a drawer in his bedroom. A few days later he discovered that his mother had taken his jeans and washed them, and came to the genuine conclusion that, in washing the jeans, she had destroyed the remaining tablets which he had not yet taken. He told the doctor what had happened and obtained a prescription for a further supply to make good the loss. In September 1970, months after the treatment had been completed, the appellant started to clear out his drawer altogether, and in the course of so doing he found the missing tablets. He took some of them and later when the police made a search of the premises they found 18 in his possession. The appellant was convicted of being in unlawful possession of dangerous drugs contrary to s1(1) of the Drugs (Prevention of Misuse) Act 1964 (now s5 of the Misuse of Drugs Act 1971) and appealed.

Held, the conviction should be quashed as: (1) where a person was in lawful possession of drugs under a doctor's prescription, the possession of those drugs which remained unconsumed did not automatically become unlawful once the treatment was concluded; (2) where a person who was in lawful possession of drugs forgot their existence, or mistakenly thought that they had been disposed of or destroyed, although in fact they remained in his custody, he did not thereby cease to be in possession of them; the continued possession remained lawful as the tablets were in the appellant's possession by virtue of the doctor's prescription. (But see *Warner v Metropolitan Police Commissioner*, which was distinguished.)

R v Byrne [1960] 3 All ER 1 (Court of Criminal Appeal)

Byrne strangled a young woman at a hostel in Birmingham and mutilated her body. From an early age he had suffered from violent perverted sexual desires which were so strong that he found it difficult, and at times impossible, to resist putting them into practice. However, except for these sexual addictions and practices, he was otherwise normal. The medical evidence established that he was a sexual psychopath and suffered from abnormality of mind which arose from either a condition of arrested or retarded development of mind or inherent causes but the trial judge withdrew the defence of diminished responsibility from the jury on the ground that the evidence was not sufficient to bring the case within the defence. Byrne was convicted of murder.

Held, a conviction for manslaughter would be substituted on the ground that the jury should have been told that inability to exercise willpower to control physical acts due to abnormality of mind is capable of constituting diminished responsibility. (See Homicide Act 1957, s2; but see *R v Egan*.)

R v Caldwell [1981] 1 All ER 961 (House of Lords)

The respondent was convicted of damaging property with intent to endanger life or being reckless whether life would be endangered contrary to s1(2) of the Criminal Damage Act 1971. He had originally pleaded guilty to a charge under s1(1) of the 1971 Act and not guilty to the charge under s1(2). He quarrelled with the owner of a hotel for whom he had done some work, got drunk and set fire to the hotel in revenge. This was put out before any serious damage was done and none of the guests was injured. He contended that he was so drunk at the time that it had never crossed his mind that anyone might have been injured. The judge directed the jury that drunkenness was not a defence to this charge. The Court of Appeal allowed the appeal on the ground that under s1(2)(b) the mental element of intention or recklessness, as far as endangering life was concerned, was a matter of specific intent and had to be established as a separate ingredient of the offence and drunkenness could be a good defence.

Held, the Crown's appeal would be dismissed. The term 'reckless' was to be used in its dictionary sense rather than as a term of legal art. 'A person charged with an offence under s1(1) of the 1971 Act is "reckless as to whether or not any property would be destroyed or damaged" if (1) he does an act which in fact creates an obvious risk that property will be destroyed or damaged and (2) when he does the act he either has not given any thought to the possibility of there being any such risk or has recognised that there was some risk involved and has none the less gone on to do it. That would be a proper direction to the jury; cases in the Court of Appeal which held otherwise should be regarded as overruled' (*per* LORD DIPLOCK). A person would be guilty under s1(2) if what he did amounted to an offence under s1(1) (if he intended or was reckless as to whether property was destroyed or damaged and was reckless as to whether another's life might be endangered). If 'intention' appeared in the charge under s1(1) or s1(2), evidence of self-induced intoxication would be relevant to the accused's defence; if the charge concerned being 'reckless', evidence of self intoxication was irrelevant. It followed that it was irrelevant that the respondent had given no thought to the risk of endangering the lives of others in the hotel because of his self-intoxication. (See also *Director of Public Prosecutions v Majewski, R v Coles* and *R v Cunningham*.)

R v Callender [1992] 3 All ER 51 (Court of Appeal)

The appellant was convicted of obtaining a pecuniary advantage by deception contrary of s16(1) of the Theft Act 1968 in that he had dishonestly obtained for himself 'the opportunity to earn remuneration in an office or employment' as an accountant by falsely representing that he had accountancy qualifications. He had agreed to prepare accounts for two businessmen and submit income tax and value added tax returns, but did not fulfil this work. He argued he was employed as an independent contractor and that the fees he received were not received 'in an office or employment'.

Held, that the appeal would be dismissed. For the purposes of the 1968 Act the businessmen had 'employed' him and he had as a result dishonestly obtained for himself 'the opportunity to earn remuneration in an office or employment'. He was guilty of deception by obtaining a pecuniary advantage 'in an office or employment'.

R v Cambridge [1994] 2 All ER 760 (Court of Appeal)

The appellant was convicted of murder. The Crown relied on the evidence of two witnesses that the appellant had been seen on top of the deceased. There was evidence that he had been involved in an argument with the deceased shortly before his death. There was no evidence that anyone had seen the knife or any stabbing movement; or that anyone else had attacked or been involved in a struggle with the deceased. The appellant contended that he had not been present when the deceased was fatally stabbed. The appellant appealed on the ground that the judge should have left the issue of provocation to the jury (see s3 of the Homicide Act 1957).

Held, the appeal would be allowed and a verdict of guilty of manslaughter substituted. If the facts revealed sufficient evidence capable of amounting to provocation, even if the defendant did not rely on provocation but maintained he was not present at the scene of the crime or that he did not kill the deceased, the trial judge was still required to leave the defence of provocation to the jury. The judge had to decide whether there was sufficient evidence on which the jury could find that the defendant was in fact provoked to lose his self-control; if there was, the jury were left with the question whether the things said or done might have caused a reasonable man to have acted similarly to the defendant, even if the judge himself believed the circumstances to be such that no reasonable man would have reacted as did the defendant. (See also *Director of Public Prosecutions v Camplin, Mancini v Director of Public Prosecutions* and *R v Rossiter*.)

R v Campbell (Mary) [1984] Crim LR 683 (Court of Appeal)

The appellant originally pleaded not guilty to a count charging forgery contrary to s1 of the Forgery and Counterfeiting Act 1981. On a ruling that on the facts she had no defence, she changed her plea to guilty. She had endorsed a cheque, handed to her by a friend, over to herself by writing on the back the name appearing on the front and her own name. The cheque was paid into her bank account. When the cheque was cleared she withdrew the amount in cash and paid it over to her friend. The friend had had no right to the cheque. Campbell appealed against her conviction.

Held, the appeal would be dismissed. The appellant had made a false instrument with the intention that the bank should accept it as genuine. Had the bank then acted to its own or another's prejudice? The bank's duty was to pay out on a valid instrument, not to honour a false one (s10(2)). Applying s10(1)(c), the appellant's act was to the bank's prejudice because it was the result of the bank having accepted a false instrument as genuine in connection with the bank's performance of any duty. The offence had been made out.

R v Campbell (1991) 93 Cr App R 350 (Court of Appeal)

The appellant was convicted of attempted robbery. Police officers, acting on information received, suspected that he was planning a robbery on a sub-post office and kept watch. He was seen loitering near the sub-post office on a number of occasions. When arrested he had with him an imitation firearm and a threatening note. The appellant claimed he had originally intended to carry out a robbery but changed his mind before he was arrested. In directing the jury on s1(1) of the Criminal Attempts Act 1981 the judge referred to the law prior to passing the 1981 Act.

Held, the appeal would be allowed. A jury could be confused if unnecessary detail was given on the law which previously applied. To convict for attempt the jury must be satisfied that the defendant intended to commit the crime and that with that intent he did an act which was more than merely preparatory to committing that offence. The appellant had not been in a position where he could carry out the offence, it could hardly be said that he had performed an act which could be properly said to be an attempt. (See also *R* v *Gullefer* and *R* v *Jones*.)

R v Campbell (No 2) [1997] 1 Cr App R 199 (Court of Appeal)

The defendant was found guilty of murder. He tried to put forward the defences of provocation and diminished responsibility. The trial judge directed the jury not to consider the latter because there was insufficient evidence. The defendant appealed on the ground that the trial judge should have left diminished responsibility to be considered by the jury; this was rejected. The defendant's case was referred to the Court of Appeal under s17(1)(a) Criminal Appeal Act 1968, there being fresh psychiatric evidence supporting a claim of diminished responsibility. Given subsequent changes in the law, he tried to argue that the trial judge's direction on provocation should be examined again since the jury may have been inclined to exclude evidence of mental abnormality when applying the test for provocation.

Held, the appeal was allowed in part. As regards the fresh evidence of diminished responsibility, the defendant should be retried on an indictment alleging murder so a jury could consider that evidence. As regards the matter or provocation, the court drew attention to a conflict of authority on the extent to which mental abnormality could be regarded as a characteristic for the purposes of the objective test – *Luc Thiet Thuan* v *The Queen* saying it was not and *R* v *Humphreys* and other cases indicating otherwise. The Court of Appeal regarded itself bound by its own previous decisions and not those of the Privy Council. However, it was not the court's practice to reopen convictions because of a subsequent change in the law and it would not allow the defendant's appeal on this basis.

R v Caresana [1996] Crim LR 67 (Court of Appeal)

The defendant was convicted on a number of counts of obtaining property by deception, and securing the execution of a valuable security by deception. He appealed against his conviction for theft on the ground that no money had been appropriated. A complex fraud was devised by the defendant and others. They used a purported sale of a consignment of sugar (when there was in fact no sugar to sell) to induce a branch of NatWest in Leeds to discount a letter of credit and pay a large sum of money in dollars into an account (in the name of a company controlled by the defendant) held with Deutsche Bank Frankfurt. The bank in Leeds had to transfer money by telex to NatWest in New York from where it was transferred to Deutsche Bank New York and then on to Deutsche Bank Frankfurt. The defendant withdrew a large percentage of the funds after the money had been credited to the Frankfurt account.

Held, the appeal was allowed on the theft point because no money had been appropriated. He had simply caused the bank in Leeds to become indebted to Deutsche Bank Frankfurt. (See also *R* v *Preddy; R* v *Slade.*)

R v Cato [1976] 1 All ER 260 (Court of Appeal)

After drinking at a public house Cato returned with a friend, Farmer, to the house that they shared. Farmer produced a bag of white powder, which he said was heroin, and some syringes, and invited Cato to have a 'fix' with him. They injected each other a number of times, following a procedure whereby each man prepared a mixture of heroin and water in the syringe to his own liking and for his own consumption and then gave it to the other to administer the injection. They continued to give each other injections throughout the night and the following morning they were both very ill. Cato was having difficulty in breathing and his life was saved by someone giving him some rudimentary first aid, but Farmer died. When it was discovered that Farmer was dead, two other men, who also lived in the said house and had themselves been injecting each other with heroin the previous night, Morris and Dudley, tried to cover up the death. Cato was convicted of manslaughter and administering a noxious thing, contrary to s23 of the Offences against the Person Act 1861, and Dudley and Morris were convicted of assisting an offender (Cato).

Held, Cato's conviction would be affirmed as: (1) although Farmer's consent to the injection of heroin was no defence to a charge of manslaughter it was something which had to be taken into account when the jury came to consider whether Cato had acted with recklessness or gross negligence; (2) there was an unlawful act, viz the injecting of Farmer with a mixture of heroin and water which at the time of the injection and for the purposes thereof Cato had unlawfully taken into his possession; (3) an 'article' is noxious within s23 if it is liable to cause injury in common use and the heroin was a 'noxious thing' within the section. (See also *R* v *Blaue, R* v *Lamb, R* v *Marcus, R* v *Dalby, R* v *Goodfellow* and *R* v *Kennedy.*)

R v Chan-Fook [1994] 2 All ER 552 (Court of Appeal)

The appellant was convicted of assault occasioning actual bodily harm contrary to s47 of the Offences against the Person Act 1861 and appealed on the grounds of a misdirection. The appellant and others interrogated the complainant, who lodged with the appellant's fiancée's family, about the disappearance of his fiancée's engagement ring. The complainant, against whom there was no evidence to support the suspicion that he had taken the ring, could not explain its disappearance; he was dragged by the appellant upstairs and locked in a second-floor room. He tried to escape through the window but was injured when he fell. It was argued that the complainant, even if he had not suffered any physical injury as a result of the assault, had been reduced to a mental state which in itself amounted to actual bodily harm; he had felt abused, humiliated and frightened. The jury were directed that an assault which caused a hysterical or nervous condition was capable of being an assault occasioning actual bodily harm.

Held, the conviction would be quashed. While 'actual bodily harm' was capable of including psychiatric injury, it did not include mere emotions such as fear, distress, panic or a hysterical or nervous condition, nor did it include states of mind that were not themselves evidence of some identifiable clinical condition. Where psychiatric injury was relied on as the basis for an allegation of bodily harm which was disputed by the defendant, the Crown should call expert evidence and, in the absence of such expert evidence, the question whether psychiatric injury had been occasioned by an assault should not be left to the jury. (See also *R* v *Baker and Wilkins* and *R* v *Ireland; R* v *Burstow*.)

R v *Cheshire* (1991) 93 Cr App R 251 (Court of Appeal)

The appellant was charged with murder and convicted. He had shot the deceased in the leg and stomach during an argument. Having been seriously wounded the deceased was taken to hospital, operated on and then placed in intensive care. He developed respiratory problems and a tracheotomy tube was used to assist his breathing, the tube remaining in place for four weeks. Complications arose and the deceased complained of breathing difficulties. Over two months after the shooting the deceased died while still in hospital. The cause of death was cardio-respiratory arrest – the windpipe had become obstructed due to a narrowing where the tracheotomy had been performed. While this condition was rare it was not an unknown complication following a tracheotomy. At the trial, the consultant surgeon gave evidence for the defence to the effect that death was caused by the negligent failure of the medical staff to diagnose and treat the deceased's respiratory condition. The leg and stomach wounds caused at the time of the shooting were no longer life threatening at the time of death. The trial judge directed the jury that the medical treatment could not be viewed as a novus actus interveniens unless the medical staff had been reckless in their treatment of the patient.

Held, the appeal would be dismissed. The jury had to be satisfied that the appellant's acts had made a significant contribution to his death. They did not have to weigh competing causes or to determine which was the dominant cause. It was therefore sufficient for the judge to direct the jury that they had to be satisfied that the Crown had proved that the acts of the accused caused the death of the deceased. Those acts did not have to be the only or even the main cause of the death. It was sufficient that they had contributed significantly to that result. Even though the treatment was negligent and this had been the immediate cause of death, the jury should not regard it as excluding the responsibility of the appellant unless such treatment was so independent of his acts and in itself so potent in causing death that they regarded the contribution made by the appellant's acts as insignificant. (See also *R* v *Malcherek; R* v *Steel*.)

R v Chrastny [1991] 1 WLR 1381 (Court of Appeal)

The appellant was charged with conspiring with her husband, and two others, to supply a Class A controlled drug, contrary to s1(1) of the Criminal Law Act 1977. She was convicted and appealed on the ground that the trial judge had erred in law in directing the jury that, although she had only conspired with her husband that the offence should be committed, s2(2)(a) of the Criminal Law Act 1977 gave no protection where she had known of the existence of the other conspirators.

Held, the appeal would be dismissed. Knowing that her husband was conspiring with others to commit an unlawful act, she, in joining the conspiracy, conspired with him and those others, even though she only agreed with her husband. (Compare *R v Griffiths*.)

R v Church [1965] 2 All ER 72 (Court of Criminal Appeal)

Church was charged with murder. He took a woman in a van near to a river in order to have sexual intercourse with her. He was unable to satisfy her, whereupon, she reproached him and slapped his face. He then attacked her and inflicted a number of injuries that were likely to cause death or grievous bodily harm and tried to strangle her. She became unconscious and, after trying for about half an hour to revive her, Church, thinking she was dead, panicked and threw her body into the river. The woman was not dead when she was thrown into the river but continued to breathe for some time and eventually died from drowning. He was acquitted of murder but convicted of manslaughter and appealed to the Court of Criminal Appeal.

Held, the conviction would be affirmed on the ground that he was guilty of criminal negligence by not endeavouring to ascertain whether or not she was still alive when he threw the body into the river and that the woman died as a result of an unlawful act which a reasonable man would regard as likely to cause harm. The court also stated that the jury could have convicted of murder, even though Church thought his blows and attempted strangulation had actually produced death when he threw the body into the river, if they regarded his behaviour from the moment he first struck her to the moment when he threw the body into the river as a series of acts designed to cause death or grievous bodily harm. (See also *Thabo Meli v R* and *R v Le Brun*.)

R v Clarke [1972] 1 All ER 219 (Court of Appeal)

The appellant went shopping at a supermarket in Leicester and selected various goods including a pound of butter, a jar of coffee and a jar of mincemeat, which she put in the wire basket provided by the shop. At some stage before she went to the checkout point the appellant transferred the sugar, coffee and mincemeat out of the wire basket and into her own shopping bag and they were not paid for. She was charged with theft and contended that she had no intention of stealing the goods. The appellant suffered from sugar diabetes and had not been feeling well on the morning in question nor for quite some time. In the previous year she had gone down with 'flu' and on the day before her husband had broken his collar-bone. She had become very depressed and on a number of occasions had become very forgetful. The appellant maintained that she had no recollection of putting the three items in her shopping bag, but must have done so in a moment of absent-mindedness. A psychiatrist and a medical practitioner testified that the appellant was suffering from depression, a minor mental illness, which produces states of absent-mindedness in which the patient would do things he would not normally do, in periods of confusion and memory lapses. The appellant had been forgetful a number of times in the past, and on one occasion she had put sugar in the refrigerator instead of in the cupboard and the sweeping brush in the dustbin and then put the dirt where the brush should have been put. The assistant recorder interpreted the evidence as constituting the defence of 'not guilty due to insanity' under the *M'Naghten* rules, and the appellant changed her plea to that of guilty.

Held, the conviction would be quashed on the ground that the assistant recorder misstated the law and the evidence fell short either of showing that the appellant suffered from a defect of reason or that the consequences of that defect of reason, if any, were that she was unable to know the nature and quality of the act she was doing. 'The *M'Naghten* rules relate to accused persons who by reason of a disease of the mind are deprived of the power of reasoning. They do not apply and never have applied to those who retain the power of reasoning but who in moments of confusion or absent-mindedness fail to use their powers to the full.' (per ACKNER J) (See *M'Naghten's* Case.)

R v Clarke [1991] Crim LR 383 (Court of Appeal)

The appellant was convicted of murder. He had hit his victim, strangled her and then placed live wires in her mouth, electrocuting her. He raised the defence of provocation. In his appeal he contended that the jury should have been directed, when considering provocation, to disregard the act of electrocuting her which could have occurred after she was dead.

Held, the application for leave to appeal would be rejected. In considering whether a reasonable man would have acted as did the accused, the jury should examine everything the accused had done.

R v Clegg [1995] 1 All ER 334 (House of Lords)

The appellant was convicted of murder. He was a British soldier based in Northern Ireland. With other members of his unit he was on night patrol. A member of the patrol stopped a stolen car at a checkpoint some way down the road. The car, having accelerated away, with headlights full on, came towards the appellant and three other members of the patrol. They opened fire, a call to stop the car having come from the checkpoint. The driver and a rear-seat passenger were killed. A bullet from the appellant's rifle was found to have hit the passenger in the back. The appellant's evidence was that he had fired three shots at the windscreen and a fourth shot at the side of the car as it passed, having thought that a colleague's life was in danger. Scientific evidence showed that the fourth shot was fired after the car had passed and was some fifty feet down the road. The judge found that the fourth shot was not fired in self-defence or in defence of a colleague since the car had gone past them. The Court of Appeal of Northern Ireland dismissed the appeal. The appellant had been rightly convicted of the unlawful killing of the passenger. However, there had been no evil motive; the appellant had acted wrongly in a situation which suddenly confronted him in the course of his duties as a soldier. Had a conviction for manslaughter been available to the court it would have better reflected the nature of the offence. The appellant appealed to the House of Lords.

Held, the appeal would be dismissed. Where a plea of self-defence to a charge of murder failed because the force used was excessive and unreasonable, the homicide could not be reduced to manslaughter. A soldier or police officer who, in the course of his duty, kills a person by firing a shot which amounts to the use of excessive and unreasonable force in self-defence, is guilty of murder, not manslaughter.

R v *Clotworthy* [1981] Crim LR 501 (Court of Appeal)

The appellant, who worked in a garage, was convicted on a charge of taking a conveyance without authority contrary to s12(1) of the Theft Act 1968. He had been asked by the garage owner to drive a customer's car to an associated garage; he held no driving licence and was uninsured. The police stopped him en route. His defence was based on s12(6) of the 1968 Act. The prosecutor submitted that the car owner would not have given his consent to an unlicensed or uninsured driver. It was also contrary to the garage's own terms of bailment to allow such a person to drive. The trial judge upheld that submission and the appellant appealed against conviction.

Held, the appeal would be allowed, the submission was invalid. It was for the jury to decide what was the appellant's state of mind, whether the defence was acceptable to them or whether they were sure he had no genuine belief. The defendant was entitled to put forward his reasonable belief that he had lawful authority or the owner's consent. The jury would decide the matter taking into account the circumstances of the case.

R v *Clouden* [1987] Crim LR 56 (Court of Appeal)

The appellant was convicted of robbery contrary to s8(1) of the Theft Act 1968. He had pulled on a lady's handbag in order to wrench it out of her hands. It was contended that force had not been used 'on any person'.

Held, the appeal would be dismissed. If property was taken from a victim without his resistance, eg by a pickpocket, such should not amount to robbery. Whether force was used 'on any person' should be left to the jury. It may be sufficient for the appellant to use force on the victim's possessions in a way which affects the victim. (See also *R* v *Dawson.*)

R v *Coady* [1996] Crim LR 518 (Court of Appeal)

The appellant was convicted of obtaining property by deception. He served himself with petrol and then told the cashier to charge his employer's account. In fact the appellant was no longer an employee of the named employer and was not entitled to charge petrol to the account. The appellant appealed on the basis that any dishonest representation by him arose after he had filled up with petrol; alternatively there was no evidence that any deception had operated on the mind of the cashier prior to the obtaining.

Held, the appeal would be allowed. The only evidence of a deception was through what happened after he had filled up with petrol. While the cashier had to press a button before petrol could be delivered, there was no direct evidence that the appellant had been aware of this or that the cashier had been persuaded to press the button by any conduct on the appellant's part.

R v Cocker [1989] Crim LR 740 (Court of Appeal)

The appellant pleaded guilty to murdering his wife having originally pleaded not guilty to murder but guilty to manslaughter by reason of provocation. The appellant's wife suffered from an incurable disease. She had become severely incapacitated and repeatedly asked her husband to end her life. One morning she demanded he kill her having woken him by clawing at his back. He placed a pillow over her face. She died from asphyxia. In evidence he stated that her final request to him to end her life and her entreaties to him had been too much for him. The judge ruled that there was no evidence that the appellant had been actuated by provocation which led to the change of plea.

Held, his appeal would be dismissed. His behaviour had not stemmed from provocation. He had acceded to what his wife had wished to happen and had not lost his self-control.

R v Cogan; R v Leak [1975] 2 All ER 1059 (Court of Appeal)

The appellants had been out drinking and went to Leak's home at about 6pm. Leak told his wife that Cogan wanted to have sexual intercourse with her and that he, Leak, was going to see that she did. Mrs Leak was a slightly built woman in her early twenties and on the previous day Leak had knocked her down and kicked her several times whilst she was on the floor when she refused to give him money. Leak made her go upstairs, took off her clothes and lowered her onto the bed. Cogan then came into the room and Leak asked him twice if he wanted to have sexual intercourse with Mrs Leak. He said 'No'. Leak had sexual intercourse with Mrs Leak in the presence of Cogan and when he finished he again asked Cogan if he wanted to have sexual intercourse with Mrs Leak. Cogan said that he did and proceeded to do so in the presence of Leak. Whilst this was going on, for most of the time Mrs Leak was sobbing; she did not struggle when Cogan was on top of her but she tried to turn away from him. Leak then had intercourse with her again, behaving in a revolting way. Cogan was convicted of rape and Leak of, inter alia, aiding and abetting rape. They appealed: Cogan contended that he had believed that Mrs Leak had consented to the intercourse with him although there were no reasonable grounds for that belief; Leak contended that his conviction could not stand if the principal offender, Cogan, was acquitted.

Held, Cogan's appeal should be allowed in view of the decision in *Director of Public Prosecutions* v *Morgan*, but Leak's conviction would be affirmed as an accused who aids and abets another man to have sexual intercourse with a woman knowing that she does not consent may be found guilty of aiding and abetting rape, notwithstanding that the other man is acquitted of rape on the ground that he mistakenly believed that the woman was consenting. It is immaterial that the accused is the woman's husband. The court stated that Leak could have been indicted and tried as a principal. 'The modern law allowed Leak to be tried and punished as a principal offender. In our judgment he could have been indicted as a principal offender. It would have been no defence for him to submit that if Cogan was an "innocent" agent, he was necessarily in the old terminology of the law a principal in the first degree, which was a legal impossibility as a man cannot rape his own wife during cohabitation. The law no longer concerns itself with niceties of degrees of participation in crime, but even if it did, Leak would still be guilty' (*per* LAWTON LJ).

R v *Cole* [1994] Crim LR 582 (Court of Appeal)

The appellant pleaded guilty to robbery following a ruling by the trial judge on the matter of duress. He had tried to adduce evidence that he had acted under duress when committing a number of robberies at building societies. He owed money to money lenders who had threatened him, his girl friend and their child with violence if the money was not repaid. The trial judge ruled that the facts did not give rise to the defence since the threats had not been directed at the commission of a particular offence, but to the repayment of the debt.

Held, the appeal would be dismissed. The defence of duress could only be made out if the person making the threats told the appellant which crime to commit. Here the appellant had been told to repay the debt; this did not necessarily involve the commission of a crime. There would have to be a more definite link between the danger to the appellant (and others) and the offence committed before the defence of duress could be relied upon. Evidence was required to show that the commission of the offence had been an immediate reaction to the threat made. (But see *DPP* v *Bell*.)

R v *Coles* [1994] Crim LR 820 (Court of Appeal)

The appellant was charged with arson, being reckless as to whether the lives of others would be endangered. He was aged 15 at the time of the alleged offence and was of lower than average mental ability. The evidence was that he had tried to set fire to some hay in a hay barn while playing there with other children. The children escaped unhurt. The trial judge rejected a submission that the *Caldwell* direction, regarding the assessment of whether or not the appellant had, by his actions, created an obvious risk that property would be destroyed or damaged and was reckless as to whether another's life might be endangered, should be made more subjective. The test was whether or not the risk would have been obvious to the reasonable prudent adult person.

Held, the appeal would be dismissed. The state of mind of the accused was irrelevant to the question of whether or not he had, by his act or omission, created an obvious risk of harm to persons or property. The first limb of the *Caldwell* direction was objective. It had been argued that the second limb should have some regard to the defendant's capacity to foresee risk. The Court of Appeal felt that this argument had failed in *Elliot* v *C* [1983] 1 WLR 939 and that that decision had been confirmed by the Court of Appeal in *R* v *Stephen Malcolm* (1984) 79 Cr App R 334. (See also *R* v *Caldwell*.)

R v *Collins* [1972] 3 WLR 243 (Court of Appeal)

The appellant had taken a lot of drink and was desirous of having sexual intercourse. He was passing the complainant's house at about 3.30 am and he saw a light on in an upstairs room which he knew was the complainant's bedroom. He fetched a ladder, put it up against the window and climbed up. He saw the complainant lying on her bed, which was just under the window, naked and asleep. He descended the ladder, stripped off his clothes, climbed back up and pulled himself onto the window sill. As he did so the complainant awoke and saw a naked male form against the window and came to the conclusion that it was her boyfriend, with whom she had spent the evening and with whom she had been on terms of regular and frequent intimacy, and that he had come to pay her an ardent nocturnal visit. She sat up in bed and beckoned him in. The appellant descended from the sill, joined the complainant and they had full sexual intercourse. After a lapse of some time the complainant became suspicious of the length of the appellant's hair; his voice as they exchanged 'love talk' and certain other features made her wonder if he was really her boyfriend. She turned on the bedside light and when she saw that it was not her boyfriend she slapped the appellant's face, bit him as he held her arm, and told him to go. The appellant was convicted of burglary with intent to commit rape, contrary to s9(1)(a) of the Theft Act 1968, after the trial judge told the jury that they had to be satisfied that the appellant had entered the room as a trespasser with intent to commit rape and that the issue of entry as a trespasser depended on the question: was the entry intentional or reckless?

Held, the conviction would be quashed since there cannot be a conviction for entering premises 'as a trespasser' within s9 of the Theft Act 1968 unless the person entering did so knowing that he was a trespasser and nevertheless deliberately entered or was reckless whether or not he was entering the premises of another without the other party's consent. The jury had not been property directed since they should have considered whether the appellant was inside or outside the window at the moment when the complainant beckoned him in. It was also stated that the crucial question for the jury was whether the Crown had established that, at the moment when he entered the bedroom, the appellant knew that he was not welcome there or, being reckless whether or not he was welcome, was nevertheless determined to enter. (Compare *R* v *Ryan*.)

R v *Conway* [1988] 3 All ER 1025 (Court of Appeal)

The appellant was convicted of reckless driving. Fearing for the safety of his car passenger, the appellant had driven recklessly to protect him from what he had believed to be an assassination attempt. A ground of the appeal was that on the evidence before the jury the defence of necessity was raised and the jury should have been, but were not, directed as to that defence.

Held, the appeal would be allowed. '… necessity can only be a defence to a charge of reckless driving where the facts establish "duress of circumstances", as in *R* v *Willer*, ie where the defendant was constrained by circumstances to drive as he did to avoid death or serious bodily harm to himself or some other person … "Duress of circumstances" is available only if from an objective standpoint the defendant can be said to be acting in order to avoid a threat of death or serious injury … [the jury] should have been directed as to the possibility that they could find the appellant not guilty because of duress of circumstances, although they were otherwise satisfied that he had driven recklessly' (*per* WOLF LJ). (See also *R* v *Willer* and *Director of Public Prosecutions* v *Bell*.)

R v *Cooke* [1986] 2 All ER 985 (House of Lords)

The defendant, a member of the BR buffet car staff, was convicted of conspiracy to defraud. He and others decided to sell food and drink to passengers which was not British Railways property and not to account to British Railways for the proceeds of sale. The appeal was on the ground that the charge involved the commission of a substantive offence under s25(1) of the Theft Act 1968 and that he and his co-defendants should have been charged under s1(1) of the Criminal Law Act 1977. The Court of Appeal allowed the appeal and certified the following point of law – 'whether conspiracy to defraud at common law may or may not be charged where the evidence discloses a conspiracy to defraud one alleged victim and in addition discloses a statutory conspiracy to commit a substantive offence and/or discloses a substantive offence against a different alleged victim having regard to ss1 and 5 of the Criminal Law Act 1977.'

Held, the Crown's appeal would be allowed. A conspiracy to defraud at common law might be charged even if the evidence pointed to a statutory conspiracy to commit a substantive offence. Per curiam: a conspiracy which involves the commission of a substantive offence and nothing more can be charged only as a statutory conspiracy to commit that offence. As to selling the food (*per* LORD BRIDGE OF HARWICH): 'Upright citizens as the ordinary run of British Rail passengers may be presumed to be, I am not prepared to assume that they would necessarily refuse to take and pay for refreshments even if they knew perfectly well, that the buffet staff were practising the kind of "fiddle" here involved.' Whether or not the element of 'cheat' under s25(1) is made out is a matter for the jury. (See also *R* v *Doukas*, *R* v *Corboz* and *R* v *Whiteside and Antoniou*.)

R v *Corbett* [1996] Crim LR 594 (Court of Appeal)

The defendant was convicted of the manslaughter of B (who was a mentally handicapped man). Both had been drinking heavily. The defendant attacked B who ran away, fell into a gutter, was struck by a passing vehicle and killed. The trial judge told the jury they had to consider whether what B had done was within the foreseeable range. B had been very drunk – had he done something that might be expected as a reaction of someone in that state? On appeal it was contended the judge should have told the jury that the Crown had to prove death occurred as *the* natural consequence of what the defendant had done. If there had been scope for any other consequence the Crown would not have discharged the burden of proof on them.

Held, the defendant's appeal would be dismissed. The test was not whether the defendant actually foresaw B's conduct but whether that conduct could have reasonably been foreseen as a consequence of what the defendant did. Following *R* v *Roberts,* the trial judge's direction had been correct. (See *R* v *Roberts* (1971) and *R* v *Dear*.)

R v *Corboz* [1984] Crim LR 629 (Court of Appeal)

The appellant, a chief steward employed by British Railways, was convicted of going equipped to cheat contrary to s25(1) of the Theft Act 1968. He had some coffee which it was alleged he was selling or intending to sell to the passengers keeping the proceeds for himself and not telling his employers. He appealed on the grounds that the judge had failed to direct the jury properly on the definition of 'cheat' and the element of dishonesty involved in the offence.

Held, the appeal would be dismissed. The summing-up fully dealt with the matters comprising the offence as laid down by GEOFFREY LANE LJ in *R v Doukas*. (See also *R v Doukas*, *R v Cooke* and *R v Whiteside and Antoniou*.)

R v Cousins [1982] 2 All ER 115 (Court of Appeal)

The defendant was found guilty of threatening to kill contrary to s16 of the Offences against the Person Act 1861 (as amended by Sch 12 to the Criminal Law Act 1977). He appealed on the ground that the trial judge had erred in withdrawing from the jury the issue whether, on the evidence, the defendant had a defence of lawful excuse. He believed that one Kelly Reed, and a cousin of his, had put a contract out to shoot him for beating up Kelly Reed's father. The defendant had gone round to Kelly's parents to make a threat. He wanted to convey that threat to them, backing it up with a gun. He wanted them to think the gun was loaded; he intended them to believe his threat which was to kill their son, Kelly, if he came anywhere near any of his family or him.

Held, the appeal against conviction would be allowed. If there was evidence of facts which could give rise to a lawful excuse, it was the duty of the judge to direct the jury to these facts and, having reminded them that the onus lay with the prosecution to prove the absence of lawful excuse, to have left it to the jury to decide whether the existence of lawful excuse had been disposed of. If there was no evidence of any facts which would give rise to a lawful excuse, it was the duty of the judge to direct the jury accordingly. Here, the judge had directed the jury that lawful excuse did not come into the matter at all, which was not the case.

R v Cox [1995] 2 Cr App R 513 (Court of Appeal)

The appellant admitted killing a young woman during a violent knife attack. The prosecution rejected his plea to plead guilty to manslaughter. His defence was that he had been suffering from diminished responsibility at the time of the attack. On appeal it was contended that although the issue of provocation had not been raised by the defence, the trial judge should have directed the jury to consider the matter given there was evidence that the killing had resulted from a loss of self-control on the appellant's part.

Held, the appeal would be dismissed. There was evidence upon which the jury could have considered the defence of provocation. There was a misdirection in that the trial judge had not dealt with the matter. However, the proviso to s2(1) Criminal Appeal Act 1968 would be applied since the court was satisfied that the jury would have concluded that a reasonable man with the accused characteristics would not have been provoked as he had.

R v Cunningham [1957] 2 All ER 412 (Court of Criminal Appeal)

The appellant was convicted of unlawfully and maliciously causing another to take a noxious thing so as to endanger life, contrary to s23 of the Offences against the Person Act 1861. He tore a gas meter from a wall in an unoccupied house stealing the money and leaving gas to escape, which seeped through the dividing wall into the next house where W came to be partially asphyxiated. The trial judge directed that 'malicious' meant 'wicked'.

Held, the appeal would be allowed. 'Malicious' did not mean 'wicked' in a statutory offence. The jury should have been left to determine whether, even if the appellant had not intended to injure W, he foresaw that the removal of the gas meter might cause injury to someone but he nonetheless removed it. (Approved in *R v Savage; R v Parmenter*; see also *Director of Public Prosecutions v Majewski* and *R v Caldwell*.)

R v *Cunningham* [1981] 2 All ER 863 (House of Lords)

The appellant was convicted of murder. He had attacked the deceased, repeatedly hitting him with a chair, who died from his injuries. The appellant claimed he did not intend to kill the deceased. The trial judge directed the jury that if the appellant was found to have intended really serious harm he ought to be convicted of murder. The Court of Appeal rejected a submission that there had been a misdirection to the jury. In the House of Lords it was contended that murder should be restricted to situations where an accused desired or foresaw the likely consequences of his act as being the death of another; an intention to kill or to endanger life should be proved.

Held, the appeal would be dismissed. It was sufficient to establish an intention to cause grievous bodily harm, even though such intention might fall short of an intention to kill or to endanger life, to prove intent in the crime of murder. (*R v Vickers, Director of Public Prosecutions v Smith* and *Hyam v Director of Public Prosecutions* approved; but see *R v Moloney* and *R v Nedrick*.)

R v *Dalby* [1982] 1 All ER 916 (Court of Appeal)

The appellant was convicted of manslaughter. He and his friend were drug addicts. The appellant supplied a controlled drug (which he had obtained on prescription) to his friend – they each injected themselves intraveneously. The friend later injected himself with another substance; the next day he was dead. The charge of manslaughter was based on the contention that the act of supplying his friend with a controlled drug was an unlawful and dangerous act which had caused his death. On appeal the appellant submitted that the act was not a dangerous one so as to constitute manslaughter; the direct cause of death was not the supply of the drug but that it had been taken in too large a quantity.

Held, the appeal would be allowed. The unlawful and dangerous act which inadvertently caused death had to be directed at the victim and be likely to cause immediate injury to constitute the actus reus of manslaughter. The supplying of the drug was not an act directed against the deceased or one likely to cause him direct injury. Not being a dangerous act it did not constitute the actus reus of manslaughter. (Compare *R v Cato*. See *R v Goodfellow*. Distinguish *Attorney-General's Reference (No 3 of 1994)*.)

R v *Davies* [1975] 1 All ER 890 (Court of Appeal)

The appellant and his wife, librarians employed at a public library at Rochester, were married in 1970. The marriage was happy until 1972 when the wife met one Stedman and began to associate with him. The appellant became very upset and jealous, showed his wife a gun and threatened to kill Stedman. The wife left the matrimonial home and went to live with her parents in Newbury. In October 1972 the appellant broke into his father-in-law's house in the middle of the night, went to his wife's bedroom and showed her a pistol and ammunition indicating that somebody's life was in danger. On 21 December, the appellant went to a house of some mutual friends where his wife was staying, saw her enter the house with Stedman at 11.10 pm and saw Stedman leave at 1.00 am. The appellant had about 17 cans of petrol in his car at the time and proceeded to spread the petrol round the house and set it on fire. On 23 January 1973 the appellant bought a double-barrelled shotgun and 50 rounds of ammunition in the Channel Islands, and on the 30th, armed with these, he went to Rochester to look for his wife. During the course of his search the appellant saw Stedman walking towards the library where his wife worked and followed him. The wife came out of the library and the appellant went up to her, called her by name and shot her, causing her death. The appellant was convicted of arson and murder and appealed contending that with regard to the charge of murder, the trial judge misdirected the jury on the defence of provocation when he told them that provocation was an act or a series of acts done by the victim or words uttered by her to the appellant which would have caused in a reasonable person, and actually caused in the appellant, 'a sudden and temporary loss of self-control rendering the appellant so subject to passion as to make him for the moment not master of his mind', and failed to tell them that they should also consider the part played by Stedman. The trial judge had also told the jury that they could review the whole course of the wife's conduct through 1972 and decide whether the appellant had been provoked to kill her.

Held, the jury, in determining whether an accused had been provoked, were entitled to consider whether acts or words emanating from a person other than the victim had been such as to provoke a reasonable man to do as the appellant had done and there had been a technical misdirection by the judge. The matter had, however, been left to the jury in such a way that they could not have failed to have taken Stedman's actions into account and the proviso to s2 of the Criminal Appeal Act 1968 would be applied. The appeal was dismissed as there had been no miscarriage of justice. (See also *R* v *Brown* (1972).)

R v *Dawson* [1976] Crim LR 692 (Court of Appeal)

The appellant was convicted of robbery contrary to s8(1) of the Theft Act 1968. Three men, including the appellant, approached the victim who was 'nudged' by one of them, causing him to lose his balance, at which point another stole his wallet. It was contended that what was done could not amount to the use of force.

Held, the appeal would be dismissed. The 1968 Act used the word 'force' as opposed to the word 'violence' which had appeared in the Larceny Act 1916. Whether nudging or jostling in this case amounted to the use of force had been left to the jury and it could not be said that they had been wrong. The question under the 1968 Act is whether force had been used in order to steal. (See also *R* v *Clouden*.)

R v Deakin [1972] 3 All ER 803 (Court of Appeal)

A wagon containing a large quantity of spirits was left in Cardiff goods yard one weekend and sometime during the Sunday and Monday night the seals were broken and some 25 cartons stolen. The thieves included two brothers, Terence and Raymond Wall, who lived at the house of a Mrs Thomas in Ninian Park Road, Cardiff. The goods were taken to Mrs Thomas's house during the night but removed early on the Monday afternoon. The police went to the house of the appellant in Port Talbot at 7.30 and 11.30 pm on the Tuesday night; on the first visit there was no answer but on the second the door was opened by the appellant who agreed to accompany them to Cardiff while they made further enquiries. While on the way to Cardiff the appellant told the police that a Mr Nott brought the thieves to his house and that he bought the stolen cartons of spirits from them and gave them to a friend for safe keeping as he heard that the police had been to his (the appellant's) house making enquiries. The appellant was convicted of handling stolen goods contrary to s22(1) of the Theft Act 1968, and appealed contending that, inter alia, as the purchaser he could not be said to have 'undertaken the realisation' of the stolen goods for the benefit of anyone.

Held, the conviction would be affirmed as 'realisation' merely involved the exchange of goods for money and he who paid for the goods was just as much involved in the realisation as he who received the payment and since the former paid the latter the realisation was clearly for the benefit of the latter, even though it might also benefit the former.

R v Dear [1996] Crim LR 595 (Court of Appeal)

The defendant was convicted of murder. He attacked P in response to his daughter's allegation that P had sexually assaulted her. P later died from his wounds. It was contended that P had either reopened his wounds, or had failed to seek medical attention for those wounds which had reopened on their own accord, and this had broken the chain of causation in law.

Held, the appeal would be dismissed. P had died from wounds inflicted by the defendant. His liability should not depend on distinctions between P's negligence or gross negligence in respect of his injuries. The defendant's stabbing of P was a cause in law of P's death even if P had deliberately reopened his wounds. (See further *R v Roberts* (1971), *R v Blaue* and *R v Corbett*; compare *R v Dalby*.)

R v Diggin [1980] Crim LR 656 (Court of Appeal)

The appellant, D, was convicted of allowing himself to be carried in a car taken without consent, contrary to s12(1) of the Theft Act 1968. D's brother had taken the car and then collected D. D, somewhat the worse for drink, thought he was in a friend's car, it being of the same make and year of manufacture. They drove to a service area on the M1, stopped for refreshments, but were seen getting back into the vehicle by the police who arrested them before the vehicle could move off. D claimed it was only when the police approached he realised the car had been taken without consent. The trial judge directed the jury that D's claim was no defence because the offence was committed by 'allowing' oneself to be carried and not by 'being carried'. The offence was committed before the ignition switch was turned on.

Held, the appeal would be allowed. The trial judge had erred in giving his direction to the jury that the offence was committed before the car moved. There must be movement to be carried.

R v Dodge and Harris [1971] 2 All ER 1523 (Court of Appeal)

Harris owed money to a man called Gold who had been led to understand that Harris was expecting a legacy of £24,000. When this was discovered by Gold to be untrue, he said he was owed this sum by the appellant Dodge. In order to discourage Gold from pursuing his writ which he had issued for the money he had loaned to Harris, the appellant Dodge agreed to sign two bonds purporting to be payable by him to Harris. The documents were quite property executed, but the statements regarding the sums of money were untrue. The appellants appealed against their conviction under s1(1) of the Forgery Act 1913 (see now ss1, 9 of the Forgery and Counterfeiting Act 1981).

Held, for a document to be a false document within the meaning of the section, it had to tell a lie about itself. The false statement contained in the bonds were lies about the intention of the parties to implement them and were not lies about the bonds themselves. The appeal would be allowed and the conviction quashed. (See also *R* v *Gambling*.)

R v Donnelly (1984) 79 Cr App R 76 (Court of Appeal)

The appellant, the manager of a jewellery shop, was convicted of forgery contrary to s1 of the Forgery and Counterfeiting Act 1981. He drew up what was purported to be a valuation certificate concerning items of jewellery which in fact did not exist. The object was to defraud an insurance company. The trial judge was of the opinion that the valuation was a false instrument within the meaning of s9(1)(g) of the 1981 Act. He directed the jury that an instrument could be false if it purported to be made in circumstances in which it was not in fact made. An appeal was made on the ground that the certificate was not capable of being a false instrument.

Held, the appeal would be dismissed. The words 'otherwise in circumstances' in s9(1)(g) expanded the ambit of the subsection beyond dates and places in *any* case in which an instrument purported to be made when in fact it was not made. In this case the certificate purported to have been made after the examination of certain jewellery which did not in fact exist. The document told a lie about itself. It was a worthless piece of paper which was a forgery. The judges' direction had been correct.

R v Doukas [1978] 1 All ER 1061 (Court of Appeal)

The appellant, a wine waiter at a hotel, was convicted of going equipped to 'cheat' contrary of s25(1) of the Theft Act 1968, which by ss25(5) and 15 of the 1968 Act meant obtaining property by deception. He would use his own wine on occasions, making out a separate bill for the customers, and keep the money. The grounds of appeal included a contention that the prosecution evidence did not prove the necessary causal link between the intended deception and getting the money from the customer.

Held, the appeal would be dismissed. A hypothetical customer being reasonably honest and intelligent would not have willingly been a party to a fraud by the waiter on his employers. The jury could conclude that his obtaining money from the customer was the result of a deception practised on that customer. GEOFFREY LANE LJ analysed the combined provisions of s25(1) and s15(1). The following have to be proved: there was an article for use in connection with the deception, a proposed deception, an intention to obtain property by means of the deception, dishonesty and that the obtaining would have been, wholly or partially, by virtue of the deception. (See also *R* v *Corboz, R* v *Cooke* and *R* v *Whiteside and Antoniou*.)

R v Dryden [1995] 4 All ER 987 (Court of Appeal)

The appellant was convicted of murder. He had built a bungalow without planning permission. C, the local planning authority's principal planning officer, along with other officers, told the appellant his property was about to be demolished. The appellant went inside, found a pistol and shot C dead. At his trial the appellant raised the defence of diminished responsibility and provocation, but he was convicted. On appeal the defendant contended that the trial judge should have drawn attention to the appellant's obsessive personality and paranoia as characteristics that should be attributed to the reasonable person for the purposes of the objective test for provocation.

Held, the appeal would be dismissed. The shot had not been fired as a result of a sudden and temporary loss of self-control. He had previously said what he would do if his property was demolished. However, that the appellant demonstrated an obsessiveness as to his right to use his land as he pleased, was something significant which attributed to him something different from others. This ought to have been put to the jury as a characteristic to be attributed to the reasonable man. (See further *R* v *Humphreys, R* v *Morhall, R* v *Stewart* and *R* v *Thornton (No 2)*.)

R v Dudley [1989] Crim LR 57 (Court of Appeal)

The appellant was charged with arson contrary to s1(1) and (2) of the Criminal Damage Act 1971. He pleaded guilty to the charge under s1(1) and there was a trial under s1(2). He had thrown a fire-bomb at a house in which there lived a family with whom he had a grievance. It caused a small fire which was put out quickly and there was little damage. The trial judge rejected a submission by the defence of no case to answer in that the jury could not properly find that the actual damage caused was intended to endanger life or was likely to do so. The defendant changed his plea to guilty – being reckless as to whether the life of another would be endangered. He appealed against conviction on the ground that the judge's ruling was wrong in law.

Held, the appeal would be dismissed. The intention to endanger life, or recklessness as to whether life would be endangered, should be looked at in the light of the harm he intended to cause and not simply at the harm he did cause. (See also *R* v *Webster and Others; R* v *Warwick*.)

R v Dudley and Stephens (1884) QBD 273

Dudley and Stephens, together with two others, Brooks and the cabin-boy Parker, were shipwrecked about 1,600 miles from the Cape of Good Hope and cast adrift in an open boat. After they had been drifting for twenty days and had been without food for nine days and without water for seven days, Dudley and Stephens, Brooks refusing to assent, decided to kill Parker and feed upon his body. Dudley killed Parker, who was the weakest of the four and who in no way assented to his death, and all three fed upon his flesh for four days when they were picked up by a passing vessel. It was proved that at the time when Parker was killed there was no ship in sight or any reasonable prospect of being rescued and that Dudley and Stephens believed that if they did not feed upon the boy or one of themselves they would all have died of starvation.

Held, they were guilty of murder. The defence of necessity could not be invoked since the fact that the killing afforded their only reasonable prospect of saving their lives was no legal justification for it.

R v Durkin [1973] 2 All ER 872 (Court of Appeal)

Durkin entered the art gallery at Middlesbrough at 1.30am one Sunday by breaking a window. He rushed upstairs, removed an L S Lowry painting which was on exhibition in the first floor gallery and then made his exit. He hid the painting inside a warehouse and then sent a note to the Teeside Council Arts Committee with four demands: that they should install an efficient alarm system in the Teeside museums and art galleries; that all museums and art galleries in Teeside should be opened on Sundays for a trial run, using unemployed men as attendants; that the local authority should give a donation of £100 to each of two named charities and that the local authority should raffle a pair of the mayor's underpants and give the proceeds to another charity. The art gallery was owned by the local authority and was opened to the public on weekdays but closed on Sundays. Only part of the collection of pictures owned by the authority was on view at any one time but the pictures were all shown at least once a year, sections of the collection being exhibited at various times of the year for short periods. He was convicted of, inter alia, removing the painting from the gallery, contrary to s11(1) of the Theft Act 1968, and appealed.

Held, the conviction would be affirmed as the words 'a collection intended for permanent exhibition to the public' within s11(2) meant simply a collection intended to be permanently available for exhibition to the public and that intention was sufficiently manifested by the local authority's settled practice of periodically displaying to the public at the art gallery the pictures in their permanent collection.

R v Egan [1992] 4 All ER 470 (Court of Appeal)

The appellant was convicted of murder. He had a mentality said to approach the border of the subnormal. Under the influence of drink he forcefully and unlawfully entered the house of an elderly widow, severely assaulted and killed her. The Crown did not accept his plea of guilty to manslaughter on the basis of diminished responsibility pursuant to s2(1) of the Homicide Act 1957 on the ground of abnormality of mind which substantially impaired his mental responsibility. The appeal was on the ground that the judge had misdirected the jury by failing to direct them to disregard the effect of alcohol and by directing their attention to questions of causation rather than the contribution of abnormality of mind to the mental responsibility for the killing.

Held, the appeal would be dismissed. The judge did direct the jury's mind to the vital question 'was the appellant's abnormality of mind such that he would have been under diminished responsibility, drink or no drink? ... There was much evidence upon which the jury could properly have rejected, as they did, the attempt to prove diminished responsibility and, in doing so, must have rejected the contention of the defence that the disinhibiting effect of alcohol was irrelevant because the defendant would have killed without it ... the judgments in *R* v *Gittens* and *R* v *Atkinson* ... should be regarded together as representing, in our opinion, the high authority on this troublesome subject of diminished responsibility where drink is a factor. We add to them, where it is maintained that alcoholism alone can establish this defence, the judgment in *R* v *Tandy* ... guidance as to the meaning of "substantial" should be explicitly provided for the jury by using one or other of the two meanings in *R* v *Lloyd*' (*per* WATKINS LJ).

R v Elbekkay [1995] Crim LR 163 (Court of Appeal)

The appellant stayed the night at the house of the complainant and her boyfriend, E. After an evening drinking E fell asleep in the room in which the appellant was going to stay. The appellant went into the complainant's bedroom and started having sexual intercourse with her. The complainant very soon realised she was not having sex with her boyfriend but with the appellant. She punched and stabbed the appellant to stop him. On behalf of the appellant it was unsuccessfully argued that the actus reus of rape had not occurred in that the complainant had initially consented. On appeal it was argued that there was no liability for rape under s1(2) of the Sexual Offences Act 1956 nor under s1(3) because instances of impersonation were limited to the defendant impersonating the complainant's husband.

Held, the appeal would be dismissed. Parliament had not intended to exclude the possibility of liability for rape arising where a defendant procured intercourse by impersonating the long standing sexual partner of an unmarried woman. (See also *R* v *R*.)

R v Ellames [1974] 3 All ER 130 (Court of Appeal)

A Ford Cortina car was stolen in Plumstead on 13 April 1973, and a robbery took place at the premises of a company in the Isle of Dogs in the afternoon. Two men, both disguised, burst into an office where the wages were being prepared for payment to the staff of the company and held up the office staff with a sawn-off shotgun. They squirted ammonia at the staff from a 'squeezy lemon squirter'. Having grabbed a drawer in which were the wage packets for the staff, and which contained a total of £850 odd, they ran out of the office and went off in the Cortina car which was driven by a third man. About 6.45 pm that evening the police found a blue tartan bag in a small hut or caravan near Shed 30 at the West India Docks and in it were the sawn-off shotgun, a pair of goggles, brown wig, two masks and the black hat used in the robbery, two 'Jif' lemons containing ammonia solution, two other shotguns, some cartridges, a pair of white gloves and other articles. The following morning the police also found a boiler suit, the wooden drawer which had contained the wage packets, some empty wage packets, 3 pairs of gloves, wage slips, two cricket balls and some other items in a locker in the amenity block. In a written statement to the police Ellames purported to admit that he had known about the robbery before it happened and that he had agreed to clear up afterwards. He said that as he was walking up and down outside Shed 32 on the afternoon of the robbery, a blue car pulled up with three men in it. One of them told him to dump the car and get rid of the articles used in the robbery. He was convicted of having articles for theft contrary to s25 of the Theft Act 1968. The trial judge had told the jury that, inter alia, a person can be convicted of an offence under s25(1) of the 1968 Act if he was in possession of the articles used in connection with theft immediately after the theft was completed. He appealed.

Held, the conviction should be quashed as there was a misdirection in the summing-up. The court stated that to establish an offence under s25(1) the prosecution must prove that the defendant was in possession of the article and intended the article to be used in the course of or in connection with some future burglary, theft or cheat, although it is not necessary to prove that he intended it to be used in connection with any specific burglary, theft or cheat.

R v Feely [1973] 1 All ER 341 (Court of Appeal)

Feely was employed as a branch manager by a firm of bookmakers. The employers sent a circular to all their managers stating the practice of borrowing from the employers' tills was to stop. A month after receiving the circular Feely took £30 from the employers' safe to give to his father. He was transferred four days later to another branch and the new manager discovered the loss. Feely gave him an IOU to cover the deficiency. In a written statement to the police the appellant said he had borrowed £30 from 'the float' and intended to pay it back, that he had given an IOU and that his employers owed him £70 in wages and commission. He was charged with theft contrary to s1(1) of the Theft Act 1968. A wages clerk gave evidence that the employers owed Feely £40 for wages and £16 by way of bonus. The judge said it was no defence for the appellant to say he intended to repay the money and had the means to repay it or that the employers owned him more than enough to cover what he had taken. He did not direct the jury to decide whether the Crown had proved that the appellant had taken the money dishonestly. He expressed his concept of dishonesty as follows: 'If someone does something deliberately knowing that his employers are not prepared to tolerate it, is that not dishonest?' Feely was convicted and appealed.

Held, the conviction should be quashed as it is a defence for a person charged with theft and proved to have appropriated money to say that the appropriation was not dishonest in that when he took the money he intended to repay it and had reasonable grounds for believing and did believe that he would be able to do so. Also it is a question of fact for the jury whether the money was appropriated dishonestly. (See also *R v O'Connell*.)

R v Feeny (1992) 94 Cr App R 1 (Court of Appeal)

The appellant, a solicitor, was convicted of two offences of obtaining property by deception, contrary to s15 of the Theft Act 1968. With two others, G and P, it was alleged that he helped to arrange a series of false sales of a property which G wanted to sell and P to purchase. Such would inflate the price and thus the amount advanced by way of mortgage to P. The appellant was said by the prosecution to have known what was going on, and to have been deliberately dishonest, acting as he was on behalf of the building society as well as the purchaser. He maintained that he had no knowledge of the fraud, and that if he had done wrong it was because of his faulty judgment, even negligence, but not dishonesty. The judge raised the issue of recklessness for the first time in his summing-up.

Held, the appeal would be allowed. The judge should have allowed counsel to address him on recklessness and deal with it before the jury. The jury must not confuse recklessness with dishonesty nor conclude that dishonesty inevitably follows recklessness. This was especially so where the defendant denied dishonesty but explained his actions as arising from a fault of his professional judgment or negligence. Dishonesty (s15(1)) had to be established as a separate and essential ingredient of the offence, even though the deception might have been made recklessly or deliberately (s15(4)). As the judge's summing-up might have led the jury to confuse recklessness with dishonesty, they might have convicted on an incorrect basis and one on which counsel had not addressed them, so the conviction would be quashed. (But see *Halstead* v *Patel*.)

R v *Fernandes* [1996] 1 Cr App R 175 (Court of Appeal)

D, a solicitor, was convicted of a number of offences, including theft. He received money on behalf of a client, which was to be held in a building society account; no withdrawals were to be made without a court order. D nonetheless withdrew money and invested it in a money-lending business run by R, his bookkeeper. D was later unable to account for the money. It was suggested that the trial judge may have misled the jury into equating the placing of P's funds into a risky investment with an intention to permanently deprive P of those funds. It was also contended that the first limb of s6(1) Theft Act 1968 was restricted to instances where D took P's property and resold, or attempted to re-sell, it to P, and that the second limb of s6(1) applied to instances where D borrowed or lent P's property in circumstances whereby it became valueless on its being returned to P (*per* observations by LORD LANE CJ in *R* v *Lloyd* (1985) 81 Cr App R 182). It was argued that D's case, at best, fell within the second limb of s6(1) and the trial judge had not directed the jury on this matter.

Held, the appeal relating to D's conviction for theft would be dismissed. Section 6(1) did not have the limited meaning put forward on D's behalf, nor did LORD LANE suggest it should be so limited. Did D intend to 'treat the thing as his own to dispose of regardless of the other's rights? ... s6 may apply to a person in possession or control of another's property who, dishonestly and for his own purpose, deals with that property in such a manner that he knows he is risking its loss' (per AULD LJ). (See also *R* v *Marshall; R* v *Coombes; R* v *Eren*.)

R v *Firth* [1990] Crim LR 326 (Court of Appeal)

The appellant, a consultant gynaecologist/obstetrician, was convicted on four counts of evading a liability by deception contrary to s2(1)(c) of the Theft Act 1978. It was alleged that he had treated private patients in an NHS hospital but failed to inform the hospital and thereby avoided being billed for those services used. He appealed on the grounds that an offence contrary to s2(1)(c) could not be committed by omission and that at the time of the alleged deception there had been no existing liability to make a payment.

Held, the appeal would be dismissed. By not informing the hospital as he should have done (presumably under his contract with the hospital) the offence could be committed by omission. Under s2(1)(c) there was no reference to any 'existing liability' as there was under s2(1)(a) and s2(1)(b). Therefore no existing liability had to be shown at the time of deception.

R v Flatt [1996] Crim LR 576 (Court of Appeal)

The appellant, a drug addict, was convicted of possession of prohibited drugs with intent to supply. He owed money to a drug dealer who had threatened to shoot the appellant's family if he did not look after a consignment of drugs. In examining the objective element of the test for duress the trial judge did not direct the jury to consider how the reasonable drug addict would have responded to the threats.

Held, the appeal would be dismissed. There had been no error in the direction by not attributing the characteristic of being a drug addict to the 'person of reasonable fortitude' in the test for duress. Either there was no reason to conclude that a drug addict would display less fortitude than any other person or the mental abnormality induced by addicts was self-induced and therefore excluded on grounds of public policy. (See *R v Bowen*; compare *R v Tandy*.)

R v Fotheringham (1989) 88 Cr App R 206 (Court of Appeal)

The appellant was charged with and convicted of rape contrary to s1 of the Sexual Offences (Amendment) Act 1976. His defence to raping a 14-year-old girl, who had been babysitting for him and his wife, was that he was so drunk at the time of the offence that he thought he was having sexual intercourse with his wife. The judge directed the jury that they consider whether there were reasonable grounds, which would be reasonable to a sober man, for the appellant to believe that he was sleeping with his wife. It was argued on appeal that the judge had erred in law in directing the jury to disregard the appellant's self-induced intoxication as a defence.

Held, the appeal would be dismissed. Self-induced intoxication was not a defence, be the issue intention, consent or mistake (as here) as to the identity of the victim. The judge had been correct in his direction of the jury.

R v Gallasso [1993] Crim LR 459 (Court of Appeal)

The appellant was convicted of the theft of a cheque for £1,800. She was a nurse caring for mentally disturbed adults and looked after her patients' financial affairs, drawing money from their accounts for their day-to-day expenses. A patient, J, received a cheque for £4,000 for which the appellant opened a second account in J's name. Later the appellant transferred

£3,000 from the second account to the patient's first account and the balance of £1,000 to her own account. A further £1,800 sent to J was used by the appellant to open a cash card account in J's name. The conviction for theft related to the £1,000 transferred to her own account and the £1,800 used to open the cash card account. The appeal was in respect of the £1,800.

Held, the appeal would be allowed and the conviction for theft of the cheque for £1,800 quashed. In this instance the appellant had acted properly in relation to the cheque, holding up J's right to the money. Her course of action did not amount to an appropriation. Any secret dishonest intent did not change this. (But see *R v Gomez*.)

R v Gambling [1974] 3 All ER 479 (Court of Appeal)

The appellant was convicted of forgery. He had paid successive visits to five different post offices in South London, opening a savings bank account in each of them. In filling in the form he gave a false name in each case, a false date of birth and a false address. He also signed the printed declaration in the names of non-existent persons. When the applications were received the suspicions of the Post Office were aroused. The police were informed and when the appellant went to collect his savings account book from one of the post offices, he was questioned by police officers. He admitted his correct name and that he was the person who had made each of five applications in names other than his own and with untrue particulars. At the trial he stated the purpose of opening accounts in different names other than his own was he wished to operate a system for betting on horses. It did not involve dishonesty but he expected to win large sums. Such success, if achieved by one person, would cause bookmakers to decline further bets with that person. He denied that he intended to defraud the Post Office or anyone else.

Held, each application was false (s1(2) Forgery Act 1913; see now ss1, 9 of the Forgery and Counterfeiting Act 1981) and the jury, properly directed, could have concluded that if the Post Office had known, for example, that the appellant had signed one of the forms in a name other than his own, it would have refused to open the account. The trial judge gave a misdirection on the words 'fictitious person', and s1(2) (see s9(1)(h), 1981 Act) above and an inadequate direction on what is forgery. The conviction would be quashed. (See also *R v Dodge and Harris*.)

R v Garwood [1987] 1 All ER 1032 (Court of Appeal)

The appellant was convicted of blackmail, making an 'unwarranted demand with menaces', contrary to s21(1) of the Theft Act 1968. The victim gave the appellant £10 after the appellant had accused him of 'doing his house over' and had demanded that the victim pay him £10 'to make it quits'; he also demanded £20 to be paid three days later and then 'he would be protected'. The appellant had also said 'Don't tell the police or your parents or I'll get you'. The appellant gave a different version of events. The appellant appealed contending that there had been a misdirection as to the meaning of the word 'menaces'.

Held, the appeal would be dismissed. Although the jury had to some extent been misdirected the court felt it was a case for the application of the proviso to s2(1) of the Criminal Appeal

Act 1968. In explaining the meaning of the word 'menaces' LORD LANE CJ stated: 'It is an ordinary word of which the meaning will be clear to any jury. As CAIRNS LJ said in *R* v *Lawrence; R* v *Pomroy* (1971) 57 Cr App R 64 at 72: "In exceptional cases where because of special knowledge in special circumstances what would be a menace to an ordinary person is not a menace to the person to whom it is addressed, or where the converse may be true, it is no doubt necessary to spell out the meaning of the word." It seems to us that there are two possible occasions on which a further direction on the meaning of the word menaces may be required. The first is where the threats might have affected the mind of an ordinary person of normal stability but did not affect the person actually addressed. In such circumstances that would amount to a sufficient menace: see *R* v *Clear* ... The second situation is where the threats in fact affected the mind of the victim, although they would not have affected the mind of a person of normal stability. In that case, in our judgment, the existence of menaces is proved provided that the accused man was aware of the likely effect of his actions on the victim.' (See also *R* v *Harvey*.)

R v Gateway Foodmarkets Ltd [1997] 3 All ER 78 (Court of Appeal)

The defendant company pleaded guilty to a charge under s2(1) Health and Safety at Work Act 1974, namely failing to ensure, so far as is reasonably practicable, the health and safety and welfare at work of employees. Such plea followed the trial judge's ruling that the offence was one of strict liability. The contact mechanism of the store's service lift exhibited recurring problems. The maintenance company used by the defendant company had shown the staff how to free the mechanism manually. A section manager went into the control room to free the contact mechanism and fell to his death through a trap door. The defendant company appealed on the ground that since it had not known of the practice at the store by which the lift mechanism was freed, it was not responsible for the failure to conform to s2(1).

Held, the appeal would be dismissed. The offence was one of strict liability. If the prosecution made out the circumstances specified in s2(1) the company was guilty. It was for the defendant company to demonstrate that all reasonable precautions had been taken by its employees. There had not been a safe system of work operated by the store management, so the company was criminally liable.

R v Geddes (1996) The Times 16 July (Court of Appeal)

The appellant was convicted of attempted kidnapping. He was found trespassing in the boys' toilet of a school having with him a rucksack in which were lengths of string, sealing wax, a knife and other items. An appeal was made on the basis that the trial judge had misdirected the jury as to what constituted an attempt in law.

Held, the appeal would be allowed. With reference to s1(1) Criminal Attempts Act 1981 an attempt is committed if it is shown that the defendant has done an act which demonstrated he was actually trying to commit the action in question rather than merely putting himself in the position of equipping himself in order to do so. There had been no contact with pupils; there was insufficient evidence to show he had tried to commit the offence.

R v Ghosh [1982] 2 All ER 689 (Court of Appeal)

The defendant was convicted of attempting to obtain, and obtaining, money by deception contrary to s15(1) of the Theft Act 1968. He was a consultant acting as a locum at a hospital; he falsely pretended that money was due to him for an operation which had been carried out by another person and/or under the National Health Service. His defence was that the money in question was properly payable to him as consultation fees; he had therefore not acted dishonestly. In directing the jury, the judge said that it was for them to decide whether or not the defendant had acted 'dishonestly' within the meaning of the Act by applying their own standards of honesty. On his appeal against conviction, the defendant contended that the judge had misdirected the jury. Was the test for 'dishonesty' a subjective one – descriptive of the defendant's state of mind (did he know he was acting dishonestly?), or an objective one characterising a course of conduct (had he in fact acted dishonestly?).

Held, the appeal would be dismissed. To determine whether an accused had acted dishonestly, the test was first whether the defendant's actions had been dishonest according to the ordinary standards of reasonable and honest persons and, if so, whether the defendant himself had realised that his actions were, according to those standards, dishonest. Dishonesty could not be determined completely objectively by the jury – dishonesty described not a course of conduct but a state of mind which had to take account of the defendant's knowledge and belief. There had been no miscarriage of justice – the jury had rejected the defendant's explanation of events and a finding of dishonesty was inevitable whichever test of dishonesty was applied. (See also *R v Lightfoot*.)

R v Gilks [1972] 3 All ER 280 (Court of Appeal)

Gilks placed a bet on a horse with a bookmaker. The horse was unplaced but the bookmaker paid him £106 in the mistaken belief that he had backed the winner. Gilks knew that the bookmaker had made a mistake and that he was not entitled to the money but nevertheless kept it. He was charged with theft and contended that in paying the money the bookmaker did not suppose, since the bet was a gaming transaction, that he was discharging a legal liability. He was, in fact, simply making a gift and accordingly at the moment of payment the money was not money 'belonging to another' for at that very moment the ownership was transferred; furthermore, s5(4) of the Theft Act 1968 had no application because the defendant had no obligation to repay the money. He was convicted and appealed.

Held, the conviction would be affirmed as at the moment of payment the sum paid was 'property belonging to another' and since at that moment he knew that the sum was being paid by mistake, he was guilty of theft in accepting it.

R v Gill (1993) 97 Cr App R 215 (Court of Appeal)

The appellant was convicted of conspiracy to offer to supply a controlled class A drug, contrary to s4(1)(b) of the Misuse of Drugs Act 1971. He had been seen taking £20 for a bag containing pills. A bag of vitamin C tablets was found on his co-defendant but nothing on him. A submission that he had been cheating his customers offering to supply ecstasy but actually supplying vitamin C tablets was rejected.

Held, the appeal would be dismissed. The offence was complete when the offer to supply the controlled drug was made; he did not have to intend to supply it. The fact that the appellant was charged with a conspiracy rather than the substantive offence made no difference.

R v Gittens [1984] 3 All ER 252 (Court of Appeal)

The appellant was charged with the murders of his wife and step-daughter. At the time of the alleged offence he had been suffering from depression and the effects of alcohol and drugs. The defence of diminished responsibility was raised at the trial under s2(1) of the Homicide Act 1957. The judge directed the jury that they had to decide whether the substantial cause of the appellant's conduct was abnormality of mind due to inherent causes or whether it was due to drink and drugs. The appellant was convicted and appealed.

Held, the appeal would be allowed and verdicts of manslaughter on the ground of diminished responsibility substituted for the convictions of murder. 'Where alcohol or drugs are factors to be considered by the jury, the best approach is that adopted by the judge and approved by this court in *R v Fenton* (1975) 61 Cr App R 261. The jury should be directed to disregard what, in their view, the effect of the alcohol or drugs on the defendant was, since abnormality of mind induced by alcohol or drugs is not, generally speaking, due to inherent causes and is not therefore within the section. Then the jury should consider whether the combined effect of the other matters which do fall within the section amounted to such abnormality of mind as substantially impaired the defendant's mental responsibility within the meaning of "substantial" set out in *R v Lloyd'* (*per* LORD LANE CJ). (See also *R v Tandy* and *R v Egan*.)

R v Gold; R v Schifreen [1988] 2 All ER 186 (House of Lords)

The respondents were charged with and convicted of contravening s1 of the Forgery and Counterfeiting Act 1981 by making a 'false instrument' (defined by s8(1) of the Act) with the intention of using it to induce a databank to accept it as genuine to the prejudice of the company operating the system. They had gained entry to the databank by 'hacking', ie by using identification numbers and passwords of other persons without permission to obtain information without payment and to alter data without authority. It was contended by the respondents that they had not made a 'false instrument' – they had not made a 'device on or in which information is recorded or stored by … electronic or other means'.

Held, affirming the Court of Appeal's decision to allow the appeals, the respondents had not made an instrument as recording and storing information was more than the computer momentarily holding the identification numbers and passwords while verifying them.

R v Gomez [1993] 1 All ER 1 (House of Lords)

The respondent, who was the assistant manager in an electrical goods shop, was charged with theft, contrary to s1(1) of the Theft Act 1968. A man named Ballay was in possession of two stolen building society cheques. Ballay asked the respondent if he would supply him electrical goods in exchange for the cheques. The respondent knew that the cheques were stolen but failed to tell his manager when he asked him if the shop would accept them.

Following the manager's approval, goods to the value of £16,000 were supplied to Ballay. The cheques were dishonoured. The respondent argued that there had been no 'appropriation' under s1(1) of the Theft Act 1968 – the manager had expressly authorised the goods to be removed. The judge rejected this submission and the respondent changed his plea to guilty. He appealed on the ground that the judge's ruling was wrong. The Court of Appeal allowed the appeal holding that there had been no appropriation because under the contract of sale there was a voidable contract between the shop and Ballay which had not been avoided at the time the goods were handed over. The Crown appealed.

Held, the appeal would be allowed. Where the owner of goods was induced by fraud, deception or a false representation to authorise goods to be taken, such could amount to an offence under s1(1) of the 1968 Act. There was a taking of goods with an intention by the respondent to assume the rights of the owner amounting to an appropriation; the deception practised on the owner made the appropriation dishonest. (*Lawrence v Commissioner of Police for the Metropolis* applied; see also *R v Morris, Dobson v General Accident Fire and Life Assurance Corp plc, R v Mazo, R v Hopkins; R v Kendrick* and *R v Hinks*; but see *R v Gallasso*.)

R v Goodfellow [1986] Crim LR 468 (Court of Appeal)

The appellant was convicted of manslaughter and arson. He had set fire to his council house hoping that he would then be rehoused by the council. His wife and children died in the blaze. The judge heard submissions as to whether the jury should be directed on the basis of the act creating an 'obvious and serious risk' or on the basis that the act was unlawful and dangerous.

Held, the appeal would be dismissed – this case was capable of falling within either or both types of manslaughter. The questions for the jury in a case such as the present are (1) was the act intentional? (2) was it unlawful? (3) was it an act which any reasonable person would realise was bound to subject some other human being to the risk of physical harm, albeit not necessarily serious harm? (4) was that act the cause of death?

R v Goodwin [1996] Crim LR 262 (Court of Appeal)

The appellant was convicted of going equipped to steal. He used Kenyan five shilling pieces (identical in dimensions to 50 pence pieces but worth approximately half the value) in gaming machines. He appealed on the basis that the coins that issued forth from the machines would have become his property, so stalling a conviction for theft.

Held, the appeal would be dismissed. The wrongful method used to cause the machines to pay out did not enable the property in the prize money to pass to him.

R v Gotts [1992] 1 All ER 833 (House of Lords)

The appellant was charged with attempted murder and wounding with intent. He stabbed his mother who was seriously injured. He said that his father had ordered him to kill his mother; if he failed to do so he would be shot. A submission that the defence of duress was as a matter of law open to the appellant in relation to the charge of attempted murder was rejected by the judge. The appellant then pleaded guilty to attempted murder; he appealed against his conviction. The Court of Appeal dismissed his appeal and certified under s33(2) of the Criminal Appeal Act 1968 that the following point of law of general public importance was involved in the decision: is the defence of duress available to a person charged with attempted murder?

Held, the appeal would be dismissed. 'The reason why duress has for so long been stated not to be available as a defence to a murder charge is that the law regards the sanctity of human life and the protection thereof as of paramount importance' (*per* LORD JAUNCEY). '... the speeches of LORD JAUNCEY OF TULLICHETTLE and LORD LOWRY both demonstrate that at the present time it is uncertain whether or not the law permits duress to be pleaded as a defence to a charge of attempted murder ... The law does not allow duress as a defence to murder itself on the policy grounds that it is not right to allow a man to take the life of another in order to save his own ... that policy reason applies equally to attempted murder. I can see no logical or policy reason for differentiating between the case of the successful and the unsuccessful would-be murderer' (*per* LORD BROWNE-WILKINSON).

R v Gould [1968] 1 All ER 849 (Court of Appeal)

The appellant was convicted of bigamy under s57 of the Offences against the Person Act 1861. At the time of the second marriage he honestly believed that his first marriage had been dissolved and had reasonable grounds for this belief. In fact the first marriage had not been dissolved and his first wife was still living.

Held, the conviction would be quashed. An honest belief on reasonable grounds was a good defence to a charge of bigamy if the consequences of that belief being true would be that an offence under s57 had not been committed. (See also *R v King*.)

R v Governor of Brixton Prison, ex parte Levin [1997] 1 Cr App R 335 (Queen's Bench Divisional Court)

The defendant was in prison pending the decision upon a US request for extradition. He had carried out a number of frauds causing US banks to transfer money to accounts controlled by his associates. Money had been withdrawn from these accounts. The defendant applied for a writ of habeus corpus on the basis that his detention was unlawful. He argued he had not committed the offence of producing a false instrument by entering a password onto a computer disk, and that any appropriation took place when he entered commands on his keyboard in Russia. The English courts, therefore, did not have jurisdiction.

Held, the application would be refused. A computer disk came within the definition of 'instrument' as the word was used in s8(1) Forgery and Counterfeiting Act 1981. By entering false instructions onto the disk it was falsified. Albeit the defendant was in St Petersburg when operating the keyboard, he was in fact operating on magnetic disks in New Jersey.

R v Grainge [1974] 1 All ER 928 (Court of Appeal)

The appellant and a co-defendant named O'Connor and a third man entered a shop in Sheffield which sold machinery and stationery. O'Connor stole a pocket calculating machine valued at £59. The loss was soon noticed and the salesman went out of the shop into the street to search for the three men. He saw them and noticed one pass the calculator to the appellant. The salesman reported the matter to a police officer who cautioned and arrested the three men. On the way to the offices of the Criminal Investigation Department the officer saw the appellant pass the calculator across towards the pocket of O'Connor. In evidence the appellant said: 'I never gave it a second thought. He is a friend of mine. I have known him two or three years. He has never been dishonest. I never even asked him about it. I just put it in my pocket. I thought it was a radio.' He was convicted of handling stolen goods.

Held, the appeal would be allowed. The recorder had spoken in his direction to the jury about suspicion that the property was stolen when it was handled as an ingredient of the offence. Section 22 of the Theft Act 1968 has clarified the law. It provides, inter alia, that if 'knowing or believing' goods to be stolen a person dishonestly receives them he is guilty of the offence of handling stolen goods. The section does not say that suspicion is enough. The recorder should have made plain that it was at that moment of receipt and not at any time during the handling thereafter that guilty knowledge had to be proved. (But see *Atwal* v *Massey*.)

R v Greatrex; R v Bates [1999] 1 Cr App R 126 (Court of Appeal)

The appellants, G and B, were convicted of murder. They and others made a concerted attack on the victim, who kicked violently. The victim was hit on the head by B using a bar, and, as a result, died. The appellants were charged with murder and affray. B admitted using the bar, striking only one blow, aimed at the victim's body in order to rescue a friend who had been fighting with the deceased. G pleaded guilty to affray; he denied any intention to do really serious harm and any knowledge that B would use a bar during the attack. The jury was directed that they had to be satisfied, in respect of each appellant, that they showed an intention to do really serious harm when together they joined in the attack on the deceased. Could G be convicted of murder if, notwithstanding his intent to cause really serious injury to the deceased, he neither intended nor foresaw the act by which death was caused, nor knew of the weapon by which it was caused.

Held, G's appeal would be allowed and his conviction for murder quashed; B's appeal would be dismissed. The trial judge failed to invite the jury to consider whether G foresaw B's use of the bar and whether it was outside the combined purpose. (See also *R* v *Powell and Daniels; R* v *English*.)

R v Griffiths [1965] 2 All ER 448 (Court of Criminal Appeal)

Griffiths, a supplier of lime to farmers, an employee of his, Booth, and a number of farmers were charged with and convicted of, inter alia, a conspiracy between all of them to defraud the Ministry of Agriculture, Fisheries and Food by inducing the Ministry to pay excessive contributions under the Agriculture Lime Scheme 1947-60 by submitting to the Ministry fraudulent claims for compensation. There was no link between any of the farmers who came from areas very far apart and had never met, or between any of them and Griffiths or Booth, other than that they had each entered into contracts with him for lime to be supplied to them and to be spread on their lands.

Held, the convictions should be quashed. Although there were a number of separate conspiracies between Griffiths, Booth and the individual farmers, Griffiths, Booth and all the farmers could not be said to have been acting in pursuance of a common criminal purpose. (Compare *R v Chrastny*.)

R v Gullefer (1990) 91 Cr App R 356 (Court of Appeal)

The appellant was convicted of contravening s1(1) of the Criminal Attempts Act 1981 by attempted theft of an £18 stake which he had wagered with a bookmaker. He had tried to distract the dogs when they were racing by climbing the fence onto the track and waving his arms. He also admitted he had tried to stop the race because the dog he had backed with £18 was losing. Had the dogs been distracted sufficiently the stewards would have declared 'no race' and he would have been able to recover his stake money from the bookmaker. Was the act of the appellant sufficiently proximate to the completed offence of theft to be capable of comprising an attempt to commit theft? Was his act more than merely preparatory to the commission of the offence?

Held, the appeal would be allowed. When the appellant jumped onto the track it could not be said that he was in the process of committing theft, stealing £18 from the bookmaker. He tried to distract the dogs, in turn he hoped the stewards would declare 'no race', in turn this would enable him to ask for the £18 he had staked with the bookmaker. This was judged to be insufficient evidence for it to be said that he had, when he jumped onto the track, gone beyond mere preparation. (See also *R v Jones (Kenneth)* and *Attorney-General's Reference (No 1 of 1992)*.)

R v Hamilton [1990] Crim LR 806 (Court of Appeal)

The appellant was convicted of obtaining or attempting to obtain property by deception contrary to s15 of the Theft Act 1968. Having forged an authorised signature on a number of stolen company cheques, he paid them into his building society account. He then withdrew cash by signing withdrawal slips. The conviction was based on the contention that he had made a false representation that the balance in his building society account was genuine and he was entitled to withdraw the sums he did. On his behalf it was contended that there had been no such representation, the demand for the return of money was not a representation, and it could therefore not be a false representation; no representation was being made as to the genuineness of the credit balance.

Held, the appeal would be dismissed. The appellant had dishonestly induced the bank to make credit entries in his favour using the stolen cheques. In signing a withdrawal slip a person is indicating his entitlement to make a withdrawal, that he is the person to whom the bank was indebted.

R v Harris [1965] 3 WLR 1040 (Court of Criminal Appeal)

A director of a firm of motor dealers was prosecuted on an indictment containing two counts for forgery of a receipt for £941 10s (£941.50) and uttering a forged instrument. He obtained two motor cars from Smiths's Motors, another firm of motor dealers, for a total cost of £941 10s 4d (£941.52p). When Smith wrote to him asking for payment by cheque or proof of the payment in cash which he said he had made, the director sent a photostat copy of a receipt to Smith stating that it was a copy of the receipt given to him by one of Smith's drivers after he had paid him the amount for the cars. He was acquitted on the charge of forgery but convicted on the second count.

Held, the conviction would be affirmed on the ground that, inter alia, forgery and uttering are separate offences so that a plea of autrefois acquit was not applicable and the making of the photostat copy of the forged receipt for the purpose of deceiving or defrauding Smith, together with its transmission to him, was a 'use' of the forgery within s6 of the Forgery Act 1913. (See now the Forgery and Counterfeiting Act 1981.)

R v Harrison [1938] 3 All ER 134 (Court of Criminal Appeal)

Four youths between the ages of 16 and 18 years were convicted of having had carnal knowledge of a girl under the age of 16. Although the girl seemed to be over 16 and the youths thought she was over 16, the girl said that at the time of the offence they did not ask her age and the evidence showed that none of them directed their minds to the question at all. The question arose whether the youths could bring themselves within the proviso to s2 of the Criminal Law Amendment Act 1922 (see now s6(3) of the Sexual Offences Act 1956) which provided that it would be a defence on the occasion of a first charge for a man under 23 to show that he had reasonable cause to believe the girl was over 16.

Held, they could not as it was necessary for them to show not only that they had reasonable cause to believe that the girl was at least 16 years of age, but also that they did in fact so believe.

R v Harvey (1981) 72 Cr App R 139 (Court of Appeal)

The appellant (and others) were convicted of making an 'unwarranted demand with menaces' contrary to s21(1) of the Theft Act 1968. He had threatened one S that considerable harm would come to S's wife and child if he, S, did not return £20,000 which had been given by the appellant to S, S deceiving him that he would supply him with a large quantity of cannabis. S had had no intention of supplying the cannabis. The appellants had already kidnapped S's wife and child, who had been released by the police after four days. They had also kidnapped S and subjected him to violence as well as making the threats in relation to his wife and child. The trial judge directed the jury that as a matter of law such threats could not be the 'proper' way of enforcing his demand for the return of the money.

Held, the appeal would be dismissed and the judge's ruling upheld. It does not matter what the reasonable man, or any man other than the defendant, would believe save in so far as that may throw light on what the defendant in fact believed. The factual question of the defendant's belief should be left to the jury. The defendant's belief must be that the use of menaces is a 'proper' means of reinforcing his demand; the appellant had been well aware that his threats if carried out would involve serious crimes. (See also *R v Garwood*.)

R v *Hegarty* [1994] Crim LR 353 (Court of Appeal)

The appellant was convicted of robbery. During the trial he sought to raise the defence of duress. He claimed he had been forced to commit the offences by some men who had looked after him when he had been 'on the run'. He sought to bring forward medical evidence to show that he suffererd from a 'grossly elevated neurotic state' to support his plea of duress and was therefore more susceptible to threats. This evidence was not admitted by the trial judge. The appellant appealed.

Held, the appeal would be dismissed. Evidence of some serious personality disorder could be relevant in explaining why the defendant had succumbed to the threats (see *R v Graham* [1982] 1 All ER 801) but the evidence in this case did not go that far and the trial judge had been right to rule such evidence inadmissible. When looking at the second (objective) stage of the test for duress, the court was very doubtful whether characteristics such as those put forward by the appellant could be attributed to the 'sober person of reasonable firmness'. (See also *R v Horne* and *R v Ali* (1995).)

R v *Hibbert* (1869) LR 1 CCR 184 (Court for Crown Cases Reserved)

A man was charged with taking a girl under the age of 16 out of the possession of her father contrary to s55 of the Offences against the Person Act 1861 (now s20 of the Sexual Offences Act 1956). He met a girl of 14 years in the street, took her to a place where he seduced her and then took her back to where he had met her. He did not inquire from the girl whether she was in the possession of her father or a guardian and did not believe her to be in anyone's possession. He was convicted but the case was reserved for the consideration of the Court for Crown Cases Reserved.

Held, the conviction should be quashed as the man did not know the girl was in anyone's possession. (But see *R v Prince*.)

R v *Hinks* [1998] Crim LR 904 (Court of Appeal)

The appellant was convicted of theft. P was a 53-year-old man of limited intelligence. P transferred a substantial sum of money from his building society account to the appellant's account. Submitting there was no case to answer, she stated the transfers of money had been gifts and so she could not be charged with theft. The submission was rejected and she appealed.

Held, the appeal would be dismissed. Property could be appropriated even when the donor consented to the defendant receiving it, and even though the transfer was a valid gift. A jury was not required to examine the validity or otherwise of any gift and the donor's state of mind was irrelevant. If the defendant believed the donor consented to the transfer, this could be relevant to dishonesty but did not have a bearing on appropriation. (See also *Lawrence v Commissioner of Police for the Metropolis*, *R v Gomez* and *R v Mazo*.)

R v *Holden* [1991] Crim LR 478 (Court of Appeal)

The appellant was convicted of theft contrary to s1 of the Theft Act 1968. He had worked for a number of branches of Kwik Fit and was due to do so again; however he was not so employed at the time of the offence. He had taken scrap tyres claiming he had seen others doing it, and had a supervisor's permission. The depot manager stated that taking the tyres or allowing others to do so would result in the sack. The trial judge directed the jury that the issue concerned dishonesty; it was no defence that others had taken tyres. The test was whether he had a reasonable belief that he had a right to take the tyres.

Held, the appeal would be allowed. Under s2(1)(a) of the 1968 Act the defendant had to show that he honestly believed he had a right to the property. Reasonable belief was not the relevant test of dishonesty. (See also *R* v *Ghosh*.)

R v *Hollinshead* [1985] 2 All ER 769 (House of Lords)

The respondents were charged with and convicted of conspiracy to defraud contrary to the common law. They agreed to make and sell to a third party devices for altering electricity meters to show that less electricity had been used than was the case. The third party, who was in fact a policeman, was expected to sell the devices to others for use in defrauding electricity boards. The indictment under which the respondents were charged stated nothing about the means by which the fraud was to be perpetrated. They appealed on the basis that their agreement to carry out a course of conduct, not of itself unlawful, would not amount to the common law offence of conspiracy to defraud even though the result would probably be a fraud committed by a stranger. The Crown contended that the activities amounted to conspiracy to defraud since the consequences of such was fraud on the electricity boards. The Court of Appeal allowed the respondents' appeal – the facts as stated could not properly be the subject of a change of conspiracy to defraud.

Held, in allowing the Crown's appeal, the agreement to make and sell devices which in their use would cause loss amounted to a common law conspiracy to defraud. It was irrelevant that the third party to whom the respondents were selling the devices was to sell them on and not use them himself.

R v *Holt and Lee* [1981] 2 All ER 854 (Court of Appeal)

The defendants were charged with and convicted of attempted deception ('with intent to make permanent default ... on [an] existing liability to make a payment ...') contrary to s2(1)(b) of the Theft Act 1978. They planned to pretend to the person asking for payment that they had already paid another person for their meal in a restaurant. Their plan was overheard by an off-duty police officer. When the defendants were presented with their bill and put forward their deception he prevented them from carrying it out. The trial judge rejected a submission that the defendants should have been charged under s2(1)(a) of the 1978 Act (attempting to secure 'the remission of the whole or part of [an] existing liability to make a payment') and not under s2(1)(b); if their attempt had been successful their liability to pay for their meals would have been 'remitted' within s2(1)(a) and not 'forgone' under s2(1)(b). It was submitted also that the term 'remitted' gave rise to different legal consequences from the term 'foregone'.

Held, the defendants had been properly charged and their appeals against conviction would be dismissed. The offences under paragraphs (a), (b) and (c) of s2(1) of the 1978 Act were separate offences, there were substantial differences in the elements of each offence albeit they had common features. Under (b) the 'intent to make permanent default' was unique. The jury, following a proper direction, had determined that the defendants' conduct had been motivated by the intent to 'make permanent default' in payment for their meals. There had also been the use of a 'deception' dishonestly to induce a creditor to forego payment.

R v Hopkins; R v Kendrick [1997] 2 Cr App R 524 (Court of Appeal)

H and K were convicted for conspiring to steal assets totalling £127,000. They ran a nursing home for the elderly. P, aged 99 and infirm, was a resident. H and K ultimately obtained an enduring power of attorney over P's affairs. A new will was drawn up under which H and K were the main beneficiaries. They sold P's shares at a disadvantageous time; the proceeds of sale were put into an account operated by K. H and K argued that P had become estranged from her daughter and transferred the property to them and they had acted in her interest and with her consent. They appealed on the basis that the trial judge had erred in directing the jury that they could be dishonest notwithstanding P had consented; the jury should have been directed that consent could be relevant to appropriation.

Held, the appeal would be dismissed. There was sufficient evidence to show P suffered from a mental incapacity that negated any purported transfer of property to H and K. (See also *R v Gomez*; compare *R v Mazo*.)

R v Horne [1994] Crim LR 584 (Court of Appeal)

The appellant was convicted of obtaining welfare benefits by deception. While he had not been directly threatened with violence, one of his co-conspirators had mentioned a drug dealer he knew who was willing to 'sort people out'. It was suggested that this had influenced his actions. The trial judge refused to admit expert psychiatric evidence which could have thrown light on the likely effect such pressure might have had upon the appellant.

Held, the appeal would be dismissed. The law had been correctly applied. The defendant was to be judged according to the standards of the person of 'reasonable firmness'. It would have been contradictory to have called expert evidence of the appellant's personal vulnerability for the jury's consideration. (See also *R v Hegarty* and *R v Ali* (1995).)

R v Horrex [1999] Crim LR 500 (Court of Appeal)

The appellant was convicted of murder. He, the deceased and G were alcoholic vagrants. The appellant had a strong emotional tie to G, she being a mother figure to him. G was having a sexual relationship with the deceased at the time of his death. She was attacked in the street by the deceased. When the appellant learnt of this, he went round to see the deceased, who said he was going to cause G some serious damage. A fight broke out. The appellant was adamant the deceased was alive when he left. He had not intended to cause grievous bodily harm to the deceased; he had acted in self defence and his actions were not the cause of death. The appellant denied losing self-control during the fight. The judge left the matter of provocation to the jury on the basis that the appellant might have lost his self-control, albeit he had given evidence that he had not. The jury was directed that they had to consider whether a reasonable person, somebody having that degree of self-control which was to be expected of the ordinary person who was somebody like the defendant, having any other characteristics of the defendant would have acted as had the defendant. On appeal it was contended that the jury should have been directed that the appellant's feelings for G were a characteristic of the appellant to be kept in mind when considering the effect of provocation on him. The judge had failed to assist the jury with an analysis of how the evidence might bear on the issue of provocation.

Held, the appeal would be dismissed. The word 'characteristic' was not to be applied to affectionate feelings that existed in any close relationship. Such feelings did not come within s3 Homicide Act 1957 as opposed to medical or other evidence that showed the defendant being distinguishable from the ordinary run of the community. However, the relationship was relevant when considering whether any provocation was enough to make a 'youngish man' of ordinary character lose control and also as to what the particular defendant had done. (*Director of Public Prosecutions v Camplin* applied; see also *R v Thornton (No 2)*.)

R v Hudson; R v Taylor [1971] 2 All ER 244 (Court of Appeal)

Hudson and Taylor, girls aged 17 and 19 respectively, were the principal witnesses for the prosecution at the trial of a person named Wright who was charged with wounding another person in a public house. At the trial they both failed to identify Wright as the assailant and testified they did not know him. As a result he was acquitted. At their trial for perjury Hudson and Taylor admitted that the evidence which they had given at Wright's trial was false, but Hudson said that before the trial she had been approached by a group of men who had threatened to 'cut her up' if she 'told on' Wright in court. She passed the warning to Taylor who said that she had been warned by other girls to be careful or she would be harmed. Hudson and Taylor said they decided to tell lies to avoid the consequences should they tell the truth and that this was strengthened when they saw a person named Farrell in the gallery of the court who had made threats to Hudson and who had a reputation for violence. They appealed against their conviction for perjury.

Held, the appeal would be allowed because, although it was essential to the defence of duress that the threat should be effective at the moment when the crime was committed, where the person threatened had no opportunity for delaying tactics but had to make his mind up whether or not to commit the criminal act, the existence at that moment of a threat sufficient to destroy his will would provide him with a defence even though the threatened injury might not follow instantly but only after an interval. The threats of Farrell were likely to be no less compelling because they could not have been carried out in the courtroom. It should have been left to the jury to decide whether the threats had overborne the will of the appellants and also any issue arising out of the appellants' failure to seek police protection. Also, duress is a defence to all offences including perjury (except treason or murder as a principal) if the will of the accused is overborne by threats of death or serious personal injury so that the commission of the alleged offence is no longer the voluntary act of the accused. It is essential to duress that the threat must be effective at the moment when the crime is committed.

R v *Humphreys* [1995] 4 All ER 1008 (Court of Appeal)

The appellant was convicted of murder. She lived with a man named Armitage (the deceased) and worked as a prostitute, encouraged by the deceased. He was a drug dealer and he abused the appellant. The appellant had a history of mental instability, particularly cutting her wrists to gain attention. When Armitage came home drunk one night he found that the appellant had cut her wrists. He told her she had not done a very good job. The appellant stabbed him to death. The trial judge directed the jury as to provocation. They had to assess the impact of the deceased's words on a woman who did not have a distorted or explosive personality.

Held, the appeal would be allowed and a conviction for manslaughter substituted. The trial judge should have directed the duty to take into account the appellant's immaturity and attention-seeking and the effect of the provocation. (See further *R v Morhall* and *R v Thornton (No 2)*.)

R v *Hurford; R v Williams* [1963] 2 All ER 254 (Court of Criminal Appeal)

Williams and Hurford were charged with obtaining a motor lorry under a forged instrument, contrary to s7 of the Forgery Act 1913 (see now ss1, 3 of the Forgery and Counterfeiting Act 1981). They went to some dealers who held re-possessed lorries on behalf of finance companies. Hurford said that he was Lunn and paid a deposit of £200 on a motor lorry. They then went to the office of a finance company and Hurford signed a hire-purchase form in the name of E Lunn. Both of the accused were associated with E Lunn but he had not authorised them to sign the proposal form in his name. The lorry was delivered to them and the finance company entered into the hire-purchase agreement at a later date after they had ascertained that E Lunn was credit-worthy; neither of the accused was credit-worthy.

Held, the conviction would be affirmed on the ground that the forged instrument had induced the company to part with the lorry.

R v *ICR Haulage Ltd* [1944] 1 All ER 691 (Court of Criminal Appeal)

ICR Haulage Ltd, a number of its employees, its managing director and another limited company, Rice & Son Ltd, were charged with conspiracy to defraud. Under a contract to deliver hardcore and ballast to Rice & Son Ltd, the materials were delivered by employees of the company and by sub-contractors who were paid by the company. The managing director of ICR Haulage Ltd, two of its drivers, two employees of Rice & Son Ltd and a number of sub-contractors agreed together to charge Rice & Son Ltd for a larger quantity of hardcore than that which was actually delivered. Most of the accused, including ICR Haulage Ltd, were convicted and their appeals dismissed. In its appeal ICR Haulage Ltd contended that a common law conspiracy to defraud could not lie against a limited company as it was not a natural person and therefore could not have the necessary mens rea.

Held, the appeal would be dismissed as the acts of the managing director were the acts of the company and his fraud that of the company.

R v Inseal [1992] Crim LR 35 (Court of Appeal)

The appellant was convicted of murder. A plea of guilty to manslaughter by reason of diminished responsibility had not been accepted. There had been a history of violence between the appellant and his woman victim, whom he strangled. He also had a history of drinking. He claimed that he had been very drunk at the time he killed his victim and his alcoholism was such as to negate any intent, but if intent was proved, he was suffering from diminished responsibility. The appellant appealed on the ground that the judge had failed to direct the jury adequately that the defence of diminished responsibility was available if the jury concluded on a balance of probabilities that the appellant's judgment and emotional responses were substantially or grossly impaired by injury to the brain.

Held, the appeal would be dismissed. There is a difference between the person who kills when alcohol has reduced his self-control and the person whose state of mind can be described as abnormal through chronic alcoholism. To succeed in the contention that there had been gross impairment of judgment and emotional responses, the jury would have to have been satisfied on a balance of probabilities that he would have acted as he did had he had no drink. The jury were satisfied that the appellant did have the necessary intent, that he could have decided not to have had one or more drinks and that therefore any abnormality of mind was not induced by alcoholism.

R v Ireland; R v Burstow [1997] 4 All ER 225 (House of Lords)

Burstow was charged under s20 Offences Against the Person Act 1861 (inflicting grievous bodily harm). He had stalked his victim by means of various activities (hate mail, malicious telephone calls, etc) and caused her to suffer grievous bodily harm of a psychiatric nature. The defence submitted that Burstow had not 'inflicted' harm upon his victim; there had been no proof of an assault or an intentional act that directly or indirectly involved the application of violent force to the victim (*R v Wilson; R v Jenkins* [1984] AC 242). The prosecution said the term 'inflicting' was wide enough to encompass the concept of harm being imposed on the victim, also citing *R v Wilson; R v Jenkins* and *R v Mandair*. The trial judge rejected the defence submissions; *R v Wilson; R v Jenkins* could not be taken as authority that infliction must involve proof of the use of direct force upon the victim and the restricted meaning argued by the defence had no justification. Burstow changed his plea to guilty and appealed in the light of this ruling. The Court of Appeal dismissed the appeal agreeing that activity which caused the victim to suffer severe psychological harm amounted to grievous bodily harm for the purposes of s20; direct physical force was not necessary to inflict an assault. Ireland was convicted under s47 Offences Against the Person Act 1861 (assault occasioning actual bodily harm). He made a number of nuisance telephone calls to women; when the call was answered he would keep silent. Expert medical evidence suggested that the women had suffered psychological harm as a result of what the appellant had done. The appellant appealed to the Court of Appeal on the ground that no assault had been made out as required by s47, but the appeal was dismissed – assault did not have to include evidence of direct physical contact in the form of a battery (*Tuberville v Savage* (1669) 1 Mod 3); actual bodily harm could take the form of psychological disturbance (*R v Chan-Fook* [1994] 1 WLR 689); there was no need for the defendant to have threatened his victim by means of an overt act for the victim to fear physical violence. In *Smith v Chief Superintendent of Woking Police Station* (1983) 76 Cr App R 234 a woman apprehended violence when the defendant looked in through the window. In *Barton v Armstrong* [1969] 2 NSWR 451 it was held in civil law that a threat made over the telephone could amount to an assault. The defendant had in the present case been in immediate contact with his victims over the telephone and they apprehended violence. A silent telephone call was just as capable of inducing fear of violence in the victim. The following questions were certified for consideration by the House of Lords: (1) whether the making of a series of silent telephone calls can amount in law to an assault; and (2) whether an offence of inflicting grievous bodily harm under s20 Offences Against the Person Act 1861 can be committed where no physical violence is applied directly or indirectly to the body of the victim.

Held, the appeals would be dismissed. The term 'bodily harm' used in the 1861 Act could be interpreted to include psychiatric illness by applying the current meaning of the statute to modern-day conditions. As to question (1) it was possible for a defendant, given an appropriate set of facts, to be charged with 'narrow' assault, on the basis he had, by his words or telephone calls, caused the victim to apprehend immediate physical violence. As to question (2) and the use of the word 'inflict' in s20, it had the same meaning as 'cause'. (*R v Mandair, R v Chan-Fook* approved; compare *R v Baker and Wilkins*.)

R v Ives [1969] 3 All ER 470 (Court of Appeal)

The appellant was convicted of murdering his wife 12 days after she had given birth to a third child. She had suffered from puerperal psychosis during the birth of her first child and this condition had apparently arisen again. She had said to her husband that she was going to get rid of the kids as she did not want them and he struck her as she sat mumbling in bed. His plea of provocation and self-defence was rejected.

Held, (1) the conviction would be affirmed although self-defence was capable of being extended not only to steps taken to defend Ives himself, but also to those taken to protect the life and safety of the baby; (2) when provocation is relied on s3 of the Homicide Act 1957 still governs the matter, notwithstanding s8 of the Criminal Justice Act 1967. If provocation is not eliminated the jury must determine whether it was enough to make a reasonable man act as the accused did; but in considering what the reaction of the accused was, s8 of the 1967 Act requires that they should establish what was the intent of the accused when he acted as he did.

R v Jackson [1983] Crim LR 617 (Court of Appeal)

The appellant was convicted of handling stolen goods contrary to s22 of the Theft Act 1968, and evading liability by deception contrary to s2(1)(a) of the Theft Act 1978. The occupants of the appellant's car presented a stolen Access credit card to pay for petrol and other goods at a number of petrol stations. It was submitted by the defence that the counts under s1(1)(a) should have been charged under s2(1)(b) and be withdrawn from the jury; however the trial judge allowed the case to proceed as charged.

Held, the appeal would be dismissed. A trader who accepted a (stolen) credit card would look to the company who issued the card for payment, not the person who tendered it. It followed that the person tendering that stolen credit card had dishonestly secured the remission of an existing liability. It was not necessary to determine whether the charge should have been made under s2(1)(b).

R v James (1997) The Times 2 October (Court of Appeal)

The defendant was convicted of wrongful imprisonment. He appealed on the ground that the trial judge had misdirected the jury on the issue of intent.

Held, the appeal would be allowed. The actus reus of false imprisonment arose where the defendant placed unlawful restrictions on P's freedom of movement. The mens rea required proof that he intended to cause such restrictions or was reckless as to whether he did so or not. If P's fear arose as an aside from the defendant's words or actions as opposed to an intentional or reckless assault, he should be acquitted. If P was fearful of what the defendant might do if she attempted to escape as opposed to being physically restrained, the jury must be directed to consider the mens rea very carefully.

R v J F Alford Transport Ltd; R v Alford; R v Payne [1997] 2 Cr App R 326 (Court of Appeal)

Drivers in the defendant company were convicted of making false entries on tachograph records contrary to s99(5) Transport Act 1988. The company, its managing director and transport manager were convicted of aiding and abetting these offences; they appealed on the ground that the trial judge had erred in directing the jury that passive acquiescence on the part of the defendants was sufficient to give rise to accessorial liability in respect of those offences committed by the drivers.

Held, the appeals would be allowed. There was insufficient evidence of the defendants having the necessary mens rea to be accomplices. To aid and abet required proof that the drivers had committed the offences; the defendants knew what the drivers were doing; and the defendants had given positive encouragement to the drivers. The defendants required knowledge of the principal offence, an ability to control the action of the offender, and a deliberate decision not to so control. If the prosecution could show that the defendants took no steps to prevent misconduct it was open to the jury, given no alternative explanation, to infer that the individual defendant, and the company, was positively encouraging what was happening.

R v Johnson [1989] 2 All ER 839 (Court of Appeal)

The appellant was convicted of murder. He made violent threats towards the deceased and his girlfriend; the latter taunted him and the deceased grabbed hold of the appellant, pinned him to a wall while holding a glass. When the deceased let the glass go the appellant stabbed him to death with a flick knife, which he said he carried to protect himself because he had been 'glassed' and mugged before. He pleaded self-defence. His counsel was not willing to raise the defence of provocation because it ran counter to the defence of self-defence. He submitted that the judge ought to leave the issue of provocation to the jury. The judge did not do so on the ground that provocation which was self-induced could not be a defence within s3 of the Homicide Act 1957.

Held, the appeal would be allowed and a verdict of manslaughter substituted. Self-induced provocation was not eliminated from consideration under s3 of the 1957 Act as '... the jury shall take into account everything both done and said ...'. This included the deceased's reaction to the appellant's behaviour and the appellant's response to that reaction which caused him to lose his self-control. If there was evidence upon which a jury might find provocation, whether self-induced or not, that defence must be left to the jury. The appellant had not had the opportunity of putting the defence of provocation to the jury. (See also *Edwards v R, Director of Public Prosecutions v Camplin, R v Ali* (1989) and *R v Ahluwalia.*)

R v Jones (Kenneth) (1990) 91 Cr App R 351 (Court of Appeal)

The appellant, a married man, was convicted of attempted murder. He sought out F, a man who was having a relationship with a woman the appellant had had an affair with. He found F, got into his car and pointed a loaded sawn-off shotgun at F, who managed to disarm the appellant. The trial judge rejected a submission that there was insufficient evidence to support the charge given that at least three more preparatory acts would have had to be carried out by the appellant before the full offence could have been completed; removing the safety catch, putting his finger on the trigger and pulling it. An appeal was made on the ground that the judge had erred in his construction of s1(1) of the Criminal Attempts Act 1981.

Held, the appeal would be dismissed. The natural meaning of the statutory words of s1(1) had to be considered. The judge had to ask whether there was evidence from which a reasonable jury could conclude that the appellant had done acts which were more than preparatory; it was for the jury to decide whether those acts were more than preparatory to the commission of the full offence. Once the appellant had entered F's car and pointed the loaded gun at him with the intention of killing him, there was sufficient evidence for the jury to consider on a charge of attempted murder, and it had been properly left to the jury. (*R v Gullefer* applied.)

R v Kanwar [1982] Crim LR 532 (Court of Appeal)

The appellant was convicted of handling stolen goods by dishonestly assisting in their retention contrary to s22(1) of the Theft Act 1968. While police were searching the appellant's house they found property which was later identified as the proceeds from burglaries and which had been brought there by her husband. She returned and on being questioned, she denied there was any stolen property and lied to questions about specific items to persuade the police that they were lawfully hers. She appealed on the ground that the verdict was unsafe and unsatisfactory.

Held, the appeal would be dismissed. Something must be done intentionally, dishonestly, knowing or believing the goods to be stolen, for the purpose of enabling the goods to be retained for the benefit of another. Oral representations identifying the goods as lawfully hers, if made dishonestly and for the benefit of another (her husband), amounted to dishonestly assisting in the retention of stolen goods.

R v *Kassim* [1991] 3 All ER 713 (House of Lords)

The appellant was charged with and convicted on 21 counts of obtaining property by deception contrary to s15 of the Theft Act 1968 and with '[procuring] the execution of a valuable security' contrary to s20(2) of the 1968 Act. He opened a number of bank accounts giving a false name and address; he also obtained cheque books and a credit card. A large number of withdrawals were made against the accounts; he also used the credit card. The accounts became overdrawn by a total of £8,338; there was also £943 owing on the credit card. In relation to the charges under s20(2) of the Act the appellant appealed to the House of Lords (the Court of Appeal having dismissed his appeal against conviction) on the ground that there was no 'execution' of a valuable security.

Held, the appeal would be allowed. 'Execution' envisaged acts done to or in connection with the document and not the giving effect to the document by carrying out the instructions which it contained, eg the delivery of goods or payment of money. There was no execution of a valuable security when a bank on which a cheque was drawn or a credit card company which received a credit voucher following a credit transaction gave effect to it by paying it. By his conduct the appellant had not procured the execution of a valuable security under s20(2).

R v *Kelly* (1993) 97 Cr App R 245 (Court of Appeal)

The appellant was convicted of aggravated burglary contrary to s10(1)(b) of the Theft Act 1968. He had used a large screwdriver to break into a house and produced it when faced by the occupier and a woman. He prodded the occupier in the stomach with it as a means of ensuring compliance with his demand that a video recorder and remote control be handed over. The question in issue was whether the prosecution had to prove that the appellant had the weapon (screwdriver) with him with intent to cause injury before the occasion to use the screwdriver had arisen.

Held, the appeal against conviction would be dismissed. 'The relevant time at which the prosecution had to prove that the appellant had an offensive weapon with him was when he actually stole. The screwdriver became an offensive weapon on proof that he intended to use it for causing injury to, or incapacitating, the occupier or the woman at the time of theft, thereby aggravating the burglary' (*per* POTTS J).

R v Kelly [1998] 3 All ER 741 (Court of Appeal)

The defendant, D, and L were convicted of theft of body parts from the Royal College of Surgeons. D, an artist, had permission to draw anatomical specimens at the College. Along with L, a technician at the College, he removed a number of body parts and made casts of them. During a police investigation into the disappearance of body parts, some were found in D's flat, some at a friend's house and some buried in a field. On appeal D and L contended that the body parts were not property under s4(1) Theft Act 1968, and that the body parts had not been in the lawful possession of the College given they had been kept for longer than two years allowed under the Anatomy Act 1832 – they could not be regarded as belonging to the College under s5(1) Theft Act 1968.

Held, the appeals would be dismissed. Body parts were property and whether or not the College had lawful possession was irrelevant. (See also *R v Turner (No 2).*)

R v Kennedy [1999] Crim LR 65 (Court of Appeal)

K was convicted of the manslaughter of B. C and B had been drinking. B told K he wanted something to help him sleep. K was seen by C to prepare and then hand a heroin-filled syringe to B who injected it intravenously. B paid K, left the house and was dead within the hour. It was argued that *R v Dalby* was relevant authority: X supplies drugs to Y who voluntarily takes them and then dies; X is not guilty of manslaughter since the supply does not constitute the actus reus. On the other hand, if the facts were distinguishable from *Dalby*, counsel for K should have been allowed to persuade the jury that B's death was caused by his own decision to take the drugs. It was also argued that the judge did not explain to the jury any break in the chain of causation if they concluded B's death was due to his own decision to inject himself.

Held, the appeal would be dismissed. If C's evidence was accepted by the jury, K had prepared the syringe and handed it to B who immediately injected himself. K's own conduct was unlawful in assisting or encouraging B to inject himself. (Distinguish *R v Dalby*. See also *R v Cato*.)

R v Khan [1990] 2 All ER 783 (Court of Appeal)

The appellants were convicted of attempted rape under s1(1) of the Criminal Attempts Act 1981 as applied to the offence of rape contained in s1(1) of the Sexual Offences (Amendment) Act 1976. The point at issue was whether the offence of attempted rape is committed when the defendant is reckless as to the woman's consent to sexual intercourse.

Held, the appeals against conviction would be dismissed. 'In our judgment an acceptable analysis of the offence of rape is as follows: (1) the intention of the offender is to have sexual intercourse with a woman; (2) the offence is committed if, but only if, the circumstances are that (a) the woman does not consent *and* (b) the defendant knows that she is not consenting or is reckless as to whether she consents. Precisely the same analysis can be made of the offence of attempted rape ... The only difference between the two offences is that in rape sexual intercourse takes place whereas in attempted rape it does not, although there has to be some act which is more than preparatory to sexual intercourse ... the intent of the defendant is precisely the same in rape as in attempted rape and the mens rea is identical, namely an intention to have intercourse plus a knowledge of or recklessness as to the woman's absence of consent. No question of attempting to achieve a reckless state of mind arises; the attempt relates to the physical activity; the mental state of the defendant is the same. A man does not recklessly have sexual intercourse, nor does he recklessly attempt it. Recklessness in rape and attempted rape arises not in relation to the physical act of the accused but only in his state of mind when engaged in the activity of having or attempting to have sexual intercourse' (*per* RUSSELL LJ). (Applied in *Attorney-General's Reference (No 3 of 1992)*.)

R v Khan (Rungzabe) (1998) The Times 7 April (Court of Appeal)

The appellant was convicted of manslaughter. He had supplied twice the amount of heroin than an experienced user might have consumed to P, a 15-year-old prostitute. She fell into a coma on the appellant's premises having consumed the heroin. The appellant left P alone and she died soon after. There was expert evidence that her life could have been saved if medical attention had been sought. A charge of murder was withdrawn from the jury through lack of evidence of mens rea. Following *R v Dalby* and *R v Goodfellow*, the trial judge also ruled that the case could not proceed as one of unlawful act of manslaughter. The appellant was convicted of manslaughter and appealed on the basis that the trial judge had not properly dealt with the issue of killing by gross negligence.

Held, the appeal would be allowed. In considering the case as one of causing death by omission, liability for manslaughter could only arise if the death has been caused by the appellants's gross negligence. The trial judge had not given any guidance as to whether or not the facts were capable of giving rise to the drug dealer being under a common law duty to summon assistance.

R v King [1963] 3 All ER 561 (Court of Criminal Appeal)

King married his first wife in 1941 and they separated in 1946. He expected her to divorce him quickly as was done in Scotland, and in April 1949, believing that he had been divorced, he went through a ceremony of marriage with Phyllis Oliver; in 1947 his first wife had divorced him but King did not know of this. Later in 1949 King's mother told him that he had been divorced and without making any inquiries he came to the conclusion that the divorce was after the second ceremony of marriage and he went through a third ceremony of marriage with Agnes Smith in September 1961, as a result of which he was charged with bigamy, contrary to the Offences against the Person Act 1861, s57. In his defence King said that because of what his mother told him he thought that his marriage to Phyllis Oliver was void since he was still validly married to his first wife when he 'married' her.

Held, the conviction would be affirmed. Although an honest belief based on reasonable grounds that a previous marriage is invalid is a good defence to a prosecution for bigamy, King did not have any reasonable grounds for this belief. (See *R v Gould*.)

R v Kingston [1994] 3 All ER 353 (House of Lords)

The respondent, who had paedophiliac homosexual tendencies, was convicted of an indecent assault on a 15-year-old boy. He claimed that before the acts took place his co-defendant, P, had drugged him. He did not remember the incident. There was no evidence to suggest that the drugs would have made the respondent do anything he would not otherwise have done. The trial judge ruled that it was not open to the jury to find the respondent not guilty if they found that the respondent had assaulted the boy by reason of an intent induced by the influence of drugs given to him by P without his knowledge, nor was it open to them to find that intoxication by drugs given to him without his knowledge negatived any intent or mens rea on the respondent's part. The trial judge directed the jury that they should acquit the defendant if they found that because he was so affected by drugs he did not intend or may not have intended to commit an indecent assault on the boy, but that if they were sure that despite the effect of any drugs he still intended to commit an indecent assault the case was proved because a drugged intent was still an intent. The Court of Appeal quashed the conviction on the grounds that if intoxicating liquor or drugs were secretly administered and caused the person to lose self-control, to then form an intent which he would not otherwise have formed, such an intent would not be criminal because mens rea would be negatived. The prosecution appealed to the House of Lords.

Held, the appeal would be allowed. In general it was not a defence to plead a loss of self-control even if that came about as a result of an act of a third party. If intoxication did not cause automatism or temporary insanity, involuntary intoxication was not a defence to a criminal charge if it was proved that the defendant had the necessary intent when the act was carried out even though the intent came about out of circumstances for which the defendant was not to blame. An offence would not be made out if the intoxication was such that the defendant could not form an intent. The trial judge had been correct in his direction to the jury. If the defendant still intended to commit the indecent assault despite the effect of any drugs, the case against him was proved. The drug had not brought about a desire that had not previously existed; it had allowed an existing desire to be released and acted upon. (Applied: *Yip Chiu-cheung* v *R*; see also *Director of Public Prosecutions* v *Majewski*.)

R v Klineberg; R v Marsden [1999] 1 Cr App R 427 (Court of Appeal)

The appellants were convicted on a number of counts of theft. The appellant, M, was a director of a company that purchased a timeshare development and marketed the timeshares; a solicitor was another director and the appellant, K, was in charge of the London office. Intending purchasers paid the company money which was to be transmitted to stakeholders to protect the purchasers until the apartments were ready for occupation. Some of the intending purchasers were told that the independent trusteeship would be via a stakeholding trust company, while others were told it would be via the solicitor's firm. Only £223 out of around half a million pounds paid by intending purchasers was transmitted to the trust company. It was argued that once the money had been paid into the company's bank account it ceased to be property belonging to the intending purchasers.

Held, the appeal would be allowed in part. Section 5(3) Theft Act 1968 was applied to overcome the problem arising from *R* v *Preddy*. Where a person was induced to enter a contract or did contract on the assumption that their money would be safe under a trusteeship, a legal obligation arose under s5(3) Theft Act 1968. Under s5(3) property or its proceeds were to be regarded as belonging to another. Where a s5(3) obligation existed in relation to the 'appropriation' element of theft, the prosecution had to prove a breach of that obligation. (See also *R* v *Preddy* [1996] 3 WLR 255.)

R v *Laing* [1995] Crim LR 395 (Court of Appeal)

The appellant was convicted of burglary contrary to s9(1)(a) Theft Act 1968 in that he was trespassing when he was found by the police in the stock room of a department store after the store had been closed to the public.

Held, the appeal would be allowed. A defendant cannot become a trespasser in a building, or part of a building, for the purposes of burglary where he has previously entered that building, or part of the building, as a lawful visitor.

R v *Lamb* [1967] 2 All ER 1282 (Court of Appeal)

The appellant, as a practical joke and with no intention to cause harm, pointed a revolver at the deceased, his best friend, when it had two bullets in the chambers. Neither bullet was in the chamber opposite the barrel. The appellant pulled the trigger, still with no intention to discharge the revolver, and his friend, who all along also regarded the matter as a joke, was killed. The pulling of the trigger rotated the cylinder and placed a bullet opposite the barrel so that it was struck by the striking pin or hammer, but the appellant was unaware that the pulling of the trigger would have had this effect and three expert witnesses for the prosecution agreed that the mistake was natural for someone who was not aware of the ways in which the revolver mechanism worked. The trial judge refused to allow the defence of accident to go to the jury and the appellant was convicted of manslaughter.

Held, the conviction should be quashed on the ground that when the gravamen of a charge is criminal negligence or recklessness of the accused, the jury must consider his state of mind, including whether or not he thought that that which he was doing was safe, and the trial judge had not directed the jury on this matter. The appellant was entitled to a direction that the jury should take into account the fact that he had indisputably formed the view that there was no danger, and that there was expert evidence as to that being an understandable mistake. Also, 'unlawful' in criminal law does not mean unlawful merely from the angle of civil liberties. (See also *R* v *Arobieke*.)

R v *Lambie* [1981] Crim LR 712 (House of Lords)

The defendant was convicted of obtaining a pecuniary advantage by deception contrary to s16(1) of the Theft Act 1968. She had been asked to return her credit card, having exceeded her credit limit. She had not done so at the material time. A shop assistant allowed her to take goods from a shop, the assistant having made the usual checks against the credit card the defendant had tendered. She appealed on the grounds that the evidence had not shown that any deception had been operative. The Court of Appeal allowed the appeal and the Crown appealed to the House of Lords.

Held, the appeal would be allowed. By tendering the credit card the customer was making a representation of actual authority to make the contract on the bank's behalf that the bank would honour the voucher on presentation by the shop. Had the assistant known that the customer did not have the authority to make such representation, there was a strong inference that she would not have allowed her to take the goods away. Even though the assistant had not been asked, there was no reason why the matter should not be left to the jury to decide on the evidence as a whole whether that inference was irresistible, as it was in the present case. (See also *Metropolitan Police Commissioner v Charles*.)

R v Laverty [1970] 3 All ER 432 (Court of Appeal)

Laverty was convicted of obtaining £65 in cash and a cheque for £165 by deception. He had sold to a Mr Bedborough a car which had originally been in bad condition, but which he had repaired, putting new number plates on it. It was alleged at the trial that there was a representation by conduct that the car being sold to Mr Bedborough was the original car to which the chassis plate and rear plate which it bore had been assigned. This representation by conduct was false, but the question which arose was whether the false representation operated on Mr Bedborough's mind so as to cause him to hand over the cheque. Mr Bedborough stated in his evidence that what induced him to part with his money was the representation by conduct that the appellant had a title to sell the car.

Held, the onus of proving that the false representation acted on the mind of the purchaser falls on the prosecution. Here, this burden had not been discharged. The conviction would be quashed.

R v Lawrence and Pomroy (1971) 57 Cr App R 64 (Court of Appeal)

Pomroy repaired the roof of a house owned by Thorn for an agreed price of £195. Thorn was not satisfied with the work but paid £125 and promised to pay the balance when the work was completed to his satisfaction. Subsequently Pomroy went to Thorn's home and enquired from him when he intended to pay the remaining £70. Thorn replied that, as the work was not satisfactory and Pomroy had not put it right, he would have to sue. Pomroy told Thorn that unless he paid him within seven days he would have to look over his shoulder before he stepped out of doors. Four days later Pomroy, accompanied by Lawrence, who was a big man, called again at Thorn's house and said to Thorn, 'I have come for the £70 you owe me.' Lawrence said, 'What about the £70?' Thorn again refused to pay whereupon Lawrence asked what was wrong with the job and added, 'Step outside the house and we will sort this matter out.' Thorn refused and Lawrence said menacingly, 'Come on mate, come outside.' A flick knife was later found in the pocket of Lawrence's overcoat. The two men were convicted of blackmail and Lawrence was also convicted of unlawful possession of an offensive weapon; they appealed.

Held, the convictions would be affirmed. With regard to the conviction for blackmail, the court stated that: The word 'menaces' is an ordinary English word which any jury can be expected to understand and only in exceptional cases where, because of special knowledge in special circumstances, what would be a menace to an ordinary person is not a menace to the person to whom it is addressed, or where the converse applies, it is necessary for the trial judge to spell out the meaning of the word.

R v Le Brun [1991] 4 All ER 673 (Court of Appeal)

The appellant was charged with murder and convicted of manslaughter. While walking home after an evening at a friend's house the appellant hit his wife on the jaw during a heated argument. She fell down unconscious. He tried to lift her body but she slipped from his grasp. Her head hit the pavement. She sustained fractures to her skull from which she died. The trial judge directed the jury that they could convict the appellant of murder or manslaughter (depending on the intention with which he had previously assaulted his wife) if they were sure that, having committed the assault with no serious injury resulting, the appellant had accidentally dropped her causing her death whilst either (1) attempting to move her to her home against her wishes, including any wishes she may have expressed prior to the previous assault, [and/or] (2) attempting to dispose of her body or otherwise cover up the previous assault. He appealed against the conviction of manslaughter on the ground that the judge had misdirected the jury.

Held, the appeal would be dismissed. '... the act which causes death and the necessary mental state to constitute manslaughter need not coincide in point of time' (LORD LANE CJ). The unlawful application of force and the eventual act causing death were parts of the same sequence of events even though the mens rea was contained in the initial unlawful assault and the actus reus was the eventual act which caused death. The interval between the two acts did not exonerate the defendant from liability for murder or manslaughter. The judge's direction in so far as it applied to manslaughter was satisfactory. (See also *Thabo Meli v R* and *R v Church*.)

R v Lightfoot [1993] Crim App R 24 (Court of Appeal)

The appellant was convicted of obtaining property by deception. It was alleged that the appellant had stolen a colleague's unsigned credit card, signed it using his colleague's name and used it to attempt to obtain goods by deception. The appellant was in debt and would not have been able to secure a credit card in his own name; he claimed that his colleague had agreed to him doing what he had done. The jury were told by the trial judge that the appellant's ignorance of the law would not afford a defence. He appealed on the ground that the judge had not given an adequate explanation of the relevance of ignorance of the law to dishonesty.

Held, the appeal would be allowed. It should have been made clear to the jury that ignorance of the law was irrelevant if the appellant was nonetheless dishonest in that he appreciated that he was doing something that reasonable and honest people would regard as dishonest. (See also *R v Ghosh*.)

R v Lincoln [1980] Crim LR 575 (Court of Appeal)

The appellant was convicted of handling stolen goods, contrary to s22(1) of the Theft Act 1968. The jury were directed that the prosecution had to prove that, at the time he received the items of stolen property dishonestly he knew or believed it to be stolen property, which could be proved in three ways, if he was aware of the theft; if he believed that the item was stolen and 'even if he suspected that it was stolen property and deliberately shut his eyes to the circumstances'. He appealed on the ground that there had been a misdirection by too literal an application of *Atwal* v *Massey*.

Held, the appeal would be allowed. Section 22(1) did not include the word suspicion. To direct a jury that the offence was committed by the person charged, suspecting that the goods were stolen, deliberately shutting his eyes to the circumstances as an alternative to knowing or believing the goods were stolen, was a misdirection. To direct them that in common sense and in law they might find that he knew or believed the goods to be stolen because he deliberately shut his eyes to the circumstances, was a proper direction. (See also *Atwal* v *Massey*.)

R v Lipman [1969] 3 All ER 410 (Court of Appeal)

Lipman and the deceased, a girl, were both drug addicts, and one evening after he had consumed a quantity of the drug LSD at her flat he began to suffer from hallucinations and had an illusion of descending to the centre of the earth and being attacked by snakes with which he fought. While in this hallucinatory state he struck her two blows on the head causing haemorrhage and crammed about eight inches of sheet into her mouth causing her to die from asphyxia. He was charged with murder and pleaded that he had no knowledge of what he was doing whilst under the influence of the drug and that he had no intention to harm the deceased. He was convicted of manslaughter and appealed.

Held, the conviction would be affirmed as for the purposes of criminal responsibility no distinction is made between the effect of drugs voluntarily taken and drunkenness voluntarily induced. As no specific intent is necessary to support a conviction of manslaughter based on a killing in the course of an unlawful act, self-induced intoxication is no defence. (See also *Director of Public Prosecutions* v *Majewski, R* v *Church* and *R* v *Lamb*.)

R v Lloyd [1966] 1 All ER 107 (Court of Criminal Appeal)

The appellant was convicted of murder. At his trial he raised the defence of diminished responsibility under s2(1) of the Homicide Act 1957. Evidence showed that he had had three fainting attacks some nine years previously but no mental explanation was established. He later made two unsuccessful attempts at suicide. The prison medical officer said the appellant was abnormal due to mental illness; he could not say that the abnormality was diminished to any substantial degree. A consultant in psychiatry also said the appellant was suffering from an abnormality of mind but could not say to what degree; it was not as low as minimal but it was not substantial. The appeal concerned the manner in which the trial judge dealt with the word 'substantially' under s2(1) of the 1957 Act.

Held, the appeal would be dismissed. In determining that there were no grounds for criticising the trial judge as to how he invited the jury to approach the word 'substantial' or 'substantially' EDMUND DAVIES J quoted from the trial judge's summing-up: 'Substantial does not mean total, that is to say, the mental responsibility need not be totally impaired, so to speak, destroyed altogether. At the other end of the scale substantial does not mean trivial or minimal. It is something in between and Parliament has left it to you and other juries to say on the evidence was the mental responsibility impaired, and, if so, was it substantially impaired?' The trial judge had also quoted from LORD PARKER CJ in *R v Byrne*: '... was the abnormality such as substantially impaired his mental responsibility for his acts in doing or being a party to the killing?' (See also *R v Gittens, R v Tandy* and *R v Egan*.)

R v Lobell [1957] 1 All ER 734 (Court of Criminal Appeal)

Lobell was charged with, inter alia, wounding Evans, and pleaded self-defence. On the day of the wounding Evans came towards Lobell uttering threats and Lobell threw a brick at him. Evans continued to advance towards Lobell in a threatening manner, and Lobell picked up a knife, which he said he had bought for his protection, and stabbed him. In his summing-up the trial judge told the jury that where self-defence is pleaded as a defence the onus of proof shifts on to the defence.

Held, the conviction would be quashed as where the defence of self-defence is raised the onus of proof does not shift on to the accused but remains on the prosecution.

R v Loukes (1995) The Times 26 December (Court of Appeal)

A truck driver was charged with causing death by dangerous driving contrary to s1 Road Traffic Act 1988 as amended by the Road Traffic Act 1991. The appellant's responsibility was to oversee the maintenance and servicing of the company's vehicles. A crash occurred in which a car driver was killed. Evidence showed that there was a defective propeller shaft on the lorry. The trial judge directed the jury to acquit the truck driver but indicated they could convict the appellant as accomplice. The appellant was convicted of causing death by dangerous driving and appealed.

Held, the appeal would be allowed. Where a principal offender was acquitted on a charge of causing death by dangerous driving, no other person could be convicted as accomplice. Given the issue around the interpretation of 'dangerous' in respect of the driving had to be determined by reference to what a competent and careful driver would have contemplated, the direction to the jury in respect of the principal offender meant there had been no actus reus. (This decision was consistent with the earlier case of *Thornton v Mitchell* [1940] 1 All ER 339.)

R v Lovesey; R v Peterson [1969] 2 All ER 1077 (Court of Appeal)

The deceased, a jeweller, arrived at his shop about 9am one morning, and 15 minutes later his wife found him handcuffed to a railing in the basement suffering from severe head injuries from which he later died. Blood was found on the ground floor and on the stairs, the shop was in disorder and some cases of valuables had been removed. There was no direct evidence as to how many men had been involved in the raid or of the parts which they had individually played. Lovesey and Peterson denied all knowledge of the affair but the prosecution sought to implicate them in the crime in the following ways: witnesses were called to prove a connection between them and a Jaguar car which was thought to have been used in the raid; the deceased's daughter said that Lovesey had visited the shop with a woman three months before and when they were arrested the two halves of a torn envelope which had come from the shop were found in their respective pockets. They were convicted of robbery with violence and murder after the trial judge, in an otherwise impeccable summing-up, told the jury that the two offences would stand or fall together. They appealed.

Held, the convictions for murder should be quashed as the summing-up contained a misdirection. The court said that the two offences did not necessarily stand or fall together as even though there was clearly a common design to rob, this would not suffice to convict of murder unless the common design included the use of whatever force was necessary to achieve the robbers' object (or to permit escape without fear of subsequent identification), even if this involved killing, or the infliction of grievous bodily harm on the victim. Also, a common design to use unlawful violence short of the infliction of grievous bodily harm, renders all the co-adventurers guilty of manslaughter if the victim's death is an unexpected consequence of the carrying out of that design, but where the victim's death is not a product of the common design but is attributable to one of the co-adventurers going beyond the scope of that design by using violence which is intended to cause grievous bodily harm, the others are not responsible for that unauthorised act. (See also *R v Anderson and Morris*.)

R v Lowe [1973] 1 All ER 805 (Court of Appeal)

Lowe, a man of low intelligence, was living with a woman with whom he had five children including a baby of nine weeks. The woman was of subnormal intelligence and one of the children had been taken into care by the local authority. The baby became ill and Lowe told the woman to take her to the doctor but she declined to do so as she was afraid that it would also be taken into care by the local authority. The baby died some ten days later of dehydration and gross emaciation. Lowe was charged with manslaughter and cruelty by wilfully neglecting the child so as to cause her unnecessary suffering or injury to health, contrary to s1(1) of the Children and Young Persons Act 1933. In his summing up the trial judge told the jury that in order to constitute the offence under s1 of the 1933 Act it was not necessary that the accused should have foreseen the probable or possible result of his failure to call a doctor, and that if they found him guilty on this count and death had resulted from the neglect they were bound to find him guilty of manslaughter. It was not necessary to prove he had been reckless. He was convicted and appealed.

Held, the conviction for wilful neglect would be affirmed but that for manslaughter should be quashed as a clear distinction was to be drawn in relation to an act of commission and an act of omission; mere neglect, even though deliberate, which caused injury to a child's health and resulted in its death, did not necessarily constitute manslaughter where the accused had failed to foresee the consequences of his neglect. 'We think there is a clear distinction between an act of omission and an act of commission likely to cause harm.

Whatever may be the position in regard to the latter it does not follow that the same is true of the former' (*per* PHILLIMORE LJ).

R v Mahmood [1994] Crim LR 368 (Court of Appeal)

The defendant and his co-accused were convicted of manslaughter having been jointly charged following the unlawful taking of a vehicle by his co-accused. The car ploughed into a pram after the defendants had jumped out of it during a police chase. The baby in the pram was killed. While it might be inferred that the defendant foresaw the possibiity of a police chase and was a party to causing it, there had been no evidence that he was a party to a plan to abandon the car, leaving it in gear without a driver. It was contended on the defendant's behalf that the judge should have withdrawn the case from the jury given no evidence of encouragement or joint enterprise.

Held, the appeal would be allowed. The judge should have asked whether the obvious risk of causing injury included a possibility that the moving car might be abandoned by its driver and so cause injury, and whether the defendant anticipated that the driver might drive recklessly given the scenario. While the defendant might be found to have contemplated reckless driving, the evidence was insufficient to support the contention that he contemplated the abandonment of the car.

R v Malcherek; R v Steel [1981] 2 All ER 422 (Court of Appeal)

The appellant in the first case and the applicant in the second case had both been convicted of murder. In the first case the appellant had stabbed his wife who required hospital treatment. Some six days later she collapsed and her heart stopped beating. After an operation to remove a blood clot from the pulmonary artery, the heart started beating again; this was after a 30 minute cessation. She was put on a life support machine. Three days later it was considered that she had suffered irretrievable brain damage. Tests were carried out to confirm the position and the next day the life support machine was disconnected and soon afterwards she was declared dead. In the second case the applicant attacked a girl causing her grave head injuries. She was taken to hospital and put on a life support machine. Two days later doctors came to the conclusion that her brain had ceased to function and the machine was disconnected, and soon afterwards she was declared dead. At both trials the judge withdrew the issue of the cause of the victim's death from the jury on the ground that at the time of death the original injuries inflicted on the victim were an operating cause of death; it was not for the jury to conclude that the accused in each case had not caused the death of the victim. The appellant appealed and the applicant sought leave to appeal against conviction on the ground that the issue of causation should not have been withdrawn from the jury; in each case the jury should have been able to consider the evidence that death came about through the switching off of the life-support machine.

Held, both matters would be dismissed. The chain of causation was not broken when, after competent and careful medical treatment, it was decided by generally accepted medical criteria that the victim, who had been put on a life support machine, was dead and the machine was disconnected. This did not exonerate the assailant from responsibility for the death if at the time of death the original injury was a continuing or operating cause of death. Disconnecting the machine did not break the chain of causation between that injury being inflicted and death. There was no evidence in either case that the injury was not still an operating factor and so the question of causation had been correctly withdrawn from the jury. (See also *Airedale NHS Trust v Bland, R v Blaue* and *R v Cheshire*.)

R v Malone [1998] Crim LR 834 (Court of Appeal)

The defendant was convicted of raping P, who had been brought home by her friends drunk. Alone with P, it was alleged he climbed on top of her as she lay in bed and started to have sexual intercourse with her. P said she kicked out at him and he went out of the room. The defendant alleged P had made sexual advances towards him and when she kicked out at him he thought she was teasing him. He appealed, claiming that the trial judge had not dealt adequately with the issue of consent, there having been no force, deceit or threat by him. Neither was there any evidence of P's resistance either by words or physical conduct.

Held, the appeal would be dismissed. Had P consented to sexual intercourse? The complainant's testimony could be sufficient to show consent was not given. There was no requirement for direct evidence of threats, deceit or force used by a defendant, or resistance from P, albeit these may be factors which would influence a jury one way or the other. (See *R v Olugboja*.)

R v Mandair [1994] 2 All ER 715 (House of Lords)

The defendant was convicted of '... causing grievous bodily harm, contrary to s20 of the [Offences against the Person Act 1861]' as an alternative count to a charge of causing grievous bodily harm with intent, contrary to s18 of the 1861 Act. The prosecution alleged that the defendant had thrown sulphuric acid at his wife, who suffered severe facial burns. There had been some doubt whether the defendant had intended to inflict the serious injury; the trial judge allowed the jury the option to return the lesser verdict of 'causing grievous bodily harm contrary to s20 of the 1861 Act' if they were satisfied that he had caused the injury to his wife but without intent to cause serious bodily harm. The defendant appealed successfully that he had been convicted of an offence not known to the law; under s20 the offence is one of 'inflicting', not 'causing' grievous bodily harm. The Crown appealed to the House of Lords.

Held, the appeal as regards the availability of an alternative verdict under s20 would be allowed. The expression 'causing grievous bodily harm' in s18 was wide enough to include 'inflicting grievous bodily harm' under s20 and therefore a jury could convict a defendant charged with causing grievous bodily harm with intent contrary to s18 of the alternative offence of inflicting grievous bodily harm contrary to s20. The verdict of 'causing grievous bodily harm, contrary to s20' could only mean causing grievous bodily harm contrary to s20 in that what the defendant did consisted of inflicting grievous bodily harm on another person. The jury had not given a verdict on an offence not known to law. (See s6(3) of the Criminal Law Act 1967; see also *R v Savage; R v Parmenter* and *R v Ireland; R v Burstow*.)

R v *Marcus* [1981] 2 All ER 833 (Court of Appeal)

The appellant was convicted of attempting to cause to be taken a noxious thing with intent to injure, aggrieve or annoy, contrary to s24 of the Offences against the Person Act 1861. She had put eight sedative and sleeping tablets into her neighbour's bottle of milk. Little harm would have resulted. The effect of the toxicity of the drugs in the milk would have caused sedation and possibly sleep. There would have been a potential danger if someone had drunk the milk and then, eg, driven a car. Whether the drugs in the milk were a 'noxious thing' was a matter of fact and degree for the jury to decide. The grounds of her appeal were (1) that the drugs in the milk were not a 'noxious thing' within s24 because they were intrinsically harmless and they could not be regarded as 'noxious' merely because the appellant had attempted to administer them in an excessive quantity; (2) in s24 the word 'noxious' meant harmful in the sense of causing injury to bodily health, and did not cover impairment of faculties, and on the evidence there was no risk of injury to bodily health.

Held, the appeal would be dismissed. The offence under s24 involved an intention 'to injure, aggrieve, or annoy' so the concept of a 'noxious thing' involved both the quality and quantity administered or attempted to be administered. Something which could be harmless in small quantities could be 'noxious' if the quantity administered injured, aggrieved or annoyed. The judge had been correct in directing the jury to look at the substance in regard to both quality and quantity. The jury had evidence before them that, had the milk been drunk, the drugs present in it posed a potential danger through a person's faculties being impaired by them.

R v *Marks* [1998] Crim LR 676 (Court of Appeal)

The defendant was convicted of murder. He belonged to a drug-dealing syndicate. The prosecution alleged he had encouraged another member of the syndicate to kill the deceased. He appealed on the ground that the trial judge should have directed the jury on the issue of provocation, albeit this issue was not raised on his behalf at his trial.

Held, the appeal would be dismissed. There being no direct evidence of provocation put forward at the trial, there had been nothing of substance to warrant the trial judge to direct the jury. The court accepted that the defence of provocation could be available to those charged with murder as an accomplice. (See *R* v *Acott*.)

R v *Marsh* [1997] Crim LR 205 (Court of Appeal)

The defendant pleaded guilty to aggravated vehicle-taking following a ruling by the trial judge that he could be convicted of the aggravated offence if he caused injury to another whilst driving the vehicle he took without consent, even though his driving was not said to be at fault. The defendant had hit a woman who had run out onto the road. He appealed against conviction on the grounds that the trial judge's ruling was wrong.

Held, the appeal would be dismissed. Proof was required only 'that, owing to the driving of the vehicle, an accident occurred by which injury was caused to any person' (s12A(2)(b) Theft Act 1968). The defendant's driving had not been in any way culpable.

R v Marshall; R v Coombes; R v Eren (1998) The Times 10 March (Court of Appeal)

The appellants were convicted for the theft of tickets. They asked travellers on the London Underground for any unwanted tickets. Where these were still valid for travel they were sold on to members of the public wanting to use the underground. The appellants appealed against conviction arguing there was no evidence of any intention to permanently deprive London Underground of the tickets; an original purchaser bought the ticket to travel on the underground which was transferred to the appellants. No such right belonged to the London Underground and so there could be no intention to permanently deprive. As to the theft of the ticket itself, it was argued it would be returned to London Underground and so there was no intention to permanently deprive.

Held, the appeals would be dismissed. When a traveller purchased a ticket a contract came into existence creating rights on both sides; the traveller to use the underground and London Underground to insist only the purchaser could use the ticket. This last right was being disregarded by the appellants. As to the theft of tangible property, the ticket itself, the court determined the appellants had treated the tickets as their own to dispose of having no regard to any rights of London Underground, irrespective of the fact that when London Underground did get the tickets back they were worthless. (See *R v Fernandes.*)

R v Martindale [1986] 3 All ER 25 (Court of Appeal)

The appellant was convicted of having a controlled drug in his possession contrary to s5(2) of the Misuse of Drugs Act 1971. When searched by police a small quantity of cannabis resin was found in a wallet in his pocket. He claimed he had been given the drug two years before in Canada and had forgotten he still had it. The appellant changed his plea to guilty after the judge had ruled that since the appellant knew what the substance was and had kept it in his possession, albeit he had forgotten about it, he had no defence to the charge. He applied for leave to appeal against conviction arguing that because he had forgotten about the drug's existence he could not be in 'possession'.

Held, the application for leave to appeal would be dismissed. The judge had been correct in his ruling. The appellant had put the substance in his wallet knowing what it was and had put the wallet in his pocket, so he had remained in possession of the drug even though his memory of its presence had faded or even disappeared altogether.

R v Mazo [1996] Crim LR 435 (Court of Appeal)

The appellant was convicted of theft. She was employed as a maid to Lady S, who over some two years made out a number of cheques in her favour totalling £37,000. Lady S affirmed her intention to pay when on one occasion the bank queried the payments. The jury was directed that they could convict if satisfied that Lady S had written the cheques while her mental state was impaired; that the appellant knew this and had been dishonest. The appeal was on the ground that there had been no adequate direction as to the validity of the transfers.

Held, the appeal would be allowed. What was Lady S's state of mind? If she was of sound mind the cheque was valid and there was no theft. If she had been of unsound mind the cheque was not valid and the issue became one of mens rea. As to this issue the direction had been inadequate. (See also *R* v *Gomez, Lawrence* v *Commissioner of Police for the Metropolis, Dobson* v *General Accident Fire and Life Assurance Corporation plc* and *R* v *Hinks*; compare *R* v *Hopkins; R* v *Kendrick*.)

R v Meech [1973] 3 All ER 939 (Court of Appeal)

A man named McCord obtained a cheque for £1,450 from a hire purchase finance company by means of a forged instrument. McCord was an undischarged bankrupt and asked Meech, whom he owed £40, to cash the cheque for him and Meech agreed to do so. At the time Meech agreed to cash the cheque he did not know of the dishonest method by which McCord had obtained it. Meech paid the cheque into his own account at a branch of Lloyds Bank at High Wycombe and a few days later, by which time the cheque had been cleared, he made a withdrawal of £1,410, having deducted the £40 he was owed by McCord. Between the paying in of the original cheque and the withdrawal Meech became aware that McCord had obtained the original cheque dishonestly and arranged with two men, Parslow and Jolliffe, that after making the withdrawal he would take the money to a prearranged destination where they were to join him and fake a robbery in order to provide an explanation to McCord for not handing over the money to him. The bogus robbery was staged and reported to the police who discovered the true facts. Meech, Parslow and Jolliffe were convicted of theft and appealed to the Court of Appeal.

Held, the convictions would be affirmed since at the time when Meech, in ignorance of the fraud, obtained the original cheque from McCord, he assumed an obligation to McCord which on the facts known to him he remained obliged to fulfil. Section 5(3) of the Theft Act 1968 looked at the time of the creation of the obligation rather than the time of its performance and accordingly the position did not change when Meech learnt of the fraud. Consequently, since Meech received the cheque from McCord under the initial obligation to deal with it in accordance with his instructions, the cheque and its proceeds were deemed by s5(3) to be McCord's property, for the purposes of theft. (See also *R* v *Gilks*.)

R v Mellor [1996] 2 Cr App R 245 (Court of Appeal)

The appellant was convicted of murder having attacked the victim, who died in hospital. The appellant contended that a substantial cause of the victim's death was the failure at the hospital to give sufficient oxygen to the victim. The question of whether or not the judge had properly directed the jury on whether or not medical treatment would break the chain of causation was raised on appeal.

Held, the appeal would be dismissed. The onus was on the Crown to prove D's act was a substantial cause of death. There was no onus on the Crown to prove that any supervening cause, eg medical treatment, was not a substantial cause of death.

R v Merrick [1995] Crim LR 802 (Court of Appeal)

The defendant offered a 'service' to property owners to remove television cabling where permission had not been granted to fix such cabling to their properties. His response to a number of charges of criminal damage as regards the removal of cables (which belonged to the television company) was that he had acted with reasonable excuse having the householders' consent. These charges were withdrawn from the jury. The defendant was further charged with criminal damage being reckless as to whether life would be endangered contrary to s1(2) of the Criminal Damage Act 1971. He had left a live mains cable exposed for some five minutes before cementing it underground. He said that he knew that the exposed wire was dangerous but he was capable of dealing with that danger and had only undertaken the work because he was competent to complete it safely. The defendant pleaded guilty when the trial judge ruled he could only refute the allegation of recklessness if there was evidence he had taken steps to eliminate the risk of endangering life before the damage was caused.

Held, the defendant's appeal would be dismissed because he had to show that precautions were taken to prevent a risk arising rather than acting to reduce the risk once he had caused a danger to arise.

R v Miller [1983] 1 All ER 978 (House of Lords)

The appellant was convicted of arson contrary to s1(1) and (3) of the Criminal Damage Act 1971. He had been sleeping in an empty house. On the night in question he returned to the house after having a few drinks. He lay down on his mattress and lit a cigarette; he fell asleep and the cigarette set the matress alight. He woke up, saw the fire, got up and went to the next room and fell asleep again. The next thing he knew was that the police and fire crews had arrived. The house was badly damaged by fire. Leave to appeal to the House of Lords on a point of law of general public importance was granted by the Court of Appeal. The question was 'Whether the actus reus of the offence of arson is present when a defendant accidentally starts a fire and thereafter, intending to destroy or damage property belonging to another or being reckless as to whether any such property would be destroyed or damaged, fails to take any steps to extinguish the fire or prevent damage to such property by that fire?'

Held, the appeal would be dismissed. 'Where the accused is initially unaware that he has done an act that in fact sets in train events which, by the time the accused becomes aware of them, would make it obvious to anyone who troubled to give his mind to them that they present a risk that property belonging to another would be damaged, a suitable direction to the jury would be that the accused is guilty of the offence under s1(1) of the 1971 Act if, when he does become aware that the events in question have happened as a result of his own act, he does not try to prevent or reduce the risk of damage by his own efforts or if necessary by sending for help from the fire brigade and the reason why he does not is either because he has not given any thought to the possibility of there being any such risk or because having recognised that there was some risk involved he has decided not to try to prevent or reduce it' (*per* LORD DIPLOCK).

R v Millward [1994] Crim LR 527 (Court of Appeal)

The appellant was convicted of procuring an offence which was one of recklessness. His employee was acquitted on a charge of causing death by reckless driving having been instructed by the appellant to tow a trailer behind a tractor on a main road. The hitch mechanism was defective, the trailer became detached and collided with a car killing a passenger. The appellant contended that given the principal offender had been acquitted, he could not be convicted of procuring the offence. Since the offence was one of recklessness, the acquittal of the principal offender implied that the actus reus had not been committed.

Held, the appeal would be dismissed. The actus reus had been taking the vehicle on the road in a defective condition. The defendant could procure the actus reus of an offence irrespective of whether or not the principal offender had the necessary mens rea.

R v Mitchell and Another [1999] Crim LR 496
(Queen's Bench Divisional Court)

FM and K were convicted of murder. They, together with MM, were in a takeaway restaurant. MM and K assaulted two other customers and MM caused damage to the restaurant. They were followed out by BA and his two sons, A and T, and other members of staff, some of whom were armed. During the ensuing fight K was beaten. Two men who had been drinking at a nearby public house joined in the fight and the restaurant staff were on the receiving end of the violence. T was injured by MM and he later died. FM, K and MM were charged with murder. It was alleged they were in a joint enterprise to do serious harm to the victim. FM and K argued that if there had been a joint enterprise to inflict violence on T, that joint enterprise had ended by the time the fatal blows were struck. The judge gave an appropriate direction on joint enterprise according to the state of the law at the date of the trial. The judge also went on to tell the jury that they might have to ask themselves whether any joint enterprise had simply come to an end before the fatal blows were administered. To withdraw from a joint enterprise there had to be established a timely communication of the intention to abandon the common purpose from those who wanted to dissociate from the contemplated crime.

Held, the appeal would be allowed. The case of *R v Powell and Daniels; R v English* was decided subsequent to the appellant's trial, so the judge's direction no longer represented the law. Summing up in a case of joint enterprise, in addition to giving general instructions, the judge had to give two further directions: the jury had to be satisfied that the fatal injuries were sustained when the joint enterprise was continuing and that the defendant was still acting within that joint enterprise; and the jury had to be satisfied that the acts which had caused the death were within the scope of the joint enterprise. In a case of spontaneous violence a direction as to the test of communication of withdrawal was inappropriate since such communication was only a necessary condition for disassociation from pre-planned violence. The direction given to the jury was inappropriate and the convictions were unsafe. (See *R v Powell and Daniels; R v English*.)

R v Modupe [1991] Crim LR 530 (Court of Appeal)

The appellant was convicted of evading a liability by deception, contrary to s2(1)(b) of the

Theft Act 1978. He gave false information to obtain finance to purchase cars. Two county court judgments were registered against him for large sums of money. He contended that since the hire-purchase agreement had been improperly executed and would need, under s65(1)(2) of the Consumer Credit Act 1974, a court order to enforce it, there was no existing liability to make payment as required under s2(1)(b).

Held, the appeal would be dismissed. There was an existing liability; it merely required certain procedures for enforcement.

R v Mohan [1975] 2 All ER 193 (Court of Appeal)

A police officer in uniform saw the appellant driving a motor car towards him at a speed which he estimated to be in excess of the permitted limit of 30 mph. He stepped into the road, held up his hand and signalled the appellant to stop. The car slowed down, but when he reached a point some ten yards from the officer the appellant suddenly increased the speed and drove straight at him. The officer leapt out of the way to avoid being struck and the appellant drove on without stopping. The appellant was convicted of driving a motor vehicle in a manner dangerous to the public and attempting to cause bodily harm to the police officer. In relation to the second offence, in his summing-up the trial judge had directed the jury that the Crown had to prove that the appellant had deliberately driven the vehicle wantonly and that he must have realised at the time that, unless he were to stop or there were some other intervening factor, such driving was likely to cause bodily harm, or that he was reckless as to whether bodily harm was caused, but that it was not necessary to prove an intention actually to cause bodily harm.

Held, the conviction should be quashed on the ground that the direction was bad in law. In order to prove the offence of attempt to commit a crime the Crown had to prove a specific intent, ie a decision by the accused to bring about, so far as it lay within his power, the commission of the offence which it was alleged that he had attempted to commit. It was not sufficient to establish that the accused knew or foresaw that the consequences of his act would, unless interrupted, be likely to be the commission of the complete offence; nor was a reckless state of mind sufficient to constitute the necessary mens rea.

R v Moloney [1985] 1 All ER 1025 (House of Lords)

The appellant was convicted of murder. He fired a single cartridge from a 12-bore shotgun, the full blast of which struck his stepfather in the side of the face at a range of about six feet, killing him instantly. The event occurred following an argument as to whether the appellant should leave the army. Both parties had had a considerable amount to drink. The stepfather claimed he could not only outshoot his stepson, but outload and outdraw him; the challenge was made, two shotguns and cartridges were collected by the stepson. The appellant had loaded the right hand barrel, closed the gun, taken off the safety catch and pulled the trigger of the left hand barrel and told his stepfather he had lost before his stepfather had inserted his cartridge. The stepfather was alleged to have said, 'I didn't think you'd got the guts, but if you have pull the trigger.' The appellant stated that he did not aim the gun, just pulled the trigger, and his stepfather was dead. The Court of Appeal, Criminal Division, dismissed his appeal against conviction of murder. The court certified that a point of law of general public importance was involved: 'Is malice aforethought in the crime of murder established by proof that when doing the act which causes the death of another the accused either: (a) intends to kill or do serious harm; or (b) foresees that death or serious harm will probably occur, whether or not he desires either of those consequences?'

Held, the appeal would be allowed, the verdict of murder would be set aside and a verdict of manslaughter substituted. LORD BRIDGE OF HARWICH, obiter, attempted some clarification and simplification on the appropriate direction to be given as to the mental element in the crime of murder. He concluded by saying 'In the rare cases in which it is necessary to direct a jury by reference to foresight of consequences, I do not believe it is necessary for the judge to do more than invite the jury to consider two questions. First, was death or really serious injury in a murder case ... a natural consequence of the defendant's voluntary act? Second, did the defendant foresee that consequence as being a natural consequence of his act? The jury should then be told that if they answer Yes to both questions it is a proper inference for them to draw that he intended that consequence.' (See *R v Nedrick* and *R v Woollin*.)

R v More [1987] 3 All ER 825 (House of Lords)

The appellant was convicted of forgery, contrary to s1 of the Forgery and Counterfeiting Act 1981. He stole a cheque made payable to 'M R Jessel' (a Michael Richard Jessel), opened a building society account in the name of Mark Richard Jessel and paid the cheque into that account. He then withdrew most of the money, completing a withdrawal form and signing it M J Jessel. It was contended he had made a false instrument by signing the withdrawal form in the name Michael Richard Jessel. On appeal it was argued that the withdrawal form was not a 'false' instrument within s9(1) of the 1981 Act. The Court of Appeal dismissed the appeal on the ground that the withdrawal form fell within s9(1)(h) of the 1981 Act because it purported to have been 'made ... by an existing person but he did not in fact exist'.

Held, the appeal would be allowed. A document was 'false' if it told a lie about itself, if it purported to be made by a person who did not make it. The withdrawal form did not tell a lie about itself. It was signed by the person who had opened the building society account, the appellant, who was a real person. The appellant had not therefore committed the offence of forgery.

R v Morhall [1995] 3 All ER 659 (House of Lords)

The appellant had an addiction to sniffing glue. He killed Denton after an argument over this addiction. At his trial for murder the defence of provocation was put forward on the appellant's behalf. The trial judge directed the jury that the characteristic of glue sniffing was something they should take into account because it was the issue to which the provocative words were related. Following his conviction for murder, he appealed on the ground that the trial judge's direction had been inadequate. The appeal was dismissed by the Court of Appeal – the attribution of a characteristic such as an addiction to glue sniffing was inconsistent with the concept of the reasonable man which had been developed in previous cases. The court certified the following point of law for the House of Lords to consider: 'When directing a jury on provocation under s3 Homicide Act 1957, and explaining to them in accordance with the model direction of LORD DIPLOCK in *Director of Public Prosecutions* v *Camplin* ... should the judge exclude from the jury's consideration characteristics and past behaviour of the defendant, at which taunts are directed, which in the judge's view are inconsistent with the concept of the reasonable man?'

Held, the appeal would be allowed and a conviction for manslaughter substituted. The deceased's words had been directed towards the appellant's habit. Nothing which was said in *Director of Public Prosecutions* v *Camplin* suggested that such a characteristic ought to be excluded from being considered. The jury should be directed towards those matters which affected the gravity of the provocation. A defendant should be judged by the standard of the ordinary person of the age and sex of the defendant, having the defendant's inclinations. (See also *Director of Public Prosecutions* v *Camplin* and *R* v *Thornton (No 2)*.)

R v *Morris; Anderton* v *Burnside* [1983] 3 All ER 288 (House of Lords)

The appellants in each case were convicted of theft contrary to s1(1) of the Theft Act 1968. They had each taken price labels from lower priced articles and substituted them for the price labels on higher priced articles. One of them paid the lower prices indicated at the checkout and was then arrested. The other was detected before he paid the lesser price for the articles and was arrested. It was determined that the switching of the price labels amounted to an 'appropriation' of the articles within s3(1) of the 1968 Act. Their appeals were dismissed by the Court of Appeal.

Held, both appeals would be dismissed. In s3(1) of the 1968 Act 'appropriates' involves an element of adverse interference with or usurpation of the rights of an owner. Changing the price labels involved a dishonest appropriation because there was an adverse interference with or usurpation of the right of the owner to determine that the goods should be sold and paid for at the higher price. (See also *Lawrence* v *Commissioner of Police for the Metropolis* and *R* v *Gomez*.)

R v *Mowatt* [1967] 3 All ER 47 (Court of Appeal)

The appellant's mate snatched a £5 note from a man and made off. The man grabbed the appellant by the lapels of his jacket and demanded to know where his mate was. The appellant knocked the man to the ground, struck him several violent blows in the face with his fist, pulled him to his feet and struck him again in the face, knocking him down and rendering him almost unconscious. The £5 note was found concealed in the appellant's hand. The appellant's defence was that he acted in self-defence. He was convicted of robbery with violence and unlawful wounding contrary to s20 of the Offences against the Person Act 1861. In his summing-up the trial judge did not give the jury any direction as to the meaning of 'maliciously' in s20 of the Act of 1861. The appellant appealed against conviction.

Held, the conviction would be affirmed on the ground that where the plea of accident or of self-defence was the only point at issue and it was clear that there was a direct assault which any ordinary person would be bound to realise was likely to cause some physical harm, it was unnecessary for the trial judge to give the jury any directions on the meaning of the word 'maliciously'. The court stated that 'maliciously' should be ignored when directing the jury on the offence under s18, and that within s20 it means an awareness by the person who unlawfully inflicts the wound that his act may have the consequence of causing physical harm to some other person. (Approved in *R* v *Savage*; *R* v *Parmenter*.)

R v Nedrick [1986] 3 All ER 1 (Court of Appeal)

The appellant was convicted of murder. He set fire to a house in which there was a woman (and her child) against whom he bore a grudge. The child died in the fire. The appellant claimed he only wanted to frighten the woman. The trial judge directed the jury before the publication of the speeches in the House of Lords in *R* v *Moloney* and *R* v *Hancock* in a way which was now clearly wrong in the light of those cases.

Held, the appeal against conviction of murder would be allowed and a verdict of manslaughter substituted. LORD LANE CJ summarised the position as follows: 'In *R* v *Hancock* the House decided that the *R* v *Moloney* guidelines require a reference to probability. Lord Scarman said: "They also require an explanation that the greater the probability of a consequence the more likely it is that the consequence was foreseen and that if that consequence was foreseen the greater the probability is that that consequence was also intended." When determining whether the defendant had the necessary intent, it may therefore be helpful for a jury to ask themselves two questions. (1) How probable was the consequence which resulted from the defendant's voluntary act? (2) Did he foresee that consequence? If he did not appreciate that death or serious harm was likely to result from his act, he cannot have intended to bring it about. If he did, but thought that the risk to which he was exposing the person killed was only slight, then it may be easy for the jury to conclude that he did not intend to bring about that result. On the other hand, if the jury are satisfied that at the material time the defendant recognised that death or serious harm would be virtually certain (barring some unforeseen intervention) to result from his voluntary act, then that is a fact from which they may find it easy to infer that he intended to kill or do serious bodily harm, even though he may not have had any desire to achieve that result'. (See also *R* v *Walker*; *R* v *Hayles* and *R* v *Woollin*.)

R v Ngan (1997) The Times 24 July (Court of Appeal)

The defendant was convicted of three counts of theft. She opened a Barclays Bank account and was issued with an account number that had been previously allocated to a debt collection agency. In error, the account was credited with over £77,000 due to the agency. After a while she signed three cheques in blank and sent them to her sister in Scotland. They were eventually presented for payment; two in Scotland, one in England. The defendant appealed against her conviction on the ground that the actus reus of the theft had not been committed within the jurisdiction of the English courts.

Held, the appeal would be allowed in respect of the cheques presented for payment in Scotland but not allowed for the cheque presented for payment in England. Signing the cheques in blank did not amount to an appropriation of the funds which belonged to the agency. An appropriation took place when the cheques were presented for payment.

R v O'Brien [1995] Crim LR 734 (Court of Appeal)

The appellant was convicted of attempted murder when he had aided and abetted one, Magee, in the commission of the offence. He appealed on the ground he should only have been convicted of attempted murder if he knew that Magee intended to kill; foresight that he might shoot to kill was insufficient.

Held, the appeal would be dismissed. The appellant could have been convicted as an accomplice if Magee had shot and killed the intended victim because he could have foreseen that death or grievous bodily harm might result from the common design being carried out. If the jury was satisfied that the principal offender was guilty of attempted murder then the same state of mind should suffice to ensure the appellant's conviction for attempted murder. (See also *R v Stewart and Scholfield*.)

R v O'Connell [1991] Crim LR 771 (Court of Appeal)

The appellant was convicted of offences of obtaining property by deception, contrary to s15(1) of the Theft Act 1968, and attempting to obtain by deception. He (and others) carried out a fraud on building societies obtaining cheques representing mortgage advances. False particulars were given in the mortgage applications. The intention was to let the properties at a rate which would allow the appellant to repay the mortgage by monthly instalments, or if the property was sold, to repay the mortgage in full from the proceeds of sale. The judge ruled that it was irrelevant that he intended to pay back the building society; the court had to consider the element of dishonesty in relation to obtaining the cheques. The appellant changed his plea to guilty and now appealed.

Held, the appeal would be dismissed. The judge was wrong to have excluded evidence concerning his intention to repay which, although it was not a defence, it might be some evidence of honesty. A jury should be trusted to give it such weight as it deserved. However, there had been no miscarriage of justice, there was no doubt that the appellant would have been convicted in any event, so the proviso to s2(1) of the Criminal Appeal Act 1968 would be applied. (See also *R v Ghosh* and *R v Feely*.)

R v O'Grady [1987] 3 All ER 420 (Court of Appeal)

The defendant was charged with murder. Both he and the deceased had consumed large quantities of alcohol. They went to the defendant's flat where they fell asleep. The defendant woke to find the deceased hitting him; he retaliated, the fight eventually subsided and he fell asleep again. When he next awoke he found that the deceased was dead; he had suffered multiple injuries of a serious nature consistent with blows from both blunt and sharp objects. The defendant claimed to have acted in self-defence. The trial judge directed the jury that he could rely on a mistake as to the existence of an attack but not as to the severity of the attack or the amount of force necessary to defend himself.

Held, the appeal against conviction of manslaughter would be dismissed. '... a defendant is not entitled to rely, so far as self-defence is concerned, on a mistake of fact which has been induced by voluntary intoxication' (*per* LORD LANE CJ). (See also *Director of Public Prosecutions v Majewski*.)

R v Olugboja [1981] 3 All ER 443 (Court of Appeal)

The appellant was convicted of rape contrary to s1 of the Sexual Offences Act 1956. Section 1(1) of the Sexual Offences (Amendment) Act 1976 defines rape as being when a man has 'unlawful sexual intercourse with a woman who at the time of the intercourse does not consent to it ...'. The appellant had sexual intercourse with J who had already been raped by L. J told the appellant that earlier L had had her in the car and asked why he could not leave her alone. She did what she was told because she was frightened. The appellant pushed her on the settee and had intercourse with her. She did not struggle, made no resistance and did not scream or cry for help until he penetrated her and when she thought he was going to ejaculate inside her; he then withdrew. J only made a complaint about L. Interviewing the appellant about the complaint against L it was put to him that L had said that he, the appellant, had had intercourse with J. The appellant admitted to having done so. Asked 'Did she consent?' he replied, 'Well, not at first but I persuaded her.' The question to be considered so far as the actus reus is concerned was: at the time of intercourse did the woman consent to it?

Held, the appeal would be dismissed. To prove a charge of rape it is necessary to show merely that the victim did not in fact consent. 'It is not necessary for the prosecution to prove that what might otherwise appear to have been consent was in reality merely submission induced by force, fear or fraud, although one or more of these factors will no doubt be present in the majority of cases of rape. [The jury] should be directed that consent, or the absence of it, is to be given its ordinary meaning and if need be, by way of example, that there is a difference between consent and submission; every consent involves a submission, but it by no means follows that a mere submission involves consent' (*per* DUNN LJ). (See *R v Malone*.)

R v Owino [1995] Crim LR 743 (Court of Appeal)

The appellant was convicted of causing actual bodily harm to his wife. He said her injuries were sustained as a result of defending himself against her assault on him. The trial judge directed the jury on the issue of self-defence – the prosecution had to prove that the appellant had not believed that the force he used was reasonable. It was contended on behalf of the appellant that the trial judge's direction on self-defence had been inadequate in the light of the Court of Appeal decision in *R v Scarlett* [1993] 4 All ER 629.

Held, the appeal would be dismissed. *R v Scarlett*, correctly interpreted, showed that a defendant could use an amount of force that would be regarded as reasonable, given the circumstances as he honestly, albeit unreasonably, believed them to be. (This interpretation emphasises the correct approach following the decision in *R v Williams (Gladstone)* – the defendant should be judged on the facts as he believes them to be.) (See *R v Williams (Gladstone)*.)

R v P & O European Ferries (Dover) Ltd (1991) 93 Cr App R 72 (Central Criminal Court)

The owners and operators of the ferry *Herald of Free Enterprise*, P&O European Ferries

(Dover) Ltd, were charged, along with seven other defendants, with the manslaughter of the passengers and crew who died as a result of the ferry capsizing whilst leaving Zeebrugge harbour. The question arose as to whether or not an indictment would lie against a corporation for the offence of manslaughter.

Held, a body corporate could be indicted for the offence of manslaughter. In the context of manslaughter, it sufficed that where a corporation, through the controlling mind of one of its agents, did an act which fulfilled the elements of the crime of manslaughter, it was able to be indicted for that crime. 'If it be accepted that manslaughter in English law is the unlawful killing of one human being by another human being (which must include both direct and indirect acts) and that a person who is the embodiment of a corporation and acting for the purposes of the corporation is doing the act or omission which caused the death, the corporation as well as the person may also be found guilty of manslaughter' (*per* TURNER J). (See also *Readhead Freight Ltd v Shulman*.)

R v Pawlicki; R v Swindell [1992] 1 WLR 827 (Court of Appeal)

The appellants were convicted of having firearms with intent to commit an indictable offence, namely robbery, contrary to s18(1) of the Firearms Act 1968. Police officers had been alerted to the possibility of a robbery and arrested both appellants who were standing close to each other in an auctioneer's showroom. A search of P's car revealed three sawn-off shotguns.

Held, the appeals would be dismissed. The words of s18(1) of the 1968 Act '... to have with him a firearm ...' indicated some closeness between the person and the weapon. Were the guns sufficiently accessible to the appellants as they embarked on the robbery? Under the circumstances there were no grounds for interfering with the conviction.

R v Peart [1970] 2 All ER 823 (Court of Appeal)

Peart secured the loan of a van for £2 by representing to the owner that he wanted to go to Alnwick urgently. He assured the owner he would be back by 7.30pm. He did not return and about 9pm he was stopped in Burnley by the police because of a defective exhaust. The issue was whether the fraud which induced the consent vitiated it so as to make the appellant liable to prosecution under s12(1) of the Theft Act 1968.

Held, the appeal would be allowed on the ground that, on the true construction of the section, the consent of the owner of a motor car to its use by another is not vitiated by the fact that consent is obtained by a false pretence as to the destination and purpose of the journey.

R v Perman [1995] Crim LR 736 (Court of Appeal)

The appellant was convicted of manslaughter. His co-accused was convicted of murder. A shop assistant was shot and killed by the co-accused in the course of an armed robbery on an off-licence. The appellant knew his co-accused had a gun, but was not aware that it was loaded. The trial judge directed the jury that if the appellant had agreed to the gun being used to frighten anyone in the shop, he could be guilty as an accomplice to manslaughter, even if he believed the gun to be unloaded.

Held, the appeal was allowed on other grounds, but the court observed that if the appellant had contemplated robbery with an unloaded gun he did not have the necessary mens rea to be an accomplice to the killing which came about by reason of the principal offender's use of the loaded gun. The defendant could have been convicted as an accomplice to manslaughter if he had contemplated the use of a loaded gun in order to frighten the shop assistant. (See also *R v Stewart and Scholfield*.)

R v Petters and Parfitt [1995] Crim LR 501 (Court of Appeal)

J died as a result of a violent attack on him by the appellants, who were charged with his murder. They had arrived at a car park separately. There was no pre-arranged plan; they kicked and punched J. The trial judge directed the jury that if the appellants adopted the same mode of attack with a common intention, even without a pre-arranged plan, there could be a joint enterprise. The appellants were convicted of manslaughter.

Held, their appeals would be allowed. In considering whether there was a joint enterprise or not a trial judge should direct a jury to consider whether those involved shared a common purpose and had, by their conduct, intimated to each other that they were acting in concert. (See also *R v Greatrex; R v Bates* and *R v Mitchell and Another*.)

R v Pigg [1982] 2 All ER 591 (Court of Appeal)

The appellant was convicted of attempted rape (as defined in s1(1) of the Sexual Offences (Amendment) Act 1976). The judge directed the jury that the appellant was 'reckless' as to whether his victim consented to sexual intercourse if he was aware of the possibility that she might not be consenting and yet went ahead regardless. It was contended that the judge had misdirected the jury in that he failed to tell them that the appellant had to be aware of a serious and obvious risk that the victim was not consenting and not merely that there was a possibility that she was not.

Held, the appeal would be dismissed. '... a man is reckless if either he was indifferent and gave no thought to the possibility that the woman might not be consenting in circumstances where if any thought had been given to the matter it would have been obvious that there was a risk she was not, or he was aware of the possibility that she might not be consenting but nevertheless persisted regardless of whether she consented or not' (per LORD LANE CJ). The judge's direction to the jury had, if anything, been too favourable to the appellant. (For the reversal of the Court of Appeal's decision on a different point, see [1983] 1 All ER 56.)

R v Podola [1959] 3 All ER 418 (Court of Criminal Appeal)

Podola killed a police officer while being arrested. At his trial he claimed that he was suffering from hysterical amnesia and could not remember what happened on the day of the killing. A jury was empanelled to consider whether his loss of memory was genuine and consequently whether he was unfit to plead. The jury found that he was not suffering from a genuine loss of memory and was fit to plead. The trial proceeded and he was convicted. Podola did not appeal but the Home Secretary referred the case to the Court of Criminal Appeal for their consideration.

Held, the conviction should be affirmed on the ground that, inter alia, even if the jury had held that Podola was suffering from a genuine loss of memory that of itself would not have rendered him insane and therefore unfit to plead. The court also laid down that if the defence alleges unfitness to plead the onus of proof lies on them to prove unfitness to plead on the balance of probabilities, but where the prosecution alleges fitness to plead then they must prove fitness to plead beyond reasonable doubt.

R v Pommell [1995] 2 Cr App R 607 (Court of Appeal)

The appellant was convicted of possessing a prohibited weapon and ammunition without a firearms certificate. He tried to raise the defence of necessity or duress of circumstance. He claimed he had taken the gun from another man who had visited him and who was going to carry out a revenge killing on a third party. The appellant intended to hand the gun over to the police the following day. The trial judge ruled that because he had not handed over the gun immediately, he had forfeited the right to raise the defence. He appealed on the ground that he had been wrongly denied the opportunity to place the defence of necessity before the jury.

Held, the appeal would be allowed and a re-trial ordered. (The defence was available for all offences save for murder, attempted murder and treason.) The defendant had to place himself in a position where he was not committing an offence as soon as he reasonably could. This would be a matter for the jury (unless in the eyes of the trial judge he had acted as soon as he reasonably could and consequently there would be no evidence for a jury to consider). The trial judge had been wrong to rule that the appellant's failure to hand over the gun at the earliest opportunity denied him the right to have the matter put before a jury.

R v Powell and Daniels; R v English [1997] 4 All ER 545
(House of Lords)

In R v *Powell and Daniels*, the appellants were convicted of being accessories to murder. They, together with a third man, went to an address in South London, to buy drugs. The deceased opened the door and was shot dead by one of them. The trial judge directed the jury that they could convict the appellants as accessories to murder if they were satisfied that they had foreseen death or grievous bodily harm as a possible incident of the common design being carried out (R v *Hyde* [1991] 1 QB 134 and *Chan Wing-Siu* v *The Queen*). They appealed unsuccessfully to the Court of Appeal. The following question was certified for consideration by the House of Lords: 'Is it sufficient to found a conviction for murder for a secondary party to a killing to have realised that the primary party might kill with intent to do so or must the secondary party have held such intention himself?'

In R v *English*, one, Weddle, was convicted of murder and the appellant was convicted of murder as an accomplice. Weddle had allegedly been involved in an assault on his girlfriend. Police officers attended his house. Weddle and the appellant became involved in a fight with the police officers. Having attacked one officer, Sgt Forth, with a fencing stave, the appellant was chased from the house and arrested by PC Hay 100 yards away. PC Hay handcuffed the appellant and at the same time Weddle pulled a knife on Sgt Forth and stabbed him to death. After an unsuccessful appeal to the Court of Appeal the following question was certified for consideration by the House of Lords: 'Is it sufficient for murder that the secondary party intends or foresees that the primary party would or may act with intent to cause grievous bodily harm, if the lethal act carried out by the primary party is fundamentally different from the acts foreseen or intended by the secondary party?

Held, the appeals of Powell and Daniels would be dismissed. Where there is a joint enterprise and the victim of an unlawful attack is killed, an accomplice can incur liability for murder where he realises that, in the course of pursuing the joint enterprise the principal offender might kill or cause grievous bodily harm with intent to produce either of those consequences. The appeal by English was allowed. The trial judge had not qualified the direction he gave to the jury on the foresight that had to be established on the part of an accomplice in a joint enterprise. He had not stressed that an accomplice who did not foresee the use of a deadly weapon by the principal offender should not be convicted of murder. (See also *Chan Wing-Siu v The Queen, R v Anderson and Morris, R v Greatrex; R v Bates* and *R v Mitchell and Another*.)

R v Preddy; R v Slade [1996] 3 All ER 481 (House of Lords)

The appellants were convicted under various counts under s15 Theft Act 1968 (obtaining property by deception). They completed a large number of application forms to building societies for mortgage advances in order to purchase properties. These forms contained deliberate falsehoods intending to deceive the lenders into granting applications. The transfer of funds was executed electronically via the 'CHAPS' system. On appeal to the Court of Appeal the appellants contended that they had not obtained property; there was no property belonging to another; and there could be no intention to permanently deprive the lender where the transfer was effected by means of an electronic transfer system. The Court of Appeal dismissed the appeal. An electronic transfer of funds came within s4(1) which applied to s15 Theft Act 1968. The money advanced belonged to another – the solicitor who acted for both appellants and lenders, held the sums on trust for the lender. There was an intention to permanently deprive since there was a transfer of funds and the appellants did not intend to repay the lenders. The Court of Appeal certified the following questions of general public importance: (1) Whether the debiting of a bank account and the corresponding credit of another's bank account brought about by dishonest misrepresentation amounts to obtaining of property within s15 of the Theft Act 1968?. (2) Is the answer to (1) above different if the account in credit is that of a solicitor acting in a mortgage transaction? (3) Where a defendant is charged with obtaining intangible property by deception, namely an advance by way of mortgage, is his intention to redeem the mortgage in full relevant to the question of permanent intention to deprive or only to dishonesty?

Held, the appeals would be allowed. The sums standing to the credit of the lending institutions in their bank accounts were property within s4 Theft Act 1968 being choses in action (debts owed by the banks where the accounts were maintained). Did they represent property belonging to another at the time the defendant's account was credited? When the lending institution's account was debited, its chose in action was extinguished (or reduced pro tanto). When the defendant's account was credited a new chose in action belonging to the defendant was created. The chose in action never existed as property belonging to another. A charge under s15 would not succeed. (See also *R v Caresana* and the Theft (Amendment) Act 1996.)

R v Prince (1875) LR 2 CCR 154 (Court for Crown Cases Reserved)

Prince was charged with taking an unmarried girl under the age of 16 years out of the possession and against the will of her father, contrary to s55 of the Offences against the Person Act 1861 (now s20 of the Sexual Offences Act 1956). At the time when he took the girl out of her father's possession, Prince knew that she was in the possession of her father but believed on reasonable grounds that she was aged 18 years.

Held, the conviction would be affirmed on the ground that at the time when he took her away Prince knew she was in her father's possession, and an honest belief on reasonable grounds that the girl was over 16 years of age was no defence. The section in question was one of the provisions of the Act forming a code for the protection of women and the guardians of young women and, having knowingly done an act, viz, taking the girl away from the lawful possession of her father against his will and in violation of his rights as guardian by nature, Prince could not say that he thought the girl was of an age beyond that prohibited by the statute. (But see *R v Hibbert*.)

R v Quick; R v Paddison [1973] 3 All ER 347 (Court of Appeal)

Quick, a charge nurse at a mental hospital, was charged with assault occasioning bodily harm and Paddison, a state enrolled nurse at the same hospital, with aiding and abetting him. About 4pm one day, Green, a paraplegic spastic patient, unable to walk, was sitting in a ward at the hospital watching television. At the time Quick was on duty and Paddison, who had gone off duty at 2pm, was still present in the ward. Half an hour later Green had sustained two black eyes, a fractured nose, a split lip and bruising of his arm and shoulders. The medical evidence showed that the injuries could not have been self-inflicted. In evidence Quick said that he had been a diabetic since the age of seven and on the morning of the day in question he had taken insulin as prescribed by his doctor; he had then had a small breakfast and no lunch. Thereafter, before the assault took place, he had been drinking, the drinks including whisky and a quarter of a bottle of rum. He pleaded not guilty on the ground of automatism but the judge ruled that the evidence could only be relied on to support a defence of insanity since it indicated that he was suffering from a defect of reason from disease of the mind, within the *McNaghten* rules, and he changed his plea to guilty. Paddison was also convicted.

Held, the convictions would be quashed. In relation to Quick: (1) in order to sustain a defence of insanity on the ground that he was suffering from a defect of reason from disease of the mind, an accused had to show a malfunctioning of the mind caused by disease; a malfunctioning of the mind of transitory effect caused by the application to the body of some external factor, such as violence, drugs, including anaesthetics, alcohol and hypnotic influences, could not be said to be due to disease. (2) The mental condition from which he had been suffering had not been caused by his diabetes but by the use of insulin prescribed by his doctor; the alleged malfunctioning of his mind had therefore been caused by an external factor and not by a bodily disorder in the nature of a disease and he was entitled to have his defence of automatism left to the jury. (See also *R* v *Clarke* and *Bratty* v *Attorney-General for Northern Ireland*.)

R v *R* [1991] 3 WLR 767 (House of Lords)

The defendant was convicted of the attempted rape of his wife and assault occasioning actual bodily harm They were married in 1984. His wife left him in 1989 to return to her parents. She intimated her intention to start divorce proceedings. The defendant visited his wife at her parent's home and attempted to have sexual intercourse with her, assaulting her in the process. The trial judge ruled that a husband could be guilty of raping his wife where she had revoked her consent to sexual intercourse.

Held, the defendant's appeal against conviction would be dismissed. Following a detailed historical survey of the court's approach to the question of marital rape, LORD KEITH OF KINKEL concluded that 'Section 1(1) of the [Sexual Offences (Amendment) Act] 1976] presents no obstacle to this House declaring that in modern times the supposed marital exception in rape forms no part of the law in England.' (See also *R* v *Elbekkay*.)

R v *Reid* [1992] 3 All ER 673 (House of Lords)

The appellant was convicted of causing death by reckless driving. He overtook another car while driving on the inside lane of a dual carriageway. His car hit a taxi drivers' rest hut which protruded some six feet into the road. His passenger received fatal injuries. The judge directed the jury in terms of LORD DIPLOCK's speech in *R* v *Lawrence*.

Held, this had been the correct approach and the appeal would be dismissed. 'The substance of Lord Diplock's formulation of a specimen jury direction is ... apt ... to cover the generality of cases. But I do not rule out that in certain cases there may be special circumstances which require it to be modified or added to, for example where the driver acted under some understandable and excusable mistake or where his capacity to appreciate risks was adversely affected by some condition not involving fault on his part. There may also be cases where the driver acted as he did in a sudden dilemma created by the actions of others. The specific certified question as to whether the jury should always be directed in the ipsissima verba of Lord Diplock's formulation I would answer in the negative. In some cases when the only relevant issue is one of disputed fact it may not be necessary to use it at all. In others it may require to be modified or adapted to suit the circumstances of the case' (*per* LORD KEITH OF KINKEL).

R v *Richards* [1973] 3 All ER 1088 (Court of Appeal)

The appellant, Mrs Richards, in the belief that her marriage was breaking down, became depressed and took to drink. In an endeavour to restore the marriage she offered £5 to two men, Bryant and Squires, to beat up her husband badly enough to put him into hospital for a month. She thought that if he were hurt he would turn to her for affection. Acting under a pre-arranged plan, as her husband left to go to work one evening she lit a candle and held it up to a window as a signal to the men. The two men, wearing balaclavas over their heads, attacked Mr Richards in a nearby lane and struck him on the back of his head. Mr Richards sustained a laceration on the top of his scalp which required two stitches, but he was not detained in hospital. The appellant was convicted of wounding with intent, contrary to s18 of the Offences against the Person Act 1861, and the two men were convicted of an offence under s20. The appellant appealed, contending that she was in the position of one who aided and abetted the other two to commit the offence and could not be guilty of a graver crime than that of which the two men were guilty, viz, an offence under s20.

Held, the appeal would be allowed and a conviction for the lesser offence of unlawful wounding substituted. The assault on the husband had been perpetrated at some distance from where the appellant was and so she was not in the position of an abettor of those who committed the assault. Only one offence had been proved, ie unlawful wounding, and it could not be said that what had been done had been done with the intention of the appellant.

R v *Richardson; R* v *Irwin* [1999] 1 Cr App R 392 (Court of Appeal)

The appellants were convicted of inflicting grievous bodily harm (s20 Offences Against the Person Act 1861). They and others had been drinking and were engaged in horseplay. The complainant was allegedly held over the edge of a balcony by the appellants and dropped some 10 to 12 feet. The case against the appellants was that they had acted unlawfully and maliciously; they both foresaw that letting the complainant go would or might cause him harm and they took the risk when they let him go. The appellants said the fall was an accident and the complainant had consented to the horseplay. The jury were directed to consider each appellant's intention on the basis of a reasonable man (not one intoxicated) and not as they were, under the influence of drink.

Held, the appeal would be allowed. The proper direction was for the jury to decide not whether the reasonable, sober man would have realised that injury might result, but whether these appellants would have foreseen that their actions might cause injury had they not been drinking. The convictions were unsafe and would be quashed. (See also *Director of Public Prosecutions* v *Majewski*.)

R v *Robert Millar (Contractors) Ltd and Robert Millar*
[1970] 1 All ER 577 (Court of Appeal)

A lorry driver employed by Robert Millar (Contractors) Ltd was sent from Scotland into England with a lorry carrying a heavy load. One of the tyres was known to be defective by the lorry driver and by Robert Millar, the company's managing director. While the lorry was in England the tyre burst and the lorry crashed into a motor car, killing six occupants. The lorry driver was convicted of dangerous driving and the appellants were convicted of counselling and procuring those offences.

Held, their appeals would be dismissed as they had knowledge of the serious risk of harm to other road users arising from the use of a heavily laden lorry with a defective tyre. It was also held that the appellants were liable to be tried in England because they had participated in the crime by the driver in England and, alternatively, they had counselled and procured the driver to drive the lorry in a dangerous state, and that counselling and procuring was a continuous act which persisted so long as the driver was driving the lorry in that condition on the road.

R v Roberts (1971) 56 Cr App R 95 (Court of Appeal)

Roberts met a girl at a party in Warrington and agreed to give her a lift to another party in the town. They left the first party at 3am and drove out of Warrington towards Runcorn. During the course of the journey Roberts made advances to the girl and tried to take off her coat. The girl opened the car door, jumped out and ran to the nearest house, arriving there in a distressed condition. She was taken to hospital, where she was treated for concussion and some grazing and was detained there for three days. Roberts was convicted of an assault occasioning her actual bodily harm and appealed. It was contended that the judge had misdirected the jury in saying they should convict if the girl jumped out of the car as a result of the above actions by Robert.

Held, the appeal would be dismissed. The direction was not open to objection as the proper test was not whether Roberts actually foresaw the conduct of the girl which resulted in the actual bodily harm, but whether that conduct could have reasonably been foreseen as a consequence of what he was saying or doing. (See also *R v Corbett* and *R v Dear*.)

R v Roberts [1993] 1 All ER 583 (Court of Appeal)

The appellant was convicted of murder and robbery. He and another man had gone to the house of the victim with the intention of robbing him. A struggle ensued between the two men and the victim in which the victim was killed by blows to the face with a blunt instrument. The two men blamed each other for the victim's death. The prosecution case was that both the accused had agreed to rob the victim, they were present together with the victim and had expressly or tacitly agreed that he should be killed or that serious bodily injury should intentionally be inflicted on him if it became necessary. The judge directed the jury that all the prosecution had to prove against the accused who did not inflict the blows was that the other accused had inflicted them with the intention of killing or causing serious bodily harm, and that the former had lent himself to the joint criminal enterprise (robbery) and that in the course of the robbery he foresaw or appreciated that the latter might kill the man or intentionally inflict really serious bodily harm on him.

Held, the appeal against conviction of murder would be dismissed. A person entering into a joint unlawful enterprise could be guilty of murder if he realised that the other person might kill or intentionally inflict serious injury and he continued to participate with the other person. The trial judge had given a clear exposition of the law to the jury. (See also *R* v *Anderson and Morris*.)

R v *Rook* [1993] 2 All ER 955 (Court of Appeal)

The appellant and two other men agreed with a fourth man to kill the fourth man's wife for £20,000. The appellant did not turn up for the killing as arranged, but it was carried out by the other two men. All four were jointly charged with murder, but the appellant maintained that he had never intended the woman to be killed, that he had hoped to get some money 'up front' and then disappear, and that he had thought that his deliberate absence would cause the other two to abandon the proposed crime.

Held, his appeal against conviction would be dismissed as it was no defence for a secondary party to say that he did not intend the victim to be killed or to suffer serious harm if he contemplated or foresaw the killing as a real or serious risk. His mere absence on the day of the crime did not amount to an unequivocal communication to the others of his withdrawal from the murder. (See also *Director of Public Prosecutions for Northern Ireland* v *Maxwell*, *R* v *Whitefield* and *R* v *Siracusa*.)

R v *Rossiter* [1994] 2 All ER 752 (Court of Appeal)

The appellant was convicted of murder. She inflicted fatal and other wounds upon her husband during a domestic argument. The evidence showed that she had been the subject of verbal abuse and physical violence from her husband that day. She suffered injuries which in part accorded with her story that there had been a 'ghastly accident' or that she had been defending herself, except when she inflicted the fatal wounds. She did not accept that she had deliberately inflicted injury on her husband. Her defence counsel was therefore unable to put forward the defence of provocation to the jury. She appealed on the ground that the judge had failed to leave the question of provocation to the jury as required by s3 of the Homicide Act 1957.

Held, the appeal would be allowed and a verdict of guilty of manslaughter substituted. Even though the appellant never accepted that she had deliberately stabbed her husband, it was possible to infer from the evidence that the appellant had lost her self-control. The jury should have been given the opportunity to consider whether the provocation had been sufficient to make a reasonable person act as she had done.

R v *Rowley* (1992) 94 Cr App R 95 (Court of Appeal)

The appellant was convicted on a number of counts of commiting an act outraging public decency and one count of attempted incitement of a child under 14 to commit an act of gross indecency, contrary to s1(1) of the Criminal Attempts Act 1981. The Crown's case was that various notes were written and left in public places. They had been designed to lure boys for immoral purposes. It had been argued for the defence that there was insufficient evidence to support a charge of outraging public decency. As far as the incitement charge was concerned, the acts done were no more than preparatory. The defence submissions were rejected and the trial judge allowed the Crown to adduce evidence from the appellant's diary which indicated his desire for sexual activity with boys; he said the jury were entitled to look at the purpose behind the notes to determine whether they were lewd or disgusting.

Held, the appeals would be allowed and the convictions quashed. The judge should not have directed the jury to consider motive, or to have allowed evidence from the diary. He should have accepted the submission that there was nothing in the notes themselves to amount to outraging public decency. One had to be concerned with the nature and effect of the act itself. Motive or intention did not bring lewdness or obscenity to the act if the act itself lacked those qualities. As to the attempt charge, the notes went no further than trying to set up a preliminary meeting and could not be regarded as being more than preparatory. (See also *R* v *Gullefer* and *R* v *Jones (Kenneth)*.)

R v *Ryan* [1996] Crim LR 320 (Court of Appeal)

The appellant was convicted of burglary contrary to s9 Theft Act 1968. His head and right arm were wedged in the window of a house at 2.30 am. He claimed he had been trying to get a baseball bat back that had been thrown through the window by a friend. In his appeal he argued he had not entered the building as required by s9.

Held, the appeal would be dismissed. Following the decision in *R* v *Brown* [1985] Crim LR 212, an entry for the purposes of s9 could be made out even where D inserted only a part of his body into the building. (Compare *R* v *Collins*.)

R v *Sagoo* [1975] 2 All ER 926 (Court of Appeal)

The appellant, a British subject born in Kenya, had a domicile of origin there and was a Sikh by religion. He married in Kenya in 1959 at a time when polygamous marriages were permitted there. In 1960 the Hindu Marriage and Divorce Ordinance of Kenya, which applied to Sikhs, was passed and prohibited polygamy; the statute did not have a retrospective effect and marriages solemnised before July 1960 remained valid even if the marriage in question had been up to that date polygamous or potentially polygamous. In 1966 the appellant and his wife came to England and in 1973 he went through a form of marriage with a single woman while his wife was still living and his marriage to her still subsisting. On a charge of bigamy contrary to s57 of the Offences against the Person Act 1861, the appellant submitted that a potentially polygamous marriage was not a valid first marriage for the purposes of founding a prosecution for bigamy, but the submission was overruled and the appellant convicted.

Held, the conviction would be affirmed since for the purposes of the criminal law the relevant time for determining the question whether the appellant was within the meaning of the words 'being married' in s57 of the 1861 Act was the time of the alleged bigamous ceremony of marriage, ie 1973. At that date his potentially polygamous marriage still subsisted but it had become monogamous in character by operation of the 1960 Kenyan ordinance and by his acquisition of an English domicile whereby monogamy had become part of his personal law.

R v Sainthouse [1980] Crim LR 506 (Court of Appeal)

The appellant was convicted of theft contrary to s1(1) of the Theft Act 1968. He was present with another man when the latter stole items (a box of tools, a can of petrol and a briefcase) from the boot of an unattended car. The appellant sold the box and tools, forced open the briefcase and helped to put some of the petrol into the car he and the other man were using. He later placed the briefcase inside a suitcase stolen by the other man. The appellant pleaded guilty to handling but such plea was not accepted. The jury were directed to return a verdict of guilty, the judge ruling that on the appellant's own account in giving evidence he was guilty. The appeal was on the grounds that the ruling was wrong; the appellant could not have appropriated property when that property had already been appropriated by the other man, subject to the exception in s22 of the 1968 Act, he could not be guilty of both stealing and handling goods by the same actions.

Held, the appeal would be allowed. It followed from s1(1) and s1(3) of the 1968 Act that when the actions of a handler amounted to a dishonest assumption by him of the rights of an owner with the intention to permanently deprive the owner of his property, the handler would also be guilty of theft. The recorder was technically correct to say that the appellant's actions could amount to a dishonest appropriation necessary to establish a charge of theft. However, the matter would have been better left to the jury. The recorder had taken too active a part in the prosecution of the case. The convictions were unsatisfactory.

R v Sanders (1991) 93 Cr App R 245 (Court of Appeal)

The appellant was convicted of murder. He attacked S, the woman with whom he had previously lived, after she had started a relationship with another man. The appellant suffered from diabetes; he had lost a toe, had become blind in one eye, the sight in the other was quite badly affected. He had come to rely upon S. When he had to retire from business he was left alone during the day since S worked. He became depressed. When he learnt that S was seeing another man he became worse. He formed an intent to kill her and later did so by way of attacking her with a hammer. He then tried, unsuccessfully, to take his own life. At his trial the appellant put forward evidence of diminished responsibility. The Crown accepted that he suffered from an abnormality of the mind but did not accept that it affected his responsibility for his actions. The appeal was on the grounds that the trial judge had failed to point out to the jury that the expert evidence regarding his state of mind was unanimous in finding that the requirements of s2(1) of the Homicide Act 1957 were satisfied.

Held, the appeal would be dismissed. Two clear principles emerged from certain cases on diminished responsibility; 'The first is that if there are no other circumstances to consider, unequivocal, uncontradicted medical evidence favourable to a defendant should be accepted by a jury and they should be so directed. The second is that where there are other circumstances to be considered the medical evidence, though it be unequivocal and uncontradicted, must be assessed in the light of the other circumstances' (*per* WATKINS LJ). Evidence of the relationship between the parties, S's attachment to another man, the attack with the hammer, the appellant having made his will and written certain letters, and his statements to the police had all been considered by the jury along with the medical evidence. The jury were entitled to reach their verdict on the evidence as a whole. (See also *R v Egan*.)

R v Savage; R v Parmenter [1991] 3 WLR 914 (House of Lords)

Savage was convicted of unlawful wounding contrary to s20 of the Offences against the Person Act 1861. There had been bad feeling between Savage and another woman. Savage had thrown the contents of an almost full pint glass of beer over her. The glass left Savage's hand and broke, and the other woman suffered cuts as a result. On appeal against conviction, the Court of Appeal, Criminal Division, held that the recorder's direction to the jury was defective in that he had omitted to direct the jury that they had to find that the defendant foresaw that some physical harm would follow as a result of what she did. The appeal against conviction under s20 was allowed but a conviction for assault occasioning actual bodily harm contrary to s47 of the Offences against the Person Act 1861 was substituted under s3 of the Criminal Appeal Act 1968.

Held, the defendant's appeal would be dismissed. Parmenter was charged with and convicted of four offences of inflicting grievous bodily harm contrary to s20 of the Offences against the Person Act 1861 in respect of injuries he had caused to his three-month-old son as a result of rough handling. At the trial it was contended that Parmenter had not had the intent required for the offence as he was inexperienced with small babies. His handling of his son would not have been inappropriate in the case of a three-or-four-year-old child but it was quite inappropriate as regards a new born baby. The trial judge directed the jury that it was 'unnecessary that the accused should have foreseen that his unlawful act might cause physical harm' of the type envisaged in s20; it was 'enough that he should have foreseen that some physical harm to some person, albeit of a minor character, might result'. The Court of Appeal, Criminal Division, allowed Parmenter's appeal against conviction. The trial judge had misdirected the jury by telling them to ask themselves not whether Parmenter actually foresaw that his acts would cause injury, but whether he ought to have foreseen it. The Court of Appeal declined to substitute a verdict under s47 of the 1861 Act under s3 of the 1968 Act.

Held, the Crown's appeal would be allowed to the extent that a verdict of guilty of assault occasioning actual bodily harm contrary to s47 would be substituted for the conviction under s20. To establish an offence under s20 of the 1861 Act the prosecution must prove either that the defendant intended or that he actually foresaw that his act would cause harm. It is enough that he should have foreseen that some physical harm to some person, albeit of a minor character, might result. The verdict of assault occasioning actual bodily harm may be returned upon proof of an assault together with proof of the fact that actual bodily harm was occasioned by the assault. The prosecution is not obliged to prove that the defendant intended to cause some actual bodily harm or was reckless as to whether such harm would be caused. (See also *R v Mandair*.)

R v Shannon [1974] 2 All ER 1009 (House of Lords)

Shannon and Tracey were charged on an indictment with, inter alia, having conspired together dishonestly to handle stolen goods. Shannon pleaded guilty but Tracey pleaded not guilty to the charge and to a count charging him with handling stolen goods. The jury were unable to agree on their verdict and Tracey was retried a few days later. He was found not guilty of handling stolen goods and the prosecution offered no evidence against him on the conspiracy charge and a formal verdict of not guilty was entered on that count. Shannon thereupon appealed, contending that as Tracey had been found not guilty of conspiring with him, his own conviction and sentence following on his plea of guilty of conspiring with Tracey could not stand. The conviction was quashed by the Court of Appeal and the Crown appealed.

Held, the conviction would be restored as, inter alia, where one of two alleged conspirators has been fairly and properly tried and, on the evidence adduced, rightly convicted, there is no reason why his conviction should be invalidated if for any reason the other alleged conspirator is acquitted at a subsequent trial.

R v Sharp [1987] 3 All ER 103 (Court of Appeal)

The appellant was charged with murder. He was a member of a gang who to his knowledge used loaded firearms to carry out robberies on sub-post offices. On one such occasion the leader of the gang shot and killed the sub-postmaster. The appellant claimed that he had not wanted to participate in the robbery once he knew that loaded firearms were to be used; he was threatened that his head would be blown off if he did not participate. He put forward the defence of duress. The trial judge ruled that the defence of duress was not available to him because he had voluntarily joined the gang knowing that they used firearms. The defendant was convicted of manslaughter.

Held, his appeal would be dismissed. '... where a person has voluntarily, and with knowledge of its nature, joined a criminal organisation or gang which he knew might bring pressure on him to commit an offence and was an active member when he was put under such pressure, he cannot avail himself of the defence of duress' (per LORD LANE CJ).

R v Sheehan, R v Moore [1975] 2 All ER 960 (Court of Appeal)

The deceased, Neary, stole a £1 note from Sheehan's pocket one night while they were at a public house and the following evening Sheehan was overheard speaking to Moore about burning someone out and buying petrol. Later that night the appellants bought a gallon of petrol in a tin, went to the derelict house where Neary lived with a number of other men, ordered the others out and set the house on fire. Neary escaped but was pursued by the appellants and caught. Sheehan punched Neary, knocking him to the ground, and as he lay there on his back, poured the petrol over him and set light to him. Neary died and the appellants were charged with murder. At the trial Sheehan pleaded drunkenness, stating that at the time when the offence was committed he was substantially affected by drink and had no recollection of the events in question; Moore asserted that he was not a party to the common enterprise to kill Neary. In his summing-up the trial judge told the jury that drunkenness is only a defence to an act which would otherwise be criminal if a person has drunk so much that he is incapable of forming the intention to do the particular act and from the evidence they might conclude that the men were perfectly capable of forming the intention either to kill or cause grievous bodily harm or to attack Neary. They were convicted and appealed.

Held, the appeals should be allowed and convictions for manslaughter substituted as what the jury should have been told to consider was whether, in the light of all the evidence, including intoxication, they felt sure that the appellants had had the intention either to kill Neary or do him grievous bodily harm, and the judge's direction was liable to have given them the erroneous impression that the onus was on the appellants to show that they were incapable of forming the intention to attack Neary. (See also *Director of Public Prosecutions* v *Beard* and *R* v *Anderson and Morris*.)

R v *Sheppard* [1980] 3 All ER 899 (House of Lords)

The appellants were charged and convicted under s1(1) of the Children and Young Persons Act 1933 with wilfully neglecting their child in a manner likely to cause him unnecessary suffering or injury to health. Their 16-month-old son died of hypothermia and malnutrition. At their trial it was alleged that the appellants, a young couple of low intelligence living in deprived conditions, had not provided their son with proper medical aid on a number of occasions, in particular in the week prior to his death. Their defence was that they had not appreciated that their child was sufficiently ill to call a doctor and that they had genuinely thought that his loss of appetite and failure to take in food was due to a minor upset which would right itself. The trial judge took the view that the offence was one of strict liability. An objective test was to be applied; would a reasonable parent, given the facts known to the appellants, have appreciated that failure to call a doctor was likely to cause the child 'unnecessary suffering or injury to health'?

Held, their appeals against conviction would be allowed. The offence under s1(1) of the 1933 Act was not an offence of strict liability to be judged by the objective test. The actus reus of the offence was the failure to provide the child with medical care when needed. The mens rea of the offence is to be found in the word 'wilfully'. While failure to provide adequate medical aid amounts to neglect under s2(a) of the 1933 Act it does not amount to 'wilful' neglect. It was for the prosecution to prove that the child needed adequate medical care and that the parents had deliberately or recklessly failed to provide such care. It was a good defence that the parents had genuinely failed to appreciate that their child needed medical care or that they had failed to provide that care through stupidity, ignorance or personal inadequacy. (See also *R* v *Lowe*.)

R v *Shivpuri* [1986] 2 All ER 334 (House of Lords)

The appellant was convicted under s1 of the Criminal Attempts Act 1981 of attempting to commit the offence of being knowingly concerned in dealing with and harbouring prohibited drugs, contrary to s170(1)(b) of the Customs and Excise Management Act 1979. The appellant believed he had prohibited drugs in his suitcase but on analysis the substance turned out to be snuff or similar harmless vegetable matter.

Held, the appeal would be dismissed. Under s1(1) of the 1981 Act a person was guilty of an attempt based on the facts as the defendant believed them to be. The defendant had done more than what was merely preparatory to dealing with a controlled drug. The sole intent of the appellant from start to finish was to defeat the customs prohibition. (But see *Haughton v Smith*.)

R v *Siracusa* [1989] Crim LR 712 (Court of Appeal)

The appellants were convicted of conspiracy to evade the prohibition on the import of cannabis resin and heroin. It was contended that the law with respect to conspiracy differed from that relating to the substantive offence (s170(2) of the Customs and Excise Management Act 1979). It was for the prosecution to prove in a conspiracy case that each defendant knew exactly what was being imported.

Held, the appeal would be dismissed. The mens rea sufficient to support the commission of a substantive offence will not necessarily be sufficient to support a charge of conspiracy to commit that offence. Where the prosecution charge is conspiracy under s170(2) of the 1979 Act by the importation of heroin, they must prove that the agreed course of conduct was indeed the importation of heroin. The court was satisfied that the trial judge had given directions which were clearly to that effect. (See also *R* v *Rook*.)

R v *Smith (David Raymond)* [1974] 1 All ER 632 (Court of Appeal)

Smith was the tenant of a flat the letting of which included a conservatory. He and his brother, who lived with him, installed some electric wiring in the conservatory for use with stereo equipment. Also, with the landlord's permission, they put up roofing material and asbestos wall panels and laid floorboards. Smith gave notice to quit and asked the landlord to allow his brother to remain as tenant of the flat. The request was refused and the next day Smith damaged the roofing, wall panels and floorboards he had installed in order, according to his brother, to gain access to and remove the wiring. When interviewed by the police he said, 'Look, how can I be done for smashing my own property? I put the flooring and that in, so if I want to pull it down it's a matter for me.' He was convicted of causing criminal damage, contrary to s1(1) of the Criminal Damage Act 1971, and appealed.

Held, the conviction should be quashed as no offence is committed under s1(1) of the Criminal Damage Act 1971 by a person who destroys or causes damage to property belonging to another if he does so in the honest but mistaken belief that the property is his own, for the existence of that belief negatives the necessary mens rea. Also, if the belief is honestly held the question whether or not it is justifiable is irrelevant.

R v *Smith (John)* [1974] 1 All ER 376 (Court of Appeal)

The appellant was a medical practitioner in general practice who also specialised in the termination of pregnancy. A young woman of 19 years who wanted an abortion was sent to him. She was pregnant but not suffering stomach pains or vaginal bleeding. The appellant did not examine her or ask her medical history. She was not seen by a second doctor as required by s1(1) of the Abortion Act 1967 (now substituted by the Human Fertilisation and Embryology Act 1990). An operation was performed in a nursing home. Later the young woman developed stomach pains and her general medical practitioner reported to the Ministry of Health the circumstances. The appellant was charged with unlawfully using an instrument to procure a miscarriage contrary to s58 of the Offences against the Person Act 1861. He appealed against conviction on the ground that the verdict was unsafe and unsatisfactory, contending that a finding of bad faith against a medical practitioner when it related to the forming of a medical opinion could not be safe or satisfactory unless supported by medical evidence pointing overwhelmingly to the lack of good faith.

Held, (1) the question of good faith was an essential one for the jury to determine on the totality of the evidence and not solely on the views put forward in evidence by expert witnesses; (2) although the recorder had been wrong in excluding the appellant's evidence of professional practice in certain hospitals with which he was familiar, that error was of no importance since the recorder had explained clearly the limitations of the medical evidence and had left to the jury the question whether the appellant had formed an honest opinion. The appeal would be dismissed. (See *R* v *Bourne, Royal College of Nursing* v *Department of Health and Social Security* and *Janaway* v *Salford Health Authority*.)

R v *Smith (Morgan)* [1998] 4 All ER 387 (Court of Appeal)

The defendant was convicted of murder. He argued with P and fatally stabbed him. The defendant raised the defence of provocation. In order to assess how a reasonable person sharing the characteristics of the accused would have reacted, he sought to have his severe depression taken into account. The trial judge ruled that the reasonable person could only be imbued with the characteristic of severe depression for the purpose of assessing the gravity of the provocation of the defendant, not for the purpose of assessing whether the reasonable person would have lost his self-control.

Held, the appeal would be allowed. His conviction for murder was quashed and a conviction for manslaughter substituted. When attributing the characteristics of the accused to the reasonable person for the purposes of the objective test in provocation, no distinction was to be drawn between characteristics that related to the gravity of the provocation and those that related to a reasonable person's reaction to the provocation. (See also *Director of Public Prosecutions* v *Camplin*. Consider *R* v *Thornton (No 2)* and *R* v *Ahluwalia*. *Luc Thiet Thuan* v *R* not followed.)

R v *Stewart* [1995] 4 All ER 999 (Court of Appeal)

The appellant killed his wife having inflicted a number of blows to her head; her death had been accidental. He had used force to stop her leaving the house believing that if she had left she would have committed suicide. She had suffered from bulimia nervosa, depression, irritability and low self-esteem. The appellant admitted that he had become 'fed-up' with his wife's illnesses, but denied he had killed her in a fit of temper. The defence of provocation was not put forward on his behalf but the trial judge ensured that the matter was left to the jury. The judge gave no specific guidance as to any evidence that might have shown that the appellant had had a sudden and temporary loss of self-control The appellant was convicted of murder and appealed.

Held, the appeal would be dismissed. The jury had rightly been left with the issue of provocation. Since the trial judge had not indicated what evidence supported the conclusion that the appellant had lost his self-control it amounted to a non-direction. But, had the trial judge brought the relevant evidence to the jury's attention, it would have shown a lack of evidence and no jury could have concluded that a reasonable man would have acted as had the appellant. The proviso to s2(1) of the Criminal Appeal Act 1968 was applied. (See further *R* v *Humphreys*.)

R v *Stewart and Scholfield* [1995] 3 All ER 159 (Court of Appeal)

Lambert, Stewart and Scholfield took part in a robbery that ended in the murder of the shopkeeper for which they all faced a murder charge. Stewart had suggested that they rob the shopkeeper and armed herself with a knife; Lambert carried a piece of scaffolding and Scholfield kept watch outside the premises. Lambert beat the shopkeeper to death with the scaffolding pole and pleaded guilty to murder and robbery. Stewart and Scholfield were convicted of manslaughter. Relying on *R* v *Anderson and Morris* they argued on appeal that they could not be convicted of manslaughter where the principal offender had gone beyond the common design (to rob the shopkeeper). It was said that Lambert had carried out the attack being motivated by racial hatred and not in his wish to rob.

Held, the appeal would be dismissed. A party to a joint enterprise who was charged with murder can only escape liability for manslaughter (where the principal defendant was convicted for murder), if the killing was not committed in the course of the joint enterprise, a question of fact, not law.

R v *Stone; R* v *Dobinson* [1977] 2 All ER 341 (Court of Appeal)

The appellants were convicted of manslaughter. The man, Stone, aged 67, was of low average intelligence and had impaired sight and hearing. He lived with his mistress, Dobinson, aged 43, who was described as 'weak and ineffectual'. Stone's sister, Fanny, an eccentric woman, who was also morbidly anxious about becoming overweight, came to live with the appellants in 1972. In early spring 1975, Fanny was found wandering in the street. The appellants attempted to find her doctor but failed and then did nothing else to seek professional help for her, although they knew she was unwell. Over the next months Fanny's condition deteriorated. Despite being urged to get a doctor, an ambulance, assistance from the social services or police, the appellants did nothing positive. Fanny died in early August. She was in bed, naked, emaciated, her body ingrained with dirt, lying in a pool of excrement. The cause of death was toxaemia from the infected bed sores and prolonged immobilisation. The Crown alleged that the appellants had voluntarily assumed responsibility for Fanny, knowing she was relying on them; Stone and Dobinson had with gross negligence, failed to perform their duty of caring for Fanny – as a result she died. The judge directed the jury that gross negligence was established if it was proved that there had been a reckless disregard by the appellants of their duty of care.

Held, the appeals against conviction would be dismissed. The appellants had been under a common law duty to care for Fanny when she had become helplessly infirm in July 1975, and would have discharged that duty by getting help or looking after her themselves. When there had been an assumption of the duty of care for an infirm person, recklessness would be established by proof that the defendant had been indifferent to an obvious risk of injury to that person's health, or had foreseen the risk of injury but had run that risk.

R v Straw [1995] 1 All ER 187 (Court of Appeal)

The applicant was found guilty of murder and sentenced to life imprisonment. She then wanted the plea of diminished responsibility to be heard and applied to the court for leave to introduce fresh evidence and for leave to appeal against her conviction. She had been charged with the murder of her husband. Medical reports showed that she was suffering from paranoid schizophrenia and medical opinion was that her responsibility for the killing was materially diminished. The applicant refused to make a plea of guilty of manslaughter on the ground of diminished responsibility or to allow such a defence to be in issue before the jury. Her instructions were that she would plead not guilty to murder. She appealed against her conviction.

Held, her application would be dismissed. On the medical evidence she had been capable of considering how she should plead to the charge of murder. Advice had been given to her with regard to a plea of manslaughter on the ground of diminished responsibility. In law she was capable of making a decision as to how her case should be presented to the court. Following conviction, it was not permissible for the applicant to change her mind and apply for leave to introduce a plea of diminished responsibility and to appeal against conviction on that basis.

R v Sullivan [1983] 2 All ER 673 (House of Lords)

The defendant was charged with, and admitted at his trial to, inflicting grievous bodily harm on P, a friend. The harm had occurred when the defendant was coming through the final stage of a minor epileptic seizure; he had no memory of, and would not be conscious of, what he had done during the course of the seizure. The trial judge ruled that his defence amounted to insanity and he would be willing to direct the jury on the defence of insanity, but not that of automatism. The defendant changed his plea to guilty of the lesser offence of assault occasioning actual bodily harm (and was so convicted), to avoid the consequences of the jury returning the special verdict of not guilty by reason of insanity (s2(1) of the Trial of Lunatics Act 1883) – the judge would then have been required to order the defendant to be detained in a special hospital (s5(1) of the Criminal Procedure (Insanity) Act 1964). He appealed against the conviction on the ground that the trial judge had wrongly denied him the opportunity to plead the defence of automatism to the original charge.

Held, the appeal would be dismissed. In putting forward a defence of insanity the defendant had to prove, under the *M'Naghten* rules, that when the criminal act was committed he was labouring under a 'defect of reason' resulting from 'disease of the mind' – 'mind' used in its ordinary sense of the mental faculties of reason, memory and understanding. If a disease impaired those faculties depriving the defendant of knowing what he was doing, or if he did know, that he did not know that it was wrong, he was legally 'insane'. It did not matter if the cause of impairment was organic, as in epilepsy, or functional or permanent or transient and intermittent, so long as it persisted at the time of the wrongful act. The special verdict of not guilty by reason of insanity was correct if an epileptic fit brought about a temporary suspension of the mental faculties of reason, memory and understanding during the course of which an offence was committed.

R v Tandy [1989] 1 All ER 267 (Court of Appeal)

The appellant, an alcoholic, was charged with and convicted of her 11-year-old daughter's murder. She sought to establish the defence of diminished responsibility under s2(1) of the Homicide Act 1957. She had drunk almost a whole bottle of vodka. The Crown contended that her abnormal state of mind at the time she strangled her daughter was due to the fact that she was drunk on vodka, having chosen that drink rather than her customary one of vermouth or barley wine; it could not therefore be said that her resultant abnormality of mind was involuntarily induced by alcoholism. The jury was directed to consider the Crown's view of whether, when her daughter was being strangled, she was suffering from an abnormality of mind in the form of grossly impaired judgment and emotional responses as a direct condition of her alcoholism, over which she had no immediate control. She appealed against conviction on the ground that the judge's direction had wrongly removed from the jury any consideration of the issue whether she had proved that she had such a craving for drink as in itself to produce an abnormality of mind under s2(1).

Held, her appeal would be dismissed. There had been no material misdirection. For there to be an abnormality of mind, within s2(1) of the 1957 Act, induced by the disease of alcoholism, the alcoholism had to have reached such a level that the defendant's brain was damaged so that there was impairment of judgment and emotional responses or the craving had to be such as to render the defendant's use of alcohol involuntary because she was no longer able to resist the impulse of drink. If, on the other hand, the defendant had simply not resisted an impulse to drink, she could not rely on the defence of diminished responsibility. (See also *R v Gittens*, *R v Lloyd*, *R v Egan* and *R v Flatt*.)

R v Thornton (No 2) [1996] 2 All ER 1023 (Court of Appeal)

The appellant was convicted of murder. Her husband was a heavy drinker, a jealous and possessive person. They met in May 1987 and, knowing his disposition, she married him in August 1988. She suffered a personality disorder. He was a violent man in the home. In May 1989 her husband committed a serious assault on the appellant leading to charges being laid. In June the appellant told a work colleague that she would kill her husband. Later that month, after a series of rows, the appellant went to the kitchen to calm down. While there she picked up a carving knife, sharpened it and went back to her husband. After a further argument the appellant made to stab her husband, expecting him to ward off the blow, but the carving knife went into his stomach fatally wounding him. She said she did not mean to kill him, it had been an accident. She was advised to base her defence on that of diminished responsibility, support coming from expert psychiatric opinion. Evidence of provocative remarks made by her husband before he was stabbed was brought forward. The judge was expected to leave the defence of manslaughter as a result of provocation to the jury as an alternative verdict. The direction the judge gave in respect of provocation was that it required evidence of some 'sudden and temporary loss of self-control' on the part of the accused which would have caused a reasonable, sober person to lose her self-control and act as had the appellant. The appeal on the grounds that the judge had misdirected the jury on provocation was dismissed. In 1995 the Home Secretary referred the case back to the Court of Appeal pursuant to the Criminal Appeal Act 1968 on the basis of further medical evidence to the effect that the appellant possessed two particular characteristics at the time of the killing; (a) her personality disorder; and (b) the effect of her husband's abuse over a period of time on her mental state. On this latter point the judge would have been required to direct the jury to consider whether a reasonable woman with these characteristics might have lost her self-control and murdered her husband.

Held, the appellant's conviction would be quashed and a re-trial ordered. In a murder trial 'battered woman syndrome' was a relevant characteristic which could be considered by a jury. A defendant could not, though, succeed in relying on provocation unless the jury considered she had suffered or might have suffered from a sudden and temporary loss of self-control at the time of the killing. Had the trial judge had the fresh evidence in relation to the appellant's personality disorder and battered woman syndrome as relevant characteristics before him, he would have directed the jury as to those two characteristics now relied on in putting forward the defence of provocation. The fresh evidence cast doubt on the jury's verdict on the specific question whether a hypothetical reasonable woman possessing the appellant's characteristics would have reacted to her husband's provocative conduct in the way the appellant did. The jury had to decide whether the appellant did or might have lost her self-control at the time of the killing. (See *R v Morhall*, *R v Humphreys* and *R v Horrex*.)

R v Tobierre [1986] 1 All ER 346 (Court of Appeal)

The appellant was convicted of using a false instrument contrary to s3 of the Forgery and Counterfeiting Act 1981. He had made claims for and received payments amounting to £4,345 by way of child allowance. He had signed a child allowance book in his wife's name. He did not tell anyone that his wife and children were, at the material times, living abroad.

Held, to establish that a person had the requisite mens rea, proof was required of two states of mind: that the defendant intended to induce another to accept the instrument as genuine, and that that other, by reason of accepting it, should act or not act to his own or another's prejudice. It was therefore not sufficient for the Crown merely to show that the defendant intended to induce another to accept the instrument as genuine. The appeal would therefore be allowed and the convictions quashed.

R v Toney; R v Ali (Tanveer) [1993] 2 All ER 409 (Court of Appeal)

In these appeals the question was whether the offence of perverting the course of justice by interfering with a potential witness could be committed where there was no evidence of any bribe, threat, undue pressure or other unlawful means.

Held, while it would obviously be easier to prove the actus reus of the offence, ie an act tending to pervert the course of justice, and the necessary intention, or mens rea, if the means were unlawful, the answer was in the affirmative. 'Take, for example, the case of a man who comes up to a witness for the prosecution as he is entering the courtroom and says: "Tell the court that the defendant had nothing to do with it." This would be evidence from which a jury could find that the man had committed the actus reus of the offence even if there was no indication of improper pressure. The gist of the offence lies in telling a potential witness what he should or should not say with the intention of influencing his evidence, not in the means adopted' (*per* LLOYD LJ).

R v Towers (1874) 12 Cox CC 530

Towers was charged with the manslaughter of a child aged four and a half months. He struck a person named Glaister, who was nursing the child, in the face and pulled her up by the hair. The woman screamed and so frightened the child that it suffered nervous shock. It screamed violently for more than an hour, suffered intermittent attacks of fits and convulsions and died 33 days later. In his summing-up the trial judge told the jury that if the assault on Glaister was entirely unconnected with the death and was not the cause of it then the offence was not committed.

Held, mere intimidation causing a person to die of fright by working upon his fancy was not murder. However, if four or more persons were to stand round a man and so threaten him and frighten him as to make him believe that his life was in danger, and he was to back away from then and tumble over a precipice to avoid them, this would constitute murder. In the event, Towers was acquitted.

R v Turner (No 2) [1971] 2 All ER 441 (Court of Appeal)

Turner took his car to Brown's garage to be repaired. When the work was done, Turner told Brown that he would return the next day to pay for the repairs and to take the car away. A few hours later, however, without telling Brown, he took the car from where it had been parked on the road near Brown's garage. The loss was reported to the police and later the car was discovered near Turner's home. Turner later admitted to the police that he had taken the car away without paying, but alleged that he had Brown's consent. At the trial the judge directed the jury that (1) the sole question was whether Brown had possession or control of the car, and (2) in order to find Turner guilty it was essential to prove he had acted dishonestly and it was immaterial that he had no basis in law for his belief that he had a claim of right to the car. Turner was convicted of the theft of the car.

Held, the jury had been properly directed and the appeal would be dismissed because (1) there was no ground for qualifying the words 'possession or control' in s5 of the Theft Act 1968, it being sufficient that the person from whom the property was appropriated was at the time in fact in possession or control; (2) the test of dishonesty was the mental element of belief and the jury were properly told that if the appellant believed that he had a right, within the meaning of s2(1) of the Act. (See also *R v Kelly*.)

R v Uddin [1998] 2 All ER 744 (Court of Appeal)

The appellant and T were convicted of murder. Other members of the group with which they were involved were convicted of manslaughter. A group attack took place on S. Some in the group were armed with poles and bars. In the course of the attack T produced a flick-knife with which he stabbed S to death. The appellant argued he had not known T had a knife, and that the trial judge had been deficient in directing the jury on the extent to which the principal offender's use of a knife amounted to a deliberate departure from a common design.

Held, the appeal would be allowed and a retrial ordered. A defendant is only guilty of murder as an accomplice if the principal's acts causing death are of a type that the defendant foresees (even if he does not intend that death or grievous bodily harm should result). The accomplice will not incur accessorial liability where the principal's actions are of an 'entirely different' type to that contemplated by the accomplice even where the accomplice foresees death or grievous bodily harm being caused by the principal, albeit by different means. The accomplice will not be a party to the killing if the principal uses a gun to kill when the accomplice did not foresee the use of any weapon by the principal. There will be liability when the use of a weapon is contemplated by the accomplice even though a different weapon is used. (See also *R v Powell and Daniels; R v English*.)

R v Vickers [1957] 2 All ER 741 (Court of Criminal Appeal)

Vickers broke into the cellar of a shop occupied by a woman aged 73 with intent to steal. On seeing the woman he struck her a number of blows and kicked her in the face; she died of shock. It was proved that the degree of forced used to inflict the injuries was slight to moderately severe. He was convicted of murder and appealed, contending that, inter alia, malice aforethought could not be implied where death resulted from an intention to cause grievous bodily harm.

Held, the conviction would be affirmed on the grounds that s1 of the Homicide Act 1957 did not abolish implied malice, ie, the implication of malice aforethought from a voluntary act inflicting grievous bodily harm and causing death. (Approved in *R v Cunningham*.)

R v Walker; R v Hayles (1990) 90 Cr App R 226 (Court of Appeal)

The appellants were convicted on a charge of attempted murder. They had been in a fight with one J and, having banged his head against a wall and threatened to kill him, they dropped him from a third-floor balcony to the ground; he survived. The jury were directed that they could draw the inference that the appellants intended to kill J if they were sure that the appellants knew that there was a 'very high degree of probability' that J would be killed. On appeal it was argued that the judge had led the jury to equate probability of death and foresight of death with an intention to kill and that the words 'virtual certainty' (see *R v Nedrick*) should have been used instead of 'high degree of probability'.

Held, the appeal would be dismissed. '... we are not persuaded that it is only when death is a virtual certainty that the jury can infer intention to kill. Providing the dividing line between intention and recklessness is never blurred, and provided it is made clear, as it was here, that it is a question for the jury to infer from the degree of probability in the particular case whether the defendant intended to kill, we would not regard the use of the words 'very high degree of probability' as a misdirection' (per LLOYD LJ).

R v Watson [1989] 2 All ER 865 (Court of Appeal)

The appellant was convicted of burglary and manslaughter. He and another man entered a house with intent to commit burglary. The occupant was an 87 year old man who had a serious heart condition. He was woken up and verbally abused by the appellant who, with his accomplice, left without stealing anything. Later the police arrived, as did council workmen to board up the window. An hour and a half after the burglary, the old man had a heart attack and died. The appellant appealed against his conviction for manslaughter. It was argued on behalf of the appellant that his counsel had been denied sufficient opportunity to address the jury as to whether or not the excitement of the arrival of the police and workmen could have taken over as the operating and substantial cause of death.

Held, the conviction for manslaughter would be quashed. The trial judge had correctly directed the jury that the unlawful act had to be dangerous in the sense that a reasonable bystander understood. 'The unlawful act in the present circumstances comprised the whole of the burglarious intrusion and did not come to an end on the appellant's foot crossing the threshold or windowsill. That being so, the appellant (and therefore the bystander) during the course of the unlawful act must have become aware of Mr Moyler's frailty and approximate age' (*per* LORD LANE CJ). However, since counsel had not been able to address the jury on the possible effect the arrival of the police and council workmen might have had on Mr Moyler the verdict of guilty of manslaughter was unsatisfactory and it would be quashed.

R v Webster and Others; R v Warwick [1995] 2 All ER 168 (Court of Appeal)

The question before the court, in two separate appeals, was whether it was appropriate to lay a charge of damaging property with intent to endanger life, contrary to s1(2) of the Criminal Damage Act 1971, if an object was deliberately or recklessly thrown causing damage which endangered the life of another. In the first case a heavy coping-stone on a railway bridge parapet had been pushed onto a passenger train. It had landed on the rear bulkhead of a carriage and a piece of the stone had penetrated the roof. While passengers had received no physical injury, they had been showered with material from the roof. The jury had been directed that they could assume in the circumstances that the appellants intended to damage the roof of the carriage and thereby to endanger the life of any passenger upon which the stone might have fallen. On appeal it was contended that the judge had misdirected the jury on the ground that it was necessary to prove that the damage caused by the appellants' act would endanger life for an offence under s1(2) to be committed; it was not sufficient to prove merely that they had intended that their act would endanger life. In the second case the appellant was convicted under s1(2) of the 1971 Act. He drove a stolen car from which a passenger threw bricks at a pursuing police car. One of the bricks went through the rear window of the police car, showering the officers in the car with broken glass. The appellant then drove his car into the police car several times. He was charged on two counts of damaging property with intent to endanger life and on two counts of recklessness as to whether life would be endangered. At the trial the appellant submitted that s1(2) did not apply to the facts proved by the Crown and that the charges should be withdrawn from the jury on the grounds that, in order to sustain a prosecution under s1(2) the actual damage created had to endanger life and not the means by which the damage was caused and that the ramming of the police car and the throwing of the bricks at the police car and showering the officers with glass were not acts which were themselves capable of endangering life. In both cases the judge held that the danger to life arose from the damage itself. The damage to the police car caused by it being rammed and the shattered glass were both sources of danger to the police officer or others on the road because either might have caused the car to run off the road. The charges were left to the jury and the appellant was convicted. The appellant contended that the facts proved did not constitute an offence under s1(2)(b) and that the judge had been wrong in allowing the counts under that section to go to the jury.

Held, on a charge of damaging property with intent to endanger life or recklessness as to whether life would be endangered under s1(2)(b) of the 1971 Act, the prosecution had to prove that the danger to life resulted from the destruction of or damage to property and it was not sufficient for the prosecution to prove that the danger to life resulted from the defendant's act which caused the destruction of the property. The 'destruction or damage' in s1(2)(b) referred to that which the defendant intended to cause or to the risk of which he was reckless, not to the destruction or damage which in fact occurred. What had to be considered was not whether and how life was in fact endangered or if there was an obvious risk of it being endangered. If a defendant pushed a stone off a bridge and intended it to crash through the carriage roof directly injuring passengers or was reckless whether it did, then s1(2) would not apply. If he intended that the stone would crash onto the carriage roof so that material from it would or might fall onto passengers or he was reckless whether it did, so endangering life, he would be guilty of an offence under s1(2). In the first case the jury's verdict showed that they had found that the appellants intended that the stone itself would crash through the carriage roof and endanger life. The conviction under s1(2) could not be upheld on that basis. However, the jury's finding implied that the appellants must have been reckless as to the danger to passengers from material falling from the roof, so a conviction under the alternative count of damaging property, being reckless as to whether life was endangered, would be substituted. In the second case, as to whether an offence under s1(2) was committed, it did not rest on whether the brick hit the windscreen but on whether the defendant intended to hit it and intended or was reckless as to whether any resulting damage would endanger life. The damage caused was capable of endangering life by causing the driver to lose control of the car. It was open to the jury to infer an intention to endanger life by damaging the car. The judge had ruled correctly and had properly left the matter to the jury. The appeal would be dismissed. (See also *R v Dudley*.)

R v Wheeler (1991) 92 Cr App R 279 (Court of Appeal)

The appellant was charged on three counts: (1) dishonestly receiving stolen goods contrary to s22 of the Theft Act 1968; (2) obtaining property by deception contrary to s15 of the 1968 Act; (3) theft contrary to s1 of the 1968 Act (an alternative to receiving). P, an antiques dealer, suffered a burglary; the property stolen included military antiques to the value of £15,000. Within a few days the appellant had purchased the bulk of the military antiques for £3,500. He had stalls at Camden Market and Covent Garden. On the morning of 19 March B agreed to purchase a medal for £150 from the appellant's Camden Market stall – the appellant kept the medal for him until later in the day when B would return and pay for it. At midday P, together with the police, visited the stall. After that visit, the appellant knew that the medal was stolen. B returned at 5.30 pm having learnt about the police visit. In response to the question whether the medal was on the police list of stolen goods, the appellant dishonestly responded that it was not. B gave him a cheque for £150. On 21 March the appellant was arrested. A search of his house revealed a large part of the rest of the stolen property; he appeared to be aware that most, if not all, of the property was stolen. On the first count it was submitted that there was insufficient evidence of guilty knowledge on the appellant's part for the case to be left to the jury. On counts 2 and 3 it was submitted as a matter of law that the appellant was not guilty. All the submissions failed. The appellant then changed his plea on counts 2 and 3 to guilty. A verdict of 'not guilty' was then entered on the first count. He appealed against his convictions on counts 2 and 3.

Held, the appeal would be allowed. The appellant was able to give a good title to B by reason of a sale in market overt; property in the goods passed to B at the time the contract was made (in the morning) (a contract for the sale of specific goods in a deliverable state). At 5.30 pm the appellant could not represent that he was the lawful owner of the medal; the particulars of the offence in count 2 were held not to be made out. Section 3(2) of the 1968 Act protected the appellant against the charge in count 3, he being a bona fide purchaser who gave value for the military antiques without any notice of defect in the transferor's title.

R v Whitchurch (1890) 24 QBD 420 (Court for Crown Cases Reserved)

Whitchurch, Howe and Elizabeth Cross were charged with conspiracy. The parties believed that Elizabeth Cross had been rendered pregnant by Howe and they agreed that Whitchurch and Howe should administer to her certain noxious drugs and use or cause to be used upon her certain instruments in order to procure an abortion. It was later established that the woman was not pregnant.

Held, the conviction would be affirmed on the ground that the agreement to do the unlawful act constituted conspiracy and it was irrelevant that the woman was not in fact pregnant.

R v White [1910] 2 KB 124 (Court of Criminal Appeal)

White was charged with attempted murder. His mother was found dead sitting upright on a sofa with a wine glass containing lemonade and a quantity of cyanide of potassium on a table beside her. The medical evidence showed that she had died from a heart attack without drinking it. Furthermore, the quantity of cyanide in the lemonade was not sufficient to kill an adult. The deceased had made a will leaving White a sum of money and, prior to her death, he had on several occasions stated that he expected her to die, although she was in a good state of health. The jury came to the conclusion that White had put the cyanide of potassium in the wine glass with intent to murder the deceased.

Held, the conviction would be affirmed on the ground that the administration of poison can constitute an attempt to murder even though the quantity of poison is not sufficient to cause death. Furthermore, he could be convicted of an attempt to murder by slow poisoning after endeavouring to administer the first dose.

R v Whitefield [1984] Crim LR 97 (Court of Appeal)

The appellant was convicted of burglary. He told the police that he had told one of two people who had been arrested for the burglary that the flat next to his was unoccupied and that he could use his flat to break in. Later he informed that other that he wished no longer to take part in the burglary. The judge, rejecting a submission of no case, ruled that the appellant's communication of withdrawal from the common enterprise was not enough. The appellant changed his plea to guilty. He appealed on the ground that the jury should have been left to decide whether what he had done was enough to withdraw.

Held, the appeal would be allowed. It was enough to tell the other person that if the burglary went ahead it was to be without the appellant's aid and assistance. When the trial judge had indicated in his ruling, in response to the submission of no case to answer, that he would withdraw that issue from the jury, a change of plea founded on that ruling could not stand. (See also *R v Rook*.)

R v Whiteley (1991) 93 Cr App R 25 (Court of Appeal)

The appellant, a computer hacker, was convicted of damaging property, contrary to s1(1) of the Criminal Damage Act 1971. He had gained unauthorised access to the Joint Academic Network (JANET), a network of connected ICL main frame computers at universities and Science and Engineering Research Council institutions. 'Property' in s1 of the 1971 Act means, under s10(1), 'property of a tangible nature'. The case against him was that through his interference he caused criminal damage to the discs, altering the state of the magnetic particles on them so as create and delete files, change the passwords of authorised users and delete the user file to remove evidence of his own use of the system, the discs and the magnetic particles on them containing the information being one entity and capable of being damaged. It was argued on the appellant's behalf that the magnetic discs on which the system's files were stored had not been damaged by his activities; the only damage was to the information stored on the discs and since such was intangible property it fell outside the scope of the offence.

Held, the appeal would be dismissed. The magnetic discs on which the files were stored were tangible property. By deleting the files the appellant had interfered with the configuration of magnetic particles on the discs; there was therefore damage to tangible property. (See also *Cox v Riley*.)

R v *Whiteside and Antoniou* [1989] Crim LR 436 (Court of Appeal)

The appellants were convicted of going equipped for cheating. They were selling counterfeit cassette tapes at a lower price than the average retail price. They said in evidence that they had never claimed that the tapes were originals and told customers, if they asked, that they were good quality tapes. On appeal they contended that there was no direct evidence from any prosecution witness that he had bought a tape believing it to be original so the prosecution could not establish an intention to cheat; that the recorder had erred in directing the jury that the obtaining could be wholly or partly as a result of the appellants' deception; that the question of a breach of copyright introduced by the recorder in his summing-up was irrelevant.

Held, in allowing the appeals the court accepted the second and third contentions, but it did hold that the tapes looked very like the genuine article and the appellants had done nothing to suggest to the public that they were other than authorised copies. In this situation the jury had been entitled to infer an intention to 'cheat' the public. (See also *R v Doukas, R v Corboz* and *R v Cooke*.)

R v *Widdowson* [1986] Crim LR 233 (Court of Appeal)

The appellant was convicted of attempting to obtain services by deception, contrary to s1 of the Theft Act 1978. The particulars of the offence included the words 'credit facilities to assist in the purchase'. He gave another person's name and address when filling in a hire-purchase form but he was given no facilities. He said that the other person had agreed that if facilities had been granted that person would have obtained the vehicle for the appellant. The appellant would then have repaid the other person. The appeal was on the grounds that a hire-purchase agreement did not amount to the obtaining of services nor to the obtaining of credit facilities.

Held, the appeal would be allowed. The indictment was bad: a hire-purchase agreement in ordinary form cannot properly be described as credit facilities; a hire-purchase agreement can be regarded as services within s1(2) of the 1978 Act, a benefit being conferred by causing or permitting the garage to deliver possession of the vehicle to the hirer; there was no evidence of an attempt to commit the crime charged. All he had done was to attempt to ascertain whether the person whose name he used was acceptable to the finance company. What he had done could not be considered as being more than merely preparatory to obtaining hire-purchase facilities.

R v *Willer* (1986) 83 Cr App R 225 (Court of Appeal)

The appellant was convicted of reckless driving. He was faced with a gang of shouting and bawling youths as he drove up an alleyway. There were some 20 to 30 of them. The youths banged on his car and one got into the car and attacked the passenger in the rear of the car. The appellant drove slowly onto the pavement and through a gap into the front of a shopping precinct; he then realised he had lost one of his companions who had got out of the car, so he turned the car round and drove back through the gap. The one youth was still in the back of the car fighting with the rear seat passenger. The appellant drove to the police station and reported the matter, but was prosecuted. One of the grounds of appeal was that the judge had erred in his ruling that the defence of necessity was not available to the appellant.

Held, the appeal would be allowed. '… it would have been for the jury to decide if necessity could have been a defence at all in those circumstances, whether the whole incident should be regarded as one, or could properly be regarded as two separate incidents so as to enable them to say that necessity applied in one instance [driving through the gap] but not in the other [coming back again]' (*per* WATKINS LJ). (See also *R v Conway* and *DPP v Bell*.)

R v Williams (Jean-Jacques) [1980] Crim LR 589 (Court of Appeal)

The appellant was convicted of theft contrary to s1(1) of the Theft Act 1968. He had taken obsolete Yugoslavian dinar banknotes, purchased at Stanley Gibbons, to a bureau de change in a department store. Asking either, 'Will you change these notes?' or 'Can I cash these in?' he received money far exceeding what he had paid for them. He was charged with obtaining property by deception, contrary to s15 of the 1968 Act, and, alternatively, theft. The appellant, who admitted dishonesty, claimed he had not made any representation about the bank notes. The judge ruled that there was a case to answer on theft even though there was no evidence on which a jury could safely find that the appellant had made any of the false representations alleged against him in the indictment. The appellant contended on appeal that there had been no appropriation of money belonging to another; the cashiers had handed over the money voluntarily.

Held, the appeal would be dismissed. When a person went to a bureau de change asking in one way or another for notes to be changed it was open to the jury to find that he was representing the notes to be genuine and currently in use in the country of origin. With the admitted dishonesty an offence under s15 of the 1968 Act had been made out. The relevant provisions for theft were ss1(1), 3(1) and 5(4). The money was the property of the department store and was appropriated when the appellant put it into his pocket. There was a dishonest intention to permanently deprive the owner of the money. The offence of theft was also made out.

R v Williams (Gladstone) [1987] 3 All ER 411 (Court of Appeal)

The appellant was convicted of assault occasioning actual bodily harm contrary to s47 of the Offences against the Person Act 1861. M had caught a youth he had seen robbing a woman in the street. The appellant was told by M that he, M, was a police officer, which was untrue, and he was not able to produce a warrant card when asked to do so by the appellant. A struggle followed in which the appellant punched M in the face. He honestly believed that M was assaulting the youth. The judge directed the jury that the appellant's state of mind on the issue of defence of another had to be both honest and reasonable.

Held, the appeal would be allowed. 'The reasonableness or unreasonableness of the defendant's belief is material to the question of whether the belief was held by the defendant at all. If the belief was in fact held, its unreasonableness, so far as guilt or innocence is concerned, is neither here nor there. It is irrelevant. … The jury should be directed, first of all, that the prosecution have the burden or duty of proving the unlawfulness of the defendant's actions, second, that if the defendant may have been labouring under a mistake as to the facts he must be judged according to his mistaken view of the facts and, third, that that is so whether the mistake was, on an objective view, a reasonable mistake or not' (*per* LORD LANE CJ). (See also *R* v *Owino*.)

R v *Williams*; R v *Davis* [1992] 1 WLR 380 (Court of Appeal)

The appellants were convicted of manslaughter and robbery. The victim, S, a hitch-hiker, had jumped out of the car driven by the appellant W, and in which D and another, B, were passengers. He received fatal injuries. The evidence suggested that W had asked S to make a contribution towards the cost of petrol. D alleged that W had threatened S with violence if he did not give W any money with the result that S jumped out of the car. W alleged that D had tried to take money from S's wallet which had driven him to jump out of the car; there had been no prior agreement to rob. B denied being involved in any plan to rob and blamed D. The appellants and B were tried on charges of manslaughter and robbery on the basis that there had been a joint enterprise to rob S, who had met his death trying to escape. The judge directed the jury on causation by referring to *Director of Public Prosecutions* v *Daley* which appeared to establish six criteria for proof of causation in 'escape' cases. B was acquitted. W and D appealed.

Held, the appeals would be allowed. What evidence there was of a joint enterprise to rob applied equally to the three defendants. To have convicted W and acquitted B the jury must, against the judge's direction, have used D's statement against him. Turning to D's appeal, on a case of death following a threat of violence the real issue was that of causation. In considering the foreseeability of harm to the victim from the threat and whether the victim's action was not so unreasonable as to break the chain of causation, the nature of the threat was important. The judge should have directed the jury to consider whether the deceased's action in jumping out of the car was proportional to the gravity of the threat. The judge had not done so. (See also *Director of Public Prosecutions* v *Daley*.)

R v *Wills* (1991) 92 Cr App R 297 (Court of Appeal)

The appellant, a financial consultant, and his assistants, were convicted of theft contrary to s1(1) of the Theft Act 1968, with particular regard to s5(3) of the 1968 Act. His assistants received moneys from clients for investment in particular schemes; it was however used for the general purpose of the business and not invested as each client had instructed. Not being present at the time the monies were paid to his assistants, the appellant contended that by virtue of s5(3) he could not be convicted; he had been unaware of the obligation that existed at the time the monies were paid. On appeal it was contended that an essential ingredient of the offence was direct knowledge of the obligation to deal with the property in a particular way.

Held, the appeal would be allowed. Section 5(3) requires a person to have knowledge of the obligation placed upon them and proof of actions contrary to the obligation was insufficient. For the purposes of s5(3) the prosecution had to prove actual knowledge by the principal of the obligation. While the appellant may have had knowledge about the general running of the business it would be expected that cheques drawn in favour of the business (as these had been) would be paid into the business account; some further evidence would be required to show how the monies should have been applied. Theft had not been sufficiently proved.

R v Wilson [1996] 3 WLR 125 (Court of Appeal)

D was convicted of an assault occasioning actual bodily harm contrary to s47 Offences Against the Person Act 1861. He had branded his initials upon his wife's (P's) buttocks with a hot knife at P's request. P's doctor reported what he later saw. The trial judge felt bound by *R v Brown* (1993) in that consent was not a defence to causing actual bodily harm even though the act had been consensual and private.

Held, the appeal would be allowed. The case came within one of the exceptional situations identified in *R v Brown* (1993) where consent to actual bodily harm, or worse, would be valid. There had been no aggressive intent on the part of the appellant; he had been motivated by his wife to do what he did. Consensual activity between husband and wife in the privacy of the matrimonial home was not a matter for criminal investigation. (Compare *R v Brown* (1993).)

R v Winson [1968] 1 All ER 197 (Court of Appeal)

The appellant was the holder of a justices' on-licence in respect of the premises of a discothèque club which was owned by a company of which he was a director. It was a term of the licence that members should not be served intoxicating liquor until a period of forty-eight hours had elapsed after they had become members. Two police officers were admitted to the premises on payment of 5s (25p) each on three occasions on each of which they were served with drinks without the forty-eight-hour period having elapsed. At the material times the premises were being run by a manager. The appellant had no knowledge that drinks were being served to persons contrary to the conditions of the licences. He was convicted under s161(1) of the Licensing Act 1964 of 'knowingly selling' intoxicating liquor to persons he was not entitled to sell it to.

Held, the appellant was rightly convicted. Even though the statute used the word 'knowingly' the holder of a justices' on-licence could not evade the responsibilities attached to that licence by absenting himself and delegating the responsibilities to another. 'A man cannot get out of the responsibilities and duties attached to a licence by absenting himself. The position of course is quite different if he remains in control. It would be only right that he should not be liable if a servant behind his back did something which contravened the terms of the licence. If, however, he wholly absents himself leaving somebody else in control, he cannot claim that what has happened has happened without his knowledge if the delegate has knowingly carried on in contravention of the licence' (*per* LORD PARKER CJ). (See also *Vane v Yiannopoullos* and *Ross v Moss*.)

R v Woollin [1998] 4 All ER 103 (House of Lords)

The defendant was convicted of murder. His three-month-old son died from head injuries having been thrown by him onto a hard surface. On the issue of whether he had intended to cause grievous bodily harm, the trial judge gave the jury a *Nedrick* direction (they were not entitled to infer the necessary intention unless they felt sure that death or serious bodily harm was a virtual certainty as a result of the defendant's actions and that he had appreciated that such was the case). The judge advised the jury that they could convict if they were sure the defendant had recognised that there was a substantial risk of grievous bodily harm resulting from his actions. He argued the judge had widened the scope of the mens rea for murder. The defendant's appeal to the Court of Appeal was dismissed. The Court held that a *Nedrick* direction was only required where evidence of intent was limited to the admitted actions of the accused and that it was unnecessary where there was other evidence. The defendant appealed to the House of Lords.

Held, the appeal would be allowed and a conviction for manslaughter substituted. The trial judge had blurred the distinction between intention and recklessness. The approach of the Court of Appeal in *R v Nedrick* was correct and not limited in its application as the Court of Appeal had suggested. (*R v Nedrick* applied; *R v Moloney* considered. See also *Attorney-General's Reference (No 3 of 1994)*.)

R v Wuyts [1969] 2 All ER 799 (Court of Appeal)

W drove a car to a garage and ordered some petrol for which he tendered a forged £5 note in payment. The pump attendant noticed the forgery and refused to accept it whereupon he found other genuine money to pay for the petrol. In due course he surrendered the £5 note in question to the police. Some 13 days later, when working as a mini-cab driver, he took a fare to Stanstead from London late at night and was paid with two forged £5 notes for which he gave four genuine £1 notes in change. He said that on his way back he noticed for the first time that the notes were forgeries and, after an unsuccessful attempt to find the man who gave them to him, he complained to the others at the mini-cab headquarters. The forged £5 notes were subsequently found in an atlas under the front seat of the car by the owners and handed over to the police. W said that he intended to hand in the forged notes to the police when he discovered that they were forgeries, but was unable to do so because he had no time and because the owners of the car had taken it away from him. He was convicted of uttering a forged banknote, against which conviction he did not appeal, and of being in possession of forged banknotes knowing them to be forged, contrary to s8 of the Forgery Act 1913 (see now ss15, 16 of the Forgery and Counterfeiting Act 1981), against which he appealed.

Held, the conviction should be set aside as the trial judge failed to leave to the jury the question whether they were satisfied on a balance of probabilities that W's sole purpose in retaining possession of the notes was to hand them over to the proper authorities. The court also held that if an accused person in the position of W is able to prove on a balance of probabilities that, although in possession of notes which he knew to be forged, he had retained possession of them solely in order to place them before the police authorities so that the previous possessors of the notes might be prosecuted, that amounts to a lawful excuse. The fact that an accused has not delivered them to the police at the first available opportunity does not prevent him from relying on the defence, the question still being one for the jury.

Readhead Freight Ltd v Shulman [1988] Crim LR 696

The appellant company was convicted of causing an employee to use a goods vehicle fitted with a tachograph contrary to s97(1) of the Transport Act 1988; records were not being completed. The company's transport manager was said to have been responsible.

Held, the appeal would be allowed. To establish a responsibility for 'causing' something to be done, there had to be something which amounted to a command or direction to do the act. Although it was clear that the appellants knew or turned a blind eye to what was happening, it did not amount to 'causing' it to happen which is what was required by the offence. (See also *R v P & O European Ferries (Dover) Ltd*; but see *Seaboard Offshore Ltd v Secretary of State for Transport*.)

Rice v Connolly [1966] 2 All ER 649 (Queen's Bench Divisional Court)

A man was prosecuted in the magistrates' court for wilfully obstructing a police officer in the execution of his duties, contrary to s51 of the Police Act 1964. At about 12.45 am one day he was seen by a uniformed police officer, in an area where a number of breaking-in offences had recently been committed, walking and looking around in a suspicious manner. The police officer kept him under observation for some time and then stopped him and asked him where he was going and for his name and address. He refused to say where he was going and, although after being asked a number of times he said that his name was Rice and he lived at Convamore Road, he refused to give his full name and address or to go to a police box to confirm his identity, saying that he would only give his full name and address or move from the spot where he was if he were arrested. He was arrested and it was found that the name and address he gave were correct although they were incomplete. He was convicted and after an unsuccessful appeal to quarter sessions he appealed to the Divisional Court.

Held, the conviction would be quashed. Although Rice had been obstructive, in the circumstances he had not been guilty of 'wilful obstruction' as no obstruction without lawful excuse had been established.

Ross v Moss [1965] 3 All ER 145 (Queen's Bench Divisional Court)

Moss, the manager of a club and holder of a justices' on-licence, was prosecuted for knowingly permitting intoxicating liquor to be supplied to persons who were not members of the club properly elected. By the rules of the club every candidate for membership had, inter alia, to be proposed by a member and the proposal seconded by another member. Police officers in plain clothes who were not members went to the club and, after filling in membership application forms and paying five shillings (25p) each, were given membership cards and allowed to buy intoxicating drinks. Also on one occasion 48 persons, who were not members or guests introduced in accordance with the rules, were supplied with intoxicating drinks. On the dates when the offences were alleged to have been committed Moss was on holiday in Scotland and had delegated the management of the premises to his father. The father knew that members of the public were being admitted to membership without having a proposer or seconder. Moss was convicted and appealed to the Divisional Court.

Held, the conviction would be affirmed on the ground that 'knowledge' in this connection is not limited to actual knowledge but includes shutting your eyes to what is going on where a person intends a course of conduct to continue and deliberately looks the other way. (But see *Vane* v *Yiannopoullos*.)

Royal College of Nursing of the United Kingdom v *Department of Health and Social Security* [1981] 1 All ER 545 (House of Lords)

The Royal College of Nursing sought a declaration against the Department of Health and Social Security that procedures being followed when terminating a pregnancy by medical induction caused nurses to contravene s58 of the Offences against the Person Act 1861. Section 1(1) of the Abortion Act 1967 (now amended by s37 of the Human Fertilisation and Embryology Act 1990) protects a registered medical practitioner when terminating a pregnancy in specified circumstances. Using the medical induction method involves a doctor inserting a catheter into the womb, followed by the nurses administering the fluid into the womb via the catheter under the doctor's instructions but in his absence, although he was on call. It was the nurses who, by administering the fluid, caused induced labour which terminated the pregnancy. The department, in issuing advice, took the view that in the circumstances the pregnancy was terminated by a registered medical practitioner within s1(1) of the 1967 Act. The judge did not find that the department's advice involved nurses in unlawful acts and granted a declaration to that effect. The Court of Appeal reversed that decision, stating that the whole process of medical induction must be carried out by a doctor. The department appealed to the House of Lords.

Held, the appeal would be allowed. So long as a doctor prescribed the treatment for the termination of pregnancy, remained in charge and accepted responsibility throughout, and the treatment was carried out according to his instructions, the pregnancy was 'terminated by a registered medical practitioner'. Section 1(1) gave protection to those taking part in the termination. (See also *R* v *Bourne*, *R* v *Smith (John)* and *Janaway* v *Salford Health Authority*.)

Scott v *Commissioner of Police for the Metropolis* [1974] 3 All ER 1032 (House of Lords)

The appellant appealed against his conviction of conspiracy to defraud. He admitted that he had agreed with employees of cinema owners temporarily to abstract, without permission of such cinema owners, and in return for payments to such employees, cinematograph films, without the knowledge or consent of the owners of the copyright and/or distribution rights in such films, for the purpose of making infringing copies and distributing the same on a commercial basis. However, he submitted that there could not be conspiracy to defraud unless there was deceit. The Court of Appeal rejected this submission but certified that a point of law of public importance was involved, namely: 'Whether, on a charge of conspiracy to defraud, the Crown must establish an agreement to deprive the owners of their property by deception; or whether it is sufficient to prove an agreement to prejudice the rights of another or others without lawful justification and in circumstances of dishonesty.'

Held, the appeal would be dismissed. It stated that the view of the Criminal Law Revision Committee in its eighth report on 'Theft and Related Offences', that an important element of larceny, embezzlement and fraudulent conversion was the dishonest appropriation of another person's property and that the words 'dishonestly appropriates' meant the same as 'fraudulently converts to his own use or benefit ...', were endorsed by Parliament in the Theft Act 1968. Section 32(1) of that Act did not abolish the offence of conspiracy to defraud. The answer to the first question was therefore in the negative. The answer to the second question, viz whether it is sufficient to prove an agreement to prejudice the rights of another or others without lawful justification and in circumstances of dishonesty, was Yes, if by 'prejudice' is meant 'injure'.

Seaboard Offshore Ltd v *Secretary of State for Transport, The Safe Carrier* [1994] 2 All ER 99 (House of Lords)

The appellants were convicted of failing to take all reasonable steps to ensure that their ship was operated in a safe manner contrary to s31 of the Merchant Shipping Act 1988. The new chief engineer had failed to properly familiarise himself with the ship. The engine broke down three times within 24 hours leaving the ship adrift at sea. The justices found that someone in the company had been at fault and that failure by anyone in the company to take reasonable steps to ensure that the vessel was operated in a safe manner amounted to an offence by the company under s31 of the 1988 Act. The Court of Appeal allowed the appeal on the ground that s31 did not impose vicarious liability on the company for the acts of its employees. The Secretary of State appealed to the House of Lords on the grounds that there had been a failure on the part of those entrusted with the exercise of the powers of the company to discharge the duty laid on them by s31; there was no system to ensure that the ship did not go to sea before the chief engineer had familiarised himself with the ship.

Held, the appeal would be dismissed. The duty under s31 on the owner, charterer or manager was a personal one and there would be criminal liability for a failure to discharge that duty. There was no criminal liability for the acts or omissions of the employees if all reasonable steps had been taken by the owner, charterer or manager. (See also *National Rivers Authority* v *Alfred McAlpine Homes East Ltd*.)

Shaw v *Director of Public Prosecutions* [1961] 2 All ER 446 (House of Lords)

The appellant published the *Ladies' Directory*, a magazine containing the names, addresses and telephone numbers of prostitutes offering their services for sexual intercourse and the practice of sexual perversions. The appellant's purpose was to assist the prostitutes to ply their trade when they were no longer able to solicit on the street as a result of the Street Offences Act 1959. The prostitutes paid for the advertisements and the appellant derived profit from the publication. He was charged with, inter alia, (1) conspiracy to corrupt public morals; (2) living on the earnings of prostitution contrary to s30 of the Sexual Offences Act 1956. He was convicted of these offences.

Held, his appeal would be dismissed. (1) The appellant was knowingly living in part on the earnings of prostitution. The words 'living on' connote 'living parasitically': *per* LORD REID. (2) A conspiracy to corrupt public morals was a common law misdemeanour and there was evidence fit to be left to a jury on which the appellant could be found guilty. It was irrelevant to this charge that s2(4) of the Obscene Publications Act 1959 might bar proceedings against the appellant if no conspiracy was alleged, for the conspiracy alleged consisted of an agreement to corrupt public morals by means of the magazine. 'There is in [the] court a residual power, where no statute has yet intervened to supersede the common law, to superintend those offences which are prejudicial to the public welfare' (*per* VISCOUNT SIMONDS). (See also *Knuller Ltd v Director of Public Prosecutions.*)

Sherras v De Rutzen [1895] 1 QB 918

The appellant, the licensee of a public house, was convicted under s16(2) of the Licensing Act 1872 of unlawfully supplying liquor to a police constable on duty without having the authority of a superior officer of such a constable for doing so. The appellant's public house was opposite the police station. It was frequented by policemen when off duty. They were sometimes in uniform when served but did not wear their armlets. The armlet was removed at the police station when a constable was dismissed at the end of his duty. In this case the constable was not wearing his armlet and had every appearance of being off duty. The appellant believed he was off duty and in that belief served him with liquor. There was no intention to do a wrongful act.

Held, the conviction would be quashed. 'The presumption is that mens rea, an evil intention or a knowledge of the wrongfulness of the act, is an essential ingredient in every offence; but that presumption is liable to be displaced either by the words of the statute creating the offence, or by the subject-matter with which it deals, and both must be considered … there must in general be guilty knowledge on the part of the defendant, or of someone whom he has put in his place to act for him generally or in the particular matter, in order to constitute an offence' (*per* WRIGHT J).

Stapylton v O'Callaghan [1973] 2 All ER 782
(Queen's Bench Divisional Court)

A flat was broken into on 6 April 1972, and a driving licence and other property stolen. On 8 April 1972, O'Callaghan was found in possession of the driving licence and when questioned by the police as to how he came into possession of it he gave two conflicting explanations. The first was that it belonged to a friend who had lent it to him, and the second was that he found it the night before. In the magistrates' court he was acquitted of handling the driving licence, contrary to s22(1) of the Theft Act 1968, and the theft of the said driving licence, contrary to s1 of the Act the magistrate treating the charges as alternative ones. The prosecution appealed.

Held, he should have been convicted of theft, and the case would be remitted to the magistrate with a direction to that effect. He had dishonestly possessed himself of a driving licence intending to keep it, he had dishonestly assumed a right to it by keeping or dealing with it as owner within s3(1) of the 1968 Act and thus dishonestly appropriated property belonging to another with the intention of permanently depriving the other of it within s1(1). (See also *Lawrence v Commissioner of Police for the Metropolis*.)

Sweet v Parsley [1969] 1 All ER 347 (House of Lords)

Police officers found a quantity of cannabis resin and other dangerous drugs at a farmhouse in the county of Oxford. The farmhouse had been let to the appellant who in turn sub-let the rooms to divers persons. The appellant retained one of the rooms for herself but subsequently went to live at another address and only visited the farmhouse occasionally to collect the rent. She had no knowledge whatsoever that the house was being used for the purpose of smoking cannabis or cannabis resin. She was convicted in the magistrates' court of being concerned in the management of premises which were used for the purpose of smoking dangerous drugs contrary to s5 of the Dangerous Drugs Act 1965 (now s8 of the Misuse of Drugs Act 1971, which contains the word 'knowingly' and therefore makes it clear that mens rea is now required). The conviction was affirmed by the Divisional Court and she appealed to the House of Lords.

Held, the conviction should be quashed on the ground that the offence is not one of absolute liability but requires proof of mens rea. 'On a fair reading of the phrase "concerned in the management of any premises used for any such purpose", a link is denoted between management and user for a purpose. To say that someone is concerned in the management of premises used for the purpose of smoking cannabis involves, in my view, that his management is with knowledge that the premises are so used. The wording of s5(b) contains positive indications that mens rea is an essential ingredient of an offence. Even if, contrary to my view, it is not affirmatively enacted that there must be mens rea I cannot read the wording as enacting that there need not be mens rea. I find it wholly impossible to say that the statute either clearly, or by necessary implication, ruled out mens rea as a constituent part of guilt' (*per* LORD MORRIS OF BORTH-Y-GEST). (See also *Warner v Metropolitan Police Commissioner* and *Sherras v De Rutzen*.)

Thabo Meli v R [1954] 1 All ER 373 (Privy Council)

Four men were charged with murder. Acting in concert with one another they agreed to kill the deceased and then make it appear that he died in an accident. Thabo Meli invited the deceased to a hut, gave him beer, and when he became partially intoxicated, struck him a blow on the head. Believing him to be dead he then rolled the body over a cliff and dressed up the scene to make the whole affair look like an accident. The medical evidence showed that the deceased did not die from the blow he received but from exposure at the bottom of the cliff. They were convicted and an appeal was brought to the Judicial Committee of the Privy Council, contending that the conviction was wrong since there were two separate acts: the attack in the hut which, though accompanied by mens rea, did not cause death, and the rolling of the body over the cliff which, although it caused death, was not accompanied by mens rea.

Held, the conviction would be affirmed on the ground that the whole matter was one transaction and could not be divided up in this way. (See also *R v Church* and *R v Le Brun*.)

Treacy v Director of Public Prosecutions [1971] 1 All ER 110 (House of Lords)

The appellant was charged with and convicted of an offence under s21(1) of the Theft Act 1968 of making an unwarranted demand with menaces. He wrote and posted a letter in England addressed to a Mrs X in Germany where she received the letter.

Held, his appeal would be dismissed. Even if the offence of blackmail were not complete until the demand was received abroad by the person to whom it was addressed, the demander could still be tried in England as it was there that the demand was made, ie, when the letter was posted.

Tuck v Robson [1970] 1 All ER 1171 (Queen's Bench Divisional Court)

Tuck was the licensee of a public house and at 11pm he called 'time' in his saloon bar and switched off the main lights. At 11.05pm he called 'glasses please', entering the public bar to clear away glasses and assist customers from that part of the premises. No consumption of intoxicating liquor was permitted by law on the premises after 11.10pm, but it was established that Tuck was aware that customers were consuming liquor in the saloon bar when the police arrived at 11.23pm. He had taken no steps to stop them since he thought all he was required to do was to call time and ask the customers to leave. He was convicted of aiding and abetting the consumption of drinks after hours and he appealed.

Held, the appeal would be dismissed because there was no question that the appellant had full knowledge of the facts which constituted the offence, and the magistrate had been entitled in all the circumstances to draw the inference that the appellant had lent passive assistance to the commission of the offence.

Tynan v Balmer [1966] 2 All ER 133 (Queen's Bench Divisional Court)

Tynan was charged with wilfully obstructing a police officer in the execution of his duties contrary to s51 of the Police Act 1964. During the course of a strike of draughtsmen at a factory, Tynan, who was the leader of the strikers and chairman of the negotiating committee, began to lead about 40 pickets moving in a circle at the main entrance, the circle extending into the public highway. A police officer requested him to stop the pickets from circling but he refused, saying that he was challenging the authority of the officer and that they intended to make a test case of it. He was convicted and, after an unsuccessful appeal to the Liverpool Crown Court, he appealed to the Divisional Court.

Held, the conviction would be affirmed on the ground that the conduct of the pickets in sealing off part of the highway was a common law nuisance since it was an unreasonable user of the highway and the position was not covered by s2 of the Trades Disputes Act 1906 (now repealed) since part of the object of the pickets was to seal off the highway and cause vehicles approaching the premises to stop, and not wholly to peacefully obtain or communicate information or peacefully persuade anyone to work or abstain from working.

Vane v Yiannopoullos [1964] 3 All ER 820 (House of Lords)

The proprietor of a restaurant who held a justices' on-licence was charged with knowingly selling intoxicating liquor to persons whom he was not permitted by the licence to serve, ie persons who did not order meals. He instructed the waitress only to serve intoxicating drinks to customers who ordered meals, but one evening she sold a glass of whisky and a glass of beer to two customers who did not order a meal. At the time when the drinks were served Yiannopoullos was in another part of the building and did not know that the two customers did not order a meal. He was acquitted, and after an unsuccessful appeal to the Divisional Court the prosecution appealed to the House of Lords.

Held, the acquittal would be affirmed on the ground that since he had no knowledge, actual or constructive, of the breach by the waitress he could not be convicted. (But see *Ross v Moss*.)

Wai Yu-tsang v The Queen [1991] 3 WLR 1006 (Privy Council)

The defendant, the chief accountant of the Hang Lung Bank, was convicted of conspiring with others to defraud the bank and its existing and potential shareholders, creditors and depositors. He had dishonestly concealed the dishonouring of certain cheques in the bank's accounts. He stated that he had been acting on the managing director's instructions; that it had been done to prevent a further run on the bank; that he believed that subsequent balancing transactions were genuine and that he was acting in the best interests of the bank. The judge directed the jury that, even if no loss was suffered and the defendant had not wished any loss to be caused, if he had been a party to an agreement with the common intention to defraud and imperil economic or proprietary interests, such was sufficient to constitute fraud.

Held, the appeal would be dismissed. The trial judge's direction had been correct. 'The question whether particular facts reveal a conspiracy to defraud depends upon what the conspirators have dishonestly agreed to do, and in particular whether they have agreed to practise a fraud on somebody. ... it is enough ... that the conspirators have dishonestly agreed to bring about a state of affairs which they realise will or may deceive the victim into so acting, or failing to act, that he will suffer economic loss or his economic interests will be put at risk ... the mere fact that [he does not wish the victim or potential victim to suffer harm] will not of itself prevent the agreement from constituting a conspiracy to defraud' (*per* LORD GOFF OF CHIEVELEY).

Warner v Metropolitan Police Commissioner [1968] 2 All ER 356 (House of Lords)

The appellant was a floor-layer who sold scent as a side-line. On the night in question he collected two boxes from a café which, according to his evidence, he believed contained scent. He was later stopped by a police officer and on examination one of the boxes was found to contain scent but the other contained certain tablets which were prohibited drugs under the Drugs (Prevention of Misuse) Act 1964. The appellant was convicted under s1 of the 1964 Act (now s5 of the Misuse of Drugs Act 1971) of being in possession of dangerous drugs. The jury were directed that it was sufficient for the prosecution to prove that the appellant was in control of the box and that his lack of knowledge of the contents was irrelevant.

Held, this was a misdirection as, although the offence under s1 was absolute, nevertheless a person was not in possession of the contents of a package if he was unaware of their existence or genuinely mistaken as to their general nature. But if he was aware of their general nature it was not a defence to show that he did not know their precise nature or qualities or that they were illicit. In the present case, however, no reasonable jury would have accepted the accused's story and the appeal would be dismissed. (But see s28 of the Misuse of Drugs Act 1971 and *R* v *Buswell* where this case was distinguished.)

Wilcox v *Jeffery* [1951] 1 All ER 464 (King's Bench Divisional Court)

W, the owner and managing editor of a monthly magazine entitled *Jazz Illustrated*, was prosecuted for aiding and abetting the contravention of a provision of the Aliens Order 1920. Hawkins, a citizen of the United States, was given permission to land in the United Kingdom on condition that he took no employment, paid or unpaid, during his stay, and W, who knew of the restrictions, met him on his arrival at London Airport and later the same afternoon attended a concert where Hawkins played the saxophone. Subsequently he published a laudatory description of the performance and several pages of photographs in his magazine. He was convicted and appealed to the Divisional Court.

Held, the conviction would be affirmed on the ground that his presence at the concert was not accidental but he had gone there with the deliberate object of encouraging or concurring with Hawkins.

Woolmington v *Director of Public Prosecutions* [1935] All ER Rep 1 (House of Lords)

Woolmington was charged with the murder of his wife. He admitted that he had shot her but alleged that the gun had gone off accidentally whilst he was endeavouring to persuade her to return to live with him by threatening to shoot himself. The judge directed the jury that once it was proved that it was the accused's act that caused the deceased's death, the law presumes malice unless the contrary is proved. Woolmington was convicted and appealed.

Held, the conviction would be quashed. Where it is proved that the accused performed the guilty act the onus remains on the prosecution to show beyond reasonable doubt that he did it with the necessary mens rea. Except in the case of insanity and subject to certain statutory exceptions, the onus of proving the absence of mens rea never shifts to the defence. 'Throughout the web of the English criminal law one golden threat is always to be seen – that it is the duty of the prosecution to prove the prisoner's guilt subject to what I have already said as to the defence of insanity and subject also to any statutory exception. If, at the end of and on the whole of the case, there is a reasonable doubt, created by the evidence given by either the prosecution or the prisoner, as to whether the prisoner killed the deceased with a malicious intention, the prosecution has not made out the case and the prisoner is entitled to an acquittal. No matter what the charge or where the trial, the principle that the prosecution must prove the guilt of the prisoner is part of the common law of England and no attempt to whittle it down can be entertained' (*per* LORD SANKEY LC).

Yip Chiu-cheung v *R* [1994] 2 All ER 924 (Privy Council)

The appellant was convicted of conspiring to traffic in heroin. He made an agreement with N, who was in fact an undercover drug enforcement officer (trying to identify the drug suppliers in Hong Kong and the dealers in Australia), whereby N would take a consignment of heroin from the appellant in Hong Kong and fly to Australia. The authorities in both countries were fully briefed and undertook to allow N free passage from Hong Kong to Australia. N did not take the flight to Hong Kong and took no further steps to carry out the plan. The jury were directed that if they found that N intended to export the heroin out of Hong Kong he was in law a co-conspirator and the appellant could be convicted of a conspiracy with him. The Court of Appeal in Hong Kong dismissed his appeal. An appeal to the Privy Council was made on the basis that N could not be a co-conspirator because in law he lacked the necessary mens rea for the offence and therefore there could be no conspiracy.

Held, the appeal would be dismissed. The Executive in Hong Kong had no power to authorise a breach in the law. Although N would not have been prosecuted had he carried out the plan, it did not mean that he did not intend to commit a criminal offence. There had therefore been a conspiracy and the appellant had been properly convicted. (Applied in *R* v *Kingston*.)

Statutes

Treason Act 1351
(25 Edw 3 Stat 5 c 2)

Declaration what offences shall be adjudged treason

Item, whereas divers opinions have been before this time in what case treason shall be said, and in what not: the King, at the request of the lords and of the commons, hath made a declaration in the manner as hereafter followeth, that is to say; when a man doth compass or imagine the death of our lord the King, or of our lady his Queen, or of their eldest son and heir; or if a man do violate the King's companion, or the King's eldest daughter unmarried, or the wife of the King's eldest son and heir; or if a man do levy war against our lord the King in his realm, or be adherent to the King's enemies in his realm, giving to them aid and comfort in the realm, or elsewhere, and thereof be probably attainted of open deed by the people of their condition and if a man slea the chancellor, treasurer, or the King's justices of the one bench or the other, justices in eyre, or justices of assise, and all other justices assigned to hear and determine, being in their places, doing their offences: and it is to be understood that in the cases above rehearsed, that ought to be judged treason which extends to our lord the King, and his royal majesty:

[As amended by the Forgery Act 1830, s31; 2 & 3 Will 4 c34 (1831–2) s1; 9 Geo 4 c31, s1; 10 Geo 4 c34, s1; Escheat (Procedure) Act 1887, Schedule; Statute Law Revision Act 1948; Criminal Law Act 1967, s10(2), Schedule 3, Pt 1; Criminal Law Act (Northern Ireland) 1967, Schedule 2, Pt 1.]

Treason Act 1702
(1 Anne Stat 2 c 21)

3 Endeavouring to hinder the succession to the crown according to the limitations of Stat Limitations stated; and attempting the same by overt act; high treason

And for the further security of her Majesties person and the succession of the crown in the protestant line and for extinguishing the hopes of the pretended Prince of Wales and all other pretenders and their open and secret abettors be it further enacted by the authority aforesaid that if any person or persons shall endeavour to deprive or hinder any person who shall be the next in succession to the crown for the time being according to the limitations in an Act intituled An Act declaring the rights and liberties of the subject and settling the succession of the crown and according to one other Act intituled An Act for the further limitation of the crown and better securing the rights and liberties of the subject from succeeding after the decease of her Majesty (whom God long preserve) to the imperial crown of this realm and the dominions and territories thereunto belonging according to the limitations in the before mentioned Acts that is to say such issue of her Majesties body as shall from time to time be next in succession to the crown if it shall please God Almighty to bless her Majesty with issue and during the time her Majesty shall have no issue the Princess Sophia Electoress and Dutchess dowager of Hanover and after the decease of the said Princess Sophia the next in succession to the crown for the time being according to the limitation of the said Acts and the same malitiously advisedly and directly shall attempt by any overt act or deed every such offence shall be adjudged high treason and the offender or offenders therein their abettors procurers and comforters knowing the said offence to be done being thereof convicted or attainted according to the laws and statutes of this realm shall be deemed and adjudged traytors and shall be liable to imprisonment for life as in cases of high treason.

[As amended by the Statute Law Revision Act 1948; Crime and Disorder Act 1998, s36(2)(c).]

Vagrancy Act 1824
(5 Geo 4 c 83)

3 Persons [wandering abroad or begging] shall be deemed idle and disorderly persons, and may be imprisoned for one month ...

Every person wandering abroad, or placing himself or herself in any public place, street, highway, court, or passage, to beg or gather alms, or causing or procuring or encouraging any child or children so to do; shall be deemed an idle and disorderly person within the true intent and meaning of this Act; and subject to section 70 of the Criminal Justice Act 1982, it shall be lawful for any justice of the peace to commit such offender (being thereof convicted before him by his own view, or by the confession of such offender, or by the evidence on oath of one or more credible witness or witnesses,) to the house of correction for any time not exceeding one calendar month.

4 Persons committing certain offences shall be deemed rogues and vagabonds and may be imprisoned for three months ...

Every person committing any of the offences hereinbefore mentioned, after having been convicted as an idle and disorderly person; every person wandering abroad and lodging in any barn or outhouse, or in any deserted or unoccupied building, or in the open air, or under a tent, or in any cart or waggon, and not giving a good account of himself or herself; every person wilfully, openly, lewdly, and obscenely exposing his person, with intent to insult any female; every person wandering abroad, and endeavouring by the exposure of wounds or deformities to obtain or gather alms; every person going about as a gatherer or collector of alms, or endeavouring to procure charitable contributions of any nature or kind, under any false or fraudulent pretence; every person being found in or upon any dwelling house, warehouse, coachhouse, stable, or outhouse, or in any inclosed yard, garden, or area for any unlawful purpose; and every person apprehended as an idle and disorderly person, and violently resisting any constable, or other peace officer so apprehending him or her, and being subsequently convicted of the offence for which he or she shall have been so apprehended; shall be deemed a rogue and vagabond, within the true intent and meaning of this Act; and subject to section 70 of the Criminal Justice Act 1982, it shall be lawful for any justice of the peace to commit such offender (being thereof convicted before him by the confession of such offender, or by the evidence on oath of one or more credible witness or witnesses,) to the house of correction for any time not exceeding three calendar months.

5 Certain offenders shall be deemed incorrigible rogues and may be committed for trial at the Crown Court

Every person committing any offence against this Act which shall subject him or her to be dealt with as a rogue and vagabond, such person having been at some former time adjudged so to be, and duly convicted thereof; shall, subject to section 70 of the Criminal Justice Act 1982, be deemed an incorrigible rogue within the true intent and meaning of this Act; and, subject to section 70 of the Criminal Justice Act 1982, it shall be lawful for any justice of the peace to commit such offender (being thereof convicted before him by the confession of such offender, or by the evidence on oath of one or more credible witness or witness,) to the Crown Court either in custody or on bail.

[As amended by the Statute Law Revision (No 1) Act 1888; Statute Law Revision (No 2) Act 1888; Criminal Justice Act 1925, ss42, 49(4)(5), Schedule 3; National Assurance Act 1948, s62, Schedule 7, Pt I; Criminal Justice Act 1948, ss1(2); 83(3), Schedule 10; Criminal Justice Act 1967, s103(1), Schedule 6, para 1; Theft Act 1968, s33(3), Schedule 3, Pt I; Courts Act 1971, s56(1), Schedule 8, Pt II, para 5(a); Indecent Displays (Control) Act 1981, s5(2), Schedule; Criminal Attempts Act 1981, ss8, 10, Schedule, Pt II; Criminal Justice Act 1982, s77, Schedule 14, para 1, 1(b); Public Order Act 1986, s40(3), Schedule 3; Statute Law (Repeals) Act 1989, Schedule 1, Pt I.]

Libel Act 1843
(6 & 7 Vict c 96)

4 False defamatory libel punishable by imprisonment and fine

If any person shall maliciously publish any defamatory libel, knowing the same to be false, every such person, being convicted thereof, shall be liable to be imprisoned in the common gaol or house of correction for any term not exceeding two years, and to pay such fine as the court shall award.

5 *Malicious defamatory libel, by imprisonment or fine*

If any person shall maliciously publish any defamatory libel, every such person, being convicted thereof, shall be liable to fine or imprisonment, or both, as the Court may award, such imprisonment not to exceed the term of one year.

6 *Proceedings upon the trial of an indictment or information for a defamatory libel*

On the trial of any indictment or information for a defamatory libel, the defendant having pleaded such plea as hereinafter mentioned, the truth of the matters charged may be inquired into, but shall not amount to a defence, unless it was for the public benefit that the said matters charged should be published; and to entitle the defendant to give evidence of the truth of such matters charged as a defence to such indictment or information it shall be necessary for the defendant, in pleading to the said indictment or information, to allege the truth of the said matters charged in the manner now required in pleading a justification to an action for defamation, and further to allege that it was for the public benefit that the said matters charged should be published, and the particular fact or facts by reason whereof it was for the public benefit that the said matters charged should be published, to which plea the prosecutor shall be at liberty to reply generally, denying the whole thereof; and if after such plea the defendant shall be convicted on such indictment or information it shall be competent to the court, in pronouncing sentence, to consider whether the guilt of the defendant is aggravated or mitigated by the said plea, and by the evidence given to prove or to disprove the same: Provided always, that the truth of the matters charged in the alleged libel complained of by such indictment or information shall in no case be inquired into without such plea of justification: Provided also, that in addition to such plea it shall be competent to the defendant to plead a plea of not guilty; Provided also, that nothing in this Act contained shall take away or prejudice any defence under the plea of not guilty which it is now competent to the defendant to make under such plea to any action or indictment or information for defamatory words or libel.

7 *Evidence to rebut prima facie case of publication by an agent*

Whensoever, upon the trial of any indictment or information for the publication of a libel, under the plea of not guilty, evidence shall have been given which shall establish a presumptive case of publication against the defendant by the act of any other person by his authority, it shall be competent to such defendant to prove that such publication was made without his authority, consent, or knowledge, and that the said publication did not arise from want of due care or caution on his part.

[As amended by the Statute Law Revision Act 1891.]

Treason Felony Act 1848
(11 & 12 Vict c 12)

3 *Offences herein mentioned declared to be felonies*

If any person whatsoever shall, within the United Kingdom or without, compass, imagine, invent, devise, or intend to deprive or depose our Most Gracious Lady the Queen, from the style, honour, or royal name of the imperial crown of the United Kingdom, or of any other of her Majesty's dominions and countries, or to levy war against her Majesty, within any part of the United Kingdom, in order by force or constraint to compel her to change her measures or counsels, or in order to put any force or constraint upon or in order to intimidate or overawe both Houses or either House of Parliament, or to move or stir any foreigner or stranger with force to invade the United Kingdom or any other of her Majesty's dominions or countries under the obeisance of her Majesty, and such compassings, imaginations, inventions, devices, or intentions, or any of them, shall express, utter, or declare, by publishing any printing or writing, or by any overt act or deed, every person so offending shall be guilty of felony, and being convicted thereof shall be liable, to be transported beyond the seas for the term of his or her natural life.

6 *Saving as to 25 Edw 3 stat 5 c2*

Provided always, that nothing herein contained shall lessen the force of or in any manner affect any thing enacted by the Treason Act 1351.

7 *Indictments for felony valid, though the facts may amount to treason*

Provided also, that if the facts or matters alleged in an indictment for any felony under this Act shall amount in law to treason, such indictment shall not by reason thereof be deemed void, erroneous, or defective; and if the facts or matters proved on the trial of any person indicted for any felony under this Act shall amount in law to treason, such person shall not by reason thereof be entitled to be acquitted of such felony; but no person tried for such felony shall be afterwards prosecuted for treason upon the same facts.

[As amended by Statute Law Revision Acts 1891 and 1892.]

Accessories and Abettors Act 1861
(24 & 25 Vict c 94)

8 *Abettors ...*

Whosoever shall aid, abet, counsel, or procure the commission of any indictable offence, whether the same be an offence at common law or by virtue of any Act passed or to be passed, shall be liable to be tried, indicted, and punished as a principal offender.

[As amended by the Criminal Law Act 1977, s65(4), Schedule 12.]

Malicious Damage Act 1861
(24 & 25 Vict c 97)

35 Placing wood, etc on railway, taking up rails, etc turning points, showing or hiding signals, etc with intent to obstruct or overthrow any engine, etc

Whosoever shall unlawfully and maliciously put, place, cast, or throw upon or across any railway any wood, stone, or other matter or thing, or shall unlawfully and maliciously take up, remove, or displace any rail, sleeper, or other matter or thing belonging to any railway, or shall unlawfully and maliciously turn, move, or divert any points or other machinery belonging to any railway, or shall unlawfully and maliciously make or show, hide or remove, any signal or light upon or near to any railway, or shall unlawfully and maliciously do or cause to be done any other matter or thing, with intent, in any of the cases aforesaid, to obstruct, upset, overthrow, injure, or destroy any engine, tender, carriage, or truck using such railway, shall be guilty of felony, and being convicted thereof shall be liable, at the discretion of the Court, to be kept in penal servitude for life or to be imprisoned.

36 Obstructing engines or carriages on railways

Whosoever, by any unlawful act, or by any wilful omission or neglect, shall obstruct or cause to be obstructed any engine or carriage using any railway, or shall aid or assist therein, shall be guilty of a misdemeanour, and being convicted thereof shall be liable, at the discretion of the court, to be imprisoned for any term not exceeding two years, with or without hard labour.

58 Malice against owner of property unnecessary

Every punishment and forfeiture by this Act imposed on any person maliciously committing any offence, whether the same be punishable upon indictment or upon summary conviction, shall equally apply and be enforced, whether the offence shall be committed from malice conceived against the owner of the property in respect of which it shall be committed, or otherwise.

[As amended by the Statute Law Revision Act 1892; Statute Law Revision (No 2) Act 1893; Criminal Justice Act 1948, s83(3), Schedule 10, Pt I.]

Offences Against the Person Act 1861
(24 & 25 Vict c 100)

4 Conspiring or soliciting to commit murder

Whosoever shall solicit, encourage, persuade or endeavour to persuade, or shall propose to any person, to murder any other person, whether he be a subject of Her Majesty or not, and whether he be within the Queen's dominions or not, shall be guilty of a misdemeanour, and being convicted thereof shall be liable to imprisonment for life

5 *Manslaughter*

Whosoever shall be convicted of manslaughter shall be liable, at the discretion of the court, to be kept in penal servitude for life.

9 *Murder or manslaughter abroad*

Where any murder or manslaughter shall be committed on land out of the United Kingdom, whether within the Queen's dominions or without, and whether the person killed were a subject of Her Majesty or not, every offence committed by any subject of Her Majesty in respect of any such case, whether the same shall amount to the offence of murder or of manslaughter, may be dealt with, inquired of, tried, determined, and punished in England or Ireland: Provided, that nothing herein contained shall prevent any person from being tried in any place out of England or Ireland for any murder or manslaughter committed out of England or Ireland, in the same manner as such person might have been tried before the passing of this Act.

16 *Threats to kill*

A person who without lawful excuse makes to another a threat, intending that that other would fear it would be carried out, to kill that other or a third person shall be guilty of an offence and liable on conviction on indictment to imprisonment for a term not exceeding ten years.

17 *Impeding a person endeavouring to save himself or another from shipwreck*

Whosoever shall unlawfully and maliciously prevent or impede any person, being on board of or having quitted any ship or vessel which shall be in distress, or wrecked, stranded, or cast on shore, in his endeavour to save his life, or shall unlawfully and maliciously prevent or impede any person in his endeavour to save the life of any such person as in this section first aforesaid, shall be guilty of felony, and being convicted thereof shall be liable to be kept in penal servitude for life.

18 *Shooting or attempting to shoot, or wounding, with intent to do grievous bodily harm, or to resist apprehension*

Whosoever shall unlawfully and maliciously by any means whatsoever wound or cause any grievous bodily harm to any person with intent to do some grievous bodily harm to any person, or with intent to resist or prevent the lawful apprehension or detainer of any person, shall be guilty of felony, and being convicted thereof shall be liable, to be kept in penal servitude for life.

20 Inflicting bodily injury, with or without weapon

Whosoever shall unlawfully and maliciously wound or inflict any grievous bodily harm upon any other person, either with or without any weapon or instrument, shall be guilty of a misdemeanour, and being convicted thereof shall be liable to be kept in penal servitude.

21 Attempting to choke, etc in order to commit or assist in the committing of any indictable offence

Whosoever shall, by any means whatsoever, attempt to choke, suffocate, or strangle any other person, or shall by any means calculated to choke, suffocate, or strangle, attempt to render any other person insensible, unconscious, or incapable of resistance, with intent in any of such cases thereby to enable himself or any other person to commit, or with intent in any of such cases thereby to assist any other person in committing any indictable offence, shall be guilty of felony, and being convicted thereof shall be liable to be kept in penal servitude for life.

22 Using chloroform, etc to commit or assist in the committing of any indictable offence

Whosoever shall unlawfully apply or administer to or cause to be taken by, or attempt to apply or administer to or attempt to cause to be administered to or taken by, any person, any chloroform, laudanum, or other stupefying or overpowering drug, matter, or thing, with intent in any of such cases thereby to enable himself or any other person to commit, or with intent in any such cases thereby to assist any other person in committing, any indictable offence, shall be guilty of felony, and being convicted thereof shall be liable to be kept in penal servitude for life.

23 Maliciously administering poison, etc so as to endanger life or inflict grievous bodily harm

Whosoever shall unlawfully and maliciously administer to or cause to be administered to or taken by any other person any poison or other destructive or noxious thing, so as thereby to endanger the life of such person, or so as thereby to inflict upon such person any grievous bodily harm, shall be guilty of felony, and being convicted thereof shall be liable to be kept in penal servitude for any term not exceeding ten years.

24 Maliciously administering poison, etc with intent to injure, aggrieve, or annoy any other person

Whosoever shall unlawfully and maliciously administer to or cause to be administered to or taken by any other person, any poison or other destructive or noxious thing, with intent to injure, aggrieve, or annoy such person, shall be guilty of a misdemeanour, and being convicted thereof shall be liable to be kept in penal servitude.

25 Person charged with felony under s23 may be found guilty of misdemeanour under s24

If, upon the trial of any person for any felony in the last but one preceding section mentioned, the jury shall not be satisfied that such person is guilty thereof, but shall be satisfied that he is guilty of any misdemeanour in the last preceding section mentioned, then and in every such case the jury may acquit the accused of such felony, and find him guilty of such misdemeanour, and thereupon he shall be liable to be punished in the same manner as if convicted upon an indictment for such misdemeanour.

32 Placing wood, etc on railway, taking up rails, turning points, showing or hiding signals, etc with intent to endanger passengers

Whosoever shall unlawfully and maliciously put or throw upon or across any railway any wood, stone, or other matter or thing, or shall unlawfully and maliciously take up, remove, or displace any rail, sleeper, or other matter or thing belonging to any railway, or shall unlawfully and maliciously turn, move, or divert any points or other machinery belonging to any railway, or shall unlawfully and maliciously make or show, hide or remove, any signal or light upon or near to any railway, or shall unlawfully and maliciously do or cause to be done any other matter or thing, with intent, in any of the cases aforesaid, to endanger the safety of any person travelling or being upon such railway, shall be guilty of felony, and being convicted thereof shall be liable, at the discretion of the court to be kept in penal servitude for life or to be imprisoned.

33 Casting stone, etc, upon a railway carriage, with intent to endanger the safety of any person therein, or in any part of the same train

Whosoever shall unlawfully and maliciously throw, or cause to fall or strike, at, against, into, or upon any engine, tender, carriage, or truck used upon any railway, any wood, stone, or other matter or thing, with intent to injury or endanger the safety of any person being in or upon such engine, tender, carriage, or truck, or in or upon any other engine, tender, carriage, or truck of any train of which such first-mentioned engine, tender, carriage, or truck shall form part, shall be guilty of felony, and being convicted thereof shall be liable to be kept in penal servitude for life.

35 Drivers of carriages injuring persons by furious driving

Whosoever, having the charge of any carriage or vehicle, shall by wanton or furious driving or racing, or other wilful misconduct, or by wilful neglect, do or cause to be done any bodily harm to any person whatsoever, shall be guilty of a misdemeanour, and being convicted thereof shall be liable, at the discretion of the court, to be imprisoned for any term not exceeding two years, with or without hard labour.

36 *Obstructing or assaulting a clergyman or other minister in the discharge of his duties in place of worship or burial place, or on his way thither*

Whosoever shall, by threats or force, obstruct or prevent or endeavour to obstruct or prevent, any clergyman or other minister in or from celebrating divine service or otherwise officiating in any church, chapel, meeting house, or other place of divine worship, or in or from the performance of his duty in the lawful burial of the dead in any churchyard or other burial place, or shall strike or offer any violence to, or shall, upon any civil process, or under the pretence of executing any civil process, arrest any clergyman or other minister who is engaged in, or to the knowledge of the offender is about to engage in, any of the rites or duties in this section aforesaid, or who to the knowledge of the offender shall be going to perform the same or returning from the performance thereof, shall be guilty of a misdemeanour, and being convicted thereof shall be liable, at the discretion of the court, to be imprisoned for any term not exceeding two years, with or without hard labour.

38 *Assault with intent to [resist or prevent arrest]*

Whosoever shall assault any person with intent to resist or prevent the lawful apprehension or detainer of himself or of any other person for any offence, shall be guilty of a misdemeanour, and being convicted thereof shall be liable, at the discretion of the court, to be imprisoned for any term not exceeding two years, with or without hard labour.

47 *Assault occasioning bodily harm ...*

Whosoever shall be convicted upon an indictment of any assault occasioning actual bodily harm shall be liable to be kept in penal servitude.

57 *Bigamy*

Whosoever, being married, shall marry any other person during the life of the former husband or wife, whether the second marriage shall have taken place in England or Ireland or elsewhere, shall be guilty of felony, and being convicted thereof shall be liable to be kept in penal servitude for any term not exceeding seven years: Provided, that nothing in this section contained shall extend to any second marriage contracted elsewhere than in England and Ireland by any other than a subject of Her Majesty, or to any person marrying a second time whose husband or wife shall have been continually absent from such person for the space of seven years then last past, and shall not have been known as such person to be living within that time, or shall extend to any person who, at the time of such second marriage, shall have been divorced from the bond of the first marriage, or to any person whose former marriage shall have been declared void by the sentence of any court of competent jurisdiction.

58 *Administering drugs or using instruments to procure abortion*

Every woman, being with child, who, with intent to procure her own miscarriage, shall unlawfully administer to herself any poison or other noxious thing, or shall unlawfully use any instrument or other means whatsoever with the like intent, and whosoever, with intent to procure the miscarriage of any woman, whether she be or be not with child, shall unlawfully administer to her or cause to be taken by her any poison or other noxious thing, or shall unlawfully use any instrument or other means whatsoever with the like intent, shall be guilty of felony, and being convicted thereof shall be liable to be kept in penal servitude for life.

59 Procuring drugs, etc to cause abortion

Whosoever shall unlawfully supply or procure any poison or other noxious thing, or any instrument or thing whatsoever, knowing that the same is intended to be unlawfully used or employed with intent to procure the miscarriage of any woman, whether she be or not with child, shall be guilty of a misdemeanour, and being convicted thereof shall be liable to be kept in penal servitude.

60 Concealing the birth of a child

If any woman shall be delivered of a child, every person who shall, by any secret disposition of the dead body of the said child, whether such child died before, at, or after its birth, endeavour to conceal the birth thereof, shall be guilty of a misdemeanour, and being convicted thereof shall be liable, at the discretion of the court, to be imprisoned for any term not exceeding two years, with or without hard labour.

64 Making or having gunpowder, etc with intent to commit or enable any person to commit any felony mentioned in this Act

Whosoever shall knowingly have in his possession, or make or manufacture, any gunpowder, explosive substance, or any dangerous or noxious thing, or any machine, engine, instrument, or thing, with intent by means thereof to commit, or for the purpose of enabling any other person to commit, any of the felonies in this Act mentioned shall be guilty of a misdemeanour, and being convicted thereof shall be liable, at the discretion of the court, to be imprisoned for any term not exceeding two years.

[As amended by the Statute Law Revision Act 1892; Statute Law Revision (No 2) Act 1893; Criminal Justice Act 1925, s49 Schedule 3; Criminal Justice Act 1948, s83(3), Schedule 10, Part I; Police Act 1964, s64(3), Schedule 10, Part I; Criminal Law Act 1967, s10(2), Schedule 2, para 13(1), Schedule 3, Part III; Criminal Law Act 1977, ss5(10) (a), (b), s65(4), (5), Schedules 12, 13; Criminal Justice Act 1988, s170(2), Schedule 16.]

Explosive Substances Act 1883
(46 & 47 Vict c 3)

2 *Causing explosion likely to endanger life or property*

A person who in the United Kingdom or (being a citizen of the United Kingdom and Colonies) in the Republic of Ireland unlawfully and maliciously causes by any explosive substance an explosion of a nature likely to endanger life or to cause serious injury to property shall, whether any injury to person or property has been actually caused or not, be guilty of an offence and on conviction on indictment shall be liable to imprisonment for life.

3 *Attempt to cause explosion, or for making or keeping explosive with intent to endanger life or property*

(1) A person who in the United Kingdom or a dependency or (being a citizen of the United Kingdom and Colonies) elsewhere unlawfully and maliciously –

    (a) does any act with intent to cause, or conspires to cause, by an explosive substance an explosion of a nature likely to endanger life or cause serious injury to property; whether in the United Kingdom or the Republic of Ireland; or

    (b) makes or has in his possession or under his control an explosive substance with intent by means thereof to endanger life, or cause serious injury to property, whether in the United Kingdom or the Republic of Ireland, or to enable any other person so to do,

shall, whether any explosion does or not take place, and whether any injury to person or property is actually caused or not, be guilty of an offence and on conviction on indictment shall be liable to imprisonment for life, and the explosive substance shall be forfeited.

(2) In this section 'dependency' means the Channel Islands, the Isle of Man and any colony, other than a colony for whose external relations a country other than the United Kingdom is responsible.

4 *Making or possession of explosive under suspicious circumstances*

(1) Any person who makes or knowingly has in his possession or under his control any explosive substance, under such circumstances as to give rise to a reasonable suspicion that he is not making it or does not have it in his possession or under his control for a lawful object, shall, unless he can show that he made it or had it in his possession or under his control for a lawful object, be guilty of felony, and, on conviction, shall be liable to penal servitude for a term not exceeding fourteen years, or to imprisonment for a term not exceeding two years with or without hard labour, and the explosive substance shall be forfeited.

[As amended by the Criminal Jurisdiction Act 1975, s7(1), (3); Criminal Law Act 1977, s65(4), Schedule 12.]

Trial of Lunatics Act 1883
(46 & 47 Vict c 38)

2 *Special verdict where accused found guilty, but insane at date of act or omission charged ...*

(1) Where in any indictment or information any act or omission is charged against any person as an offence, and it is given in evidence on the trial of such person for that offence that he was insane, so as not to be responsible, according to law, for his actions at the time when the act was done or omission made, then, if it appears to the jury before whom such person is tried that he did the act or made the omission charged, but was insane as aforesaid at the time when he did or made the same, the jury shall return a special verdict that the accused is not guilty by reason of insanity.

[As amended by the Criminal Procedure (Insanity) Act 1964, s1.]

Public Meeting Act 1908
(8 Edw 7 c 66)

1 *Penalty on endeavour to break up public meeting*

(1) Any person who at a lawful public meeting acts in a disorderly manner for the purpose of preventing the transaction of the business for which the meeting was called together shall be guilty of an offence and shall on summary conviction be liable to imprisonment for a term not exceeding six months or to a fine not exceeding level 5 on the standard scale or to both.

(2) Any person who incites others to commit an offence under this section shall be guilty of a like offence.

(3) If any constable reasonably suspects any person of committing an offence under the foregoing provisions of this section, he may if requested so to do by the chairman of the meeting require that person to declare to him immediately his name and address and, if that person refuses or fails so to declare his name and address or gives a false name and address he shall be guilty of an offence under this subsection and liable on summary conviction thereof to a fine not exceeding level 1 on the standard scale.

(4) This section does not apply as respects meetings to which section 97 of the Representation of the People Act 1983 applies.

[As amended by the Public Order Act 1936, s6; Representation of the People Act 1949, s175(1), Schedule 9; Public Order Act 1963 s1(2); Criminal Law Act 1977 ss15(1)(a), 30, Schedule 1; Representation of the People Act 1983, s206, Schedule 8, para 1; Police and Criminal Evidence Act 1984, ss26(1), 119(2), Schedule 7, Part I.]

Perjury Act 1911
(1 & 2 Geo 5 c 6)

1 Perjury

(1) If any person lawfully sworn as a witness or as an interpreter in a judicial proceedings wilfully makes a statement material in that proceeding, which he knows to be false or does not believe to be true, he shall be guilty of perjury, and shall, on conviction thereof on indictment, be liable to penal servitude for a term not exceeding seven years, or to imprisonment with or without hard labour for a term not exceeding two years, or to a fine or to both such penal servitude or imprisonment and fine.

(2) The expression 'judicial proceeding' includes a proceeding before any court, tribunal, or person having by law power to hear, receive, and examine evidence on oath.

(3) Where a statement made for the purposes of a judicial proceeding is not made before the tribunal itself, but is made on oath before a person authorised by law to administer an oath to the person who makes the statement, and to record or authenticate the statement, it shall, for the purposes of this section, be treated as having been made in a judicial proceeding.

(4) A statement made by a person lawfully sworn in England for the purposes of a judicial proceeding –

    (a) in another part of His Majesty's dominions; or
    (b) in a British tribunal lawfully constituted in any place by sea or land outside His Majesty's dominions; or
    (c) in a tribunal of any foreign state,

shall, for the purposes of this section, be treated as a statement made in a judicial proceeding in England.

(5) Where, for the purposes of a judicial proceeding in England, a person is lawfully sworn under the authority of an Act of Parliament –

    (a) in any other part of His Majesty's dominions; or
    (b) before a British tribunal or a British officer in a foreign country, or within the jurisdiction of the Admiralty of England;

a statement made by such person so sworn as aforesaid (unless the Act of Parliament under which it was made otherwise specifically provides) shall be treated for the purposes of this section as having been made in the judicial proceedings in England for the purposes whereof it was made.

(6) The question whether a statement on which perjury is assigned was material is a question of law to be determined by the court of trial.

1A False unsworn statement under Evidence (Proceedings in Other Jurisdictions) Act 1975

If any person, in giving any testimony (either orally or in writing) otherwise than on oath, where required to do so by an order under section 2 of the Evidence (Proceedings in Other Jurisdictions) Act 1975, makes a statement –

(a) which he knows to be false in a material particular, or

(b) which is false in a material particular and which he does not believe to be true,

he shall be guilty of an offence and shall be liable on conviction on indictment to imprisonment for a term not exceeding two years or a fine or both.

2 False statements on oath made otherwise than in a judicial proceeding

If any person –

(1) being required or authorised by law to make any statement on oath for any purpose, and being lawfully sworn (otherwise than in a judicial proceeding) wilfully makes a statement which is material for that purpose and which he knows to be false or does not believe to be true; or

(2) wilfully uses any false affidavit for the purposes of the Bills of Sale Act 1878, as amended by any subsequent enactment,

he shall be guilty of a misdemeanour, and, on conviction thereof on indictment shall be liable to penal servitude for a term not exceeding seven years or to imprisonment, with or without hard labour, for a term not exceeding two years, or to a fine or to both such penal servitude or imprisonment and fine.

3 False statements, etc with reference to marriage

(1) If any person –

(a) for the purpose of procuring a marriage, or a certificate or licence for marriage, knowingly and wilfully makes a false oath, or makes or signs a false declaration, notice or certificate required under any Act of Parliament for the time being in force relating to marriage; or

(b) knowingly and wilfully makes, or knowingly and wilfully causes to be made, for the purpose of being inserted in any register of marriage, a false statement as to any particular required by law to be known and registered relating to any marriage; or

(c) forbids the issue of any certificate or licence for marriage by falsely representing himself to be a person whose consent to the marriage is required by law knowing such representation to be false; or

(d) with respect to a declaration made under section 16(1A) or 27B(2) of the Marriage Act 1949 –

(i) enters a caveat under subsection (2) of the said section 16, or

(ii) makes a statement mentioned in subsection(4) of the said 27B, which he knows to be false in a material particular,

he shall be guilty of a misdemeanour, and, on conviction thereof on indictment, shall be liable to penal servitude for a term not exceeding seven years or to imprisonment, with or without hard labour, for a term not exceeding two years, or to a fine or to both such penal servitude or imprisonment and fine and on summary conviction thereof shall be liable to a penalty not exceeding the prescribed sum.

(2) No prosecution for knowingly and wilfully making a false declaration for the purpose of procuring any marriage out of the district in which the parties or one of them dwell shall take place after the expiration of eighteen months from the solemnisation of the marriage to which the declaration refers.

4 False statements, etc as to births or deaths

(1) If any person –

(a) wilfully makes any false answer to any question put to him by any registrar of births or deaths relating to the particulars required to be registered concerning any birth or death, or wilfully gives to any such registrar any false information concerning any birth or death or the cause of any death; or

(b) wilfully makes any false certificate or declaration under or for the purposes of any Act relating to the registration of births or deaths, or, knowing any such certificate or declaration to be false,uses the same as true or gives or sends the same as true to any person; or

(c) wilfully makes, gives or uses any false statement or declaration as to a child born alive as having been still-born, or as to the body of a deceased person or a still-born child in any coffin, or falsely pretends that any child born alive was still-born; or

(d) makes any false statement with intent to have the same inserted in any register of births or deaths;

he shall be guilty of a misdemeanour and shall be liable –

(i) on conviction thereof on indictment, to penal servitude for a term not exceeding seven years, or to imprisonment, with or without hard labour, for a term not exceeding two years, or to a fine instead of either of the said punishments; and

(ii) on summary conviction thereof, to a penalty not exceeding the prescribed sum.

(2) A prosecution on indictment for an offence against this section shall not be commenced more than three years after the commission of the offence.

5 False statutory declarations and other false statements without oath

If any person knowingly and wilfully makes (otherwise than on oath) a statement false in a material particular and the statement is made –

(a) in a statutory declaration; or

(b) in an abstract, account, balance sheet, book, certificate, declaration, entry, estimate, inventory, notice, report, return, or other document which he is authorised or required to make, attest or verify, by any public general Act of Parliament for the time being in force; or

(c) in any oral declaration or oral answer which he is required to make by, under, or in pursuance of any public general Act of Parliament for the time being in force,

he shall be guilty of misdemeanour and shall be liable on conviction thereof on indictment to imprisonment, with or without hard labour, for any term not exceeding two years, or to a fine or to both such imprisonment and fine.

6 False declarations, etc to obtain registration, etc for carrying on a vocation

If any person –

(a) procures or attempts to procure himself to be registered on any register or roll kept under or in pursuance of any public general Act of Parliament for the time being in force of persons qualified by law to practise any vocation or calling; or
(b) procures or attempts to procure a certificate of the registration of any person on any such register or roll as aforesaid,

by wilfully making or producing or causing to be made or produced either verbally or in writing, any declaration, certificate, or representation which he knows to be false or fraudulent, he shall be guilty of misdemeanour and shall be liable on conviction thereof on indictment to imprisonment for any term not exceeding twelve months, or to a fine, or to both such imprisonment and fine.

7 Aiders, abettors, suborners, etc

(1) Every person who aids, abets, counsels, procures, or suborns another person to commit an offence against this Act shall be liable to be proceeded against, indicted, tried and punished as if he were a principal offender.

(2) Every person who incites another person to commit an offence against this Act shall be guilty of a misdemeanour, and, on conviction thereof on indictment, shall be liable to imprisonment, or to a fine, or to both such imprisonment and fine.

15 Interpretation, etc

(1) For the purposes of this Act, the forms and ceremonies used in administering an oath are immaterial, if the court or person before whom the oath is taken has power to administer an oath for the purpose of verifying the statements in question, and if the oath has been administered in a form and with ceremonies which the person taking the oath has accepted without objection, or has declared to be binding on him.

(2) In this Act –

The expression 'oath' includes 'affirmation' and 'declaration' and the expression 'swear' includes 'affirm' and 'declare'; and
The expression 'statutory declaration' means a declaration made by virtue of the Statutory Declarations Act 1835, or of any Act, Order in Council, rule or regulation applying or extending the provisions thereof.

[As amended by the Criminal Justice Act 1925, s28(1); Criminal Law Act 1967, s10(2), Schedule 3 Part III; Evidence (Proceedings in Other Jurisdictions) Act 1975, s8(1), Schedule 1; Administration of Justice Act 1977, ss8(3), 32(4), Schedule 5, Part III; Magistrates' Courts Act 1980, s32(2); Marriage (Prohibited Degrees of Relationship) Act 1986 s4.]

Official Secrets Act 1911
(1 & 2 Geo 5 c 28)

1 *Penalties for spying*

(1) If any person for any purpose prejudicial to the safety or interests of the State –

(a) approaches, inspects, passes over, or is in the neighbourhood of, or enters any prohibited place within the meaning of this Act; or

(b) makes any sketch, plan, model, or note which is calculated to be or might be or is intended to be directly or indirectly useful to an enemy; or

(c) obtains, collects, records, or publishes, or communicates to any other person any secret official code word, or pass word, or any sketch, plan, model, article or note, or other document or information which is calculated to be or might be or is intended to be directly or indirectly useful to an enemy;

he shall be guilty of felony.

(2) On a prosecution under this section, it shall not be necessary to show that the accused person was guilty of any particular act tending to show a purpose prejudicial to the safety or interests of the State, and, notwithstanding that no such act is proved against him, he may be convicted if, from the circumstances of the case, or his conduct, or his known character as proved, it appears that his purpose was a purpose prejudicial to the safety or interests of the State; and if any sketch, plan, model, article, note, document, or information relating to or used in any prohibited place within the meaning of this Act, or anything in such a place or any secret official code word or pass word, is made, obtained, collected, recorded, published, or communicated by any person other than a person acting under lawful authority, it shall be deemed to have been made, obtained, collected, recorded, published or communicated for a purpose prejudicial to the safety or interests of the State unless the contrary is proved.

3 *Definition of prohibited place*

For the purposes of this Act, the expression 'prohibited place' means –

(a) any work of defence, arsenal, naval or air force establishment or station, factory, dockyard, mine, minefield, camp, ship, or aircraft belonging to or occupied by or on behalf of His Majesty, or any telegraph, telephone, wireless or signal station, or office so belonging or occupied, and any place belonging to or occupied by or on behalf of His Majesty and used for the purpose of building, repairing, making or storing any munitions of war, or any sketches, plans, models, or documents relating thereto, or for the purpose of getting any metals, oil, or minerals of use in time of war; and

(b) any place not belonging to His Majesty where any munitions of war, or any sketches, models, plans or documents relating thereto, are being made, repaired, gotten, or stored under contract with, or with any person on behalf of, His Majesty, or otherwise on behalf of His Majesty; and

(c) any place belonging to or used for the purposes of His Majesty which is for the time being declared by order of a Secretary of State to be a prohibited place for the purposes of this section on the ground that information with respect thereto, or damage thereto, would be useful to an enemy; and

(d) any railway, road, way, or channel, or other means of communication by land or water (including any works or structures being part thereof or connected therewith), or any place used for gas, water, or electricity works or other works for purposes of a public character,or any place where any munitions of war, or any sketches, models, plans or documents relating thereto, are being made, repaired, or stored otherwise than on behalf of His Majesty, which is for the time being declared by order of a Secretary of State to be a prohibited place for the purposes of this section, on the ground that information with respect thereto, or the destruction or obstruction thereof, or interference therewith, would be useful to an enemy.

7 Penalty for harbouring spies

If any person knowingly harbours any person whom he knows, or has reasonable grounds for supposing, to be a person who is about to commit or has committed an offence under this Act, or knowingly permits to meet or assemble in any premises in his occupation or under his control any such persons, or if any person having harboured any such person, or permitted to meet or assemble in any premises in his occupation or under his control any such persons, wilfully omits or refuses to disclose to a superintendent of police any information which it is in his power to give in relation to any such person he shall be guilty of a misdemeanour.

[As amended by the Official Secrets Act 1920, ss10, 11(2), Schedules 1, 2.]

Official Secrets Act 1920
(10 & 11 Geo 5 c 75)

1 Unauthorised use of uniforms; falsification of reports ... personation, and false documents

(1) If any person for the purpose of gaining admission, or of assisting any other person to gain admission, to a prohibited place, within the meaning of the Official Secrets Act 1911 (hereinafter referred to as 'the principal Act'), or for any other purpose prejudicial to the safety or interests of the State within the meaning of the said Act –

(a) uses or wears, without lawful authority, any naval, military, air-force, police, or other official uniform, or any uniform so nearly resembling the same as to be calculated to deceive, or falsely represent himself to be a person who is or has been entitled to use or wear any such uniform; or

(b) orally, or in writing in any declaration or application, or in any document signed by him or on his behalf, knowingly makes or connives at the making of any false statement or any omission; or

(c) tampers with any passport or any naval, military, air-force, police, or official pass, permit, certificate, licence, or other document of a similar character (hereinafter in this section referred to as an official document), or has in his possession any forged, altered, or irregular official document; or

(d) personates, or falsely represents himself to be a person holding, or in the employment of a person holding office under His Majesty, or to be or not to be a person to whom an official document or secret official code word, or pass word, has been duly issued or communicated, or with intent to obtain an official document, secret official code word or pass word, whether for himself or any other person, knowingly makes any false statement; or

(e) uses, or has in his possession or under his control, without the authority of the Government Department or the authority concerned, any die, seal, or stamp of or belonging to, or used, made or provided by any Government Department, or by any diplomatic, naval, military, or air force authority appointed by or acting under the authority of His Majesty, or any die, seal or stamp so nearly resembling any such die, seal or stamp as to be calculated to deceive, or counterfeits any such die, seal or stamp, or uses, or has in his possession, or under his control, any such counterfeited die, seal or stamp;

he shall be guilty of a misdemeanour.

(2) If any person –

(a) retains for any purpose prejudicial to the safety or interests of the State any official document, whether or not completed or issued for use, when he has no right to retain it or when it is contrary to his duty to retain it, or fails to comply with any directions issued by any Government Department or any person authorised by such department with regard to the return or disposal thereof; or

(b) allows any other person to have possession of any official document issued for his use alone, or communicates any secret official code word or pass word so issued, or, without lawful authority or excuse, has in his possession any official document or secret official code word or pass word issued for the use of some person other than himself, or on obtaining possession of any official document by finding or otherwise, neglects or fails to restore it to the person or authority by whom or for whose use it was issued, or to a police constable; or

(c) without lawful authority or excuse, manufactures or sells, or has in his possession for sale any such die, seal or stamp as aforesaid;

he shall be guilty of a misdemeanour.

(3) In the case of any prosecution under this section involving the proof of a purpose prejudicial to the safety or interests of the State, subsection (2) of section one of the principal Act shall apply in like manner as it applies to prosecutions under that section.

3 Interfering with officers of the police or members of His Majesty's forces

No person in the vicinity of any prohibited place shall obstruct, knowingly mislead or otherwise interfere with or impede, the chief officer or a superintendent or other officer of police, or any member of His Majesty's forces engaged on guard, sentry, patrol, or other similar duty in relation to the prohibited place, and, if any person acts in contravention of, or fails to comply with, this provision, he shall be guilty of a misdemeanour.

6 Duty of giving information as to commission of offences

(1) Where a chief officer of police is satisfied that there is reasonable ground for suspecting that an offence under section 1 of the principal Act has been committed and for believing that any person is able to furnish information as to the offence or suspected offence, he may apply to a Secretary of State for permission to exercise the powers conferred by this subsection and, if such permission is granted, he may authorise a superintendent of police, or any police officer not below the rank of inspector, to require the person believed to be able to furnish information to give any information in his power relating to the offence or suspected offence, and, if so required and on tender of his reasonable expenses, to attend at such reasonable time and place as may be specified by the superintendent or other officer; and if a person required in pursuance of such an authorisation to give information, or to attend as aforesaid, fails to comply with any such requirement or knowingly gives false information, he shall be guilty of a misdemeanour.

(2) Where a chief officer of police has reasonable grounds to believe that the case is one of great emergency and that in the interest of the State immediate action is necessary, he may exercise the powers conferred by the last foregoing subsection without applying for or being granted the permission of a Secretary of State, but if he does so shall forthwith report the circumstances to the Secretary of State.

(3) References in this section to a chief officer of police shall be construed as including references to any other officer of police expressly authorised by a chief officer of police to act on his behalf for the purposes of this section when by reason of illness, absence, or other cause he is unable to do so.

7 Attempts, incitements, etc

Any person who attempts to commit any offence under the principal Act or this Act, or solicits or incites or endeavours to persuade another person to commit an offence, or aids or abets and does any act preparatory to the commission of an offence under the principal Act or this Act, shall be guilty of a felony or a misdemeanour or a summary offence according as the offence in question is a felony, a misdemeanour or a summary offence, and on conviction shall be liable to the same punishment, and to be proceeded against in the same manner, as if he had committed the offence.

[As amended by the Official Secrets Act 1939, s1; Forgery and Counterfeiting Act 1981, s30, Schedule, Part I.]

Infant Life (Preservation) Act 1929
(19 & 29 Geo 5 c 34)

1 Punishment for child destruction

(1) Subject as hereinafter in this subsection provided, any person who, with intent to destroy the life of a child capable of being born alive, by any wilful act causes a child to die before it has an existence independent of its mother, shall be guilty of felony, to wit, of child destruction, and shall be liable on conviction thereof on indictment to penal servitude for life:

Provided that no person shall be found guilty of an offence under this section unless it is proved that the act which caused the death of the child was not done in good faith for the purpose only of preserving the life of the mother.

(2) For the purposes of this Act, evidence that a woman had at any material time been pregnant for a period of twenty-eight weeks or more shall be prima facie proof that she was at that time pregnant of a child capable of being born alive.

2 Prosecution of offences

(2) Where upon the trial of any person for the murder or manslaughter of any child, or for infanticide, or for an offence under section 58 of the Offences against the Person Act 1861 (which relates to administering drugs or using instruments to procure abortion), the jury are of opinion that the person charged is not guilty of murder, manslaughter or infanticide, or of an offence under the said section 58, as the case may be, but that he is shown by the evidence to be guilty of the felony of child destruction, the jury may find him guilty of that felony, and thereupon the person convicted shall be liable to be punished as if he had been convicted upon an indictment for child destruction.

(3) Where upon the trial of any person for the felony of child destruction the jury are of opinion that the person charged is not guilty of that felony, but that he is shown by the evidence to be guilty of an offence under the said section 58 of the Offences against the Person Act 1861, the jury may find him guilty of that offence, and thereupon the person convicted shall be liable to be punished as if he had been convicted upon an indictment under that section.

[As amended by the Criminal Law Act 1967, s10(2), Schedule 3, Pt II; Police and Criminal Evidence Act 1984, s119(2), Schedule 7, Pt V.]

Children and Young Persons Act 1933
(23 Geo 5 c 12)

1 Cruelty to persons under sixteen

(1) If any person who has attained the age of sixteen years and has responsibility for any child or young person under that age, wilfully assaults, ill-treats, neglects, abandons, or

exposes him, or causes or procures him to be assaulted, ill-treated, neglected, abandoned, or exposed, in a manner likely to cause him unnecessary suffering or injury to health (including injury to or loss of sight or hearing, or limb, or organ of the body, and any mental derangement), that person shall be guilty of a misdemeanour, and shall be liable –

(a) on conviction on indictment, to a fine, or alternatively, or in addition thereto, to imprisonment for any term not exceeding ten years;

(b) on summary conviction, to a fine not exceeding the prescribed sum, or alternatively, or in addition thereto, to imprisonment for any term not exceeding six months.

(2) For the purposes of this section –

(a) a parent or other person legally liable to maintain a child or young person, or the legal guardian of a child or young person, shall be deemed to have neglected him in a manner likely to cause injury to his health if he has failed to provide adequate food, clothing, medical aid or lodging for him, or if, having been unable otherwise to provide such food, clothing, medical aid or lodging, he has failed to take steps to procure it to be provided under the enactments applicable in that behalf;

(b) where it is proved that the death of an infant under three years of age was caused by suffocation (not being suffocation caused by disease or the presence of any foreign body in the throat or air passages of the infant) while the infant was in bed with some other person who has attained the age of sixteen years, that other person shall, if he was, when he went to bed, under the influence of drink, be deemed to have neglected the infant in a manner likely to cause injury to its health.

(3) A person may be convicted of an offence under this section –

(a) notwithstanding that actual suffering or injury to health, or the likelihood of actual suffering or injury to health was obviated by the action of another person;

(b) notwithstanding the death of the child or young person in question.

(7) Nothing in this section shall be construed as affecting the right of any parent, or (subject to section 548 of the Education Act 1996) any other person, having the lawful control or charge of a child or young person to administer punishment to him.

38 Evidence of child of tender years

(2) If any child whose evidence is received unsworn in any proceedings for an offence by virtue of section 52 of the Criminal Justice Act 1991 wilfully gives false evidence in such circumstances that he would, if the evidence had been given on oath, have been guilty of perjury, he shall be liable on summary conviction to be dealt with as if he had been summarily convicted of an indictable offence punishable in the case of an adult with imprisonment.

50 Age of criminal responsibility

It shall be conclusively presumed that no child under the age of ten years can be guilty of any offence.

53 *Punishment of certain grave crimes*

(1) A person convicted of an offence who appears to the court to have been under the age of eighteen years at the time the offence was committed shall not, if he is convicted of murder, be sentenced to imprisonment for life, nor shall sentence of death be pronounced on or recorded against any such person; but in lieu thereof the court shall (notwithstanding anything in this or any other Act) sentence him to be detained during Her Majesty's pleasure, and if so sentenced he shall be liable to be detained in such place and under such conditions –

(a) as the Secretary of State may direct, or
(b) as the Secretary of State may arrange with any person.

(2) Subsection (3) below applies –

(a) where a person of at least 10 but not more than 17 years is convicted on indictment of –

(i) any offence punishable in the case of an adult with imprisonment for fourteen years or more, not being an offence the sentence for which is fixed by law, or
(ii) an offence under section 14 of the Sexual Offences Act 1956 (indecent assault on a woman);

(b) where a young person is convicted of –

(i) an offence under section 1 of the Road Traffic Act 1988 (causing death by dangerous driving), or
(ii) an offence under section 3A of the Road Traffic Act 1988 (causing death by careless driving while under influence of drink or drugs).

(3) Where this subsection applies, then, if the court is of opinion that none of the other methods in which the case may legally be dealt with is suitable, the court may sentence the offender to be detained for such period not exceeding the maximum term of imprisonment with which the offence is punishable in the case of an adult as may be specified in the sentence; and where such a sentence has been passed the child or young person shall, during that period, be liable to be detained in such place and on such conditions –

(a) as the Secretary of State may direct, or
(b) as the Secretary of State may arrange with any person.

(4) A person detained pursuant to the directions or arrangements made by the Secretary of State under this section shall, while so detained, be deemed to be in legal custody.

[As amended by the National Assistance (Adaptation of Enactments) Regulations 1950, the Children and Young Persons Act 1963, ss16(1), 64(1), (3), Schedule 3, para 1, Schedule 5; Murder (Abolition of Death Penalty) Act 1965, s1(5), (4); Criminal Law Act 1967, s10, Schedule 2, para 13(1), Schedule 3, Part III; Children Act 1975, s108(1)(b), Schedule 4, Part III; Magistrates' Courts Act 1980, s32(2); Criminal Justice Act 1988, ss34(1), 45, 170(2), Schedule 16; Children Act 1989, s108(4), (5), Schedule 12, para 2, Schedule 13, para 2; Criminal Justice Act 1991, s100, Schedule 11, para 1; Criminal Justice and Public Order Act 1994, s16; School Standards and Framework Act 1998, s140(1), Schedule 30, para 1.]

Incitement to Disaffection Act 1934
(24 & 25 Geo 5 c 56)

1 Penalty on persons endeavouring to seduce members of His Majesty's forces from their duty or allegiance

If any person maliciously and advisedly endeavours to seduce any members of His Majesty's forces from his duty or allegiance to His Majesty, he shall be guilty of an offence under this Act.

Vagrancy Act 1935
(25 & 26 Geo 5 c 20)

1 Amendment of 5 Geo 4 c 38, s4

(1) So much of section 4 of the Vagrancy Act 1824, as enacts that a person wandering abroad and lodging in any barn or outhouse, or in any deserted or unoccupied building, or in the open air, or under a tent, or in any cart or waggon, not having any visible means of subsistence, and not giving a good account of himself, shall be deemed a rogue and vagabond within the meaning of that Act, shall have effect subject to the following provisions of this section.

(3) A person wandering abroad and lodging as aforesaid shall not be deemed by virtue of the said enactment a rogue and vagabond within the meaning of the said Act unless it is proved either –

(a) that, in relation to the occasion on which he lodged as aforesaid, he had been directed to a reasonably accessible place of shelter and failed to apply for, or refused, accommodation there;

(b) that he is a person who persistently wanders abroad and, notwithstanding that a place of shelter is reasonably accessible, lodges or attempts to lodge as aforesaid; or

(c) that by, or in the course of, lodging as aforesaid he caused damage to property, infection with vermin, or other offensive consequence, or that he lodged as aforesaid in such circumstances as to appear to be likely so to do.

In this subsection the expression 'a place to shelter' means a place where provision is regularly made for giving (free of charge) accommodation for the night to such persons as apply therefor.

(4) The reference in the said enactment to a person lodging under a tent or in a cart or waggon shall not be deemed to include a person lodging under a tent or in a cart or waggon with or in which he travels.

[As amended by the State Law Revision Act 1950.]

Infanticide Act 1938
(1 & 2 Geo 6 c 36)

1 Offence of infanticide

(1) Where a woman by any wilful act or omission causes the death of her child being a child under the age of twelve months, but at the time of the act or omission the balance of her mind was disturbed by reason of her not having fully recovered from the effect of giving birth to the child or by reason of the effect of lactation consequent upon the birth of the child, then, notwithstanding that the circumstances were such that but for this Act the offence would have amounted to murder, she shall be guilty of felony, to wit of infanticide, and may for such offence be dealt with and punished as if she had been guilty of the offence of manslaughter of the child.

(2) Where upon the trial of a woman for the murder of her child, being a child under the age of twelve months, the jury are of opinion that she by any wilful act or omission caused its death, but that at the time of the act or omission the balance of her mind was disturbed by reason of her not having fully recovered from the effect of giving birth to the child or by reason of the effect of lactation consequent upon the birth of the child, then the jury may, notwithstanding that the circumstances were such that but for the provisions of this Act they might have returned a verdict of murder, return in lieu thereof a verdict of infanticide

(3) Nothing in this Act shall affect the power of the jury upon an indictment for the murder of a child to return a verdict of manslaughter, or a verdict of guilty but insane.

[As amended by the Criminal Law Act 1967, s10(2), Schedule 3, Part III.]

Marriage Act 1949
(12, 13 & 14 Geo 6 c 76)

75 Offences relating to solemnisation of marriages

(1) Any person who knowingly and wilfully –

(a) solemnises a marriage at any other time than between the hours of eight in the forenoon and six in the afternoon (not being a marriage by special licence, a marriage according to the usages of the Society of Friends or a marriage between two persons professing the Jewish religion according to the usages of the Jews);
(b) solemnises a marriage to the rites of the Church of England without banns of matrimony having been duly published (not being a marriage solemnised on the authority of a special licence, a common licence or a certificate of a superintendent registrar);
(c) solemnises a marriage according to the said rites (not being a marriage by special licence or a marriage in pursuance of section 26(1)(dd) of this Act) in any place other than a church or other building in which banns may be published;
(d) solemnises a marriage according to the said rites falsely pretending to be in Holy Orders;

shall be guilty of felony and shall be liable to imprisonment for a term not exceeding fourteen years.

(2) Any person who knowingly and wilfully –

(a) solemnises a marriage (not being a marriage by special licence, a marriage according to the usages of the Society of Friends or a marriage between two persons professing the Jewish religion according to the usages of the Jews) in any place other than –

(i) a church or other building in which marriages may be solemnised according to the rites of the Church of England, or

(ii) the registered building, office, approved premises or person's residence specified as the place where the marriage was to be solemnised in the notice of marriage and certificate required under Part III of this Act;

(aa) solemnises a marriage purporting to be in pursuance of section 26(1)(bb) of this Act on premises that are not approved premises;

(b) solemnises a marriage in any such registered building as aforesaid (not being a marriage in the presence of an authorised person) in the absence of a registrar of the district in which the registered building is situated;

(bb) solemnises a marriage in pursuance of section 26(1)(dd) of this Act, otherwise than according to the rites of the Church of England, in the absence of a registrar of the registration district in which the place where the marriage is solemnised is situated;

(c) solemnises a marriage in the office of a superintendent registrar in the absence of a registrar of the district in which the office is situated;

(cc) solemnises a marriage on approved premises in pursuance of section 26(1)(bb) of this Act in the absence of a registrar of the district in which the premises are situated;

(d) solemnises a marriage on the authority of a certificate of a superintendent registrar (not being a marriage by licence) within twenty-one days after the day on which the notice of marriage was entered in the marriage notice book; or

(e) solemnises a marriage on the authority of a certificate of a superintendent registrar after the expiration of the period which is, in relation to that marriage, the applicable period for the purposes of section 33 of this Act;

shall be guilty of felony and shall be liable to imprisonment for a term not exceeding five years.

(3) A superintendent registrar who knowingly and wilfully –

(a) issues any certificate for marriage (not being a marriage by licence) before the expiration of twenty-one days from the day on which the notice of marriage was entered in the marriage notice book, or issues a certificate for marriage by licence before the expiration of one whole day from the said day on which the notice was entered as aforesaid;

(b) issues any certificate or licence for marriage after the expiration of the period which is, in relation to that marriage, the applicable period for the purposes of section 33 of this Act;

(c) issues any certificate the issue of which has been forbidden under section 30 of this Act by any person entitled to forbid the issue of such a certificate; or

(d) solemnises or permits to be solemnised in his office or, in the case of a marriage in pursuance of s26(1)(bb) or (dd) of this Act, in any other place any marriage which is void by virtue of any of the provisions of Part III of this Act;

shall be guilty of felony and shall be liable to imprisonment for a term not exceeding five years.

(4) No prosecution under this section shall be commenced after the expiration of three years from the commission of the offence.

(5) Any reference in subsection (2) of this section to a registered building shall be construed as including a reference to any chapel registered under section 70 of this Act.

[**NB** Section 26(1)(bb) refers to a marriage on approved premises, ie premises approved by a local authority for the solemnisation of marriages. Section 26(1)(dd) refers to a marriage, other than a marriage according to the usages of the Society of Friends or a marriage between two person professing the Jewish religion according to the usages of the Jews, of a person who is house-bound or is a detained person at the place where he or she usually resides.]

76 *Offences relating to registration of marriages*

(1) Any person who refuses or without reasonable cause omits to register any marriage which he is required by this Act to register, and any person having the custody of a marriage register book or a certified copy of a marriage register book or part thereof who carelessly loses or injures the said book or copy or carelessly allows the said book or copy to be injured while in his keeping, shall be liable on summary conviction to a fine not exceeding level 3 of the standard scale.

(2) Where any person who is required under Part IV of this Act to make and deliver to a superintendent registrar a certified copy of entries made in the marriage register book kept by him, or a certificate that no entries have been made therein since the date of the last certified copy, refuses to deliver any such copy or certificate, or fails to deliver any such copy or certificate during any month in which he is required to do so, he shall be liable on summary conviction to a fine not exceeding level 1 on the standard scale.

(3) Any registrar who knowingly and wilfully registers any marriage which is void by virtue of any of the provisions of Part III of this Act shall be guilty of felony and shall be liable to imprisonment for a term not exceeding five years ...

(5) Subject as may be prescribed, a superintendent registrar may prosecute any person guilty of an offence under either of the said subsections committed within his district ...

(6) No prosecution under subsection (3) of this section shall be commenced after the expiration of three years from the commission of the offence.

[As amended by the Criminal Justice Act 1982, ss38, 46; Marriage Act 1983, s1(7), Schedule 1, para 20; Marriage Act 1994, s1(3), Schedule, para 7; Deregulation (Validity of Civil Preliminaries to Marriage) Order 1997, art 2(1), (4).]

Prevention of Crime Act 1953
(1 & 2 Eliz 2 c 14)

1 Prohibition of the carrying of offensive weapons without lawful authority or reasonable excuse

(1) Any person who without lawful authority or reasonable excuse, the proof whereof shall lie on him, has with him in any public place any offensive weapon shall be guilty of an offence, and shall be liable –

(a) on summary conviction, to imprisonment for a term not exceeding six months or a fine not exceeding the prescribed sum, or both;

(b) on conviction on indictment, to imprisonment for a term not exceeding four years or a fine or both.

(2) Where any person is convicted of an offence under subsection (1) of this section the court may make an order for the forfeiture or disposal of any weapon in respect of which the offence was committed.

(4) In this section 'public place' includes any highway and any other premises or place to which at the material time the public have or are permitted to have access, whether on payment or otherwise; and 'offensive weapon' means any article made or adapted for use for causing injury to the person, or intended by the person having it with him for such use by him or by some other person.

[As amended by the Criminal Law Act 1977, s32(1); Magistrates' Courts Act 1980, s32(2); Police and Criminal Evidence Act 1984, ss26(1), 119(2), Schedule 7, Part I; Public Order Act 1986, s40(2), Schedule 2, para 2; Criminal Justice Act 1988, s46(1), (3); Offensive Weapons Act 1996, s2(1), (4).]

Sexual Offences Act 1956
(4 & 5 Eliz 2 c 69)

1 Rape of woman or man

(1) It is an offence for a man to rape a woman or another man.

(2) A man commits rape if –

(a) he has sexual intercourse with a person (whether vaginal or anal) who at the time of the intercourse does not consent to it; and

(b) at the time he knows that the person does not consent to the intercourse or is reckless as to whether that person consents to it.

(3) A man also commits rape if he induces a married woman to have sexual intercourse with him by impersonating her husband.

(4) Subsection (2) applies for the purpose of any enactment.

2 Procurement of woman by threats

(1) It is an offence for a person to procure a woman, by threats or intimidation, to have sexual intercourse in any part of the world.

3 Procurement of woman by false pretences

(1) It is an offence for a person to procure a woman, by false pretences or false representations, to have sexual intercourse in any part of the world.

4 Administering drugs to obtain or facilitate intercourse

(1) It is an offence for a person to apply or administer to, or cause to be taken by, a woman any drug, matter or thing with intent to stupefy or overpower her so as thereby to enable any man to have unlawful sexual intercourse with her.

5 Intercourse with girl under thirteen

It is a felony for a man to have unlawful sexual intercourse with a girl under the age of thirteen.

6 Intercourse with girl [under] sixteen

(1) It is an offence, subject to the exceptions mentioned in this section, for a man to have unlawful sexual intercourse with a girl under the age of sixteen.

(2) Where a marriage is invalid under section 2 of the Marriage Act 1949, or section 1 of the Age of Marriage Act 1929 (the wife being a girl under the age of sixteen), the invalidity does not make the husband guilty of an offence under this section because he has sexual intercourse with her, if he believes her to be his wife and has reasonable cause for the belief.

(3) A man is not guilty of an offence under this section because he has unlawful sexual intercourse with a girl under the age of sixteen, if he is under the age of twenty-four and has not previously been charged with a like offence, and he believes her to be of the age of sixteen or over and has reasonable cause for the belief.

In this subsection, 'a like offence' means an offence under this section or an attempt to commit one, or an offence under paragraph (1) of section 5 of the Criminal Law Amendment Act 1885 (the provision replaced for England and Wales by this section).

7 Intercourse with defective

(1) It is an offence, subject to the exception mentioned in this section, for a man to have unlawful sexual intercourse with a woman who is a defective.

(2) A man is not guilty of an offence under this section because he had unlawful sexual intercourse with a woman if he does not know and has no reason to suspect her to be a defective.

9 Procurement of defective

(1) It is an offence, subject to the exception mentioned in this section, for a person to procure a woman who is a defective to have unlawful sexual intercourse in any part of the world.

(2) A person is not guilty of an offence under this section because he procures a defective to have unlawful sexual intercourse, if he does not know and has no reason to suspect her of being a defective.

10 Incest by a man

(1) It is an offence for a man to have sexual intercourse with a woman whom he knows to be his grand-daughter, daughter, sister or mother.

(2) In the foregoing subsection 'sister' includes half-sister, and for the purposes of that subsection any expression importing a relationship between two people shall be taken to apply notwithstanding that the relationship is not traced through lawful wedlock.

11 Incest by a woman

(1) It is an offence for a woman of the age of sixteen or over to permit a man whom she knows to be her grandfather, father, brother or son to have sexual intercourse with her by her consent.

(2) In the foregoing subsection 'brother' includes half-brother, and for the purposes of that subsection any expression importing a relationship between two people shall be taken to apply notwithstanding that the relationship is not traced through lawful wedlock.

12 Buggery

(1) It is felony for a person to commit buggery with another person otherwise than in the circumstances described in subsection (1A) below or with an animal.

(1A) The circumstances referred to in subsection (1) are that the act of buggery takes place in private and both parties have attained the age of eighteen.

(1B) An act of buggery by one man with another shall not be treated as taking place in private if it takes place –

(a) when more than two persons take part or are present; or
(b) in a lavatory to which the public have or are permitted to have access, whether on payment or otherwise.

(1C) In any proceedings against a person for buggery with another person it shall be for the prosecutor to prove that the act of buggery took place otherwise than in private or that one of the parties to it had not attained the age of eighteen.

13 Indecency between men

It is an offence for a man to commit an act of gross indecency with another man, whether in public or private, or to be a party to the commission by a man of an act of gross indecency with another man, or to procure the commission by a man of an act of gross indecency with another man.

14 Indecent assault on a woman

(1) It is an offence, subject to the exception mentioned in subsection (3) of this section, for a person to make an indecent assault on a woman.

(2) A girl under the age of sixteen cannot in law give any consent which would prevent an act being an assault for the purposes of this section.

(3) Where a marriage is invalid under section 2 of the Marriage Act 1949 or section 1 of the Age of Marriage Act 1929 (the wife being a girl under the age of sixteen), the invalidity does not make the husband guilty of any offence under this section by reason of her incapacity to consent while under that age, if he believes her to be his wife and has reasonable cause for the belief.

(4) A woman who is a defective cannot in law give any consent which would prevent an act being an assault for the purposes of this section, but a person is only to be treated as guilty of an indecent assault on a defective by reason of that incapacity to consent, if that person knew or had reason to suspect her to be a defective.

15 Indecent assault on a man

(1) It is an offence for a person to make an indecent assault on a man.

(2) A boy under the age of sixteen cannot in law give any consent which would prevent an act being an assault for the purposes of this section.

(3) A man who is a defective cannot in law give any consent which would prevent an act being an assault for the purposes of this section, but a person is only to be treated as guilty of an indecent assault on a defective by reason of that incapacity to consent, if that person knew or had reason to suspect him to be a defective.

16 Assault with intent to commit buggery

(1) It is an offence for a person to assault another person with intent to commit buggery.

17 Abduction of woman by force or for the sake of her property

(1) It is felony for a person to take away or detain a woman against her will with the intention that she shall marry or have unlawful sexual intercourse with that or any other person, if she is so taken away or detained either by force or for the sake of her property or expectations of property.

(2) In the foregoing subsection, the reference to a woman's expectations of property relates to property of a person to whom she is next of kin or one of the next of kin, and 'property' includes any interest in property.

19 Abduction of unmarried girl under eighteen from parent or guardian

(1) It is an offence, subject to the exception mentioned in this section, for a person to take an unmarried girl under the age of eighteen out of the possession of her parent or guardian against his will, if she is so taken with the intention that she shall have unlawful sexual intercourse with men or with a particular man.

(2) A person is not guilty of an offence under this section because he takes such a girl out of the possession of her parent or guardian as mentioned above, if he believes her to be of the age of eighteen or over and has reasonable cause for the belief.

(3) In this section 'guardian' means any person having parental responsibility for or care of the girl.

20 Abduction of unmarried girl under sixteen from parent or guardian

(1) It is an offence for a person acting without lawful authority or excuse to take an unmarried girl under the age of sixteen out of the possession of her parent or guardian against his will.

(2) In the foregoing subsection 'guardian' means any person having parental responsibility for or care of the girl.

21 Abduction of defective from parent or guardian

(1) It is an offence, subject to the exception mentioned in this section, for a person to take a woman who is a defective out of the possession of her parent or guardian against his will, if she is so taken with the intention that she shall have unlawful sexual intercourse with men or with a particular man.

(2) A person is not guilty of an offence under this section because he takes such a woman out of the possession of her parent or guardian as mentioned above, if he does not know and has no reason to suspect her to be a defective.

(3) In this section 'guardian' means any person having parental responsibility for or care of the woman.

22 Causing prostitution of women

(1) It is an offence for a person –
    (a) to procure a woman to become, in any part of the world, a common prostitute; or
    (b) to procure a woman to leave the United Kingdom, intending her to become an inmate of or frequent a brothel elsewhere; or
    (c) to procure a woman to leave her usual place of abode in the United Kingdom, intending her to become an inmate of or frequent a brothel in any part of the world for the purposes of prostitution.

23 *Procuration of girl under twenty-one*

(1) It is an offence for a person to procure a girl under the age of twenty-one to have unlawful sexual intercourse in any part of the world with a third person.

24 *Detention of woman in brothel or other premises*

(1) It is an offence for a person to detain a woman against her will on any premises with the intention that she shall have unlawful sexual intercourse with men or with a particular man, or to detain a woman against her will in a brothel.

(2) Where a woman is on any premises for the purpose of having unlawful sexual intercourse or is in a brothel, a person shall be deemed for the purpose of the foregoing subsection to detain her there if, with the intention of compelling or inducing her to remain there, he either withholds from her her clothes or any other property belonging to her or threatens her with legal proceedings in the event of her taking away clothes provided for her by him or on his directions.

(3) A woman shall not be liable to any legal proceedings, whether civil or criminal, for taking away or being found in possession of any clothes she needed to enable her to leave premises on which she was for the purpose of having unlawful sexual intercourse or to leave a brothel.

25 *Permitting girl under thirteen to use premises for intercourse*

It is a felony for a person who is the owner or occupier of any premises, or who has, or acts or assists in, the management or control of any premises, to induce or knowingly suffer a girl under the age of thirteen to resort to or be on those premises for the purpose of having unlawful sexual intercourse with men or with a particular man.

26 *Permitting girl [under] sixteen to use premises for intercourse*

It is an offence for a person who is the owner or occupier of any premises, or who has, or acts or assists in, the management or control of any premises, to induce or knowingly suffer a girl under the age of sixteen, to resort to or be on those premises for the purpose of having unlawful sexual intercourse with men or with a particular man.

27 *Permitting defective to use premises for intercourse*

(1) It is an offence, subject to the exception mentioned in this section, for a person who is the owner or occupier of any premises, or who has, or acts or assists in, the management or control of any premises, to induce or knowingly suffer a woman who is a defective to resort to or be on those premises for the purpose of having unlawful intercourse with men or with a particular man.

(2) A person is not guilty of an offence under this section because he induces or knowingly suffers a defective to resort to or be on any premises for the purpose mentioned, if he does not know and has no reason to suspect her to be a defective.

28 Causing or encouraging prostitution of, intercourse with or indecent assault on, girl under sixteen

(1) It is an offence for a person to cause or encourage the prostitution of, or the commission of unlawful sexual intercourse with, or of an indecent assault on, a girl under the age of sixteen for whom he is responsible.

(2) Where a girl has become a prostitute, or has unlawful sexual intercourse, or has been indecently assaulted, a person shall be deemed for the purposes of this section to have caused or encouraged it, if he knowingly allowed her to consort with, or to enter or continue in the employment of, any prostitute or person of known immoral character.

(3) The persons who are to be treated for the purposes of this section as responsible for a girl are (subject to subsection (4) of this section) –

(a) her parents;
(b) any person who is not a parent of hers but who has parental responsibility for her; and
(c) any person who has care of her.

(4) An individual falling within subsection 3(a) or (b) of this section is not to be treated as responsible for a girl if –

(a) a residence order under the Children Act 1989 is in force with respect to her and he is not named in the order as the person with whom she is to live; or
(b) a care order under that Act is in force with respect to her.

(5) If, on a charge of an offence against a girl under this section, the girl appears to the court to have been under the age of sixteen at the time of the offence charged, she shall be presumed for the purposes of this section to have been so, unless the contrary is proved.

29 Causing or encouraging prostitution of defective

(1) It is an offence, subject to the exception mentioned in this section, for a person to cause or encourage the prostitution in any part of the world of a woman who is a defective.

(2) A person is not guilty of an offence under this section because he causes or encourages the prostitution of such a woman, if he does not know and has no reason to suspect her to be a defective.

30 Man living on earnings of prostitution

(1) It is an offence for a man knowingly to live wholly or in part on the earnings of prostitution.

(2) For the purposes of this section a man who lives with or is habitually in the company of a prostitute, or who exercises control, direction or influence over a prostitute's movements in a way which shows he is aiding, abetting or compelling her prostitution with others, shall be presumed to be knowingly living on the earnings of prostitution, unless he proves the contrary.

31 Woman exercising control over prostitute

It is an offence for a woman for purposes of gain to exercise control, direction or influence over a prostitute's movement in a way which shows she is aiding, abetting or compelling her prostitution.

32 Solicitation by men

It is an offence for a man persistently to solicit or importune in a public place for immoral purposes.

33 Keeping a brothel

It is an offence for a person to keep a brothel, or to manage, or act or assist in the management of, a brothel.

34 Landlord letting premises for use as brothel

It is an offence for the lessor or landlord of any premises or his agent to let the whole or part of the premises with the knowledge that it is to be used, in whole or in part, as a brothel, or, where the whole or part of the premises is used as a brothel, to be wilfully a party to that use continuing.

35 Tenant permitting premises to be used as brothel

(1) It is an offence for the tenant or occupier, or person in charge, of any premises knowingly to permit the whole or part of the premises to be used as a brothel.

(2) Where the tenant or occupier of any premises is convicted (whether under this section or, for an offence committed before the commencement of this Act, under section 13 of the Criminal Law Amendment Act 1885) of knowingly permitting the whole or part of the premises to be used as a brothel, the First Schedule of this Act shall apply to enlarge the rights of the lessor or landlord with respect to the assignment or determination of the lease or other contract under which the premises are held by the person convicted.

(3) Where the tenant or occupier of any premises is so convicted, or was so convicted under the said section 13 before the commencement of this Act, and either –

(a) the lessor or landlord, after having the conviction brought to his notice, fails or failed to exercise his statutory rights in relation to the lease or contract under which the premises are or were held by the person convicted; or

(b) the lessor or landlord, after exercising his statutory rights so as to determine that lease or contract, grants or granted a new lease or enters or entered into a new contract of tenancy of the premises to, with or for the benefit of the same person, without having all reasonable provisions to prevent the recurrence of the offence inserted in the new lease or contract;

then, if subsequently an offence under this section is committed in respect of the premises during the subsistence of the lease or contract referred to in paragraph (a) of this subsection or (where paragraph (b) applies) during the subsistence of the new lease or contract, the lessor landlord shall be deemed to be a party to that offence unless he shows that he took all reasonable steps to prevent the recurrence of the offence.

Reference in this subsection to the statutory rights of a lessor or landlord refer to his rights under the First Schedule to this Act or under subsection (1) of section 5 of the Criminal Law Amendment Act 1912 (the provision replaced for England and Wales by that Schedule).

36 Tenant permitting premises to be used for prostitution

It is an offence for the tenant or occupier of any premises knowingly to permit the whole or part of the premises to be used for the purposes of habitual prostitution.

44 Meaning of 'sexual intercourse'

Where, on the trial of any offence under this Act, it is necessary to prove sexual intercourse (whether natural or unnatural), it shall not be necessary to prove the completion of the intercourse by the emission of seed, but the intercourse shall be deemed complete upon proof of penetration only.

45 Meaning of defective

In this Act 'defective' means a person suffering from a state of arrested or incomplete development of mind which includes severe impairment of intelligence and social functioning.

46 Use of words 'man', 'boy', 'woman' and 'girl'

The use in any provision of this Act of the word 'man' without the addition of the word 'boy', or vice versa, shall not prevent the provision applying to any person to whom it would have applied if both words had been used, and similarly with the words 'woman' and 'girl'.

46A Meaning of 'parental responsibility'

In this Act 'parental responsibility' has the same meaning as in the Children Act 1989.

[NB 'Parental responsibility' is defined in s3 of the 1989 Act. Section 3(1) stipulates: 'In this Act "parental responsibility" means all the rights, duties, powers, responsibilities and authority which by law a parent of a child has in relation to the child and his property.']

47 Proof of exceptions

Where in any of the foregoing sections the description of an offence is expressed to be subject to exceptions mentioned in the section, proof of the exception is to lie on the person relying on it.

[As amended by the Mental Health Act 1959, s127(1)(a), (b); Criminal Law Act 1967, s10(1), Schedule 2, para 14; Children Act 1975, s108(1)(b), Schedule 4, Part I; Mental

Health (Amendment) Act 1982, s65(1), Schedule 3, Part I, para 29; Children Act 1989, s108(4), Schedule 12, paras 11, 12, 13, 17; Criminal Justice and Public Order Act 1994, ss142, 143, 168(1), (3), Schedule 9, para 2, Schedule 11.]

Homicide Act 1957
(5 & 6 Eliz 2 c 11)

1 Abolition of 'constructive malice'

(1) Where a person kills another in the course or furtherance of some other offence, the killing shall not amount to murder unless done with the same malice aforethought (express or implied) as is required for a killing to amount to murder when not done in the course or furtherance of another offence.

(2) For the purpose of the foregoing subsection, a killing done in the course or for the purpose of resisting an officer of justice, or of resisting or avoiding or preventing a lawful arrest, or of affecting or assisting an escape or rescue from legal custody, shall be treated as a killing in the course or furtherance of an offence.

2 Persons suffering from diminished responsibility

(1) Where a person kills or is a party to a killing of another, he shall not be convicted of murder if he was suffering from such abnormality of mind (whether arising from a condition of arrested or retarded development or mind or any inherent causes or induced by disease or injury) as substantially impaired his mental responsibility for his acts and omissions in doing or being a party to the killing.

(2) On a charge of murder, it shall be for the defence to prove that the person charged is by virtue of this section not liable to be convicted of murder.

(3) A person who but for this section would be liable, whether as principal or as accessory, to be convicted of murder shall be liable instead to be convicted of manslaughter.

(4) The fact that one party to a killing is by virtue of this section not liable to be convicted of murder shall not affect the question whether the killing amounted to murder in the case of any other party to it.

3 Provocation

Where on a charge of murder there is evidence on which the jury can find that the person charged was provoked (whether by things done or by things said or by both together) to lose his self-control, the question whether the provocation was enough to make a reasonable man do as he did shall be left to be determined by the jury; and in determining that question the jury shall take into account everything both done and said according to the effect which, in their opinion, it would have on a reasonable man.

4 Suicide pacts

(1) It shall be manslaughter, and shall not be murder, for a person acting in pursuance of a suicide pact between him and another to kill the other or be a party to the other being killed by a third person.

(2) Where it is shown that a person charged with the murder of another killed the other or was a party to his being killed, it shall be for the defence to prove that the person charged was acting in pursuance of a suicide pact between him and the other.

(3) For the purposes of this section 'suicide pact' means a common agreement between two or more persons having for its object the death of all of them, whether or not each is to take his own life, but nothing done by a person who enters into a suicide pact shall be treated as done by him in pursuance of the pact unless it is done while he has the settled intention of dying in pursuance of the pact.

[As amended by the Suicide Act 1961, s3(2), Schedule 2.]

Restriction of Offensive Weapons Act 1959
(7 & 8 Eliz 2 c 37)

1 Penalties for offences in connection with dangerous weapons

(1) Any person who manufactures, sells or hires or offers for sale or hire, or exposes or has in his possession for the purpose of sale or hire, or lends or gives to any other person –

(a) any knife which has a blade which opens automatically by hand pressure applied to a button, spring or other device in or attached to the handle of the knife, sometimes known as a 'flick knife' or 'flick gun'; or

(b) any knife which has a blade which is released from the handle or sheath thereof by the force of gravity or the application of centrifugal force and which, when released, is locked in place by means of a button, spring, lever, or other device, sometimes known as a 'gravity knife',

shall be guilty of an offence and shall be liable on summary conviction to imprisonment for a term not exceeding six months or to a fine not exceeding level 5 on the standard scale or to both such imprisonment and fine.

(2) The importation of any such knife as is described in the foregoing subsection is hereby prohibited.

[As amended by the Restriction of Offensive Weapons Act 1961, s1; Criminal Justice Act 1988, s46(2), (3).]

Street Offences Act 1959
(7 & 8 Eliz 2 c 57)

1 *Loitering or soliciting for purposes of prostitution*

(1) It shall be an offence for a common prostitute to loiter or solicit in a street or public place for the purpose of prostitution.

(2) A person guilty of an offence under this section shall be liable, on summary conviction, to a fine of an amount not exceeding level 2 on the standard scale or, for an offence committed after a previous conviction, to a fine of an amount not exceeding level 3 on that scale.

(3) A constable may arrest without warrant anyone he finds in a street or public place and suspects, with reasonable cause, to be committing an offence under this section.

(4) For the purposes of this section 'street' includes any bridge, road, lane, footway, subway, square, court, alley or passage, whether a thoroughfare or not, which is for the time being open to the public; and the doorways and entrances of premises abutting on a street (as hereinbefore defined), and any ground adjoining and open to a street, shall be treated as forming part of the street.

[As amended by the Criminal Justice Act 1982, s71; Statute Law (Repeals) Acts 1989 and 1993.]

Obscene Publications Act 1959
(7 & 8 Eliz 2 c 66)

1 *Test of obscenity*

(1) For the purposes of this Act an article shall be deemed to be obscene if its effect or (where the article comprises two or more distinct items) the effect of any one of its items, is, if taken as a whole, such as to tend to deprave and corrupt persons who are likely, having regard to all relevant circumstances, to read, see or hear the matter contained or embodied in it.

(2) In this Act 'article' means any description of article containing or embodying matter to be read or looked at or both, any sound record, and any film or other record of a picture or pictures.

(3) For the purposes of this Act a person publishes an article who –

(a) distributes, circulates, sells, lets on hire, gives, or lends it or who offers it for sale or for letting on hire; or

(b) in the case of an article containing or embodying matter to be looked at or a record, shows, plays or projects it or, where the matter is data stored electronically, transmits that data.

(4) For the purposes of this Act a person also publishes an article to the extent that any matter recorded on it is included by him in a programme included in a programme service.

(5) Where the inclusion of any matter in a programme so included would, if that matter were recorded matter, constitute the publication of an obscene article for the purposes of this Act by virtue of subsection (4) above, this Act shall have effect in relation to the inclusion of that matter in that programme as if it were recorded matter.

(6) In this section 'programme' and 'programme service' have the same meaning as in the Broadcasting Act 1990.

2 Prohibition of publication of obscene matter

(1) Subject as hereinafter provided, any person who, whether for gain or not, publishes an obscene article or who has an obscene article for publication for gain (whether gain to himself or gain to another) shall be liable –

(a) on summary conviction to a fine not exceeding the prescribed sum or to imprisonment for a term not exceeding six months;
(b) on conviction on indictment to a fine or to imprisonment for a term not exceeding three years or both.

(3) A prosecution for an offence against this section shall not be commenced more than two years after the commission of the offence.

(3A) Proceedings for an offence under this section shall not be instituted except by or with the consent of the Director of Public Prosecutions in any case where the article in question is a moving picture film of a width of not less than sixteen millimetres and the relevant publication or the only other publication which followed or could reasonably have been expected to follow from the relevant publication took place or (as the case may be) was to take place in the course of a film exhibition and in this subsection 'the relevant publication' means –

(a) in the case of any proceedings under this section for publishing an obscene article, the publication in respect of which the defendant would be charged if the proceedings were brought; and
(b) in the case of any proceedings under this section for having an obscene article for publication for gain, the publication which, if the proceedings were brought, the defendant would be alleged to have had in contemplation.

(4) A person publishing an article shall not be proceeded against for an offence at common law consisting of the publication of any matter contained or embodied in the article where it is of the essence of the offence that the matter is obscene.

(4A) Without prejudice to subsection (4) above, a person shall not be proceeded against for an offence at common law –

(a) in respect of a film exhibition or anything said or done in the course of a film exhibition, where it is of the essence of the common law offence that the exhibition or, as the case may be, what was said or done was obscene, indecent, offensive, disgusting or injurious to morality; or
(b) in respect of an agreement to give a film exhibition or to cause anything to be said or done in the course of such an exhibition where the common law offence consists of

conspiring to corrupt public morals or to do any act contrary to public morals or decency.

(5) A person shall not be convicted of an offence against this section if he proves that he had not examined the article in respect of which he is charged and had no reasonable cause to suspect that it was such that his publication of it would make him liable to be convicted of an offence against this section.

(6) In any proceedings against a person under this section the question whether an article is obscene shall be determined without regard to any publication by another person unless it could reasonably have been expected that the publication by the other person would follow from publication by the person charged.

(7) In this section 'film exhibition' has the same meaning as in the Cinemas Act 1985.

4 Defence of public good

(1) Subject to subsection 1A of this section a person shall not be convicted of an offence against section 2 of this Act, and an order for forfeiture shall not be made under the foregoing section, if it is proved that publication of the article in question is justified as being for the public good on the ground that it is in the interests of science, literature, art or learning, or of other objects of general concern.

(1A) Subsection (1) of this section shall not apply where the article in question is a moving picture film or soundtrack, but –

(a) a person shall not be convicted of an offence against section 2 of this Act in relation to any such film or soundtrack, and
(b) an order for forfeiture of any such film or soundtrack shall not be made under section 3 of this Act,

if it is proved that publication of the film or soundtrack is justified as being for the public good on the ground that it is in the interests of drama, opera, ballet or any other art, or of literature or learning.

(2) It is hereby declared that the opinion of experts as to the literary, artistic, scientific or other merits of an article may be admitted in any proceedings under this Act either to establish or to negative the said ground.

(3) In this section 'moving picture soundtrack' means any sound record designed for playing with a moving picture film, whether incorporated with the film or not.

[As amended by the Obscene Publications Act 1964, s1(1); Criminal Law Act 1977, s53(1), (6), (7), 65(5), Schedule 13; Magistrates' Courts Act 1980, s32(2); Cinemas Act 1985, s24(1), Schedule 2, para 6; Broadcasting Act 1990, ss162; 203(3), Schedule 21; Criminal Justice and Public Order Act 1994, s168(1), Schedule 9, para 3.]

Indecency with Children Act 1960
(8 & 9 Eliz 2 c 33)

1 Indecent conduct towards young child

(1) Any person who commits an act of gross indecency with or towards a child under the age of fourteen, or who incites a child under that age to such an act with him or another, shall be liable on conviction on indictment to imprisonment for a term not exceeding ten years, or on summary conviction to imprisonment for a term not exceeding six months, to a fine not exceeding the prescribed sum, or to both. ...

2 Length of imprisonment for certain offences against young girls

(1) The maximum term of imprisonment to which a person is liable under the Sexual Offences Act 1956 of conviction under indictment of an attempt to have unlawful sexual intercourse with a girl under the age of thirteen, shall be seven years. ...

[As amended by the Magistrates' Courts Act 1980, s32(2); Police and Criminal Evidence Act 1984, s119(2), Schedule 7, Part V; Sexual Offences Act 1985, s5(2)(5); Crime (Sentences) Act 1997, s52.]

Suicide Act 1961
(9 & 10 Eliz 2 c 60)

1 Suicide to cease to be a crime

The rule of law whereby it is a crime for a person to commit suicide is hereby abrogated.

2 Criminal liability for complicity in another's suicide

(1) A person who aids, abets, counsels or procures the suicide of another, or an attempt by another to commit suicide, shall be liable on conviction on indictment to imprisonment for a term not exceeding fourteen years.

(2) If on the trial of an indictment for murder or manslaughter it is proved that the accused aided, abetted, counselled or procured the suicide of the person in question, the jury may find him guilty of that offence. ...

(4) No proceedings shall be instituted for an offence under this section except by or with the consent of the Director of Public Prosecutions.

[As amended by the Criminal Law Act 1967, s10(2), Schedule 3, Pt II; Criminal Jurisdiction Act 1975, s14(5), Schedule 6, Pt I.]

Obscene Publications Act 1964
(1964 c 74)

1 *Obscene articles intended for publication for gain ...*

(2) For the purpose of any proceedings for an offence against the said section 2 [of the Obscene Publications Act 1959] a person shall be deemed to have an article for publication for gain if with a view to such publication he had the article in his ownership, possession or control.

(3) In proceedings brought against a person under the said section 2 for having an obscene article for publication for gain the following provisions shall apply in place of subsections (5) and (6) of that section, that is to say –

    (a) he shall not be convicted of that offence if he proves that he had not examined the article and had no reasonable cause to suspect that it was such that his having it would make him liable to be convicted of an offence against that section; and

    (b) the question whether the article is obscene shall be determined by reference to such publication for gain of the article as in the circumstances it may reasonably be inferred he had in contemplation and to any further publication that could reasonably be expected to follow from it, but not to any other publication.

(4) Where articles are seized under section 3 of the Obscene Publications Act 1959 (which provides for the seizure and forfeiture of obscene articles kept for publication for gain), and a person is convicted under section 2 of that Act of having them for publication for gain, the Court on his conviction shall order the forfeiture of those articles:

Provided that an order made by virtue of this subsection (including an order so made on appeal) shall not take effect until the expiration of the ordinary time within which an appeal in the matter of the proceedings in which the order was made may be instituted or, where such an appeal is duly instituted, until the appeal is finally decided or abandoned; and for this purpose –

    (a) an application for a case to be stated or for leave to appeal shall be treated as the institution of an appeal; and

    (b) where a decision on appeal is subject to a further appeal, the appeal shall not be deemed to be finally decided until the expiration of the ordinary time within which a further appeal may be instituted or, where a further appeal is duly instituted, until the further appeal is finally decided or abandoned.

(5) References in section 3 of the Obscene Publications Act 1959 and this section to publication for gain shall apply to any publication with a view to gain, whether the gain is to accrue by way of consideration for the publication or in any other way.

2 *Negatives, etc for production of obscene articles*

(1) The Obscene Publications Act 1959 (as amended by this Act) shall apply in relation to anything which is intended to be used, either alone or as one of a set, for the reproduction or manufacture therefrom of articles containing or embodying matter to be read, looked at

or listened to, as if it were an article containing or embodying that matter so far as that matter is to be derived from it or from the set.

(2) For the purposes of the Obscene Publications Act 1959 (as so amended) an article shall be deemed to be had or kept for publication if it is had or kept for the reproduction or manufacture therefrom of articles for publication; and the question whether an article so had or kept is obscene shall –

(a) for purposes of section 2 of the Act be determined in accordance with section 1(3)(b) above as if any reference there to publication of the article were a reference to publication of articles reproduced or manufactured from it; and
(b) for purposes of section 3 of the Act be determined on the assumption that articles reproduced or manufactured from it would be published in any manner likely having regard to the circumstances in which it was found, but in no other manner.

Criminal Procedure (Insanity) Act 1964
(1964 c 84)

1 Acquittal on grounds of insanity

The special verdict required by section 2 of the Trial of Lunatics Act 1883 (hereinafter referred to as a 'special verdict') shall be that the accused is not guilty by reason of insanity.

4 Finding of unfitness to plead

(1) This section applies where on the trial of a person the question arises (at the instance of the defence or otherwise) whether the accused is under a disability, that is to say, under any disability such that apart from this Act it would constitute a bar to his being tried.

(2) If, having regard to the nature of the supposed disability, the court are of opinion that it is expedient to do so and in the interests of the accused, they may postpone consideration of the question of fitness to be tried until any time up to the opening of the case for the defence.

(3) If, before the question of fitness to be tried falls to be determined, the jury return a verdict of acquittal on the count or each of the counts on which the accused is being tried, that question shall not be determined.

(4) Subject to subsection (2) and (3) above, the question of fitness to be tried shall be determined as soon as it arises.

(5) The question of fitness to be tried shall be determined by a jury and –

(a) where it falls to be determined on the arraignment of the accused and the trial proceeds, the accused shall be tried by a jury other than that which determined that question;
(b) where it falls to be determined at any later time, it shall be determined by a separate jury or by the jury by whom the accused is being tried, as the court may direct.

(6) A jury shall not make a determination under subsection (5) above except on the written

or oral evidence of two or more registered medical practitioners at least one of whom is duly approved.

4A Finding that the accused did the act or made the omission charged against him

(1) This section applies where in accordance with section 4(5) above it is determined by a jury that the accused is under a disability.

(2) The trial shall not proceed or further proceed but it shall be determined by a jury –

(a) on the evidence (if any) already given in the trial; and

(b) on such evidence as may be adduced or further adduced by the prosecution, or adduced by a person appointed by the court under this section to put the case for the defence,

whether they are satisfied, as respects the count or each of the counts on which the accused was to be or was being tried, that he did the act or made the omission charged against him as the offence.

(3) If as respects that count or any of those counts the jury are satisfied as mentioned in subsection (2) above, they shall make a finding that the accused did the act or made the omission charged against him.

(4) If as respects that count or any of those counts the jury are not so satisfied, they shall return a verdict of acquittal as if on the count in question the trial had proceeded to a conclusion.

(5) A determination under subsection (2) above shall be made –

(a) where the question of disability was determined on the arraignment of the accused, by a jury other than that which determined that question; and

(b) where that question was determined at any later time, by the jury by whom the accused was being tried.

5 Powers to deal with persons not guilty by reason of insanity or unfit to plead, etc

(1) This section applies where –

(a) a special verdict is returned that the accused is not guilty by reason of insanity; or

(b) findings are recorded that the accused is under a disability and that he did the act or made the omission charged against him.

(2) Subject to subsection (3)below, the court shall either –

(a) make an order that the accused be admitted, in accordance with the provisions of Schedule 1 to the Criminal Procedure (Insanity and Unfitness to Plead) Act 1991, to such hospital as may be specified by the Secretary of State; or

(b) where they have the power to do so by virtue of section 5 of that Act, make in respect of the accused such one of the following orders as they think most suitable in all the circumstances of the case, namely –

(i) a guardianship order within the meaning of the Mental Health Act 1983;

(ii) a supervision and treatment order within the meaning of Schedule 2 to the said Act of 1991; an

(iii) an order for his absolute discharge.

(3) Paragraph (b) of subsection (2) above shall not apply where the offence to which the special verdict or findings relate is an offence the sentence of which is fixed by law.

6 Evidence by prosecution of insanity or diminished responsibility

Where on a trial for murder the accused contends –

(a) that at the time of the alleged offence he was insane so as not to be responsible according to law for his actions; or

(b) that at that time he was suffering from such abnormality of mind as is specified in subsection (1) of section 2 of the Homicide Act 1957 (diminished responsibility),

the court shall allow the prosecution to adduce or elicit evidence tending to prove the other of those contentions, and may give directions as to the stage of the proceedings at which the prosecution may adduce such evidence.

[As amended by the Criminal Procedure (Insanity and Unfitness to Plead) Act 1991, ss2, 3, 8(1), (3), Schedule 4.]

Murder (Abolition of Death Penalty) Act 1965
(1965 c 71)

1 Abolition of death penalty for murder

(1) No person shall suffer death for murder, and a person convicted of murder shall, subject to subsection (5) below, be sentenced to imprisonment for life.

(2) On sentencing any person convicted of murder to imprisonment for life the court may at the same time declare the period which it recommends to the Secretary of State as the minimum period which in its view should elapse before the Secretary of State orders the release of that person on licence under [section 35(2), (3) of the Criminal Justice Act 1991].

(3) For the purpose of any proceedings on or subsequent to a person's trial on a charge of capital murder that charge and any plea or finding of guilty of capital murder shall be treated as being or having been a charge, or a plea or finding of guilty, of murder only; and if at the commencement of this Act a person is under sentence of death for murder, the sentence shall have effect as a sentence of imprisonment for life.

(4) In the foregoing subsections any reference to murder shall include an offence of 'or corresponding to murder under s70 of the Army Act 1955 or of the Air Force Act 1955 or under section 42 of the Naval Discipline Act 1957, and any reference to capital murder shall be construed accordingly. …

Criminal Law Act 1967
(1967 c 58)

1 Abolition of distinction between felony and misdemeanour

(1) All distinctions between felony and misdemeanour are hereby abolished.

(2) Subject to the provisions of this Act, on all matters on which a distinction has previously been made between felony and misdemeanour, including mode of trial, the law and practice in relation to all offences cognisable under the law of England and Wales (including piracy) shall be the law and practice applicable at the commencement of this Act in relation to misdemeanour.

3 Use of force in making arrest, etc

(1) A person may use such force as is reasonable in the circumstances in the prevention of crime, or in effecting or assisting in the lawful arrest of offenders or suspected offenders or of persons unlawfully at large.

(2) Subsection (1) above shall replace the rules of the common law on the questions when force used for a purpose mentioned in the subsection is justified by that purpose.

4 Penalties for assisting offenders

(1) Where a person has committed an arrestable offence, any other person who, knowing or believing him to be guilty of the offence or of some other arrestable offence, does without lawful authority or reasonable excuse any act with intent to impede his apprehension or prosecution shall be guilty of an offence.

(1A) In this section and section 5 below 'arrestable offence' has the meaning assigned to it by section 24 of the Police and Criminal Evidence Act 1984.

(2) If on the trial of an indictment for an arrestable offence the jury are satisfied that the offence charged (or some other offence of which the accused might on that charge be found guilty) was committed, but find the accused not guilty of it, they may find him guilty of any offence under subsection (1) above of which they are satisfied that he is guilty in relation to the offence charged (or that other offence).

(3) A person committing an offence under subsection (1) above with intent to impede another person's apprehension or prosecution shall on conviction on indictment be liable to imprisonment according to the gravity of the other person's offence, as follows –

  (a) if that offence is one for which the sentence is fixed by law, he shall be liable to ·imprisonment for not more than ten years;
  (b) if it is one for which a person (not previously convicted) may be sentenced to imprisonment for a term of fourteen years, he shall be liable to imprisonment for not more than seven years;

(c) if it is not one included above but is one for which a person (not previously convicted) may be sentenced to imprisonment for a term of ten years, he shall be liable to imprisonment for not more than five years;

(d) in any other case, he shall be liable to imprisonment for not more than three years.

(4) No proceedings shall be instituted for an offence under subsection (1) above except by or with the consent of the Director of Public Prosecutions.

5 Penalties for concealing offences or giving false information

(1) Where a person has committed an arrestable offence, any other person who, knowing or believing that the offence or some other arrestable offence has been committed, and that he has information which might be of material assistance in securing the prosecution or conviction of an offender for it, accepts or agrees to accept for not disclosing that information any consideration other than the making of good or loss or injury caused by the offence, or the making of reasonable compensation for that loss or injury, shall be liable on conviction on indictment to imprisonment for not more than two years.

(2) Where a person causes any wasteful employment of the police by knowingly making to any person a false report tending to show that an offence has been committed, or to give rise to apprehension for the safety of any persons or property, or tending to show that he has information material to any police inquiry, he shall be liable on summary conviction to imprisonment for not more than six months or to a fine of not more than level 4 on the standard scale or to both.

(3) No proceedings shall be instituted for an offence under this section except by or with the consent of the Director of Public Prosecutions.

(5) The compounding of an offence other than treason shall not be an offence otherwise than under this section.

6 Trial of offences

(1) Where a person is arraigned on an indictment –

(a) he shall in all cases be entitled to make a plea of not guilty in addition to any demurrer or special plea;

(b) he may plead not guilty of the offence specifically charged in the indictment but guilty of another offence of which he might be found guilty on that indictment;

(c) if he stands mute of malice or will not answer directly to the indictment, the court may order a plea of not guilty to be entered on his behalf, and he shall then be treated as having pleaded not guilty.

(2) On an indictment for murder a person found not guilty of murder may be found guilty –

(a) of manslaughter, or of causing grievous bodily harm with intent to do so; or

(b) of any offence of which he may be found guilty under an enactment specifically so providing, or under section 4(2) of this Act; or

(c) of an attempt to commit murder, or of an attempt to commit any other offence of which he might be found guilty;

but may not be found guilty of any offence not included above.

(3) Where, on a person's trial on indictment for any offence except treason or murder, the jury find him not guilty of the offence specifically charged in the indictment, but the allegations in the indictment amount to or include (expressly or by implication) an allegation of another offence falling within the jurisdiction of the court of trial, the jury may find him guilty of that other offence or of an offence of which he could be found guilty on an indictment specifically charging that other offence.

(4) For purposes of subsection (3) above any allegation of an offence shall be taken as including an allegation of attempting to commit that offence; and where a person is charged on indictment with attempting to commit an offence or with any assault or other act preliminary to an offence, but not with the completed offence, then (subject to the discretion of the court to discharge the jury with a view to the preferment of an indictment for the completed offence) he may be convicted of the offence charged notwithstanding that he is shown to be guilty of the completed offence.

(5) Where a person arraigned on an indictment pleads not guilty of an offence charged in the indictment but guilty of some offence of which he might be found guilty on that charge, and he is convicted on that plea of guilty without trial for the offence of which he had pleaded not guilty, then (whether or not the two offences are separately charged in distinct counts) his conviction of the one offence shall be an acquittal of the other.

(6) Any power to bring proceedings for an offence by criminal information in the High Court is hereby abolished.

(7) Subsections (1) to (3) above shall apply to an indictment containing more than one count as if each count were a separate indictment.

13 Abolition of certain offences, and consequential repeals

(1) The following offences are hereby abolished, that is to say –

(a) any distinct offence under the common law in England and Wales of maintenance (including champerty, but not embracery), challenging to fight, eavesdropping or being a common barrator, a common scold or a common night walker; and

(b) any offence under an enactment mentioned in Part I of Schedule 4 to this Act, to the extent to which the offence depends on any section or part of a section included in the third column of that Schedule. ...

[As amended by the Criminal Jurisdiction Act 1975, s14(5), Schedule 6, Pt I; Criminal Justice Act 1982, ss38, 46; Police and Criminal Evidence Act 1984, s119(1), Schedule 6, Part I, para 17.]

Sexual Offences Act 1967
(1967 c 60)

1 Amendment of law relating to homosexual acts in private

(1) Notwithstanding any statutory or common law provision, a homosexual act in private shall not be an offence provided that the parties consent thereto and have attained the age of eighteen years.

(2) An act which would otherwise be treated for the purposes of this Act as being done in private shall not be so treated if done –

(a) when more than two persons take part or are present; or
(b) in a lavatory to which the public have or are permitted to have access, whether on payment or otherwise.

(3) A man who is suffering from severe mental handicap cannot in law give any consent which, by virtue of subsection (1) of this section, would prevent a homosexual act from being an offence, but a person shall not be convicted, on account of the incapacity of such a man to consent, of an offence consisting of such an act if he proves that he did not know and had no reason to suspect that man to be suffering from severe mental handicap.

(3A) In subsection (3) of this section 'severe mental handicap' means a state of arrested or incomplete development of mind which includes severe impairment of intelligence and social functioning. ...

(6) It is hereby declared that where in any proceedings it is charged that a homosexual act is an offence the prosecutor shall have the burden of proving that the act was done otherwise than in private or otherwise than with the consent of the parties or that any of the parties had not attained the age of eighteen years.

(7) For the purposes of this section a man shall be treated as doing a homosexual act if, and only if, he commits buggery with another man or commits an act of gross indecency with another man or is a party to the commission by a man of such an act.

4 Procuring others to commit homosexual acts

(1) A man who procures another man to commit with a third man an act of buggery which by reason of section 1 of this Act is not an offence shall be liable on conviction on indictment to imprisonment for a term not exceeding two years.

(3) It shall not be an offence under section 13 of the [Sexual Offences Act] of 1956 for a man to procure the commission by another man of an act of gross indecency with the first-mentioned man which by reason of section 1 of this Act is not an offence under the said section 13.

5 Living on earnings of male prostitute

(1) A man or woman who knowingly lives wholly or in part on the earnings of prostitution of another man shall be liable –

(a) on summary conviction to imprisonment for a term not exceeding six months; or

(b) on conviction on indictment to imprisonment for a term not exceeding seven years.

(3) Anyone may arrest without a warrant a person found committing an offence under this section.

6 *Premises resorted to for homosexual practices*

Premises shall be treated for purposes of sections 33 to 35 of the Act of 1956 as a brothel if people resort to it for the purpose of lewd homosexual practices in circumstances in which resort thereto for lewd heterosexual practices would have led to its being treated as a brothel for the purposes of those sections.

[As amended by the Mental Health (Amendment) Act 1982, s65(1), (2), Schedule 3, Part I, para 34(a), (b), Schedule 4, Part 1; Criminal Justice and Public Order Act 1994, ss145, 146, 168(3), Schedule 11.]

Criminal Justice Act 1967
(1967 c 80)

8 *Proof of criminal intent*

A court or jury, in determining whether a person has committed an offence, –

(a) shall not be bound in law to infer that he intended or foresaw a result of his actions by reason only of its being a natural and probable consequence of those actions; but

(b) shall decide whether he did intend or foresee that result by reference to all the evidence, drawing such inferences from the evidence as appear proper in the circumstances.

Abortion Act 1967
(1967 c 87)

1 *Medical termination of pregnancy*

(1) Subject to the provisions of this section, a person shall not be guilty of an offence under the law relating to abortion when a pregnancy is terminated by a registered medical practitioner if two registered medical practitioners are of the opinion, formed in good faith –

(a) that the pregnancy has not exceeded its twenty-fourth week and that the continuance of the pregnancy would involve risk, greater than if the pregnancy were terminated, of injury to the physical or mental health of the pregnant woman or any existing children of her family; or

(b) that the termination is necessary to prevent grave permanent injury to the physical or mental health of the pregnant woman; or

(c) that the continuance of the pregnancy would involve risk to the life of the pregnant woman, greater than if the pregnancy were terminated; or

(d) that there is a substantial risk that if the child were born it would suffer form such physical or mental abnormalities as to be seriously handicapped.

(2) In determining whether the continuance of a pregnancy would involve such risk of injury to health as is mentioned in paragraph (a) or (b) of subsection (1) of this section, account may be taken of the pregnant woman's actual or reasonably foreseeable environment.

(3) Except as provided by subsection (4) of this section, any treatment for the termination of pregnancy must be carried out in a hospital vested in the Secretary of State for the purposes of his functions under the National Health Service Act 1977 or the National Health Service (Scotland) Act 1978, or in a hospital vested in a National Health Service trust, or in a place approved for the purposes of this section by the Secretary of State.

(3A) The power under subsection (3) of this section to approve a place includes power, in relation to treatment consisting primarily in the use of such medicines as may be specified in the approval and carried out in such manner as may be so specified, to approve a class of places'.

(4) Subsection (3) of this section, and so much of subsection (1) as relates to the opinion of two registered medical practitioners, shall not apply to the termination of a pregnancy by a registered medical practitioner in a case where he is of the opinion, formed in good faith, that the termination is immediately necessary to save the life or to prevent grave permanent injury to the physical or mental health of the pregnant woman.

4 Conscientious objection to participation in treatment

(1) Subject to subsection (2) of this section, no person shall be under any duty, whether by contract or by any statutory or other legal requirement, to participate in any treatment authorised by this Act to which he has a conscientious objection: Provided that in any legal proceedings the burden of proof of conscientious objection shall rest on the person claiming to rely on it.

(2) Nothing in subsection (1) of this section shall affect any duty to participate in treatment which is necessary to save the life or to prevent grave permanent injury to the physical or mental health of a pregnant woman. ...

5 Supplementary provisions

(1) No offence under the Infant Life (Preservation) Act 1929 shall be committed by a registered medical practitioner who terminates a pregnancy in accordance with the provisions of this Act.

(2) For the purposes of the law relating to abortion, anything done with intent to procure a woman's miscarriage (or, in the case of a woman carrying more than one foetus, her miscarriage of any foetus) is unlawfully done unless authorised by section 1 of this Act and, in the case of a woman carrying more than one foetus, anything done with intent to procure her miscarriage of any foetus is authorised by that section if –

   (a) the ground for termination for the pregnancy specified in subsection (1)(d) of that section applies in relation to any foetus and the thing is done for the purpose of procuring the miscarriage of that foetus, or

(b) any of the other grounds for termination of the pregnancy specified in that section applies.

6 Interpretation

In this Act, the following expressions have meanings hereby assigned to them:

'the law relating to abortion' means sections 58 and 59 of the Offences against the Person Act 1861, and any rule of law relating to the procurement of abortion.

[As amended by the Health Service Act 1980 ss1, 2, 25(4), Schedule 1, para 17(1), Schedule 7; Human Fertilisation and Embryology Act 1990, s37 (1), (2), (4), (5); National Health Service and Community Care Act 1990, s66(1), Schedule 9, para 8.]

Criminal Appeal Act 1968
(1968 c 19)

1 Right of appeal

(1) Subject to subsection (3) below, a person convicted of an offence on indictment may appeal to the Court of Appeal against his conviction.

(2) An appeal under this section lies only –

(a) with the leave of the Court of Appeal; or

(b) if the judge of the court of trial grants a certificate that the case is fit for appeal.

(3) Where a person is convicted before the Crown Court of a scheduled offence it shall not be open to him to appeal to the Court of Appeal against the conviction on the ground that the decision of the court which transferred proceedings against him for trial as to the value involved was mistaken.

(4) In subsection (3) above 'scheduled offence' and 'the value involved' have the same meanings as they have in section 22 of the Magistrates' Courts Act 1980 (certain offences against property to be tried summarily if value of property or damage is small).

2 Grounds for allowing an appeal under s1

(1) Subject to the provisions of this Act, the Court of Appeal –

(a) shall allow an appeal against conviction if they think that the conviction is unsafe; and

(b) shall dismiss such an appeal in any other case.

(2) In the case of an appeal against conviction the court shall, if they allow the appeal, quash the conviction.

(3) An order of the Court of Appeal quashing a conviction shall, except when under section 7

below the appellant is ordered to be retried, operate as a direction to the court of trial to enter, instead of the record of conviction, a judgment and verdict of acquittal.

3 Power to substitute conviction of alternative offence

(1) This section applies on an appeal against conviction, where the appellant has been convicted of an offence and the jury could on the indictment have found him guilty of some other offence, and on the finding of the jury it appears to the Court of Appeal that the jury must have been satisfied of facts which proved him guilty of the other offence.

(2) The court may, instead of allowing or dismissing the appeal, substitute for the verdict found by the jury a verdict of guilty of the other offence, and pass such sentence in substitution for the sentence passed at the trial as may be authorised by law for the other offence, not being a sentence of greater severity.

4 Sentence when appeal allowed on part of an indictment

(1) This section applies where, on an appeal against conviction on an indictment containing two or more counts, the Court of Appeal allow the appeal in respect of part of the indictment.

(2) Except as provided by subsection (3) below, the court may in respect of any count on which the appellant remains convicted pass such sentence, in substitution for any sentence passed thereon at the trial, as they think proper and is authorised by law for the offence of which he remains convicted on that count.

(3) The court shall not under this section pass any sentence such that the appellant's sentence on the indictment as a whole will, in consequence of the appeal, be of greater severity than the sentence (taken as a whole) which was passed at the trial for all offences of which he was convicted on the indictment.

5 Disposal of appeal against conviction on special verdict

(1) This section applies on an appeal against conviction in a case where the jury have found a special verdict.

(2) If the Court of Appeal consider that a wrong conclusion has been arrived at by the court of trial on the effect of the jury's verdict they may, instead of allowing the appeal, order such conclusion to be recorded as appears to them to be in law required by the verdict, and pass such sentence in substitution for the sentence passed at the trial as may be authorised by law.

6 Substitution of finding of insanity or findings of unfitness to plead, etc

(1) This section applies where, on an appeal against conviction, the Court of Appeal, on the written or oral evidence of two or more registered medical practitioners at least one of whom is duly approved, are of opinion –

(a) that the proper verdict would have been one of not guilty by reason of insanity; or

(b) that the case is not one where there should have been a verdict of acquittal, but there should have been findings that the accused was under a disability and that he did the act or made the omission charged against him.

(2) Subject to subsection (3) below, the Court of Appeal shall either –

(a) make an order that the appellant be admitted, in accordance with the provisions of Schedule 1 to the Criminal Procedure (Insanity and Unfitness to Plead) Act 1991, to such hospital as may be specified by the Secretary of State; or

(b) where they have the power to do so by virtue of section 5 of that Act, make in respect of the appellant such one of the following orders as they think most suitable in all the circumstances of the case, namely –

(i) a guardianship order within the meaning of the Mental Health Act 1983;

(ii) a supervision and treatment order within the meaning of Schedule 2 to the said Act of 1991; and

(iii) an order for his absolute discharge.

(3) Paragraph (b) of subsection (2) above shall not apply where the offence to which the appeal relates is an offence the sentence for which is fixed by law.

7 Power to order retrial

(1) Where the Court of Appeal allow an appeal against conviction and it appears to the court that the interests of justice so require, they may order the appellant to be retried.

(2) A person shall not under this section be ordered to be retried for any offence other than –

(a) the offence of which he was convicted at the original trial and in respect of which his appeal is allowed as mentioned in subsection (1) above;

(b) an offence of which he could have been convicted at the original trial on an indictment for the first-mentioned offence; or

(c) an offence charged in an alternative count of the indictment in respect of which the jury were discharged from giving a verdict in consequence of convicting him of the first-mentioned offence.

12 Appeal against verdict of not guilty by reason of insanity

A person in whose case there is returned a verdict of not guilty by reason of insanity may appeal to the Court of Appeal against the verdict –

(a) with the leave of the Court of Appeal; or

(b) if the judge of the court of trial grants a certificate that the case is fit for appeal.

13 Disposal of appeal under s12

(1) Subject to the provisions of this section, the Court of Appeal –

(a) shall allow an appeal under section 12 of this Act if they think that the verdict is unsafe; and

(b) shall dismiss the appeal in any other case.

(3) Where apart from this subsection –

(a) an appeal under section 12 of this Act would fall to be allowed; and

(b) none of the grounds for allowing it relates to the question of the insanity of the accused,

the Court of Appeal may dismiss the appeal if they are of opinion that, but for the insanity of the accused, the proper verdict would have been that he was guilty of an offence other than the offence charged.

(4) Where an appeal under section 12 of this Act is allowed, the following provisions apply:

(a) if the ground, or one of the grounds, for allowing the appeal is that the finding of the jury as to the insanity of the accused ought not to stand and the Court of Appeal are of opinion that the proper verdict would have been that he was guilty of an offence (whether the offence charged or any other offence of which the jury could have found him guilty), the court –

(i) shall substitute for the verdict of not guilty by reason of insanity a verdict of guilty of that offence; and

(ii) shall, subject to subsection (5) below, have the like powers of punishing or otherwise dealing with the appellant, and other powers, as the court of trial would have had if the jury had come to the substituted verdict; and

(b) in any other case, the Court of Appeal shall substitute for the verdict of the jury a verdict of acquittal.

(5) The Court of Appeal shall not by virtue of subsection (4)(a) above sentence any person to death; but where under that paragraph they substitute a verdict of guilty of an offence for which apart from this subsection they would be required to sentence the appellant to death, their sentence shall (whatever the circumstances) be one of imprisonment for life.

(6) An order of the Court of Appeal allowing an appeal in accordance with this section shall operate as a direction to the court of trial to amend the record to conform with the order.

14 Substitution of findings of unfitness to plead, etc

(1) This section applies where, on an appeal under section 12 of this Act, the Court of Appeal, on the written or oral evidence of two or more registered medical practitioners at least one of whom is duly approved, are of opinion that –

(a) the case is not one where there should have been a verdict of acquittal; but

(b) there should have been findings that the accused was under a disability and that he did the act or made the omission charged against him.

(2) Subject to subsection (3) below, the Court of Appeal shall either –

(a) make an order that the appellant be admitted, in accordance with the provisions of

Schedule 1 to the Criminal Procedure (Insanity and Unfitness to Plead) Act 1991, to such hospital as may be specified by the Secretary of State; or

(b) where they have the power to do so by virtue of section 5 of that Act, make in respect of the appellant such one of the following orders as they think most suitable in all the circumstances of the case, namely –

(i) a guardianship order within the meaning of the Mental Health Act 1983;

(ii) a supervision and treatment order within the meaning of Schedule 2 to the said Act of 1991; and

(iii) an order for his absolute discharge.

(3) Paragraph (b) of subsection (2) above shall not apply where the offence to which the appeal relates is an offence the sentence for which is fixed by law.

14A Substitution of verdict of acquittal

(1) This section applies where, in accordance with section 13(4)(b) of this Act, the Court of Appeal substitute a verdict of acquittal and the Court, on the written or oral evidence of two or more registered medical practitioners at least one of whom is duly approved, are of opinion –

(a) that the appellant is suffering from mental disorder of a nature or degree which warrants his detention in a hospital for assessment (or for assessment followed by medical treatment) for at least a limited period; and

(b) that he ought to be so detained in the interests of his own health or safety or with a view to the protection of other persons.

(2) The Court of Appeal shall make an order that the appellant be admitted for assessment, in accordance with the provisions of Schedule 1 to the Criminal Procedure (Insanity and Unfitness to Plead) Act 1991, to such hospital as may be specified by the Secretary of State.

15 Right of appeal against finding of disability

(1) Where there has been a determination under section 4 of the Criminal Procedure (Insanity) Act 1964 of the question of a person's fitness to be tried, and the jury has returned findings that he is under disability and that he did the act or made the omission charged against him, the person may appeal to the Court of Appeal against either or both of those findings.

(2) An appeal under this section lies only –

(a) with the leave of the Court of Appeal; or

(b) if the judge of the court of trial grants a certificate that the case is fit for appeal.

16 Disposal of appeal under s15

(1) The Court of Appeal –

(a) shall allow an appeal under section 15 of this Act against a finding if they think that the finding is unsafe; and

(b) shall dismiss such an appeal in any other case.

(3) Where the Court of Appeal allow an appeal under section 15 of this Act against a finding that the appellant is under a disability –

(a) the appellant may be tried accordingly for the offence with which he was charged; and

(b) the court may, subject to section 25 of the Criminal Justice and Public Order Act 1994 [no bail for defendants charged with or convicted of homicide or rape after previous conviction of such offences], make such orders as appear to them necessary or expedient pending any such trial for this custody, release on bail or continued detention under the Mental Health Act 1983;

and Schedule 3 to this Act has effect for applying provisions in Part III of that Act to persons in whose case an order is made by the court under this subsection.

(4) Where, otherwise than in a case falling within subsection (3) above, the Court of Appeal allow an appeal under section 15 of this Act against a finding that the appellant did the act or made the omission charged against him, the court shall, in addition to quashing the finding, direct a verdict of acquittal to be recorded (but not a verdict of not guilty by reason of insanity).

33 Right of appeal to House of Lords

(1) An appeal lies to the House of Lords, at the instance of the defendant or the prosecutor, from any decision of the Court of Appeal on an appeal to that court under Part I of this Act or section 9 (preparatory hearings) of the Criminal Justice Act 1987 or section 35 of the Criminal Procedure and Investigations Act 1996.

(2) The appeal lies only with the leave of the Court of Appeal or the House of Lords; and leave shall not be granted unless it is certified by the Court of Appeal that a point of law of general public importance is involved in the decision and it appears to the Court of Appeal or the House of Lords (as the case may be) that the point is one which ought to be considered by that House.

(3) Except as provided by this Part of this Act and section 13 of the Administration of Justice Act 1960 (appeal in cases of contempt of court), no appeal shall lie from any decision of the criminal division of the Court of Appeal.

49 Saving for prerogative of mercy

Nothing in this Act is to be taken as affecting Her Majesty's prerogative of mercy.

[As amended by the Bail Act 1976, s12(1), Schedule 2, para 39; Criminal Law Act 1977, s44; Magistrates' Courts Act 1980 s154(1), Schedule 7, para 71; Supreme Court Act 1981, s152(1), Schedule 5; Mental Health Act 1983, s148(1), Schedule 4, para 23(f); Criminal Justice Act 1987, s15, Schedule 2, para 3; Criminal Justice Act 1988, ss43(1), (2), 170(2), Schedule 16; Criminal Procedure (Insanity and Unfitness to Plead) Act 1991, ss4(1), (2), 7, 8(2), (3), Schedule 3, paras 2, 3, 4, Schedule 4; Criminal Justice and Public Order Act 1994, ss44(3), 168(2), Schedule 4, Pt II, para 16, Schedule 10, para 12; Criminal Appeal Act 1995, ss1(1), (3), (5), 2(1), (3), (5), 29(1), Schedule 2, para 4(1), (2); Criminal Procedure and Investigations Act 1996, s36(1)(a).]

Firearms Act 1968
(1968 c 27)

1 Requirement of firearm certificate

(1) Subject to any exemption under this Act, it is an offence for a person –

(a) to have in his possession, or to purchase or acquire, a firearm to which this section applies without holding a firearm certificate in force at the time, or otherwise than as authorised by such a certificate;

(b) to have in his possession, or to purchase or acquire, any ammunition to which this section applies without holding a firearm certificate in force at the time, or otherwise than as authorised by such a certificate, or in quantities in excess of those so authorised.

(2) It is an offence for a person to fail to comply with a condition subject to which a firearm certificate is held by him.

(3) This section applies to every firearm except –

(a) a shot gun within the meaning of this Act, that is to say a smooth-bore gun (not being an air gun) which –

(i) has a barrel not less than 24 inches in length and does not have any barrel with a bore exceeding 2 inches in diameter;

(ii) either has no magazine or has a non-detachable magazine incapable of holding more than two cartridges; and

(iii) is not a revolver gun; and

(b) an air weapon (that is to say, an air rifle, air gun or air pistol not of a type declared by rules made by the Secretary of State under section 53 of this Act to be specially dangerous)

(3A) A gun which has been adapted to have such a magazine as is mentioned in subsection (3)(a)(ii) above shall not be regarded as falling within that provision unless the magazine bears a mark approved by the Secretary of State for denoting that fact and that mark has been made, and the adaptation has been certified in writing as having been carried out in a manner approved by him, either by one of the two companies mentioned in section 58(1) of this Act or by such other person as may be approved by him for that purpose.

(4) This section applies to any ammunition for a firearm, except the following articles, namely –

(a) cartridges containing five or more shot, none of which exceeds .36 inch in diameter;

(b) ammunition for an air gun, air rifle or air pistol; and

(c) blank cartridges not more than one inch in diameter measured immediately in front of the rim or cannelure of the base of the cartridge.

2 Requirement of certificate for possession of shot guns

(1) Subject to any exemption under this Act, it is an offence for a person to have in his possession, or to purchase or acquire, a shot gun without holding a certificate under this Act authorising him to possess shot guns.

(2) It is an offence for a person to fail to comply with a condition subject to which a shot gun certificate is held by him.

3 Business and other transactions with firearms and ammunition

(1) A person commits an offence if, by way of trade or business, he –

(a) manufactures, sells, transfers, repairs, tests or proves any firearm or ammunition to which section 1 of this Act applies, or a shot gun; or
(b) exposes for sale or transfer, or has in his possession for sale, transfer, repair, test or proof any such firearm or ammunition, or a shot gun,

without being registered under this Act as a firearms dealer.

(2) It is an offence for a person to sell or transfer to any other person in the United Kingdom, other than a registered firearms dealer, any firearm or ammunition to which section 1 of this Act applies, or a shot gun, unless that other produces a firearm certificate authorising him to purchase or acquire it or, as the case may be, his shot gun certificate, or shows that he is by virtue of this Act entitled to purchase or acquire it without holding a certificate.

(3) It is an offence for a person to undertake the repair, test or proof of a firearm or ammunition to which section 1 of this Act applies, or of a shot gun, for any other person in the United Kingdom other than a registered firearms dealer as such, unless that other produces or causes to be produced a firearm certificate authorising him to have possession of the firearm or ammunition or, as the case may be, his shot gun certificate, or shows that he is by virtue of this Act entitled to have possession of it without holding a certificate.

(4) Subsections (1) to (3) above have effect subject to any exemption under subsequent provisions of this Part of this Act.

(5) A person commits an offence if, with a view to purchasing or acquiring, or procuring the repair, test or proof of, any firearm or ammunition to which section 1 of this Act applies, or a shot gun, he produces a false certificate or a certificate in which any false entry has been made, or personates a person to whom a certificate has been granted, or knowingly or recklessly makes a statement false in any material particular.

(6) It is an offence for a pawnbroker to take in pawn any firearm or ammunition to which section 1 of this Act applies, or a shot gun.

4 Conversion of weapons

(1) Subject to this section, it is an offence to shorten the barrel of a shot gun to a length less than 24 inches.

(2) It is not an offence under subsection (1) above for a registered firearms dealer to shorten the barrel of a shot gun for the sole purpose of replacing a defective part of the barrel so as to produce a barrel not less than 24 inches in length.

(3) It is an offence for a person other than a registered firearms dealer to convert into a firearm anything which, though having the appearance of being a firearm, is so constructed as to be incapable of discharging any missile through its barrel.

(4) A person who commits an offence under section 1 of this Act by having in his possession, or purchasing or acquiring, a shot gun which has been shortened contrary to subsection (1) above or a firearm which has been converted as mentioned in subsection (3) above (whether by a registered firearms dealer or not), without holding a firearm certificate authorising him to have it in his possession, or to purchase or acquire it, shall be treated for the purposes of provisions of this Act relating to the punishment of offences as committing that offence in an aggravated form.

5 Weapons subject to general prohibition

(1) A person commits an offence if, without the authority of the Defence Council, he has in his possession, or purchases or acquires, or manufactures, sells or transfers –

(a) any firearm which is so designed or adapted that two or more missiles can be successively discharged without repeated pressure on the trigger;

(ab) any self-loading or pump-action rifled gun other than one which is chambered for .22 rim-fire cartridges;

(aba) any firearm which either has a barrel less than 30 centimetres in length or is less than 60 centimetres in length overall, other than air weapon, a muzzle-loading gun or a firearm designed as signalling apparatus;

(ac) any self-loading or pump-action smooth-bore gun which is not an air weapon or chambered for .22 rim-fire cartridges and either has a barrel less than 24 inches in length or is less than 40 inches in length overall;

(ad) any smooth-bore revolver gun other than one which is chambered for 9mm rim-fire cartridges or a muzzle-loading gun;

(ae) any rocket launcher, or any mortar, for projecting a stabilised missile, other than a launcher or mortar designed for line-throwing or pyrotechnic purposes or as signalling apparatus;

(b) any weapon of whatever description designed or adapted for the discharge of any noxious liquid, gas or other thing; and

(c) any cartridge with a bullet designed to explode on or immediately before impact, any ammunition containing or designed or adapted to contain any such noxious thing as is mentioned in paragraph (b) above and, if capable of being used with a firearm of any description, any grenade, bomb (or other like missile), or rocket or shell designed to explode as aforesaid.

(1A) Subject to section 5A of this Act, a person commits an offence if, without the authority of the Secretary of State, he has in his possession, or purchases or acquires or sells or transfers –

(a) any firearm which is disguised as another object;

(b) any rocket or ammunition not falling within paragraph (c) of subsection (1) of this section which consists in or incorporates a missile designed to explode on or immediately before impact and is for military use;

(c) any launcher or other projecting apparatus not falling within paragraph (ae) of that subsection which is designed to be used with any rocket or ammunition falling within paragraph (b) above or with ammunition which would fall within that paragraph but for its being ammunition falling within paragraph (c) of that subsection;

(d) any ammunition which incorporates a missile designed or adapted to expand on impact;

(e) any ammunition for military use which consists in or incorporates a missile designed, on account of its having a jacket and hard-core, to penetrate armour plating, armour screening or body armour;

(f) any ammunition which is designed to be used with a pistol and incorporates a missile designed or adapted to expand on impact;

(g) anything which is designed to be projected as a missile from any weapon and is designed to be, or has been, incorporated in –

(i) any ammunition falling within any of the preceding paragraphs; or

(ii) any ammunition which would fall within any of those paragraphs but for it being specified in subsection (1) of this section.

(2) The weapons and ammunition specified in subsections (1) and (1A) of this section (including, in the case of ammunition, any missiles falling within subsection (1A)(g) of this section) are referred to in this Act as 'prohibited weapons' and 'prohibited ammunition' respectively.

(3) An authority given to a person by the Defence Council under this section shall be in writing and be subject to conditions specified therein.

(4) The conditions of the authority shall include such as the Defence Council, having regard to the circumstances of each particular case, think fit to impose for the purpose of securing that the prohibited weapon or ammunition to which the authority relates will not endanger the public safety or the peace.

(5) It is an offence for a person to whom an authority is given under this section to fail to comply with any condition of the authority.

(6) The Defence Council may at any time, if they think fit, revoke an authority given to a person under this section by notice in writing requiring him to deliver up the authority to such person as may be specified in the notice within twenty-one days from the date of the notice; and it is an offence for him to fail to comply with that requirement.

(7) For the purposes of this section and section 5A of this Act –

(a) any rocket or ammunition which is designed to be capable of being used with a military weapon shall be taken to be for military use;

(b) references to a missile designed so that a substance contained in the missile will ignite on or immediately before impact include references to any missile containing a substance that ignites on exposure to air; and

(c) references to a missile's expanding on impact include references to its deforming in any predictable manner on or immediately after impact.

(8) For the purposes of subsection (1)(aba) and (ac) above, any detachable, folding, rectractable or other movable butt-stock shall be disregarded in measuring the length of any firearm.

(9) Any reference in this section to a muzzle-loading gun is a reference to a gun which is designed to be loaded at the muzzle end of the barrel or chamber with a loose charge and a separate ball (or other missile).

5A Exemptions from requirement of authority under s5

(1) Subject to subsection (2) below, the authority of the Secretary of State shall not be required by virtue of subsection (1A) of section 5 of this Act for any person to have in his possession, or to purchase, acquire, sell or transfer, any prohibited weapon or ammunition if he is authorised by a certificate under this Act to possess, purchase or acquire that weapon or ammunition subject to a condition that he does so only for the purpose of it being kept or exhibited as part of a collection.

(2) No sale or transfer may be made under subsection (1) above except to a person who –

(a) produces the authority of the Secretary of State under section 5 of this Act for his purchase or acquisition; or
(b) shows that he is, under this section or a licence under the Schedule to the Firearms (Amendment) Act 1988 (museums etc) entitled to make the purchase or acquisition without the authority of the Secretary of State.

(3) The authority of the Secretary of State shall not be required by virtue of subsection (1A) of section 5 of this Act for any person to have in his possession, or to purchase or acquire, any prohibited weapon or ammunition if his possession, purchase or acquisition is exclusively in connection with the carrying on of activities in respect of which –

(a) that person; or
(b) the person on whose behalf he has possession, or makes the purchase or acquisition,

is recognised, for the purposes of the law of another member State relating to firearms, as a collector of firearms or a body concerned in the cultural or historical aspects of weapons.

(4) The authority of the Secretary of State shall not be required by virtue of subsection (1A) of section 5 of this Act for any person to have in his possession, or to purchase or acquire, or to sell or transfer, any expanding ammunition or the missile for any such ammunition if –

(a) he is authorised by a firearm certificate to possess, purchase or acquire ammunition; and
(b) the certificate contains a condition prohibiting the use of expanding ammunition for purposes not authorised by the European weapons directive.

(5) The authority of the Secretary of State shall not be required by virtue of subsection (1A) of section 5 of this Act for any person to have in his possession any expanding ammunition or the missile for any such ammunition if –

(a) he is authorised by a firearm certificate or visitor's firearm permit to possess, or purchase or acquire, any expanding ammunition; and

(b) the certificate or permit is subject to a condition restricting the use of any expanding ammunition to use in connection with any one or more of the following, namely –

(i) the lawful shooting of deer;

(ii) the shooting of vermin or, in the course of carrying on activities in connection with the management of any estate, other wildlife;

(iii) the humane killing of animals;

(iv) the shooting of animals for the protection of other animals or humans.

(6) The authority of the Secretary of State shall not be required by virtue of subsection (1A) of section 5 of this Act for the sale or transfer of any expanding ammunition or the missile for any such ammunition to any person who produces a certificate by virtue of which he is authorised under subsection (4) above to purchase or acquire it without the authority of the Secretary of State.

(7) The authority of the Secretary of State shall not be required by virtue of subsection (1A) of section 5 of this Act for a person carrying on the business of a firearms dealer, or any servant of his, to have in his possession, or to purchase, acquire, sell or transfer, any expanding ammunition or the missile for any such ammunition in the ordinary course of that business.

(8) In this section –

(a) references to expanding ammunition are references to any ammunition which incorporates a missile which is designed to expand on impact; and

(b) references to the missile for any such ammunition are references to anything which, in relation to any such ammunition, falls within section 5(1A)(g) of this Act.

16 Possession of firearm with intent to injure

It is an offence for a person to have in his possession any firearm or ammunition with intent by means thereof to endanger life or to enable another person by means thereof to endanger life whether any injury has been caused or not.

16A Possession of firearm with intent to cause fear of violence

It is an offence for a person to have in his possession any firearm or imitation firearm with intent –

(a) by means thereof to cause, or

(b) to enable another person by means thereof to cause,

any person to believe that unlawful violence will be used against him or another person.

17 Use of firearm to resist arrest

(1) It is an offence for a person to make or attempt to make any use whatsoever of a firearm

or imitation firearm with intent to resist or prevent the lawful arrest or detention of himself or another person.

(2) If a person, at the time of his committing or being arrested for an offence specified in Schedule 1 to this Act, has in his possession a firearm or imitation firearm, he shall be guilty of an offence under this subsection unless he shows that he had it in his possession for a lawful object.

(4) For purposes of this section, the definition of 'firearm' in section 57(1) of this Act shall apply without paragraphs (b) and (c) of that subsection, and 'imitation firearm' shall be construed accordingly. ...

18 Carrying firearm with criminal intent

(1) It is an offence for a person to have with him a firearm or imitation firearm with intent to commit an indictable offence, or to resist arrest or prevent the arrest of another, in either case while he has the firearm or imitation firearm with him.

(2) In proceedings for an offence under this section proof that the accused had a firearm or imitation firearm with him and intended to commit an offence or to resist or prevent arrest, is evidence that he intended to have it with him while doing so. ...

19 Carrying firearm in a public place

A person commits an offence if, without lawful authority or reasonable excuse (the proof whereof lies on him) he has with him in a public place a loaded shot gun or loaded air weapon, or any other firearm (whether loaded or not) together with ammunition suitable for use in that firearm.

20 Trespassing with firearm

(1) A person commits an offence if, while he has a firearm or imitation firearm with him, he enters or is in any building or part of a building as a trespasser and without reasonable excuse (the proof whereof lies on him).

(2) A person commits an offence if, while he has a firearm or imitation firearm with him, he enters or is on any land as a trespasser and without reasonable excuse (the proof whereof lies on him).

(3) In subsection (2) of this section the expression 'land' includes land covered with water.

21 Possession of firearms by persons previously convicted of crime

(1) A person who has been sentenced to custody for life or to preventive detention, or to imprisonment or to corrective training for a term of three years or more or to youth custody or detention in a young offender institution for such a term, or who has been sentenced to be detained for such a term in a young offenders institution in Scotland, shall not at any time have a firearm or ammunition in his possession.

(2) A person who has been sentenced to imprisonment for a term of three months or more but less than three years or to youth custody or detention in a young offender institution for such a term, or who has been sentenced to be detained for such a term in a detention centre or in a young offenders institution in Scotland or who has been subject to a secure training order, shall not at any time before the expiration of the period of five years from the date of his release have a firearm or ammunition in his possession.

(2A) For the purposes of subsection (2) above, 'the date of his release' means –

(a) in the case of a person sentenced to imprisonment with an order under section 47(1) of the Criminal Law Act 1977 (prison sentence partly served and partly suspended), the date on which he completes service of so much of the sentence as was by that order required to be served in prison;

(b) in the case of a person who has been subject to a secure training order –

(i) the date on which he is released from detention under the order;

(ii) the date on which he is released from detention ordered under section 4 of the Criminal Justice and Public Order Act 1994; or

(iii) the date halfway through the total period specified by the court in making the order, whichever is the later.

(3) A person who –

(a) is the holder of a licence issued under section 53 of the Children and Young Persons Act 1933 or section 57 of the Children and Young Persons (Scotland) Act 1937 (which sections provide for the detention of children and young persons convicted of serious crime, but enable them to be discharged on licence by the Secretary of State); or

(b) is subject to a recognisance to keep the peace or to be of good behaviour, a condition of which is that he shall not possess, use or carry a firearm, or is subject to a probation order containing a requirement that he shall not possess, use or carry a firearm; or

(c) has, in Scotland, been ordained to find caution a condition of which is that he shall not possess, use or carry a firearm;

shall not, at any time during which he holds the licence or is so subject or has been so ordained, have a firearm or ammunition in his possession.

(3A) Where by section 19 of the Firearms Act (Northern Ireland) 1969, or by any other enactment for the time being in force in Northern Ireland and corresponding to this section, a person is prohibited in Northern Ireland from having a firearm or ammunition in his possession, he shall also be so prohibited in Great Britain at any time when to have it in his possession in Northern Ireland would be a contravention of the said section 19 or corresponding enactment.

(4) It is an offence for a person to contravene any of the foregoing provisions of this section.

(5) It is an offence for a person to sell or transfer a firearm or ammunition to, or to repair, test or prove a firearm or ammunition for, a person whom he knows or has reasonable ground for believing to be prohibited by this section from having a firearm or ammunition in his possession.

(6) A person prohibited under subsection (1), (2), (3) or (3A) of this section from having in

his possession a firearm or ammunition may apply to the Crown Court or, in Scotland, in accordance with Act of Sederunt to the sheriff for a removal of the prohibition; and if the application is granted that prohibition shall not then apply to him.

(7) Schedule 3 to this Act shall have effect with respect to the courts with jurisdiction to entertain an application under this section and to the procedure appertaining thereto.

22 Acquisition and possession of firearms by minors

(1) It is an offence for a person under the age of seventeen to purchase or hire any firearm or ammunition.

(1A) Where a person under the age of eighteen is entitled, as the holder of a certificate under this Act, to have a firearm in his possession, it is an offence for that person to use that firearm for a purpose not authorised by the European weapons directive.

(2) It is an offence for a person under the age of fourteen to have in his possession any firearm or ammunition to which section 1 of this Act or section 15 of the Firearms (Amendment) Act 1988 applies, except in circumstances where under section 11(1), (3) or (4) of this Act he is entitled to have possession of it without holding a firearm certificate.

(3) It is an offence for a person under the age of fifteen to have with him an assembled shot gun except while under the supervision of a person of or over the age of twenty-one, or while the shot gun is so covered with a securely fastened gun cover that it cannot be fired.

(4) Subject to section 23 below, it is an offence for a person under the age of fourteen to have with him an air weapon or ammunition for an air weapon.

(5) Subject to section 23 below, it is an offence for a person under the age of seventeen to have an air weapon with him in a public place, except an air gun or air rifle which is so covered with a securely fastened gun cover that it cannot be fired.

23 Exceptions from s22(4) and (5)

(1) It is not an offence under section 22(4) of this Act for a person to have with him an air weapon or ammunition while he is under the supervision of a person of or over the age of twenty-one; but where a person has with him an air weapon on any premises in circumstances where he would be prohibited from having it with him but for this subsection, it is an offence –

    (a) for him to use it for firing any missile beyond those premises; or
    (b) for the person under whose supervision he is to allow him so to use it.

(2) It is not an offence under section 22(4) or (5) of this Act for a person to have with him an air weapon or ammunition at a time when –

    (a) being a member of a rifle club or miniature rifle club for the time being approved by the Secretary of State for the purposes of this section or section 15 of the Firearms (Amendment) Act 1988, he is engaged as such a member in connection with target shooting; or

(b) he is using the weapon or ammunition at a shooting gallery where the only firearms used are either air weapons or miniature rifles not exceeding .23 inch calibre.

24 Supplying firearms to minors

(1) It is an offence to sell or let on hire any firearm or ammunition to a person under the age of seventeen.

(2) It is an offence –

(a) to make a gift of or lend any firearm or ammunition to which section 1 of this Act applies to a person under the age of fourteen; or
(b) to part with the possession of any such firearm or ammunition to a person under that age, except in circumstances where that person is entitled under section 11(1), (3) or (4) of this Act to have possession thereof without holding a firearm certificate.

(3) It is an offence to make a gift of a shot gun or ammunition for a shot gun to a person under the age of fifteen.

(4) It is an offence –

(a) to make a gift of an air weapon or ammunition for an air weapon to a person under the age of fourteen; or
(b) to part with the possession of an air weapon or ammunition for an air weapon to a person under that age except where by virtue of section 23 of this Act or section 15 of the Firearms (Amendment) Act 1988 the person is not prohibited from having it with him.

(5) In proceedings for an offence under any provision of this section it is a defence to prove that the person charged with the offence believed the other person to be of or over the age mentioned in that provision and had reasonable ground for the belief.

25 Supplying firearm to person drunk or insane

It is an offence for a person to sell or transfer any firearm or ammunition to, or to repair, prove or test any firearm or ammunition for, another person whom he knows or has reasonable cause for believing to be drunk or of unsound mind.

57 Interpretation

(1) In this Act, the expression 'firearm' means a lethal barrelled weapon of any description from which any shot, bullet or other missile can be discharged and includes –

(a) any prohibited weapon, whether it is such a lethal weapon as aforesaid or not; and
(b) any component part of such a lethal or prohibited weapon; and
(c) any accessory to any such weapon designed or adapted to diminish the noise or flash caused by firing the weapon;

and so much of section 1 of this Act as excludes any description of firearm from the category of firearms to which that section applies shall be construed as also excluding component parts of, and accessories to, firearms of that description.

(2) In this Act, the expression 'ammunition' means ammunition for any firearm and includes grenades, bombs and other like missiles, whether capable of use with a firearm or not, and also includes prohibited ammunition.

(2A) In this Act 'self-loading' and 'pump-action' in relation to any weapon mean respectively that it is designed or adapted (otherwise than as mentioned in section 5(1)(a)) so that it is automatically reloaded or that it is so designed or adapted that it is reloaded by the manual operation of the fore-end or forestock of the weapon.

(2B) In this Act 'revolver', in relation to a smooth-bore gun, means a gun containing a series of chambers which revolve when the gun is fired. ...

Schedule 1
Offences to Which Section 17(2) Applies

1 Offences under section 1 of the Criminal Damage Act 1971.

2 Offences under any of the following provisions of the Offences Against the Person Act 1861 –

  sections 20 to 22 (inflicting bodily injury; garrotting; criminal use of stupefying drugs);
  section 30 (laying explosive to buildings, etc);
  section 32 (endangering railway passengers by tampering with track);
  section 38 (assault with intent to commit felony or resist arrest);
  section 47 (criminal assaults);

2A Offences under Part 1 of the Child Abduction Act 1984 (abduction of children)

4 Theft, robbery, burglary, blackmail, and any offence under section 12(1) (taking of motor vehicle or other conveyance without owner's consent) of the Theft Act 1968.

5 Offences under section 89(1) of the Police Act 1996 or section 41 of the Police (Scotland) Act 1967 (assaulting constable in execution of his duty).

5A An offence under section 90(1) of the Criminal Justice Act 1991 (assaulting prisoner custody officer).

5B An offence under section 13(1) of the Criminal Justice and Public Order Act 1994 (assaulting secure training centre custody officer).

6 Offences under any of the following provisions of the Sexual Offences Act 1956 –

  section 1 (rape);
  sections 17, 18 and 20 (abduction of women).

8 Aiding and abetting the commission of any offence specified in paragraphs 1 to 6 of this Schedule.

9 Attempting to commit any offence so specified.

[As amended by the Theft Act 1968, s33(2), Schedule 2, Part III; Criminal Damage Act 1971, s11(7), (8), Schedule, Part I; Courts Act 1971, s56(2), Schedule 9, Part II; Criminal Justice Act 1972, s29; Criminal Law Act 1977, s47, Schedule 9, para 9; Criminal Justice Act 1982, s77, Schedule 14, para 24; Child Abduction Act 1984, s11(2); Criminal Justice Act 1988, s123(6), Schedule 8, Part I, para 6, s170(2), Schedule 16; Firearms (Amendment) Act 1988, ss1(1), (2), (3), 2, 23(1) (4), 25(1), (2); Firearms Acts (Amendment) Regulations 1992, regs 3, 4(1); Firearms (Amendment) Act 1994, ss1(1), 2(1); Criminal Justice and Public Order Act 1994, s168(1), (2), Schedule 9, para 8, Schedule 10, para 24(1), (2); Police Act 1996, s103(1), Schedule 7, Pt II, para 16; Firearms (Amendment) Act 1997, ss1(1)–(6), 9, 10, 52(1), (2), Schedule 2, paras 1, 2(1), 3, Schedule 3; Firearms (Amendment) (No 2) Act 1997, ss1, 2(7), Schedule.]

Theft Act 1968
(1968 c 60)

1 Basic definition of theft

(1) A person is guilty of theft if he dishonestly appropriates property belonging to another with the intention of permanently depriving the other of it; and 'thief' and 'steal' shall be construed accordingly.

(2) It is immaterial whether the appropriation is made with a view to gain, or is made for the thief's own benefit.

(3) The five following sections of this Act shall have effect as regards the interpretation and operation of this section (and, except as otherwise provided by this Act, shall apply only for purposes of this section).

2 'Dishonestly'

(1) A person's appropriation of property belonging to another is not to be regarded as dishonest –

(a) if he appropriates the property in the belief that he has in law the right to deprive the other of it, on behalf of himself or of a third person; or

(b) if he appropriates the property in the belief that he would have the other's consent if the other knew of the appropriation and the circumstances of it; or

(c) (except where the property came to him as trustee or personal representative) if he appropriates the property in the belief that the person to whom the property belongs cannot be discovered by taking reasonable steps.

(2) A person's appropriation of property belonging to another may be dishonest notwithstanding that he is willing to pay for the property.

3 'Appropriates'

(1) Any assumption by a person of the rights of an owner amounts to an appropriation, and this includes, where he has come by the property (innocently or not) without stealing it, any later assumption of a right to it by keeping or dealing with it as owner.

(2) Where property or a right or interest in property is or purports to be transferred for value to a person acting in good faith, no later assumption by him of rights which he

believed himself to be acquiring shall, by reason of any defect in the transferor's title, amount to theft of the property.

4 'Property'

(1) 'Property' includes money and all other property, real or personal, including things in action and other intangible property.

(2) A person cannot steal land, or things forming part of land and severed from it by him or by his directions, except in the following cases, that is to say –

(a) when he is a trustee or personal representative, or is authorised by power of attorney, or as liquidator of a company; or otherwise, to sell or dispose of land belonging to another, and he appropriates the land or anything forming part of it by dealing with it in breach of the confidence reposed in him; or

(b) when he is not in possession of the land and appropriates anything forming part of the land by severing it or causing it to be severed, or after it has been severed; or

(c) when, being in possession of the land under a tenancy, he appropriates the whole or part of any fixture or structure let to be used with the land.

For purposes of this subsection 'land' does not include incorporeal hereditaments, 'tenancy' means a tenancy for years or any less period and includes an agreement for such a tenancy, but a person who after the end of a tenancy remains in possession as statutory tenant or otherwise is to be treated as having possession under the tenancy, and 'let' shall be construed accordingly.

(3) A person who picks mushrooms growing wild on any land, or who picks flowers, fruit or foliage from a plant growing wild on any land, does not (although not in possession of the land) steal what he picks, unless he does it for reward or for sale or other commercial purpose.

For purposes of this subsection 'mushroom' includes any fungus, and 'plant' includes any shrub or tree.

(4) Wild creatures, tamed or untamed, shall be regarded as property; but a person cannot steal a wild creature not tamed nor ordinarily kept in captivity, or the carcass of any such creature, unless either it has been reduced into possession by or on behalf of another person and possession of it has not since been lost or abandoned, or another person is in course of reducing it into possession.

5 'Belonging to another'

(1) Property shall be regarded as belonging to any person having possession or control of it, or having in it any proprietary right or interest (not being an equitable interest arising only from an agreement to transfer or grant an interest).

(2) Where property is subject to a trust, the persons to whom it belongs shall be regarded as including any person having a right to enforce the trust, and an intention to defeat the trust shall be regarded accordingly as an intention to deprive of the property any person having that right.

(3) Where a person receives property from or on account of another, and is under an obligation to the other to retain and deal with that property or its proceeds in a particular way, the property or proceeds shall be regarded (as against him) as belonging to the other.

(4) Where a person gets property by another's mistake, and is under an obligation to make restoration (in whole or in part) of the property or its proceeds or of the value thereof, then to the extent of that obligation the property or proceeds shall be regarded (as against him) as belonging to the person entitled to restoration, and an intention not to make restoration shall be regarded accordingly as an intention to deprive that person of the property or proceeds.

(5) Property of a corporation sole shall be regarded as belonging to the corporation notwithstanding a vacancy in the corporation.

6 'With the intention of permanently depriving the other of it'

(1) A person appropriating property belonging to another without meaning the other permanently to lose the thing itself is nevertheless to be regarded as having the intention of permanently depriving the other of it if his intention is to treat the thing as his own to dispose of regardless of the other's rights; and a borrowing or lending of it may amount to so treating it if, but only if, the borrowing or lending is for a period and in circumstances making it equivalent to an outright taking or disposal.

(2) Without prejudice to the generality of subsection (1) above, where a person, having possession or control (lawfully or not) of property belonging to another, parts with the property under a condition as to its return which he may not be able to perform, this (if done for purposes of his own and without the other's authority) amounts to treating the property as his own to dispose of regardless of the other's rights.

7 Theft

A person guilty of theft shall on conviction on indictment be liable to imprisonment for a term not exceeding seven years.

8 Robbery

(1) A person is guilty of robbery if he steals, and immediately before or at the time of doing so, and in order to do so, he uses force on any person or puts or seeks to put any person in fear of being then and there subjected to force.

(2) A person guilty of robbery, or of an assault with intent to rob, shall on conviction on indictment be liable to imprisonment for life.

9 Burglary

(1) A person is guilty of burglary if –

   (a) he enters any building or part of a building as a trespasser and with intent to commit any such offence as is mentioned in subsection (2) below; or

(b) having entered any building or part of a building as a trespasser he steals or attempts to steal anything in the building or that part of it or inflicts or attempts to inflict on any person therein any grievous bodily harm.

(2) The offences referred to in subsection (1)(a) above are offences of stealing anything in the building or part of a building in question, of inflicting on any person, therein any grievous bodily harm or raping any person therein, and of doing unlawful damage to the building or anything therein.

(3) A person guilty of burglary shall on conviction on indictment be liable to imprisonment for a term not exceeding –

(a) where the offence was committed in respect of a building or part of a building which is a dwelling, fourteen years;
(b) in any other case, ten years.

(4) References in subsections (1) and (2) above to a building, and the reference in subsection (3) above to a building which is a dwelling, shall apply also to an inhabited vehicle or vessel, and shall apply to any such vehicle or vessel at times when the person having a habitation in it is not there as well as at times when he is.

10 Aggravated burglary

(1) A person is guilty of aggravated burglary if he commits any burglary and at the time has with him any firearm or imitation firearm, any weapon of offence, or any explosive; and for this purpose –

(a) 'firearm' includes an airgun or air pistol, and 'imitation firearm' means anything which has the appearance of being a firearm, whether capable of being discharged or not; and
(b) 'weapon of offence' means any article made or adapted for use for causing injury to or incapacitating a person, or intended by the person having it with him for such use; and
(c) 'explosive' means any article manufactured for the purpose of producing a practical effect by explosion, or intended by the person having it with him for that purpose.

(2) A person guilty of aggravated burglary shall on conviction on indictment be liable to imprisonment for life.

11 Removal of articles from places open to the public

(1) Subject to subsections (2) and (3) below, where the public have access to a building in order to view the building or part of it, or a collection or part of a collection housed in it, any person who without lawful authority removes from the building or its grounds the whole or part of any article displayed or kept for display to the public in the building or that part of it or in its grounds shall be guilty of an offence.

For this purpose 'collection' includes a collection got together for a temporary purpose, but references in this section to a collection do not apply to a collection made or exhibited for the purpose of effecting sales or other commercial dealings.

(2) It is immaterial for purposes of subsection (1) above, that the public's access to a building is limited to a particular period or particular occasion; but where anything removed from a building or its grounds is there otherwise than as forming part of, or being on loan for exhibition with, a collection intended for permanent exhibition to the public, the person removing it does not thereby commit an offence under this section unless he removes it on a day when the public have access to the building as mentioned in subsection (1) above.

(3) A person does not commit an offence under this section if he believes that he has lawful authority for the removal of the thing in question or that he would have it if the person entitled to give it knew of the removal of the circumstances of it.

(4) A person guilty of an offence under this section shall, on conviction on indictment be liable to imprisonment for a term not exceeding five years.

12 Taking motor vehicle or other conveyance without authority

(1) Subject to subsections (5) and (6) below, a person shall be guilty of an offence if, without having the consent of the owner or other lawful authority, he takes any conveyance for his own or another's use or, knowing that any conveyance has been taken without such authority, drives it or allows himself to be carried in or on it.

(2) A person guilty of an offence under subsection (1) above shall be liable on summary conviction to fine not exceeding level 5 on the standard scale, to imprisonment for a term not exceeding six months, or to both.

(4) If on the trial of an indictment for theft the jury are not satisfied that the accused committed theft, but it is proved that the accused committed an offence under subsection (1) above, the jury may find him guilty of the offence under subsection (1) and if he is found guilty of it, he shall be liable as he would have been liable under subsection (2) above on summary conviction.

(5) Subsection (1) above shall not apply in relation to pedal cycles; but, subject to subsection (6) below, a person who, without having the consent of the owner or other lawful authority, takes a pedal cycle for his own or another's use, or rides a pedal cycle knowing it to have been taken without such authority, shall on summary conviction be liable to a fine not exceeding level 3 on the standard scale.

(6) A person does not commit an offence under this section by anything done in the belief that he has lawful authority to do it or that he would have the owner's consent if the owner knew of his doing it and the circumstances of it.

(7) For purposes of this section –

(a) 'conveyance' means any conveyance constructed or adapted for the carriage of a person or person whether by land, water or air, except that it does not include a conveyance constructed or adapted for use only under the control of a person not carried in or on it, and 'drive' shall be construed accordingly; and

(b) 'owner', in relation to a conveyance which is the subject of a hiring agreement or hire-purchase agreement, means the person in possession of the conveyance under that agreement.

12A Aggravated vehicle-taking

(1) Subject to subsection (3) below, a person is guilty of aggravated taking of a vehicle if –

(a) he commits an offence under section 12(1) above (in this section referred to as a 'basic offence') in relation to a mechanically propelled vehicle; and

(b) it is proved that, at any time after the vehicle was unlawfully taken (whether by him or another) and before it was recovered, the vehicle was driven, or injury or damage was caused, in one or more of the circumstances set out in paragraphs (a) to (d) of subsection (2) below.

(2) The circumstances referred to in subsection (1)(b) above are –

(a) that the vehicle was driven dangerously on a road or other public place;

(b) that, owing to the driving of the vehicle, an accident occurred by which injury was caused to any person;

(c) that, owing to the driving of the vehicle, an accident occurred by which damage was caused to any property, other than the vehicle;

(d) that damage was caused to the vehicle.

(3) A person is not guilty of an offence under this section if he proves that, as regards any such proven driving, injury or damage as is referred to in subsection (1)(b) above, either –

(a) the driving, accident or damage referred to in subsection (2) above occurred before he committed the basic offence; or

(b) he was neither in nor on nor in the immediate vicinity of the vehicle when that driving, accident or damage occurred.

(4) A person guilty of an offence under this section shall be liable on conviction on indictment to imprisonment for a term not exceeding two years or, if it is proved that, in circumstances falling within subsection (2)(b) above, the accident caused the death of the person concerned, five years.

(5) If a person who is charged with an offence under this section is found not guilty of that offence but it is proved that he committed a basic offence, he may be convicted of the basic offence.

(6) If by virtue of subsection (5) above a person is convicted of a basic offence before the Crown Court, that court shall have the same powers and duties as a magistrates' court would have had on convicting him of such an offence.

(7) For the purposes of this section a vehicle is driven dangerously if –

(a) it is driven in a way which falls far below what would be expected of a competent and careful driver; and

(b) it would be obvious to a competent and careful driver that driving the vehicle in that way would be dangerous.

(8) For the purposes of this section a vehicle is recovered when it is restored to its owner or to other lawful possession or custody; and in this subsection 'owner' has the same meaning as in section 12 above.

13 Abstracting of electricity

A person who dishonestly uses without due authority, or dishonestly causes to be wasted or diverted, any electricity shall on conviction on indictment be liable to imprisonment for a term not exceeding five years.

14 Extension to thefts from mails outside England and Wales, and robbery, etc on such a theft

(1) Where a person –

(a) steals or attempts to steal any mail bag or postal packet in the course of transmission as such between places in different jurisdictions in the British postal area, or any of the contents of such a mail bag or postal packet; or

(b) in stealing or with intent to steal any such mail bag or postal packet or any of its contents, commits any robbery, attempted robbery or assault with intent to rob;

then, notwithstanding that he does so outside England and Wales, he shall be guilty of committing or attempting to commit the offence against this Act as if he had done so in England or Wales, and he shall accordingly be liable to be prosecuted, tried and punished in England and Wales without proof that the offence was committed there.

(2) In subsection (1) above the reference to different jurisdictions in the British postal area is to be construed as referring to the several jurisdictions of England and Wales, of Scotland, of Northern Ireland, of the Isle of Man and of the Channel Islands.

(3) For purposes of this section 'mail bag' includes any article serving the purpose of a mail bag.

15 Obtaining property by deception

(1) A person who by any deception dishonestly obtains property belonging to another, with the intention of permanently depriving the other of it, shall on conviction on indictment be liable to imprisonment for a term not exceeding ten years.

(2) For purposes of this section a person is to be treated as obtaining property if he obtains ownership, possession or control of it, and 'obtain' includes obtaining for another or enabling another to obtain or to retain.

(3) Section 6 above shall apply for purposes of this section, with the necessary adaptation of the reference to appropriating, as it applies for purposes of section 1.

(4) For purposes of this section 'deception' means any deception (whether deliberate or reckless) by words or conduct as to fact or as to law, including a deception as to the present intentions of the person using the deception or any other person.

15A Obtaining a money transfer by deception

(1) A person is guilty of an offence if by any deception he dishonestly obtains a money transfer for himself or another.

(2) A money transfer occurs when –

(a) a debit is made to one account,
(b) a credit is made to another, and
(c) the credit results from the debit or the debit results from the credit.

(3) Reference to a credit and to a debit are to a credit of an amount of money and to a debit of an amount of money.

(4) It is immaterial (in particular) –

(a) whether the amount credited is the same as the amount debited;
(b) whether the money transfer is effected on presentment of a cheque or by another method;
(c) whether any delay occurs in the process by which the money transfer is effected;
(d) whether any intermediate credits or debits are made in the course of the money transfer;
(e) whether either of the accounts is overdrawn before or after the money transfer is effected.

(5) A person guilty of an offence under this section shall be liable on conviction on indictment to imprisonment for a term not exceeding ten years.

15B Section 15A: supplementary

(1) The following provisions have effect for the interpretation of section 15A of this Act.

(2) 'Deception' has the same meaning as in section 15 of this Act.

(3) 'Account' means an account kept with –

(a) a bank; or
(b) a person carrying on a business which falls within subsection (4) below.

(4) A business falls within this subsection if –

(a) in the course of the business money received by way of deposit is lent to others; or
(b) any other activity of the business is financed, wholly or to any material extent, out of the capital of or the interest on money received by way of deposit;

and 'deposit' here has the same meaning as in section 35 of the Banking Act 1987 (fraudulent inducement to make a deposit).

(5) For the purposes of subsection (4) above –

(a) all the activities which a person carries on by way of business shall be regarded as a single business carried on by him; and
(b) 'money' includes money expressed in a currency other than sterling or in the European currency unit (as defined in Council Regulation No 3320/94/EC or any Community instrument replacing it).

16 Obtaining pecuniary advantage by deception

(1) A person who by any deception dishonestly obtains for himself or another any pecuniary

advantage shall on conviction on indictment be liable to imprisonment for a term not exceeding five years.

(2) The cases in which a pecuniary advantage within the meaning of this section is to be regarded as obtained for a person are cases where –

(b) he is allowed to borrow by way of overdraft, or to take out any policy of insurance or annuity contract, or obtains an improvement of the terms on which he is allowed to do so; or

(c) he is given the opportunity to earn remuneration or greater remuneration in an office or employment, or to win money by betting.

(3) For purposes of this section 'deception' has the same meaning as in section 15 of this Act.

17 False accounting

(1) Where a person dishonestly, with a view to gain for himself or another or with intent to cause loss to another –

(a) destroys, defaces, conceals or falsifies any account or any record or document made or required for any accounting purpose; or

(b) in furnishing information for any purpose produces or makes use of any account, or any such record or document as aforesaid, which to his knowledge is or may be misleading, false or deceptive in a material particular;

he shall, on conviction on indictment, be liable to imprisonment for a term not exceeding seven years.

(2) For purposes of this section a person who makes or concurs in making in an account or other document an entry which is or may be misleading, false or deceptive in a material particular, or who omits or concurs in omitting a material particular from an account or other document, is to be treated as falsifying the account or document.

18 Liability of company officers for certain offences by company

(1) Where an offence committed by a body corporate under sections 15, 16 or 17 of this Act is proved to have been committed with the consent or connivance of any director, manager, secretary or other similar officer of the body corporate or any person who was purporting to act in any such capacity, he as well as the body corporate shall be guilty of that offence, and shall be liable to be proceeded against and punished accordingly.

(2) Where the affairs of a body corporate are managed by its members, this section shall apply in relation to the acts and defaults of a member in connection with his functions of management as if he were a director of the body corporate.

19 False statements by company directors, etc

(1) Where an officer of a body corporate or unincorporated association (or person purporting to act as such), with intent to deceive members or creditors of the body

corporate or association about its affairs, publishes or concurs in publishing a written statement or account which to his knowledge is or may be misleading, false or deceptive in a material particular, he shall on conviction on indictment be liable to imprisonment for a term not exceeding seven years.

(2) For purposes of this section a person who has entered into a security for the benefit of a body corporate or association is to be treated as a creditor of it.

(3) Where the affairs of a body corporate or association are managed by its members, this section shall apply to any statement which a member publishes or concurs in publishing in connection with his functions of management as if he were an officer of the body corporate or association.

20 Suppression, etc of documents

(1) A person who dishonestly, with a view to gain for himself or another or with intent to cause loss to another, destroys, defaces or conceals any valuable security, any will or other testamentary document or any original document of or belonging to, or filed or deposited in, any court of justice or any government department shall on conviction on indictment be liable to imprisonment for a term not exceeding seven years.

(2) A person who dishonestly, with a view to gain for himself or another or with intent to cause loss to another, by any deception procures the execution of a valuable security shall on conviction on indictment be liable to imprisonment for a term not exceeding seven years; and this subsection shall apply in relation to the making, acceptance, indorsement, alteration, cancellation or destruction in whole or in part of a valuable security, and in relation to the signing or sealing of any paper or other material in order that it may be made or converted into, or used or dealt with as, a valuable security, as if that were the execution of a valuable security.

(3) For purposes of this section 'deception' has the same meaning as in section 15 of this Act, and 'valuable security' means any document creating, transferring, surrendering or releasing any right to, in or over property, or authorising the payment of money or delivery of any property, or evidencing the creation, transfer, surrender or release of any such right, or the payment of money or delivery of any property, or the satisfaction of any obligation.

21 Blackmail

(1) A person is guilty of blackmail if, with a view to gain for himself or another or with intent to cause loss to another, he makes any unwarranted demand with menaces; and for this purpose this demand with menaces is unwarranted unless the person making it does so in belief –

   (a) that he has reasonable grounds for making the demand; and
   (b) that the use of the menaces is a proper means of reinforcing the demand.

(2) The nature of the act or omission demanded is immaterial, and it is also immaterial whether the menaces relate to action to be taken by the person making the demand.

(3) A person guilty of blackmail shall on conviction on indictment be liable to imprisonment for a term not exceeding fourteen years.

22 Handling stolen goods

(1) A person handles stolen goods if (otherwise than in the course of the stealing) knowing or believing them to be stolen goods he dishonestly receives the goods or dishonestly undertakes or assists in their retention, removal, disposal or realisation by or for the benefit of another person, or if he arranges to do so.

(2) A person guilty of handling stolen goods shall on conviction on indictment be liable to imprisonment for a term not exceeding fourteen years.

23 Advertising rewards for return of goods stolen or lost

Where any public advertisement of a reward for the return of any goods which have been stolen or lost uses any words to the effect that no question will be asked, or that the person producing the goods will be safe from apprehension or inquiry, or that any money paid for the purchase of the goods or advanced by way of loan on them will be repaid, the person advertising the reward and any person who prints or publishes the advertisement shall on summary conviction be liable to a fine not exceeding level 3 on the standard scale.

24 Scope of offences relating to stolen goods

(1) The provisions of this Act relating to goods which have been stolen shall apply whether the stealing occurred in England or Wales or elsewhere, and whether it occurred before or after the commencement of this Act, provided that the stealing (if not an offence under this Act) amounted to an offence where and at the time when the goods were stolen; and references to stolen goods shall be construed accordingly.

(2) For purposes of those provisions references to stolen goods shall include, in addition to the goods originally stolen and parts of them (whether in their original state or not) –

(a) any other goods which directly or indirectly represent or have at any time represented the stolen goods in the hands of the thief as being the proceeds of any disposal or realisation of the whole or part of the goods stolen or of goods so representing the stolen goods; and

(b) any other goods which directly or indirectly represent or have at any time represented the stolen goods in the hands of a handler of the stolen goods or any part of them as being the proceeds of any disposal or realisation of the whole or part of the stolen goods handled by him or of goods so representing them.

(3) But no goods shall be regarded as having continued to be stolen goods after they have been restored to the person from whom they were stolen or to other lawful possession or custody, or after that person or any other person claiming through him have otherwise ceased as regards those goods to have any right to restitution in respect of the theft.

(4) For purposes of the provisions of this Act relating to goods which have been stolen (including subsections (1) to (3) above) goods obtained in England or Wales or elsewhere

either by blackmail or in the circumstances described in section 15(1) of this Act shall be regarded as stolen; and 'steal', 'theft' and 'thief' shall be construed accordingly.

24A Dishonestly retaining a wrongful credit

(1) A person is guilty of an offence if –

(a) a wrongful credit has been made to an account kept by him or in respect of which he has any right or interest;
(b) he knows or believes that the credit is wrongful; and
(c) he dishonestly fails to take such steps as are reasonable in the circumstances to secure that the credit is cancelled.

(2) References to a credit are to a credit of an amount of money.

(3) A credit to an account is wrongful if it is the credit side of a money transfer obtained contrary to section 15A of this Act.

(4) A credit to an account is also wrongful to the extent that it derives from –

(a) theft;
(b) an offence under section 15A of this Act;
(c) blackmail; or
(d) stolen goods.

(5) In determining whether a credit to an account is wrongful, it is immaterial (in particular) whether the account is overdrawn before or after the credit is made.

(6) A person guilty of an offence under this section shall be liable on conviction on indictment to imprisonment for a term not exceeding ten years.

(7) Subsection (8) below applies for purposes of provisions of this Act relating to stolen goods (including subsection (4) above).

(8) References to stolen goods include money which is dishonestly withdrawn from an account to which a wrongful credit has been made, but only to the extent that the money derives from the credit.

(9) In this section 'account' and 'money' shall be construed in accordance with section 15B of this Act.

25 Going equipped for stealing, etc

(1) A person shall be guilty of an offence if, when not at his place of abode, he has with him any article for use in the course of or in connection with any burglary, theft or cheat.

(2) A person guilty of an offence under this section shall on conviction on indictment be liable to imprisonment for a term not exceeding three years.

(3) Where a person is charged with an offence under this section, proof that he had with him any article made or adapted for use in committing a burglary, theft or cheat shall be evidence that he had it with him for such use.

(4) Any person may arrest without warrant anyone who is, or whom he, with reasonable cause, suspects to be, committing an offence under this section.

(5) For purposes of this section an offence under section 12(1) of this Act of taking a conveyance shall be treated as theft, and 'cheat' means an offence under section 15 of this Act.

26 Search for stolen goods

(1) If it is made to appear by information on oath before a justice of the peace that there is reasonable cause to believe that any person has in his custody or possession or on his premises any stolen goods, the justice may grant a warrant to search for and seize the same; but no warrant to search for stolen goods shall be addressed to a person other than a constable except under the authority of an enactment expressly so providing.

(3) Where under this section a person is authorised to search premises for stolen goods, he may enter and search the premises accordingly, and may seize any goods he believes to be stolen goods.

(5) This section is to be construed in accordance with section 24 of this Act.

30 Husband and wife

(1) This Act shall apply in relation to the parties to a marriage, and to property belonging to the wife or husband whether or not by reason of an interest derived from the marriage, as it would apply if they were not married and any such interest subsisted independently of the marriage.

(2) Subject to subsection (4) below, a person shall have the same right to bring proceedings against that person's wife or husband for any offence (whether under this Act or otherwise) as if they were not married, and a person bringing any such proceedings shall be competent to give evidence for the prosecution at every stage of the proceedings.

(4) Proceedings shall not be instituted against a person for any offence of stealing or doing unlawful damage to property which at the time of the offence belongs to that person's wife or husband, or for any attempt, incitement or conspiracy to commit such an offence, unless the proceedings are instituted by or with the consent of the Director of Public Prosecutions:

Provided that –

   (a) this subsection shall not apply to proceedings against a person for an offence –

      (i) if that person is charged with committing the offence jointly with the wife or husband; or
      (ii) if by virtue of any judicial decree or order (wherever made) that person and the wife or husband are at the time of the offence under no obligation to cohabit.

(5) Notwithstanding section 6 of the Prosecution of Offences Act 1979 subsection (4) of this section shall apply –

   (a) to an arrest (if without warrant) made by the wife or husband, and
   (b) to a warrant of arrest issued on an information laid by the wife or husband.

32 Effect on existing law and construction of references to offences

(1) The following offences are hereby abolished for all purposes not relating to offences committed before the commencement of this Act, that is to say –

(a) any offence at common law of larceny, robbery, burglary, receiving stolen property, obtaining property by threats, extortion by colour of office or franchise, false accounting by public officers, concealment of treasure trove and, except as regards offences relating to the public revenue, cheating; and

(b) any offences under an enactment mentioned in Part I of Schedule 3 to this Act, to the extent to which the offence depends on any section or part of a section included in column 3 of that Schedule;

but so that the provisions in Schedule 1 to this Act (which preserve with modifications certain offences under the Larceny Act 1861 of taking or killing deer and taking or destroying fish) shall have effect as there set out.

(2) Except as regards offences committed before the commencement of this Act, and except in so far as the context otherwise requires, –

(a) references in any enactment passed before this Act to an offence abolished by this Act shall, subject to any express amendment or repeal made by this Act, have effect as references to the corresponding offence under this Act, and in any such enactment the expression 'receive' (when it relates to an offence of receiving) shall mean handle, and 'receiver' shall be construed accordingly; and

(b) without prejudice to paragraph (a) above, references in any enactment, whenever passed, to theft or stealing (including references to stolen goods), and references to robbery, blackmail, burglary, aggravated burglary or handling stolen goods, shall be construed in accordance with the provisions of this Act including those of section 24.

34 Interpretation

(1) Sections 4(1) and 5(1) of this Act shall apply generally for purposes of this Act as they apply for purposes of section 1.

(2) For purposes of this Act –

(a) 'gain' and 'loss' are to be construed as extending only to gain or loss in money or other property, but as extending to any such gain or loss whether temporary or permanent; and –

(i) 'gain' includes a gain by keeping what one has, as well as a gain by getting what one has not; and

(ii) 'loss' includes a loss by not getting what one might get, as well as a loss by parting with what one has;

(b) 'goods', except in so far as the context otherwise requires, includes money and every other description of property except land, and includes things severed from the land by stealing.

Schedule 1

Taking or destroying fish

2. – (1) Subject to subparagraph (2) below, a person who unlawfully takes or destroys, or attempts to take or destroy, any fish in water which is private property or in which there is any private right of fishery shall on summary conviction be liable to imprisonment for a term not exceeding three months or to a fine not exceeding level 3 on the standard scale or to both.

(2) Subparagraph (1) above shall not apply to taking or destroying fish by angling in the daytime (that is to say, in the period beginning one hour before sunrise and ending one hour after sunset); but a person who by angling in the daytime unlawfully takes or destroys, or attempts to take or destroy, any fish in water which is private property or in which there is any private right of fishery shall on summary conviction be liable to a fine not exceeding level 1 on the standard scale.

(3) The court by which a person is convicted of an offence under this paragraph may order the forfeiture of anything which, at the time of the offence, he had with him for use for taking or destroying fish.

(4) Any persons may arrest without warrant anyone who is, or whom he, with reasonable cause, suspects to be, committing an offence under subparagraph (1) above, and may seize from any person who is, or whom he, with reasonable cause, suspects to be, committing any offence under this paragraph anything which on that person's conviction of the offence would be liable to be forfeited under subparagraph (3) above.

[As amended by the Criminal Jurisdiction Act 1975, s14(4), Schedule 5, para 2; Theft Act 1978 s5(5); Prosecution of Offences Act 1979, s11(1), Schedule 1; Criminal Justice Act 1982, ss35, 38, 46; Criminal Justice Act 1988, s37(1); Criminal Justice Act 1991, s26(1), (2); Aggravated Vehicle-Taking Act 1992, s1(1); Criminal Justice and Public Order Act 1994, s168(2), Schedule 10, para 26; Theft (Amendment) Act 1996, ss1, 2.]

Genocide Act 1969
(1969 c 12)

1 Genocide

(1) A person commits an offence of genocide if he commits any act falling within the definition of 'genocide' in Article II of the Genocide Convention as set out in the Schedule to this Act.

(2) A person guilty of an offence of genocide shall on conviction on indictment –

   (a) if the offence consists of the killing of any person, be sentenced to imprisonment for life;
   (b) in any other case, be liable to imprisonment for a term not exceeding fourteen years.

(3) Proceedings for an offence of genocide shall not be instituted in England or Wales except by or with the consent of the Attorney General ...

Schedule

In the present Convention, genocide means any of the following acts committed with intent to destroy, in whole or in part, a national, ethical, racial or religious group, as such:

(a) Killing members of the group;
(b) Causing serious bodily or mental harm to members of the group;
(c) Deliberately inflicting on the group conditions of life calculated to bring about its physical destruction in whole or in part;
(d) Imposing measures intended to prevent births within the group;
(e) Forcibly transferring children of the group to another group.

[As amended by the Suppression of Terrorism Act 1978, s9(2), Schedule 2; Criminal Justice Act 1988, s170(1), Schedule 15, para 34, s170(2), Schedule 16; Extradition Act 1989, ss36(2), 37, Schedule 2.]

Tattooing of Minors Act 1969
(1969 c 24)

1 Prohibition of tattooing of minors

It shall be an offence to tattoo a person under the age of eighteen except when the tattoo is performed for medical reasons by a duly qualified medical practitioner or by a person working under his direction, but it shall be a defence for a person charged to show that the time the tattoo was performed he had reasonable cause to believe that the person tattooed was of or over the age of eighteen and did in fact so believe.

2 Penalties

Any person committing such an offence shall be liable on summary conviction to a fine not exceeding level 3 on the standard scale.

[As amended by the Criminal Justice Act 1982, ss38, 46.]

Late Night Refreshment Houses Act 1969
(1969 c 53)

9 Illegal and disorderly conduct

(1) If the licensee of a late night refreshment house knowingly permits unlawful gaming therein or knowingly permits prostitutes, thieves, or drunken and disorderly persons to assemble at, or continue in or upon, his premises, he shall be guilty of an offence.

(2) In subsection (1) of this section the reference to unlawful gaming is to the playing of any

game in such circumstances that an offence is committed under Part II of the Betting, Gaming and Lotteries Act 1963.

(4) If a person who is drunk, riotous, quarrelsome or disorderly in a late night refreshment house licensed under this Act refuses or neglects to leave it on being requested to do so by the manager or occupier, or his agent or servant, or by any constable, he shall be guilty of an offence.

Auctions (Bidding Agreements) Act 1969
(1969 c 56)

1 Offences under Auctions (Bidding Agreements) Act 1927 to be indictable as well as triable summarily, and extension of time for bringing summary proceedings

(1) Offences under section 1 of the Auctions (Bidding Agreements) Act 1927 (which, as amended by the Criminal Justice Act 1967, renders a dealer who agrees to give, or gives, or offers a gift or consideration to another as an inducement or reward for abstaining, or for having abstained, for bidding at a sale by auction punishable on summary conviction with a fine not exceeding £5,000 or imprisonment for a term not exceeding six months, or both, and renders similarly punishable a person who agrees to accept, or accepts, or attempts to obtain from a dealer any such gift or consideration as aforesaid) shall be triable on indictment as well as summarily; and the penalty that may be imposed on a person on conviction on indictment of an offence under that section shall be imprisonment for a term not exceeding two years or a fine or both.

2 Persons convicted not to attend or participate in auctions

(1) On any such summary conviction or conviction on indictment as is mentioned in section 1 above, the court may order that the person so convicted or that person and any representative of him shall not (without leave of the court) for a period from the date of such conviction –

    (a) in the case of a summary conviction, of not more than one year, or
    (b) in the case of a conviction on indictment, of not more than three years,

enter upon any premises where goods intended for sale by auction are on display or to attend or participate in any way in any sale by auction.

(2) In the event of a contravention of an order under this section, the person who contravenes it (and, if he is the representative of another, that other also) shall be guilty of an offence and liable –

    (a) on summary conviction, to a fine not exceeding the prescribed sum;
    (b) on conviction on indictment, to imprisonment for a term not exceeding two years or to a fine or to both.

(3) In any proceedings against a person in respect of a contravention of an order under this

section consisting in the entry upon premises where goods intended for sale by auction were on display, it shall be a defence for him to prove that he did not know, and had no reason to suspect, that goods so intended were on display on the premises, and in any proceedings against a person in respect of a contravention of such an order consisting in his having done something as the re-presentative of another, it shall be a defence for him to prove that he did not know, and had no reason to suspect, that that other was the subject of such an order.

(4) A person shall not be guilty of an offence under this section by reason only of his selling property by auction or causing it to be so sold.

3 Rights of seller of goods by auction where agreement subsists that some person shall abstain from bidding for the goods

(1) Where goods are purchased at an auction by a person who has entered into an agreement with another or others that the other or the others (or some of them) shall abstain from bidding for the goods (not being an agreement to purchase the goods bona fide on a joint account) and he or the other party, or one of the other parties, to the agreement is a dealer, the seller may avoid the contract under which the goods are purchased.

(2) Where a contract is avoided by virtue of the foregoing subsection, then, if the purchaser has obtained possession of the goods and restitution thereof is not made, the persons who were parties to the agreement that one or some of them should abstain from bidding for the goods the subject of the contract shall be jointly and severally liable to make good to the seller the loss (if any) he sustained by reason of the operation of the agreement.

(3) Subsection (1) above applies to a contract made after the commencement of this Act whether the agreement as to the abstention of a person or persons from bidding for the goods the subject of the contract was made before or after that commencement.

(4) Section 2 of the Auctions (Bidding Agreements) Act 1927 (right of vendors to treat certain sales as fraudulent) shall not apply to a sale the contract for which is made after the commencement of this Act.

(5) In this section 'dealer' has the meaning assigned to it by section 1(2) of the Auctions (Bidding Agreements) Act 1927.

4 Copy of Act to be exhibited at sale

Section 3 of the Auctions (Bidding Agreements) Act 1927 (copy of Act to be exhibited at sale) shall have effect, as if the reference to that Act included a reference to this Act.

[As amended by the Criminal Law Act 1977, s65(5), Schedule 13; Magistrates' Courts Act 1980, s32(9).]

Coinage Act 1971
(1971 c 24)

9 Prohibition of coins and tokens not issued by authority

(1) No piece of gold, silver, copper, or bronze, or of any metal or mixed metal, of any value whatever, shall be made or issued except with the authority of the Treasury, as a coin or a token for money, or as purporting that the holder thereof is entitled to demand any value denoted thereon.

(2) Every person who acts in contravention of this section shall be liable on summary conviction to a fine not exceeding level 2 on the standard scale.

10 Restrictions on melting or breaking of metal coins

(1) No person shall, except under the authority of a licence granted by the Treasury melt down or break up any metal coin which is for the time being current in the United Kingdom or which, having been current there, has at any time after 16 May 1969 ceased to be so.

(2) Any person who contravenes subsection (1) of this section shall be liable –

(a) on summary conviction, to a fine not exceeding the prescribed sum;
(b) on conviction on indictment, to a fine or to imprisonment for a term not exceeding two years, or both.

(3) If any condition attached to a licence granted under subsection (1) of this section is contravened or not complied with, the person to whom the licence was granted shall be liable on summary conviction to a fine not exceeding level 5 on the standard scale unless he proves that the contravention or non-compliance occurred without his consent or connivance and that he exercised all due diligence to prevent it.

(4) The court by or before which any person is convicted of an offence under this section may, whether or not it imposes any other punishment, order the articles in respect of which the offence was committed to be forfeited to Her Majesty.

(5) Where an offence under this section committed by a body corporate is proved to have been committed with the consent or connivance of, or to be attributable to any neglect on the part of, any director, manager, secretary or other similar officer of the body corporate or any person who was purporting to act in any such capacity, he as well as the body corporate shall be guilty of that offence and shall be liable to be proceeded against and punished accordingly.

[As amended by the Government Trading Funds Act 1973, s7(4); Magistrates' Courts Act 1980, s32(2); Criminal Justice Act 1982, ss37, 46.]

Unsolicited Goods and Services Act 1971
(1971 c 30)

2 Demands and threats regarding payment

(1) A person who, not having reasonable cause to believe there is a right to payment, in the course of any trade or business makes a demand for payment, or asserts a present or prospective right to payment, for what he knows are unsolicited goods sent (after the commencement of this Act) to another person with a view to his acquiring them, shall be guilty of an offence and on summary conviction shall be liable to a fine not exceeding level 4 on the standard scale.

(2) A person who, not having reasonable cause to believe there is a right to payment, in the course of any trade or business and with a view to obtaining any payment for what he knows are unsolicited goods sent as aforesaid –

(a) threatens to bring any legal proceedings; or
(b) places or causes to be placed the name of any person on a list of defaulters or debtors or threatens to do so; or
(c) invokes or causes to be invoked any other collection procedure or threatens to do so,

shall be guilty of an offence and shall be liable on summary conviction to a fine not exceeding level 5 on the standard scale.

3 Directory entries

(1) A person shall not be liable to make any payment, and shall be entitled to recover any payment made by him, by way of charge for including or arranging for the inclusion in a directory of an entry relating to that person or his trade or business, unless there has been signed by him or on his behalf an order complying with this section or a note complying with this section of his agreement to the charge and, in the case of a note of agreement to the charge, before the note was signed, a copy of it was supplied, for retention by him, to him or to a person acting on his behalf.

(2) A person shall be guilty of an offence punishable on summary conviction with a fine not exceeding the prescribed sum if, in a case where a payment in respect of a charge would, in the absence of an order or note of agreement to the charge complying with this section, be recoverable from him in accordance with the terms of subsection (1) above, he demands payment, or asserts a present or prospective right to payment, of the charge or any part of it, without knowing or having reasonable cause to believe that the entry to which the charge relates was ordered in accordance with this section or a proper note of agreement has been duly signed.

(3) For the purpose of subsection (1) above, an order for an entry in a directory must be made by means of an order form or other stationery belonging to the person to whom, or to whose trade or business, the entry is to relate and bearing, in print, the name and address (or one or more of the addresses) of that person; and the note required by this section of a

person's agreement to a charge must state the amount of the charge immediately above the place for signature, and –

(a) must identify the directory or proposed directory, and give the following particulars of it –

(i) the proposed date of publication of the directory or of the issue in which the entry is to be included and the name and address of the person producing it;
(ii) if the directory or that issue is to be put on sale, the price at which it is to be offered for sale and the minimum number of copies which are to be available for sale;
(iii) if the directory or that issue is to be distributed free of charge (whether or not it is also to be put on sale), the minimum number of copies which are to be so distributed; and

(b) must set out or give reasonable particulars of the entry in respect of which the charge would be payable.

(4) Nothing in this section shall apply to a payment due under a contract entered into before the commencement of this Act, or entered into by the acceptance of an offer made before that commencement.

3A Contents and form of notes of agreement, invoices and similar documents

(1) For the purposes of this Act, the Secretary of State may make regulations as to the contents and form of notes of agreement, invoices and similar documents; and, without prejudice to the generality of the foregoing, any such regulations may –

(a) require specified information to be included,
(b) prescribe the manner in which specified information is to be included,
(c) prescribe such other requirements (whether as to presentation, type, size, colour or disposition of lettering, quality or colour of paper or otherwise) as the Secretary of State may consider appropriate for securing that specified information is clearly brought to the attention of the recipient of any note of agreement, invoice or similar document,
(d) make different provision for different classes or descriptions of notes of agreement, invoices or similar documents or for the same class description in different circumstances,
(e) contain such supplementary and incidental provisions as the Secretary of State may consider appropriate.

(2) Any reference in this section to a note of agreement includes any such copy as is mentioned in section 3(1) of this Act.

(3) Regulations under this section shall be made by statutory instrument and shall be subject to annulment in pursuance of a resolution of either House of Parliament.

4 Unsolicited publications

(1) A person shall be guilty of an offence if he sends or causes to be sent to another person any book, magazine or leaflet (or advertising material for any such publication) which he

knows or ought reasonably to know is unsolicited and which describes or illustrates human sexual techniques.

(2) A person found guilty of an offence under this section shall be liable on summary conviction to a fine not exceeding level 5 on the standard scale.

(3) A prosecution for an offence under this section shall not in England and Wales be instituted except by, or with the consent of, the Director of Public Prosecutions.

[As amended by the Unsolicited Goods and Services (Amendment) Act 1975, ss1, 4(4); Magistrates' Courts Act 1980, s32(2); Criminal Justice Act 1982, ss38, 46.]

Misuse of Drugs Act 1971
(1971 c 38)

4 Restriction of production and supply of controlled drugs

(1) Subject to any regulations under section 7 of this Act for the time being in force, it shall not be lawful for a person –

(a) to produce a controlled drug; or
(b) to supply or offer to supply a controlled drug to another.

(2) Subject to section 28 of this Act, it is an offence for a person –

(a) to produce a controlled drug in contravention of subsection (1) above; or
(b) to be concerned in the production of such a drug in contravention of that subsection by another.

(3) Subject to section 28 of this Act, it is an offence for a person –

(a) to supply or offer to supply a controlled drug to another in contravention of subsection (1) above; or
(b) to be concerned in the supplying of such a drug to another in contravention of that subsection; or
(c) to be concerned in the making to another in contravention of that subsection of an offer to supply such a drug.

5 Restriction of possession of controlled drugs

(1) Subject to any regulations under section 7 of this Act for the time being in force it shall not be lawful for a person to have a controlled drug in his possession.

(2) Subject to section 28 of this Act and to subsection (4) below, it is an offence for a person to have a controlled drug in his possession in contravention of subsection (1) above.

(3) Subject to section 28 of this Act, it is an offence for a person to have a controlled drug in his possession, whether lawfully or not, with intent to supply it to another in contravention of section 4(1) of this Act.

(4) In any proceedings for an offence under subsection (2) above in which it is proved that the accused had a controlled drug in his possession, it shall be a defence for him to prove –

(a) that, knowing or suspecting it to be a controlled drug, he took possession of it for the purpose of preventing another from committing or continuing to commit an offence in connection with that drug and that as soon as possible after taking possession of it he took all such steps as were reasonably open to him to destroy the drug or to deliver it into the custody of a person lawfully entitled to take custody of it; or

(b) that, knowing or suspecting it to be a controlled drug, he took possession of it for the purpose of delivering it into the custody of a person lawfully entitled to take custody of it and that as soon as possible after taking possession of it he took all such steps as were reasonably open to him to deliver it into the custody of such a person.

(6) Nothing in subsection (4) above shall prejudice any defence which it is open to a person charged with an offence under this section to raise apart from that subsection.

6 Restrictions of cultivation of cannabis plant

(1) Subject to any regulations under section 7 of this Act for the time being in force, it shall not be lawful for a person to cultivate any plants of the genus Cannabis.

(2) Subject to section 28 of this Act, it is an offence to cultivate any such plant in contravention of subsection (1) above.

8 Occupiers, etc of premises to be punishable for permitting certain activities to take place there

A person commits an offence if, being the occupier or concerned in the management of any premises, he knowingly permits or suffers any of the following activities to take place on those premises, that is to say –

(a) producing or attempting to produce a controlled drug in contravention of section 4(1) of this Act;

(b) supplying or attempting to supply a controlled drug to another in contravention of section 4(1) of this Act, or offering to supply a controlled drug to another in contravention of section 4(1);

(c) preparing opium for smoking;

(d) smoking cannabis, cannabis resin or prepared opium.

9 Prohibition of certain activities, etc relating to opium

Subject to section 28 of this Act, it is an offence for a person –

(a) to smoke or otherwise use prepared opium; or

(b) to frequent a place used for the purpose of opium smoking; or

(c) to have in his possession –

(i) any pipes or other utensils made or adapted for use in connection with the smoking of opium, being pipes or utensils which have been used by him or with his knowledge and permission in that connection or which he intends to use or permit others to use in that connection; or

(ii) any utensils which have been used by him or with his knowledge and permission in connection with the preparation of opium for smoking.

9A Prohibition of supply, etc of articles for administering or preparing controlled drugs

(1) A person who supplies or offers to supply any article which may be used or adapted to be used (whether by itself or in combination with another article or other articles) in the administration by any person of a controlled drug to himself or another, believing that the article (or the article as adapted) is to be so used in circumstances where the administration is unlawful, is guilty of an offence.

(2) It is not an offence under subsection (1) above to supply or offer to supply a hypodermic syringe, or any part of one.

(3) A person who supplies or offers to supply any article which may be used to prepare a controlled drug for administration by any person to himself or another believing that the article is to be so used in circumstances where the administration is unlawful is guilty of an offence.

(4) For the purposes of this section, any administration of a controlled drug is unlawful except –

(a) the administration by any person of a controlled drug to another in circumstances where the administration of the drug is not unlawful under section 4(1) of this Act, or
(b) the administration by any person of a controlled drug to himself in circumstances where having the controlled drug in his possession is not unlawful under section 5(1) of this Act.

(5) In this section, references to administration by any person of a controlled drug to himself include a reference to his administering it to himself with the assistance of another.

28 Proof of lack of knowledge, etc to be a defence in proceedings for certain offences

(1) This section applies to offences under any of the following provisions of this Act, that is to say section 4(2) and (3), section 5(2) and (3), section 6(2) and section 9.

(2) Subject to subsection (3) below, in any proceedings for an offence to which this section applies it shall be a defence for the accused to prove that he neither knew of nor suspected nor had reason to suspect the existence of some fact alleged by the prosecution which it is necessary for the prosecution to prove if he is to be convicted of the offence charged.

(3) Where in any proceedings for an offence to which this section applies it is necessary, if the accused is to be convicted of the offence charged, for the prosecution to prove that some substance or product involved in the alleged offence was the controlled drug which the prosecution alleges it to have been, and it is proved that the substance or product in question was that controlled drug, the accused –

(a) shall not be acquitted of the offence charged by reason only of proving that he neither knew nor suspected nor had reason to suspect that the substance or product in question was the particular controlled drug alleged; but

(b) shall be acquitted thereof –

(i) if he proves that he neither believed nor suspected nor had reason to suspect that the substance or product in question was a controlled drug; or

(ii) if he proves that he believed the substance or product in question to be a controlled drug, or a controlled drug of a description, such that, if it had in fact been that controlled drug or a controlled drug of that description, he would not at the material time have been committing any offence to which this section applies.

(4) Nothing in this section shall prejudice any defence which it is open to a person charged with an offence to which this section applies to raise apart from this section.

[As amended by the Criminal Attempts Act 1981, s10, Schedule, Part I; Drug Trafficking Offences Act 1986, s34(1).]

Criminal Damage Act 1971
(1971 c 48)

1 *Destroying or damaging property*

(1) A person who without lawful excuse destroys or damages any property belonging to another intending to destroy or damage any such property or being reckless as to whether any such property would be destroyed or damaged shall be guilty of an offence.

(2) A person who without lawful excuse destroys or damages any property, whether belonging to himself or another –

(a) intending to destroy or damage any property or being reckless as to whether any property would be destroyed or damaged; and

(b) intending by the destruction or damage to endanger the life of another or being reckless as to whether the life of another would be thereby endangered;

shall be guilty of an offence.

(3) An offence committed under this section by destroying or damaging property by fire shall be charged as arson.

2 *Threats to destroy or damage property*

A person who without lawful excuse makes to another a threat, intending that that other would fear it would be carried out –

(a) to destroy or damage any property belonging to that other or a third person; or

(b) to destroy or damage his own property in a way which he knows is likely to endanger the life of that other or a third person;

shall be guilty of an offence.

3 Possessing anything with intent to destroy or damage property

A person who has anything in his custody or under his control intending without lawful excuse to use it or cause or permit another to use it –

(a) to destroy or damage any property belonging to some other person; or

(b) to destroy or damage his own or the user's property in a way which he knows is likely to endanger the life of some other person;

shall be guilty of an offence.

4 Punishment of offences

(1) A person guilty of arson under section 1 above or of an offence under section 1(2) above (whether arson or not) shall on conviction on indictment be liable to imprisonment for life.

(2) A person guilty of any other offence under this Act shall on conviction on indictment be liable to imprisonment for a term not exceeding ten years.

5 'Without lawful excuse'

(1) This section applies to any offence under section 1(1) above and any offence under section 2 or 3 above other than one involving a threat by the person charged to destroy or damage property in a way which he knows is likely to endanger the life of another or involving an intent by the person charged to use or cause or permit the use of something in his custody or under his control so to destroy or damage property.

(2) A person charged with an offence to which this section applies shall, whether or not he would be treated for those purposes as having a lawful excuse apart from this subsection, be treated for those purposes as having a lawful excuse –

(a) if at the time of the act or acts alleged to constitute the offence he believed that the person or persons whom he believed to be entitled to consent to the destruction of or damage to the property in question had so consented, or would have so consented to it if he or they had known of the destruction or damage and its circumstances, or

(b) if he destroyed or damaged or threatened to destroy or damage the property in question or, in the case of a charge of an offence under section 3 above, intended to use or cause or permit the use of something to destroy or damage it, in order to protect property belonging to himself or another or a right or interest in property which was or which he believed to be vested in himself or another, and at the time of the act or acts alleged to constitute the offence he believed –

(i) that the property, right or interest was in immediate need of protection; and

(ii) that the means of protection adopted or proposed to be adopted were or would be reasonable having regard to all the circumstances.

(3) For the purposes of this section it is immaterial whether a belief is justified or not if it is honestly held.

(4) For the purposes of subsection (2) above a right or interest in property includes any right or privilege in or over land, whether created by grant, licence or otherwise.

(5) This section shall not be construed as casting doubt on any defence recognised by law as a defence to criminal charges.

10 Interpretation

(1) In this Act 'property' means property of a tangible nature, whether real or personal, including money and –

(a) including wild creatures which have been tamed or are ordinarily kept in captivity, and any other wild creatures or their carcasses if, but only if, they have been reduced into possession which has not been lost or abandoned or are in the course of being reduced into possession; but

(b) not including mushrooms growing wild on any land or flowers, fruit or foliage of a plant growing wild in any land.

For the purposes of this subsection 'mushroom' includes any fungus and 'plant' includes any shrub or tree.

(2) Property shall be treated for the purposes of this Act as belonging to any person –

(a) having the custody or control of it;

(b) having in it any proprietary right or interest (not being an equitable interest arising only from an agreement to transfer or grant an interest); or

(c) having a charge on it.

(3) Where property is subject to a trust, the persons to whom it belongs shall be so treated as including any person having a right to enforce the trust.

(4) Property of a corporation sole shall be so treated as belonging to the corporation notwithstanding a vacancy in the corporation.

Sex Discrimination Act 1975
(1975 c 65)

37 Discriminatory practices

(1) In this section 'discriminatory practice' means the application of a requirement or condition which results in an act of discrimination which is unlawful by virtue of any provision of Part II or III taken with section 1(1)(b) or 3(1)(b) or which would be likely to result in such an act of discrimination if the person to whom it is applied were not all of one sex.

(2) A person acts in contravention of this section if and so long as –

(a) he applies a discriminatory practice, or

(b) he operates practices or other arrangements which in any circumstances would call for the application by him of a discriminatory practice.

(3) Proceedings in respect of a contravention of this section shall be brought only by the Commission in accordance with sections 67 to 71 of this Act.

38 *Discriminatory advertisements*

(1) It is unlawful to publish or cause to be published an advertisement which indicates, or might reasonably be understood as indicating, an intention by a person to do any act which is or might be unlawful by virtue of Part II or III.

(2) Subsection (1) does not apply to an advertisement if the intended act would not in fact be unlawful.

(3) For the purposes of subsection (1), use of a job description with a sexual connotation (such as 'waiter', 'salesgirl', 'postman' or 'stewardess') shall be taken to indicate an intention to discriminate, unless the advertisement contains an indication to the contrary.

(4) The publisher of an advertisement made unlawful by subsection (1) shall not be subject to any liability under that subsection in respect of the publication of the advertisement if he proves –

(a) that the advertisement was published in reliance on a statement made to him by the person who caused it to be published to the effect that, by reason of the operation of subsection (2), the publication would not be unlawful, and
(b) that it was reasonable for him to rely on the statement.

(5) A person who knowingly or recklessly makes a statement such as is referred to in subsection (4) which in a material respect is false or misleading commits an offence, and shall be liable on summary conviction to a fine not exceeding level 5 on the standard scale.

39 *Instructions to discriminate*

It is unlawful for a person –

(a) who has authority over another person, or
(b) in accordance with whose wishes that other person is accustomed to act,

to instruct him to do any act which is unlawful by virtue of Part II or III, or procure or attempt to procure the doing by him of any such act.

40 *Pressure to discriminate*

(1) It is unlawful to induce, or attempt to induce, a person to do any act which contravenes Part II or III by –

(a) providing or offering to provide him with any benefit, or
(b) subjecting or threatening to subject him to any detriment.

(2) An offer or threat is not prevented from falling within subsection (1) because it is not made directly to the person in question, if it is made in such a way that he is likely to hear of it.

41 *Liability of employers and principals*

(1) Anything done by a person in the course of his employment shall be treated for the purposes of this Act as done by his employer as well as by him, whether or not it was done with the employer's knowledge or approval.

(2) Anything done by a person as agent for another person with the authority (whether express or implied, and whether precedent or subsequent) of that other person shall be treated for the purpose of this Act as done by that other person as well as by him.

(3) In proceedings brought under this Act against any person in respect of an act alleged to have been done by an employee of his it shall be a defence for that person to prove that he took such steps as were reasonably practicable to prevent the employee from doing that act, or from doing in the course of his employment acts of that description.

42 Aiding unlawful acts

(1) A person who knowingly aids another person to do an act made unlawful by this Act shall be treated for the purpose of this Act as himself doing an unlawful act of the like description.

(2) For the purposes of subsection (1) an employee or agent for whose act the employer or principal is liable under section 41 (or would be so liable but for section 41 (3)) shall be deemed to aid the doing of the act by the employer or principal.

(3) A person does not under this section knowingly aid another to do an unlawful act if –

(a) he acts in reliance on a statement made to him by that other person that, by reason of any provision of this Act, the act which he aids would not be unlawful, and
(b) it is reasonable for him to rely on the statement.

(4) A person who knowingly or recklessly makes a statement such as is referred to in subsection (3)(a) which in a material respect is false or misleading commits an offence, and shall be liable on summary conviction to a fine not exceeding level 5 on the standard scale.

[As amended by the Criminal Justice Act 1982, ss38, 46.]

Sexual Offences (Amendment) Act 1976
(1976 c 82)

1 Meaning of 'rape', etc

(2) It is hereby declared that if at a trial for a rape offence the jury has to consider whether a man believed that a woman or man was consenting to sexual intercourse, the presence or absence of reasonable grounds for such a belief is a matter to which the jury is to have regard, in conjunction with any other relevant matters, in considering whether he so believed.

2 Restrictions on evidence at trials for rape, etc

(1) If at a trial any person is for the time being charged with a rape offence to which he pleads not guilty, then, except with the leave of the judge, no evidence and no question in cross-examination shall be adduced or asked at the trial, by or on behalf of any defendant at the trial, about any sexual experience of a complainant with a person other than that defendant.

(2) The judge shall not give leave in pursuance of the preceding subsection for any evidence

or question except on an application made to him in the absence of the jury by or on behalf of the defendant; and on such an application the judge shall give leave if and only if he is satisfied that it would be unfair to that defendant to refuse to allow the evidence to be adduced or the question to be asked.

(3) In subsection (1) of this section 'complainant' means a woman or man upon whom, in a charge for a rape offence to which the trial in question relates, it is alleged that rape was committed, attempted or proposed.

(4) Nothing in this section authorises evidence to be adduced or a question to be asked which cannot be adduced or asked apart from this section.

3 Application of s2 to committal proceedings, courts-martial and summary trials

(1) Where a magistrates' court inquires into a rape offence as examining justices, then, except with the consent of the court, no restricted matter shall be raised; and for this purpose a restricted matter is a matter as regards which evidence could not be adduced and a question could not be asked without leave in pursuance of section 2 of this Act if –

(a) the inquiry were a trial at which a person is charged as mentioned in section 2(1) of this Act, and
(b) each of the accused at the inquiry were charged at a trial with the offence or offences of which he is accused at the inquiry.

(2) On an application for consent in pursuance of the preceding subsection for any matter the court shall –

(a) refuse the consent unless the court is satisfied that leave in respect of the matter would be likely to be given at a relevant trial; and
(b) give the consent if the court is so satisfied.

(3) Where a person charged with a rape offence is tried for that offence either by court-martial or summarily before a magistrates' court in pursuance of section 24(1) of the Magistrates' Courts Act 1980 (which provides for the summary trial in certain cases of persons under the age of 17 who are charged with indictable offences) the preceding section shall have effect in relation to the trial as if –

(a) the words 'in the absence of the jury' in subsection (2) were omitted or (in the case of a trial by court-martial for which a judge advocate is appointed) were substituted by the words 'in the absence of the court'; and
(b) for any reference to the judge there were substituted –

(i) in the case of a trial by court-martial for which a judge advocate is appointed, a reference to the judge advocate, and
(ii) in any other case, a reference to the court.

4 Anonymity of complainants in rape, etc cases

(1) Except as authorised by a direction given in pursuance of this section –

(a) after an allegation that a woman or man has been the victim of a rape offence has been made by the woman or man or by any other person, neither the name nor the address of the woman or man nor a still or moving picture of her or him shall during that person's lifetime –

(i) be published in England and Wales in a written publication available to the public; or

(ii) be included in a relevant programme for reception in England and Wales,

if that is likely to lead members of the public to identify that person as an alleged victim of such an offence; and

(b) after a person is accused of a rape offence, no matter likely to lead members of the public to identify a woman or man as the complainant in relation to that accusation shall during that person's lifetime –

(i) be published in England and Wales in a written publication available to the public; or

(ii) be included in a relevant programme for reception in England and Wales;

but nothing in this subsection prohibits the publication or inclusion in a relevant programme of matter consisting only of a report of criminal proceedings other than proceedings at, or intended to lead to, or on an appeal arising out of, a trial at which the accused is charged with the offence.

(1A) In subsection (1) above 'picture' includes a likeness however produced.

(2) If, before the commencement of a trial at which a person is charged with a rape offence, he or another person against whom the complainant may be expected to give evidence at the trial applies to a judge of the Crown Court for a direction in pursuance of this subsection and satisfies the judge –

(a) that the direction is required for the purpose of inducing persons to come forward who are likely to be needed as witnesses at the trial; and

(b) that the conduct of the applicant's defence at the trial is likely to be substantially prejudiced if the direction is not given,

the judge shall direct that the preceding subsection shall not, by virtue of the accusation alleging the offence aforesaid, apply in relation to the complainant.

(3) If at a trial the judge is satisfied that the effect of subsection (1) of this section is to impose a substantial and unreasonable restriction upon the reporting of proceedings at the trial and that it is in the public interest to remove or relax the restriction, he shall direct that that subsection shall not apply to such matter as is specified in the direction; but a direction shall not be given in pursuance of this subsection by reason only of the outcome of the trial.

(4) If a person who has been convicted of an offence and given notice of appeal to the Court of Appeal against the conviction, or notice of an application for leave so to appeal, applies to the Court of Appeal for a direction in pursuance of this subsection and satisfies the court –

(a) that the direction is required for the purpose of obtaining evidence in support of the appeal; and

(b) that the applicant is likely to suffer substantial injustice if the direction is not given,

the court shall direct that subsection (1) of this section shall not, by virtue of an accusation which alleges a rape offence and is specified in the direction, apply in relation to a complainant so specified.

(5) If any matter is published or included in a relevant programme in contravention of subsection (1) of this section, the following persons, namely –

(a) in the case of a publication in a newspaper or periodical, any proprietor, any editor and any publisher of the newspaper or periodical;
(b) in the case of any other publication, the person who publishes it; and
(c) in the case of matter included in a relevant programme, any body corporate which is engaged in providing the service in which the programme is included and any person having functions in relation to the programme corresponding to those of an editor of a newspaper,

shall be guilty of an offence and liable on summary conviction to a fine not exceeding level 5 on the standard scale.

(5A) Where a person is charged with an offence under subsection (5) of this section in respect of the publication of any matter or the inclusion of any matter in a relevant programme, it shall be a defence, subject to subsection (5B) below, to prove that the publication or programme in which the matter appeared was one in respect of which the woman or man had given written consent to the appearance of matter of that description.

(5B) Written consent is not a defence if it is proved that any person interfered unreasonably with the peace or comfort of the woman or man with intent to obtain the consent.

(6) For the purposes of this section a person is accused of a rape offence if –

(a) an information is laid alleging that he has committed a rape offence; or
(b) he appears before a court charged with a rape offence; or
(c) a court before which he is appearing transfers proceedings against him for trial for a new charge alleging a rape offence; or
(d) a bill of indictment charging him with a rape offence is preferred before a court in which he may lawfully be indicted for an offence,

and references in this section and section 7(5) of this Act to an accusation alleging a rape offence shall be construed accordingly; and in this section –

'complainant', in relation to a person accused of a rape offence or an accusation alleging a rape offence, means the woman or man against whom the offence is alleged to have been committed; and
'relevant programme' means a programme included in a programme service (within the meaning of the Broadcasting Act 1990); and
'written publication' includes a film, a sound track and any other record in permanent form but does not include an indictment or other document prepared for use in particular legal proceedings.

(6A) For the purposes of this section, where it is alleged or there is an accusation that an offence of incitement to rape or conspiracy to rape has been committed, the person who is alleged to have been the intended victim of the rape shall be regarded as the alleged victim of the incitement or conspiracy or, in the case of an accusation, as the complainant.

(7) Nothing in this section –

(b) affects any prohibition or restriction imposed by virtue of any other enactment upon a publication or upon matter included in a relevant programme;

and a direction in pursuance of this section does not affect the operation of subsection (1) of this section at any time before the direction is given.

7 Citation, interpretation, commencement and extent

(2) In this Act –

'a rape offence' means any of the following, namely rape, attempted rape, aiding, abetting, counselling and procuring rape or attempted rape, incitement to rape, conspiracy to rape and burglary with intent to rape; and
section 46 of the Sexual Offences Act 1956 (which relates to the meaning of 'man' and 'woman' in this Act) shall have effect as if the reference to that Act included a reference to this Act.

[As amended by the Magistrates' Courts Act 1980, s154(1), Schedule 7, para 148; Armed Forces Act 1981, s11, Schedule 2, para 9; Criminal Justice Act 1988, ss158(1)-(4), s170(2), Schedule 15, para 53, Schedule 16; Broadcasting Act 1990, s203(1), (3), Schedule 20, para 26(1)(a)–(e), Schedule 21; Criminal Justice and Public Order Act 1994, ss44(3), 168(1), (2), Schedule 4, Pt II, paras 26, 27, Schedule 9, para 13, Schedule 10, paras 35, 36; Criminal Procedure and Investigations Act 1996, s47, Schedule 1, Pt II, para 23, Pt III, para 39.]

Criminal Law Act 1977
(1977 c 45)

1 The offence of conspiracy

(1) Subject to the following provisions of this Part of this Act, if a person agrees with any other person or persons that a course of conduct shall be pursued which, if the agreement is carried out in accordance with their intentions, either –

(a) will necessarily amount to or involve the commission of any offence or offences by one or more of the parties to the agreement, or
(b) would do so but for the existence of facts which render the commission of the offence or any of the offences impossible,

he is guilty of conspiracy to commit the offence or offences in question.

(2) Where liability for any offence may be incurred without knowledge on the part of the person committing it of any particular fact or circumstance necessary for the commission of the offence, a person shall nevertheless not be guilty of conspiracy to commit that offence by virtue of subsection (1) above unless he and at least one other party to the agreement intend

or know that that fact or circumstance shall or will exist at the time when the conduct constituting the offence is to take place.

(4) In this Part of this Act 'offence' means an offence triable in England and Wales.

1A Conspiracy to commit offences outside the United Kingdom

(1) Where each of the following conditions is satisfied in the case of an agreement, this Part of this Act has effect in relation to the agreement as it has effect in relation to an agreement falling within section 1(1) above.

(2) The first condition is that the pursuit of the agreed course of conduct would at some stage involve –

    (a) an act by one or more of the parties, or
    (b) the happening of some other event.

intended to take place in a country or territory outside the United Kingdom.

(3) The second condition is that that act or other event constitutes an offence under the law in force in that country or territory.

(4) The third condition is that the agreement would fall within section 1(1) above as an agreement relating to the commission of an offence but for the fact that the offence would not be an offence triable in England and Wales if committed in accordance with the parties' intentions.

(5) The fourth condition is that –

    (a) a party to the agreement, or a party's agent, did anything in England and Wales in relation to the agreement before its formation, or
    (b) a party to the agreement became a party in England and Wales (by joining it either in person or through an agent), or
    (c) a party to the agreement, or a party's agent, did or omitted anything in England and Wales in pursuance of the agreement.

(6) In the application of this Part of this Act to an agreement in the case of which each of the above conditions is satisfied, a reference to an offence is to be read as a reference to what would be the offence in question but for the fact that it is not an offence triable in England and Wales.

(7) Conduct punishable under the law in force in any country or territory is an offence under that law for the purposes of this section, however it is described in that law.

(8) Subject to subsection (9) below, the second condition is to be taken to be satisfied unless, not later than rules of court may provide, the defence serve on the prosecution a notice –

    (a) stating that, on the facts as alleged with respect to the agreed course of conduct, the condition is not in their opinion satisfied,
    (b) showing their grounds for that opinion, and
    (c) requiring the prosecution to show that it is satisfied.

(9) The court may permit the defence to require the prosecution to show that the second condition is satisfied without the prior service of a notice under subsection (8) above.

(10) In the Crown Court the question whether the second condition is satisfied shall be decided by the judge alone, and shall be treated as a question of law for the purposes of –

(a) section 9(3) of the Criminal Justice Act 1987 (preparatory hearing in fraud cases), and
(b) section 31(3) of the Criminal Procedure and Investigations Act 1996 (preparatory hearing in other cases).

(11) Any act done by means of a message (however communicated) is to be treated for the purposes of the fourth condition as done in England and Wales if the message is sent or received in England and Wales.

(12) In any proceedings in respect of an offence triable by virtue of this section, it is immaterial to guilt whether or not the accused was a British citizen at the time of any act or other event proof of which is required for conviction of the offence.

(13) References to any enactment, instrument or document (except those in this Part of this Act) to an offence of conspiracy to commit an offence include an offence triable in England and Wales as such a conspiracy by virtue of this section (without prejudice to subsection (6) above).

(14) Nothing in this section –

(a) applies to an agreement entered into before the day on which the Criminal Justice (Terrorism and Conspiracy) Act 1998 was passed, or
(b) imposes criminal liability on any person acting on behalf of, or holding office under, the Crown.

2 Exemptions from liability for conspiracy

(1) A person shall not by virtue of section 1 above be guilty of conspiracy to commit any offence if he is an intended victim of that offence.

(2) A person shall not by virtue of section 1 above be guilty of conspiracy to commit any offence or offences if the only other person or persons with whom he agrees are (both initially and at all times during the currency of the agreement) persons of any one or more of the following descriptions, that is to say –

(a) his spouse;
(b) a person under the age of criminal responsibility; and
(c) an intended victim of that offence or of each of those offences.

(3) A person is under the age of criminal responsibility for the purposes of subsection (2)(b) above so long as it is conclusively presumed, by virtue of section 50 of the Children and Young Persons Act 1933, that he cannot be guilty of any offence.

3 Penalties for conspiracy

(1) A person guilty by virtue of section 1 above of conspiracy to commit any offence or offences shall be liable on conviction on indictment –

(a) in a case falling within subsection (2) or (3) below, to imprisonment for a term related in accordance with that subsection to the gravity of the offence or offences in question (referred to below in this section as the relevant offence or offences); and

(b) in any other case, to a fine.

Paragraph (b) above shall not be taken as prejudicing the application of section 30(1) of the Powers of Criminal Courts Act 1973 (general power of court to fine offender convicted on indictment) in a case falling within subsection (2) or (3) below.

(2) Where the relevant offence or any of the relevant offences is an offence of any of the following descriptions, that is to say –

(a) murder, or any other offence the sentence for which is fixed by law;

(b) an offence for which a sentence extending to imprisonment for life is provided; or

(c) an indictable offence punishable with imprisonment for which no maximum term of imprisonment is provided,

the person convicted shall be liable to imprisonment for life.

(3) Where in a case other than one to which subsection (2) above applies the relevant offence or any of the relevant offences is punishable with imprisonment, the person convicted shall be liable to imprisonment for a term not exceeding the maximum term provided for that offence or (where more than one such offence is in question) for any one of those offences (taking the longer or the longest term as the limit for the purposes of this section where the terms provided differ).

In the case of an offence triable either way the references above in this subsection to the maximum term provided for that offence are references to the maximum term so provided on conviction on indictment.

4 Restrictions on the institution of proceedings for conspiracy

(1) Subject to subsection (2) below proceedings under section 1 above for conspiracy to commit any offence or offences shall not be instituted against any person except by or with the consent of the Director of Public Prosecutions if the offence or (as the case may be) each of the offences in question is a summary offence.

(2) In relation to the institution of proceedings under section 1 above for conspiracy to commit –

(a) an offence which is subject to a prohibition by or under any enactment on the institution of proceedings otherwise than by, or on behalf or with the consent of, the Attorney General, or

(b) two or more offences of which at least one is subject to such a prohibition,

subsection (1) above shall have effect with the substitution of a reference to the Attorney General for the reference to the Director of Public Prosecutions.

(3) Any prohibition by or under any enactment on the institution of proceedings for any offence which is not a summary offence otherwise than by, or on behalf or with the consent of, the Director of Public Prosecutions or any other person shall apply also in relation to proceedings under section 1 above for conspiracy to commit that offence.

(4) Where –

(a) an offence has been committed in pursuance of any agreement; and
(b) proceedings may not be instituted for that offence because any time limit applicable to the institution of any such proceedings has expired,

proceedings under section 1 above for conspiracy to commit that offence shall not be instituted against any person on the basis of that agreement.

(5) Subject to subsection (6) below, no proceedings for an offence triable by virtue of section 1A above may be instituted except by or with the consent of the Attorney General.

(6) The Secretary of State may by order provide that subsection (5) above shall not apply, or shall not apply to any case of a description specified in the order.

(7) An order under subsection (6) above –

(a) shall be made by statutory instrument, and
(b) shall not be made unless a draft has been laid before, and approved by resolution of, each House of Parliament.

5 Abolitions, savings, transitional provisions, consequential amendment and repeals

(1) Subject to the following provisions of this section, the offence of conspiracy at common law is hereby abolished.

(2) Subsection (1) above shall not affect the offence of conspiracy at common law so far as relates to conspiracy to defraud.

(3) Subsection (1) above shall not affect the offence of conspiracy at common law if and in so far as it may be committed by entering into an agreement to engage in conduct which –

(a) tends to corrupt public morals or outrages public decency; but
(b) would not amount to or involve the commission of an offence if carried out by a single person otherwise than in pursuance of an agreement. ...

(6) The rules laid down by sections 1 and 2 above shall apply for determining whether a person is guilty of an offence of conspiracy under any enactment other than section 1 above, but conduct which is an offence under any such other enactment shall not also be an offence under section 1 above.

(7) Incitement to commit the offence of conspiracy (whether the conspiracy incited would be an offence at common law or under section 1 above or any other enactment) shall cease to be offences.

(8) The fact that the person or persons who, so far as appears from the indictment on which any person has been convicted of conspiracy, were the only other parties to the agreement on which his conviction was based, have been acquitted of conspiracy by reference to that agreement (whether after being tried with the person convicted or separately) shall not be a ground for quashing his conviction unless under all the circumstances of the case his conviction is inconsistent with the acquittal of the other person or persons in question.

(9) Any rule of law or practice inconsistent with the provisions of subsection (8) above is hereby abolished. …

6 *Violence for securing entry*

(1) Subject to the following provisions of this section, any person who, without lawful authority, uses or threatens violence for the purpose of securing entry into any premises for himself or for any other person is guilty of an offence, provided that –

(a) there is someone present on those premises at the time who is opposed to the entry which the violence is intended to secure; and
(b) the person using or threatening the violence knows that this is the case.

(1A) Subsection (1) above does not apply to a person who is a displaced residential occupier or a protected intending occupier of the premises in question or who is acting on behalf of such an occupier; and if the accused adduces sufficient evidence that he was, or was acting on behalf of, such an occupier he shall be presumed to be, or to be acting on behalf of, such an occupier unless the contrary is proved by the prosecution.

(2) Subject to subsection (1A) above, the fact that a person has any interest in or right to possession or occupation of any premises shall not for the purposes of subsection (1) above constitute lawful authority for the use or threat of violence by him or anyone else for the purpose of securing his entry into those premises.

(4) It is immaterial for the purposes of this section –

(a) whether the violence in question is directed against the person or against property; and
(b) whether the entry which the violence is intended to secure is for the purpose of acquiring possession of the premises in question or for any other purpose.

(5) A person guilty of an offence under this section shall be liable on summary conviction to imprisonment for a term not exceeding six months or to a fine not exceeding level 5 on the standard scale or to both.

(6) A constable in uniform may arrest without warrant anyone who is, or whom he, with reasonable cause, suspects to be, guilty of an offence under this section.

(7) Section 12 below contains provisions which apply for determining when any person is to be regarded for the purposes of this Part of this Act as a displaced residential occupier of any premises or of any access to any premises and section 12A below contains provisions which apply for determining when any person is to be regarded for the purposes of this Part of this Act as a protected intending occupier of any premises or of any access to any premises.

7 *Adverse occupation of residential premises*

(1) Subject to the following provisions of this section and to section 12A(9) below, any person who is on any premises as a trespasser after having entered as such is guilty of an offence if he fails to leave those premises on being required to do so by or on behalf of –

(a) a displaced residential occupier of the premises; or

(b) an individual who is a protected intending occupier of the premises.

(2) In any proceedings for an offence under this section it shall be a defence for the accused to prove that he believed that the person requiring him to leave the premises was not a displaced residential occupier or protected intending occupier of the premises or a person acting on behalf of a displaced residential occupier or protected intending occupier.

(3) In any proceedings for an offence under this section it shall be a defence for the accused to prove –

(a) that the premises in question are or form part of premises used mainly for non-residential purposes; and
(b) that he was not on any part of the premises used wholly or mainly for residential purposes.

(4) Any reference in the preceding provisions of this section to any premises includes a reference to any access to them, whether or not any such access itself constitutes premises, within the meaning of this Part of this Act.

(5) A person guilty of an offence under this section shall be liable on summary conviction to imprisonment for a term not exceeding six months or to a fine not exceeding level 5 on the standard scale or to both.

(6) A constable in uniform may arrest without warrant anyone who is, or whom he, with reasonable cause, suspects to be, guilty of an offence under this section.

(7) Section 12 below contains provisions which apply for determining when any person is to be regarded for the purposes of this Part of this Act as a displaced residential occupier of any premises or of any access to any premises and section 12A below contains provisions which apply for determining when any person is to be regarded for the purposes of this Part of this Act as a protected intending occupier of any premises or of any access to any premises.

8 Trespassing with a weapon of offence

(1) A person who is on any premises as a trespasser, after having entered as such, is guilty of an offence if, without lawful authority or reasonable excuse, he has with him on the premises any weapon of offence.

(2) In subsection (1) above 'weapon of offence' means any article made or adapted for use for causing injury to or incapacitating a person, or intended by the person having it with him for such use.

(3) A person guilty of an offence under this section shall be liable on summary conviction to imprisonment for a term not exceeding three months or to a fine not exceeding level 5 on the standard scale or both.

(4) A constable in uniform may arrest without warrant anyone who is, or whom he, with reasonable cause, suspects to be, in the act of committing an offence under this section.

12 *Supplementary provisions*

(1) In this Part of this Act –

(a) 'premises' means any building, any part of a building under separate occupation, any land ancillary to a building, the site comprising any building or buildings together with any land ancillary thereto, and (for the purposes only of sections 10 and 11 above) any other place; and

(b) 'access' means, in relation to any premises, any part of any site or building within which those premises are situated which constitutes an ordinary means of access to those premises (whether or not that is its sole or primary use).

(2) References in this section to a building shall apply also to any structure other than a movable one, and to any movable structure, vehicle or vessel designed or adapted for use for residential purposes; and for the purposes of subsection (1) above –

(a) part of a building is under separate occupation if anyone is in occupation or entitled to occupation of that part as distinct from the whole; and

(b) land is ancillary to a building if it is adjacent to it and used (or intended for use) in connection with the occupation of that building or any part of it.

(3) Subject to subsection (4) below, any person who was occupying any premises as a residence immediately before being excluded from occupation by anyone who entered those premises, or any access to those premises, as a trespasser is a displaced residential occupier of the premises for the purposes of this Part of this Act so long as he continues to be excluded from occupation of the premises by the original trespasser or by any subsequent trespasser.

(4) A person who was himself occupying the premises in question as a trespasser immediately before being excluded from occupation shall not by virtue of subsection (3) above be a displaced residential occupier of the premises for the purposes of this Part of this Act.

(5) A person who by virtue of subsection (3) above is a displaced residential occupier of any premises shall be regarded for the purposes of this Part of this Act as a displaced residential occupier also of any access to those premises.

(6) Anyone who enters or is on or in occupation of any premises by virtue of –

(a) any title derived from a trespasser; or

(b) any licence or consent given by a trespasser or by a person deriving title from a trespasser,

shall himself be treated as a trespasser for the purposes of this Part of this Act (without prejudice to whether or not he would be a trespasser apart from this provision); and references in this Part of this Act to a person's entering or being on or occupying any premises as a trespasser shall be construed accordingly.

(7) Anyone who is on any premises as a trespasser shall not cease to be a trespasser for the purposes of this Part of this Act by virtue of being allowed time to leave the premises, nor shall anyone cease to be a displaced residential occupier of any premises by virtue of any such allowance of time to a trespasser.

(8) No rule of law ousting the jurisdiction of magistrates' courts to try offences where a dispute of title to property is involved shall preclude magistrates' courts from trying offences under this Part of this Act.

12A Protected intending occupiers: supplementary provisions

(1) For the purposes of this Part of this Act an individual is a protected intending occupier of any premises at any time if at that time he falls within subsection (2), (4) or (6) below.

(2) An individual is a protected intending occupier of any premises if –

(a) he has in those premises a freehold interest or a leasehold interest with not less than two years still to run;
(b) he requires the premises for his own occupation as a residence;
(c) he is excluded from occupation of the premises by a person who entered them, or any access to them, as a trespasser; and
(d) he or a person acting on his behalf holds a written statement –

(i) which specifies his interest in the premises;
(ii) which states that he requires the premises for occupation as a residence for himself; and
(iii) with respect to which the requirements in subsection (3) below are fulfilled.

(3) The requirements referred to in subsection (2)(d)(iii) above are –

(a) that the statement is signed by the person whose interest is specified in it in the presence of a justice of the peace or commissioner for oaths; and
(b) that the justice of the peace or commissioner for oaths has subscribed his name as a witness to the signature.

(4) An individual is also a protected intending occupier of any premises if –

(a) he has a tenancy of those premises (other than a tenancy falling within subsection (2)(a) above or (6)(a) below) or a licence to occupy those premises granted by a person with a freehold interest or a leasehold interest with not less than two years still to run in the premises;
(b) he requires the premises for his own occupation as a residence;
(c) he is excluded from occupation of the premises by a person who entered them, or any access to them, as a trespasser; and
(d) he or a person acting on his behalf holds a written statement –

(i) which states that he has been granted a tenancy of those premises or a licence to occupy those premises;
(ii) which specifies the interest in the premises of the person who granted that tenancy or licence to occupy ('the landlord');
(iii) which states that he requires the premises for occupation as a residence for himself; and
(iv) with respect to which the requirements in subsection (5) below are fulfilled.

(5) The requirements referred to in subsection (4)(d)(iv) above are –

(a) that the statement is signed by the landlord and by the tenant or licensee in the presence of a justice of the peace or commissioner for oaths;
(b) that the justice of the peace or commissioner for oaths has subscribed his name as a witness to the signatures.

(6) An individual is also a protected intending occupier of any premises if –

(a) he has a tenancy of those premises (other than a tenancy falling within subsection (2)(a) or (4)(a) above) or a licence to occupy those premises granted by an authority to which this subsection applies;
(b) he requires the premises for his own occupation as a residence;
(c) he is excluded from occupation of the premises by a person who entered the premises, or any access to them, as a trespasser; and
(d) there has been issued to him by or on behalf of the authority referred to in paragraph (a) above a certificate stating that –

(i) he has been granted a tenancy of those premises or a licence to occupy those premises as a residence by the authority; and
(ii) the authority which granted that tenancy or licence to occupy is one to which this subsection applies, being of a description specified in the certificate.

(7) Subsection (6) above applies to the following authorities –

(a) any body mentioned in section 14 of the Rent Act 1977 (landlord's interest belonging to local authority etc);
(b) the Housing Corporation; and
(d) a registered social landlord within the meaning of the Housing Act 1985 (see section 5(4) and (5) of that Act).

(7A) Subsection (6) also applies to the Secretary of State if the tenancy or licence is granted by him under Part III of the Housing Associations Act 1985.

(8) A person is guilty of an offence if he makes a statement for the purposes of subsection (2)(d) or (4)(d) above which he knows to be false in a material particular or if he recklessly makes such a statement which is false in a material particular.

(9) In any proceedings for an offence under section 7 of this Act where the accused was requested to leave the premises by a person claiming to be or to act on behalf of a protected intending occupier of the premises –

(a) it shall be a defence for the accused to prove that, although asked to do so by the accused at the time the accused was requested to leave, that person failed at that time to produce to the accused such a statement as is referred to in subsection (2)(d) or (4)(d) above or such a certificate as is referred to in subsection (6)(d) above; and
(b) any document purporting to be a certificate under subsection (6)(d) above shall be received in evidence and, unless the contrary is proved, shall be deemed to have been issued by or on behalf of the authority stated in the certificate.

(10) A person guilty of an offence under subsection (8) above shall be liable on summary

conviction to imprisonment for a term not exceeding six months or to a fine not exceeding level 5 on the standard scale or to both.

(11) A person who is a protected intending occupier of any premises shall be regarded for the purposes of this Part of this Act as a protected intending occupier also of any access to those premises.

51 Bomb hoaxes

(1) A person who –

(a) places any article in any place whatever; or
(b) dispatches any article by post, rail or any other means whatever of sending things from one place to another,

with the intention (in either case) of inducing in some other person a belief that it is likely to explode or ignite and thereby cause personal injury or damage to property is guilty of an offence.

In this subsection 'article' includes substance.

(2) A person who communicates any information which he knows or believes to be false to another person with the intention of inducing in him or any other person a false belief that a bomb or other thing liable to explode or ignite is present in any place or location whatever is guilty of an offence.

(3) For a person to be guilty of an offence under subsection (1) or (2) above it is not necessary for him to have any particular person in mind as the person in whom he intends to induce the belief mentioned in that subsection.

(4) A person guilty of an offence under this section shall be liable –

(a) on summary conviction, to imprisonment for a term not exceeding six months or to a fine not exceeding the prescribed sum, or both;
(b) on conviction on indictment, to imprisonment for a term not exceeding seven years.

[As amended by the Magistrates' Courts Act 1980, s32(2); Criminal Attempts Act 1981, ss5, 10, Schedule, Pt I; Criminal Justice Act 1982, ss38, 46; Housing (Consequential Provisions) Act 1985, s4, Schedule 2, para 36; Criminal Justice Act 1987, s12(2); Housing Act 1988, s140(1), Schedule 17, Part II, para 101; Criminal Justice Act 1991, s26(4); Trade Union and Labour Relations (Consolidation) Act 1992, s300(1), Schedule 1; Criminal Justice and Public Order Act 1994, ss72, 73, 74, 168(3), Schedule 11; Housing Act 1996 (Consequential Provisions) Order 1996, art 5, Schedule 2, para 8; Criminal Justice (Terrorism and Conspiracy) Act 1998, ss5(1), (2), 9, Schedule 1, Pt II, para 4, Schedule 2, Pt II; Government of Wales Act 1998, ss140, 141, 152, Schedule 16, para 3, Schedule 18, Pt VI.]

Theft Act 1978
(1978 c 31)

1 Obtaining services by deception

(1) A person who by any deception dishonestly obtains services from another shall be guilty of an offence.

(2) It is an obtaining of services where the other is induced to confer a benefit by doing some act, or causing or permitting some act to be done, on the understanding that the benefit has been or will be paid for.

(3) Without prejudice to the generality of subsection (2) above, it is an obtaining of services where the other is induced to make a loan, or to cause or permit a loan to be made, on the understanding that any payment (whether by way of interest or otherwise) will or has been made in respect of the loan.

2 Evasion of liability by deception

(1) Subject to subsection (2) below, where a person by any deception –

    (a) dishonestly secures the remission of the whole or part of any existing liability to make a payment, whether his own liability or another's; or

    (b) with intent to make permanent default in whole or in part on any existing liability to make a payment, or with intent to let another do so, dishonestly induces the creditor or any person claiming payment on behalf of the creditor to wait for payment (whether or not the due date for payment is deferred) or to forgo payment; or

    (c) dishonestly obtains any exemption from or abatement of liability to make a payment;

he shall be guilty of an offence.

(2) For purposes of this section 'liability' means legally enforceable liability; and subsection (1) shall not apply in relation to a liability that has not been accepted or established to pay compensation for a wrongful act or omission.

(3) For purposes of subsection (1)(b) a person induced to take in payment a cheque or other security for money by way of conditional satisfaction of a pre-existing liability is to be treated not as being paid but as being induced to wait for payment.

(4) For purposes of subsection (1)(c) 'obtains' includes obtaining for another or enabling another to obtain.

3 Making off without payment

(1) Subject to subsection (3) below, a person who, knowing that payment on the spot for any goods supplied or service done is required or expected from him, dishonestly makes off without having paid as required or expected and with intent to avoid payment of the amount due shall be guilty of an offence.

(2) For purposes of this section 'payment on the spot' includes payment at the time of collecting goods on which work has been done or in respect of which service has been provided.

(3) Subsection (1) above shall not apply where the supply of the goods or the doing of the service is contrary to law, or where the service done is such that payment is not legally enforceable.

(4) Any person may arrest without warrant anyone who is, or whom he, with reasonable cause, suspects to be, committing or attempting to commit an offence under this section.

4 Punishments

(1) Offences under this Act shall be punishable either on conviction on indictment or on summary conviction.

(2) A person convicted on indictment shall be liable –

(a) for an offence under section 1 or section 2 of this Act, to imprisonment for a term not exceeding five years; and
(b) for an offence under section 3 of this Act, to imprisonment for a term not exceeding two years.

(3) A person convicted summarily of any offence under this Act shall be liable –

(a) to imprisonment for a term not exceeding six months; or
(b) to a fine not exceeding the prescribed sum for the purposes of section 32 of the Magistrates' Courts Act 1980 (punishment on summary conviction of offences triable either way: £5,000 or other sum substituted by order under that Act),

or to both.

5 Supplementary

(1) For purposes of sections 1 and 2 above 'deception' has the same meaning as in section 15 of the Theft Act 1968, that is to say, it means any deception (whether deliberate or reckless) by words or conduct as to fact or as to law, including a deception as to the present intentions of the person using the deception or any other person; and section 18 of that Act (liability of company officers for offences by the company) shall apply in relation to sections 1 and 2 above as it applies in relation to section 15 of that Act.

(2) Sections 30(1) (husband and wife), 31(1) (effect on civil proceedings) and 34 (interpretation) of the Theft Act 1968, so far as they are applicable in relation to this Act, shall apply as they apply in relation to that Act.

[As amended by the Magistrates' Courts Act 1980, s154(1), Schedule 7, para 170, Criminal Justice Act 1991, s17(2)(c); Theft (Amendment) Act 1996, s4.]

Magistrates' Courts Act 1980
(1980 c 43)

32 Penalties on summary conviction for offences triable either way

(1) On summary conviction of any of the offences triable either way listed in Schedule 1 to this Act a person shall be liable to imprisonment for a term not exceeding six months or to a fine not exceeding the prescribed sum or both, except that –

(a) a magistrates' court shall not have power to impose imprisonment for an offence so listed if the Crown Court would not have that power in the case of an adult convicted of it on indictment;

(b) on summary conviction of an offence consisting in the incitement to commit an offence triable either way a person shall not be liable to any greater penalty than he would be liable to on summary conviction of the last-mentioned offence.

(2) For any offence triable either way which is not listed in Schedule 1 to this Act, being an offence under a relevant enactment, the maximum fine which may be imposed on summary conviction shall by virtue of this subsection be the prescribed sum unless the offence is one for which by virtue of an enactment other than this subsection a larger fine may be imposed on summary conviction.

(3) Where, by virtue of any relevant enactment, a person summarily convicted of an offence triable either way would, apart from this section, be liable to a maximum fine of one amount in the case of a first conviction and of a different amount in the case of a second or subsequent conviction, subsection (2) above shall apply irrespective of whether the conviction is a first, second or subsequent one.

(9) In this section –

'fine' includes a pecuniary penalty but does not include a pecuniary forfeiture or pecuniary compensation;

'the prescribed sum' means £5,000 or such sum as is for the time being substituted in this definition by an order in force under section 143(1) below;

'relevant enactment' means an enactment contained in the Criminal Law Act 1977 or in any Act passed before, or in the same Session as, that Act.

33 Maximum penalties on summary conviction in pursuance of section 22

(1) Where in pursuance of subsection (2) of section 22 above a magistrates' court proceeds to the summary trial of an information, then, if the accused is summarily convicted of the offence –

(a) subject to subsection (3) below the court shall not have power to impose on him in respect of that offence imprisonment for more than three months or a fine greater than level 4 on the standard scale; and

(b) section 38 below shall not apply as regards that offence.

(2) In subsection (1) above 'fine' includes a pecuniary penalty but does not include a pecuniary forfeiture or pecuniary compensation.

(3) Paragraph (a) of subsection (1) above does not apply to an offence under section 12A of the Theft Act 1968 (aggravated vehicle-taking).

36 Restriction on fines in respect of young persons

(1) Where a person under 18 years of age is found guilty by a magistrates' court of an offence for which, apart from this section, the court would have power to impose a fine of an amount exceeding £1,000, the amount of any fine imposed by the court shall not exceed £1,000.

(2) In relation to a person under the age of 14 subsection (1) above shall have effect as if for the words '£1,000', in both places where they occur, there were substituted the words '£250'.

44 Aiders and abettors

(1) A person who aids, abets, counsels or procures the commission by another person of a summary offence shall be guilty of the like offence and may be tried (whether or not he is charged as a principal) either by a court having jurisdiction to try that other person or by a court having by virtue of his own offence jurisdiction to try him.

(2) Any offence consisting in aiding, abetting, counselling or procuring the commission of an offence triable either way (other than an offence listed in Schedule 1 to this Act) shall by virtue of this subsection be triable either way.

45 Incitement

(1) Any offence consisting in the incitement to commit a summary offence shall be triable only summarily.

(2) Subsection (1) above is without prejudice to any other enactment by virtue of which any offence is triable only summarily.

(3) On conviction of an offence consisting in the incitement to commit a summary offence a person shall be liable to the same penalties as he would be liable to on conviction of the last-mentioned offence.

[As amended by the Criminal Justice Act 1991, ss17(2)(a), (b), (c), 68, 101(2), Schedule 4, Pt II, Schedule 8, para 6(1)(c), Schedule 13; Aggravated Vehicle-Taking Act 1992, s2(3).]

Highways Act 1980
(1980 c 66)

131 Penalty for damaging highway, etc

(1) If a person, without lawful authority or excuse –

(a) makes a ditch or excavation in a highway which consists of or comprises a carriageway, or

(b) removes any soil or turf from any part of a highway, except for the purpose of improving the highway and with the consent of the highway authority for the highway, or

(c) deposits anything whatsoever on a highway so as to damage the highway, or

(d) lights any fire, or discharges any firearm or firework, within 50 feet from the centre of a highway which consists of or comprises a carriageway, and in consequence thereof the highway is damaged,

he is guilty of an offence.

(2) If a person without lawful authority or excuse pulls down or obliterates a traffic sign placed on or over a highway, or a milestone or direction post (not being a traffic sign) so placed, he is guilty of an offence; but it is a defence in any proceedings under this subsection to show that the traffic sign, milestone or post was not lawfully so placed.

(3) A person guilty of an offence under this section is liable to a fine not exceeding level 3 on the standard scale.

131A Disturbance of surface of certain highways

(1) A person who, without lawful authority or excuse, so disturbs the surface of –

(a) a footpath,
(b) a bridleway, or
(c) any other highway which consists of or comprises a carriageway other than a made-up carriageway,

as to render it inconvenient for the exercise of the public right of way is guilty of an offence and liable to a fine not exceeding level 3 on the standard scale.

(2) Proceedings for an offence under this section shall be brought only by the highway authority or the council of the non-metropolitan district, parish or community in which the offence is committed; and, without prejudice to section 130 (protection of public rights) above, it is the duty of the highway authority to ensure that where desirable in the public interest such proceedings are brought.

132 Unauthorised marks on highways

(1) A person who, without either the consent of the highway authority for the highway in question or an authorisation given by or under an enactment or a reasonable excuse, paints or otherwise inscribes or affixes any picture, letter, sign or other mark upon the surface of a highway or upon any tree, structure or works on or in a highway is guilty of an offence and liable to a fine not exceeding level 4 on the standard scale.

(2) The highway authority for a highway may, without prejudice to their powers apart from this subsection and whether or not proceedings in respect of the matter have been taken in pursuance of subsection (1) above, remove any picture, letter, sign or other mark which has, without either the consent of the authority or an authorisation given by or under an enactment, been painted or otherwise inscribed or affixed upon the surface of the highway or upon any tree, structure or works on or in the highway.

137 Penalty for wilful obstruction

(1) If a person, without lawful authority or excuse, in any way wilfully obstructs the free passage along a highway he is guilty of an offence and liable to a fine not exceeding level 3 on the standard scale.

138 Penalty for erecting building, etc in highway

If a person, without lawful authority or excuse, erects a building or fence, or plants a hedge, in a highway which consists of or comprises a carriageway he is guilty of an offence and liable to a fine not exceeding level 3 on the standard scale.

148 Penalty for depositing things or pitching booths, etc on highway

If, without lawful authority or excuse –

(a) a person deposits on a made-up carriageway any dung, compost or other material for dressing land, or any rubbish, or

(b) a person deposits on any highway that consists of or comprises a made-up carriageway any dung, compost or other material for dressing land, or any rubbish, within 15 feet from the centre of that carriageway, or

(c) a person deposits any thing whatsoever on a highway to the interruption of any user of the highway, or

(d) a hawker or other itinerant trader pitches a booth, stall or stand, or encamps, on a highway,

he is guilty of an offence and liable to a fine not exceeding level 3 of the standard scale.

155 Penalties in connection with straying animals

(1) If any horses, cattle, sheep, goats or swine are at any time found straying or lying on or at the side of a highway their keeper is guilty of an offence; but this subsection does not apply in relation to a part of a highway passing over any common, waste or unenclosed ground. In this section 'keeper', in relation to any animals, means a person in whose possession they are.

(2) A person guilty of an offence under this section is liable to a fine not exceeding level 3 on the standard scale.

(3) A person guilty of an offence under this section is also liable to pay the reasonable expenses of removing any animal so found straying or lying to the premises of their keeper, or to the common pound, or to such other place as may have been provided for the purpose, and any person who incurs such expenses is entitled to recover them summarily as a civil debt. For the purposes of this subsection 'expenses', in a case where an animal has been removed to the common pound, includes the usual fees and charges of the authorised keeper of the pound.

(4) If a person, without lawful authority or excuse, releases any animal seized for the

purpose of being impounded under this section from the pound or other place where it is impounded, or on the way to or from any such place, or damages any such place, he is guilty of an offence and liable to a fine not exceeding level 2 on the standard scale.

(5) Nothing in this section prejudices or affects any right of pasture on the side of a highway.

161 *Penalties for causing certain kinds of danger or annoyance*

(1) If a person, without lawful authority or excuse, deposits any thing whatsoever on a highway in consequence of which a user of the highway is injured or endangered, that person is guilty of an offence and liable to a fine not exceeding level 3 on the standard scale.

(2) If a person, without lawful authority or excuse –

(a) lights any fire on or over a highway which consists of or comprises a carriageway; or
(b) discharges any firearm or firework within 50 feet of the centre of such a highway,

and in consequence a user of the highway is injured, interrupted or endangered, that person is guilty of an offence and liable to a fine not exceeding level 3 on the standard scale.

(3) If a person plays at football or any other game on a highway to the annoyance of a user of the highway he is guilty of an offence and liable to a fine not exceeding level 1 on the standard scale.

(4) If a person, without lawful authority or excuse, allows any filth, dirt, lime or other offensive matter or thing to run or flow on to a highway from any adjoining premises, he is guilty of an offence and liable to a fine not exceeding level 1 on the standard scale.

161A *Danger or annoyance caused by fires lit otherwise than on highways*

(1) If a person –

(a) lights a fire on any land not forming part of a highway which consists of or comprises a carriageway; or
(b) directs or permits a fire to be lit on any such land,

and in consequence a user of any highway which consists of or comprises a carriageway is injured, interrupted or endangered by, or by smoke from, that fire or any other fire caused by that fire, that person is guilty of an offence and liable to a fine not exceeding level 5 on the standard scale.

(2) In any proceedings for an offence under this section it shall be a defence for the accused to prove –

(a) that at the time the fire was lit he was satisfied on reasonable grounds that it was unlikely that users of any highway consisting of or comprising a carriageway would be injured, interrupted or endangered by, or by smoke from, that fire or any other fire caused by that fire; and
(b) either –

(i) that both before and after the fire was lit he did all he reasonably could to prevent users of any such highway from being so injured, interrupted or endangered, or

(ii) that he had a reasonable excuse for not doing so.

162 Penalty for placing rope, etc across highway

A person who for any purpose places any rope, wire or other apparatus across a highway in such a manner as to be likely to cause danger to persons using the highway is, unless he proves that he had taken all necessary means to give adequate warning of the danger, guilty of an offence and liable to a fine not exceeding level 3 on the standard scale.

163 Prevention of water falling on or flowing on to highway

(1) A competent authority may, by notice to the occupier of premises adjoining a highway, require him within 28 days from the date of service of the notice to construct or erect and thereafter to maintain such channels, gutters or downpipes as may be necessary to prevent –

(a) water from the roof or any other part of the premises falling upon persons using the highway, or

(b) so far as is reasonably practicable, surface water from the premises flowing on to, or over, the footway of the highway.

For the purposes of this section the competent authorities, in relation to any highway, are the highway authority and also (where they are not the highway authority) the local authority for the area in which the highway is situated.

(2) A notice under subsection (1) above may, at the option of the authority, be served on the owner of the premises in question instead of on the occupier or may be served on both the owner and the occupier of the premises.

(3) A person aggrieved by a requirement under this section may appeal to a magistrates' court.

(4) Subject to any order made on appeal, if a person on whom a notice is served under this section fails to comply with the requirement of the notice within the period specified in subsection (1) above he is guilty of an offence and liable to a fine not exceeding level 1 on the standard scale; and if the offence is continued after conviction he is guilty of a further offence and liable to a fine not exceeding £2 for each day on which the offence is so continued.

[As amended by the Criminal Justice Act 1982, ss38, 46; Highways (Amendment) Act 1986, s1(2)(3); Rights of Way Act 1990, s1(2).]

Forgery and Counterfeiting Act 1981
(1981 c 45)
Part I

1 The offence of forgery

A person is guilty of forgery if he makes a false instrument, with the intention that he or another shall use it to induce somebody to accept it as genuine, and by reason of so accepting it to do or not to do some act to his own or any other person's prejudice.

2 The offence of copying a false instrument

It is an offence for a person to make a copy of an instrument which is, and which he knows or believes to be, a false instrument, with the intention that he or another shall use it to induce somebody to accept it as a copy of a genuine instrument, and by reason of so accepting it to do or not to do some act to his own or any other person's prejudice.

3 The offence of using a false instrument

It is an offence for a person to use an instrument which is, and which he knows or believes to be, false, with the intention of inducing somebody to accept it as genuine, and by reason of so accepting it to do or not to do some act to his own or any other person's prejudice.

4 The offence of using a copy of a false instrument

It is an offence for a person to use a copy of an instrument which is, and which he knows or believes to be, a false instrument, with the intention of inducing somebody to accept it as a copy of a genuine instrument, and by reason of so accepting it to do or not to do some act to his own or any other person's prejudice.

5 Offences relating to money orders, share certificates, passports, etc

(1) It is an offence for a person to have in his custody or under his control an instrument to which this section applies which is, and which he knows or believes to be, false, with the intention that he or another shall use it to induce somebody to accept it as genuine, and by reason of so accepting it to do or not to do some act to his own or any other person's prejudice.

(2) It is an offence for a person to have in his custody or under his control, without lawful authority or excuse, an instrument to which this section applies which is, and which he knows or believes to be, false.

(3) It is an offence for a person to make or to have in his custody or under his control a machine or implement, or paper or any other material, which to his knowledge is or has been specially designed or adapted for the making of an instrument to which this section

applies, with the intention that he or another shall make an instrument to which this section applies which is false and that he or another shall use the instrument to induce somebody to accept it as genuine, and by reason of so accepting it to do or not to do some act to his own or any other person's prejudice.

(4) It is an offence for a person to make or to have in his custody or under his control any such machine, implement, paper or material, without lawful authority or excuse.

(5) The instruments to which this section applies are –

(a) money orders;
(b) postal orders;
(c) United Kingdom postage stamps;
(d) Inland Revenue stamps;
(e) share certificates;
(f) passports and documents which can be used instead of passports;
(g) cheques;
(h) travellers' cheques;
(j) cheque cards;
(k) credit cards;
(l) certified copies relating to an entry in a register of births, adoptions, marriages or deaths and issued by the Registrar General, the Registrar General for Northern Ireland, a registration officer or a person lawfully authorised to register marriages; and
(m) certificates relating to entries in such registers.

(6) In subsection (5)(e) above 'share certificate' means an instrument entitling or evidencing the title of a person to a share or interest –

(a) in any public stock, annuity, fund or debt of any government or state, including a state which forms part of another state; or
(b) in any stock, fund or debt of a body (whether corporate or unincorporated) established in the United Kingdom or elsewhere.

6 Penalties for offences under Part I

(1) A person guilty of an offence under this Part of this Act shall be liable on summary conviction –

(a) to a fine not exceeding the statutory maximum; or
(b) to imprisonment for a term not exceeding six months; or
(c) to both.

(2) A person guilty of an offence to which this subsection applies shall be liable on conviction on indictment to imprisonment for a term not exceeding ten years.

(3) The offences to which subsection (2) above applies are offences under the following provisions of this Part of this Act –

(a) section 1;
(b) section 2;
(c) section 3;

(d) section 5;
(e) section5(1); and
(f) section 5(3).

(4) A person guilty of an offence under section 5(2) or (4) above shall be liable on conviction on indictment to imprisonment for a term not exceeding two years.

8 Meaning of 'instrument'

(1) Subject to subsection (2) below, in this Part of this Act 'instrument' means –

(a) any document, whether of a formal or informal character;
(b) any stamp issued or sold by the Post Office;
(c) any Inland Revenue stamp; and
(d) any disc, tape, sound track or other device on or in which information is recorded or stored by mechanical, electronic or other means.

(2) A currency note within the meaning of Part II of this Act is not an instrument for the purposes of this Part of this Act.

(3) A mark denoting payment of postage which the Post Office authorise to be used instead of an adhesive stamp is to be treated for the purposes of this Part of this Act as if it were a stamp issued by the Post Office.

(4) In this Part of this Act 'Inland Revenue stamp' means a stamp as defined in section 27 of the Stamp Duties Management Act 1891.

9 Meaning of 'false' and 'making'

(1) An instrument is false for the purposes of this Part of this Act –

(a) if it purports to have been made in the form in which it is made by a person who did not in fact make it in that form; or
(b) if it purports to have been made in the form in which it is made on the authority of a person who did not in fact authorise its making in that form; or
(c) if it purports to have been made in the terms in which it is made by a person who did not in fact make it in those terms; or
(d) if it purports to have been made in the terms in which it is made on the authority of a person who did not in fact authorise its making in those terms; or
(e) if it purports to have been altered in any respect by a person who did not in fact alter it in that respect; or
(f) if it purports to have been altered in any respect on the authority of a person who did not in fact authorise the alteration in that respect; or
(g) if it purports to have been made or altered on a date on which, or at a place at which, or otherwise in circumstances in which, it was not in fact made or altered; or
(h) if it purports to have been made or altered by an existing person but he did not in fact exist.

(2) A person is to be treated for the purposes of this Part of this Act as making a false

instrument if he alters an instrument so as to make it false in any respect (whether or not it is false in some other respect apart from that alteration).

10 Meaning of 'prejudice' and 'induce'

(1) Subject to subsections (2) and (4) below, for the purposes of this Part of this Act an act or omission intended to be induced is to a person's prejudice if, and only if, it is one which, if it occurs –

(a) will result –

(i) in his temporary or permanent loss of property; or
(ii) in his being deprived of an opportunity to earn remuneration or greater remuneration; or
(iii) in his being deprived of an opportunity to gain a financial advantage otherwise than by way of remuneration; or

(b) will result in somebody being given an opportunity –

(i) to earn remuneration or greater remuneration from him; or
(ii) to gain a financial advantage from him otherwise than by way of remuneration; or

(c) will be the result of his having accepted a false instrument as genuine, or a copy of a false instrument as a copy of a genuine one, in connection with his performance of any duty.

(2) An act which a person has an enforceable duty to do and an omission to do an act which a person is not entitled to do shall be disregarded for the purposes of this Part of this Act.

(3) In this Part of this Act references to inducing somebody to accept a false instrument as genuine, or a copy of a false instrument as a copy of a genuine one, include references to inducing a machine to respond to the instrument or copy as if it were a genuine instrument or, as the case may be, a copy of a genuine one.

(4) Where subsection (3) above applies, the act or omission intended to be induced by the machine responding to the instrument or copy shall be treated as an act or omission to a person's prejudice.

(5) In this section 'loss' includes not getting what one might get as well as parting with what one has.

13 Abolition of offence of forgery at common law

The offence of forgery at common law is hereby abolished for all purposes not relating to offences committed before the commencement of this Act.

Part II

14 Offences of counterfeiting notes and coins

(1) It is an offence for a person to make a counterfeit of a currency note or of a protected coin, intending that he or another shall pass or tender it as genuine.

(2) It is an offence for a person to make a counterfeit of a currency note or of a protected coin without lawful authority or excuse.

15 Offences of passing, etc counterfeit notes and coins

(1) It is an offence for a person –

(a) to pass or tender as genuine any thing which is, and which he knows or believes to be, a counterfeit of a currency note or of a protected coin; or
(b) to deliver to another any thing which is, and which he knows or believes to be, such a counterfeit, intending that the person to whom it is delivered or another shall pass or tender it as genuine.

(2) It is an offence for a person to deliver to another, without lawful authority or excuse, any thing which is, and which he knows or believes to be, a counterfeit of a currency note or of a protected coin.

16 Offences involving the custody or control of counterfeit notes and coins

(1) It is an offence for a person to have in his custody or under his control any thing which is, and which he knows or believes to be, a counterfeit of a currency note or of a protected coin, intending either to pass or tender it as genuine or to deliver it to another with the intention that he or another shall pass or tender it as genuine.

(2) It is an offence for a person to have in his custody or under his control, without lawful authority or excuse, any thing which is, and which he knows or believes to be, a counterfeit of a currency note or of a protected coin.

(3) It is immaterial for the purposes of subsections (1) and (2) above that a coin or note is not in a fit state to be passed or tendered or that the making or counterfeiting of a coin or note has not been finished or perfected.

17 Offences involving the making or custody or control of counterfeiting materials and implements

(1) It is an offence for a person to make, or to have in his custody or under his control, any thing which he intends to use, or to permit any other person to use, for the purpose of making a counterfeit of a currency note or of a protected coin with the intention that it be passed or tendered as genuine.

(2) It is an offence for a person without lawful authority or excuse –

(a) to make; or

(b) to have in his custody or under his control,

any thing which, to his knowledge, is or has been specially designed or adapted for the making of a counterfeit of a currency note.

(3) Subject to subsection (4) below, it is an offence for a person to make, or to have in his custody or under his control, any implement which, to his knowledge, is capable of imparting to any thing a resemblance –

(a) to the whole or part of either side of a protected coin; or

(b) to the whole or part of the reverse of the image on either side of a protected coin.

(4) It shall be defence for a person charged with an offence under subsection (3) above to show –

(a) that he made the implement or, as the case may be, had it in his custody or under his control, with the written consent of the Treasury; or

(b) that he had lawful authority otherwise than by virtue of paragraph (a) above, or a lawful excuse, for making it or having it in his custody or under his control.

18 The offence of reproducing British currency notes

(1) It is an offence for any person, unless the relevant authority has previously consented in writing, to reproduce on any substance whatsoever, and whether or not on the correct scale, any British currency note or any part of a British currency note.

(2) In this section –

'British currency note' means any note which –

(a) has been lawfully issued in England and Wales, Scotland or Northern Ireland; and

(b) is or has been customarily used as money in the country where it was issued; and

(c) is payable on demand; and

'the relevant authority', in relation to a British currency note of any particular description, means the authority empowered by law to issue notes of that description.

19 Offences of making, etc imitation British coins

(1) It is an offence for a person –

(a) to make an imitation British coin in connection with a scheme intended to promote the sale of any product or the making of contracts for the supply of any service; or

(b) to sell or distribute imitation British coins in connection with any such scheme, or to have imitation British coins in his custody or under his control with a view to such sale or distribution,

unless the Treasury have previously consented in writing to the sale or distribution of such imitation British coins in connection with that scheme.

(2) In this section –

'British coin' means any coin which is legal tender in any part of the United Kingdom; and 'imitation British coin' means any thing which resembles a British coin in shape, size and the substance of which it is made.

20 Prohibition of importation of counterfeit notes and coins

The importation, landing or unloading of a counterfeit of a currency note or of a protected coin without the consent of the Treasury is hereby prohibited.

21 Prohibition of exportation of counterfeit notes and coins

(1) The exportation of a counterfeit of a currency note or of a protected coin without the consent of the Treasury is hereby prohibited.

(2) A counterfeit of a currency note or of a protected coin which is removed to the Isle of Man from the United Kingdom shall be deemed to be exported from the United Kingdom –

(a) for the purposes of this section; and
(b) for the purposes of the customs and excise Acts, in their application to the prohibition imposed by this section.

22 Penalties for offences under Part II

(1) A person guilty of an offence to which this subsection applies shall be liable –

(a) on summary conviction –

(i) to a fine not exceeding the statutory maximum; or
(ii) to imprisonment for a term not exceeding six months; or
(iii) to both; or

(b) on conviction on indictment –

(i) to a fine; or
(ii) to imprisonment for a term not exceeding ten years; or
(iii) to both.

(2) The offences to which subsection (1) above applies are offences under the following provisions of this Part of this Act –

(a) section 14(1);
(b) section 15(1);
(c) section 16(1); and
(d) section 17(1).

(3) A person guilty of an offence to which this subsection applies shall be liable –

(a) on summary conviction –

(i) to a fine not exceeding the statutory maximum; or
(ii) to imprisonment for a term not exceeding six months; or
(iii) to both; and

(b) on conviction on indictment –

(i) to a fine; or
(ii) to imprisonment for a term not exceeding two years; or
(iii) to both.

(4) The offences to which subsection (3) above applies are offences under the following provisions of this Part of this Act –

(a) section 14(2);
(b) section 15(2);
(c) section 16(2);
(d) section 17(2); and
(e) section 17(3).

(5) A person guilty of an offence under section 18 or 19 above shall be liable –

(a) on summary conviction, to a fine not exceeding the statutory maximum; and
(b) on conviction on indictment, to a fine.

27 Meaning of 'currency note' and 'protected coin'

(1) In this Part of this Act –

'currency note' means –

(a) any note which –

(i) has been lawfully issued in England and Wales, Scotland, Northern Ireland, any of the Channel Islands, the Isle of Man or the Republic of Ireland; and
(ii) is or has been customarily used as money in the country where it was issued; and
(iii) is payable on demand; or

(b) any note which –

(i) has been lawfully issued in some country other than those mentioned in paragraph (a)(i) above; and
(ii) is customarily used as money in that country; and

'protected coin' means any coin which –

(a) is customarily used as money in any country; or
(b) is specified in an order made by the Treasury for the purposes of this Part of this Act.

(2) The power to make an order conferred on the Treasury by subsection (1) above shall be exercisable by statutory instrument.

(3) A statutory instrument containing such an order shall be laid before Parliament after being made.

28 Meaning of 'counterfeit'

(1) For the purposes of this Part of this Act a thing is a counterfeit of a currency note or of a protected coin –

(a) if it is not a currency note or a protected coin but resembles a currency note or protected coin (whether on one side only or on both) to such an extent that it is reasonably capable of passing for a currency note or protected coin of that description; or
(b) if it is a currency note or protected coin which has been so altered that it is reasonably capable of passing for a currency note or protected coin of some other description.

(2) For the purposes of this Part of this Act –

(a) a thing consisting of one side only of a currency note, with or without the addition of other material, is a counterfeit of such a note;
(b) a thing consisting –

(i) of parts of two or more currency notes; or
(ii) of parts of a currency note, or of parts of two or more currency notes, with the addition of other material,

is capable of being a counterfeit of a currency note.

(3) References in this Part of this Act to passing or tendering a counterfeit of a currency note or a protected coin are not to be construed as confined to passing or tendering it as legal tender.

[As amended by the Fines and Penalties (Northern Ireland) Order 1984, art 19(1), Schedule 6, paras 20, 21, Schedule 7; Criminal Justice Act 1991, s17(2)(c); Statute Law (Repeals) Act 1993.]

Criminal Attempts Act 1981
(1981 c 47)

1 Attempting to commit an offence

(1) If, with intent to commit an offence to which this section applies, a person does an act which is more than merely preparatory to the commission of the offence, he is guilty of attempting to commit the offence.

(1A) Subject to section 8 of the Computer Misuse Act 1990 (relevance of external law), if this subsection applies to an act, what the person doing it had in view shall be treated as an offence to which this section applies.

(1B) Subsection (1A) above applies to an act if –

(a) it is done in England and Wales; and
(b) it would fall within subsection (1) above as more than merely preparatory to the commission of an offence under section 3 of the Computer Misuse Act 1990 but for the fact that the offence, if completed, would not be an offence triable in England and Wales.

(2) A person may be guilty of attempting to commit an offence to which this section applies even though the facts are such that the commission of the offence is impossible.

(3) In any case where –

(a) apart from this subsection a person's intention would not be regarded as having amounted to an intent to commit an offence; but

(b) if the facts of the case had been as he believed them to be, his intention would be so regarded,

then, for the purposes of subsection (1) above, he shall be regarded as having had an intent to commit that offence.

(4) This section applies to any offence which, if it were completed, would be triable in England and Wales as an indictable offence, other than –

(a) conspiracy (at common law or under section 1 of the Criminal Law Act 1977 or any other enactment);

(b) aiding, abetting, counselling, procuring or suborning the commission of an offence;

(c) offences under section 4(1) (assisting offenders) or 5(1) (accepting or agreeing to accept consideration for not disclosing information about an arrestable offence) of the Criminal law Act 1967.

1A Extended jurisdiction in relation to certain attempts

(1) If this section applies to an act, what the person doing the act had in view shall be treated as an offence to which section 1(1) above applies.

(2) This section applies to an act if –

(a) it is done in England and Wales, and

(b) it would fall within section 1(1) above as more than merely preparatory to the commission of a Group A offence but for the fact that that offence, if completed, would not be an offence triable in England and Wales.

(3) In this section 'Group A offence' has the same meaning as in Part I of the Criminal Justice Act 1993.

(4) Subsection (1) above is subject to the provisions of section 6 of the Act of 1993 (relevance of external law).

(5) Where a person does any act to which this section applies, the offence which he commits shall for all purposes be treated as the offence of attempting to commit the relevant Group A offence.

2 Application of procedural and other provisions to offences under s1

(1) Any provision to which this section applies shall have effect with respect to an offence under section 1 above of attempting to commit an offence as it has effect with respect to the offence attempted.

(2) This section applies to provisions of any of the following descriptions made by or under any enactment (whenever passed) –

(a) provisions whereby proceedings may not be instituted or carried on otherwise than by, or on behalf or with the consent of, any person (including any provisions which also make other exceptions to the prohibition);

(b) provisions conferring power to institute proceedings;

(c) provisions as to the venue of proceedings;

(d) provisions whereby proceedings may not be instituted after the expiration of a time limit;

(e) provisions conferring a power of arrest or search;

(f) provisions conferring a power of seizure and detention of property;

(g) provisions whereby a person may not be convicted or committed for trial on the uncorroborated evidence of one witness (including any provision requiring the evidence of not less than two credible witnesses);

(h) provisions conferring a power of forfeiture, including any power to deal with anything liable to be forfeited;

(i) provisions whereby, if an offence committed by a body corporate is proved to have been committed with the consent or connivance of another person, that person also is guilty of the offence.

3 Offences of attempt under other enactments

(1) Subsections (2) to (5) below shall have effect, subject to subsection (6) below and to any inconsistent provision in any other enactment, for the purpose of determining whether a person is guilty of an attempt under a special statutory provision.

(2) For the purposes of this Act an attempt under a special statutory provision is an offence which –

(a) is created by an enactment other than section 1 above, including an enactment passed after this Act; and

(b) is expressed as an offence of attempting to commit another offence (in this section referred to as 'the relevant full offence').

(3) A person is guilty of an attempt under a special statutory provision if, with intent to commit the relevant full offence, he does an act which is more than merely preparatory to the commission of that offence.

(4) A person may be guilty of an attempt under a special statutory provision even though the facts are such that the commission of the relevant full offence is impossible.

(5) In any case where –

(a) apart from this subsection a person's intention would not be regarded as having amounted to an intent to commit the relevant full offence; but

(b) if the facts of the case had been as he believed them to be, his intention would be so regarded,

then, for the purposes of subsection (3) above, he shall be regarded as having had an intent to commit that offence.

(6) Subsections (2) to (5) above shall not have effect in relation to an act done before the commencement of this Act.

4 *Trial and penalties*

(1) A person guilty by virtue of section 1 above of attempting to commit an offence shall –

(a) if the offence attempted is murder or any other offence the sentence for which is fixed by law, be liable on conviction on indictment to imprisonment for life; and

(b) if the offence attempted is indictable but does not fall within paragraph (a) above, be liable on conviction on indictment to any penalty to which he would have been liable on conviction on indictment of that offence; and

(c) if the offence attempted is triable either way, be liable on summary conviction to any penalty to which he would have been liable on summary conviction of that offence.

(2) In any case in which a court may proceed to summary trial of an information charging a person with an offence and an information charging him with an offence under section 1 above of attempting to commit it or an attempt under a special statutory provision, the court may, without his consent, try the informations together.

(3) Where, in proceedings against a person for an offence under section 1 above, there is evidence sufficient in law to support a finding that he did not act falling within subsection (1) of that section, the question whether or not this act fell within that subsection is a question of fact.

(4) Where, in proceedings against a person for an attempt under a special statutory provision, there is evidence sufficient in law to support a finding that he did an act falling within subsection (3) of section 3 above, the question whether or not his act fell within that subsection is a question of fact.

(5) Subsection (1) above shall have effect –

(a) subject to section 37 of and Schedule 2 to the Sexual Offences Act 1956 (mode of trial of and penalties for attempts to commit certain offences under that Act); and

(b) notwithstanding anything –

(i) in section 32(1) (no limit to fine on conviction on indictment) of the Criminal Law Act 1977; or

(ii) in section 31(1) and (2) (maximum of six months' imprisonment on summary conviction unless express provision made to the contrary) of the Magistrates' Courts Act 1980.

6 *Effect of Part I on common law*

(1) The offence of attempt at common law and any offence at common law of procuring materials for crime are hereby abolished for all purposes not relating to acts done before the commencement of this Act.

(2) Except as regards offences committed before the commencement of this Act, references in any enactment passed before this Act which fall to be construed as references to the offence of attempt at common law shall be construed as references to the offence under section 1 above.

8 Abolition of offence of loitering, etc with intent

The provisions of section 4 of the Vagrancy Act 1824 which apply to suspected persons and reputed thieves frequenting or loitering about the places described in that section with the intent there specified shall cease to have effect.

9 Interference with vehicles

(1) A person is guilty of the offence of vehicle interference if he interferes with a motor vehicle or trailer or with anything carried in or on a motor vehicle or trailer with the intention that an offence specified in subsection (2) below shall be committed by himself or some other person.

(2) The offences mentioned in subsection (1) above are –

(a) theft of the motor vehicle or trailer or part of it;
(b) theft of anything carried in or on the motor vehicle or trailer; and
(c) an offence under section 12(1) of the Theft Act 1968 (taking and driving away without consent);

and, if it is shown that a person accused of an offence under this section intended that one of those offences should be committed, it is immaterial that it cannot be shown which it was.

(3) A person guilty of an offence under this section shall be liable on summary conviction to imprisonment for a term not exceeding three months or to a fine not exceeding level 4 on the standard scale or to both.

(5) In this section 'motor vehicle' and 'trailer' have the meanings assigned to them by section 185(1) of the Road Traffic Act 1988.

[As amended by the Criminal Justice Act 1982, ss38, 46; Road Traffic (Consequential Provisions) Act 1988, s4, Schedule 3, para 23; Computer Misuse Act 1990, s7(3); Criminal Justice Act 1993, s5(2).]

Taking of Hostages Act 1982
(1982 c 28)

1 Hostage-taking

(1) A person, whatever his nationality, who, in the United Kingdom or elsewhere, –

(a) detains any other person ('the hostage'), and
(b) in order to compel a State, international governmental organisation or person to do or abstain from doing any act, threatens to kill, injure or continue to detain the hostage,

commits an offence.

(2) A person guilty of an offence under this Act shall be liable, on conviction on indictment, to imprisonment for life.

2 Prosecution of offences

(1) Proceedings for an offence under this Act shall not be instituted –

(a) in England and Wales, except by or with the consent of the Attorney General ...

Firearms Act 1982
(1982 c 31)

1 Control of imitation firearms readily convertible into firearms to which section 1 of the 1968 Act applies

(1) This Act applies to an imitation firearm if –

(a) it has the appearance of being a firearm to which section 1 of the 1968 Act (firearms requiring a firearm certificate) applies; and

(b) it is so construed or adapted as to be readily convertible into a firearm to which that section applies.

(2) Subject to section 2(2) of this Act and the following provisions of this section, the 1968 Act shall apply in relation to an imitation firearm to which this Act applies as it applies in relation to a firearm to which section 1 of that Act applies.

(3) Subject to the modifications in subsection (4) below, any expression given a meaning for the purposes of the 1968 Act has the same meaning in this Act.

(4) For the purposes of this section and the 1968 Act, as it applies by virtue of this section –

(a) the definition of air weapon in section 1(3)(b) of that Act (air weapons excepted from requirement of firearm certificate) shall have effect without the exclusion of any type declared by rules made by the Secretary of State under section 53 of that Act to be specially dangerous; and

(b) the definition of firearm in sections 57(1) of that Act shall have effect without paragraphs (b) and (c) of that subsection (component parts and accessories).

(5) In any proceedings brought by virtue of this section for an offence under the 1968 Act involving an imitation firearm to which this Act applies, it shall be a defence for the accused to show that he did not know and had no reason to suspect that the imitation firearm was so constructed or adapted as to be readily convertible into a firearm to which section 1 of that Act applies.

(6) For the purposes of this section an imitation firearm shall be regarded as readily convertible into a firearm to which section 1 of the 1968 Act applies if –

(a) it can be so converted without any special skill on the part of the person converting it in the construction or adaptation of firearms of any description; and

(b) the work involved in converting it does not require equipment or tools other than such as are in common use by persons carrying out works of construction and maintenance in their own homes.

2 *Provisions supplementary to section 1*

(1) Subject to subsection (2) below, references in the 1968 Act, and in any order made under section 6 of that Act (orders prohibiting movement of firearms or ammunition) before this Act comes into force –

(a) to firearms (without qualification); or
(b) to firearms to which section 1 of that Act applies;

shall be read as including imitation firearms to which this Act applies.

(2) The following provisions of the 1968 Act do not apply by virtue of this Act to an imitation firearm to which this Act applies, that is to say –

(a) section 4(3) and (4) (offence to convert anything having appearance of firearm into a firearm and aggravated offence under section 1 involving a converted firearm); and
(b) the provisions of that Act which relate to, or to the enforcement of control over, the manner in which a firearm is used or the circumstances in which it is carried;

but without prejudice, in the case of the provisions mentioned in paragraph (b) above, to the application to such an imitation firearm of such of those provisions as apply to imitation firearms apart from this Act.

(3) The provisions referred to in subsection (2)(b) are sections 16 to 20 and section 47.

Aviation Security Act 1982
(1982 c 36)

1 *Hijacking*

(1) A person on board an aircraft in flight who unlawfully, by the use of force or by threats of any kind, seizes the aircraft or exercises control of it commits the offence of hijacking, whatever his nationality, whatever the State in which the aircraft is registered and whether the aircraft is in the United Kingdom or elsewhere, but subject to subsection (2) below.

(2) If –

(a) the aircraft is used in military, customs or police service, or
(b) both the place of take-off and the place of landing are in the territory of the State in which the aircraft is registered,
subsection (1) above shall not apply unless –

(i) the person seizing or exercising control of the aircraft is a United Kingdom national; or
(ii) his act is committed in the United Kingdom; or
(iii) the aircraft is registered in the United Kingdom or is used in the military or customs service of the United Kingdom or in the service of any police force in the United Kingdom.

(3) A person who commits the offence of hijacking shall be liable, on conviction on indictment, to imprisonment for life.

(4) If the Secretary of State by order made by statutory instrument declares –

(a) that any two or more States named in the order have established an organisation or agency which operates aircraft; and
(b) that one of those States has been designated as exercising, for aircraft so operated, the powers of the State of registration,

the State declared under paragraph (b) of this subsection shall be deemed for the purposes of this section to be the State in which any aircraft so operated is registered; but in relation to such an aircraft subsection (2)(b) above shall have effect as if it referred to the territory of any one of the States named in the order.

(5) For the purposes of this section the territorial waters of any State shall be treated as part of its territory.

2 *Destroying, damaging or endangering safety of aircraft*

(1) It shall, subject to subsection (4) below, be an offence for any person unlawfully and intentionally–

(a) to destroy an aircraft in service or so to damage such an aircraft as to render it incapable of flight or as to be likely to endanger its safety in flight; or
(b) to commit on board an aircraft in flight any act of violence which is likely to endanger the safety of the aircraft.

(2) It shall also, subject to subsection (4) below, be an offence for any person unlawfully and intentionally to place, or cause to be placed, on an aircraft in service any device or substance which is likely to destroy the aircraft, or is likely so to damage it as to render it incapable of flight or as to be likely to endanger its safety in flight; but nothing in this subsection shall be construed as limiting the circumstances in which the commission of any act –

(a) may constitute an offence under subsection (1) above, or
(b) may constitute attempting or conspiring to commit, or aiding, abetting, counselling or procuring, or being art and part in, the commission of such an offence.

(3) Except as provided by subsection (4) below, subsections (1) and (2) above shall apply whether any such act as is therein mentioned is committed in the United Kingdom or elsewhere, whatever the nationality of the person committing the act and whatever the State in which the aircraft is registered.

(4) Subsections (1) and (2) above shall not apply to any act committed in relation to an aircraft used in military, customs or police service unless –

(a) the act is committed in the United Kingdom, or
(b) where the act is committed outside the United Kingdom, the person committing it is a United Kingdom national.

(5) A person who commits an offence under this section shall be liable, on conviction on indictment, to imprisonment for life.

(6) In this section 'unlawfully' –

(a) in relation to the commission of an act in the United Kingdom, means so as (apart from this Act) to constitute an offence under the law of the part of the United Kingdom in which the act is committed, and

(b) in relation to the commission of an act outside the United Kingdom, means so that the commission of the act would (apart from this Act) have been an offence under the law of England and Wales if it had been committed in England and Wales or of Scotland if it had been committed in Scotland.

(7) In this section 'act of violence' means –

(a) any act done in the United Kingdom which constitutes the offence of murder, attempted murder, manslaughter, culpable homicide or assault or an offence under sections 18, 20, 21, 22, 23, 24, 28 or 29 of the Offences against the Person Act 1861 or under section 2 of the Explosive Substances Act 1883, and

(b) any act done outside the United Kingdom which, if done in the United Kingdom, would constitute such an offence as is mentioned in paragraph (a) above.

3 Other acts endangering or likely to endanger safety of aircraft

(1) It shall, subject to subsection (5) and (6) below, be an offence for any person unlawfully and intentionally to destroy or damage any property to which this subsection applies, or to interfere with the operation of any such property, where the destruction, damage or interference is likely to endanger the safety of aircraft in flight.

(2) Subsection (1) above applies to any property used for the provision of air navigation facilities, including any land, building or ship so used, and including any apparatus or equipment so used, whether it is on board an aircraft or elsewhere.

(3) It shall also, subject to subsections (4) and (5) below, be an offence for a person intentionally to communicate any information which is false, misleading or deceptive in a material particular, where the communication of the information endangers the safety of an aircraft or is likely to endanger the safety of aircraft in flight.

(4) It shall be a defence for a person charged with an offence under subsection (3) above to prove –

(a) that he believed, and had reasonable grounds for believing, that the information was true; or

(b) that, when he communicated the information, he was lawfully employed to perform duties which consisted of or included the communication of information and that he communicated the information in good faith in the performance of those duties.

(5) Subsections (1) and (3) above shall not apply to the commission of any act unless either the act is committed in the United Kingdom, or, where it is committed outside the United Kingdom –

(a) the person committing it is a United Kingdom national; or

(b) the commission of the act endangers or is likely to endanger the safety in flight of a civil aircraft registered in the United Kingdom or chartered by demise to a lessee whose principal place of business, or (if he has no place of business) whose permanent residence, is in the United Kingdom; or

(c) the act is committed on board a civil aircraft which is so registered or so chartered; or

(d) the act is committed on board a civil aircraft which lands in the United Kingdom with the person who committed the act still on board.

(6) Subsection (1) above shall also not apply to any act committed outside the United Kingdom and so committed in relation to property which is situated outside the United Kingdom and is not used for the provision of air navigation facilities in connection with international air navigation, unless the person committing the act is a United Kingdom national.

(7) A person who commits an offence under this section shall be liable, on conviction on indictment, to imprisonment for life.

(8) In this section 'civil aircraft' means any aircraft other than an aircraft used in military, customs or police service and 'unlawfully' has the same meaning as in section 2 of this Act.

4 *Offences in relation to certain dangerous articles*

(1) It shall be an offence for any person without lawful authority or reasonable excuse (the proof of which shall lie on him) to have with him –

(a) in any aircraft registered in the United Kingdom, whether at a time when the aircraft is in the United Kingdom or not, or

(b) in any other aircraft at a time when it is in, or in flight over, the United Kingdom, or

(c) in any part of an aerodrome in the United Kingdom, or

(d) in any air navigation installation in the United Kingdom which does not form part of an aerodrome,

any article to which this section applies.

(2) This section applies to the following articles, that is to say –

(a) any firearm, or any article having the appearance of being a firearm, whether capable of being discharged or not;

(b) any explosive, any article manufactured or adapted (whether in the form of a bomb, grenade or otherwise) so as to have the appearance of being an explosive, whether it is capable of producing a practical effect by explosion or not, or any article marked or labelled so as to indicate that it is or contains an explosive; and

(c) any article (not falling within either of the preceding paragraphs) made or adapted for use for causing injury to or incapacitating a person or for destroying or damaging property, or intended by the person having it with him for such use, whether by him or by any other person.

(3) For the purposes of this section a person who is for the time being in an aircraft, or in part of an aerodrome, shall be treated as having with him in the aircraft, or in that part of the aerodrome, as the case may be, an article to which this section applies if –

(a) where he is in an aircraft, or an article in which it is contained, is in the aircraft and has been caused (whether by him or by any other person) to be brought there as being, or as forming part of, his baggage on a flight in the aircraft or has been caused by him to be brought there as being, or as forming part of, any other property to be carried on such a flight, or

(b) where he is in part of an aerodrome (otherwise than in an aircraft), the article, or an article in which it is contained, is in that or any other part of the aerodrome and has been caused (whether by him or by any other person) to be brought into the aerodrome as being, or as forming part of, his baggage on a flight from that aerodrome or has been caused by him to be brought there as being, or as forming part of, any other property to be carried on such a flight on which he is also to be carried,

notwithstanding that the circumstances may be such that (apart from this subsection) he would not be regarded as having the article with him in the aircraft or in a part of the aerodrome, as the case may be.

(4) A person guilty of an offence under this section shall be liable –

(a) on summary conviction, to a fine not exceeding the statutory maximum or to imprisonment for a term not exceeding three months or to both;
(b) on conviction on indictment, to a fine or to imprisonment for a term not exceeding five years or to both.

(5) Nothing in subsection (3) above shall be construed as limiting the circumstances in which a person would, apart from that subsection, be regarded as having an article with him as mentioned in subsection (1) above.

8 Prosecution of offences and proceedings

(1) Proceedings for an offence under any of the preceding provisions of this Part of this Act (other than sections 4 and 7) shall not be instituted –

(a) in England and Wales, except by, or with the consent of, the Attorney General ...

38 Interpretation, etc

(3) For the purposes of this Act –

(a) the period during which an aircraft is in flight shall be deemed to include any period from the moment when all its external doors are closed following embarkation until the moment when any such door is opened for disembarkation, and, in the case of a forced landing, any period until the competent authorities take over responsibility for the aircraft and for persons and property on board; and
(b) an aircraft shall be taken to be in service during the whole of the period which begins with the pre-flight preparation of the aircraft for a flight and ends 24 hours after the aircraft lands having completed that flight, and also at any time (not falling within that period) while, in accordance with the preceding paragraph, the aircraft is in flight,

and anything done on board an aircraft while in flight over any part of the United Kingdom shall be treated as done in that part of the United Kingdom. ...

Criminal Justice Act 1982
(1982 c 48)

37 *The standard scale of fines for summary offences*

(1) There shall be a standard scale of fines for summary offences, which shall be known as 'the standard scale'.

(2) The standard scale is shown below –

Level on the scale	Amount of fine
1	£200
2	£500
3	£1,000
4	£2,500
5	£5,000

(3) Where any enactment (whether contained in an Act passed before or after this Act) provides –

(a) that a person convicted of a summary offence shall be liable on conviction to a fine or a maximum fine by reference to a specified level on the standard scale; or

(b) confers power by subordinate instrument to make a person liable on conviction of a summary offence (whether or not created by the instrument) to a fine or maximum fine by reference to a specified level on the standard scale,

it is to be construed as referring to the standard scale for which this section provides as that standard scale has effect from time to time by virtue either of this section or of an order under section 143 of the Magistrates' Courts Act 1980.

70 *Vagrancy offences*

(1) Where a person is convicted –

(a) under section 3 or 4 of the Vagrancy Act 1824, of wandering abroad, or placing himself in any public place, street, highway, court, or passage, to beg or gather alms; or

(b) under section 4 of that Act, –

(i) of wandering abroad and lodging in any barn or outhouse, or in any deserted or unoccupied building, or in the open air, or under a tent, or in any cart or waggon, and not giving a good account of himself; or

(ii) of wandering abroad, and endeavouring by the exposure of wounds and deformities to obtain or gather alms,

the court shall not have power to sentence him to imprisonment but shall have the same power to fine him as if this section had not been enacted.

(2) If a person deemed a rogue and vagabond by virtue of section 4 of the Vagrancy Act 1824 is thereafter guilty of an offence mentioned in subsection (1) above, he shall be convicted of that offence under section 4 of that Act and accordingly –

(a) shall not be deemed an incorrigible rogue; and
(b) shall not be committed to the Crown Court,

by reason only of that conviction.

(3) This section applies to offences committed before as well as after it comes into effect.

[As amended by the Criminal Justice Act 1991, ss17(1), 101(1), Schedule 12, para 6.]

Representation of the People Act 1983
(1983 c 2)

97 Disturbances at election meetings

(1) A person who at a lawful public meeting to which this section applies acts, or incites others to act, in a disorderly manner for the purpose of preventing the transaction of the business for which the meeting was called together shall be guilty of an illegal practice.

(2) This section applies to –

(a) a political meeting held in any constituency between the date of the issue of a writ for the return of a Member of Parliament for the constituency and the date at which a return to the writ is made;
(b) a meeting held with reference to a local government election in the electoral area for that election in the period beginning with the last date on which notice of the election may be published in accordance with rules made under section 36 or, in Scotland, section 42 above and ending with the day of election.

(3) If a constable reasonably suspects any person of committing an offence under subsection (1) above, he may if requested so to do by the chairman of the meeting require that person to declare to him immediately his name and address and, if that person refuses or fails so to declare his name and address or gives a false name and address, he shall be liable on summary conviction to a fine not exceeding level 1 on the standard scale. ...

[As amended by the Police and Criminal Evidence Act 1984, ss26(1), 119(2), Schedule 7, Part I; Representation of the People Act 1985, s24, Schedule 4, para 39.]

Child Abduction Act 1984
(1984 c 37)

1 Offences of abduction of child by parent, etc

(1) Subject to subsections (5) and (8) below, a person connected with a child under the age of sixteen commits an offence if he takes or sends the child out of the United Kingdom without the appropriate consent.

(2) A person is connected with a child for the purposes of this section if –

(a) he is a parent or guardian of the child; or
(b) in the case of a child whose parents were not married to each other at the time of his birth, there are reasonable grounds for believing that he is the father of the child; or
(c) he is a guardian of the child; or
(d) he is a person in whose favour a residence order is in force with respect to the child; or
(e) he has custody of the child.

(3) In this section 'the appropriate consent', in relation to a child, means –

(a) the consent of each of the following –

(i) the child's mother;
(ii) the child's father, if he has parental responsibility for him;
(iii) any guardian of the child;
(iv) any person in whose favour a residence order is in force with respect to the child;
(v) any person who has custody of the child; or

(b) the leave of the court granted under or by virtue of any provision of Part II of the Children Act 1989; or
(c) if any person has custody of the child, the leave of the court which awarded custody to him.

(4) A person does not commit an offence under this section by taking or sending a child out of the United Kingdom without obtaining the appropriate consent if –

(a) he is a person in whose favour there is a residence order in force with respect to the child, and
(b) he takes or sends him out of the United Kingdom for a period of less than one month.

(4A) Subsection (4) above does not apply if the person taking or sending the child out of the United Kingdom does so in breach of an order under Part II of the Children Act 1989.

(5) A person does not commit an offence under this section by doing anything without the consent of another person whose consent is required under the foregoing provisions if –

(a) he does it in the belief that the other person –

(i) has consented; or
(ii) would consent if he was aware of all the relevant circumstances; or

(b) he has taken all reasonable steps to communicate with the other person but has been unable to communicate with him; or
(c) the other person has unreasonably refused to consent.

(5A) Subsection (5)(c) above does not apply if –

(a) the person who refused to consent is a person–

(i) in whose favour there is a residence order in force with respect to the child; or
(ii) who has custody of the child; or

(b) the person taking or sending the child out of the United Kingdom is, by so acting, in breach of an order made by a court in the United Kingdom.

(6) Where, in proceedings for an offence under this section, there is sufficient evidence to raise an issue as to the application of subsection (5) above, it shall be for the prosecution to prove that that subsection does not apply.

(7) For the purposes of this section –

(a) 'guardian of a child', 'residence order' and 'parental responsibility' have the same meaning as in the Children Act 1989; and

(b) a person shall be treated as having custody of a child if there is in force an order of a court in the United Kingdom awarding him (whether solely or jointly with another person) custody, legal custody or care and control of the child.

(8) This section shall have effect subject to the provisions of the Schedule to this Act in relation to a child who is in the care of a local authority, detained in a place of safety, remanded to a local authority accommodation or the subject of proceedings or an order relating to adoption.

2 Offence of abduction of child by other persons

(1) Subject to subsection (3) below, a person, other than one mentioned in subsection (2) below commits an offence if, without lawful authority or reasonable excuse, he takes or detains a child under the age of sixteen –

(a) so as to remove him from the lawful control of any person having lawful control of the child; or

(b) so as to keep him out of the lawful control of any person entitled to lawful control of the child.

(2) The persons are –

(a) where the father and mother of the child in question were married to each other at the time of his birth, the child's father and mother;

(b) where the father and mother of the child in question were not married to each other at the time of his birth, the child's mother; and

(c) any other person mentioned in section 1(2)(c) to (e) above.

(3) In proceedings against any person for an offence under this section, it shall be a defence for that person to prove –

(a) where the father and mother of the child in question were not married to each other at the time of his birth –

(i) that he is the child's father; or

(ii) that, at the time of the alleged offence, he believed, on reasonable grounds, that he was the child's father; or

(b) that, at the time of the alleged offence, he believed that the child had attained the age of sixteen.

3 Construction of references to taking, sending and detaining

For the purposes of this Part of this Act –

(a) a person shall be regarded as taking a child if he causes or induces the child to accompany him or any other person or causes the child to be taken;

(b) a person shall be regarded as sending a child if he causes the child to be sent;

(c) a person shall be regarded as detaining a child if he causes the child to be detained or induces the child to remain with him or any other person; and

(d) references to a child's parents and to a child whose parents were (or were not) married to each other at the time of his birth shall be construed in accordance with section 1 of the Family Law Reform Act 1987 (which extends their meaning).

4 Penalties and prosecutions

(1) A person guilty of an offence under this Part of this Act shall be liable –

(a) on summary conviction, to imprisonment for a term not exceeding six months or to a fine not exceeding the statutory maximum, or to both such imprisonment and fine;

(b) on conviction on indictment, to imprisonment for a term not exceeding seven years.

(2) No prosecution for an offence under section 1 above shall be instituted except by or with the consent of the Director of Public Prosecutions.

5 Restriction on prosecutions for offence of kidnapping

Except by or with the consent of the Director of Public Prosecutions no prosecution shall be instituted for an offence of kidnapping if it was committed –

(a) against a child under the age of sixteen; and

(b) by a person connected with the child, within the meaning of section 1 above.

[As amended by the Family Law Act 1986, s65; Children Act 1989, s108(4), (7), Schedule 12, paras 37(1)–(5), 38, 39, Schedule 15.]

Police and Criminal Evidence Act 1984
(1984 c 60)

24 Arrest without warrant for arrestable offences

(1) The powers of summary arrest conferred by the following subsections shall apply –

(a) to offences for which the sentence is fixed by law;

(b) to offences for which a person of 21 years of age or over (not previously convicted) may be sentenced to imprisonment for a term of five years (or might be so sentenced but for the restrictions imposed by section 33 of the Magistrates' Courts Act 1980); and

(c) to the offences to which subsection (2) below applies,

and in this Act 'arrestable offence' means any such offence.

(2) The offences to which this subsection applies are –

(a) offences for which a person may be arrested under the customs and excise Acts, as defined in section 1(1) of the Customs and Excise Management Act 1979;

(b) offences under the Official Secrets Acts 1911 and 1920 that are not arrestable offences by virtue of the term of imprisonment for which a person may be sentenced in respect of them;

(bb) offences under any provision of the Official Secrets Act 1989 except section 8(1), (4) or (5);

(c) offences under section 22 (causing prostitution of women) or 23 (procuration of girl under 21) of the Sexual Offences Act 1956;

(d) offences under section 12(1) (taking motor vehicle or other conveyance without authority etc) or 25(1) (going equipped for stealing, etc) of the Theft Act 1968; and

(e) any offence under the Football (Offences) Act 1991.

(f) an offence under section 2 of the Obscene Publications Act 1959 (publication of obscene matter);

(g) an offence under section 1 of the Protection of Children Act 1978 (indecent photographs and pseudo-photographs of children);

(h) an offence under section 166 of the Criminal Justice and Public Order Act 1994 (sale of tickets by unauthorised persons);

(i) an offence under section 19 of the Public Order Act 1986 (publishing, etc material intended or likely to stir up racial hatred);

(j) an offence under section 167 of the Criminal Justice and Public Order Act 1994 (touting for hire car services);

(k) an offence under section 1(1) of the Prevention of Crime Act 1953 (prohibition of the carrying of offensive weapons without lawful authority or reasonable excuse);

(l) an offence under section 139(1) of the Criminal Justice Act 1988 (offence of having article with blade or point in public place);

(m) an offence under section 139A(1) or (2) of the Criminal Justice Act 1988 (offence of having article with blade or point (or offensive weapon) on school premises);

(n) an offence under section 2 of the Protection from Harassment Act 1997 (harassment);

(o) an offence under section 60(8)(b) of the Criminal Justice and Public Order Act 1994 (failing to comply with requirement to remove mask etc);

(p) an offence falling within sections 32(1)(a) of the Crime and Disorder Act 1998 (racially-aggravated harassment);

(q) an offence under section 16(4) of the Football Spectators Act 1989 (failure to comply with reporting duty imposed by restriction order);

(r) an offence under section 32(3) of the Public Order Act 1986 (entering premises in breach of domestic football banning order).

(3) Without prejudice to section 2 of the Criminal Attempts Act 1981, the powers of summary arrest conferred by the following subsections shall also apply to the offences of –

(a) conspiring to commit any of the offences mentioned in subsection (2) above;

(b) attempting to commit any such offence other than an offence under section 12(1) of the Theft Act 1968;

(c) inciting, aiding, abetting, counselling or procuring the commission of any such offence;

and such offences are also arrestable offences for the purposes of this Act.

(4) Any person may arrest without a warrant –

(a) anyone who is in the act of committing an arrestable offence;
(b) anyone whom he has reasonable grounds for suspecting to be committing such an offence.

(5) Where an arrestable offence has been committed, any person may arrest without a warrant –

(a) anyone who is guilty of the offence;
(b) anyone whom he has reasonable grounds for suspecting to be guilty of it.

(6) Where a constable has reasonable grounds for suspecting that an arrestable offence has been committed, he may arrest without a warrant anyone whom he has reasonable grounds for suspecting to be guilty of the offence.

(7) A constable may arrest without a warrant –

(a) anyone who is about to commit an arrestable offence;
(b) anyone whom he has reasonable grounds for suspecting to be about to commit an arrestable offence.

25 General arrest conditions

(1) Where a constable has reasonable grounds for suspecting that any offence which is not an arrestable offence has been committed or attempted, or is being committed or attempted, he may arrest the relevant person if it appears to him that service of a summons is impracticable or inappropriate because any of the general arrest conditions is satisfied.

(2) In this section 'the relevant person' means any person whom the constable has reasonable grounds to suspect of having committed or having attempted to commit the offence or of being in the course of committing or attempting to commit it.

(3) The general arrest conditions are –

(a) that the name of the relevant person is unknown to, and cannot be readily ascertained by, the constable;
(b) that the constable has reasonable grounds for doubting whether a name furnished by the relevant person as his name is his real name;
(c) that –

(i) the relevant person has failed to furnish a satisfactory address for service; or
(ii) the constable has reasonable grounds for doubting whether an address furnished by the relevant person is a satisfactory address for service;

(d) that the constable has reasonable grounds for believing that arrest is necessary to prevent the relevant person –

(i) causing physical injury to himself or any other person;
(ii) suffering physical injury;

(iii) causing loss or damage to property;

(iv) committing an offence against public decency; or

(v) causing an unlawful obstruction of the highway;

(e) that the constable has reasonable grounds for believing that arrest is necessary to protect a child or other vulnerable person from the relevant person.

(4) For the purposes of subsection (3) above an address is a satisfactory address for service if it appears to the constable –

(a) that the relevant person will be at it for a sufficiently long period for it to be possible to serve him with a summons; or

(b) that some other person specified by the relevant person will accept service of a summons for the relevant person at it.

(5) Nothing in subsection (3)(d) above authorises the arrest of a person under sub-paragraph (iv) of that paragraph except where members of the public going about their normal business cannot reasonably be expected to avoid the person to be arrested.

(6) This section shall not prejudice any power of arrest conferred apart from this section.

28 Information to be given on arrest

(1) Subject to subsection (5) below, where a person is arrested, otherwise than by being informed that he is under arrest, the arrest is not lawful unless the person arrested is informed that he is under arrest as soon as is practicable after his arrest.

(2) Where a person is arrested by a constable, subsection (1) above applies regardless of whether the fact of the arrest is obvious.

(3) Subject to subsection (5) below, no arrest is lawful unless the person arrested is informed of the ground for the arrest at the time of, or as soon as is practicable after, the arrest.

(4) Where a person is arrested by a constable, subsection (3) above applies regardless of whether the ground for the arrest is obvious.

(5) Nothing in this section is to be taken to require a person to be informed –

(a) that he is under arrest; or

(b) of the ground for the arrest,

if it was not reasonably practicable for him to be so informed by reason of his having escaped from arrest before the information could be given.

117 Power of constable to use reasonable force

Where any provision of this Act –

(a) confers a power on a constable; and

(b) does not provide that the power may only be exercised with the consent of some person, other than a police officer,

the officer may use reasonable force, if necessary, in the exercise of the power.

[As amended by the Criminal Justice Act 1988, s170(11), Schedule 15, paras 97, 98; Official Secrets Act 1989, s11(1); Football (Offences) Act 1991, s5(1); Criminal Justice and Public Order Act 1994, ss85(1), (2), 155, 166(4), 167(7); Offensive Weapons Act 1996, s1(1); Protection from Harassment Act 1997, s2(3); Crime and Disorder Act 1998, ss27(1), 32(2), 84(2), 120(1), Schedule 9, para 9; Football (Offences and Disorder) Act 1999, s8(3).]

Intoxicating Substances (Supply) Act 1985
(1985 c 26)

1 Offence of supply of intoxicating substance

(1) It is an offence for a person to supply or offer to supply a substance other than a controlled drug –

(a) to a person under the age of eighteen whom he knows, or has reasonable cause to believe, to be under that age; or

(b) to a person –

(i) who is acting on behalf of a person under that age; and

(ii) whom he knows, or has reasonable cause to believe, to be so acting,

if he knows or has reasonable cause to believe that the substance is, or its fumes are, likely to be inhaled by the person under the age of eighteen for the purpose of causing intoxication.

(2) In proceedings against any person for an offence under subsection (1) above it is a defence for him to show that at the time he made the supply or offer he was under the age of eighteen and was acting otherwise than in the course or furtherance of a business.

(3) A person guilty of an offence under this section shall be liable on summary conviction to imprisonment for a term not exceeding six months or to a fine not exceeding level 5 on the standard scale, or to both.

(4) In this section 'controlled drug' has the same meaning as in the Misuse of Drugs Act 1971.

Sexual Offences Act 1985
(1985 c 44)

1 Kerb-crawling

(1) A man commits an offence if he solicits a woman (or different women) for the purpose of prostitution –

(a) from a motor vehicle while it is in a street or public place; or

(b) in a street or public place while in the immediate vicinity of a motor vehicle that he has just got out of or off,

persistently or in such manner or in such circumstances as to be likely to cause annoyance to the woman (or any of the women) solicited, or nuisance to other persons in the neighbourhood.

(2) A person guilty of an offence under this section shall be liable on summary conviction to a fine not exceeding level 3 on the standard scale.

(3) In this section 'motor vehicle' has the same meaning as in the Road Traffic Act 1988.

2 Persistent soliciting of women for the purpose of prostitution

(1) A man commits an offence if in a street or public place he persistently solicits a woman (or different women) for the purpose of prostitution.

(2) A person guilty of an offence under this section shall be liable on summary conviction to a fine not exceeding level 3 on the standard scale.

[As amended by the Road Traffic (Consequential Provisions) Act 1988, s4, Schedule 3, para 29.]

Sporting Events (Control of Alcohol, etc) Act 1985
(1985 c 57)

1 Offences in connection with alcohol on coaches and trains

(1) This section applies to a vehicle which –

(a) is a public service vehicle or railway passenger vehicle, and
(b) is being used for the principal purpose of carrying passengers for the whole or part of a journey to or from a designated sporting event.

(2) A person who knowingly causes or permits intoxicating liquor to be carried on a vehicle to which this section applies is guilty of an offence –

(a) if the vehicle is a public service vehicle and he is the operator of the vehicle or the servant or agent of the operator, or
(b) if the vehicle is a hired vehicle and he is the person to whom it is hired or the servant or agent of that person.

(3) A person who has intoxicating liquor in his possession while on a vehicle to which this section applies is guilty of offence.

(4) A person who is drunk on a vehicle to which this section applies is guilty of an offence.

(5) In this section 'public service vehicle' and 'operator' have the same meaning as in the Public Passenger Vehicles Act 1981.

1A Alcohol on certain other vehicles

(1) This section applies to a motor vehicle which –

(a) is not a public service vehicle but is adapted to carry more than 8 passengers, and

(b) is being used for the principal purpose of carrying two or more passengers for the whole or part of a journey to or from a designated sporting event.

(2) A person who knowingly causes or permits intoxicating liquor to be carried on a motor vehicle to which this section applies is guilty of an offence –

(a) if he its driver, or

(b) if he is not its driver but is its keeper, the servant or agent of its keeper, a person to whom it is made available (by hire, loan or otherwise) by its keeper or the keeper's servant or agent, or the servant or agent of a person to whom it is so made available.

(3) A person who has intoxicating liquor in his possession while on a motor vehicle to which this section applies is guilty of an offence.

(4) A person who is drunk on a motor vehicle to which this section applies is guilty of an offence.

(5) In this section –

'keeper', in relation to a vehicle, means the person having the duty to take out a licence for it under the Vehicle Excise and Registration Act 1994,

'motor vehicle' means a mechanically propelled vehicle intended or adapted for use on roads, and

'public service vehicle' has the same meaning as in the Public Passenger Vehicles Act 1981.

2 Offences in connection with alcohol, containers, etc at sports grounds

(1) A person who has intoxicating liquor or an article to which this section applies in his possession –

(a) at any time during the period of a designated sporting event when he is in any area of a designated sports ground from which the event may be directly viewed, or

(b) while entering or trying to enter a designated sports ground at any time during a period of a designated sporting event at that ground,

is guilty of an offence.

(1A) Subsection (1)(a) above has effect subject to section 5A(1) [private facilities for viewing events] of this Act.

(2) A person who is drunk in a designated sports ground at any time during the period of a designated sporting event at that ground or is drunk while entering or trying to enter such a ground at any time during the period of a designated sporting event at that ground is guilty of an offence.

(3) This section applies to any article capable of causing injury to a person struck by it, being –

(a) a bottle, can or other portable container (including such an article when crushed or broken) which –

(i) is for holding any drink, and

(ii) is of a kind which, when empty, is normally discarded or returned to, or left to be recovered by, the supplier, or

(b) part of an article falling within paragraph (a) above;

but does not apply to anything that is for holding any medicinal product (within the meaning of the Medicines Act 1968).

2A Fireworks, etc

(1) A person is guilty of an offence if he has an article or substance to which this section applies in his possession –

(a) at any time during the period of a designated sporting event when he is in any area of a designated sports ground from which the event may be directly viewed, or

(b) while entering or trying to enter a designated sports ground at any time during the period of a designated sporting event at the ground.

(2) It is a defence for the accused to prove that he had possession with lawful authority.

(3) This section applies to any article or substance whose main purpose is the emission of a flare for purposes of illuminating or signalling (as opposed to igniting or heating) or the emission of smoke or a visible gas; and in particular it applies to distress flares, fog signals, and pellets and capsules intended to be used as fumigators or for testing pipes, but not to matches, cigarette lighters or heaters.

(4) This section also applies to any article which is a firework.

6 Closure of bars

(1) If at any time during the period of a designated sporting event at any designated sports ground it appears to a constable in uniform that the sale or supply of intoxicating liquor at any bar within the ground is detrimental to the orderly conduct or safety of spectators at that event, he may require any person having control of the bar to close it and keep it closed until the end of that period.

(2) A person who fails to comply with a requirement imposed under subsection (1) above is guilty of an offence, unless he shows that he took all reasonable steps to comply with it.

7 Powers of enforcement

(1) A constable may, at any time during the period of a designated sporting event at any designated sports ground, enter any part of the ground for the purpose of enforcing the provisions of this Act.

(2) A constable may search a person he has reasonable grounds to suspect is committing or has committed an offence under this Act, and may arrest such a person.

(3) A constable may stop a public service vehicle (within the meaning of section 1 of this Act) or a motor vehicle to which section 1A of this Act applies and may search such a vehicle or a railway passenger vehicle if he has reasonable grounds to suspect that an offence under that section is being or has been committed in respect of the vehicle.

8 Penalties for offences

A person guilty of an offence under this Act shall be liable on summary conviction –

(a) in the case of an offence under section 1(2) or 1A(2), to a fine not exceeding level 4 on the standard scale,

(b) in the case of an offence under section 1(3), 1A(3), 2(1), 2A(1), 3(10), 5B(2), 5C(3), 5D(2) or 6(2), to a fine not exceeding level 3 on the standard scale or to imprisonment for a term not exceeding three months or both,

(c) in the case of an offence under section 1(4), 1A(4) or 2(2), to a fine not exceeding level 2 on the standard scale. ...

9 Interpretation

(1) The following provisions shall have effect for the interpretation of this Act.

(2) 'Designated sports ground' means any place –

(a) used (wholly or partly) for sporting events where accommodation is provided for spectators, and

(b) for the time being designated, or of a class designated, by order made by the Secretary of State;

and an order under this subsection may include provision for determining for the purposes of this Act the outer limit of any designated sports ground.

(3) 'Designated sporting event' –

(a) means a sporting event or proposed sporting event for the time being designated, or of a class designated, by order made by the Secretary of State, ...

and an order under this subsection may apply to events or proposed events outside Great Britain as well as those in England and Wales.

(4) The period of a designated sporting event is the period beginning two hours before the start of the event or (if earlier) two hours before the time at which it is advertised to start and ending one hour after the end of the event, but –

(a) where an event advertised to start at a particular time on a particular day is postponed to a later day, the period includes the period in the day on which it is advertised to take place beginning two hours before and ending one hour after that time, and

(b) where an event advertised to start at a particular time on a particular day does not take place, the period is the period referred to in paragraph (a) above. ...

(6) This Act does not apply to any sporting event or proposed sporting event –

(a) where all competitors are to take part otherwise than for reward, and

(b) to which all spectators are to be admitted free of charge.

(7) Expressions used in this Act and in the Licensing Act 1964 have the same meaning as in that Act, and section 58(2) of that Act (meaning of chief officer of police) applies for the purposes of this Act as it applies for the purposes of Part II of that Act.

(8) Any power to make an order under this section shall be exercisable by statutory

instrument subject to annulment in pursuance of a resolution of either House of Parliament.

[As amended by the Public Order Act 1986, s40(1), (3), Schedule 1, Part 1, paras 1, 2, 3, 5, 6, 7; Schedule 3; Vehicle Excise and Registration Act 1994, s63, Schedule 3, para 20.]

Public Order Act 1986
(1986 c 64)
Part I
New Offences

1 Riot

(1) Where 12 or more persons who are present together use or threaten unlawful violence for a common purpose and the conduct of them (taken together) is such as would cause a person of reasonable firmness present at the scene to fear for his personal safety, each of the persons using unlawful violence for the common purpose is guilty of riot.

(2) It is immaterial whether or not the 12 or more use or threaten unlawful violence simultaneously.

(3) The common purpose may be inferred from conduct.

(4) No person of reasonable firmness need actually be, or be likely to be, present at the scene.

(5) Riot may be committed in private as well as in public places.

(6) A person guilty of riot is liable on conviction on indictment to imprisonment for a term not exceeding ten years or a fine or both.

2 Violent disorder

(1) Where three or more persons who are present together use or threaten unlawful violence and the conduct of them (taken together) is such as would cause a person of reasonable firmness present at the scene to fear for his personal safety, each of the persons using or threatening unlawful violence is guilty of violent disorder.

(2) It is immaterial whether or not the three or more use or threaten unlawful violence simultaneously.

(3) No person of reasonable firmness need actually be, or be likely to be, present at the scene.

(4) Violent disorder may be committed in private as well as in public places.

(5) A person guilty of violent disorder is liable on conviction on indictment to imprisonment for a term not exceeding five years or a fine or both, or on summary conviction to imprisonment for a term not exceeding six months or a fine not exceeding the statutory maximum or both.

3 Affray

(1) A person is guilty of affray if he uses or threatens unlawful violence towards another and his conduct is such as would cause a person of reasonable firmness present at the scene to fear for his personal safety.

(2) Where two or more persons use or threaten the unlawful violence, it is the conduct of them taken together that must be considered for the purposes of subsection (1).

(3) For the purposes of this section a threat cannot be made by the use of words alone.

(4) No person of reasonable firmness need actually be, or be likely to be, present at the scene.

(5) Affray may be committed in private as well as in public places.

(6) A constable may arrest without warrant anyone he reasonably suspects is committing affray.

(7) A person guilty of affray is liable on conviction on indictment to imprisonment for a term not exceeding three years or a fine or both, or on summary conviction to imprisonment for a term not exceeding six months or a fine not exceeding the statutory maximum or both.

4 Fear or provocation of violence

(1) A person is guilty of an offence if he –

(a) uses towards another person threatening, abusive or insulting words or behaviour, or
(b) distributes or displays to another person any writing, sign or other visible representation which is threatening, abusive or insulting,

with intent to cause that person to believe that immediate unlawful violence will be used against him or another by any person, or to provoke the immediate use of unlawful violence by that person or another, or whereby that person is likely to believe that such violence will be used or it is likely that such violence will be provoked.

(2) An offence under this section may be committed in a public or a private place, except that no offence is committed where the words or behaviour are used, or the writing, sign or other visible representation is distributed or displayed, by a person inside a dwelling and the other person is also inside that or another dwelling.

(3) A constable may arrest without warrant anyone he reasonably suspects is committing an offence under this section.

(4) A person guilty of an offence under this section is liable on summary conviction to imprisonment for a term not exceeding six months or a fine not exceeding level 5 on the standard scale or both.

4A Intentional harassment, alarm or distress

(1) A person is guilty of an offence if, with intent to cause a person harassment, alarm or distress, he –

(a) uses threatening, abusive or insulting words or behaviour, or disorderly behaviour, or

(b) displays any writing, sign or other visible representation which is threatening, abusive or insulting,

thereby causing that or another person harassment, alarm or distress.

(2) An offence under this section may be committed in a public or a private place, except that no offence is committed where the words or behaviour are used, or the writing, sign or other visible representation is displayed, by a person inside a dwelling and the person who is harassed, alarmed or distressed is also inside that or another dwelling.

(3) It is a defence for the accused to prove –

(a) that he was inside a dwelling and had no reason to believe that the words or behaviour used, or the writing, sign or other visible representation displayed, would be heard or seen by a person outside that or any other dwelling, or

(b) that his conduct was reasonable.

(4) A constable may arrest without warrant anyone he reasonably suspects is committing an offence under this section.

(5) A person guilty of an offence under this section is liable on summary conviction to imprisonment for a term not exceeding 6 months or a fine not exceeding level 5 on the standard scale or both.

5 Harassment, alarm or distress

(1) A person is guilty of an offence if he –

(a) uses threatening, abusive or insulting words or behaviour, or disorderly behaviour, or

(b) displays any writing, sign or other visible representation which is threatening, abusive or insulting,

within the hearing or sight of a person likely to be caused harassment, alarm or distress thereby.

(2) An offence under this section may be committed in a public or a private place, except that no offence is committed where the words or behaviour are used, or the writing, sign or other visible representation is displayed, by a person inside a dwelling and the other person is also inside that or another dwelling.

(3) It is a defence for the accused to prove –

(a) that he had no reason to believe that there was any person within hearing or sight who was likely to be caused harassment, alarm or distress, or

(b) that he was inside a dwelling and had no reason to believe that the words or behaviour used, or the writing, sign or other visible representation displayed, would be heard or seen by a person outside that or any other dwelling, or

(c) that his conduct was reasonable.

(4) A constable may arrest a person without warrant if –

(a) he engages in offensive conduct which a constable warns him to stop, and

(b) he engages in further offensive conduct immediately or shortly after the warning.

(5) In subsection (4) 'offensive conduct' means conduct the constable reasonably suspects to constitute an offence under this section, and the conduct mentioned in paragraph (a) and the further conduct need not be of the same nature.

(6) A person guilty of an offence under this section is liable on summary conviction to a fine not exceeding level 3 on the standard scale.

6 Mental element: miscellaneous

(1) A person is guilty of riot only if he intends to use violence or is aware that his conduct may be violent.

(2) A person is guilty of violent disorder or affray only if he intends to use or threaten violence or is aware that his conduct may be violent or threaten violence.

(3) A person is guilty of an offence under section 4 only if he intends his words or behaviour, or the writing, sign or other visible representation, to be threatening, abusive or insulting, or is aware that it may be threatening, abusive or insulting.

(4) A person is guilty of an offence under section 5 only if he intends his words or behaviour, or the writing, sign or other visible representation, to be threatening, abusive or insulting, or is aware that it may be threatening, abusive or insulting or (as the case may be) he intends his behaviour to be or is aware that it may be disorderly.

(5) For the purposes of this section a person whose awareness is impaired by intoxication shall be taken to be aware of that of which he would be aware if not intoxicated, unless he shows either that his intoxication was not self-induced or that it was caused solely by the taking or administration of a substance in the course of medical treatment.

(6) In subsection (5) 'intoxication' means any intoxication, whether caused by drink, drugs or other means, or by a combination of means.

(7) Subsections (1) and (2) do not affect the determination for the purposes of riot or violent disorder of the number of persons who use or threaten violence.

7 Procedure: miscellaneous

(1) No prosecution for an offence of riot or incitement to riot may be instituted except by or with the consent of the Director of Public Prosecutions.

(2) For the purposes of the rules against charging more than one offence in the same count or information, each of sections 1 to 5 creates one offence.

(3) If on the trial on indictment of a person charged with violent disorder or affray the jury find him not guilty of the offence charged, they may (without prejudice to section 6(3) of the Criminal Law Act 1967) find him guilty of an offence under section 4.

(4) The Crown Court has the same powers and duties in relation to a person who is by virtue of subsection (3) convicted before it of an offence under section 4 as a magistrates' court would have on convicting him of the offence.

8 Interpretation

In this Part –

'dwelling' means any structure or part of a structure occupied as a person's home or as other living accommodation (whether the occupation is separate or shared with others) but does not include any part not so occupied, and for this purpose 'structure' includes a tent, caravan, vehicle, vessel or other temporary or movable structure;

'violence' means any violent conduct, so that –

(a) except in the context of affray, it includes violent conduct towards property as well as violent conduct towards persons, and
(b) it is not restricted to conduct causing or intended to cause injury or damage but includes any other violent conduct (for example, throwing at or towards a person a missile of a kind capable of causing injury which does not hit or falls short).

9 Offences abolished

(1) The common law offences of riot, rout, unlawful assembly and affray are abolished. ...

Part II

Processions and Assemblies

11 Advance notice of public processions

(1) Written notice shall be given in accordance with this section of any proposal to hold a public procession intended –

(a) to demonstrate support for or opposition to the views or actions of any person or body of persons,
(b) to publicise a cause or campaign, or
(c) to mark or commemorate an event,

unless it is not reasonably practicable to give any advance notice of the procession.

(2) Subsection (1) does not apply where the procession is one commonly or customarily held in the police area (or areas) in which it is proposed to be held or is a funeral procession organised by a funeral director acting in the normal course of his business.

(3) The notice must specify the date when it is intended to hold the procession, the time when it is intended to start it, its proposed route, and the name and address of the person (or of one of the persons) proposing to organise it.

(4) Notice must be delivered to a police station –

(a) in the police area in which it is proposed the procession will start, or
(b) where it is proposed the procession will start in Scotland and cross into England, in the first police area in England on the proposed route.

(5) If delivered not less than six clear days before the date when the procession is intended to be held, the notice may be delivered by post by the recorded delivery service; but section 7

of the Interpretation Act 1978 (under which a document sent by post is deemed to have been served when posted and to have been delivered in the ordinary course of post) does not apply.

(6) If not delivered in accordance with subsection (5), the notice must be delivered by hand not less than six clear days before the date when the procession is intended to be held or, if that is not reasonably practicable, as soon as delivery is reasonably practicable.

(7) Where a public procession is held, each of the persons organising it is guilty of an offence if –

(a) the requirements of this section as to notice have not been satisfied, or
(b) the date when it is held, the time when it starts, or its route, differs from the date, time or route specified in the notice.

(8) It is a defence for the accused to prove that he did not know of, and neither suspected nor had reason to suspect, the failure to satisfy the requirements or (as the case maybe) the difference of date, time or route.

(9) To the extent that an alleged offence turns on a difference of date, time or route, it is a defence for the accused to prove that the difference arose from circumstances beyond his control or from something done with the agreement of a police officer or by his direction.

(10) A person guilty of an offence under subsection (7) is liable on summary conviction to a fine not exceeding level 3 on the standard scale.

12 *Imposing conditions on public processions*

(1) If the senior police officer, having regard to the time or place at which and the circumstances in which any public procession is being held or is intended to be held and to its route or proposed route, reasonably believes that –

(a) it may result in serious public disorder, serious damage to property or serious disruption to the life of the community, or
(b) the purpose of the persons organising it is the intimidation of others with a view to compelling them not to do an act they have a right to do, or to do an act they have a right not to do,

he may give directions imposing on the persons organising or taking part in the procession such conditions as appear to him necessary to prevent such disorder, damage, disruption or intimidation, including conditions as to the route of the procession or prohibiting it from entering any public place specified in the directions.

(2) In subsection (1) 'the senior police officer' means –

(a) in relation to a procession being held, or to a procession intended to be held in a case where persons are assembling with a view to taking part in it, the most senior in rank of the police officers present at the scene, and
(b) in relation to a procession intended to be held in a case where paragraph (a) does not apply, the chief officer of police.

(3) A direction given by a chief officer of police by virtue of subsection (2)(b) shall be given in writing.

(4) A person who organises a public procession and knowingly fails to comply with a condition imposed under this section is guilty of an offence, but it is a defence for him to prove that the failure arose from circumstances beyond his control.

(5) A person who takes part in a public procession and knowingly fails to comply with a condition imposed under this section is guilty of an offence, but it is a defence for him to prove that the failure arose from circumstances beyond his control.

(6) A person who incites another to commit an offence under subsection (5) is guilty of an offence.

(7) A constable in uniform may arrest without warrant anyone he reasonably suspects is committing an offence under subsection(4), (5) or (6).

(8) A person guilty of an offence under subsection (4) is liable on summary conviction to imprisonment for a term not exceeding three months or a fine not exceeding level 4 on the standard scale or both.

(9) A person guilty of an offence under subsection (5) is liable on summary conviction to a fine not exceeding level 3 on the standard scale.

(10) A person guilty of an offence under subsection (6) is liable on summary conviction to imprisonment for a term not exceeding three months or a fine not exceeding level 4 on the standard scale or both, notwithstanding section 45(3) of the Magistrates' Courts Act 1980 (inciter liable to same penalty as incited). ...

13 Prohibiting public processions

(1) If at any time the chief officer of police reasonably believes that, because of particular circumstances existing in any district or part of a district, the powers under section 12 will not be sufficient to prevent the holding of public processions in that district or part from resulting in serious public disorder, he shall apply to the council of the district for an order prohibiting for such period not exceeding three months as may be specified in the application the holding of all public processions (or of any class of public procession so specified) in the district or part concerned.

(2) On receiving such an application, a council may with the consent of the Secretary of State make an order either in the terms of the application or with such modifications as may be approved by the Secretary of State.

(3) Subsection (1) does not apply in the City of London or the metropolitan police district.

(4) If at any time the Commissioner of Police for the City of London or the Commissioner of Police of the Metropolis reasonably believes that, because of particular circumstances existing in his police area or part of it, the powers under section 12 will not be sufficient to prevent the holding of public processions in that area or part from resulting in serious public disorder, he may with the consent of the Secretary of State make an order prohibiting for such period not exceeding three months as may be specified in the order the holding of

all public processions (or of any class of public procession so specified) in the area or part concerned.

(5) An order made under this section may be revoked or varied by a subsequent order made in the same way, that is, in accordance with subsections (1) and (2) or subsection (4), as the case may be.

(6) Any order under this section shall, if not made in writing, be recorded in writing as soon as practicable after being made.

(7) A person who organises a public procession the holding of which he knows is prohibited by virtue of an order under this section is guilty of an offence.

(8) A person who takes part in a public procession the holding of which he knows is prohibited by virtue of an order under this section is guilty of an offence.

(9) A person who incites another to commit an offence under subsection (8) is guilty of an offence.

(10) A constable in uniform may arrest without warrant anyone he reasonably suspects is committing an offence under subsection (7), (8) or (9).

(11) A person guilty of an offence under subsection (7) is liable on summary conviction to imprisonment for a term not exceeding three months or a fine not exceeding level 4 on the standard scale or both.

(12) A person guilty of an offence under subsection (8) is liable on summary conviction to a fine not exceeding level 3 on the standard scale.

(13) A person guilty of an offence under subsection (9) is liable on summary conviction to imprisonment for a term not exceeding three months or a fine not exceeding level 4 on the standard scale or both, notwithstanding section 45(3) of the Magistrates' Courts Act 1980.

14 Imposing conditions on public assemblies

(1) If the senior police officer, having regard to the time or place at which and the circumstances in which any public assembly is being held or is intended to be held, reasonably believes that –

(a) it may result in serious public disorder, serious damage to property or serious disruption to the life of the community, or
(b) the purpose of the persons organising it is the intimidation of others with a view to compelling them not to do an act they have a right to do, or to do an act they have a right not to do,

he may give directions imposing on the persons organising or taking part in the assembly such conditions as to the place at which the assembly may be (or continue to be) held, its maximum duration, or the maximum number of persons who may constitute it, as appear to him necessary to prevent such disorder, damage, disruption or intimidation.

(2) In subsection (1) 'the senior police officer' means –

(a) in relation to an assembly being held, the most senior in rank of the police officers present at the scene, and

(b) in relation to an assembly intended to be held, the chief officer of police.

(3) A direction given by a chief officer of police by virtue of subsection (2)(b) shall be given in writing.

(4) A person who organises a public assembly and knowingly fails to comply with a condition imposed under this section is guilty of an offence, but it is a defence for him to prove that the failure arose from circumstances beyond his control.

(5) A person who takes part in a public assembly and knowingly fails to comply with a condition imposed under this section is guilty of an offence, but it is a defence for him to prove that the failure arose from circumstances beyond his control.

(6) A person who incites another to commit an offence under subsection (5) is guilty of an offence.

(7) A constable in uniform may arrest without warrant anyone he reasonably suspects is committing an offence under subsection (4), (5) or (6).

(8) A person guilty of an offence under subsection (4) is liable on summary conviction to imprisonment for a term not exceeding 3 months or a fine not exceeding level 4 on the standard scale or both.

(9) A person guilty of an offence under subsection (5) is liable on summary conviction to a fine not exceeding level 3 on the standard scale.

(10) A person guilty of an offence under subsection (6) is liable on summary conviction to imprisonment for a term not exceeding three months or a fine not exceeding level 4 on the standard scale or both, notwithstanding section 45(3) of the Magistrates' Courts Act 1980.

14A Prohibiting trespassory assemblies

(1) If at any time the chief officer of police reasonably believes that an assembly is intended to be held in any district at a place on land to which the public has no right of access or only a limited right of access and that the assembly –

(a) is likely to be held without the permission of the occupier of the land or to conduct itself in such a way as to exceed the limits of any permission of his or the limits of the public's right of access, and
(b) may result –

(i) in serious disruption to the life of the community, or
(ii) where the land, or a building or monument on it, is of historical, architectural, archaeological or scientific importance, in significant damage to the land, building or monument,

he may apply to the council of the district for an order prohibiting for a specified period the holding of all trespassory assemblies in the district or a part of it, as specified.

(2) On receiving such an application, a council may –

(a) in England and Wales, with the consent of the Secretary of State make an order either in the terms of the application or with such modifications as may be approved by the Secretary of State; ...

(3) Subsection (1) does not apply in the City of London or the metropolitan police district.

(4) If at any time the Commissioner of Police for the City of London or the Commissioner of Police of the Metropolis reasonably believes that an assembly is intended to be held at a place on land to which the public has no right of access or only a limited right of access in his police area and that the assembly –

(a) is likely to be held without the permission of the occupier of the land or to conduct itself in such a way as to exceed the limits of any permission of his or the limits of the public's right of access, and

(b) may result –

(i) in serious disruption to the life of the community, or

(ii) where the land, or a building or monument on it, is of historical, architectural, archaeological or scientific importance, in significant damage to the land, building or monument,

he may with the consent of the Secretary of State make an order prohibiting for a specified period the holding of all trespassory assemblies in the area or a part of it, as specified.

(5) An order prohibiting the holding of trespassory assemblies operates to prohibit any assembly which –

(a) is held on land to which the public has no right of access or only a limited right of access, and

(b) takes place in the prohibited circumstances, that is to say, without the permission of the occupier of the land or so as to exceed the limits of any permission of his or the limits of the public's right of access.

(6) No order under this section shall prohibit the holding of assemblies for a period exceeding 4 days or in an area exceeding an area represented by a circle with a radius of 5 miles from a specified centre.

(7) An order made under this section may be revoked or varied by a subsequent order made in the same way, that is, in accordance with subsection (1) and (2) or subsection (4), as the case may be.

(8) Any order under this section shall, if not made in writing, be recorded in writing as soon as practicable after being made.

(9) In this section and sections 14B and 14C –

'assembly' means an assembly of 20 or more persons;

'land' means land in the open air;

'limited', in relation to a right of access by the public to land, means that their use of it is restricted to use for a particular purpose (as in the case of a highway or road) or is subject to other restrictions;

'occupier' means –

(a) in England and Wales, the person entitled to possession of the land by virtue of an estate or interest held by him; …

and in subsections (1) and (4) includes the person reasonably believed by the authority applying for or making the order to be the occupier;

'public' includes a section of the public; and
'specified' means specified in an order under this section.

(11) In relation to Wales, the references in subsection (1) above to a district and to the council of the district shall be construed, as respects applications on and after 1 April 1996, as references to a county or county borough and to the council for that county or county borough.

14B Offences in connection with trespassory assemblies and arrest therefor

(1) A person who organises an assembly the holding of which he knows is prohibited by an order under section 14A is guilty of an offence.

(2) A person who takes part in an assembly which he knows is prohibited by an order under section 14A is guilty of an offence.

(3) In England and Wales, a person who incites another to commit an offence under subsection (2) is guilty of an offence.

(4) A constable in uniform may arrest without a warrant anyone he reasonably suspects to be committing an offence under this section.

(5) A person guilty of an offence under subsection (1) is liable on summary conviction to imprisonment for a term not exceeding 3 months or a fine not exceeding level 4 on the standard scale or both.

(6) A person guilty of an offence under subsection (2) is liable on summary conviction to a fine not exceeding level 3 on the standard scale.

(7) A person guilty of an offence under subsection (3) is liable on summary conviction to imprisonment for a term not exceeding 3 months or a fine not exceeding level 4 on the standard scale or both, notwithstanding section 45(3) of the Magistrates' Courts Act 1980. ...

14C Stopping persons from proceeding to trespassory assemblies

(1) If a constable in uniform reasonably believes that a person is on his way to an assembly within the area to which an order under section 14A applies which the constable reasonably believes is likely to be an assembly which is prohibited by that order, he may, subject to subsection (2) below –

   (a) stop that person, and
   (b) direct him not to proceed in the direction of the assembly.

(2) The power conferred by subsection (1) may only be exercised within the area to which the order applies.

(3) A person who fails to comply with a direction under subsection (1) which he knows has been given to him is guilty of an offence.

(4) A constable in uniform may arrest without a warrant anyone he reasonably suspects to be committing an offence under this section.

(5) A person guilty of an offence under subsection (3) is liable on summary conviction to a fine not exceeding level 3 on the standard scale.

16 Interpretation

In this Part – ...

'public assembly' means an assembly of 20 or more persons in a public place which is wholly or partly open to the air,
'public place' means –

(a) any highway, ... and
(b) any place to which at the material time the public or any section of the public has access, on payment or otherwise, as of right or by virtue of express or implied permission;

'public procession' means a procession in a public place.

Part III

Racial Hatred

17 Meaning of 'racial hatred'

In this Part 'racial hatred' means hatred against a group of persons in Great Britain defined by reference to colour, race, nationality (including citizenship) or ethnic or national origins.

18 Use of words or behaviour or display of written material

A person who uses threatening, abusive or insulting words or behaviour, or displays any written material which is threatening, abusive or insulting, is guilty of an offence if –

(a) he intends thereby to stir up racial hatred, or
(b) having regard to all the circumstances racial hatred is likely to be stirred up thereby.

(2) An offence under this section may be committed in a public or a private place, except that no offence is committed where the words or behaviour are used, or the written material is displayed, by a person inside a dwelling and are not heard or seen except by other persons in that or another dwelling.

(3) A constable may arrest without warrant anyone he reasonably suspects is committing an offence under this section.

(4) In proceedings for an offence under this section it is a defence for the accused to prove that he was inside a dwelling and had no reason to believe that the words or behaviour used, or the written material displayed, would be heard or seen by a person outside that or any other dwelling.

(5) A person who is not shown to have intended to stir up racial hatred is not guilty of an offence under this section if he did not intend his words or behaviour, or the written material, to be, and was not aware that it might be, threatening, abusive or insulting.

(6) This section does not apply to words or behaviour used, or written material displayed, solely for the purpose of being included in a programme service.

19 Publishing or distributing written material

(1) A person who publishes or distributes written material which is threatening, abusive or insulting is guilty of an offence if –

(a) he intends thereby to stir up racial hatred, or
(b) having regard to all the circumstances racial hatred is likely to be stirred up thereby.

(2) In proceedings for an offence under this section it is a defence for an accused who is not shown to have intended to stir up racial hatred to prove that he was not aware of the content of the material and did not suspect, and had no reason to suspect, that it was threatening, abusive or insulting.

(3) References in this Part to the publication or distribution of written material are to its publication or distribution to the public or a section of the public.

20 Public performance of play

(1) If a public performance of a play is given which involves the use of threatening, abusive or insulting words or behaviour, any person who presents or directs the performance is guilty of an offence if –

(a) he intends thereby to stir up racial hatred, or
(b) having regard to all the circumstances (and, in particular, taking the performance as a whole) racial hatred is likely to be stirred up thereby.

(2) If a person presenting or directing the performance is not shown to have intended to stir up racial hatred, it is a defence for him to prove –

(a) that he did not know and had no reason to suspect that the performance would involve the use of the offending words or behaviour, or
(b) that he did not know and had no reason to suspect that the offending words or behaviour were threatening, abusive or insulting, or
(c) that he did not know and had no reason to suspect that the circumstances in which the performance would be given would be such that racial hatred would be likely to be stirred up.

(3) This section does not apply to a performance given solely or primarily for one or more of the following purposes –

(a) rehearsal,
(b) making a recording of the performance, or
(c) enabling the performance to be included in a programme service;

but if it is proved that the performance was attended by persons other than those directly connected with the giving of the performance or the doing in relation to it of the things mentioned in paragraph (b) or (c), the performance shall, unless the contrary is shown, be taken not to have been given solely or primarily for the purposes mentioned above.

(4) For the purposes of this section –

(a) a person shall not be treated as presenting a performance of a play by reason only of his taking part in it as a performer,

(b) a person taking part as a performer in a performance directed by another shall be treated as a person who directed the performance if without reasonable excuse he performs otherwise than in accordance with that person's direction, and

(c) a person shall be taken to have directed a performance of a play given under his direction notwithstanding that he was not present during the performance;

and a person shall not be treated as aiding or abetting the commission of an offence under this section by reason only of his taking part in a performance as a performer.

(5) In this section 'play' and 'public performance' have the same meaning as in the Theatres Act 1968.

(6) The following provisions of the Theatres Act 1968 apply in relation to an offence under this section as they apply to an offence under section 2 of that Act –

section 9 (script as evidence of what was performed),

section 10 (power to make copies of script),

section 15 (power of entry and inspection).

21 Distributing, showing or playing a recording

(1) A person who distributes, or shows or plays, a recording of visual images or sounds which are threatening, abusive or insulting is guilty of an offence if –

(a) he intends thereby to stir up racial hatred, or

(b) having regard to all the circumstances racial hatred is likely to be stirred up thereby.

(2) In this Part 'recording' means any record from which visual images or sounds may, by any means, be reproduced; and references to the distribution, showing or playing of a recording are to its distribution, showing or playing to the public or a section of the public.

(3) In proceedings for an offence under this section it is a defence for an accused who is not shown to have intended to stir up racial hatred to prove that he was aware of the content of the recording and did not suspect, and had no reason to suspect, that it was threatening, abusive or insulting.

(4) This section does not apply to the showing or playing of a recording solely for the purpose of enabling the recording to be included in a programme service.

22 Broadcasting or including programme in cable programme service

(1) If a programme involving threatening, abusive or insulting visual images or sounds is included in a programme service, each of the persons mentioned in subsection (2) is guilty of an offence if –

(a) he intends thereby to stir up racial hatred, or

(b) having regard to all the circumstances racial hatred is likely to be stirred up thereby.

(2) The persons are –

(a) the person providing the programme service,

(b) any person by whom the programme is produced or directed, and

(c) any person by whom offending words or behaviour are used.

(3) If the person providing the service, or a person by whom the programme was produced or directed, is not shown to have intended to stir up racial hatred, it is a defence for him to prove that –

(a) he did not know and had no reason to suspect that the programme would involve the offending material, and

(b) having regard to the circumstances in which the programme was included in a programme service, it was not reasonably practicable for him to secure the removal of the material.

(4) It is a defence for a person by whom the programme was produced or directed who is shown to have intended to stir up racial hatred to prove that he did not know and had no reason to suspect –

(a) that the programme would be included in a programme service, or

(b) that the circumstances in which the programme would be so included would be such that racial hatred would be likely to be stirred up.

(5) It is a defence for a person by whom offending words or behaviour were used and who is not shown to have intended to stir up racial hatred to prove that he did not know and had no reason to suspect –

(a) that a programme involving the use of the offending material would be included in a programme service, or

(b) that the circumstances in which a programme involving the use of the offending material would be so included, or in which a programme so included would involve the use of the offending material, would be such that racial hatred would be likely to be stirred up.

(6) A person who is not shown to have intended to stir up racial hatred is not guilty of an offence under this section if he did not know, and had no reason to suspect, that the offending material was threatening, abusive or insulting.

23 Possession of racially inflammatory material

(1) A person who has in his possession written material which is threatening, abusive or insulting, or a recording of visual images or sounds which are threatening, abusive or insulting, with a view to –

(a) in the case of written material, its being displayed, published, distributed, or included in a programme service, whether by himself or another, or

(b) in the case of a recording, its being distributed, shown, played, or included in a programme service, whether by himself or another, is guilty of an offence if he intends racial hatred to be stirred up thereby or, having regard to all the circumstances, racial hatred is likely to be stirred up thereby.

(2) For this purpose regard shall be had to such display, publication, distribution, showing, playing, or inclusion in a programme service as he has, or it may reasonably be inferred that he has, in view.

(3) In proceedings for an offence under this section it is a defence for an accused who is not shown to have intended to stir up racial hatred to prove that he was not aware of the content of the written material or recording and did not suspect, and had no reason to suspect, that it was threatening, abusive or insulting.

Part V
Miscellaneous and General

38 Contamination of or interference with goods with intention of causing public alarm or anxiety, etc

(1) It is an offence for a person, with the intention –

(a) of causing public alarm or anxiety, or
(b) of causing injury to members of the public consuming or using the goods, or
(c) of causing economic loss to any person by reason of the goods being shunned by members of the public, or
(d) of causing economic loss to any person by reason of steps taken to avoid any such alarm or anxiety, injury or loss,

to contaminate or interfere with goods, or make it appear that goods have been contaminated or interfered with, or to place goods which have been contaminated or interfered with, or which appear to have been contaminated or interfered with, in a place where goods of that description are consumed, used, sold or otherwise supplied.

(2) It is also an offence for a person, with any such intention as is mentioned in paragraph (a), (c) or (d) of subsection (1), to threaten that he or another will do, or to claim that he or another has done, any of the acts mentioned in that subsection.

(3) It is an offence for a person to be in possession of any of the following articles with a view to the commission of an offence under subsection (1) –

(a) materials to be used for contaminating or interfering with goods or making it appear that goods have been contaminated or interfered with, or
(b) goods which have been contaminated or interfered with, or which appear to have been contaminated or interfered with.

(4) A person guilty of an offence under this section is liable –

(a) on conviction on indictment to imprisonment for a term not exceeding 10 years or a fine or both, or
(b) on summary conviction to imprisonment for a term not exceeding six months or a fine not exceeding the statutory maximum or both.

(5) In this section 'goods' includes substances whether natural or manufactured and whether or not incorporated in or mixed with other goods.

(6) The reference in subsection (2) to a person claiming that certain acts have been committed does not include a person who in good faith reports or warns that such acts have been, or appear to have been, committed.

[As amended by the Broadcasting Act 1990, ss164(1), (2)(b)(c), (3), (4), 203(3), Schedule 21; Criminal Justice and Public Order Act 1994, ss70, 71, 154; Public Order (Amendment) Act 1996, s1.]

Crossbows Act 1987
(1987 c 32)

1 Sale and letting on hire

A person who sells or lets on hire a crossbow to a person under the age of seventeen is guilty of an offence, unless he believes him to be seventeen years of age or older and has reasonable ground for the belief.

2 Purchase and hiring

A person under the age of seventeen who buys or hires a crossbow or a part of a crossbow is guilty of an offence.

3 Possession

A person under the age of seventeen who has with him –

(a) a crossbow which is capable of discharging a missile, or
(b) parts of a crossbow which together (and without any other parts) can be assembled to form a crossbow capable of discharging a missile,

is guilty of an offence, unless he is under the supervision of a person who is twenty-one years of age or older.

5 Exception

This Act does not apply to crossbows with a draw weight of less than 1.4 kilograms.

6 Punishments

(1) A person guilty of an offence under section 1 shall be liable, on summary conviction, to imprisonment for a term not exceeding six months, to a fine not exceeding level 5 on the standard scale, or to both.

(2) A person guilty of an offence under section 2 or 3 shall be liable, on summary conviction, to a fine not exceeding level 3 on the standard scale.

(3) The court by which a person is convicted of an offence under this Act may make such order as it thinks fit as to the forfeiture or disposal of any crossbow or part of a crossbow in respect of which the offence was committed.

Criminal Justice Act 1987
(1987 c 38)

12 Charges of and penalty for conspiracy to defraud

(1) If –

(a) a person agrees with any other person or persons that a course of conduct shall be pursued; and

(b) that course of conduct will necessarily amount to or involve the commission of any offence or offences by one or more of the parties to the agreement if the agreement is carried out in accordance with their intentions,

the fact that it will do so shall not preclude a charge of conspiracy to defraud being brought against any of them in respect of the agreement. ...

(3) A person guilty of conspiracy to defraud is liable on conviction on indictment to imprisonment for a term not exceeding 10 years or a fine or both.

Malicious Communications Act 1988
(1988 c 27)

1 Offence of sending letters, etc with intent to cause distress or anxiety

(1) Any person who sends to another person –

(a) a letter or other article which conveys –

(i) a message which is indecent or grossly offensive;

(ii) a threat; or

(iii) information which is false and known or believed to be false by the sender; or

(b) any other article which is, in whole or part, of an indecent or grossly offensive nature,

is guilty of an offence if his purpose, or one of his purposes, in sending it is that it should, so far as falling within paragraph (a) or (b) above, cause distress or anxiety to the recipient or to any other person to whom he intends that it is or its contents or nature should be communicated.

(2) A person is not guilty of an offence by virtue of subsection (1)(a)(ii) above if he shows –

(a) that the threat was used to reinforce a demand which he believed he had reasonable grounds for making; and

(b) that he believed that the use of the threat was a proper means of reinforcing the demand.

(3) In this section references to sending include references to delivering and to causing to be sent or delivered and 'sender' shall be construed accordingly.

(4) A person guilty of an offence under this section shall be liable on summary conviction to a fine not exceeding level 4 on the standard scale.

Criminal Justice Act 1988
(1988 c 33)

39 Common assault and battery to be summary offences

Common assault and battery shall be summary offences and a person guilty of either of them shall be liable to a fine not exceeding level 5 on the standard scale, to imprisonment for a term not exceeding six months, or to both.

93A Assisting another to retain the benefit of criminal conduct

(1) Subject to subsection (3) below, if a person enters into or is otherwise concerned in an arrangement whereby –

(a) the retention or control by or on behalf of another ('A') of A's proceeds of criminal conduct is facilitated (whether by concealment, removal from the jurisdiction, transfer to nominees or otherwise); or
(b) A's proceeds of criminal conduct –

(i) are used to secure that funds are placed at A's disposal; or
(ii) are used for A's benefit to acquire property by way of investment,

knowing or suspecting that A is a person who is or has been engaged in criminal conduct or has benefited from criminal conduct, he is guilty of an offence.

(2) In this section, references to any person's proceeds of criminal conduct include a reference to any property which in whole or in part directly or indirectly represented in his hands his proceeds of criminal conduct.

(3) Where a person discloses to a constable a suspicion or belief that any funds or investments are derived from or used in connection with criminal conduct or discloses to a constable any matter on which such a suspicion or belief is based –

(a) the disclosure shall not be treated as a breach of any restriction upon the disclosure of information imposed by statute or otherwise; and
(b) if he does any act in contravention of subsection (1) above and the disclosure relates to the arrangement concerned, he does not commit an offence under this section if –

(i) the disclosure is made before he does the act concerned and the act is done with the consent of the constable; or
(ii) the disclosure is made after he does the act, but is made on his initiative and as soon as it is reasonable for him to make it.

(4) In proceedings against a person for an offence under this section, it is a defence to prove –

(a) that he did not know or suspect that the arrangement related to any person's proceeds of criminal conduct; or

(b) that he did not know or suspect that by the arrangement the retention or control by or on behalf of A of any property was facilitated or, as the case may be, that by the arrangement any property was used, as mentioned in subsection (1) above; or

(c) that –

(i) he intended to disclose to a constable such a suspicion, belief or matter as is mentioned in subsection (3) above in relation to the arrangement; but

(ii) there is reasonable excuse for his failure to make disclosure in accordance with subsection (3)(b) above.

(5) In the case of a person who was in employment at the relevant time, subsections (3) and (4) above shall have effect in relation to disclosures, and intended disclosures, to the appropriate person in accordance with the procedure established by his employer for the making of such disclosures as they have effect in relation to disclosures, and intended disclosures, to a constable.

(6) A person guilty of an offence under this section shall be liable –

(a) on summary conviction, to imprisonment for a term not exceeding six months or a fine not exceeding the statutory maximum or to both; or

(b) on conviction on indictment, to imprisonment for a term not exceeding fourteen years or a fine or to both.

(7) In this Part of this Act 'criminal conduct' means conduct which constitutes an offence to which this Part of this Act applies or would constitute such an offence if it had occurred in England and Wales or (as the case may be) Scotland.

93B Acquisition, possession or use of proceeds of criminal conduct

(1) A person is guilty of an offence if, knowing that any property is, or in whole or in part directly or indirectly represents, another person's proceeds of criminal conduct, he acquires or uses that property or has possession of it.

(2) It is a defence to a charge of committing an offence under this section that the person charged acquired or used the property or had possession of it for adequate consideration.

(3) For the purposes of subsection (2) above –

(a) a person acquires property for inadequate consideration if the value of the consideration is significantly less than the value of the property; and

(b) a person uses or has possession of property for inadequate consideration if the value of the consideration is significantly less than the value of his use or possession of the property.

(4) The provision for any person of services or goods which are of assistance to him in criminal conduct shall not be treated as consideration for the purposes of subsection (2) above.

(5) Where a person discloses to a constable a suspicion or belief that any property is, or in whole or in part directly or indirectly represents, another person's proceeds of criminal conduct or discloses to a constable any matter on which such a suspicion or belief is based –

(a) the disclosure shall not be treated as a breach of any restriction upon the disclosure of information imposed by statute or otherwise; and

(b) if he does any act in relation to that property in contravention of subsection (1) above, he does not commit an offence under this section if –

(i) the disclosure is made before he does the act concerned and the act is done with the consent of the constable; or

(ii) the disclosure is made after he does the act, but on his initiative and as soon as it is reasonable for him to make it.

(6) For the purposes of this section, having possession of any property shall be taken to be doing an act in relation to it.

(7) In proceedings against a person for an offence under this section, it is a defence to prove that –

(a) he intended to disclose to a constable such a suspicion, belief or matter as is mentioned in subsection (5) above; but

(b) there is reasonable excuse for his failure to make the disclosure in accordance with paragraph (b) of that subsection.

(8) In the case of a person who was in employment at the relevant time, subsections (5) and (7) above shall have effect in relation to disclosures, and intended disclosures, to the appropriate person in accordance with the procedure established by his employer for the making of such disclosures as they have effect in relation to disclosures, and intended disclosures, to a constable.

(9) A person guilty of an offence under this section is liable –

(a) on summary conviction, to imprisonment for a term not exceeding six months or a fine not exceeding the statutory maximum or to both; or

(b) on conviction on indictment, to imprisonment for a term not exceeding fourteen years or a fine or to both.

(10) No constable or other person shall be guilty of an offence under this section in respect of anything done by him in the course of acting in connection with the enforcement, or intended enforcement, of any provision of this Act or of any other enactment relating to criminal conduct or the proceeds of such conduct.

93C *Concealing or transferring proceeds of criminal conduct*

(1) A person is guilty of an offence if he –

(a) conceals or disguises any property which is, or in whole or in part directly or indirectly represents, his proceeds of criminal conduct; or

(b) converts or transfers that property or removes it from the jurisdiction, for the purpose of avoiding prosecution for an offence to which this Part of this Act applies or the making or enforcement in this case of a confiscation order.

(2) A person is guilty of an offence if, knowing or having reasonable grounds to suspect that any property is, or in whole or in part directly or indirectly represents, another person's proceeds of criminal conduct, he –

(a) conceals or disguises that property; or
(b) converts or transfers that property or removes it from the jurisdiction,

for the purpose of assisting any person to avoid prosecution for an offence to which this Part of this Act applies or the making or enforcement in his case of a confiscation order.

(3) In subsections (1) and (2) above, the references to concealing or disguising any property include references to concealing or disguising its nature, source, location, disposition, movement or ownership or any rights with respect to it.

(4) A person guilty of an offence under this section is liable –

(a) on summary conviction, to imprisonment for a term not exceeding six months or a fine not exceeding the statutory maximum or to both; or
(b) on conviction on indictment, to imprisonment for a term not exceeding fourteen years or a fine or to both.

93D Tipping-off

(1) A person is guilty of an offence if –

(a) he knows or suspects that a constable is acting, or is proposing to act, in connection with an investigation which is being, or is about to be, conducted into money laundering; and
(b) he discloses to any other person information or any other matter which is likely to prejudice that investigation, or proposed investigation.

(2) A person is guilty of an offence if –

(a) he knows or suspects that a disclosure ('the disclosure') has been made to a constable under section 93A or 93B above; and
(b) he discloses to any other person information or any other matter which is likely to prejudice any investigation which might be conducted following the disclosure.

(3) A person is guilty of an offence if –

(a) he knows or suspects that a disclosure of a kind mentioned in section 93A(5) or 93B(8) above ('the disclosure') has been made; and
(b) he discloses to any person information or any other matter which is likely to prejudice any investigation which might be conducted following the disclosure.

(4) Nothing in subsections (1) to (3) above makes it an offence for a professional legal adviser to disclose any information or other matter –

(a) to, or to a representative of, a client of his in connection with the giving by the adviser of legal advice to the client; or
(b) to any person –

(i) in contemplation of, or in connection with, legal proceedings, and

(ii) for the purpose of those proceedings.

(5) Subsection (4) above does not apply in relation to any information or other matter which is disclosed with a view to furthering any criminal purpose.

(6) In proceedings against a person for an offence under subsection (1), (2) or (3) above, it is a defence to prove that he did not know or suspect that the disclosure was likely to be prejudicial in the way mentioned in that subsection.

(7) In this section 'money laundering' means doing any act which constitutes an offence under section 93A, 93B or 93C above or, in the case of an act done otherwise than in England and Wales or Scotland, would constitute such an offence if done in England and Wales or (as the case may be) Scotland.

(8) For the purposes of subsection (7) above, having possession of any property shall be taken to be doing an act in relation to it.

(9) A person guilty of an offence under this section shall be liable –

(a) on summary conviction, to imprisonment for a term not exceeding six months or a fine not exceeding the statutory maximum or to both; or

(b) on conviction on indictment, to imprisonment for a term not exceeding five years or a fine or to both.

(10) No constable or other person shall be guilty of an offence under this section in respect of anything done by him in the course of acting in connection with the enforcement, or intended enforcement, of any provision of this Act or of any other enactment relating to an offence to which this Part of this Act applies.

134 Torture

(1) A public official or person acting in an official capacity, whatever his nationality, commits the offence of torture if in the United Kingdom or elsewhere he intentionally inflicts severe pain or suffering on another in the performance or purported performance of his official duties.

(2) A person not falling within subsection (1) above commits the offence of torture, whatever his nationality, if –

(a) in the United Kingdom or elsewhere he intentionally inflicts severe pain or suffering on another at the instigation or with the consent or acquiescence –

(i) of a public official; or

(ii) of a person acting in an official capacity; and

(b) the official or other person is performing or purporting to perform his official duties when he instigates the commission of the offence or consents to or acquiesces in it.

(3) It is immaterial whether the pain or suffering is physical or mental and whether it is caused by an act or an omission.

(4) It shall be a defence for a person charged with an offence under this section in respect of any conduct of his to prove that he had lawful authority, justification or excuse for that conduct.

(5) For the purposes of this section 'lawful authority, justification or excuse' means –

(a) in relation to pain or suffering inflicted in the United Kingdom, lawful authority, justification or excuse under the law of the part of the United Kingdom where it was inflicted;

(b) in relation to pain or suffering inflicted outside the United Kingdom –

(i) if it was inflicted by a United Kingdom official acting under the law of the United Kingdom or by a person acting in an official capacity under that law, lawful authority, justification or excuse under that law;

(ii) if it was inflicted by a United Kingdom official acting under the law of any part of the United Kingdom or by a person acting in an official capacity under such law, lawful authority, justification or excuse under the law of the part of the United Kingdom under whose law he was acting; and

(iii) in any other case, lawful authority, justification or excuse under the law of the place where it was inflicted.

(6) A person who commits the offence of torture shall be liable on conviction on indictment to imprisonment for life.

139 *Offence of having article with blade or point in public place*

(1) Subject to subsections (4) and (5) below, any person who has an article to which this section applies with him in a public place shall be guilty of an offence.

(2) Subject to subsection (3) below, this section applies to any article which has a blade or is sharply pointed except a folding penknife.

(3) This section applies to a folding pocketknife if the cutting edge of its blade exceeds three inches.

(4) It shall be a defence for a person charged with an offence under this section to prove that he had good reason or lawful authority for having the article with him in a public place.

(5) Without prejudice to the generality of subsection (4) above, it shall be a defence for a person charged with an offence under this section to prove that he had the article with him –

(a) for use at work;
(b) for religious reasons; or
(c) as part of any national costume.

(6) A person guilty of an offence under subsection (1) above shall be liable –

(a) on summary conviction, to imprisonment for a term not exceeding six months, or a fine not exceeding the statutory maximum, or both;

(b) on conviction on indictment, to imprisonment for a term not exceeding two years, or to a fine, or both.

(7) In this section 'public place' includes any place to which at the material time the public have or are permitted access, whether on payment or otherwise.

(8) This section shall not have effect in relation to anything done before it comes into force.

[As amended by the Criminal Justice Act 1993, ss29(1), 30, 31 and 32; Offensive Weapons Act 1996, s3.]

Firearms (Amendment) Act 1988
(1988 c 45)

5 Restriction on sale of ammunition for smooth-bore guns

(1) This section applies to ammunition to which section 1 of the [Firearms Act 1968] does not apply and which is capable of being used in a shot gun or in a smooth-bore gun to which that section applies.

(2) It is an offence for a person to sell any such ammunition to another person in the United Kingdom who is neither a registered firearms dealer nor a person who sells such ammunition by way of trade or business unless that other person –

(a) produces a certificate authorising him to possess a gun of a kind mentioned in subsection (1) above; or
(b) shows that he is by virtue of that Act or this Act entitled to have possession of such a gun without holding a certificate; or
(c) produces a certificate authorising another person to possess such a gun, together with that person's written authority to purchase the ammunition on his behalf.

(3) An offence under this section shall be punishable on summary conviction with imprisonment for a term not exceeding six months or a fine not exceeding level 5 on the standard scale or both.

6 Shortening of barrels

(1) Subject to subsection (2) below, it is an offence to shorten to a length less than 24 inches the barrel of any smooth-bore gun to which section 1 of the principal Act applies other than one which has a barrel with a bore exceeding two inches in diameter; and that offence shall be punishable –

(a) on summary conviction, with imprisonment for a term not exceeding six months or a fine not exceeding the statutory maximum or both;
(b) on indictment, with imprisonment for a term not exceeding five years or a fine or both.

(2) It is not an offence under this section for a registered firearms dealer to shorten the barrel of a gun for the sole purpose of replacing a defective part of the barrel so as to produce a barrel not less than 24 inches in length.

7 Conversion not to affect classification

(1) Any weapon which –

(a) has at any time (whether before or after the passing of the Firearms (Amendment) Act

1997) been a weapon of a kind described in section 5(1) or (1A) of the principal Act (including any amendments to section 5(1) made under section 1(4) of this Act);

(b) is not a self-loading or pump-action smooth-bore gun which has at any such time been such a weapon by reason only of having had a barrel less than 24 inches in length,

shall be treated as a prohibited weapon notwithstanding anything done for the purpose of converting it into a weapon of a different kind.

(2) Any weapon which –

(a) has at any time since the coming into force of section 2 above been a weapon to which section 1 of the principal Act applies; or

(b) would at any previous time have been such a weapon if those sections had then been in force,

shall, if it has, or at any time has had, a rifled barrel less than 24 inches in length, be treated as a weapon to which section 1 of the principal Act applies notwithstanding anything done for the purpose of converting it into a shot gun or an air weapon.

(3) For the purposes of subsection (2) above there shall be disregarded the shortening of a barrel by a registered firearms dealer for the sole purpose of replacing part of it so as to produce a barrel not less than 24 inches in length.

8 De-activated weapons

For the purposes of the principal Act and this Act it shall be presumed, unless the contrary is shown, that a firearm has been rendered incapable of discharging any shot, bullet or other missile, and has consequently ceased to be a firearm within the meaning of those Acts, if –

(a) it bears a mark which has been approved by the Secretary of State for denoting that fact and which has been made either by one or the two companies mentioned in section 58(1) of the principal Act or by such other person as may be approved by the Secretary of State for the purposes of this section; and

(b) that company or person has certified in writing that work has been carried out on the firearm in a manner approved by the Secretary of State for rendering it incapable of discharging any shot, bullet or other missile.

25 Interpretation of supplementary provisions

(1) In this Act 'the principal Act' means the Firearms Act 1968 and any expression which is also used in that Act has the same meaning as in that Act. ...

[As amended by the Firearms (Amendment) Act 1997, s52(1), Schedule 2, paras 15, 16.]

Road Traffic Act 1988
(1988 c 52)

1 Causing death by dangerous driving

A person who causes the death of another person by driving a mechanically propelled vehicle dangerously on a road or other public place is guilty of an offence.

2 Dangerous driving

A person who drives a mechanically propelled vehicle dangerously on a road or other public place is guilty of an offence.

2A Meaning of dangerous driving

(1) For the purposes of sections 1 and 2 above a person is to be regarded as driving dangerously if (and, subject to subsection (2) below, only if) –

(a) the way he drives falls far below what would be expected of a competent and careful driver, and

(b) it would be obvious to a competent and careful driver that driving in that way would be dangerous.

(2) A person is also to be regarded as driving dangerously for the purposes of sections 1 and 2 above if it would be obvious to a competent and careful driver that driving the vehicle in its current state would be dangerous.

(3) In subsections (1) and (2) above 'dangerous' refers to danger either of injury to any person or of serious damage to property; and in determining for the purposes of those subsections what would be expected of, or obvious to, a competent and careful driver in a particular case, regard shall be had not only to the circumstances of which he could be expected to be aware but also to any circumstances shown to have been within the knowledge of the accused.

(4) In determining for the purposes of subsection (2) above the state of a vehicle, regard may be had to anything attached to or carried on or in it and to the manner in which it is attached or carried.

3 Careless, and inconsiderate, driving

If a person drives a mechanically propelled vehicle on a road or other public place without due care and attention, or without reasonable consideration for other persons using the road or place, he is guilty of an offence.

3A Causing death by careless driving when under the influence of drink or drugs

(1) If a person causes the death of another person by driving a mechanically propelled

vehicle on a road or other public place without due care and attention, or without reasonable consideration for other persons using the road or place, and –

(a) he is, at the time when he is driving, unfit to drive through drink or drugs, or

(b) he has consumed so much alcohol that the proportion of it in his breath, blood or urine at that time exceeds the prescribed limit, or

(c) he is, within 18 hours after that time, required to provide a specimen in pursuance of section 7 of this Act, but without reasonable excuse fails to provide it,

he is guilty of an offence.

(2) For the purposes of this section a person shall be taken to be unfit to drive at any time when his ability to drive properly is impaired.

(3) Subsection (1)(b) and (c) above shall not apply in relation to a person driving a mechanically propelled vehicle other than a motor vehicle.

4 Driving, or being in charge, when under influence of drink or drugs

(1) A person who, when driving or attempting to drive a mechanically propelled vehicle on a road or other public place, is unfit to drive through drink or drugs is guilty of an offence.

(2) Without prejudice to subsection (1) above, a person who, when in charge of a mechanically propelled vehicle which is on a road or other public place, is unfit to drive through drink or drugs is guilty of an offence.

(3) For the purposes of subsection (2) above, a person shall be deemed not to have been in charge of a mechanically propelled vehicle if he proves that at the material time the circumstances were such that there was no likelihood of his driving it so long as he remained unfit to drive through drinks or drugs.

(4) The court may, in determining whether there was such a likelihood as is mentioned in subsection (3) above, disregard any injury to him and any damage to the vehicle.

(5) For the purposes of this section, a person shall be taken to be unfit to drive if his ability to drive properly is for the time being impaired.

(6) A constable may arrest a person without warrant if he has reasonable cause to suspect that that person is or has been committing an offence under this section.

(7) For the purpose of arresting a person under the power conferred by subsection (6) above, a constable may enter (if need be by force) any place where that person is or where the constable, with reasonable cause, suspects him to be.

(8) Subsection (7) above does not extend to Scotland, and nothing in that subsection affects any rule of law in Scotland concerning the right of a constable to enter any premises for any purposes.

5 Driving or being in charge of a motor vehicle with alcohol concentration above prescribed limit

(1) If a person –

(a) drives or attempts to drive a motor vehicle on a road or other public place, or

(b) is in charge of a motor vehicle on a road or other public place,

after consuming so much alcohol that the proportion of it in his breath, blood or urine exceeds the prescribed limit he is guilty of an offence,

(2) It is a defence for a person charged with an offence under subsection (1)(b) above to prove that at the time he is alleged to have committed the offence the circumstances were such that there was no likelihood of his driving the vehicle whilst the proportion of alcohol in his breath, blood or urine remained likely to exceed the prescribed limit.

(3) The court may, in determining whether there was such a likelihood as is mentioned of subsection (2) above, disregard any injury to him and any damage to the vehicle.

6 *Breath tests*

(1) Where a constable in uniform has reasonable cause to suspect –

(a) that a person driving or attempting to drive or in charge of a motor vehicle on a road or other public place has alcohol in his body or has committed a traffic offence whilst the vehicle was in motion, or

(b) that a person has been driving or attempting to drive or been in charge of a motor vehicle on a road or other public place with alcohol in his body and that that person still has alcohol in his body, or

(c) that a person has been driving or attempting to drive or been in charge of a motor vehicle on a road or other public place and has committed a traffic offence whilst the vehicle was in motion,

he may, subject to section 9 of this Act, require him to provide a specimen of breath for a breath test.

(2) If an accident occurs owing to the presence of a motor vehicle on a road or other public place, a constable may, subject to section 9 of this Act, require any person who he has reasonable cause to believe was driving or attempting to drive or in charge of the vehicle at the time of the accident to provide a specimen of breath for a breath test.

(3) A person may be required under subsection (1) or subsection (2) above to provide a specimen either at or near the place where the requirement is made or, if the requirement is made under subsection (2) above and the constable making the requirement thinks fit, at a police station specified by the constable.

(4) A person who, without reasonable excuse, fails to provide a specimen of breath when required to do so in pursuance of this section is guilty of an offence.

(5) A constable may arrest a person without warrant if –

(a) as a result of a breath test he has reasonable cause to suspect that the proportion of alcohol in that person's breath or blood exceeds the prescribed limit, or

(b) that person has failed to provide a specimen of breath for a breath test when required to do so in pursuance of this section and the constable has reasonable cause to suspect that he has alcohol in his body, but a person shall not be arrested by virtue of this subsection when he is at a hospital as a patient.

(6) A constable may, for the purpose of requiring a person to provide a specimen of breath under subsection (2) above in a case where he has reasonable cause to suspect that the accident involved injury to another person or of arresting him in such a case under subsection (5) above, enter (if need be by force) any place where that person is or where the constable, with reasonable cause, suspects him to be. ...

(8) In this section 'traffic offence' means an offence under –

(a) any provision of part II of the Public Passenger Vehicles Act 1981,
(b) any provision of the Road Traffic Regulation Act 1984,
(c) any provision of the Road Traffic Offenders Act 1988 except Part III, or
(d) any provision of this Act except Part V.

7 Provision of specimens for analysis

(1) In the course of an investigation into whether a person has committed an offence under section 3A, 4 or 5 of this Act a constable may, subject to the following provisions of this section and section 9 of this Act, require him –

(a) to provide two specimens of breath for analysis by means of a device of a type approved by the Secretary of State, or
(b) to provide a specimen of blood or urine for a laboratory test.

(2) A requirement under this section to provide specimens of breath can only be made at a police station.

(3) A requirement under this section to provide a specimen of blood or urine can only be made at a police station or at a hospital; and it cannot be made at a police station unless –

(a) the constable making the requirement has reasonable cause to believe that for medical reasons a specimen of breath cannot be provided or should not be required, or
(b) at the time the requirement is made a device or a reliable device of the type mentioned in subsection (1)(a) above is not available at the police station or it is then for any other reason not practicable to use such a device there, or
(bb) a device of the type mentioned in subsection (1)(a) above has been used at the police station but the constable who required the specimens of breath has reasonable cause to believe that the device has not produced a reliable indication of the proportion of alcohol in the breath of the person concerned, or
(c) the suspected offence is one under section 3A or 4 of this Act and the constable making the requirement has been advised by a medical practitioner that the condition of the person required to provide the specimen might be due to some drug;

but may then be made notwithstanding that the person required to provide the specimen has already provided or been required to provide two specimens of breath.

(4) If the provision of a specimen other than a specimen of breath may be required in pursuance of this section the question whether it is to be a specimen of blood or a specimen of urine shall be decided by the constable making the requirement, but if a medical

practitioner is of the opinion that for medical reasons a specimen of blood cannot or should not be taken the specimen shall be a specimen of urine.

(5) A specimen of urine shall be provided within one hour of the requirement for its provision being made and after the provision of a previous specimen of urine.

(6) A person who, without reasonable excuse, fails to provide a specimen when required to do so in pursuance of this section is guilty of an offence.

(7) A constable must, on requiring any person to provide a specimen in pursuance of this section, warn him that a failure to provide it may render him liable to prosecution.

8 Choice of specimens of breath

(1) Subject to subsection (2) below, of any two specimens of breath provided by any person in pursuance of section 7 of this Act that with the lower proportion of alcohol in the breath shall be used and the other shall be disregarded.

(2) If the specimen with the lower proportion of alcohol contains no more than 50 microgrammes of alcohol in 100 millilitres of breath, the person who provided it may claim that it should be replaced by such specimen as may be required under section 7(4) of this Act and, if he then provides such a specimen, neither specimen of breath shall be used.

(3) The Secretary of State may by regulations substitute another proportion of alcohol in the breath for that specified in subsection (2) above.

9 Protection for hospital patients

(1) While a person is at a hospital as a patient he shall not be required to provide a specimen of breath for a breath test or to provide a specimen for a laboratory test unless the medical practitioner in immediate charge of his case has been notified of the proposal to make the requirement; and –

(a) if the requirement is then made, it shall be for the provision of a specimen at the hospital, but
(b) if the medical practitioner objects on the ground specified in subsection (2) below, the requirement shall not be made.

(2) The ground on which the medical practitioner may object is that the requirement or the provision of a specimen or, in the case of a specimen of blood or urine, the warning required under section 7(7) of this Act, would be prejudicial to the proper care and treatment of the patient.

10 Detention of persons affected by alcohol or a drug

(1) Subject to subsections (2) and (3) below, a person required to provide a specimen of breath, blood or urine may afterwards be detained at a police station until it appears to the constable that, were that person then driving or attempting to drive a mechanically propelled vehicle on a road, he would not be committing an offence under section 4 or 5 of this Act.

(2) A person shall not be detained in pursuance of this section if it appears to a constable that there is no likelihood of his driving or attempting to drive a mechanically propelled vehicle whilst his ability to drive properly is impaired or whilst the proportion of alcohol in his breath, blood or urine exceeds the prescribed limit.

(3) A constable must consult a medical practitioner on any question arising under this section whether a person's ability to drive properly is or might be impaired through drugs and must act on the medical practitioner's advice.

11 Interpretation of sections 4 to 10

(1) The following provisions apply for the interpretation of sections 3A to 10 of this Act.

(2) In those sections –

'breath test' means a preliminary test for the purpose of obtaining, by means of a device of a type approved by the Secretary of State, an indication whether the proportion of alcohol in a person's breath or blood is likely to exceed the prescribed limit,

'drug' includes any intoxicant other than alcohol,

'fail' includes refuse,

'hospital' means an institution which provides medical or surgical treatment for in-patients or out-patients,

'the prescribed limit' means, as the case may require –

(a) 35 microgrammes of alcohol in 100 millilitres of breath,
(b) 80 milligrammes of alcohol in 100 millilitres of blood, or
(c) 107 milligrammes of alcohol in 100 millilitres of urine,

or such other proportion as may be prescribed by regulations made by the Secretary of State.

(3) A person does not provide a specimen of breath for a breath test or for analysis unless the specimen –

(a) is sufficient to enable the test or the analysis to be carried out, and
(b) is provided in such a way as to enable the objective of the test or analysis to be satisfactorily achieved.

(4) A person provides a specimen of blood if and only if he consents to its being taken by a medical practitioner and it is so taken.

[As amended by the Road Traffic (Consequential Provisions) Act 1988, s4, Schedule 2, Part III, para 31; Road Traffic Act 1991, ss1, 2, 3, 4, 48, Schedule 4, paras 32, 43, 44; Criminal Procedure and Investigations Act 1996, s63(1), (3).]

Prevention of Terrorism (Temporary Provisions) Act 1989
(1989 c 4)

1 Proscribed organisations

(1) Any organisation for the time being specified in Schedule 1 to this Act is a proscribed organisation for the purposes of this Act; and any organisation which passes under a name mentioned in that Schedule shall be treated as proscribed whatever relationship (if any) it has to any other organisation of the same name.

(2) The Secretary of State may by order made by statutory instrument –

(a) add to Schedule 1 to this Act any organisation that appears to him to be concerned in, or in promoting or encouraging, terrorism occurring in the United Kingdom and connected with the affairs of Northern Ireland;
(b) remove an organisation from that Schedule.

(3) No order shall be made under this section unless –

(a) a draft of the order has been laid before and approved by a resolution of each House of Parliament; or
(b) it is declared in the order that it appears to the Secretary of State that by reason of urgency it is necessary to make the order without a draft having been so approved.

(4) An order under this section of which a draft has not been approved under subsection (3) above –

(a) shall be laid before Parliament; and
(b) shall cease to have effect at the end of the period of forty days beginning with the day on which it was made unless, before the end of that period, the order has been approved by a resolution of each House of Parliament, but without prejudice to anything previously done or to the making of a new order.

(5) In reckoning for the purposes of subsection (4) above any period of forty days, no account shall be taken of any period during which Parliament is dissolved or prorogued or during which both Houses are adjourned for more than four days.

(6) In this section 'organisation' includes any association or combination of persons.

2 Membership, support and meetings

(1) Subject to subsection (3) below, a person is guilty of an offence if he –

(a) belongs or professes to belong to a proscribed organisation;
(b) solicits or invites support for a proscribed organisation other than support with money or other property; or
(c) arranges or assists in the arrangement or management of, or addresses, any meeting of three or more persons (whether or not it is a meeting to which the public are admitted) knowing that the meeting is –

(i) to support a proscribed organisation;

(ii) to further the activities of such an organisation; or

(iii) to be addressed by a person belonging or professing to belong to such an organisation.

(2) A person guilty of an offence under subsection (1) above is liable –

(a) on conviction on indictment, to imprisonment for a term not exceeding ten years or a fine or both;

(b) on summary conviction, to imprisonment for a term not exceeding six months or a fine not exceeding the statutory maximum or both.

(3) A person belonging to a proscribed organisation is not guilty of an offence under this section by reason of belonging to the organisation if he shows –

(a) that he became a member when it was not a proscribed organisation under the current legislation; and

(b) that he has not since he became a member taken part in any of its activities at any time while it was a proscribed organisation under that legislation.

(4) In subsection (3) above 'the current legislation', in relation to any time, means whichever of the following was in force at that time –

(a) the Prevention of Terrorism (Temporary Provisions) Act 1974;

(b) the Prevention of Terrorism (Temporary Provisions) Act 1976;

(c) the Prevention of Terrorism (Temporary Provisions) Act 1984; or

(d) this Act.

(5) The reference in subsection (3) above to a person becoming a member of an organisation is a reference to the only or last occasion on which he became a member.

3 Display of support in public

(1) Any person who in a public place –

(a) wears any item of dress; or

(b) wears, carries or displays any article,

in such a way or in such circumstances as to arouse reasonable apprehension that he is a member or supporter of a proscribed organisation, is guilty of an offence and liable on summary conviction to imprisonment for a term not exceeding six months or a fine not exceeding level 5 on the standard scale or both. ...

(3) In this section 'public place' includes any highway or, in Scotland, any road within the meaning of the Roads (Scotland) Act 1984 and any premises to which at the material time the public have, or are permitted to have, access, whether on payment or otherwise.

9 Contributions towards acts of terrorism

(1) A person is guilty of an offence if he –

(a) solicits or invites any other person to give, lend or otherwise make available, whether for consideration or not, any money or other property;

(b) receives or accepts from any other person, whether for consideration or not, any money or other property; or

(c) uses or has possession of, whether for consideration or not, any money or other property,

intending that it shall be applied or used for the commission of, or in furtherance of or in connection with, acts of terrorism to which this section applies or having reasonable cause to suspect that it may be so used or applied.

(2) A person is guilty of an offence if he –

(a) gives, lends or otherwise makes available to any other person, whether for consideration or not, any money or other property; or

(b) enters into or is otherwise concerned in an arrangement whereby money or other property is or is to be made available to another person,

knowing or having reasonable cause to suspect that it will or may be applied or used as mentioned in subsection (1) above.

(3) The acts of terrorism to which this section applies are –

(a) acts of terrorism connected with the affairs of Northern Ireland; and

(b) subject to subsection (4) below, acts of terrorism of any other description except acts connected solely with the affairs of the United Kingdom or any part of the United Kingdom other than Northern Ireland.

(4) Subsection (3)(b) above does not apply to an act done or to be done outside the United Kingdom unless it constitutes or would constitute an offence triable in the United Kingdom.

(5) In proceedings against a person for an offence under this section in relation to an act within subsection (3)(b) above done or to be done outside the United Kingdom –

(a) the prosecution need not prove that that person knew or had reasonable cause to suspect that the act constituted or would constitute such an offence as is mentioned in subsection (4) above; but

(b) it shall be a defence to prove that he did not know and had no reasonable cause to suspect that the facts were such that the act constituted or would constitute such an offence.

10 Contributions to resources of proscribed organisations

(1) A person is guilty of an offence if he –

(a) solicits or invites any other person to give, lend or otherwise make available, whether for consideration or not, any money or other property for the benefit of a proscribed organisation;

(b) gives, lends or otherwise makes available or receives or accepts or uses or has possession of, whether for consideration or not, any money or other property for the benefit of such an organisation; or

(c) enters into or is otherwise concerned in an arrangement whereby money or other property is or is to be made available for the benefit of such an organisation.

(2) In proceedings against a person for an offence under subsection (1)(b) above it is a defence to prove that he did not know and had no reasonable cause to suspect that the money or property was for the benefit of a proscribed organisation; and in proceedings against a person for an offence under subsection (1)(c) above it is a defence to prove that he did not know and had no reasonable cause to suspect that the arrangement related to a proscribed organisation.

(3) In this section and sections 11 and 13 below 'proscribed organisation' includes a proscribed organisation for the purposes of section 30 of the Northern Ireland (Emergency Provisions) Act 1996.

11 Assisting in retention or control of terrorist funds

(1) A person is guilty of an offence if he enters into or is otherwise concerned in an arrangement whereby the retention or control by or on behalf of another person of terrorist funds if facilitated, whether by concealment, removal from the jurisdiction, transfer to nominees or otherwise.

(2) In proceedings against a person for an offence under this section it is a defence to prove that he did not know and had no reasonable cause to suspect that the arrangement related to terrorist funds.

(3) In this section and section 12 below 'terrorist funds' means –

(a) funds which may be applied or used for the commission of, or in furtherance of or in connection with, acts of terrorism to which section 9 above applies;
(b) the proceeds of the commission of such acts of terrorism or of activities engaged in furtherance of or in connection with such acts; and
(c) the resources of a proscribed organisation.

(4) Paragraph (b) of subsection (3) includes any property which in whole or in part directly or indirectly represents such proceeds as are mentioned in that paragraph; and paragraph (c) of that subsection includes any money or other property which is or is to be applied or made available for the benefit of a proscribed organisation.

12 Disclosure of information about terrorist funds

(1) A person may notwithstanding any restriction on the disclosure of information imposed by statute or otherwise disclose to a constable a suspicion or belief that any money or other property is or is derived from terrorist funds or any matter on which such a suspicion or belief is based.

(2) A person who enters into or is otherwise concerned in any such transaction or arrangement as is mentioned in section 9, 10 or 11 above does not commit an offence under that section if he is acting with the express consent of a constable or if –

(a) he discloses to a constable his suspicion or belief that the money or other property concerned is or is derived from terrorist funds or any matter on which such a suspicion or belief is based; and
(b) the disclosure is made after he enters into or otherwise becomes concerned in the

transaction or arrangement in question but is made on his own initiative and as soon as it is reasonable for him to make it,

but paragraphs (a) and (b) above do not apply in a case where, having disclosed any such suspicion, belief or matter to a constable and having been forbidden by a constable to enter into or otherwise be concerned in the transaction or arrangement in question, he nevertheless does so.

(2A) For the purposes of subsection (2) above a person who uses or has possession of money or other property shall be taken to be concerned in a transaction or arrangement.

(3) In proceedings against a person for an offence under section 9(1)(b) or (c) or (2), 10(1)(b) or (c) or 11 above it is a defence to prove –

(a) that he intended to disclose to a constable such a suspicion, belief or matter as is mentioned in paragraph (a) of subsection (2) above; and
(b) that there is a reasonable excuse for his failure to make the disclosure as mentioned in paragraph (b) of that subsection.

(4) In the case of a person who was in employment at the relevant time, subsections (1) to (3) above shall have effect in relation to disclosures, and intended disclosures, to the appropriate person in accordance with the procedure established by his employer for the making of such disclosures as they have effect in relation to disclosures, and intended disclosures, to a constable.

(5) No constable or other person shall be guilty of an offence under section 9(1)(b) or (c) or (2) or 10(1)(b) or (c) above in respect of anything done by him in the course of acting in connection with the enforcement, or intended enforcement, of any provision of this Act or of any other enactment relating to terrorism or the proceeds or resources of terrorism.

(6) For the purposes of subsection (5) above, having possession of any property shall be taken to be doing an act in relation to it.

13 Penalties and forfeiture

(1) A person guilty of an offence under section 9, 10 or 11 above is liable –

(a) on conviction on indictment, to imprisonment for a term not exceeding fourteen years or a fine or both;
(b) on summary conviction, to imprisonment for a term not exceeding six months or a fine not exceeding the statutory maximum or both.

(2) Subject to the provisions of this section, the court by or before which a person is convicted of an offence under section 9(1) or (2)(a) above may order the forfeiture of any money or other property –

(a) which, at the time of the offence, he had in his possession or under his control; and
(b) which, at that time –

(i) in the case of an offence under subsection (1) of section 9, he intended should be applied or used, or had reasonable cause to suspect might be applied or used, as mentioned in that subsection;

(ii) in the case of an offence under subsection (2)(a) of that section, he knew or had reasonable cause to suspect would or might be applied or used as mentioned in subsection (1) of that section.

(3) Subject to the provisions of this section, the court by or before which a person is convicted of an offence under section 9(2)(b), 10(1)(c) or 11 above may order the forfeiture of the money or other property to which the arrangement in question related and which, in the case of an offence under section 9(2)(b), he knew or had reasonable cause to suspect would or might be applied or used as mentioned in section 9(1) above.

(4) Subject to the provisions of this section, the court by or before which a person is convicted of an offence under section 10(1)(a) or (b) above may order the forfeiture of any money or other property which, at the time of the offence, he had in his possession or under his control for the use or benefit of a proscribed organisation.

(5) The court shall not under this section make an order forfeiting any money or other property unless the court considers that the money or property may, unless forfeited, be applied or used as mentioned in section 9(1) above but the court may, in the absence of evidence to the contrary, assume that any money or property may be applied or used as there mentioned.

(6) Where a person other than the convicted person claims to be the owner of or otherwise interested in anything which can be forfeited by an order under this section, the court shall, before making such an order in respect of it, give him an opportunity to be heard. ...

16A Possession of articles for suspected terrorist purposes

(1) A person is guilty of an offence if he has any article in his possession in circumstances giving rise to a reasonable suspicion that the article is in his possession for a purpose connected with the commission, preparation or instigation of acts of terrorism to which this section applies.

(2) The acts of terrorism to which this section applies are –

(a) acts of terrorism connected with the affairs of Northern Ireland; and
(b) acts of terrorism of any other description except acts connected solely with the affairs of the United Kingdom or any part of the United Kingdom other than Northern Ireland.

(3) It is a defence for a person charged with an offence under this section to prove that at the time of the alleged offence the article in question was not in his possession for such a purpose as is mentioned in subsection (1) above.

(4) Where a person is charged with an offence under this section and it is proved that at the time of the alleged offence –

(a) he and that article were both present in any premises; or
(b) the article was in premises of which he was the occupier or which he habitually used otherwise than as a member of the public,

the court may accept the fact proved as sufficient evidence of his possessing that article at that time unless it is further proved that he did not at that time know of its presence in the premises in question, or, if he did know, that he had no control over it.

(5) A person guilty of an offence under this section is liable –

(a) on conviction on indictment, to imprisonment for a term not exceeding ten years or a fine or both;
(b) on summary conviction, to imprisonment for a term not exceeding six months or a fine not exceeding the statutory maximum or both.

(6) This section applies to vessels, aircraft and vehicles as it applies to premises.

16B Unlawful collection, etc of information

(1) No person shall, without lawful authority or reasonable excuse (the proof of which lies on him) –

(a) collect or record any information which is of such a nature as is likely to be useful to terrorists in planning or carrying out any act of terrorism to which this section applies; or
(b) have in his possession any record or document containing any such information as is mentioned in paragraph (a) above.

(2) The acts of terrorism to which this section applies are –

(a) acts of terrorism connected with the affairs of Northern Ireland; and
(b) acts of terrorism of any other description except acts connected solely with the affairs of the United Kingdom or any part of the United Kingdom other than Northern Ireland.

(3) In subsection (1) above the reference to recording information includes a reference to recording it by means of photography or by any other means.

(4) Any person who contravenes this section is guilty of an offence and liable –

(a) on conviction on indictment, to imprisonment for a term not exceeding ten years or a fine or both;
(b) on summary conviction, to imprisonment for a term not exceeding six months or a fine not exceeding the statutory maximum or both.

(5) The court by or before which a person is convicted of an offence under this section may order the forfeiture of any record or document mentioned in subsection (1) above which is found in his possession.

18 Information about acts of terrorism

(1) A person is guilty of an offence if he has information which he knows or believes might be of material assistance –

(a) in preventing the commission by any other person of an act of terrorism connected with the affairs of Northern Ireland; or
(b) in securing the apprehension, prosecution or conviction of any other person for an offence involving the commission, preparation or instigation of such an act,
and fails without reasonable excuse to disclose that information as soon as reasonably practicable –

(i) in England and Wales, to a constable; or ...

(iii) in Northern Ireland, to a constable or a member of Her Majesty's Forces.

(2) A person guilty of an offence under this section is liable –

(a) on conviction on indictment, to imprisonment for a term not exceeding five years or a fine or both;

(b) on summary conviction, to imprisonment for a term not exceeding six months or a fine not exceeding the statutory maximum or both.

(3) Proceedings for an offence under this section may be taken, and the offence may for the purposes of those proceedings be treated as having been committed, in any place where the person to be charged is or has at any time been since he first knew or believed that the information might be of material assistance as mentioned in subsection (1) above.

18A Failure to disclose knowledge or suspicion of offences under ss9 to 11

(1) A person is guilty of an offence if –

(a) he knows, or suspects, that another person is providing financial assistance for terrorism;

(b) the information, or other matter, on which that knowledge or suspicion is based came to his attention in the course of his trade, profession, business or employment; and

(c) he does not disclose the information or other matter to a constable as soon as is reasonably practicable after it comes to his attention.

(2) Subsection (1) above does not make it an offence for a professional legal adviser to fail to disclose any information or other matter which has come to him in privileged circumstances.

(3) It is a defence to a charge of committing an offence under this section that the person charged has a reasonable excuse for not disclosing the information or other matter in question.

(4) Where a person discloses to a constable –

(a) his suspicion or belief that another person is providing financial assistance for terrorism; or

(b) any information or other matter on which that suspicion or belief is based;

the disclosure shall not be treated as a breach of any restriction imposed by statute or otherwise.

(5) Without prejudice to subsection (3) or (4) above, in the case of a person who was in employment at the relevant time, it is a defence to a charge of committing an offence under this section that he disclosed the information or other matter in question to the appropriate person in accordance with the procedure established by his employer for the making of such disclosures.

(6) A disclosure to which subsection (5) above applies shall not be treated as a breach of any restriction imposed by statute or otherwise.

(7) In this section 'providing financial assistance for terrorism' means doing any act which constitutes an offence under section 9, 10 or 11 above or, in the case of an act done otherwise than in the United Kingdom, which would constitute such an offence if done in the United Kingdom.

(8) For the purposes of subsection (7) above, having possession of any property shall be taken to be doing an act in relation to it.

(9) For the purposes of this section, any information or other matter comes to a professional legal adviser in privileged circumstances if it is communicated, or given, to him –

(a) by, or by a representative of, a client of his in connection with the giving by the adviser of legal advice to the client;

(b) by, or by a representative of, a person seeking legal advice from the adviser; or

(c) by any person –

(i) in contemplation of, or in connection with, legal proceedings; and

(ii) for the purpose of those proceedings.

(10) No information or other matter shall be treated as coming to a professional legal adviser in privileged circumstances if it is communicated or given with a view to furthering any criminal purpose.

(11) A person guilty of an offence under this section shall be liable –

(a) on summary conviction, to imprisonment for a term not exceeding six months or a fine not exceeding the statutory maximum or to both; or

(b) on conviction on indictment, to imprisonment for a term not exceeding five years or a fine or to both.

[As amended by the Criminal Justice Act 1993, ss49(1), (2), (3)–(6), 51, 79(14), Schedule 6, Part I; Criminal Justice and Public Order Act 1994, s82(1); Northern Ireland (Emergency Provisions) Act 1996, s63(6), Schedule 6, paras 4, 5.]

Official Secrets Act 1989
(1989 c 6)

1 Security and intelligence

(1) A person who is or has been –

(a) a member of the security and intelligence services; or

(b) a person notified that he is subject to the provisions of this subsection,

is guilty of an offence if without lawful authority he discloses any information, document or other article relating to security or intelligence which is or has been in his possession by virtue of his position as a member of any of those services or in the course of his work while the notification is or was in force.

(2) The reference in subsection (1) above to disclosing information relating to security or intelligence includes a reference to making any statement which purports to be a disclosure

of such information or is intended to be taken by those to whom it is addressed as being such a disclosure.

(3) A person who is or has been a Crown servant or government contractor is guilty of an offence if without lawful authority he makes a damaging disclosure of any information, document or other article relating to security or intelligence which is or has been in his possession by virtue of his position as such but otherwise than as mentioned in subsection (1) above.

(4) For the purposes of subsection (3) above a disclosure is damaging if –

(a) it causes damage to the work of, or of any part of, the security and intelligence services; or
(b) it is of information or a document or other article which is such that its unauthorised disclosure would be likely to cause such damage or which falls within a class or description of information or articles the unauthorised disclosure of which would be likely to have that effect.

(5) It is a defence for a person charged with an offence under this section to prove that at the time of the alleged offence he did not know, and has no reasonable cause to believe, that the information, document or article in question related to security or intelligence or, in the case of an offence under subsection (3), that the disclosure would be damaging within the meaning of that subsection.

(6) Notification that a person is subject to subsection (1) above shall be effected by a notice in writing served on him by a Minister of the Crown; and such a notice may be served if, in the Minister's opinion, the work undertaken by the person in question is or includes work connected with the security and intelligence services and its nature is such that the interests of national security require that he should be subject to the provisions of that subsection.

(7) Subject to subsection (8) below, a notification for the purposes of subsection (1) above shall be in force for the period of five years beginning with the day on which it is served but may be renewed by further notices under subsection (6) above for periods of five years at a time.

(8) A notification for the purposes of subsection (1) above may at any time be revoked by a further notice in writing served by the Minister on the person concerned; and the Minister shall serve such a further notice as soon as, in his opinion, the work undertaken by that person ceases to be such as is mentioned in subsection (6) above.

(9) In this section 'security or intelligence' means the work of, or in support of, the security and intelligence services or any part of them, and references to information relating to security or intelligence include references to information held or transmitted by those services or by persons in support of, or of any part of, them.

2 Defence

(1) A person who is or has been a Crown servant or government contractor is guilty of an offence if without lawful authority he makes a damaging disclosure of any information,

document or other article relating to defence which is or has been in his possession by virtue of his position as such.

(2) For the purposes of subsection (1) above a disclosure is damaging if –

(a) it damages the capability of, or of any part of, the armed forces of the Crown to carry out their tasks or leads to loss of life or injury to members of those forces or serious damage to the equipment or installation of those forces; or

(b) otherwise than as mentioned in paragraph (a) above, it endangers the interests of the United Kingdom abroad, seriously obstructs the promotion or protection by the United Kingdom of those interests or endangers the safety of British citizens abroad; or

(c) it is of information or of a document or article which is such that its unauthorised disclosure would be likely to have any of those effects.

(3) It is a defence for a person charged with an offence under this section to prove that at the time of the alleged offence he did not know, and had no reasonable cause to believe, that the information, document or article in question related to defence or that its disclosure would be damaging within the meaning of subsection (1) above.

(4) In this section 'defence' means –

(a) the size, shape, organisation, logistics, order of battle, deployment, operations, state of readiness and training of the armed forces of the Crown;

(b) the weapons, stores or other equipment of those forces and the invention, development, production and operation of such equipment and research relating to it;

(c) defence policy and strategy and military planning and intelligence;

(d) plans and measures for the maintenance of essential supplies and services that are or would be needed in time of war.

3 International relations

(1) A person who is or has been a Crown servant or government contractor is guilty of an offence if without lawful authority he makes a damaging disclosure of –

(a) any information, document or other article relating to international relations; or

(b) any confidential information, document or other article which was obtained from a State other than the United Kingdom or an international organisation,

being information or a document or article which is or has been in his possession by virtue of his position as a Crown servant or government contractor.

(2) For the purposes of subsection (1) above a disclosure is damaging if –

(a) it endangers the interests of the United Kingdom abroad, seriously obstructs the promotion or protection by the United Kingdom of those interests or endangers the safety of British citizens abroad; or

(b) it is of information or of a document or article which is such that its unauthorised disclosure would be likely to have any of those effects.

(3) In the case of information or a document or article within subsection (1)(b) above –

(a) the fact that it is confidential, or

(b) its nature or contents,

may be sufficient to establish for the purposes of subsection (2)(b) above that the information, document or article is such that its unauthorised disclosure would be likely to have any of the effects there mentioned.

(4) It is a defence for a person charged with an offence under this section to prove that at the time of the alleged offence he did not know, and had no reasonable cause to believe, that the information, document or article in question was such as is mentioned in subsection (1) above or that its disclosure would be damaging within the meaning of that subsection.

(5) In this section 'international relations' means the relations between States, between international organisations or between one or more States and one or more such organisations and includes any matter relating to a State other than the United Kingdom or to an international organisation which is capable of affecting the relations of the United Kingdom with another State or with an international organisation.

(6) For the purposes of this section any information, document or article obtained from a State or organisation is confidential at any time while the terms on which it was obtained require it to be held in confidence or while the circumstances in which it was obtained make it reasonable for the State or organisation to expect that it would be so held.

4 *Crime and special investigation powers*

(1) A person who is or has been a Crown servant or government contractor is guilty of an offence if without lawful authority it discloses any information, document or other article to which this section applies and which is or has been in his possession by virtue of his position as such.

(2) This section applies to any information, document or other article –

(a) the disclosure of which –

(i) results in the commission of an offence; or
(ii) facilitates an escape from legal custody or the doing of any other act prejudicial to the safekeeping of person in legal custody; or
(iii) impedes the prevention or detection of offences or the apprehension or prosecution of suspected offenders; or

(b) which is such that its unauthorised disclosure would be likely to have any of those effects.

(3) This section also applies to –

(a) any information obtained by reason of the interception of any communication in obedience to a warrant issued under section 2 of the Interception of Communications Act 1985, any information relating to the obtaining of information by reason of any such interception and any document or other article which is or has been used or held for use in, or has been obtained by reason of, any such interception; and

(b) any information obtained by reason of action authorised by a warrant issued under section 3 of the Security Service Act 1989 or under section 5 of the Intelligence Services Act 1994 or by an authorisation given under section 7 of that Act, any information relating to the obtaining of information by reason of any such action and any document or other article which is or has been used or held for use in, or has been obtained by reason of, any such action.

(4) It is a defence for a person charged with an offence under this section in respect of a disclosure falling within subsection (2)(a) above to prove that at the time of the alleged offence he did not know, and had no reasonable cause to believe, that the disclosure would have any of the effects there mentioned.

(5) It is a defence for a person charged with an offence under this section in respect of any other disclosure to prove that at the time of the alleged offence he did not know, and had no reasonable cause to believe, that the information, document or article in question was information or a document or article to which this section applies.

(6) In this section 'legal custody' includes detention in pursuance of any enactment or any instrument made under an enactment.

5 Information resulting from unauthorised disclosures or entrusted in confidence

(1) Subsection (2) below applies where –

(a) any information, document or other article protected against disclosure by the foregoing provisions of this Act has come into a person's possession as a result of having been –

(i) disclosed (whether to him or another) by a Crown servant or government contractor without lawful authority; or

(ii) entrusted to him by a Crown servant or government contractor on terms requiring it to be held in confidence or in circumstances in which the Crown servant or government contractor could reasonably expect that it would be so held; or

(iii) disclosed (whether to him or another) without lawful authority by a person to whom it was entrusted as mentioned in sub-paragraph (ii) above; and

(b) the disclosure without lawful authority of the information, document or article by the person into whose possession it has come is not an offence under any of those provisions.

(2) Subject to subsections (3) and (4) below, the person into whose possession the information, document or article has come is guilty of an offence if he discloses it without lawful authority knowing, or having reasonable cause to believe, that it is protected against disclosure by the foregoing provisions of this Act and that it has come into his possession as mentioned in subsection (1) above.

(3) In the case of information or a document or article protected against disclosure by sections 1 to 3 above, a person does not commit an offence under subsection (2) above unless –

(a) the disclosure by him is damaging; or

(b) he makes it knowing, or having reasonable cause to believe, that it would be damaging;

and the question whether a disclosure is damaging shall be determined for the purposes of this subsection as it would be in relation to a disclosure of that information, document or article by a Crown servant in contravention of section 1(3), 2(1) or 3(1) above.

(4) A person does not commit an offence under subsection (2) above in respect of information or a document or other article which has come into his possession as a result of having been disclosed –

(a) as mentioned in subsection (1)(a)(i) above by a government contractor; or
(b) as mentioned in subsection (1)(a)(iii) above,

unless that disclosure was by a British citizen or took place in the United Kingdom, in any of the Channel Islands or in the Isle of Man or a colony.

(5) For the purposes of this section information or a document or article is protected against disclosure by the foregoing provisions of this Act if –

(a) it relates to security or intelligence, defence or international relations within the meaning of section 1, 2 or 3 above or is such as is mentioned in section 3(1)(b) above; or
(b) it is information or a document or article to which section 4 above applies;

and information or a document or article is protected against disclosure by sections 1 to 3 above if it falls within paragraph (a) above.

(6) A person is guilty of an offence if without lawful authority he discloses any information, document or other article which he knows, or has reasonable cause to believe, to have come into his possession as a result of a contravention of section 1 of the Official Secrets Act 1911.

6 *Information entrusted in confidence to other States or international organisations*

(1) This section applies where –

(a) any information, document or other article which –

(i) relates to security or intelligence, defence or international relations; and
(ii) has been communicated in confidence by or on behalf of the United Kingdom to another State or to an international organisation,

has come into a person's possession as a result of having been disclosed (whether to him or another) without the authority of that State or organisation or, in the case of an organisation, of a member of it; and

(b) the disclosure without lawful authority of the information, document or article by the person into whose possession it has come is not an offence under any of the foregoing provisions of this Act.

(2) Subject to subsection (3) below, the person into whose possession the information, document or article has come is guilty of an offence if he makes a damaging disclosure of it knowing, or having reasonable cause to believe, that it is such as is mentioned in subsection (1) above, that it has come into his possession as there mentioned and that its disclosure would be damaging.

(3) A person does not commit an offence under subsection (2) above if the information,

document or article is disclosed by him with lawful authority or has previously been made available to the public with the authority of the State or organisation concerned or, in the case of an organisation, of a member of it.

(4) For the purposes of this section 'security or intelligence', 'defence' and 'international relations' have the same meaning as in sections 1, 2 and 3 above and the question whether a disclosure is damaging shall be determined as it would be in relation to a disclosure of the information, document or article in question by a Crown servant in contravention of section 1(3), 2(1) and 3(1) above.

(5) For the purposes of this section information or a document or article is communicated in confidence if it is communicated on terms requiring it to be held in confidence or in circumstances in which the person communicating it could reasonably expect that it would be so held.

7 *Authorised disclosures*

(1) For the purposes of this Act a disclosure by –

(a) a Crown servant; or
(b) a person, not being a Crown servant or government contractor, in whose case a notification for the purposes of section 1(1) above is in force,

is made with lawful authority if, and only if, it is made in accordance with his official duty.

(2) For the purposes of this Act a disclosure by a government contractor is made with lawful authority if, and only if, it is made –

(a) in accordance with an official authorisation; or
(b) for the purposes of the functions by virtue of which he is a government contractor and without contravening an official restriction.

(3) For the purposes of this Act a disclosure made by any other person is made with lawful authority of, and only if, it is made –

(a) to a Crown servant for the purposes of his functions as such; or
(b) in accordance with an official authorisation.

(4) It is a defence for a person charged with an offence under any of the foregoing provisions of this Act to prove that at the time of the alleged offence he believed that he had lawful authority to make the disclosure in question and had no reasonable cause to believe otherwise.

(5) In this section 'official authorisation' and 'official restriction' mean, subject to subsection (6) below, an authorisation or restriction duly given or imposed by a Crown servant or government contractor or by or on behalf of a prescribed body or a body of a prescribed class.

(6) In relation to subsection 5 above 'official authorisation' includes an authorisation duly given by or on behalf of the State or organisation concerned or, in the case of an organisation, a member of it.

8 Safeguarding of information

(1) Where a Crown servant or government contractor, by virtue of his position as such, has in his possession or under his control any document or other article which it would be an offence under any of the foregoing provisions of this Act for him to disclose without lawful authority he is guilty of an offence if –

(a) being a Crown servant, he retains the document or article contrary to his official duty; or

(b) being a government contractor, he fails to comply with an official direction for the return or disposal of the document or article,

or if he fails to take such care to prevent the unauthorised disclosure of the document or article as a person in his position may reasonably be expected to take.

(2) It is a defence for a Crown servant charged with an offence under subsection (1)(a) above to prove that at the time of the alleged offence he believed that he was acting in accordance with his official duty and had no reasonable cause to believe otherwise.

(3) In subsections (1) and (2) above references to a Crown servant include any person, not being a Crown servant or government contractor, in whose case a notification for the purposes of section 1(1) above is in force.

(4) Where a person has in his possession or under his control any document or other article which it would be an offence under section 5 above for him to disclose without lawful authority, he is guilty of an offence if –

(a) he fails to comply with an official direction for his return or disposal; or

(b) where he obtained it from a Crown servant or government contractor on terms requiring it to be held in confidence or in circumstances in which that servant or contractor could reasonably expect that it would be so held, he fails to take such care to prevent its unauthorised disclosure as a person in his position may reasonably be expected to take.

(5) Where a person has in his possession or under his control any document or other article which it would be an offence under section 6 above for him to disclose without lawful authority, he is guilty of an offence if he fails to comply with an official direction for its return or disposal.

(6) A person is guilty of an offence if he discloses any official information, document or other article which can be used for the purpose of obtaining access to any information, document or other article protected against disclosure by the foregoing provisions of this Act and the circumstances in which it is disclosed are such that it would be reasonable to expect that it might be used for that purpose without authority.

(7) For the purposes of subsection (6) above a person discloses information or a document or article which is official if –

(a) he had or has had it in his possession by virtue of his position as a Crown servant or government contractor; or

(b) he knows or has reasonable cause to believe that a Crown servant or government contractor has or has had it in his possession by virtue of his position as such.

(8) Subsection (5) of section 5 above applies for the purposes of subsection (6) above as it applies for the purposes of that section.

(9) In this section 'official direction' means a direction duly given by a Crown servant or government contractor or by or on behalf of a prescribed body or a body of a prescribed class.

13 Other interpretation provisions

(1) In this Act –

'disclose' and 'disclosure', in relation to a document or other article, include parting with possession of it; ...

[As amended by the Intelligence Services Act 1994, s11(2), Schedule 4, para 4.]

Extradition Act 1989
(1989 c 33)

23 Genocide, etc

(1) For the purposes of this Act, no offence which, if committed in the United Kingdom, would be punishable as an offence of genocide or as an attempt, conspiracy or incitement to commit such an offence shall be regarded as an offence of a political character, and no proceedings in respect of such an offence shall be regarded as a criminal matter of a political character.

(2) It shall not be an objection to any proceedings against a person under this Act in respect of an offence which, if committed in the United Kingdom, would be punishable as an offence of genocide or as an attempt, conspiracy or incitement to commit such an offence that under the law in force at the time when and in the place where he is alleged to have committed the act of which he is accused or of which he was convicted he could not have been punished for it.

Computer Misuse Act 1990
(1990 c 18)

1 Unauthorised access to computer material

(1) A person is guilty of an offence if –

(a) he causes a computer to perform any function with intent to secure access to any program or data held in any computer;
(b) the access he intends to secure is unauthorised; and
(c) he knows at the time when he causes the computer to perform the function that that is the case.

(2) The intent a person has to have to commit an offence under this section need not be directed at –

(a) any particular program or data;
(b) a program or data of any particular kind; or
(c) a program or data held in any particular computer.

(3) A person guilty of an offence under this section shall be liable on summary conviction to imprisonment for a term not exceeding six months or to a fine not exceeding level 5 on the standard scale or to both.

2 Unauthorised access with intent to commit or facilitate commission of further offences

(1) A person is guilty of an offence under this section if he commits an offence under section 1 above ('the unauthorised access offence') with intent –

(a) to commit an offence to which this section applies; or
(b) to facilitate the commission of such an offence (whether by himself or by any other person);

and the offence he intends to commit or facilitate is referred to below in this section as the further offence.

(2) This section applies to offences –

(a) for which the sentence is fixed by law; or
(b) for which a person of twenty-one years of age or over (not previously convicted) may be sentenced to imprisonment for a term of five years (or, in England and Wales, might be so sentenced but for the restrictions imposed by section 33 of the Magistrates' Courts Act 1980).

(3) It is immaterial for the purposes of this section whether the further offence is to be committed on the same occasion as the unauthorised access offence or on any future occasion.

(4) A person may be guilty of an offence under this section even though the facts are such that the commission of the further offence is impossible.

(5) A person guilty of an offence under this section shall be liable –

(a) on summary conviction, to imprisonment for a term not exceeding six months or to a fine not exceeding the statutory maximum or to both; and
(b) on conviction on indictment, to imprisonment for a term not exceeding five years or to a fine or to both.

3 Unauthorised modification of computer material

(1) A person is guilty of an offence if –

(a) he does any act which causes an unauthorised modification of the contents of any computer; and

(b) at the time when he does the act he has the requisite intent and the requisite knowledge.

(2) For the purposes of subsection (1)(b) above the requisite intent is an intent to cause a modification of the contents of any computer and by so doing –

(a) to impair the operation of any computer;
(b) to prevent or hinder access to any program or data held in any computer; or
(c) to impair the operation of any such program or the reliability of any such data.

(3) The intent need not be directed at –

(a) any particular computer;
(b) any particular program or data or a program or data of any particular kind; or
(c) any particular modification or a modification of any particular kind.

(4) For the purposes of subsection (1)(b) above the requisite knowledge is knowledge that any modification he intends to cause is unauthorised.

(5) It is immaterial for the purposes of this section whether an unauthorised modification or any intended effect of it of a kind mentioned in subsection (2) above is, or is intended to be, permanent or merely temporary.

(6) For the purposes of the Criminal Damage Act 1971 a modification of the contents of a computer shall not be regarded as damaging any computer or computer storage medium unless its effect on that computer or computer storage medium impairs its physical condition.

(7) A person guilty of an offence under this section shall be liable –

(a) on summary conviction, to imprisonment for a term not exceeding six months or to a fine not exceeding the statutory maximum or to both; and
(b) on conviction on indictment, to imprisonment for a term not exceeding five years or to a fine or to both.

4 Territorial scope of offences under this Act

(1) Except as provided below in this section, it is immaterial for the purposes of any offence under section 1 or 3 above –

(a) whether any act or other event proof of which is required for conviction of the offence occurred in the home country concerned; or
(b) whether the accused was in the home country concerned at the time of any such act or event.

(2) Subject to subsection (3) below, in the case of such an offence at least one significant link with domestic jurisdiction must exist in the circumstances of the case for the offence to be committed.

(3) There is no need for any such link to exist for the commission of an offence under section 1 above to be established in proof of an allegation to that effect in proceedings for an offence under section 2 above.

(4) Subject to section 8 below, where –

(a) any such link does in fact exist in the case of an offence under section 1 above; and

(b) commission of that offence is alleged in proceedings for an offence under section 2 above;

section 2 above shall apply as if anything the accused intended to do or facilitate in any place outside the home country concerned which would be an offence to which section 2 applies if it took place in the home country concerned were the offence in question. ...

(6) References in this Act to the home country concerned are references –

(a) in application of this Act to England and Wales, to England and Wales;

(b) in application of this Act to Scotland, to Scotland; and

(c) in the application of this Act to Northern Ireland, to Northern Ireland.

5 Significant links with domestic jurisdiction

(1) The following provisions of this section apply for the interpretation of section 4 above.

(2) In relation to an offence under section 1, either of the following is a significant link with domestic jurisdiction –

(a) that the accused was in the home country concerned at the time when he did the act which caused the computer to perform the function; or

(b) that any computer containing any program or data to which the accused secured or intended to secure unauthorised access by doing that act was in the home country concerned at that time.

(3) In relation to an offence under section 3, either of the following is a significant link with domestic jurisdiction –

(a) that the accused was in the home country concerned at the time when he did the act which caused the unauthorised modification; or

(b) that the unauthorised modification took place in the home country concerned.

6 Territorial scope of inchoate offences related to offences under this Act

(1) On a charge of conspiracy to commit an offence under this Act the following questions are immaterial to the accused's guilt –

(a) the question where any person became a party to the conspiracy; and

(b) the question whether any act, omission or other event occurred in the home country concerned.

(2) On a charge of attempting to commit an offence under section 3 above the following questions are immaterial to the accused's guilt –

(a) the question where the attempt was made; and

(b) the question whether it had an effect in the home country concerned.

(3) On a charge of incitement to commit an offence under this Act the question where the incitement took place is immaterial to the accused's guilt. ...

7 Territorial scope of inchoate offences related to offences under external law corresponding to offences under this Act ...

(4) Subject to section 8 below, if any act done by a person in England and Wales would amount to the offence of incitement to commit an offence under this Act but for the fact that what he had in view would not be an offence triable in England and Wales –

(a) what he had in view shall be treated as an offence under this Act for the purposes of any charge of incitement brought in respect of that act; and
(b) any such charge shall accordingly be triable in England and Wales.

8 Relevance of external law

(1) A person is guilty of an offence triable by virtue of section 4(4) above only if what he intended to do or facilitate would involve the commission of an offence under the law in force where the whole or any part of it was intended to take place.

(3) A person is guilty of an offence triable by virtue of section 1(1A) of the Criminal Attempts Act 1981 or by virtue of section 7(4) above only if what he had in view would involve the commission of an offence under the law in force where the whole or any part of it was intended to take place.

(4) Conduct punishable under the law in force in any place is an offence under that law for the purposes of this section, however it is described in that law.

(5) Subject to subsection (7) below, a condition specified in subsection (1) or (3) above shall be taken to be satisfied unless not later than rules of court may provide the defence serve on the prosecution a notice –

(a) stating that, on the facts as alleged with respect to the relevant conduct, the condition is not in their opinion satisfied;
(b) showing their grounds for that opinion; and
(c) requiring the prosecution to show that it is satisfied.

(6) In subsection (5) above 'the relevant conduct' means –

(a) where the condition in subsection (1) above is in question, what the accused intended to do or facilitate; and
(c) where the condition in subsection (3) above is in question, what the accused had in view.

(7) The court, if it thinks fit, may permit the defence to require the prosecution to show that the condition is satisfied without the prior service of a notice under subsection (5) above. ...

(9) In the Crown Court the question whether the condition is satisfied shall be decided by the judge alone. ...

9 British citizenship immaterial

(1) In any proceedings brought in England and Wales in respect of any offence to which this section applies it is immaterial to guilt whether or not the accused was a British citizen at

the time of any act, omission or other event proof of which is required for conviction of the offence.

(2) This section applies to the following offences –

   (a) any offence under this Act;

   (c) any attempt to commit an offence under section 3 above; and

   (d) incitement to commit an offence under this Act.

10 Saving for certain law enforcement powers

Section 1(1) above has effect without prejudice to the operation –

   (a) in England and Wales of any enactment relating to powers of inspection, search or seizure; ...

and nothing designed to indicate a withholding of consent to access to any program or data from persons as enforcement officers shall have effect to make access unauthorised for the purposes of the said section 1(1).

In this section 'enforcement officer' means a constable or other person charged with the duty of investigating offences; and withholding consent from a person 'as' an enforcement officer of any description includes the operation, by the person entitled to control access, of rules whereby enforcement officers of that description are, as such, disqualified from membership of a class of persons who are authorised to have access.

12 Conviction of an offence under s1 in proceedings for an offence under s2 or 3

(1) If on the trial on indictment of a person charged with –

   (a) an offence under section 2 above; or

   (b) an offence under section 3 above or any attempt to commit such an offence;

the jury find him not guilty of the offence charged, they may find him guilty of an offence under section 1 above if on the facts shown he could have been found guilty of that offence in proceedings for that offence brought before the expiry of any time limit under section 11 above applicable to such proceedings. ...

(3) This section is without prejudice to section 6(3) of the Criminal Law Act 1967 (conviction of alternative indictable offence on trial on indictment). ...

17 Interpretation

(1) The following provisions of this section apply for the interpretation of this Act.

(2) A person secures access to any program or data held in a computer if by causing a computer to perform any function he –

   (a) alters or erases the program or data;

   (b) copies or moves it to any storage medium other than that in which it is held or to a different location in the storage medium in which it is held;

(c) uses it; or

(d) has it output from the computer in which it is held (whether by having it displayed or in any other manner);

and references to access to a program or data (and to an intent to secure such access) shall be read accordingly.

(3) For the purposes of subsection (2)(c) above a person uses a program if the function he causes the computer to perform –

(a) causes the program to be executed; or

(b) is itself a function of the program.

(4) For the purposes of subsection (2)(d) above –

(a) a program is output if the instructions of which it consists are output; and

(b) the form in which any such instructions or any other data is output (and in particular whether or not it represents a form in which, in the case of instructions, they are capable of being executed or, in the case of data, it is capable of being processed by a computer) is immaterial.

(5) Access of any kind by any person to any program or data held in a computer is unauthorised if –

(a) he is not himself entitled to control access of the kind in question to the program or data; and

(b) he does not have consent to access by him of the kind in question to the program or data from any person who is so entitled,

but this subsection is subject to section 10.

(6) References to any program or data held in a computer include references to any program or data held in any removable storage medium which is for the time being in the computer; and a computer is to be regarded as containing any program or data held in any such medium.

(7) A modification of the contents of any computer takes place if, by the operation of any function of the computer concerned or any other computer –

(a) any program or data held in the computer concerned is altered or erased; or

(b) any program or data is added to its contents;

and any act which contributes towards causing such a modification shall be regarded as causing it.

(8) Such a modification is unauthorised if –

(a) the person whose act causes it is not himself entitled to determine whether the modification should be made; and

(b) he does not have consent to the modification from any person who is so entitled.

(9) References to the home country concerned shall be read in accordance with section 4(6) above.

(10) References to a program include references to part of a program.

[As amended by the Criminal Justice and Public Order Act 1994, s162(1), (2); Criminal Justice (Terrorism and Conspiracy) Act 1998, s9, Schedule 1, Pt II, para 6(1), (2), Schedule 2, Pt II.]

Environmental Protection Act 1990
(1990 c 43)

86 Preliminary

(1) The following provisions have effect for the purposes of this Part.

(2) In England and Wales the following are 'principal litter authorities' –

  (a) a county council,
  (aa) a county borough council,
  (b) a district council,
  (c) a London borough council,
  (d) the Common Council of the City of London, and
  (e) the Council of the Isles of Scilly;

but the Secretary of State may, by order, designate other descriptions of local authorities as litter authorities for the purposes of this Part; and any such authority shall also be a principal litter authority. ...

(4) Subject to subsection (8) below, land is 'relevant land' of a principal litter authority if, not being relevant land falling within subsection (7) below, it is open to the air and is land (but not a highway or in Scotland a public road) which is under the direct control of such an authority to which the public are entitled or permitted to have access with or without payment. ...

(7) Subject to subsection (8) below, land is 'relevant land' of a designated educational institution if it is open to the air and is land which is under the direct control of the governing body of or, in Scotland, of such body or of the education authority responsible for the management of, any educational institution or educational institution of any description which may be designated by the Secretary of State, by order, for the purposes of this Part.

(8) The Secretary of State may, by order, designate descriptions of land which are not to be treated as relevant Crown land or as relevant land of principal litter authorities, of designated statutory undertakers or of designated educational institutions or of any description of any of them.

(9) Every highway maintainable at the public expense other than a trunk road which is a special road is a 'relevant highway' and the local authority which is, for the purposes of this Part, 'responsible' for so much of it as lies within its area is, subject to any other under subsection (11) below –

  (a) in Greater London, the council of the London borough or the Common Council of the City of London;
  (b) in England, outside Greater London, the council of the district;
  (bb) in Wales, a county council or county borough council;

(c) the Council of the Isles of Scilly....

(11) The Secretary of State may, by order, as respects relevant highways or relevant roads, relevant highways or relevant roads of any class or any part of a relevant highway or relevant road specified in the order, transfer the responsibility for the discharge of the duties imposed by section 89 below from the local authority to the highway or roads authority ...

(13) A place on land shall be treated as 'open to the air' notwithstanding that it is covered if it is open to the air on at least one side.

(14) The Secretary of State may, by order, apply the provisions of this Part which apply to refuse to any description of animal droppings in all or any prescribed circumstances subject to such modifications as appear to him to be necessary.

(15) Any power under this section may be exercised differently as respects different areas, different descriptions of land or for different circumstances.

87 *Offence of leaving litter*

(1) If any person throws down, drops or otherwise deposits in, into or from any place to which this section applies, and leaves, any thing whatsoever in such circumstances as to cause, or contribute to, or tend to lead to, the defacement by litter of anyplace to which this section applies, he shall, subject to subsection (2) below, be guilty of an offence.

(2) No offence is committed under this section where the depositing and leaving of the thing was –

(a) authorised by law, or
(b) done with the consent of the owner, occupier or other person or authority having control of the place in or into which that thing was deposited.

(3) This section applies to any public open place and, in so far as the place is not a public open place, also to the following places –

(a) any relevant highway or relevant road and any trunk road which is a special road;
(b) any place on relevant land of a principal litter authority;
(c) any place on relevant Crown land;
(d) any place on relevant land of any designated statutory undertaker;
(e) any place on relevant land of any designated educational institution;
(f) any place on relevant land within a litter control area of a local authority.

(4) In this section 'public open place' means a place in the open air to which the public are entitled or permitted to have access without payment; and any covered place open to the air on at least one side and available for public use shall be treated as a public open place.

(5) A person who is guilty of an offence under this section shall be liable on summary conviction to a fine not exceeding level 4 on the standard scale.

(6) A local authority, with a view to promoting the abatement of litter, may take such steps as the authority think appropriate for making the effect of subsection (5) above known to the public in their area. ...

88 *Fixed penalty notices for leaving litter*

(1) Where on any occasion an authorised officer of a litter authority finds a person who he has reason to believe has on that occasion committed an offence under section 87 above in the area of that authority, he may give that person a notice offering him the opportunity of discharging any liability to conviction for that offence by payment of a fixed penalty.

(2) Where a person is given a notice under this section in respect of an offence –

(a) no proceedings shall be instituted for that offence before the expiration of fourteen days following the date of the notice; and

(b) he shall not be convicted of that offence if he pays the fixed penalty before the expiration of that period.

(3) A notice under this section shall give such particulars of the circumstances alleged to constitute the offence as are necessary for giving reasonable information of the offence and shall state –

(a) the period during which, by virtue of subsection (2) above, proceedings will not be taken for the offence;

(b) the amount of the fixed penalty; and

(c) the person to whom and the address at which the fixed penalty may be paid;

and, without prejudice to payment by any other method, payment of the fixed penalty may be made by pre-paying and posting to that person at that address a letter containing the amount of the penalty (in cash or otherwise).

(4) Where a letter is sent in accordance with subsection (3) above payment shall be regarded as having been made at the time at which that letter would be delivered in the ordinary course of post.

(5) The form of notices under this section shall be such as the Secretary of State may by order prescribe.

(6) The fixed penalty payable to a litter authority in pursuance of a notice under this section shall, subject to subsection (7) below, be £25; and as respects the sums received by the authority, those sums –

(a) if received by an authority in England and Wales, shall be paid to the Secretary of State; ...

(7) The Secretary of State may by order substitute a different amount for the amount for the time being specified as the amount of the fixed penalty in subsection (6) above.

(8) In any proceedings a certificate which –

(a) purports to be signed by or on behalf of –

(i) in England and Wales, the chief finance officer of the litter authority; ... and

(b) states that payment of a fixed penalty was or was not received by a date specified in the certificate,

shall be evidence of the facts stated.

(9) For the purposes of this section the following are 'litter authorities' –

(a) any principal litter authority, other than an English county council or a joint board;

(b) any English county council or joint board designated by the Secretary of State, by order, in relation to such area as is specified in the order (not being an area in a National Park); and

(e) the Broads Authority. ...

[As amended by the Local Government (Wales) Act 1994, s22(3), Schedule 9, para 17(6)–(8); Environment Act 1995, s120(3), Schedule 24; Litter (Fixed Penalty) Order 1996.]

War Crimes Act 1991
(1991 c 13)

1 Jurisdiction over certain war crimes

(1) Subject to the provisions of this section, proceedings for murder, manslaughter or culpable homicide may be brought against a person in the United Kingdom irrespective of his nationality at the time of the alleged offence if that offence –

(a) was committed during the period beginning with 1 September 1939 and ending with 5 June 1945 in a place which at the time was part of Germany or under German occupation; and

(b) constituted a violation of the laws and customs of war.

(2) No proceedings shall by virtue of this section be brought against any person unless he was on 8 March 1990, or has subsequently become, a British citizen or resident in the United Kingdom, the Isle of man or any of the Channel Islands.

(3) No proceedings shall by virtue of this section be brought in England and Wales or in Northern Ireland except by or with the consent of the Attorney General, or, as the case may be, the Attorney General for Northern Ireland.

[As amended by the Criminal Procedure and Investigations Act 1996, ss46(1)(a), 79(4), 80, Schedule 4, paras 1–3, 19, Schedule 5(2).]

Football (Offences) Act 1991
(1991 c 19)

1 Designated football matches

(1) In this Act a 'designated football match' means an association football match designated, or of a description designated, for the purposes of this Act by order of the Secretary of State.

Any such order shall be made by statutory instrument which shall be subject to annulment in pursuance of a resolution of either House of Parliament.

(2) References in this Act to things done at a designated football match include anything done at the ground –

(a) within the period beginning two hours before the start of the match or (if earlier) two hours before the time at which it is advertised to start and ending one hour after the end of the match; or

(b) where the match is advertised to start at a particular time on a particular day but does not take place on that day, within the period beginning two hours before and ending one hour after the advertised starting time.

2 *Throwing of missiles*

It is an offence for a person at a designated football match to throw anything at or towards –

(a) the playing area, or any area adjacent to the playing area to which spectators are not generally admitted, or

(b) any area in which spectators or other persons are or may be present,

without lawful authority or lawful excuse (which shall be for him to prove).

3 *Indecent or racialist chanting*

(1) It is an offence to engage or take part in chanting of an indecent or racialist nature at a designated football match.

(2) For this purpose –

(a) 'chanting' means the repeated uttering of any words or sounds (whether alone or in concert with one or more others); and

(b) 'of a racialist nature' means consisting of or including matter which is threatening, abusive or insulting to a person by reason of his colour, race, nationality (including citizenship) or ethnic or national origins.

4 *Going onto the playing area*

It is an offence for a person at a designated football match to go onto the playing area, or any area adjacent to the playing area to which spectators are not generally admitted, without lawful authority or lawful excuse (which shall be for him to prove).

5 *Supplementary provisions ...*

(2) A person guilty of an offence under this Act is liable on summary conviction to a fine not exceeding level 3 on the standard scale. ...

[As amended by the Football (Offences and Disorder) Act 1999, s9.]

Criminal Procedure
(Insanity and Unfitness to Plead) Act 1991
(1991 c 25)

1 Acquittals on grounds of insanity

(1) A jury shall not return a special verdict under section 2 of the Trial of Lunatics Act 1883 (acquittal on ground of insanity) except on the written or oral evidence of two or more registered medical practitioners at least one of whom is duly approved.

(2) Subsections (2) and (3) of section 54 of the Mental Health Act 1983 ('the 1983 Act') shall have effect with respect to proof of the accused's mental condition for the purposes of the said section 2 as they have effect with respect to proof of an offender's mental condition for the purposes of section 37(2)(a) of that Act.

Sexual Offences (Amendment) Act 1992
(1992 c 34)

1 Anonymity of victims of certain offences

(1) Where all allegation has been made that an offence to which this Act applies has been committed against a person, neither the name nor address, and no still or moving picture, of that person shall during that person's lifetime –

(a) be published in England and Wales in a written publication available to the public; or
(b) be included in a relevant programme for reception in England and Wales,

if it is likely to lead members of the public to identify that person as the person against whom the offence is alleged to have been committed.

(2) Where a person is accused of an offence to which this Act applies, no matter likely to lead members of the public to identify a person as the person against whom the offence is alleged to have been committed ('the complainant') shall during the complainant's lifetime –

(a) be published in England and Wales in a written publication available to the public; or
(b) be included in a relevant programme for reception in England and Wales.

(3) Subsections (1) and (2) are subject to any direction given under section 3.

(4) Nothing in this section prohibits the publication or inclusion in a relevant programme of matter consisting only of a report of criminal proceedings other than proceedings at, or intended to lead to, or on an appeal arising out of, a trial at which the accused is charged with the offence.

2 Offences to which this Act applies

(1) This Act applies to the following offences –

(a) any offence under any of the provisions of the Sexual Offences Act 1956 mentioned in subsection (2);

(b) any offence under section 128 of the Mental Health Act 1959 (intercourse with mentally handicapped person by hospital staff etc);

(c) any offence under section 1 of the Indecency with Children Act 1960 (indecent conduct towards young child);

(d) any offence under section 54 of the Criminal Law Act 1977 (incitement by man of his grand-daughter, daughter or sister under the age of 16 to commit incest with him);

(e) any attempt to commit any of the offences mentioned in paragraphs (a) to (d);

(f) any conspiracy to commit any of those offences;

(g) any incitement of another to commit any of those offences.

(2) The provisions of the Act of 1956 are –

(a) section 2 (procurement of a woman by threats);

(b) section 3 (procurement of a woman by false pretences);

(c) section 4 (administering drugs to obtain intercourse with a woman)'

(d) section 5 (intercourse with a girl under the age of 13);

(e) section 6 (intercourse with a girl between the ages of 13 and 16);

(f) section 7 (intercourse with a mentally handicapped person);

(g) section 9 (procurement of a mentally handicapped person);

(h) section 10 (incest by a man);

(i) section 11 (incest by a woman);

(j) section 12 (buggery);

(k) section 14 (indecent assault on a woman);

(l) section 15 (indecent assault on a man);

(m) section 16 (assault with intent to commit buggery).

3 Power to displace s1

(1) If, before the commencement of a trial at which a person is charged with an offence to which this Act applies, he or another person against whom the complainant may be expected to give evidence at the trial, applies to the judge for a direction under this subsection and satisfies the judge –

(a) that the direction is required for the purpose of inducing persons who are likely to be needed as witnesses at the trial to come forward; and

(b) that the conduct of the applicant's defence at the trial is likely to be substantially prejudiced if the direction is not given,

the judge shall direct that section 1 shall not, by virtue of the accusation alleging the offence in question, apply in relation to the complainant.

(2) If at a trial the judge is satisfied –

(a) that the effect of section 1 is to impose a substantial and unreasonable restriction upon the reporting of proceedings at the trial, and

(b) that it is in the public interest to remove or relax the restriction,

he shall direct that that section shall not apply to such matter as is specified in the direction.

(3) A direction shall not be given under subsection (2) by reason only of the outcome of the trial.

(4) If a person who has been convicted of an offence and has given notice of appeal against the conviction, or notice of an application for leave so to appeal, applies to the appellate court for a direction under this subsection and satisfies the court –

(a) that the direction is required for the purpose of obtaining evidence in support of the appeal; and

(b) that the applicant is likely to suffer substantial injustice if the direction is not given,

the court shall direct that section 1 shall not, by virtue of an accusation which alleges an offence to which this Act applies and is specified in the direction, apply in relation to a complainant so specified.

(5) A direction given under any provision of this section does not affect the operation of section 1 at any time before the direction is given.

(6) In subsections (1) and (2), 'judge' means –

(a) in the case of an offence which is to be tried summarily or for which the mode of trial has not been determined, any justice of the peace acting for the petty sessions area concerned; and

(b) in any other case, any judge of the Crown Court.

(7) If, after the commencement of a trial at which a person is charged with an offence to which this Act applies, a new trial of the person for that offence is ordered, the commencement of any previous trial shall be disregarded for the purposes of subsection (1).

4 *Special rules for cases of incest or buggery*

(1) In this section –

'section 10 offence' means an offence under section 10 of the Sexual Offences Act 1956 (incest by a man) or an attempt to commit that offence;

'section 11 offence' means an offence under section 11 of that Act (incest by a woman) or an attempt to commit that offence;

'section 12 offence' means an offence under section 12 of that Act (buggery) or an attempt to commit that offence.

(2) Section 1 does not apply to a woman against whom a section 10 offence is alleged to have been committed if she is accused of having committed a section 11 offence against the man who is alleged to have committed the section 10 offence against her.

(3) Section 1 does not apply to a man against whom a section 11 offence is alleged to have been committed if he is accused of having committed a section 10 offence against the woman who is alleged to have committed the section 11 offence against him.

(4) Section 1 does not apply to a person against whom a section 12 offence is alleged to have been committed if that person is accused of having committed a section 12 offence against the person who is alleged to have committed the section 12 offence against him.

(5) Subsection (2) does not affect the operation of this Act in relation to anything done at any time before the woman is accused.

(6) Subsection (3) does not affect the operation of this Act in relation to anything done at any time before the man is accused.

(7) Subsection (4) does not affect the operation of this Act in relation to anything done at any time before the person mentioned first in that subsection is accused.

5 Offences

(1) If any matter is published or included in a relevant programme in contravention of section 1, the following persons shall be guilty of an offence and liable on summary conviction to a fine not exceeding level 5 on the standard scale –

    (a) in the case of publication in a newspaper or periodical, any proprietor, any editor and any publisher of the newspaper or periodical;

    (b) in the case of publication in any other form, the person publishing the matter; and

    (c) in the case of matter included in a relevant programme –

        (i) any body corporate engaged in providing the service in which the programme is included; and

        (ii) any person having functions in relation to the programme corresponding to those of an editor of a newspaper.

(2) Where a person is charged with an offence under this section in respect of the publication of any matter or the inclusion of any matter in a relevant programme, it shall be a defence, subject to subsection (3), to prove that the publication or programme in which the matter appeared was one in respect of which the person against whom the offence mentioned in section 1 is alleged to have been committed had given written consent to the appearance of matter of that description.

(3) Written consent is not a defence if it is proved that any person interfered unreasonably with the peace or comfort of the person giving the consent, with intent to obtain it.

(4) Proceedings for an offence under this section shall not be instituted except by or with the consent of the Attorney General.

(5) Where a person is charged with an offence under this section it shall be a defence to prove that at the time of the alleged offence he was not aware, and neither suspected nor had reason to suspect, that the publication or programme in question was of, or (as the case may be) included, the matter in question.

(6) Where an offence under this section committed by a body corporate is proved to have been committed with the consent or connivance of, or to be attributable to any neglect on the part of –

    (a) a director, manager, secretary or other similar officer of the body corporate, or

    (b) a person purporting to act in any such capacity,

he as well as the body corporate shall be guilty of the offence and liable to be proceeded against and punished accordingly.

(7) In relation to a body corporate whose affairs are managed by its members 'director', in subsection (6), means a member of the body corporate.

6 *Interpretation, etc*

(1) In this Act –

'complainant' has the meaning given in section 1(2);

'picture' includes a likeness however produced;

'relevant programme' means a programme included in a programme service, within the meaning of the Broadcasting Act 1990; and

'written publication' includes a film, a sound track and any other record in permanent form but does not include an indictment or other document prepared for use in particular legal proceedings.

(2) For the purposes of this Act –

(a) where it is alleged that an offence to which this Act applies has been committed, the fact that any person has consented to an act which, on any prosecution for that offence, would fall to be proved by the prosecution, does not prevent that person from being regarded as a person against whom the alleged offence was committed; and

(b) where a person is accused of an offence of incest or buggery, the other party to the act in question shall be taken to be a person against whom the offence was committed even though he consented to that act.

(2A) For the purpose of this Act, where it is alleged or there is an accusation that an offence of conspiracy or incitement of another to commit an offence mentioned in section 2(1)(a) to (d) has been committed, the person against whom the substantive offence is alleged to have been intended to be committed shall be regarded as the person against whom the conspiracy or incitement is alleged to have been committed. In this subsection, 'the substantive offence' means the offence to which the alleged conspiracy or incitement related.

(3) For the purposes of this Act, a person is accused of an offence if –

(a) an information is laid alleging that he has committed the offence,

(b) he appears before a court charged with the offence,

(c) a court before which he is appearing commits him for trial on a new charge alleging the offence, or

(d) a bill of indictment charging him with the offence is preferred before a court in which he may lawfully be indicted for the offence,

and references in subsection (2A) and in section 3 to an accusation alleging an offence shall be construed accordingly.

(4) Nothing in this Act affects any prohibition or restriction imposed by virtue of any other enactment upon a publication or upon matter included in a relevant programme.

[As amended by the Criminal Justice and Public Order Act 1994, ss44(3), 168(1), Schedule 4, Part II, para 74, Schedule 9, para 52.]

Trade Union and Labour Relations (Consolidation) Act 1992
(1992 c 52)

242 Restriction of offence of conspiracy: England and Wales

(1) Where in pursuance of any such agreement as is mentioned in section 1(1) of the Criminal Law Act 1977 (which provides for the offence of conspiracy) the acts in question in relation to an offence are to be done in contemplation or furtherance of a trade dispute, the offence shall be disregarded for the purposes of that subsection if it is a summary offence which is not punishable with imprisonment.

(2) This section extends to England and Wales only.

Sexual Offences Act 1993
(1993 c 30)

1 Abolition of presumption of sexual incapacity

The presumption of criminal law that a boy under the age of fourteen is incapable of sexual intercourse (whether natural or unnatural) is hereby abolished.

Criminal Justice Act 1993
(1993 c 36)

1 Offences to which this Part applies

(1) This Part applies to two groups of offences –

    (a) any offence mentioned in subsection (2) (a 'Group A offence'); and
    (b) any offence mentioned in subsection (3) (a 'Group B offence').

(2) The Group A offences are –

    (a) an offence under any of the following provisions of the Theft Act 1968 –

        section 1 (theft);
        section 15 (obtaining property by deception);
        section 15A (obtaining a money transfer by deception);
        section 16 (obtaining pecuniary advantage by deception);
        section 17 (false accounting);
        section 19 (false statements by company directors, etc);
        section 20(2) (procuring execution of valuable security by deception);
        section 21 (blackmail);
        section 22 (handling stolen goods);
        section 24A (retaining credits from dishonest sources, etc);

(b) an offence under either of the following provisions of the Theft Act 1978 –

section 1 (obtaining services by deception);
section 2 (avoiding liability by deception);

(c) an offence under any of the following provisions of the Forgery and Counterfeiting Act 1981 –

section 1 (forgery);
section 2 (copying a false instrument);
section 3 (using a false instrument);
section 4 (using a copy of a false instrument);
section 5 (offences which relate to money orders, share certificates, passports, etc);

(d) the common law offence of cheating in relation to the public revenue.

(3) The Group B offences are –

(a) conspiracy to commit a Group A offence;
(b) conspiracy to defraud;
(c) attempting to commit a Group A offence;
(d) incitement to commit a Group A offence.

(4) The Secretary of State may by order amend subsection (2) or (3) by adding or removing any offence. ...

5 Conspiracy, attempt and incitement ...

(3) A person may be guilty of conspiracy to defraud if –

(a) a party to the agreement constituting the conspiracy, or a party's agent, did anything in England and Wales in relation to the agreement before its formation, or
(b) a party to it because a party in England and Wales (by joining it either in person or through an agent), or
(c) a party to it, or a party's agent, did or omitted anything in England and Wales in pursuance of it,

and the conspiracy would be triable in England and Wales but for the fraud which the parties to it had in view not being intended to take place in England and Wales.

(4) A person may be guilty of incitement to commit a Group A offence if the incitement –

(a) takes place in England and Wales; and
(b) would be triable in England and Wales but for what the person charged had in view not being an offence triable in England and Wales.

(5) Subsections (3) and (4) are subject to section 6.

6 Relevance of external law

(1) A person is guilty of an offence triable by virtue of section 5(3), only if the pursuit of the agreed course of conduct would at some stage involve –

(a) an act or omission by one or more of the parties, or

(b) the happening of some other event,

constituting an offence under the law in force where the act, omission or other event was intended to take place.

(2) A person is guilty of an offence triable by virtue of section 1A of the Criminal Attempts Act 1981, or by virtue of section 5(4), only if what he had in view would involve the commission of an offence under the law in force where the whole or any part of it was intended to take place.

(3) Conduct punishable under the law in force in any place is an offence under that law for the purposes of this section, however it is described in that law. ...

[As amended by the Theft (Amendment) Act 1996, s3; Criminal Justice (Terrorism and Conspiracy) Act 1998, s9, Schedule 1, Pt II, para 7, Schedule 2, Pt II.]

Criminal Justice and Public Order Act 1994
(1994 c 33)

61 *Power to remove trespassers on land*

(1) If the senior police officer present at the scene reasonably believes that two or more persons are trespassing on land and are present there with the common purpose of residing there for any period, that reasonable steps have been taken by or on behalf of the occupier to ask them to leave and –

(a) that any of those persons has caused damage to the land or to property on the land or used threatening, abusive or insulting words or behaviour towards the occupier, a member of his family or an employee or agent of his, or
(b) that those persons have between them six or more vehicles on the land,

he may direct those persons, or any of them, to leave the land and to remove any vehicles or other property they have with them on the land.

(2) Where the persons in question are reasonably believed by the senior police officer to be persons who were not originally trespassers but have become trespassers on the land, the officer must reasonably believe that the other conditions specified in subsection (1) are satisfied after those persons became trespassers before he can exercise the power conferred by that subsection.

(3) A direction under subsection (1) above, if not communicated to the persons referred to in subsection (1) by the police officer giving the direction, may be communicated to them by any constable at the scene.

(4) If a person knowing that a direction under subsection (1) above has been given which applies to him –

(a) fails to leave the land as soon as reasonably practicable, or
(b) having left again enters the land as a trespasser within the period of three months beginning with the day on which the direction was given,

he commits an offence and is liable on summary conviction to imprisonment for a term not exceeding three months or a fine not exceeding level 4 on the standard scale, or both.

(5) A constable in uniform who reasonably suspects that a person is committing an offence under this section may arrest him without a warrant.

(6) In proceedings for an offence under this section it is a defence for the accused to show –

(a) that he was not trespassing on the land, or

(b) that he had a reasonable excuse for failing to leave the land as soon as reasonably practicable or, as the case may be, for again entering the land as a trespasser.

(7) In its application in England and Wales to common land this section has effect as if in the preceding subsections of it –

(a) references to trespassing or trespassers were references to acts and persons doing acts which constitute either a trespass as against the occupier or an infringement of the commoners' rights; and

(b) references to 'the occupier' included the commoners or any of them or, in the case of common land to which the public has access, the local authority as well as any commoner.

(8) Subsection (7) above does not –

(a) require action by more than one occupier; or

(b) constitute persons trespassers as against any commoner or the local authority if they are permitted to be there by the other occupier.

(9) In this section –

'common land' means common land as defined in section 22 of the Commons Registration Act 1965;

'commoner' means a person with rights of common as defined in section 22 of the Commons Registration Act 1965;

'land' does not include –

(a) buildings other than –

(i) agricultural buildings within the meaning of, in England and Wales, paragraphs 3 to 8 of Schedule 5 to the Local Government Finance Act 1988 or, in Scotland, section 7(2) of the Valuation and Rating (Scotland) Act 1956, or

(ii) scheduled monuments within the meaning of the Ancient Monuments and Archaeological Areas Act 1979;

(b) land forming part of –

(i) a highway unless it falls within the classifications in section 54 of the Wildlife and Countryside Act 1981 (footpath, bridleway or byway open to all traffic or road used as a public path) or is a cycle track under the Highways Act 1980 or the Cycle Tracks Act 1984; ...

'the local authority', in relation to common land, means any local authority which has powers in relation to the land under section 9 of the Commons Registration Act 1965;

'occupier' (and in subsection (8) 'the other occupier') means –

(a) in England and Wales, the person entitled to possession of the land by virtue of an estate or interest held by him; ...

'property', in relation to damage to property on land, means –

(a) in England and Wales, property within the meaning of section 10(1) of the Criminal Damage Act 1971; ...

and 'damage' includes the deposit of any substance capable of polluting the land;

'trespass' means, in the application of this section –

(a) in England and Wales, subject to the extensions effected by subsection (7) above, trespass as against the occupier of the land;

'trespassing' and 'trespasser' shall be construed accordingly; ...

'vehicle' includes –

(a) any vehicle, whether or not it is in a fit state for use on roads, and includes any chassis or body, with or without wheels, appearing to have formed part of such a vehicle, and any load carried by, and anything attached to, such a vehicle; and

(b) a caravan as defined in section 29(1) of the Caravan Sites and Control of Development Act 1960;

and a person may be regarded for the purposes of this section as having a purpose of residing in a place notwithstanding that he has a home elsewhere.

62 Supplementary powers of seizure

(1) If a direction has been given under section 61 and a constable reasonably suspects that any person to whom the direction applies has, without reasonable excuse –

(a) failed to remove any vehicle on the land which appears to the constable to belong to him or to be in his possession or under his control; or

(b) entered the land as a trespasser with a vehicle within the period of three months beginning with the day on which the direction was given,

the constable may seize and remove that vehicle.

(2) In this section, 'trespasser' and 'vehicle' have the same meaning as in section 61.

63 Powers to remove persons attending or preparing for a rave

(1) This section applies to a gathering on land in the open air of 100 or more persons (whether or not trespassers) at which amplified music is played during the night (with or without intermissions) and is such as, by reason of its loudness and duration and the time at which it is played, is likely to cause serious distress to the inhabitants of the locality; and for this purpose

(a) such a gathering continues during intermissions in the music and, where the gathering extends over several days, throughout the period during which amplified music is played at night (with or without intermissions); and

(b) 'music' includes sounds wholly or predominantly characterised by the emission of a succession of repetitive beats.

(2) If, as respects any land in the open air, a police officer of at least the rank of superintendent reasonably believes that –

(a) two or more persons are making preparations for the holding there of a gathering to which this section applies,

(b) ten or more persons are waiting for such a gathering to begin there, or

(c) ten or more persons are attending such a gathering which is in progress,

he may give a direction that those persons and any other persons who come to prepare or wait for or to attend the gathering are to leave the land and remove any vehicles or other property which they have with them on the land.

(3) A direction under subsection (2) above, if not communicated to the persons referred to in subsection (2) by the police officer giving the direction, may be communicated to them by any constable at the scene.

(4) Persons shall be treated as having had a direction under subsection (2) above communicated to them if reasonable steps have been taken to bring it to their attention.

(5) A direction under subsection (2) above does not apply to an exempt person.

(6) If a person knowing that a direction has been given which applies to him –

(a) fails to leave the land as soon as reasonably practicable, or

(b) having left again enters the land within the period of 7 days beginning with the day on which the direction was given,

he commits an offence and is liable on summary conviction to imprisonment for a term not exceeding three months or a fine not exceeding level 4 on the standard scale, or both.

(7) In proceedings for an offence under this section it is a defence for the accused to show that he had a reasonable excuse for failing to leave the land as soon as reasonably practicable or, as the case may be, for again entering the land.

(8) A constable in uniform who reasonably suspects that a person is committing an offence under this section may arrest him without a warrant.

(9) This section does not apply –

(a) in England and Wales, to a gathering licensed by an entertainment licence; ...

(10) In this section –

'entertainment licence' means a licence granted by a local authority under –

(a) Schedule 12 to the London Government Act 1963;

(b) section 3 of the Private Places of Entertainment (Licensing) Act 1967; or

(c) Schedule 1 to the Local Government (Miscellaneous Provisions) Act 1982;

'exempt person', in relation to land (or any gathering on land), means the occupier, any member of his family and any employee or agent of his and any person whose home is situated on the land;

'land in the open air' includes a place partly open to the air;

'local authority' means –

(a) in Greater London, a London borough council or the Common Council of the City of London;

(b) in England outside Greater London, a district council or the council of the Isles of Scilly;

(c) in Wales, a county council or county borough council; and

'occupier', 'trespasser' and 'vehicle' have the same meaning as in section 61. ...

64 Supplementary powers of entry and seizure

(1) If a police officer of at least the rank of superintendant reasonably believes that circumstances exist in relation to any land which would justify the giving of a direction under section 63 in relation to a gathering to which that section applies he may authorise any constable to enter the land for any of the purposes specified in subsection (2) below:

(2) Those purposes are –

(a) to ascertain whether such circumstances exist; and

(b) to exercise any power conferred on a constable by section 63 or subsection (4) below.

(3) A constable who is so authorised to enter land for any purpose may enter the land without a warrant.

(4) If a direction has been given under section 63 and a constable reasonably suspects that any person to whom the direction applies has, without reasonable excuse –

(a) failed to remove any vehicle or sound equipment on the land which appears to the constable to belong to him or to be in his possession or under his control; or

(b) entered the land as a trespasser with a vehicle or sound equipment within the period of 7 days beginning with the day on which the direction was given,

the constable may seize and remove that vehicle or sound equipment.

(5) Subsection (4) above does not authorise the seizure of any vehicle or sound equipment of an exempt person.

(6) In this section –

'exempt person' has the same meaning as in section 63;

'sound equipment' means equipment designed or adapted for amplifying music and any equipment suitable for use in connection with such equipment, and 'music' has the same meaning as in section 63; and

'vehicle' has the same meaning as in section 61.

65 Raves: power to stop persons from proceeding

(1) If a constable in uniform reasonably believes that a person is on his way to a gathering to which section 63 applies in relation to which a direction under section 63(2) is in force, he may, subject to subsections (2) and (3) below –

(a) stop that person, and

(b) direct him not to proceed in the direction of the gathering.

(2) The power conferred by subsection (1) above may only be exercised at a place within 5 miles of the boundary of the site of the gathering.

(3) No direction may be given under subsection (1) above to an exempt person.

(4) If a person knowing that a direction under subsection (1) above has been given to him fails to comply with that direction, he commits an offence and is liable on summary conviction to a fine not exceeding level 3 on the standard scale.

(5) A constable in uniform who reasonably suspects that a person is committing an offence under this section may arrest him without a warrant.

(6) In this section 'exempt person' has the same meaning as in section 63.

66 *Power of court to forfeit sound equipment*

(1) Where a person is convicted of an offence under section 63 in relation to a gathering to which that section applies and the court is satisfied that any sound equipment which has been seized from him under section 64(4), or which was in his possession or under his control at the relevant time, has been used at the gathering the court may make an order for forfeiture under this subsection in respect of that property.

(2) The court may make an order under subsection (1) above whether or not it also deals with the offender in respect of the offence in any other way and without regard to any restrictions on forfeiture in any enactment.

(3) In considering whether to make an order under subsection (1) above in respect of any property a court shall have regard –

   (a) to the value of the property; and
   (b) to the likely financial and other effects on the offender of the making of the order (taken together with any other order that the court contemplates making).

(4) An order under subsection (1) above shall operate to deprive the offender of his rights, if any, in the property to which it relates, and the property shall (if not already in their possession) be taken into the possession of the police.

(5) Except in a case to which subsection (6) below applies, where any property has been forfeited under subsection (1) above, a magistrates' court may, on application by a claimant of the property, other than the offender from whom it was forfeited under subsection (1) above, make an order for delivery of the property to the applicant if it appears to the court that he is the owner of the property.

(6) In a case where forfeiture under subsection (1) above has been by order of a Scottish court, a claimant such as is mentioned in subsection (5) above may, in such manner as may be prescribed by act of adjournal, apply to that court for an order for the return of the property in question.

(7) No application shall be made under subsection (5), or by virtue of subsection (6), above by any claimant of the property after the expiration of 6 months from the date on which an order under subsection (1) above was made in respect of the property.

(8) No such application shall succeed unless the claimant satisfies the court either that he had not consented to the offender having possession of the property or that he did not know, and had no reason to suspect, that the property was likely to be used at a gathering to which section 63 applies.

(9) An order under subsection (5), or by virtue of subsection (6), above shall not affect the right of any person to take, within the period of 6 months from the date of an order under subsection (5), or as the case may be by virtue of subsection (6), above, proceedings for the recovery of the property from the person in possession of it in pursuance of the order, but on the expiration of that period the right shall cease.

(10) The Secretary of State may make regulations for the disposal of property, and for the application of the proceeds of sale of property, forfeited under subsection (1) above where no application by a claimant of the property under subsection (5), or by virtue of subsection (6), above has been made within the period specified in subsection (7) above or no such application has succeeded.

(11) The regulations may also provide for the investment of money and for the audit of accounts.

(12) The power to make regulations under subsection (10) above shall be exercisable by statutory instrument which shall be subject to annulment in pursuance of a resolution of either House of Parliament.

(13) In this section –

'relevant time', in relation to a person –

(a) convicted in England and Wales of an offence under section 63, means the time of his arrest for the offence or of the issue of a summons in respect of it; ...

'sound equipment' has the same meaning as in section 64.

67 *Retention and charges for seized property*

(1) Any vehicles which have been seized and removed by a constable under section 62(1) or 64(4) may be retained in accordance with regulations made by the Secretary of State under subsection (3) below.

(2) Any sound equipment which has been seized and removed by a constable under section 64(4) may be retained until the conclusion of proceedings against the person from whom it was seized for an offence under section 63.

(3) The Secretary of State may make regulations –

(a) regulating the retention and safe keeping and the disposal and the destruction in prescribed circumstances of vehicles; and
(b) prescribing charges in respect of the removal, retention, disposal and destruction of vehicles.

(4) Any authority shall be entitled to recover from a person from whom a vehicle has been seized such charges as may be prescribed in respect of the removal, retention, disposal and destruction of the vehicle by the authority.

(5) Regulations under subsection (3) above may make different provisions for different classes of vehicles or for different circumstances.

(6) Any charges under subsection (4) above shall be recoverable as a simple contract debt.

(7) Any authority having custody of vehicles under regulations under subsection (3) above shall be entitled to retain custody until any charges under subsection (4) are paid.

(8) The power to make regulations under subsection (3) above shall be exercisable by statutory instrument which shall be subject to annulment in pursuance of a resolution of either House of Parliament.

(9) In this section –

'conclusion of proceedings' against a person means –

(a) his being sentenced or otherwise dealt with for the offence or his acquittal;
(b) the discontinuance of the proceedings; or
(c) the decision not to prosecute him,
whichever is the earlier;

'sound equipment' has the same meaning as in section 64; and
'vehicle' has the same meaning as in section 61.

68 Offence of aggravated trespass

(1) A person commits the offence of aggravated trespass if he trespasses on land in the open air and, in relation to any lawful activity which persons are engaging in or are about to engage in on that or adjoining land in the open air, does there anything which is intended by him to have the effect –

(a) of intimidating those persons or any of them so as to deter them or any of them from engaging in the activity,
(b) of obstructing that activity, or
(c) of disrupting that activity.

(2) Activity on any occasion on the part of a person or persons on land is 'lawful' for the purposes of this section if he or they may engage in the activity on the land on that occasion without committing an offence or trespassing on the land.

(3) A person guilty of an offence under this section is liable on summary conviction to imprisonment for a term not exceeding three months or a fine not exceeding level 4 on the standard scale, or both.

(4) A constable in uniform who reasonably suspects that a person is committing an offence under this section may arrest him without a warrant.

(5) In this section 'land' does not include –

(a) the highways and roads excluded from the application of section 61 by paragraph (b) of the definition of 'land' in subsection (9) of that section; or
(b) a road within the meaning of the Roads (Northern Ireland) Order 1993.

69 Powers to remove persons committing or participating in aggravated trespass

(1) If the senior police officer present at the scene reasonably believes –

(a) that a person is committing, has committed or intends to commit the offence of aggravated trespass on land in the open air; or

(b) that two or more persons are trespassing on land in the open air and are present there with the common purpose of intimidating persons so as to deter them from engaging in a lawful activity or of obstructing or disrupting a lawful activity,

he may direct that person or (as the case may be) those persons (or any of them) to leave the land.

(2) A direction under subsection (1) above, if not communicated to the persons referred to in subsection (1) by the police officer giving the direction, may be communicated to them by any constable at the scene.

(3) If a person knowing that a direction under subsection (1) above has been given which applies to him –

(a) fails to leave the land as soon as practicable, or

(b) having left again enters the land as a trespasser within the period of three months beginning with the day on which the direction was given,

he commits an offence and is liable on summary conviction to imprisonment for a term not exceeding three months or a fine not exceeding level 4 on the standard scale, or both.

(4) In proceedings for an offence under subsection (3) it is a defence for the accused to show –

(a) that he was not trespassing on the land, or

(b) that he had a reasonable excuse for failing to leave the land as soon as practicable or, as the case may be, for again entering the land as a trespasser.

(5) A constable in uniform who reasonably suspects that a person is committing an offence under this section may arrest him without a warrant.

(6) In this section 'lawful activity' and 'land' have the same meaning as in section 68.

75 Interim possession orders: false or misleading statements

(1) A person commits an offence if, for the purpose of obtaining an interim possession order, he –

(a) makes a statement which he knows to be false or misleading in a material particular; or

(b) recklessly makes a statement which is false or misleading in a material particular.

(2) A person commits an offence if, for the purpose of resisting the making of an interim possession order, he –

(a) makes a statement which he knows to be false or misleading in a material particular; or

(b) recklessly makes a statement which is false or misleading in a material particular.

(3) A person guilty of an offence under this section shall be liable –

(a) on conviction on indictment, to imprisonment for a term not exceeding two years or a fine or both;

(b) on summary conviction, to imprisonment for a term not exceeding six months or a fine not exceeding the statutory maximum or both.

(4) In this section –

'interim possession order' means an interim possession order (so entitled) made under rules of court for the bringing of summary proceedings for possession of premises which are occupies by trespassers;

'premises' has the same meaning as in Part II of the Criminal Law Act 1977 (offences relating to entering and remaining on property); and

'statement', in relation to an interim possession order, means any statement, in writing or oral and whether as to fact or belief, made in or for the purposes of the proceedings.

76 *Interim possession orders: trespassing during currency of order*

(1) This section applies where an interim possession order has been made in respect of any premises and served in accordance with rules of court; and references to 'the order' and 'the premises' shall be construed accordingly.

(2) Subject to subsection (3), a person who is present on the premises as a trespasser at any time during the currency of the order commits an offence.

(3) No offence under subsection (2) is committed by a person if –

(a) he leaves the premises within 24 hours of the time of service of the order and does not return; or

(b) a copy of the order was not fixed to the premises in accordance with rules of court.

(4) A person who was in occupation of the premises at the time of service of the order but leaves them commits an offence if he re-enters the premises as a trespasser or attempts to do so after the expiry of the order but within the period of one year beginning with the day on which it was served.

(5) A person guilty of an offence under this section shall be liable on summary conviction to imprisonment for a term not exceeding six months or a fine not exceeding level 5 on the standard scale or both.

(6) A person who is in occupation of the premises at the time of service of the order shall be treated for the purposes of this section as being present as a trespasser.

(7) A constable in uniform may arrest without a warrant anyone who is, or whom he reasonably suspects to be, guilty of an offence under this section.

(8) In this section –

'interim possession order' has the same meaning as in section 75 above and 'rules of court' is to be construed accordingly; and

'premises' has the same meaning as in that section, that is to say, the same meaning as in Part II of the Criminal Law Act 1977 (offences relating to entering and remaining on property).

77 Power of local authority to direct unauthorised campers to leave land

(1) If it appears to a local authority that persons are for the time being residing in a vehicle or vehicles within the authority's area –

(a) on any land forming part of a highway;

(b) on any other unoccupied land; or

(c) on any occupied land without the consent of the occupier,

the authority may give a direction that those persons and any others with them are to leave the land and remove the vehicle or vehicles and any other property they have with them on the land.

(2) Notice of a direction under subsection (1) must be served on the persons to whom the direction applies, but it shall be sufficient for this purpose for the direction to specify the land and (except where the direction applies to only one person) to be addressed to all occupants of the vehicles on the land, without naming them.

(3) If a person knowing that a direction under subsection (1) above has been given which applies to him –

(a) fails, as soon as practicable, to leave the land or remove from the land any vehicle or other property which is the subject of the direction, or

(b) having removed any such vehicle or property again enters the land with a vehicle within the period of three months beginning with the day on which the direction was given,

he commits an offence and is liable on summary conviction to a fine not exceeding level 3 on the standard scale.

(4) A direction under subsection (1) operates to require persons who re-enter the land within the said period with vehicles or other property to leave and remove the vehicles or other property as it operates in relation to the persons and vehicles or other property on the land when the direction was given.

(5) In proceedings for an offence under this section it is a defence for the accused to show that this failure to leave or to remove the vehicle or other property as soon as practicable or his re-entry with a vehicle was due to illness, mechanical breakdown or other immediate emergency.

(6) In this section –

'land' means land in the open air;

'local authority' means –

(a) in Greater London, a London borough or the Common Council of the City of London;

(b) in England outside Greater London, a county council, a district council or the Council of the Isles of Scilly;

(c) in Wales, a county council or a county borough council;

'occupier' means the person entitled to possession of the land by virtue of an estate or interest held by him;

'vehicle' includes –

    (a) any vehicle, whether or not it is in a fit state for use on roads, and includes any body, with or without wheels, appearing to have formed part of such a vehicle, and any load carried by, and anything attached to, such a vehicle; and

    (b) a caravan as defined in section 19(1) of the Caravan Sites and Control of Development Act 1960;

and a person may be regarded for the purposes of this section as residing on any land notwithstanding that he has a home elsewhere.

(7) Until 1 April 1996, in this section 'local authority' means, in Wales, a county council or a district council.

78 Orders for removal of persons and their vehicles unlawfully on land

(1) A magistrates' court may, on a complaint made by a local authority, if satisfied that persons and vehicles in which they are residing are present on land within that authority's area in contravention of a direction given under section 77, make an order requiring the removal of any vehicle or other property which is so present on the land and any person residing in it.

(2) An order under this section may authorise the local authority to take such steps as are reasonably necessary to ensure that the order is complied with and, in particular, may authorise the authority, by its officers and servants –

    (a) to enter upon the land specified in the order; and

    (b) to take, in relation to any vehicle or property to be removed in pursuance of the order, such steps for securing entry and rendering it suitable for removal as may be so specified.

(3) The local authority shall not enter upon any occupied land unless they have given to the owner and occupier at least 24 hours notice of their intention to do so, or unless after reasonable inquiries they are unable to ascertain their names and addresses.

(4) A person who wilfully obstructs any person in the exercise of any power conferred on him by an order under this section commits an offence and is liable on summary conviction to a fine not exceeding level 3 on the standard scale.

(5) Where a complaint is made under this section, a summons issued by the court requiring the person or persons to whom it is directed to appear before the court to answer to the complaint may be directed –

    (a) to the occupant of a particular vehicle on the land in question; or

    (b) to all occupants of vehicles on the land in question, without naming him or them.

(6) Section 55(2) of the Magistrates' Courts Act 1980 (warrant for arrest of defendant failing to appear) does not apply to proceedings on a complaint made under this section.

(7) Section 77(6) of this Act applies also for the interpretation of this section.

79 *Provisions as to directions under s77 and orders under s78*

(1) The following provisions apply in relation to the service of notice of a direction under section 77 and of a summons under section 78, referred to in those provisions as a 'relevant document'.

(2) Where it is impracticable to serve a relevant document on a person named in it, the document shall be treated as duly served on him if a copy of it is fixed in a prominent place to the vehicle concerned; and where a relevant document is directed to the unnamed occupants of vehicles, it shall be treated as duly served on those occupants if a copy of it is fixed in a prominent place to every vehicle on the land in question at the time when service is thus effected.

(3) A local authority shall take such steps as may be reasonably practicable to secure that a copy of any relevant document is displayed on the land in question (otherwise than by being fixed to a vehicle) in a manner designed to ensure that it is likely to be seen by any person camping on the land.

(4) Notice of any relevant document shall be given by the local authority to the owner of the land in question and to any occupier of that land unless, after reasonable inquiries, the authority is unable to ascertain the name and address of the owner or occupier; and the owner of any such land and any occupier of such land shall be entitled to appear and to be heard in the proceedings.

(5) Section 77(6) applies also for the interpretation of this section.

166 *Sale of tickets by unauthorised persons*

(1) It is an offence for an unauthorised person to sell, or offer or expose for sale, a ticket for a designated football match in any public place or place to which the public has access or, in the course of a trade or business, in any other place.

(2) For this purpose –

(a) a person is 'unauthorised' unless he is authorised in writing to sell tickets for the match by the home club or by the organisers of the match;
(b) a 'ticket' means anything which purports to be a ticket; and
(c) a 'designated football match' means a football match of a description, or a particular football match, for the time being designated for the purposes of Part I or Part II of the Football Spectators Act 1989.

(3) A person guilty of an offence under this section is liable on summary conviction to a fine not exceeding level 5 on the standard scale. ...

[As amended by the Football (Offences and Disorder) Act 1999, s10.]

Drug Trafficking Act 1994
(1994 c 37)

1 Meaning of 'drug trafficking' and 'drug trafficking offence'

(1) In this Act 'drug trafficking' means, subject to subsection (2) below, doing or being concerned in any of the following, whether in England and Wales or elsewhere –

(a) producing or supplying a controlled drug where the production or supply contravenes section 4(1) of the Misuse of Drugs Act 1971 or a corresponding law;

(b) transporting or storing a controlled drug where possession of the drug contravenes section 5(1) of that Act or a corresponding law;

(c) importing or exporting a controlled drug where the importation or exportation is prohibited by section 3(1) of that Act or a corresponding law;

(d) manufacturing or supplying a scheduled substance within the meaning of section 12 of the Criminal Justice (International Co-operation) Act 1990 where the manufacture or supply is an offence under that section or would be such an offence if it took place in England and Wales;

(e) using any ship for illicit traffic in controlled drugs in circumstances which amount to the commission of an offence under section 19 of that Act;

(f) conduct which is an offence under section 49 of this Act or which would be such an offence if it took place in England and Wales;

(g) acquiring, having possession of or using property in circumstances which amount to the commission of an offence under section 51 of this Act or which would amount to such an offence if it took place in England and Wales.

(2) 'Drug trafficking' also includes a person doing the following, whether in England and Wales or elsewhere, that is to say, entering into or being otherwise concerned in an arrangement whereby –

(a) the retention or control by or on behalf of another person of the other person's proceeds of drug trafficking is facilitated; or

(b) the proceeds of drug trafficking by another person are used to secure that funds are placed at the other person's disposal or are used for the other person's benefit to acquire property by way of investment.

(3) In this Act 'drug trafficking offence' means any of the following –

(a) an offence under section 4(2) or (3) or 5(3) of the Misuse of Drugs Act 1971 (production, supply and possession for supply of controlled drugs);

(b) an offence under section 20 of that Act (assisting in or inducing commission outside United Kingdom of offence punishable under a corresponding law);

(c) an offence under –

(i) section 50(2) or (3) of the Customs and Excise Management Act 1979 (improper importation),

(ii) section 68(2) of that Act (exportation), or

(iii) section 170 of that Act (fraudulent evasion),

in connection with a prohibition or restriction on importation or exportation having effect by virtue of section 3 of the Misuse of Drugs Act 1971;

(d) an offence under section 12 of the Criminal Justice (International Co-operation) Act 1990 (manufacture or supply of substance specified in Schedule 2 to that Act);

(e) an offence under section 19 of that Act (using ship for illicit traffic in controlled drugs);

(f) an offence under section 49, 50 or 51 of this Act or section 14 of the Criminal Justice (International Co-operation) Act 1990 (which makes, in relation to Scotland and Northern Ireland, provision corresponding to section 49 of this Act);

(g) an offence under section 1 of the Criminal Law Act 1977 of conspiracy to commit any of the offences in paragraphs (a) to (f) above;

(h) an offence under section 1 of the Criminal Attempts Act 1981 of attempting to commit any of those offences; and

(i) an offence of inciting another person to commit any of those offences, whether under section 19 of the Misuse of Drugs Act 1971 or at common law;

and includes aiding, abetting, counselling or procuring the commission of any of the offences in paragraphs (a) to (f) above.

(4) In this section 'corresponding law' has the same meaning as in the Misuse of Drugs Act 1971. ...

49 Concealing or transferring proceeds of drug trafficking

(1) A person is guilty of an offence if he –

(a) conceals or disguises any property which is, or in whole or in part directly or indirectly represents, his proceeds of drug trafficking, or

(b) converts or transfers that property or removes it from the jurisdiction,

for the purpose of avoiding prosecution for a drug trafficking offence or the making or enforcement in his case of a confiscation order.

(2) A person is guilty of an offence, if, knowing or having reasonable grounds to suspect that any property is, or in whole or in part directly or indirectly represents, another person's proceeds of drug trafficking, he –

(a) conceals or disguises that property, or

(b) converts or transfers that property or removes it from the jurisdiction,

for the purpose of assisting any person to avoid prosecution for a drug trafficking offence or the making or enforcement of a confiscation order.

(3) In subsections (1)(a) and (2)(a) above the references to concealing or disguising any property include references to concealing or disguising its nature, source, location, disposition, movement or ownership or any rights with respect to it.

50 Assisting another person to retain the benefit of drug trafficking

(1) Subject to subsection (3) below, a person is guilty of an offence if he enters into or is otherwise concerned in an arrangement whereby –

(a) the retention or control by or on behalf of another person (call him 'A') of A's proceeds of drug trafficking is facilitated (whether by concealment, removal from the jurisdiction, transfer to nominees or otherwise), or
(b) A's proceeds of drug trafficking –

(i) are used to secure that funds are placed at A's disposal, or
(ii) are used for A's benefit to acquire property by way of investment,

and he knows or suspects that A is a person who carries on or has carried on drug trafficking or has benefited from drug trafficking.

(2) In this section, references to any person's proceeds of drug trafficking include a reference to any property which in whole or in part directly or indirectly represented in his hands his proceeds of drug trafficking.

(3) Where a person discloses to a constable a suspicion or belief that any funds or investments are derived from or used in connection with drug trafficking, or discloses to a constable any matter on which such a suspicion or belief is based –

(a) the disclosure shall not be treated as a breach of any restriction upon the disclosure of information imposed by statute or otherwise; and
(b) if he does any act in contravention of subsection (1) above and the disclosure relates to the arrangement concerned, he does not commit an offence under this section if –

(i) the disclosure is made before he does the act concerned and the act is done with the consent of the constable; or
(ii) the disclosure is made after he does the act, but is made on his initiative and as soon as it is reasonable for him to make it.

(4) In proceedings against a person for an offence under this section, it is a defence to prove –

(a) that he did not know or suspect that the arrangement related to any person's proceeds of drug trafficking;
(b) that he did not know or suspect that by the arrangement the retention or control by or on behalf of A of any property was facilitated or, as the case may be, that by the arrangement any property was used as mentioned in subsection (1)(b) above; or
(c) that –

(i) he intended to disclose to a constable such a suspicion, belief or matter as is mentioned in subsection (3) above in relation to the arrangement, but
(ii) there is reasonable excuse for his failure to make any such disclosure in the manner mentioned in paragraph (b)(i) or (ii) of that subsection.

(5) In the case of a person who was in employment at the time in question, subsections (3) and (4) above shall have effect in relation to disclosures, and intended disclosures, to the appropriate person in accordance with the procedure established by his employer for the

making of such disclosures as they have effect in relation to disclosures, and intended disclosures, to a constable.

51 Acquisition, possession or use of proceeds of drug trafficking

(1) A person is guilty of an offence if, knowing that any property is, or in whole or in part directly or indirectly represents, another person's proceeds of drug trafficking, he acquires or uses that property or has possession of it.

(2) It is a defence to a charge of committing an offence under this section that the person charged acquired or used the property or had possession of it for adequate consideration.

(3) For the purposes of subsection (2) above –

(a) a person acquires property for inadequate consideration if the value of the consideration is significantly less than the value of the property; and

(b) a person uses or has possession of property for inadequate consideration if the value of the consideration is significantly less than the value of his use or possession of the property.

(4) The provision for any person of services or goods which are of assistance to him in drug trafficking shall not be treated as consideration for the purposes of subsection (2) above.

(5) Where a person discloses to a constable a suspicion or belief that any property is, or in whole or in part directly or indirectly represents, another person's proceeds of drug trafficking, or discloses to a constable any matter on which such a suspicion or belief is based –

(a) the disclosure shall not be treated as a breach of any restriction upon the disclosure of information imposed by statute or otherwise; and

(b) if he does any act in relation to the property in contravention of subsection (1) above, he does not commit an offence under this section if –

(i) the disclosure is made before he does the act concerned and the act is done with the consent of the constable; or

(ii) the disclosure is made after he does the act, but is made on his initiative and as soon as it is reasonable for him to make it.

(6) For the purposes of this section, having possession of any property shall be taken to be doing an act in relation to it.

(7) In proceedings against a person for an offence under this section, it is a defence to prove that –

(a) he intended to disclose to a constable such a suspicion, belief or matter as is mentioned in subsection (5) above, but

(b) there is reasonable excuse for his failure to make any such disclosure in the manner mentioned in paragraph (b)(i) or (ii) of that subsection.

(8) In the case of a person who was in employment at the time in question, subsections (5) and (7) above shall have effect in relation to disclosures, and intended disclosures, to the appropriate person in accordance with the procedure established by his employer for the

making of such disclosures as they have effect in relation to disclosures, and intended disclosures, to a constable.

(9) No constable or other person shall be guilty of an offence under this section in respect of anything done by him in the course of acting in connection with the enforcement, or intended enforcement, of any provision of this Act or of any other enactment relating to drug trafficking or the proceeds of drug trafficking.

52 *Failure to disclose knowledge or suspicion of money laundering*

(1) A person is guilty of an offence if –

(a) he knows or suspects that another person is engaged in drug money laundering,
(b) the information, or other matter, on which that knowledge or suspicion is based came to his attention in the course of his trade, profession, business or employment, and
(c) he does not disclose the information or other matter to a constable as soon as is reasonably practicable after it comes to his attention.

(2) Subsection (1) above does not make it an offence for a professional legal adviser to fail to disclose any information or other matter which has come to him in privileged circumstances.

(3) It is a defence to a charge of committing an offence under this section that the person charged had a reasonable excuse for not disclosing the information or other matter in question.

(4) Where a person discloses to a constable –

(a) his suspicion or belief that another person is engaged in drug money laundering, or
(b) any information or other matter on which that suspicion or belief is based,

the disclosure shall not be treated as a breach of any restriction imposed by statute or otherwise.

(5) Without prejudice to subsection (3) or (4) above, in the case of a person who was in employment at the time in question, it is a defence to a charge of committing an offence under this section that he disclosed the information or other matter in question to the appropriate person in accordance with the procedure established by his employer for the making of such disclosures.

(6) A disclosure to which subsection (5) above applies shall not be treated as a breach of any restriction imposed by statute or otherwise.

(7) In this section 'drug money laundering' means doing any act –

(a) which constitutes an offence under sections 49, 50 or 51 of this Act; or
(b) in the case of an act done otherwise than in England and Wales, which would constitute such an offence if done in England and Wales;

and for the purposes of this subsection, having possession of any property shall be taken to be doing an act in relation to it.

(8) For the purposes of this section, any information or other matter comes to a professional legal adviser in privileged circumstances if it is communicated, or given, to him –

(a) by, or by a representative of, a client of his in connection with the giving by the adviser of legal advice to the client;

(b) by, or by a representative of, a person seeking legal advice from the adviser; or

(c) by any person –

(i) in contemplation of, or in connection with, legal proceedings; and

(ii) for the purpose of those proceedings.

(9) No information or other matter shall be treated as coming to a professional legal adviser in privileged circumstances if it is communicated or given with a view to furthering any criminal purpose.

53 Tipping-off

(1) A person is guilty of an offence if –

(a) he knows or suspects that a constable is acting, or is proposing to act, in connection with an investigation which is being, or is about to be, conducted into drug money laundering, and

(b) he discloses to any other person information or any other matter which is likely to prejudice that investigation or proposed investigation.

(2) A person is guilty of an offence if –

(a) he knows or suspects that a disclosure has been made to a constable under section 50, 51 or 52 of that Act ('the disclosure'), and

(b) he discloses to any other person information or any other matter which is likely to prejudice any investigation which might be conducted following the disclosure.

(3) A person is guilty of an offence if –

(a) he knows or suspects that a disclosure of a kind mentioned in sections 50(5), 51(8) or 52(5) of this Act ('the disclosure') has been made, and

(b) he discloses to any person information or any other matter which is likely to prejudice any investigation which might be conducted following the disclosure.

(4) Nothing in subsections (1) to (3) above makes it an offence for a professional legal adviser to disclose any information or other matter –

(a) to, or to a representative of, a client of his in connection with the giving by the adviser of legal advice to the client; or

(b) to any person –

(i) in contemplation of, or in connection with, legal proceedings; and

(ii) for the purpose of those proceedings.

(5) Subsection (4) above does not apply in relation to any information or other matter which is disclosed with a view to furthering any criminal purpose.

(6) In proceedings against a person for an offence under subsection (1), (2) or (3) above, it is

a defence to prove that he did not know or suspect that the disclosure was likely to be prejudicial in the way mentioned in that subsection.

(7) No constable or other person shall be guilty of an offence under this section in respect of anything done by him in the course of acting in connection with the enforcement, or intended enforcement, of any provision of this Act or of any other enactment relating to drug trafficking or the proceeds of drug trafficking.

(8) In this section 'drug money laundering' has the same meaning as in section 52 of this Act.

54 Penalties

(1) A person guilty of an offence under section 49, 50 or 51 of this Act shall be liable –

(a) on summary conviction, to imprisonment for a term not exceeding six months or to a fine not exceeding the statutory maximum or to both; and
(b) on conviction on indictment, to imprisonment for a term not exceeding fourteen years or to a fine or to both.

(2) A person guilty of an offence under section 52 or 53 of this Act shall be liable –

(a) on summary conviction, to imprisonment for a term not exceeding six months or to a fine not exceeding the statutory maximum or to both; or
(b) on conviction on indictment, to imprisonment for a term not exceeding five years or to a fine or to both.

Criminal Appeal Act 1995
(1995 c 35)
Part II
The Criminal Cases Review Commission

8 The Commission

(1) There shall be a body corporate to be known as the Criminal Cases Review Commission.
...

(3) The Commission shall consist of not fewer than eleven members.

(4) The members of the Commission shall be appointed by Her Majesty on the recommendation of the Prime Minister. ...

(7) Schedule 1 (further provisions with respect to the Commission) shall have effect

9 Cases dealt with on indictment in England and Wales

(1) Where a person has been convicted of an offence on indictment in England and Wales, the Commission –

(a) may at any time refer the conviction to the Court of Appeal, and

(b) (whether or not they refer the conviction) may at any time refer to the Court of Appeal any sentence (not being a sentence fixed by law) imposed on, or in subsequent proceedings relating to, the conviction.

(2) A reference under subsection (1) of a person's conviction shall be treated for all purposes as an appeal by the person under section 1 of the [Criminal Appeal Act 1968] against the conviction.

(3) A reference under subsection (1) of a sentence imposed on, or in subsequent proceedings relating to, a person's conviction on an indictment shall be treated for all purposes as an appeal by the person under section 9 of the 1968 Act [appeal against sentence following conviction on indictment] against –

(a) the sentence, and
(b) any other sentence (not being a sentence fixed by law) imposed on, or in subsequent proceedings relating to, the conviction or any other conviction on the indictment.

(4) On a reference under subsection (1) of a person's conviction on an indictment the Commission may give notice to the Court of Appeal that any other conviction on the indictment which is specified in the notice is to be treated as referred to the Court of Appeal under subsection (1).

(5) Where a verdict of not guilty by reason of insanity has been returned in England and Wales in the case of a person, the Commission may at any time refer the verdict to the Court of Appeal; and a reference under this subsection shall be treated for all purposes as an appeal by the person under section 12 of the 1968 Act against the verdict.

(6) Where a jury in England and Wales has returned findings that a person is under a disability and that he did the act or made the omission charged against him, the Commission may at any time refer either or both of those findings to the Court of Appeal; and a reference under this subsection shall be treated for all purposes as an appeal by the person under section 15 of the 1968 Act against the finding or findings referred.

11 Cases dealt with summarily in England and Wales

(1) Where a person has been convicted of an offence by a magistrates' court in England and Wales, the Commission –

(a) may at any time refer the conviction to the Crown Court, and
(b) (whether or not they refer the conviction) may at any time refer to the Crown Court any sentence imposed on, or in subsequent proceedings relating to, the conviction.

(2) A reference under subsection (1) of a person's conviction shall be treated for all purposes as an appeal by the person under section 108(1) of the Magistrates' Courts Act 1980 [right of appeal to the Crown Court] against the conviction (whether or not he pleaded guilty).

(3) A reference under subsection (1) of a sentence imposed on, or in subsequent proceedings relating to, a person's conviction shall be treated for all purposes as an appeal by the person under section 108(1) of the Magistrates' Courts Act 1980 against –

(a) the sentence, and

(b) any other sentence imposed on, or in subsequent proceedings relating to, the conviction or any related conviction.

(4) On a reference under subsection (1) of a person's conviction the Commission may give notice to the Crown Court that any related conviction which is specified in the notice is to be treated as referred to the Crown Court under subsection (1).

(5) For the purposes of this section convictions are related if they are convictions of the same person by the same court on the same day.

(6) On a reference under this section the Crown Court may not award any punishment more severe than that awarded by the court whose decision is referred.

(7) The Crown Court may grant bail to a person whose conviction or sentence has been referred under this section; and any time during which he is released on bail shall not count as part of any term of imprisonment or detention under his sentence.

13 Conditions for making of references

(1) A reference of a conviction, verdict, finding or sentence shall not be made under any of sections 9 to 12 unless –

    (a) the Commission consider that there is a real possibility that the conviction, verdict, finding or sentence would not be upheld were the reference to be made,

    (b) the Commission so consider –

        (i) in the case of a conviction, verdict or finding, because of an argument, or evidence, not raised in the proceedings which led to it or on any appeal or application for leave to appeal against it, or

        (ii) in the case of a sentence, because of an argument on a point of law, or information, not so raised, and

    (c) an appeal against the conviction, verdict, finding or sentence has been determined or leave to appal against it has been refused.

(2) Nothing in subsection (1)(b)(i) or (c) shall prevent the making of a reference if it appears to the Commission that there are exceptional circumstances which justify making it.

14 Further provisions about references

(1) A reference of a conviction, verdict, finding or sentence may be made under any of sections 9 to 12 either after an application has been made by or on behalf of the person to whom it relates or without an application having been so made.

(2) In so considering whether to make a reference of a conviction, verdict, finding or sentence under any of sections 9 to 12 the Commission shall have regard to –

    (a) any application or representations made to the Commission by or on behalf of the person to whom it relates,

    (b) any other representations made to the Commission in relation to it, and

    (c) any other matters which appear to the Commission to be relevant.

(3) In considering whether to make a reference under section 9 or 10 the Commission may

at any time refer any point on which they desire the assistance of the Court of Appeal to that Court for the Court's opinion on it; and on a reference under this subsection the Court of Appeal shall consider the point referred and furnish the Commission with the Court's opinion on the point.

(4) Where the Commission make a reference under any of sections 9 to 12 the Commission shall –

(a) give to the court to which the reference is made a statement of the Commission's reasons for making the reference, and

(b) send a copy of the statement to every person who appears to the Commission to be likely to be a party to any proceedings on the appeal arising from the reference.

(5) Where a reference under any of sections 9 to 12 is treated as an appeal against any conviction, verdict, finding or sentence, the appeal may be on any ground relating to the conviction, verdict, finding or sentence (whether or not the ground is related to any reason given by the Commission for making the reference).

(6) In every case in which –

(a) an application has been made to the Commission by or on behalf of any person for the reference under any of sections 9 to 12 of any conviction, verdict, finding or sentence, but

(b) the Commission decide not to make a reference of the conviction, verdict, finding or sentence,

the Commission shall give a statement of the reasons for their decision to the person who made the application.

15 Investigations for Court of Appeal

(1) Where a direction is given by the Court of Appeal under section 23A(1) of the 1968 Act … the Commission shall investigate the matter specified in the direction in such manner as the Commission think fit.

(2) Where, in investigating a matter specified in such a direction, it appears to the Commission that –

(a) another matter (a 'related matter') which is relevant to the determination of the case by the Court of Appeal ought, if possible, to be resolved before the case is determined by that Court, and

(b) an investigation of the related matter is likely to result in the Court's being able to resolve it,

the Commission may also investigate the related matter.

(3) The Commission shall –

(a) keep the Court of Appeal informed as to the progress of the investigation of any matter specified in a direction under section 23A(1) of the 1968 Act … , and

(b) if they decide to investigate any related matter, notify the Court of Appeal of their decision and keep the Court informed as to the progress of the investigation.

(4) The Commission shall report to the Court of Appeal on the investigation of any matter specified in a direction under section 23A(1) of the 1968 Act ... when –

(a) they complete the investigation of that matter and of any related matter investigated by them, or
(b) they are directed to do so by the Court of Appeal,

whichever happens first.

(5) A report under subsection (4) shall include details of any inquiries made by or for the Commission in the investigation of the matter specified in the direction or any related matter investigated by them.

(6) Such a report shall be accompanied –

(a) by any statements and opinions received by the Commission in the investigation of the matter specified in the direction or any related matter investigated by them, and
(b) subject to subsection (7), by any reports so received.

(7) Such a report need not be accompanied by any reports submitted to the Commission under section 20(6) by an investigating officer.

16 *Assistance in connection with prerogative of mercy*

(1) Where the Secretary of State refers to the Commission any matter which arises in the consideration of whether to recommend the exercise of Her Majesty's prerogative of mercy in relation to a conviction and on which he desires their assistance, the Commission shall –

(a) consider the matter referred, and
(b) give to the Secretary of State a statement of their conclusions on it;

and the Secretary of State shall, in considering whether so to recommend, treat the Commission's statement as conclusive of the matter referred.

(2) Where in any case the Commission are of the opinion that the Secretary of State should consider whether to recommend the exercise of Her Majesty's prerogative of mercy in relation to the case they shall give him the reasons for their opinion.

19 *Power to require appointment of investigating officers*

(1) Where the Commission believe that inquiries should be made for assisting them in the exercise of any of their functions in relation to any case they may require the appointment of an investigating officer to carry out the inquiries.

(2) Where any offence to which the case relates was investigated by persons serving in a public body, a requirement under this section may be imposed –

(a) on the person who is the appropriate person in relation to the public body, or
(b) where the public body has ceased to exist, on any chief officer of police or on the person who is the appropriate person in relation to any public body which appears to the Commission to have functions which consist of or include functions similar to any of those of the public body which has ceased to exist.

(3) Where no offence to which the case relates was investigated by persons serving in a public body, a requirement under this section may be imposed on any chief officer of police. ...

20 *Inquiries by investigating officers*

(1) A person appointed as the investigating officer in relation to a case shall undertake such inquiries as the Commission may from time to time reasonably direct him to undertake in relation to the case. ...

(4) The Commission may take any steps which they consider appropriate for supervising the undertaking of inquiries by an investigating officer. ...

(6) When a person appointed as the investigating officer in relation to a case has completed the inquiries which he has been directed by the Commission to undertake in relation to the case, he shall –

    (a) prepare a report of his findings,
    (b) submit it to the Commission, and
    (c) send a copy of it to the person by whom he was appointed.

(7) When a person appointed as the investigating officer in relation to a case submits to the Commission a report of his findings he shall also submit to them any statements, opinions and reports received by him in connection with the inquiries which he was directed to undertake in relation to the case.

22 *Meaning of 'public body' etc*

(1) In sections 17 [power to obtain documents, etc], 19 and 20 and this section 'public body' means –

    (a) any police force.
    (b) any government department, local authority or other body constituted for purposes of the public service, local government or the administration of justice, or
    (c) any other body whose members are appointed by Her Majesty, any Minister or any government department or whose revenues consist wholly or mainly of money provided by Parliament or appropriated by Measure of the Northern Ireland Assembly. ...

Schedule 1

The Commission: Further Provisions

1. Her Majesty shall, on the recommendation of the Prime Minister, appoint one of the members of the Commission to be the chairman of the Commission.

2. – (1) Subject to the following provisions of this paragraph, a person shall hold and vacate office as a member of the Commission, or as chairman of the Commission, in accordance with the terms of his appointment. ...

(5) No person may hold office as a member of the Commission for a continuous period which is longer than ten years. ...

(8) If the chairman of the Commission ceases to be a member of the Commission he shall also cease to be chairman.

Police Act 1996
(1996 c 16)

89 Assaults on constables

(1) Any person who assaults a constable in the execution of his duty, or a person assisting a constable in the execution of his duty, shall be guilty of an offence and liable on summary conviction to imprisonment for a term not exceeding six months or to a fine not exceeding level 5 on the standard scale, or to both.

(2) Any person who resists or wilfully obstructs a constable in the execution of his duty, or a person assisting a constable in the execution of his duty, shall be guilty of an offence and liable on summary conviction to imprisonment for a term not exceeding one month or to a fine not exceeding level 3 on the standard scale, or to both.

(3) This section also applies to a constable who is a member of a police force maintained in Scotland or Northern Ireland when he is executing a warrant, or otherwise acting in England or Wales, by virtue of any enactment conferring powers on him in England and Wales.

90 Impersonation, etc

(1) Any person who with intent to deceive impersonates a member of a police force or special constable, or makes any statement or does any act calculated falsely to suggest that he is such a member or constable, shall be guilty of an offence and liable on summary conviction to imprisonment for a term not exceeding six months or to a fine not exceeding level 5 on the standard scale, or to both.

(2) Any person who, not being a constable, wears any article of police uniform in circumstances where it gives him an appearance so nearly resembling that of a member of a police force as to be calculated to deceive shall be guilty of an offence and liable on summary conviction to a fine not exceeding level 3 on the standard scale.

(3) Any person who, not being a member of a police force or special constable, has in his possession any article of police uniform shall, unless he proves that he obtained possession of that article lawfully and has possession of it for a lawful purpose, be guilty of an offence and liable on summary conviction to a fine not exceeding level 1 on the standard scale.

(4) In this section –

(a) 'article of police uniform' means any article of uniform or any distinctive badge or mark or document of identification usually issued to members of police forces or special constables, or anything having the appearance of such an article, badge, mark or document, and

(b) 'special constable' means a special constable appointed for a police area.

91 Causing disaffection

(1) Any person who causes, or attempts to cause, or does any act calculated to cause, disaffection amongst the members of any police force, or induces or attempts to induce, or does any act calculated to induce, any member of a police force to withhold his services, shall be guilty of an offence and liable –

(a) on summary conviction, to imprisonment for a term not exceeding six months or to a fine not exceeding the statutory maximum, or to both;

(b) on conviction on indictment, to imprisonment for a term not exceeding two years or to a fine, or to both.

(2) This section applies to special constables appointed for a police area as it applies to members of a police force.

Law Reform (Year and a Day Rule) Act 1996
(1996 c 19)

1 Abolition of 'year and a day' rule

The rule known as the 'year and a day rule' (that is, the rule that, for the purposes of offences involving death and of suicide, an act or omission is conclusively presumed not to have caused a person's death if more than a year and a day elapsed before he died) is abolished for all purposes.

2 Restriction on institution of proceedings for a fatal offence

(1) Proceedings to which this section applies may only be instituted by or with the consent of the Attorney General.

(2) This section applies to proceedings against a person for a fatal offence if –

(a) the injury alleged to have caused the death was sustained more than three years before the death occurred, or

(b) the person has previously been convicted of an offence committed in circumstances alleged to be connected with the death.

(3) In subsection (2) 'fatal offence' means –

(a) murder, manslaughter, infanticide or any other offence of which one of the elements is causing a person's death, or

(b) the offence of aiding, abetting, counselling or procuring a person's suicide.

(4) No provision that proceedings may be instituted only by or with the consent of the Director of Public Prosecutions shall apply to proceedings to which this section applies. ...

Dogs (Fouling of Land) Act 1996
(1996 c 20)

1 Land to which Act applies

(1) Subject to subsections (2) to (4) below, this Act applies to any land which is open to the air and to which the public are entitled or permitted to have access (with or without payment).

(2) This Act does not apply to land comprised in or running alongside a highway which comprises a carriageway unless the driving of motor vehicles on the carriageway is subject, otherwise than temporarily, to a speed limit of 40 miles per hour or less.

(3) This Act does not apply to land of any of the following descriptions, namely –

(a) land used for agriculture or for woodlands;
(b) land which is predominantly marshland, moor or heath; and
(c) common land to which the public are entitled or permitted to have access otherwise than by virtue of section 193(1) of the Law of Property Act 1925 (right of access to urban common land). ...

(5) For the purposes of this section, any land which is covered shall be treated as land which is "open to the air" if it is open to the air on at least one side. ...

2 Designation of such land

(1) A local authority may by order designate for the purposes of this Act any land in their area which is land to which this Act applies; and in this Act 'designated land' means land to which this Act applies which is for the time being so designated. ...

3 Offence

(1) If a dog defecates at any time on designated land and a person who is in charge of the dog at that time fails to remove the faeces from the land forthwith, that person shall be guilty of an offence unless –

(a) he has a reasonable excuse for failing to do so; or
(b) the owner, occupier or other person or authority having control of the land has consented (generally or specifically) to his failing to do so.

(2) A person who is guilty of an offence under this section shall be liable on summary conviction to a fine not exceeding level 3 on the standard scale.

(3) Nothing in this section applies to a person registered as a blind person in a register compiled under section 29 of the National Assistance Act 1948.

(4) For the purposes of this section –

(a) a person who habitually has a dog in his possession shall be taken to be in charge of the dog at any time unless at that time some other person is in charge of the dog;

(b) placing the faeces in a receptacle on the land which is provided for the purpose, or for the disposal of waste, shall be a sufficient removal from the land; and

(c) being unaware of the defecation (whether by reason of not being in the vicinity or otherwise), or not having a device for or other suitable means of removing the faeces, shall not be a reasonable excuse for failing to remove the faeces.

Criminal Procedure and Investigations Act 1996
(1996 c 25)

54 *Acquittals tainted by intimidation, etc*

(1) This section applies where –

(a) a person has been acquitted of an offence, and

(b) a person has been convicted of an administration of justice offence involving interference with or intimidation of a juror or a witness (or potential witness) in any proceedings which led to the acquittal.

(2) Where it appears to the court before which the person was convicted that –

(a) there is a real possibility that, but for the interference or intimidation, the acquitted person would not have been acquitted, and

(b) subsection (5) does not apply,

the court shall certify that it so appears.

(3) Where a court certifies under subsection (2) an application may be made to the High Court for an order quashing the acquittal, and the Court shall make the order if (but shall not do so unless) the four conditions in section 55 are satisfied.

(4) Where an order is made under subsection (3) proceedings may be taken against the acquitted person for the offence of which he was acquitted.

(5) This subsection applies if, because of lapse of time or for any other reason, it would be contrary to the interests of justice to take proceedings against the acquitted person for the offence of which he was acquitted.

(6) For the purposes of this section the following offences are administration of justice offences –

(a) the offence of perverting the course of justice;

(b) the offence under section 51(1) of the Criminal Justice and Public Order Act 1994 (intimidation, etc. of witnesses, jurors and others);

(c) an offence of aiding, abetting, counselling, procuring, suborning or inciting another person to commit an offence under section 1 of the Perjury Act 1911.

(7) This section applies in relation to acquittals in respect of offences alleged to be committed on or after the appointed day.

(8) The reference in subsection (7) to the appointed day is to such day as is appointed for the purposes of this section by the Secretary of State by order.

55 Conditions for making order

(1) The first condition is that it appears to the High Court likely that, but for the interference or intimidation, the acquitted person would not have been acquitted.

(2) The second condition is that it does not appear to the Court that, because of lapse of time or for any other reason, it would be contrary to the interests of justice to take proceedings against the acquitted person for the offence of which he was acquitted.

(3) The third condition is that it appears to the Court that the acquitted person has been given a reasonable opportunity to make written representations to the Court.

(4) The fourth condition is that it appears to the Court that the conviction for the administration of justice offence will stand.

(5) In applying subsection (4) the Court shall –

(a) take into account all the information before it, but
(b) ignore the possibility of new factors coming to light.

(6) Accordingly, the fourth condition has the effect that the Court shall not make an order under section 54(3) if (for instance) it appears to the Court that any time allowed for giving notice of appeal has not expired or that an appeal is pending.

56 Time limits for proceedings

(1) Where –

(a) an order is made under section 54(3) quashing an acquittal,
(b) by virtue of section 54(4) it is proposed to take proceedings against the acquitted person for the offence of which he was acquitted, and
(c) apart from this subsection, the effect of an enactment would be that the proceedings must be commenced before a specified period calculated by reference to the commission of the offence,

in relation to the proceedings the enactment shall have effect as if the period were instead one calculated by reference to the time the order is made under section 54(3).

(2) Subsection (1)(c) applies however the enactment is expressed so that (for instance) it applies in the case of –

(a) paragraph 10 of Schedule 2 to the Sexual Offences Act 1956 (prosecution for certain offences may not be commenced more than 12 months after offence);
(b) section 127(1) of the Magistrates' Courts Act 1980 (magistrates' court not to try information unless it is laid within 6 months from time when offence committed);
(c) an enactment that imposes a time limit only in certain circumstances (as where proceedings are not instituted by or with the consent of the Director of Public Prosecutions).

Sexual Offences (Conspiracy and Incitement) Act 1996
(1996 c 29)

2 Incitement to commit certain sexual acts outside the United Kingdom

(1) This section applies where –

(a) any act done by a person in England and Wales would amount to the offence of incitement to commit a listed sexual offence but for the fact that what he had in view would not be an offence triable in England and Wales,

(b) the whole or part of what he had in view was intended to take place in a country or territory outside the United Kingdom, and

(c) what he had in view would involve the commission of an offence under the law in force in that country or territory.

(2) Where this section applies –

(a) what he had in view is to be treated as that listed sexual offence for the purposes of any charge of incitement brought in respect of that act, and

(b) any such charge is accordingly triable in England and Wales.

(3) Any act of incitement by means of a message(however communicated) is to be treated as done in England and Wales if the message is sent or received in England and Wales.

3 Section ... 2: supplementary

(1) Conduct punishable under the law in force in any country or territory is an offence under that law for the purposes of section 2, however it is described in that law.

(2) Subject to subsection(3), a condition in section 2(1)(c) is to be taken to be satisfied unless, not later than rules of court may provide, the defence serve on the prosecution a notice –

(a) stating that, on the facts as alleged with respect to what the accused had in view, the condition is not in their opinion satisfied,

(b) showing their grounds for that opinion, and

(c) requiring the prosecution to show that it is satisfied.

(4) The court, if it thinks fit, may permit the defence to require the prosecution to show that the condition is satisfied without the prior service of a notice under subsection(2).

(5) In the Crown Court the question whether the condition is satisfied is to be decided by the judge alone.

(6) In any proceedings in respect of any offence triable by virtue of section 2, it is immaterial to guilt whether or not the accused was a British citizen at the time of any act or other event proof of which is required for conviction of the offence.

(8) References to an offence of incitement to commit a listed sexual offence include an

offence triable in England and Wales as such an incitement by virtue of section 2(without prejudice to subsection(2) of that section).

(9) Subsection (8) applies to references in any enactment, instrument or document(except those in sections 2 of this Act and in Part I of the Criminal Law Act 1977).

5 Interpretation

In this Act 'listed sexual offence' has the meaning given by the Schedule.

[As amended by the Criminal Justice (Terrorism and Conspiracy) Act 1998, s9, Schedule 1, Pt II, para 9(1), (2), Schedule 2, Pt II.]

Schedule
Listed Sexual Offences

1 – (1) In relation to England and Wales, the following are listed sexual offences:

(a) offences under the following provisions of the Sexual Offences Act 1956 –

(i) section 1 (rape),

(ii) section 5 (intercourse with girl under the age of thirteen),

(iii) section 6 (intercourse with girl under the age of sixteen),

(iv) section 12 (buggery),

(v) section 14 (indecent assault on a girl), and

(vi) section 15 (indecent assault on a boy),

(b) an offence under section 1 of the Indecency with Children Act 1960(indecent conduct towards young child).

(2) In sub-paragraph(1)(a), sub-paragraphs (i),(iv),(v) and(vi) do not apply where the victim of the offence has attained the age of sixteen years.

Firearms (Amendment) Act 1997
(1997 c 5)

Part I

Prohibition of Weapons and Ammunition and Control of Small-Calibre Pistols

1 Extension of s5 of the 1968 Act to prohibit certain small firearms, etc ...

(7) The general prohibition by section 5 of the [Firearms Act 1968] of firearms falling within subsection (1)(aba) of that section is subject to the special exemptions in sections 2 to 8 below.

(8) In sections 2 to 8 below any reference to a firearm certificate shall include a reference to a visitor's firearm permit. ...

2 Slaughtering instruments ...

3 Firearms used for humane killing of animals ...

4 Shot pistols used for shooting vermin ...

5 Races at athletic meetings ...

6 Trophies of war ...

7 Firearms of historic interest ...

8 Weapons and ammunition used for treating animals ...

Part III
Regulation of Firearms and Ammunition

32 Transfers firearms, etc to be in person

(1) This section applies where, in Great Britain –

(a) a firearm or ammunition to which section 1 of the 1968 Act applies is sold, let on hire, lent or given by any person, or

(b) a shot gun is sold, let on hire or given, or lent for a period of more than 72 hours by any person,

to another person who is neither a registered firearms dealer nor a person who is entitled to purchase or acquire the firearm or ammunition without holding a firearm or shot gun certificate or a visitor's firearm or shot gun permit.

(2) Where a transfer to which this section applies takes place-

(a) the transferee must produce to the transferor the certificate or permit entitling him to purchase or acquire the firearm or ammunition being transferred;

(b) the transferor must comply with any instructions contained in the certificate or permit produced by the transferee;

(c) the transferor must hand the firearm or ammunition to the transferee, and the transferee must receive it, in person.

(3) A failure by the transferor or transferee to comply with subsection (2) above shall be an offence.

36 Penalty for offences under ss32 to 35

An offence under section 32, 33 [notification of transfers involving firearms], 34 [notification of de-activation, destruction or loss of firearms, etc] or 35 [notification of events taking place outside Great Britain involving firearms, etc] above shall –

(a) if committed in relation to a transfer or other event involving a firearm or ammunition to which section 1 of the 1968 Act applies be punishable –

(i) on summary conviction with imprisonment for a term not exceeding six months or a fine not exceeding the statutory maximum or both;

(ii) on conviction on indictment with imprisonment for a term not exceeding five years or a fine or both;

(b) if committed in relation to a transfer or other event involving a shot gun be punishable on summary conviction with imprisonment for a term not exceeding six months or a fine not exceeding level 5 on the standard scale or both.

39 Register of holders of shot gun and firearm certificates

(1) There shall be established a central register of all persons who have applied for a firearm or shot gun certificate or to whom a firearm or shot gun certificate has been granted or whose certificate has been renewed.

(2) The register shall –

(a) record a suitable identifying number for each person to whom a certificate is issued; and

(b) be kept by means of a computer which provides access on-line to all police forces.

48 Firearms powered by compressed carbon dioxide

Any reference to an air rifle, air pistol or air gun –

(a) in the Firearms Acts 1968 to 1997; or

(b) in the Firearms (Dangerous Air Weapons) Rules 1969 ...,

shall include a reference to a rifle, pistol or gun powered by compressed carbon dioxide.

Part IV

Final Provisions

50 Interpretation and supplementary provisions ...

(2) Any expression used in this Act which is also used in the 1968 Act or the [Firearms (Amendment) Act 1988] has the same meaning as in that Act.

(3) Any reference in the 1968 Act to a person who is by virtue of that Act entitled to possess, purchase or acquire any weapon or ammunition without holding a certificate shall include a reference to a person who is so entitled by virtue of any provision of this Act. ...

(6) The provisions of this Act shall be treated as contained in the 1968 Act for the purposes of the Firearms Act 1982 (imitation firearms readily convertible into firearms to which section 1 of the 1968 Act applies).

Knives Act 1997
(1997 c 21)

1 Unlawful marketing of knives

(1) A person is guilty of an offence if he markets a knife in a way which –

(a) indicates, or suggests, that it is suitable for combat; or
(b) is otherwise likely to stimulate or encourage violent behaviour involving the use of the knife as a weapon.

(2) 'Suitable for combat' and 'violent behaviour' are defined in section 10.

(3) For the purposes of this Act, an indication or suggestion that a knife is suitable for combat may, in particular, be given or made by a name or description –

(a) applied to the knife;
(b) on the knife or on any packaging in which it is contained; or
(c) included in any advertisement which, expressly or by implication, relates to the knife.

(4) For the purposes of this Act, a person markets a knife if –

(a) he sells or hires it;
(b) he offers, or exposes, it for sale or hire; or
(c) he has it in his possession for the purpose of sale or hire.

(5) A person who is guilty of an offence under this section is liable –

(a) on summary conviction to imprisonment for a term not exceeding six months or to a fine not exceeding the statutory maximum, or to both;
(b) on conviction on indictment to imprisonment for a term not exceeding two years or to a fine, or to both.

2 Publications

(1) A person is guilty of an offence if he publishes any written, pictorial or other material in connection with the marketing of any knife and that material –

(a) indicates, or suggests, that the knife is suitable for combat; or
(b) is otherwise likely to stimulate or encourage violent behaviour involving the use of the knife as a weapon.

(2) A person who is guilty of an offence under this section is liable –

(a) on summary conviction to imprisonment for a term not exceeding six months or to a fine not exceeding the statutory maximum, or to both;
(b) on conviction on indictment to imprisonment for a term not exceeding two years or to a fine, or to both.

3 *Exempt trades*

(1) It is a defence for a person charged with an offence under section 1 to prove that –

(a) the knife was marketed –

(i) for use by the armed forces of any country;
(ii) as an antique or curio; or
(iii) as falling within such other category (if any) as may be prescribed;

(b) it was reasonable for the knife to be marketed in that way; and
(c) there were no reasonable grounds for suspecting that a person into whose possession the knife might come in consequence of the way in which it was marketed would use it for an unlawful purpose.

(2) It is a defence for a person charged with an offence under section 2 to prove that –

(a) the material was published in connection with marketing a knife –

(i) for use by the armed forces of any country;
(ii) as an antique or curio; or
(iii) as falling within such other category (if any) as may be prescribed;

(b) it was reasonable for the knife to be marketed in that way; and
(c) there were no reasonable grounds for suspecting that a person into whose possession the knife might come in consequence of the publishing of the material would use it for an unlawful purpose.

(3) In this section 'prescribed' means prescribed by regulations made by the Secretary of State.

4 *Other defences*

(1) It is a defence for a person charged with an offence under section 1 to prove that he did not know or suspect, and had no reasonable grounds for suspecting, that the way in which the knife was marketed –

(a) amounted to an indication or suggestion that the knife was suitable for combat; or
(b) was likely to stimulate or encourage violent behaviour involving the use of the knife as a weapon.

(2) It is a defence for a person charged with an offence under section 2 to prove that he did not know or suspect, and had no reasonable grounds for suspecting, that the material –

(a) amounted to an indication or suggestion that the knife was suitable for combat; or
(b) was likely to stimulate or encourage violent behaviour involving the use of the knife as a weapon.

(3) It is a defence for a person charged with an offence under section 1 or 2 to prove that he took all reasonable precautions and exercised all due diligence to avoid committing the offence.

9 Offences by bodies corporate

(1) If an offence under this Act committed by a body corporate is proved –

(a) to have been committed with the consent or connivance of an officer, or

(b) to be attributable to any neglect on his part, he as well as the body corporate is guilty of the offence and liable to be proceeded against and punished accordingly.

(2) In subsection (1) 'officer', in relation to a body corporate, means a director, manager, secretary or other similar officer of the body, or a person purporting to act in any such capacity.

(3) If the affairs of a body corporate are managed by its members, subsection (1) applies in relation to the acts and defaults of a member in connection with his functions of management as if he were a director of the body corporate. ...

10 Interpretation

In this Act –

'the court' means –

(a) in relation to England and Wales or Northern Ireland, the Crown Court or a magistrate's court;

(b) in relation to Scotland, the sheriff;

'knife' means an instrument which has a blade or is sharply pointed;

'marketing' and related expressions are to be read with section 1(4);

'publication' includes a publication in electronic form and, in the case of a publication which is, or may be, produced from electronic data, any medium on which the data are stored;

'suitable for combat' means suitable for use as a weapon for inflicting injury on a person or causing a person to fear injury;

'violent behaviour' means an unlawful act inflicting injury on a person or causing a person to fear injury.

Confiscation of Alcohol (Young Persons) Act 1997
(1997 c 33)

1 Confiscation intoxicating liquor

(1) Where a constable reasonably suspects of that a person in a relevant place is in possession of intoxicating liquor and that either –

(a) he is under the age of 18; or

(b) he intends that any of the liquor should be consumed by a person under the age of 18 in that or any other relevant place; or

(c) a person under the age of 18 who is, or has recently been, with him has recently consumed intoxicating liquor in that or any other relevant place, the constable may require him to surrender anything in his possession which is, or which the constable reasonably believes to be, intoxicating liquor and to state his name and address.

(2) A constable may dispose of anything surrendered to him under subsection (1) in such manner as he considers appropriate.

(3) A person who fails without reasonable excuse to comply with a requirement imposed on him under subsection (1) commits an offence and is liable on summary conviction to a fine not exceeding level 2 on the standard scale.

(4) A constable who imposes a requirement on a person under subsection (1) shall inform him of his suspicion and that failing without reasonable excuse to comply with a requirement imposed under that subsection is an offence.

(5) A constable may arrest without warrant a person who fails to comply with a requirement imposed on him under subsection (1).

(6) In subsection (1) 'relevant place', in relation to a person, means –

(a) any public place, other than licensed premises; or
(b) any place, other than a public place, to which the person has unlawfully gained access;

and for this purpose a place is a public place if at the material time the public or any section of the public has access to it, on payment or otherwise, as of right or by virtue of express or implied permission.

(7) In this section 'intoxicating liquor' and 'licensed premises', in relation to England and Wales, have the same meanings as in the Licensing Act 1964 ...

2 Short title, commencement and extent ...

(2) Section 1 shall not come into force until such day as the Secretary of State may by order made by statutory instrument appoint. ...

Protection from Harassment Act 1997
(1997 c 40)

1 Prohibition of harassment

(1) A person must not pursue a course of conduct –

(a) which amounts to harassment of another, and
(b) which he knows or ought to know amounts to harassment of the other.

(2) For the purposes of this section, the person whose course of conduct is in question ought to know that it amounts to harassment of another if a reasonable person in possession of the same information would think the course of conduct amounted to harassment of the other.

(3) Subsection (1) does not apply to a course of conduct if the person who pursued it shows –

(a) that it was pursued for the purpose of preventing or detecting crime,

(b) that it was pursued under any enactment or rule of law or to comply with any condition or requirement imposed by any person under any enactment, or

(c) that in the particular circumstances the pursuit of the course of conduct was reasonable.

2 Offence of harassment

(1) A person who pursues a course of conduct in breach of section 1 is guilty of an offence.

(2) A person guilty of an offence under this section is liable on summary conviction to imprisonment for a term not exceeding six months, or a fine not exceeding level 5 on the standard scale, or both. ...

4 Putting people in fear of violence

(1) A person whose course of conduct causes another to fear, on at least two occasions, that violence will be used against him is guilty of an offence if he knows or ought to know that his course of conduct will cause the other so to fear on each of those occasions.

(2) For the purposes of this section, the person whose course of conduct is in question ought to know that it will cause another to fear that violence will be used against him on any occasion if a reasonable person in possession of the same information would think the course of conduct would cause the other so to fear on that occasion.

(3) It is a defence for a person charged with an offence under this section to show that –

(a) his course of conduct was pursued for the purpose of preventing or detecting crime,

(b) his course of conduct was pursued under any enactment or rule of law or to comply with any condition or requirement imposed by any person under any enactment, or

(c) the pursuit of his course of conduct was reasonable for the protection of himself or another or for the protection of his or another's property.

(4) A person guilty of an offence under this section is liable –

(a) on conviction on indictment, to imprisonment for a term not exceeding five years, or a fine, or both, or

(b) on summary conviction, to imprisonment for a term not exceeding six months, or a fine not exceeding the statutory maximum, or both.

(5) If on the trial on indictment of a person charged with an offence under this section the jury find him not guilty of the offence charged, they may find him guilty of an offence under section 2.

(6) The Crown Court has the same powers and duties in relation to a person who is by virtue of subsection (5) convicted before it of an offence under section 2 as a magistrates' court would have on convicting him of the offence.

5 Restraining orders

(1) A court sentencing or otherwise dealing with a person ('the defendant') convicted of an

offence under section 2 or 4 may (as well as sentencing him or dealing with him in any other way) make an order under this section.

(2) The order may, for the purpose of protecting the victim of the offence, or any other person mentioned in the order, from further conduct which –

(a) amounts to harassment, or
(b) will cause a fear of violence, prohibit the defendant from doing anything described in the order.

(3) The order may have effect for a specified period or until further order.

(4) The prosecutor, the defendant or any other person mentioned in the order may apply to the court which made the order for it to be varied or discharged by a further order.

(5) If without reasonable excuse the defendant does anything which he is prohibited from doing by an order under this section, he is guilty of an offence.

(6) A person guilty of an offence under this section is liable –

(a) on conviction on indictment, to imprisonment for a term not exceeding five years, or a fine, or both, or
(b) on summary conviction, to imprisonment for a term not exceeding six months, or a fine not exceeding the statutory maximum, or both.

7 Interpretation of this group of sections

(1) This section applies for the interpretation of sections 1 to 5.

(2) References to harassing a person include alarming the person or causing the person distress.

(3) A 'course of conduct' must involve conduct on at least two occasions.

(4) 'Conduct' includes speech.

12 National security, etc

(1) If the Secretary of State certifies that in his opinion anything done by a specified person on a specified occasion related to –

(a) national security,
(b) the economic well-being of the United Kingdom, or
(c) the prevention or detection of serious crime,

and was done on behalf of the Crown, the certificate is conclusive evidence that this Act does not apply to any conduct of that person on that occasion.

(2) In subsection (1), 'specified' means specified in the certificate in question.

(3) A document purporting to be a certificate under subsection (1) is to be received in evidence and, unless the contrary is proved, be treated as being such a certificate.

Crime (Sentences) Act 1997
(1997 c 43)

2 *Mandatory life sentence for second serious offence*

(1) This section applies where –

(a) a person is convicted of a serious offence committed after the commencement of this section; and

(b) at the time when that offence was committed, he was 18 or over and had been convicted in any part of the United Kingdom of another serious offence.

(2) The court shall impose a life sentence, that is to say –

(a) where the person is 21 or over, a sentence of imprisonment for life;

(b) where he is under 21, a sentence of custody for life under section 8(2) of the Criminal Justice Act 1982 ('the 1982 Act'),

unless the court is of the opinion that there are exceptional circumstances relating to either of the offences or to the offender which justify its not doing so.

(3) Where the court does not impose a life sentence, it shall state in open court that it is of that opinion and what the exceptional circumstances are.

(4) An offence the sentence for which is imposed under subsection (2) above shall not be regarded as an offence the sentence for which is fixed by law.

(5) An offence committed in England and Wales is a serious offence for the purposes of this section if it is any of the following, namely –

(a) an attempt to commit murder, a conspiracy to commit murder or an incitement to murder;

(b) an offence under section 4 of the Offences Against the Person Act 1861 (soliciting murder);

(c) manslaughter;

(d) an offence under section 18 of the Offences Against the Person Act 1861 (wounding, or causing grievous bodily harm, with intent);

(e) rape or an attempt to commit rape;

(f) an offence under section 5 of the Sexual Offences Act 1956 (intercourse with a girl under 13);

(g) an offence under section 16 (possession of a firearm with intent to injure), section 17 (use of a firearm to resist arrest) or section 18 (carrying a firearm with criminal intent) of the Firearms Act 1968; and

(h) robbery where, at some time during the commission of the offence, the offender had in his possession a firearm or imitation firearm within the meaning of that Act. ...

3 *Minimum of seven years for third class A drug trafficking offence.*

(1) This section applies where –

(a) a person is convicted of a class A drug trafficking offence committed after the commencement of this section;

(b) at the time when that offence was committed, he was 18 or over and had been convicted in any part of the United Kingdom of two other class A drug trafficking offences; and

(c) one of those other offences was committed after he had been convicted of the other.

(2) The court shall impose a custodial sentence for a term of at least seven years except where the court is of the opinion that there are particular circumstances which –

(a) relate to any of the offences or to the offender; and

(b) would make it unjust to do so in all the circumstances.

(3) Where the court does not impose such a sentence, it shall state in open court that it is of that opinion and what the particular circumstances are.

(4) Where –

(a) a person is charged with a class A drug trafficking offence (which, apart from this subsection, would be triable either way); and

(b) the circumstances are such that, if he were convicted of the offence, he could be sentenced for it under subsection (2) above,

the offence shall be triable only on indictment.

(5) In this section 'class A drug trafficking offence' means a drug trafficking offence committed in respect of a class A drug; and for this purpose –

'class A drug' has the same meaning as in the Misuse of Drugs Act 1971;

'drug trafficking offence' means a drug trafficking offence within the meaning of the Drug Trafficking Act 1994 ...

(6) In this section and section 4 below 'custodial sentence' means –

(a) in relation to a person who is 21 or over, a sentence of imprisonment;

(b) in relation to a person who is under 21, a sentence of detention in a young offender institution.

4 Minimum of three years for third domestic burglary

(1) This section applies where –

(a) a person is convicted of a domestic burglary committed after the commencement of this section;

(b) at the time when that burglary was committed, he was 18 or over and had been convicted in England and Wales of two other domestic burglaries; and

(c) one of those other burglaries was committed after he had been convicted of the other, and both of them were committed after the commencement of this section.

(2) The court shall impose a custodial sentence for a term of at least three years except where the court is of the opinion that there are particular circumstances which –

(a) relate to any of the offences or to the offender; and

(b) would make it unjust to do so in all the circumstances.

(3) Where the court does not impose such a sentence, it shall state in open court that it is of that opinion and what the particular circumstances are.

(4) Where –

(a) a person is charged with a domestic burglary which, apart from this subsection, would be triable either way; and
(b) the circumstances are such that, if he were convicted of the burglary, he could be sentenced for it under subsection (2) above,

the burglary shall be triable only on indictment.

(5) In this section 'domestic burglary' means a burglary committed in respect of a building or part of a building which is a dwelling.

5 *Appeals where previous convictions set aside*

(1) This section applies where –

(a) a sentence has been imposed on any person under subsection (2) of section 2, 3 or 4 above; and
(b) any previous conviction of his without which that section would not have applied has been subsequently set aside on appeal.

(2) Notwithstanding anything in section 18 of the Criminal Appeal Act 1968, notice of appeal against the sentence may be given at any time within 28 days from the date on which the previous conviction was set aside.

NB Section 4, above, came into force on 1 December 1999.

[As amended by the Crime and Disorder Act 1998, s106, Schedule 7, paras 48, 49.]

Sex Offenders Act 1997
(1997 c 51)
Part II
Sexual Offences Committed outside the United Kingdom

7 *Extension of jurisdiction: England and Wales and Northern Ireland*

(1) Subject to subsection (2) below, any act done by a person in a country or territory outside the United Kingdom which –

(a) constituted an offence under the law in force in that country or territory; and
(b) would constitute a sexual offence to which this section applies if it had been done in England and Wales, or in Northern Ireland,

shall constitute that sexual offence under the law of that part of the United Kingdom.

(2) No proceedings shall by virtue of this section be brought against any person unless he was at the commencement of this section, or has subsequently become, a British citizen or resident in the United Kingdom.

(3) An act punishable under the law in force in any country or territory constitutes an offence under that law for the purposes of this section, however it is described in that law.

(4) Subject to subsection (5) below, the condition in subsection (1)(a) above shall be taken to be satisfied unless, not later than rules of court may provide, the defence serve on the prosecution a notice –

(a) stating that, on the facts as alleged with respect to the act in question, the condition is not in their opinion satisfied;
(b) showing their grounds for that opinion; and
(c) requiring the prosecution to show that it is satisfied.

(5) The court, if it thinks fit, may permit the defence to require the prosecution to show that the condition is satisfied without the prior service of a notice under subsection (4) above.

(6) In the Crown Court the question whether the condition is satisfied is to be decided by the judge alone.

(7) Schedule 2 to this Act (which lists the sexual offences to which this section applies) shall have effect.

Schedule 2
Sexual Offences to Which Section 7 Applies

1. – (1) In relation to England and Wales, the following are sexual offences to which section 7 of this Act applies, namely –

(a) offences under the following provisions of the Sexual Offences Act 1956 –

(i) section 1 (rape);
(ii) section 5 (intercourse with girl under 13);
(iii) section 6 (intercourse with girl between 13 and 16);
(iv) section 12 (buggery);
(v) section 14 (indecent assault on a girl);
(vi) section 15 (indecent assault on a boy); and
(vii) section 16 (assault with intent to commit buggery);

(b) an offence under section 1 of the Indecency with Children Act 1960 (indecent conduct towards young child); and
(c) an offence under section 1 of the Protection of Children Act 1978 (indecent photographs of children).

(2) In sub-paragraph (1)(a) above, sub-paragraphs (i) and (iv) to (vii) do not apply where the victim of the offence was 16 or over at the time of the offence. ...

3. Any reference in paragraph 1(1) ... above to an offence includes –

(a) a reference to any attempt, conspiracy or incitement to commit that offence; and

(b) a reference to aiding and abetting, counselling or procuring the commission of that offence.

Crime and Disorder Act 1998

(1998 c 37)

Part I

Prevention of Crime and Disorder

Chapter I

England and Wales

1 *Anti-social behaviour orders*

(1) An application for an order under this section may be made by a relevant authority if it appears to the authority that the following conditions are fulfilled with respect to any person aged 10 or over, namely –

(a) that the person has acted, since the commencement date, in an anti-social manner, that is to say, in a manner that caused or was likely to cause harassment, alarm or distress to one or more persons not of the same household as himself; and

(b) that such an order is necessary to protect persons in the local government area in which the harassment, alarm or distress was caused or was likely to be caused from further anti-social acts by him;

and in this section 'relevant authority' means the council for the local government area or any chief officer of police any part of whose police area lies within that area.

(2) A relevant authority shall not make such an application without consulting each other relevant authority.

(3) Such an application shall be made by complaint to the magistrates' court whose commission area includes the place where it is alleged that the harassment, alarm or distress was caused or was likely to be caused.

(4) If, on such an application, it is proved that the conditions mentioned in subsection (1) above are fulfilled, the magistrates' court may make an order under this section (an 'anti-social behaviour order') which prohibits the defendant from doing anything described in the order.

(5) For the purpose of determining whether the condition mentioned in subsection (1)(a) above is fulfilled, the court shall disregard any act of the defendant which he shows was reasonable in the circumstances.

(6) The prohibitions that may be imposed by an anti-social behaviour order are those necessary for the purpose of protecting from further anti-social acts by the defendant –

(a) persons in the local government area; and

(b) persons in any adjoining local government area specified in the application for the order;

and a relevant authority shall not specify an adjoining local government area in the application without consulting the council for that area and each chief officer of police any part of whose police area lies within that area.

(7) An anti-social behaviour order shall have effect for a period (not less than two years) specified in the order or until further order.

(8) Subject to subsection (9) below, the applicant or the defendant may apply by complaint to the court which made an anti-social behaviour order for it to be varied or discharged by a further order.

(9) Except with the consent of both parties, no anti-social behaviour order shall be discharged before the end of the period of two years beginning with the date of service of the order.

(10) If without reasonable excuse a person does anything which he is prohibited from doing by an anti-social behaviour order, he shall be liable –

(a) on summary conviction, to imprisonment for a term not exceeding six months or to a fine not exceeding the statutory maximum, or to both; or
(b) on conviction on indictment, to imprisonment for a term not exceeding five years or to a fine, or to both.

(11) Where a person is convicted of an offence under subsection (10) above, it shall not be open to the court by or before which he is so convicted to make an order under subsection (1)(b) (conditional discharge) of section 1A of the Powers of Criminal Courts Act 1973 ('the 1973 Act') in respect of the offence.

(12) In this section –

'the commencement date' means the date of the commencement of this section;
'local government area' means –

(a) in relation to England, a district or London borough, the City of London, the Isle of Wight and the Isles of Scilly;
(b) in relation to Wales, a county or county borough.

2 Sex offender orders

(1) If it appears to a chief officer of police that the following conditions are fulfilled with respect to any person in his police area, namely –

(a) that the person is a sex offender; and
(b) that the person has acted, since the relevant date, in such a way as to give reasonable cause to believe that an order under this section is necessary to protect the public from serious harm from him,

the chief officer may apply for an order under this section to be made in respect of the person.

(2) Such an application shall be made by complaint to the magistrates' court whose commission area includes any place where it is alleged that the defendant acted in such a way as is mentioned in subsection (1)(b) above.

(3) If, on such an application, it is proved that the conditions mentioned in subsection (1) above are fulfilled, the magistrates' court may make an order under this section (a 'sex offender order') which prohibits the defendant from doing anything described in the order.

(4) The prohibitions that may be imposed by a sex offender order are those necessary for the purpose of protecting the public from serious harm from the defendant.

(5) A sex offender order shall have effect for a period (not less than five years) specified in the order or until further order; and while such an order has effect, Part I of the Sex Offenders Act 1997 shall have effect as if –

(a) the defendant were subject to the notification requirements of that Part; and
(b) in relation to the defendant, the relevant date (within the meaning of that Part) were the date of service of the order.

(6) Subject to subsection (7) below, the applicant or the defendant may apply by complaint to the court which made a sex offender order for it to be varied or discharged by a further order.

(7) Except with the consent of both parties, no sex offender order shall be discharged before the end of the period of five years beginning with the date of service of the order.

(8) If without reasonable excuse a person does anything which he is prohibited from doing by a sex offender order, he shall be liable –

(a) on summary conviction, to imprisonment for a term not exceeding six months or to a fine not exceeding the statutory maximum, or to both; or
(b) on conviction on indictment, to imprisonment for a term not exceeding five years or to a fine, or to both.

(9) Where a person is convicted of an offence under subsection (8) above, it shall not be open to the court by or before which he is so convicted to make an order under subsection (1)(b) (conditional discharge) of section 1A of the 1973 Act in respect of the offence.

3 Sex offender orders: supplemental

(1) In section 2 above and this section 'sex offender' means a person who –

(a) has been convicted of a sexual offence to which Part I of the Sex Offenders Act 1997 applies;
(b) has been found not guilty of such an offence by reason of insanity, or found to be under a disability and to have done the act charged against him in respect of such an offence;
(c) has been cautioned by a constable, in England and Wales or Northern Ireland, in respect of such an offence which, at the time when the caution was given, he had admitted; or
(d) has been punished under the law in force in a country or territory outside the United Kingdom for an act which –

(i) constituted an offence under that law; and
(ii) would have constituted a sexual offence to which that Part applies if it had been done in any part of the United Kingdom.

(2) In subsection (1) of section 2 above 'the relevant date', in relation to a sex offender, means –

(a) the date or, as the case may be, the latest date on which he has been convicted, found, cautioned or punished as mentioned in subsection (1) above; or

(b) if later, the date of the commencement of that section. ….

(4) In subsections (1) and (2) above, any reference to a person having been cautioned shall be construed as including a reference to his having been reprimanded or warned (under section 65 below) as a child or young person.

(5) An act punishable under the law in force in any country or territory outside the United Kingdom constitutes an offence under that law for the purposes of subsection (1) above, however it is described in that law.

(6) Subject to subsection (7) below, the condition in subsection (1)(d)(i) above shall be taken to be satisfied unless, not later than rules of court may provide, the defendant serves on the applicant a notice –

(a) stating that, on the facts as alleged with respect to the act in question, the condition is not in his opinion satisfied;

(b) showing his grounds for that opinion; and

(c) requiring the applicant to show that it is satisfied.

(7) The court, if it thinks fit, may permit the defendant to require the applicant to show that the condition is satisfied without the prior service of a notice under subsection (6) above.

4 Appeals against orders

(1) An appeal shall lie to the Crown Court against the making by a magistrates' court of an anti-social behaviour order or sex offender order.

(2) On such an appeal the Crown Court –

(a) may make such orders as may be necessary to give effect to its determination of the appeal; and

(b) may also make such incidental or consequential orders as appear to it to be just.

(3) Any order of the Crown Court made on an appeal under this section (other than one directing that an application be re-heard by a magistrates' court) shall, for the purposes of section 1(8) or 2(6) above, be treated as if it were an order of the magistrates' court from which the appeal was brought and not an order of the Crown Court.

Part II

Criminal Law

28 Meaning of 'racially aggravated'

(1) An offence is racially aggravated for the purposes of sections 29 to 32 below if –

(a) at the time of committing the offence, or immediately before or after doing so, the offender demonstrates towards the victim of the offence hostility based on the victim's membership (or presumed membership) of a racial group; or

(b) the offence is motivated (wholly or partly) by hostility towards members of a racial group based on their membership of that group.

(2) In subsection (1)(a) above –

'membership', in relation to a racial group, includes association with members of that group;
'presumed' means presumed by the offender.

(3) It is immaterial for the purposes of paragraph (a) or (b) of subsection (1) above whether or not the offender's hostility is also based, to any extent, on –

(a) the fact or presumption that any person or group of persons belongs to any religious group; or
(b) any other factor not mentioned in that paragraph.

(4) In this section 'racial group' means a group of persons defined by reference to race, colour, nationality (including citizenship) or ethnic or national origins.

29 Racially-aggravated assaults

(1) A person is guilty of an offence under this section if he commits –

(a) an offence under section 20 of the Offences Against the Person Act 1861 (malicious wounding or grievous bodily harm);
(b) an offence under section 47 of that Act (actual bodily harm); or
(c) common assault,

which is racially aggravated for the purposes of this section.

(2) A person guilty of an offence falling within subsection (1)(a) or (b) above shall be liable –

(a) on summary conviction, to imprisonment for a term not exceeding six months or to a fine not exceeding the statutory maximum, or to both;
(b) on conviction of indictment, to imprisonment for a term not exceeding seven years or to a fine, or to both.

(3) A person guilty of an offence falling within subsection (1)(c) above shall be liable –

(a) on summary conviction, to imprisonment for a term not exceeding six months or to a fine not exceeding the statutory maximum, or to both;
(b) on conviction on indictment, to imprisonment for a term not exceeding two years or to a fine, or to both.

30 Racially-aggravated criminal damage

(1) A person is guilty of an offence under this section if he commits an offence under section 1(1) of the Criminal Damage Act 1971 (destroying or damaging property belonging to another) which is racially aggravated for the purposes of this section.

(2) A person guilty of an offence under this section shall be liable –

(a) on summary conviction, to imprisonment for a term not exceeding six months or to a fine not exceeding the statutory maximum, or to both;

(b) on conviction on indictment, to imprisonment for a term not exceeding fourteen years or to a fine or to both.

(3) For the purposes of this section, section 28(1)(a) above shall have effect as if the person to whom the property belongs or is treated as belonging for the purposes of that Act were the victim of the offence.

31 Racially-aggravated public order offences

(1) A person is guilty of an offence under this section if he commits –

(a) an offence under section 4 of the Public Order Act 1986 (fear or provocation of violence);

(b) an offence under section 4A of that Act (intentional harassment, alarm or distress); or

(c) an offence under section 5 of that Act (harassment, alarm or distress), which is racially aggravated for the purposes of this section.

(2) A constable may arrest without warrant anyone whom he reasonably suspects to be committing an offence falling within subsection (1)(a) or (b) above.

(3) A constable may arrest a person without a warrant if –

(a) he engages in conduct which a constable reasonably suspects to constitute an offence falling within (1)(c) above;

(b) he is warned by that constable to stop; and

(c) he engages in further such conduct immediately or shortly after the warning.

The conduct mentioned in paragraph (a) above and the further conduct need not be of the same nature.

(4) A person guilty of an offence falling within subsection (1)(a) or (b) above shall be liable –

(a) on summary conviction, to imprisonment for a term not exceeding six months or to a fine not exceeding the statutory maximum, or to both;

(b) on conviction on indictment, to imprisonment for a term not exceeding two years or to a fine, or to both.

(5) A person guilty of an offence falling within subsection (1)(c) above shall be liable on summary conviction to a fine not exceeding level 4 on the standard scale.

(6) If, on the trial on indictment of a person charged with an offence falling within subsection (1)(a) or (b) above, the jury find him not guilty of the offence charged, they may find him guilty of the basic offence mentioned in that provision.

(7) For the purposes of subsection (1)(c) above, section 28(1)(a) above shall have effect as if the person likely to be caused harassment, alarm or distress were the victim of the offence.

32 Racially-aggravated harassment, etc

(1) A person is guilty of an offence under this section if he commits –

(a) an offence under section 2 of the Protection from Harassment Act 1997 (offence of harassment); or

(b) an offence under section 4 of that Act (putting people in fear of violence),

which is racially aggravated for the purposes of this section. ...

(3) A person guilty of an offence falling within subsection (1)(a) above shall be liable –

(a) on summary conviction, to imprisonment for a term not exceeding six months or to a fine not exceeding the statutory maximum, or to both;

(b) on conviction on indictment, to imprisonment for a term not exceeding two years or to a fine, or to both.

(4) A person guilty of an offence falling within subsection (1)(b) above shall be liable –

(a) on summary conviction, to imprisonment for a term not exceeding six months or to a fine not exceeding the statutory maximum, or to both;

(b) on conviction on indictment, to imprisonment for a term not exceeding seven years or to a fine, or to both.

(5) If, on the trial on indictment of a person charged with an offence falling within subsection (1)(a) above, the jury find him not guilty of the offence charged, they may find him guilty of the basic offence mentioned in that provision.

(6) If, on the trial on indictment of a person charged with an offence falling within subsection (1)(b) above, the jury find him not guilty of the offence charged, they may find him guilty of an offence falling within subsection (1)(a) above. ...

34 Abolition of rebuttal presumption that a child is doli incapax

The rebuttable presumption of criminal law that a child aged 10 or over is incapable of committing an offence is hereby abolished.

Part IV
Dealing with Offenders
Chapter I
England and Wales ...

80 Sentencing guidelines

(1) This section applies where the Court –

(a) is seised of an appeal against, or a reference under section 36 of the Criminal Justice Act 1988 with respect to, the sentence passed for an offence; or

(b) receives a proposal under section 81 below in respect of a particular category of offence;

and in this section 'the relevant category' means any category within which the offence falls or, as the case may be, the category to which the proposal relates.

(2) The Court shall consider –

(a) whether to frame guidelines as to the sentencing of offenders for offences of the relevant category; or
(b) where such guidelines already exist, whether it would be appropriate to review them.

(3) Where the Court decides to frame or revise such guidelines, the Court shall have regard to –

(a) the need to promote consistency in sentencing;
(b) the sentences imposed by courts in England and Wales for offences of the relevant category;
(c) the cost of different sentences and their relative effectiveness in preventing re-offending;
(d) the need to promote public confidence in the criminal justice system; and
(e) the views communicated to the Court, in accordance with section 81(4)(b) below, by the Sentencing Advisory Panel.

(4) Guidelines framed or revised under this section shall include criteria for determining the seriousness of offences, including (where appropriate) criteria for determining the weight to be given to any previous convictions of offenders or any failures of theirs to respond to previous sentences.

(5) In a case falling within subsection (1)(a) above, guidelines framed or revised under this section shall, if practicable, be included in the Court's judgment in the appeal.

(6) Subject to subsection (5) above, guidelines framed or revised under this section shall be included in a judgment of the Court at the next appropriate opportunity (having regard to the relevant category of offence).

(7) For the purposes of this section, the Court is seised of an appeal against a sentence if –

(a) the Court or a single judge has granted leave to appeal against the sentence under section 9 or 10 of the Criminal Appeal Act 1968; or
(b) in a case where the judge who passed the sentence granted a certificate of fitness for appeal under section 9 or 10 of that Act, notice of appeal has been given,

and (in either case) the appeal has not been abandoned or disposed of.

(8) For the purposes of this section, the Court is seised of a reference under section 36 of the Criminal Justice Act 1988 if it has given leave under subsection (1) of that section and the reference has not been disposed of.

(9) In this section and section 81 below –

'the Court' means the criminal division of the Court of Appeal;
'offence' means an indictable offence.

81 *The Sentencing Advisory Panel*

(1) The Lord Chancellor, after consultation with the Secretary of State and the Lord Chief Justice, shall constitute a sentencing panel to be known as the Sentencing Advisory Panel ('the Panel') and appoint one of the members of the Panel to be its chairman.

(2) Where, in a case falling within subsection (1)(a) of section 80 above, the Court decides to frame or revise guidelines under that section for a particular category of offence, the Court shall notify the Panel.

(3) The Panel may at any time, and shall if directed to do so by the Secretary of State, propose to the Court that guidelines be framed or revised under section 80 above for a particular category of offence.

(4) Where the Panel receives a notification under subsection (2) above or makes a proposal under subsection (3) above, the Panel shall –

(a) obtain and consider the views on the matters in issue of such persons or bodies as may be determined, after consultation with the Secretary of State and the Lord Chief Justice, by the Lord Chancellor;
(b) formulate its own views on those matters and communicate them to the Court; and
(c) furnish information to the Court as to the matters mentioned in section 80(3)(b) and (c) above.

(5) The Lord Chancellor may pay to any member of the Panel such remuneration as he may determine.

82 Increase in sentences for racial aggravation

(1) This section applies where a court is considering the seriousness of an offence other than one under sections 29 to 32 above.

(2) If the offence was racially aggravated, the court –

(a) shall treat that fact as an aggravating factor (that is to say, a factor that increases the seriousness of the offence); and
(b) shall state in open court that the offence was so aggravated.

(3) Section 28 above applies for the purposes of this section as it applies for the purposes of sections 29 to 32 above.

Criminal Cases Review (Insanity) Act 1999
(1999 c 25)

1 Reference of former verdict of guilty but insane

(1) Where a verdict was returned in England and Wales ... to the effect that a person was guilty of the act or omission charged against him but was insane at the time, the Criminal Cases Review Commission may at any time refer the verdict to the Court of Appeal if subsection (2) below applies.

(2) This subsection applies if the Commission consider that there is a real possibility that the verdict would not be upheld were the reference to be made and either –

(a) the Commission so consider because of an argument, or evidence, not raised in the proceedings which led to the verdict, or

(b) it appears to the Commission that there are exceptional circumstances which justify the making of the reference.

(3) Section 14 of the Criminal Appeal Act 1995 (supplementary provision about the reference of a verdict) shall apply in relation to a reference under subsection (1) above as it applies in relation to references under section 9 or 10 of that Act.

2 *Reference treated as appeal: England and Wales*

(1) A reference under section 1(1) above of a verdict returned in England and Wales in the case of a person shall be treated for all purposes as an appeal by the person under section 12 of the Criminal Appeal Act 1968.

(2) In their application to such a reference by virtue of subsection (1) above, sections 13 and 14 of that Act shall have effect –

(a) as if references to the verdict of not guilty by reason of insanity were to the verdict referred under section 1(1) above, and
(b) as if, in section 14(1)(b), for the words from the beginning to 'that he' there were substituted 'the accused was under a disability and'.

Glossary
of Latin and other words and phrases

Ab extra. From outside.

Ab inconvenienti. *See* ARGUMENTUM

Ab initio. From the beginning.

Accessio. Addition; appendage. The combination of two chattels belonging to different persons into a single article.

Acta exteriora indicant interiora secreta. A man's outward actions are evidence of his innermost thoughts and intentions.

Actio personalis moritur cum persona. A personal right of action dies on the death of the person by or against whom it could be enforced.

Actio quanti minoris. Action for how much less.

Actus non facit reum, nisi mens sit rea. The act itself does not make a man guilty, unless he does it with a guilty intention.

Ad colligenda bona. To collect the goods.

Ad hoc. Arranged for this purpose; special.

Ad idem. *See* CONSENSUS.

Ad infinitum. To infinity; without limit; for ever.

Ad litem. For the purpose of the law suit.

Ad opus. For the benefit of: on behalf of.

Ad valorem. Calculated in proportion to the value or price of the property.

Adversus extraneos vitiosa possessio prodesse solet. Possession, though supported only by a defective title, will prevail over the claims of strangers other than the true owner.

A fortiori (ratione). For a stronger reason; by even more convincing reasoning.

Aliter. Otherwise; the result would be different, if …; (also, used of a judge who thinks differently from his fellow judges).

Aliud est celare; aliud est tacere; neque enim id est celare quicquid reticeas. Mere silence is one thing but active concealment is quite another thing; for it is not disguising something when you say nothing about it.

Aliunde. From elsewhere; from other sources.

A mensa et thoro. A separation from the 'table and bed' of one's spouse.

Amicus curiae. A friend of the court.

Animo contrahendi. With the intention of contracting.

Animo revocandi. With the intention of revoking.

Animus deserendi. The intention of deserting.

Animus donandi. The intention of giving.

Animus possidendi. The intention of possessing.

Animus revertendi. The intention of returning.

Animus testandi. The intention of making a will.

Ante. Before; (also used of a case referred to earlier on a page or in a book).

A posteriori. From effect to cause; inductively; from subsequent conclusions.

A priori. From cause to effect; deductively; from previous assumptions or reasoning.

Argumentum ab inconvenienti. An argument devised because of the existence of an awkward problem so as to provide an explanation for it.

Asportatio. The act of carrying away.

Assensus. *See* CONSENSUS.

Assensus ad idem. Agreement as to the same terms.

Assumpsit (super se). He undertook.

Ats. (ad sectam). At the suit of. (The opposite of VERSUS.)

Autrefois acquit. Formerly acquitted.

Autrefois convict. Formerly convicted.

Bis dat qui cito dat. He gives doubly who gives swiftly; a quick gift is worth two slow ones.

Bona fide. In good faith; sincere.

Bona vacantia. Goods without an owner.

Brutum fulmen. A silent thunderbolt; an empty threat.

Cadit quaestio. The matter admits of no further argument.

Caeterorum. Of the things which are left.

Capias ad satisfaciendum. A writ commanding the sheriff to take the body of the defendant in order that he may make satisfaction for the plaintiff's claim.

Causa causans. The immediate cause of something; the last link in the chain of causation.

Causa proxima non remota spectatur. Regard is paid to the immediate, not to the remote cause.

Causa sine qua non. A preceding link in the chain of causation without which the causa causans could not be operative.

Caveat emptor. The buyer must look out for himself.

Cessante ratione legis, cessat lex ipsa. When the reason for its existence ceases, the law itself ceases to exist.

Cestui(s) que trust. A person (or persons) for whose benefit property is held on trust; a beneficiary (beneficiaries).

Cestui que vie. Person for the duration of whose life an estate is granted to another person.

Chose in action. Intangible personal property or rights, which can be enjoyed or enforced only by legal action, and not by taking physical possession (eg debts).

Chose jugée. Thing it is idle to discuss.

Coitus interruptus. Interrupted sexual intercourse, ie withdrawal before emission.

Colore officii. Under the pretext of a person's official position.

Commorientes. Persons who die at the same time.

Confusio. A mixture; union. The mixture of things of the same nature, but belonging to different persons so that identification of the original things becomes impossible.

Consensu. By general consent; unanimously.

Consensus ad idem. Agreement as to the same thing.

Consortium. Conjugal relations with and companionship of a spouse.

Contra. To the contrary. (Used of a case in which the decision was contrary to the doctrine or cases previously cited; also of a judge who delivers a dissenting judgment.)

Contra bonos mores. Contrary to good morals.

Contra mundum. Against the world.

Contra proferentem. Against the party who puts forward a clause in a document.

Cor. (coram). In the presence of; before (a judge).

Coram non judice. Before one who is not a judge. Corpus. Body; capital.

Corpus. Body; capital.

Coverture. Marriage.

Cri de coeur. Heartfelt cry.

Cujus est solum, ejus est usque ad coelum et ad inferos. Whosoever owns the soil also owns everything above it as far as the heavens and everything below it as far as the lower regions of the earth.

Culpa. Wrongful default.

Cum onere. Together with the burden.

Cum testamento annexo. With the will annexed.

Cur. adv. vult. (curia advisari vult). The court wishes time to consider the matter.

Cy-pres. For a purpose resembling as nearly as possible the purpose originally proposed.

Damage feasant. *See* DISTRESS.

Damnosa hereditas. An insolvent inheritance.

Damnum. Loss; damage.

Damnum absque injuria. *See* DAMNUM SINE INJURIA.

Damnum emergens. A loss which arises.

Damnum fatale. Damage resulting from the workings of fate for which human negligence is not to blame.

Damnum sine (or absque) injuria. Damage which is not the result of a legally remediable wrong.

De bene esse. Evidence or action which a court allows to be given or done provisionally, subject to further consideration at a later stage.

Debitor non praesumitur donare. A debtor is presumed to give a legacy to a creditor to discharge his debt and not as a gift.

Debitum in praesenti. A debt which is due at the present time.

Debitum in futuro solvendum. A debt which will be due to be paid at a future time.

De bonis asportatis. Of goods carried away.

De bonis non administratis. Of the assets which have not been administered .

De die in diem. From day to day.

De facto. In fact.

De futuro. Regarding the future; in the future; about something which will exist in the future.

Dehors. Outside (the document or matter in question); irrelevant.

De integro. As regards the whole; entirely.

De jure. By right; rightful.

Del credere agent. An agent who for an extra commission guarantees the due performance of contracts by persons whom he introduces to his principal.

Delegatus non potest delegare. A person who is entrusted with a duty has no right to appoint another person to perform it in his place.

De minimis non curat lex. The law does not concern itself with trifles.

De novo. Anew; starting afresh.

Deodand. A chattel which caused the death of a human being and was forfeited to the Crown.

De praerogativa regis. Concerning the royal prerogative.

De son tort. Of his wrong.

Deus est procurator fatuorum. God is the protector of the simpleminded.

Devastavit. Where an executor 'has squandered' the estate.

Dictum. Saying. *See* OBITER DICTUM.

Dies non (jurisdicus). Day on which no legal business can be transacted.

Dissentiente. Delivering a dissenting judgment.

Distress damage feasant. The detention by a landowner of an animal or chattel while it is doing damage on his land.

Distringas. That you may distrain.

Doli incapax. Incapable of crime.

Dolus qui dat locum contractui. A deception which clears the way for the other party to enter into a contract.

Dominium. Ownership.

Dominus litis. The principal in a suit.

Dominus pro tempore. The master for the time being.

Donatio mortis causa. A gift made in contemplation of death and conditional thereon.

Dubitante. Doubting the correctness of the decision.

Durante absentia. During an executor's absence abroad.

Durante minore aetate. While an executor remains an infant.

Durante viduitate. During widowhood.

Ei incumbit probatio qui dicit, non qui negat. The onus of proving a fact rests upon the man who asserts its truth, not upon the man who denies it.

Ejusdem generis. General words following a list of specific things are construed as relating to things 'of the same kind' as those specifically listed.

Enceinte. Pregnant.

En ventre sa mère. Conceived but not yet born.

Eodem modo quo oritur, eodem modo dissolvitur. What has been created by a certain method may be extinguished by the same method.

Eo instanti. At that instant.

Escrow. A document delivered subject to a condition which must be fulfilled before it becomes a deed.

Estoppel. A rule of evidence which applies in certain circumstances and stops a person from denying the truth of a statement previously made by him.

Estoppel in pais. Estoppel by matter or conduct; equitable estoppel.

Et cetera (etc). And other things of that sort.

Et seq (et sequentes). And subsequent pages.

Ex. From; by virtue of.

Ex abundanti cautela. From an abundance of caution.

Ex aequo et bono. According to what is just and equitable.

Ex cathedra. From his seat of office: an authoritative statement made by someone in his official capacity.

Ex concessis. In view of what has already been accepted.

Ex contractu. Arising out of contract.

Ex converso. Conversely.

Ex debito justitiae. That which is due as of right; which the court has no discretion to refuse.

Ex delicto. Arising out of a wrongful act or tort.

Ex dolo malo non oritur actio. No right of action arises out of a fraud.

Ex facie. On the face of it; ostensibly.

Ex gratia. Out of the kindness. Gratuitous; voluntary.

Ex hypothesi. In view of what has already been assumed.

Ex improviso. Unexpectedly, without forethought.

Ex officio. By virtue of one's official position.

Ex pacto illicito non oritur actio. No action can be brought on an unlawful contract.

Ex parte. Proceedings brought on behalf of one interested party without notice to, and in the absence of, the other.

Ex post facto. By reason of a subsequent act; acting retrospectively.

Ex relatione. An action instituted by the Attorney-General on behalf of the Crown on the information of a member of the public who is interested in the matter (the relator).

Expressio unius est exclusio alterius. When one thing is expressly specified, then it prevents anything else being implied.

Expressum facit cessare tacitum. Where terms are expressed, no other terms can be implied.

Ex turpi causa non oritur actio. No action can be brought where the parties are guilty of illegal or immoral conduct.

Faciendum. Something which is to be done.

Factum. Deed; that which has been done; statement of facts or points in issue.

Fait accompli. An accomplished fact.

Falsa demonstratio non nocet cum de corpore constat. Where the substance of the property in question is clearly identified, the addition of an incorrect description of the property does no harm.

Falsus in ono, falsus in omnibus. False in one, false in all.

Fecundatio ab extra. Conception from outside, ie where there has been no penetration.

Feme covert. A married woman.

Feme sole. An unmarried woman.

Ferae naturae. Animals which are by nature dangerous to man.

Fieri facias. A writ addressed to the sheriff: 'that you cause to be made' from the defendant's goods the sum due to the plaintiff under the judgment.

Force majeure. Irresistible compulsion.

Fructus industriales. Cultivated crops.

Fructus naturales. Vegetation which grows naturally without cultivation.

Functus officio. Having discharged his duty; having exhausted its powers.

Genus numquam perit. Particular goods which have been identified may be destroyed, but 'a category or type of article can never perish'.

Habeas corpus (ad subjiciendum). A writ addressed to one who detains another in custody, requiring him 'that you produce the prisoner's body to answer' to the court.

Habitue. A frequent visitor to a place.

Ibid. (ibidem). In the same place, book, or source.

Id certum est quod certum reddi potest. That which is capable of being reduced to a certainty is already a certainty.

Idem. The same thing, or person.

Ideo consideratum est per. Therefore it is considered by the court.

Ignorantia juris haud (neminem) (non) excusat, ignorantia facti excusat. A man may be excused for mistaking facts, but not for mistaking the law.

Ignorantia juris non excusat. Ignorance of the law is no excuse.

Imperitia culpae adnumeratur. Lack of skill is accounted a fault.

In aequali jure melior est conditio possidentis. Where the legal rights of the parties are equal, the party with possession is in the stronger position.

In articulo mortis. On the point of death.

In bonis. In the goods (or estate) of a deceased person.

In capite. In chief; holding as tenant directly under the Crown.

In consimili casu. In a similar case.

In custodia legis. In the keeping of the law.

Indebitatus assumpsit. A form of action in which the plaintiff alleges the defendant 'being already indebted to the plaintiff undertook' to do something.

In delicto. At fault.

Indicia. Signs; marks.

Indicium. Indication; sign; mark.

In esse. In existence.

In expeditione. On actual military service.

In extenso. At full length.

In fieri. In the course of being performed or established.

In flagrante delicto. In the act of committing the offence.

In forma pauperis. In the character of a poor person.

Infra. Below; lower down on a page; later in a book. In futuro. In the future.

In futuro. In the future.

In hac re. In this matter; in this particular aspect.

In jure non remota causa sed proxima spectatur. In law it is the immediate and not the remote cause which is considered.

Injuria. A wrongful act for which the law provides a remedy.

Injuria sine damno. A wrongful act unaccompanied by any damage yet actionable at law.

In lieu of. In place of.

In limine. On the threshold; at the outset.

In loco parentis. In the place of a parent.

In minore delicto. A person who is 'less at fault'.

In omnibus. In every respect.

Inops consilii. Lacking facilities for legal advice.

In pari delicto, potior est conditio defendentis (or possidentis). Where both parties are equally at fault, the defendant (or the party in possession) is in the stronger position.

In pari materia. In an analogous case or position.

In personam. *See* JUS IN PERSONAM.

In pleno. In full.

In praesenti. At the present time.

In propria persona. In his own capacity. In re. In the matter of. In rem. *See* JUS IN REM.

In re. In the matter of.

In rem. *See* JUS IN REM.

In situ. In its place.

In specie. In its own form; not converted into anything else.

In statu quo ante. In the condition in which it, or a person, was before.

Inter alia. Amongst other things.

Inter alios. Amongst other persons.

Interest reipublicae ut sit finis litium. It is in the interests of the community that every law suit should reach a final conclusion (and not be reopened later).

Interim. In the meanwhile; temporary.

Inter partes. Between (the) parties.

In terrorem. As a warning; as a deterrent.

Inter se. Between themselves.

Inter vivos. Between persons who are alive.

In toto. In its entirety; completely.

In transitu. In passage from one place to another.

Intra vires. Within the powers recognised by law as belonging to the person or body in question.

In utero. In the womb.

In vacuo. In the abstract; without considering the circumstances.

In vitro. In glass; in a test tube.

Ipsissima verba. 'The very words' of a speaker.

Ipso facto. By that very fact.

Jura. Rights.

Jura mariti. By virtue of the right of a husband to the goods of his wife.

Jus. A right which is recognised in law.

Jus accrescendi. The right of survivorship; the right of joint tenants to have their interests in the joint property increased by inheriting the interests of the deceased joint tenants until the last survivor inherits the entire property.

Jus in personam. A right which can be enforced against a particular person only.

Jus in rem. A right which can be enforced over the property in question against all other persons.

Jus naturale. Natural justice.

Jus neque in re neque ad rem. A right which is enforceable neither over the property in question against all the world nor against specific persons only.

Jus quaesitum tertio. A right vested in a third party (who is not a party to the contract).

Jus tertii. *See* JUS QUAESITUM TERTIO

Laches. Slackness or delay in pursuing a legal remedy which disentitles a person from action at a later date.

Laesio fidei. Breach of faith.

Laissez faire. 'Let him do what he likes'; permissive.

Lapsus linguae. Slip of the tongue.

Lex domicilii. The law of domicile.

Lex fori. The law of the court in which the case is being heard.

Lex loci celebrationis. The law of the place where the marriage was celebrated.

Lex loci contractus. The law of the place where the contract was made.

Lex loci delicti. The law of the place where the wrong was committed.

Lex loci situs. *See* LEX SITUS.

Lex loci solutionis. The law of the place where the contract is to be performed.

Lex situs. The law of the place where the thing in question is situated.

Lien. The rights to retain possession of goods, deeds or other property belonging to another as security for payment of money.

Lis pendens. Pending action.

Loc. cit. (loco citato). In the passage previously mentioned.

Locus classicus. Authoritative passage in a book or judgment; the principal authority or source for the subject.

Locus in quo. Scene of the event.

Locus poenitentiae. Scope or opportunity for repentance.

Locus standi. Recognised position or standing; the right to appear in court.

Lucrum cessans. A benefit which is terminated.

Magnum opus. A great work of literature.

Mala fide(s). (In) bad faith.

Malitia supplet aetatem. Malice supplements the age of an infant wrongdoer who would (in the absence of malice) be too young to be responsible for his acts.

Malum in se. An act which in itself is morally wrong, eg murder.

Malum prohibitum. An act which is wrong because it is prohibited by human law but is not morally wrong.

Malus animus. Evil intent.

Mansuetae naturae. Animals which are normally of a domesticated disposition.

Mesne. Intermediate; middle; dividing.

Mesne profits. Profits of land lost by the plaintiff while the defendant remained wrongfully in possession.

Mobilia sequuntur personam. The domicile of movable property follows the owner's personal domicile.

Molliter manus imposuit. Gently laid his hand upon the other party.

Mutatis mutandis. With the necessary changes of detail being made.

Natura negotii. The nature of the transaction.

Negotiorum gestio. Handling of other people's affairs.

Nemo dat quod non habet. No one has power to transfer the ownership of that which he does not own.

Nemo debet bis vexari, si constat curiae quod sit pro una et eadem causa. No one ought to be harassed with proceedings twice, if it appears to the court that it is for one and the same cause.

Nemo est haeres viventis. No one can be the heir of a person who is still living.

Nexus. Connection; bond.

Nisi. Unless; (also used of a decree or order which will later be made absolute 'unless' good cause be shown to the contrary); provisional.

Nisi prius. Cases which were directed to be tried at Westminster only if the justices of assize should 'not' have tried them in the country 'previously'.

Nocumenta infinita sunt. There is no limit to the types of situations which constitute nuisances.

Nomen collectivum. A collective name, noun or description; a word descriptive of a class.

Non compos mentis. Not of sound mind and understanding.

Non constat. It is not certain.

Non est factum. That the document in question was not his deed.

Non haec in foedera veni. This is not the agreement which I came to sign.

Non omnibus dormio. I do not turn a blind eye on every instance of misconduct.

Non sequitur. It does not follow; an inconsistent statement.

Noscitur a sociis. The meaning of a word is known from the company it keeps (ie from its context).

Nova causa interveniens. An independent cause which intervenes between the alleged wrong and the damage in question.

Novus actus interveniens. A fresh act of someone other than the defendant which intervenes between the alleged wrong and the damage in question.

Nudum pactum. A bare agreement (unsupported by consideration).

Nullius filius. No man's son; a bastard.

Obiter dictum (dicta). Thing(s) said by the way; opinions expressed by judges in passing, on issues not essential for the decision in the case.

Obligatio quasi ex contractu. An obligation arising out of an act or event, as if from a contract, but independently of the consent of the person bound.

Omnia praesumuntur contra spoliatorem. Every presumption is raised against a wrongdoer.

Omnia praesumuntur rite et solemniter esse acta donec probetur in contrarium. All things are presumed to have been performed with all due formalities until it is proved to the contrary.

Omnis ratihabitio retrotrahitur et mandato priori aequiparatur. Every ratification of a previous act is carried back and made equivalent to a previous command to do it.

Onus probandi. The burden of proving.

Op. cit. (opere citato). In the book referred to previously.

Orse. Otherwise.

Par delictum. Equal fault.

Parens patriae. Parent of the nation.

Pari materia. With equal substance.

Pari passu. On an equal footing; equally; in step with.

Pari ratione. By an equivalent process of reasoning.

Parol. By word of mouth, or unsealed document.

Participes criminis. Accomplices in the crime.

Pater est quem nuptiae demonstrant. He is the father whom the marriage indicates to be so.

Passim. Generally; referred to throughout the book or source in question.

Patrimonium. Beneficial ownership.

Pendente lite. While a law suit is pending.

Per. By; through; in the opinion of a judge.

Per capita. Divided equally between all the persons filling the description.

Per curiam. In the opinion of the court.

Per formam doni. Through the form of wording of the gift or deed.

Per incuriam. Through carelessness or oversight.

Per quod. By reason of which.

Per quod consortium et servitium amisit. By reason of which he has lost the benefit of her company and services.

Per quod servitium amisit. By reason of which he has lost the benefit of his service.

Per se. By itself.

Persona(e) designata(e). A person(s) specified as an individual(s), not identified as a member(s) of a class nor as fulfilling a particular qualification.

Per stirpes. According to the stocks of descent; one share for each line of descendants; where the descendants of a deceased person (however many they may be) inherit between them only the one share which the deceased would have taken if alive.

Per subsequens matrimonium. Legitimation of a child 'by subsequent marriage' of the parents.

Plene administravit. A plea by an executor 'that he has fully administered' all the assets which have come into his hands and that no assets remain out of which the plaintiff's claim could be satisfied.

Plus quam tolerabile. More than can be endured.

Post. After; mentioned in a subsequent passage or page.

Post mortem. After death.

Post nuptial. Made after marriage.

Post obit bond. Agreement or bond by which a borrower agrees to pay the lender a sum larger than the loan on or after the death of a person on whose death he expects to inherit property.

Post obitum. After the death of a specified person.

Pour autrui. On behalf of another.

Prima facie. At first sight.

Primae impressionis. Of first impression.

Pro bono publico. For the public good.

Profit a prendre. The right to enter the land of another and take part of its produce.

Pro hac vice. For this occasion.

Pro privato commodo. For private benefit.

Pro rata. In proportion.

Pro rata itineris. At the same rate per mile as was agreed for the whole journey.

Pro tanto. So far; to that extent.

Pro tempore. For the time being.

Publici juris. Of public right.

Puisne. Inferior; lower in rank; not secured by deposit of deeds; of the High Court.

Punctum temporis. Moment, or point of time.

Pour autre vie. During the life of another person.

q.v. (quod vide). Which see.

Qua. As; in the capacity of.

Quaere. Consider whether it is correct.

Quaeritur. The question is raised.

Quantum. Amount; how much.

Quantum meruit. As much as he has earned.

Quantum valebant. As much as they were worth.

Quare clausum fregit. Because he broke into the plaintiff's enclosure.

Quasi. As if; seemingly.

Quasi ex contractu. *See* OBLIGATIO.

Quatenus. How far; in so far as; since.

Quia timet. Because he fears what he will suffer in the future.

Quicquid plantatur solo solo cedit. Whatever is planted in the soil belongs to the soil.

Quid pro quo. Something for something; consideration.

Qui facit per alium facit per se. He who employs another person to do something does it himself.

Qui prior est tempore potior est jure. He who is earlier in point of time is in the stronger position in law.

Quoad. Until; as far as; as to.

Quoad hoc. As far as this matter is concerned.

Quo animo. With what intention.

Quot judices tot sententiae. There were as many different opinions as there were judges.

Quousque. Until the time when.

Ratio decidendi. The reason for a decision; the principle on which a decision is based.

Ratione domicilii. By reason of a person's domicile.

Re. In the matter of; by the thing or transaction.

Renvoi. Reference to or application of the rules of a foreign legal system in a different country's courts.

Res. Thing; affair; matter; circumstance.

Res extincta. The thing which was intended to be the subject matter of a contract but had previously been destroyed.

Res gestae. Things done; the transaction.

Res integra. A point not covered by the authority of a decided case which must therefore be decided upon principle alone.

Res inter alios acta alteri nocere non debet. A man ought not to be prejudiced by what has taken place between other persons.

Res ipsa loquitur. The thing speaks for itself, ie is evidence of negligence in the absence of an explanation by the defendant.

Res judicata. A matter on which a court has previously reached a binding decision; a matter which cannot be questioned.

Res nova. A matter which has not previously been decided.

Res nullius. Nobody's property.

Respondeat superior. A principal must answer for the acts of his subordinates.

Res sua. Something which a man believes to belong to another when it in fact is 'his own property'.

Restitutio in integrum. Restoration of a party to his original position; full restitution.

Res vendita. The article which was sold.

Rex est procurator fatuorum. The King is the protector of the simple minded.

Rigor aequitatis. The inflexibility of equity.

Sc. *See* SCILICET.

Sciens. Knowing.

Scienter. Knowingly; with knowledge of an animal's dangerous disposition.

Scienti non fit injuria. A man who is aware of the existence of a danger has no remedy if it materialises.

Scilicet. To wit; namely; that is to say.

Scintilla. A spark; trace; or moment.

Scire facias. A writ; that you cause to know.

Scriptum praedictum non est factum suum. A plea that the aforesaid document is not his deed.

Secundum formam doni. In accordance with the form of wording in the gift or deed.

Secus. It is otherwise; the legal position is different.

Sed. But.

Sed quaere. But inquire; look into the matter; consider whether the statement is correct.

Semble. It appears; apparently.

Sentit commodum et periculum rei. He both enjoys the benefit of the thing and bears the risk of its loss.

Seriatim. In series; one by one; point by point.

Serivitium. Service.

Sic. So; in such a manner; (also used to emphasise wording copied or quoted from another source: 'such was the expression used in the original source').

Sic utere tuo ut alienum non laedas. So use your own property as not to injure the property of your neighbour.

Similiter. Similarly; in like manner.

Simplex commendatio non obligat. Mere praise of goods by the seller imposes no liability upon him.

Simpliciter. Simply; merely; alone; without any further action; without qualification.

Sine animo revertendi. Without the intention of returning.

Sine die. Without a day being appointed; indefinitely.

Solatium. Consolation; relief; compensation.

Sotto volce. In an undertone.

Specificatio. The making of a new article out of the chattel of one person by the labour of another.

Spes successionis. The hope of inheriting property on the death of another.

Spondes peritiam artis. If skill is inherent in your profession, you guarantee that you will display it.

Stare decisis. To stand by what has been dedided.

Status quo (ante). The previous position; the position in which things were before; unchanged position.

Stet. Let it stand; do not delete.

Stricto sensu. In the strict sense.

Sub colore officii. Under pretext of someone's official position.

Sub modo. Within limits; to a limited extent.

Sub nom. (sub nomine). Under the name of.

Sub silentio. In silence.

Sub tit. (sub titulo). Under the title of.

Suggestio falsi. The suggestion of something which is untrue.

Sui generis. Of its own special kind; unique.

Sui juris. Of his own right; possessed of full legal capacity.

Sup. *See* SUPRA.

Suppressio veri. The suppression of the truth.

Supra. (Sup.) Above; referred to higher up the page; previously.

Talis qualis. Such as it is.

Tam ... quam. As well ... as.

Toties quoties. As often as occasion shall require; as often as something happens.

Transit in rem judicatam. A right of action merges in the judgment recovered upon it.

Turpis causa. Immoral conduct which constitutes the subject matter of an action.

Uberrima fides. Most abundant good faith.

Ubi jus ibi remedium. Where there is a legally recognised right there is also a remedy.

Ubi supra. In the passage or reference mentioned previously.

Ultimus heres. The ultimate heir who is last in order of priority of those who may be entitled to claim the estate of an intestate.

Ultra vires. Outside the powers recognised by law as belonging to the person or body in question.

Uno flatu. With one breath; at the same moment.

Ut res magis valeat quam pereat. Words must be construed so as to support the validity of the contract rather than to destroy it.

v. (versus). Against.

Verba fortius accipiuntur contra proferentem. Ambiguous wording is construed adversely against the party who introduced it into the document.

Vera copula. True sexual unity.

Verbatim. Word by word; exactly; word for word.

Vice versa. The other way round; in turn.

Vide. See.

Vi et armis (et contra pacem domini regis). By force of arms (and in breach of the King's peace).

Vigilantibus et non dormientibus jura subveniunt (or jus succurrit). The law(s) assist(s) those who are vigilant, not those who doze over their rights.

Vinculum juris. Legal tie; that which binds the parties with mutual obligations.

Virgo intacta. A virgin with hymen intact.

Virtute officii. By virtue of a person's official position.

Vis-a-vis. Face to face; opposite to.

Vis major. Irresistible force.

Viva voce. Orally; oral examination.

Viz. (videlicet). Namely; that is to say.

Voir dire. Examination of a witness before he gives evidence, to ascertain whether he is competent to tell the truth on oath; trial within a trial.

Volens. Willing.

Volenti non fit injuria. In law no wrong is done to a man who consents to undergo it.

Index

Sado-masochism, *46*
Self-defence, *6, 56, 109,112*
  battery, in, *11*
  manslaughter, in, *111*
  murder, in, *87*
  proof of, *98*
  property, of, *8*
Sentencing Advisory Panel, *424*
Sex discrimination, *249*
Sex offender order, *418*
Sexual offences, *182, 367, 403, 415. See also*
  CHILD; PROCUREMENT; RAPE
  abduction, *184, 185*
  brothels, *186, 188, 204*
  buggery, *183, 184, 367, 368, 404, 416*
  girl under 13, *182, 195, 367, 404, 416*
  girl under 16, *80, 81, 117, 182, 187, 404, 416*
  homosexual acts, private, *203*
  incest, *183, 367, 368*
  indecency, *183*
  indecent assault, *184, 367, 404, 416*
  intercourse, defective, with, *182, 187*
  kerb-crawling, *301*
  prostitution, living on, *146, 187, 203*
  'sexual intercourse', *189*
  soliciting, *192, 301, 302*
  outside UK, *415*
Spying, *170*
Suicide, *195, 399. See also* MANSLAUGHTER
Summary conviction,
  penalties on, *268, 293*

Tattooing,
  minors, of, *238*
Terrorism, *338*
Theft, *30, 103, 136, 141, 147, 223, 266, 371.*
  See also BURGLARY; ROBBERY
  accounting, false, *231, 371*
  appropriation, dishonest, *17, 26, 69, 71, 75, 81, 82, 93, 109, 123, 223*
  articles for, *69*
  avoiding payment, *33, 44, 82, 266*
  blackmail. *See* BLACKMAIL
  body parts, *91*
  cheat, equipped to, *60, 65, 139*
  credit card, *87, 94, 96*
  deception, by, *21, 35, 38, 51, 56, 65, 70, 74, 79, 95, 96, 106, 111, 116, 139, 229, 371*
   evading liability, *266*

Theft, deception, by (*contd.*)
  obtaining services, *266*
  definition, *223*
  documents, suppression etc of, *90*
  electricity, *229*
  fish, *237*
  going equipped, *76, 234*
  husband and wife, *235*
  intention to steal, *2, 39*
  mails, from, *229*
  menace, demand with, *80, 95*
  painting, of, *67*
  partner, by, *41*
  pecuniary advantage, deception, by, *14, 15, 29, 35, 41, 49, 94, 230, 371*
   employment, in, *49*
  'permanently depriving', *70, 225*
  property belonging to another, *34, 74, 93, 104, 116, 140, 224*
  record, falsifying, *18, 232*
  stolen goods, handling, *6, 21, 40, 42, 44, 64, 78, 87, 89, 90, 97, 124, 233, 371*
  tickets, of, *103*
  vehicle taking, *40, 56, 64, 113, 227, 286*
   aggravated, *10, 102, 228*
  wrongful credit, *234, 371*
Threat,
  destroy property, to, *247*
  kill, to, *61, 159*
  payment, regarding, *242*
  violence, *307*
Tipping-off, *327, 391*
Torture, *328*
Treason, *153, 157*
Trespass, *260. See also* OFFENSIVE
  WEAPONS
  aggravated, *380*
  removal of trespasser, *373*

Unsound mind. *See* DIMINISHED
  RESPONSIBILITY; INSANITY

Vagrancy, *154, 177, 286, 293*
Vehicle taking. *See* THEFT
Violent disorder, *306*

War crimes, *364*
Wounding, *23, 119*
  unlawful, *36, 38, 109, 160*
Wrongful imprisonment, *88*

The Practitioner's Handbook

The primary aim of The Practitioner's Handbook is to provide barristers' chambers and firms of solicitors with a distinctive compendium of recent developments enabling practitioners to keep up to date in a time-efficient manner. The ten main areas of legal practice covered are:

- Civil Litigation
- Commercial Property
- Company Law
- Conveyancing
- Criminal Law and Procedure
- Employment Law
- European Union Law
- Matrimonial and Child Care Law
- Residential Tenancies
- Wills and Probate

The text is distinctive in that it views 'recent developments' expansively, both as to range (covering relevant practice developments in addition to changes in statutes and case law) and time span (key developments over the last two to three years are included). The text is, however, much more than a summary of recent cases and legislation, as a discernible emphasis has been placed upon evaluating issues from a practitioner's perspective. The style and format are designed to facilitate quick reference by busy practitioners and material is presented clearly and concisely.

ISBN: 1 85836 371 3
800 pages approx
Price £54.95
Due May 2000

For further information on contents, please contact:

Mail Order
Old Bailey Press
200 Greyhound Road
London
W14 9RY
Telephone No: 00 44 (0) 20 7385 3377   Fax No: 00 44 (0) 20 7381 3377

Law Update 2000

Law Update 2001 edition – due March 2001

An annual review of the most recent developments in specific legal subject areas, useful for law students at degree and professional levels, others with law elements in their courses and also practitioners seeking a quick update.

Published around March every year, the Law Update summarises the major legal developments during the course of the previous year. In conjunction with Old Bailey Press textbooks it gives the student a significant advantage when revising for examinations.

Contents

Administrative Law • Civil and Criminal Procedure • Company Law • Conflict of Laws • Constitutional Law • Contract Law • Conveyancing • Criminal Law • Criminology • English Legal System • Equity and Trusts • European Union Law • Evidence • Family Law • Jurisprudence • Land Law • Law of International Trade • Public International Law • Revenue Law • Succession • Tort

For further information on contents, please contact:

Mail Order
Old Bailey Press
200 Greyhound Road
London
W14 9RY
United Kingdom

Telephone No: 00 44 (0) 20 7385 3377
Fax No: 00 44 (0) 20 7381 3377

ISBN 1 85836 347 0
Soft cover 246 x 175 mm
392 pages   £9.95
Published March 2000

Old Bailey Press

The Old Bailey Press integrated student library is planned and written to help you at every stage of your studies. Each of our range of Textbooks, Casebooks, Revision WorkBooks and Statutes are all designed to work together and are regularly revised and updated.

We are also able to offer you Suggested Solutions which provide you with past examination questions and solutions for most of the subject areas listed below.

You can buy Old Bailey Press books from your University Bookshop or your local Bookshop, or in case of difficulty, order direct using this form.

Here is the selection of modules covered by our series:

Administrative Law; Commercial Law; Company Law (no Single Paper 1997); Conflict of Laws (no Suggested Solutions Pack); Constitutional Law: The Machinery of Government; Obligations: Contract Law; Conveyancing (no Revision Workbook); Criminology (Sourcebook in place of a Casebook or Revision WorkBook); Criminal Law; English Legal System; Equity and Trusts; Law of The European Union; Evidence; Family Law; Jurisprudence: The Philosophy of Law (Sourcebook in place of a Casebook); Land: The Law of Real Property; Law of International Trade; Legal Skills and System (Textbook only); Public International Law; Revenue Law (no Casebook); Succession: The Law of Wills and Estates; Obligations: The Law of Tort.

Mail order prices:

Textbook £11.95

Casebook £9.95

Revision WorkBook £7.95

Statutes £9.95

Suggested Solutions Pack (1991–1995) £6.95

Single Paper 1996 £3.00

Single Paper 1997 £3.00

To complete your order, please fill in the form below:

Module	Books required	Quantity	Price	Cost
		Postage		
		TOTAL		

For Europe, add 15% postage and packing (£20 maximum).
For the rest of the world, add 40% for airmail.

ORDERING

By telephone to Mail Order at 020 7385 3377, with your credit card to hand.

By fax to 020 7381 3377 (giving your credit card details).

By post to:

Old Bailey Press, 200 Greyhound Road, London W14 9RY.

When ordering by post, please enclose full payment by cheque or banker's draft, or complete the credit card details below.

We aim to despatch your books within 3 working days of receiving your order.

Name

Address

Postcode   Telephone

Total value of order, including postage: £

I enclose a cheque/banker's draft for the above sum, or

charge my   ☐ Access/Mastercard   ☐ Visa   ☐ American Express
Card number

☐☐☐☐ ☐☐☐☐ ☐☐☐☐ ☐☐☐☐

Expiry date   ☐☐☐☐

Signature: ....Date: ....